Robust Speech Recognition and Understanding

Edited by

Michael Grimm and Kristian Kroschel

Robust Speech Recognition and Understanding
Edited by Michael Grimm and Kristian Kroschel

Republished by InTech
Janeza Trdine 9, 51000 Rijeka, Croatia

Technical Editor Teodora Smiljanic

Cover Designer Dino Smrekar

Additional hard copies can be obtained from orders@intechopen.com

Robust Speech Recognition and Understanding,
Edited by Michael Grimm and Kristian Kroschel
p. cm.
ISBN 978-3-902613-08-0

For EU product safety concerns:
IN TECH d.o.o., Prolaz Marije Krucifikse Kozulić 3, 51000 Rijeka, Croatia,
info@intechopen.com or visit our website at intechopen.com.

Preface

Digital speech processing is a major field in current research all over the world. In particular for automatic speech recognition (ASR), very significant achievements have been made since the first attempts of digit recognizers in the 1950's and 1960's when spectral resonances were determined by analogue filters and logical circuits. As Prof. Furui pointed out in his review on 50 years of automatic speech recognition at the 32nd IEEE International Conference on Acoustics, Speech, and Signal Processing (ICASSP), 2007, we may now see speech recognition systems in their 3.5th generation. Although there are many excellent systems for continuous speech recognition, speech translation and information extraction, ASR systems need to be improved for spontaneous speech. Furthermore, robustness under noisy conditions is still a goal that has not been achieved entirely if distant microphones are used for speech input. The automated recognition of emotion is another aspect in voice-driven systems that has gained much importance in recent years. For natural language understanding in general, and for the correct interpretation of a speaker's recognized words, such paralinguistic information may be used to improve future speech systems.
This book on Robust Speech Recognition and Understanding brings together many different aspects of the current research on automatic speech recognition and language understanding. The first four chapters address the task of voice activity detection which is considered an important issue for all speech recognition systems. The next chapters give several extensions to state-of-the-art HMM methods. Furthermore, a number of chapters particularly address the task of robust ASR under noisy conditions. Two chapters on the automatic recognition of a speaker's emotional state highlight the importance of natural speech understanding and interpretation in voice-driven systems. The last chapters of the book address the application of conversational systems on robots, as well as the autonomous acquisition of vocalization skills.
We want to express our thanks to all authors who have contributed to this book by the best of their scientific work. We hope you enjoy reading this book and get many helpful ideas for your own research or application of speech technology.

Editors

Michael Grimm and Kristian Kroschel
Universität Karlsruhe (TH)
Germany

Contents

1

Voice Activity Detection. Fundamentals and Speech Recognition System Robustness

J. Ramírez, J. M. Górriz and J. C. Segura
University of Granada
Spain

1. Introduction

An important drawback affecting most of the speech processing systems is the environmental noise and its harmful effect on the system performance. Examples of such systems are the new wireless communications voice services or digital hearing aid devices. In speech recognition, there are still technical barriers inhibiting such systems from meeting the demands of modern applications. Numerous noise reduction techniques have been developed to palliate the effect of the noise on the system performance and often require an estimate of the noise statistics obtained by means of a precise voice activity detector (VAD).

Speech/non-speech detection is an unsolved problem in speech processing and affects numerous applications including robust speech recognition (Karray and Marting, 2003; Ramirez et al. 2003), discontinuous transmission (ITU, 1996; ETSI, 1999), real-time speech transmission on the Internet (Sangwan et al., 2002) or combined noise reduction and echo cancellation schemes in the context of telephony (Basbug et al., 2004; Gustafsson et al., 2002). The speech/non-speech classification task is not as trivial as it appears, and most of the VAD algorithms fail when the level of background noise increases. During the last decade, numerous researchers have developed different strategies for detecting speech on a noisy signal (Sohn et al., 1999; Cho and Kondoz, 2001; Gazor and Zhang, 2003, Armani et al., 2003) and have evaluated the influence of the VAD effectiveness on the performance of speech processing systems (Bouquin-Jeannes and Faucon, 1995). Most of the approaches have focussed on the development of robust algorithms with special attention being paid to the derivation and study of noise robust features and decision rules (Woo et al., 2000; Li et al., 2002; Marzinzik and Kollmeier, 2002). The different VAD methods include those based on energy thresholds (Woo et al., 2000), pitch detection (Chengalvarayan, 1999), spectrum analysis (Marzinzik and Kollmeier, 2002), zero-crossing rate (ITU, 1996), periodicity measure (Tucker, 1992), higher order statistics in the LPC residual domain (Nemer et al., 2001) or combinations of different features (ITU, 1993; ETSI, 1999; Tanyer and Özer, 2000).

This chapter shows a comprehensive approximation to the main challenges in voice activity detection, the different solutions that have been reported in a complete review of the state of the art and the evaluation frameworks that are normally used. The application of VADs for speech coding, speech enhancement and robust speech recognition systems is shown and discussed. Three different VAD methods are described and compared to standardized and recently reported strategies by assessing the speech/non-speech discrimination accuracy and the robustness of speech recognition systems.

2. Applications

VADs are employed in many areas of speech processing. Recently, VAD methods have been described in the literature for several applications including mobile communication services (Freeman et al. 1989), real-time speech transmission on the Internet (Sangwan et al., 2002) or noise reduction for digital hearing aid devices (Itoh and Mizushima, 1997). As an example, a VAD achieves silence compression in modern mobile telecommunication systems reducing the average bit rate by using the discontinuous transmission (DTX) mode. Many practical applications, such as the Global System for Mobile Communications (GSM) telephony, use silence detection and comfort noise injection for higher coding efficiency. This section shows a brief description of the most important VAD applications in speech processing: coding, enhancement and recognition.

2.1 Speech coding

VAD is widely used within the field of speech communication for achieving high speech coding efficiency and low-bit rate transmission. The concepts of silence detection and comfort noise generation lead to dual-mode speech coding techniques. The different modes of operation of a speech codec are: *i*) the active speech codec, and *ii*) the silence suppression and comfort noise generation modes. The International Telecommunication Union (ITU) adopted a toll-quality speech coding algorithm known as G.729 to work in combination with a VAD module in DTX mode. Figure 1 shows a block diagram of a dual mode speech codec. The full rate speech coder is operational during active voice speech, but a different coding scheme is employed for the inactive voice signal, using fewer bits and resulting in a higher overall average compression ratio. As an example, the recommendation G.729 Annex B (ITU, 1996) uses a feature vector consisting of the linear prediction (LP) spectrum, the full-band energy, the low-band (0 to 1 KHz) energy and the zero-crossing rate (ZCR). The standard was developed with the collaboration of researchers from France Telecom, the University of Sherbrooke, NTT and AT&T Bell Labs and the effectiveness of the VAD was evaluated in terms of subjective speech quality and bit rate savings (Benyassine et al., 1997). Objective performance tests were also conducted by hand-labeling a large speech database and assessing the correct identification of voiced, unvoiced, silence and transition periods. Another standard for DTX is the ETSI (Adaptive Multi-Rate) AMR speech coder (ETSI, 1999) developed by the Special Mobile Group (SMG) for the GSM system. The standard specifies two options for the VAD to be used within the digital cellular telecommunications system. In option 1, the signal is passed through a filterbank and the level of signal in each band is calculated. A measure of the SNR is used to make the VAD decision together with the output of a pitch detector, a tone detector and the correlated complex signal analysis module. An enhanced version of the original VAD is the AMR option 2 VAD, which uses parameters of the speech encoder, and is more robust against environmental noise than AMR1 and G.729. The dual mode speech transmission achieves a significant bit rate reduction in digital speech coding since about 60% of the time the transmitted signal contains just silence in a phone-based communication.

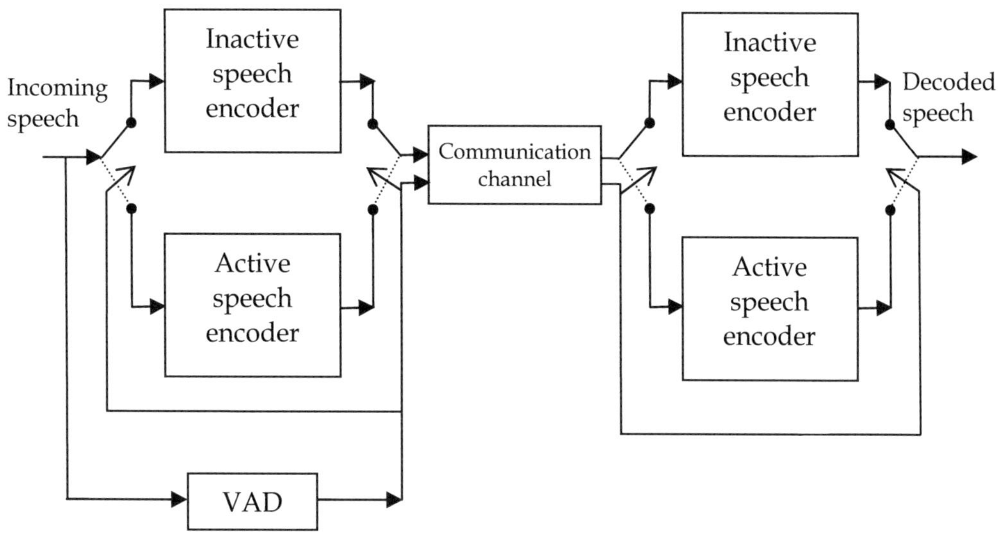

Figure 1. Speech coding with VAD for DTX.

2.2 Speech enhancement

Speech enhancement aims at improving the performance of speech communication systems in noisy environments. It mainly deals with suppressing background noise from a noisy signal. A difficulty in designing efficient speech enhancement systems is the lack of explicit statistical models for the speech signal and noise process. In addition, the speech signal, and possibly also the noise process, are not strictly stationary processes. Speech enhancement normally assumes that the noise source is additive and not correlated with the clean speech signal. One of the most popular methods for reducing the effect of background (additive) noise is spectral subtraction (Boll, 1979). The popularity of spectral subtraction is largely due to its relative simplicity and ease of implementation. The spectrum of noise N(f) is estimated during speech inactive periods and subtracted from the spectrum of the current frame $X(f)$ resulting in an estimate of the spectrum $S(f)$ of the clean speech:

$$|S(f)| = |X(f)| - |N(f)| \tag{1}$$

There exist many refinements of the original method that improve the quality of the enhanced speech. As an example, the modified spectral subtraction enabling an over-subtraction factor α and maximum attenuation β for the noise is given by:

$$|S(f)| = \max\{|X(f)| - \alpha|N(f)|, \beta|X(f)|\} \quad (2)$$

Generally, spectral subtraction is suitable for stationary or very slow varying noises so that the statistics of noise could be updated during speech inactive periods. Another popular method for speech enhancement is the Wiener filter that obtains a least squares estimate of the clean signal $s(t)$ under stationary assumptions of speech and noise. The frequency response of the Wiener filter is defined to be:

$$W(f) = \frac{\Phi_{ss}(f)}{\Phi_{ss}(f) + \Phi_{nn}(f)} \quad (3)$$

and requires an estimate of the power spectrum $\Phi_{ss}(f)$ of the clean speech and the power spectrum $\Phi_{nn}(f)$ of the noise.

2.3 Speech recognition

Performance of speech recognition systems is strongly influenced by the quality of the speech signal. Most of these systems are based on complex hidden Markov models (HMM) that are trained using a training speech database. The mismatch between the training conditions and the testing conditions has a deep impact on the accuracy of these systems and represents a barrier for their operation in noisy environments. Fig. 2 shows an example of the degradation of the word accuracy for the AURORA2 database and speech recognition task when the ETSI recommendation (ETSI, 2000) not including noise compensation algorithm is used as feature extraction process. Note that, when the HMMs are trained using clean speech, the recognizer performance rapidly decreases when the level of background noise increases. Better results are obtained when the HMMs are trained using a collection of clean and noisy speech records.

VAD is a very useful technique for improving the performance of speech recognition systems working in these scenarios. A VAD module is used in most of the speech recognition systems within the feature extraction process for speech enhancement. The noise statistics such as its spectrum are estimated during non-speech periods in order to apply the speech enhancement algorithm (spectral subtraction or Wiener filter). On the other hand, non-speech frame-dropping (FD) is also a frequently used technique in speech recognition to reduce the number of insertion errors caused by the noise. It consists on dropping non-speech periods (based on the VAD decision) from the input of the speech recognizer. This reduces the number of insertion errors due to the noise that can be a serious error source under high mismatch training/testing conditions. Fig. 3 shows an example of a typical robust speech recognition system incorporating spectral noise reduction and non-speech frame-dropping. After the speech enhancement process is applied, the Mel frequency cepstral coefficients and its first- and second-order derivatives are computed in a frame by frame basis to form a feature vector suitable for recognition. Figure 4 shows the improvement provided by a speech recognition system incorporating the VAD presented in (Ramirez et al., 2005) within an enhanced feature extraction process based on a Wiener filter and non-speech frame dropping for the AURORA 2 database and tasks. The relative improvement over (ETSI, 2000) is about 27.17% in multicondition and 60.31% in clean condition training/testing.

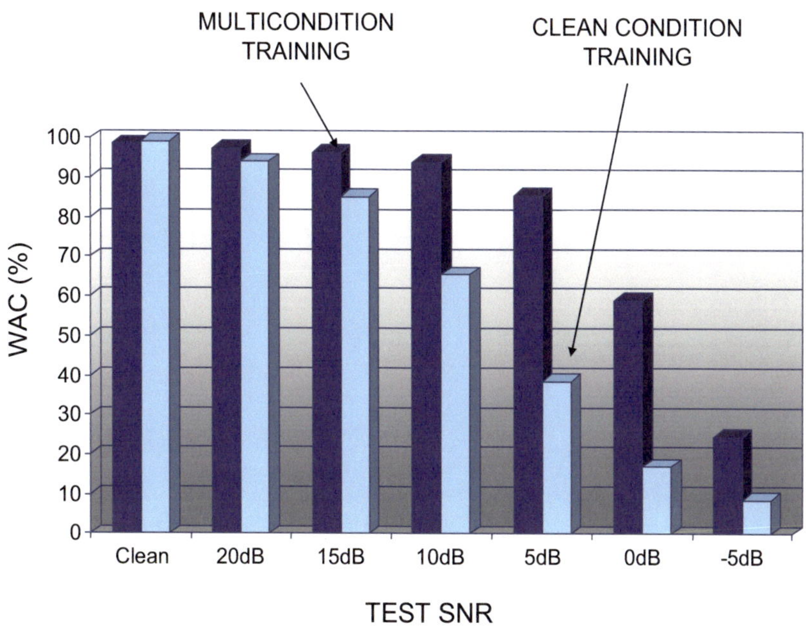

Figure 2. Speech recognition performance for the AURORA-2 database and tasks.

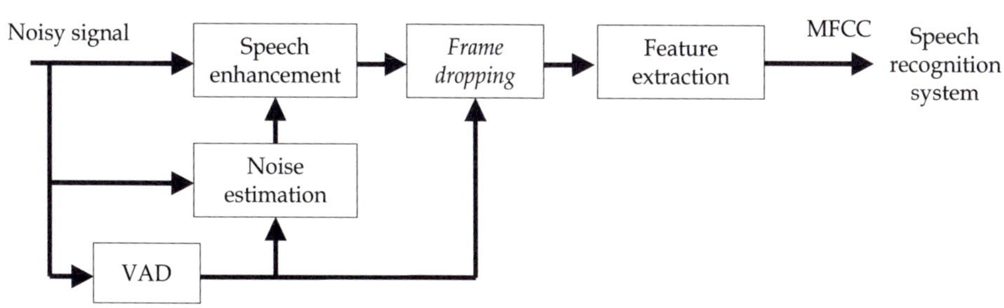

Figure 3. Feature extraction with spectral noise reduction and non-speech frame-dropping.

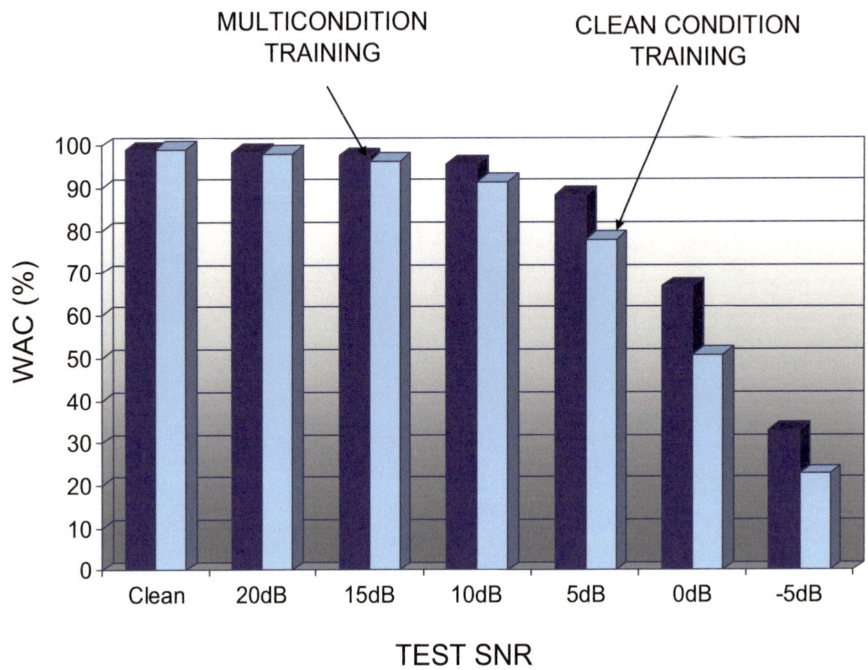

Figure 4. Results obtained for an enhanced feature extraction process incorporating VAD-based Wiener filtering and non-speech frame-dropping.

3. Voice activity detection in noisy environments

An important problem in many areas of speech processing is the determination of presence of speech periods in a given signal. This task can be identified as a statistical hypothesis problem and its purpose is the determination to which category or class a given signal belongs. The decision is made based on an observation vector, frequently called feature vector, which serves as the input to a decision rule that assigns a sample vector to one of the given classes. The classification task is often not as trivial as it appears since the increasing level of background noise degrades the classifier effectiveness, thus leading to numerous detection errors. Fig. 5 illustrates the challenge of detecting speech presence in a noisy signal when the level of background noise increases and the noise completely masks the speech signal. The selection of an adequate feature vector for signal detection and a robust decision rule is a challenging problem that affects the performance of VADs working under noise conditions. Most algorithms are effective in numerous applications but often cause detection errors mainly due to the loss of discriminating power of the decision rule at low SNR levels (ITU, 1996; ETSI, 1999). For example, a simple energy level detector can work satisfactorily in high signal-to-noise ratio (SNR) conditions, but would fail significantly when the SNR drops. VAD results more critical in non-stationary noise environments since it is needed to update the constantly varying noise statistics affecting a misclassification error strongly to the system performance.

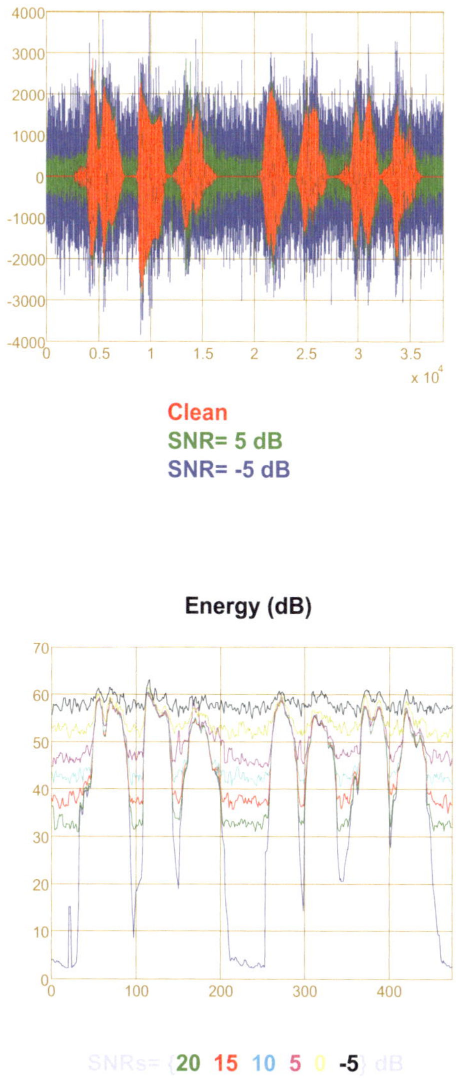

Figure 5. Energy profile of a speech utterance corrupted by additive backgorund noise at decreasing SNRs.

3.1 Description of the problem

The VAD problem considers detecting the presence of speech in a noisy signal. The VAD decision is normally based on a feature vector **x**. Assuming that the speech signals and the noise are additive, the VAD module has to decide in favour of the two hypotheses:

$$\begin{array}{lcl} H_0 & : & \mathbf{x} = \mathbf{n} \\ H_1 & : & \mathbf{x} = \mathbf{n} + \mathbf{s} \end{array} \tag{4}$$

A block diagram of VAD is shown in figure 6. It consists of: *i*) the feature extraction process, *ii*) the decision module, and *iii*) the decision smoothing stage.

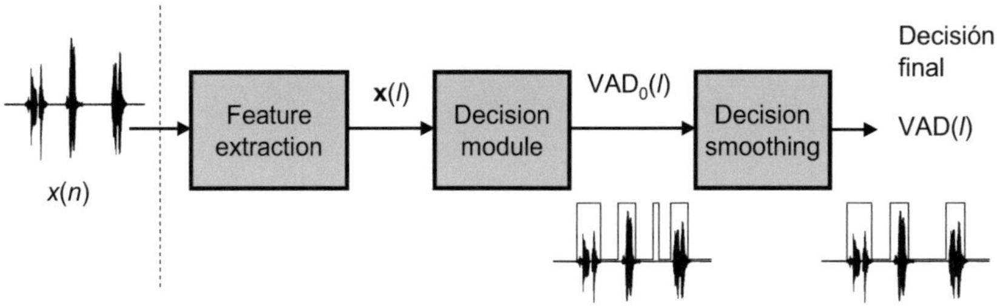

Figure 6. Block diagram of a VAD.

3.2 Feature extraction

The objective of feature extraction process is to compute discriminative speech features suitable for detection. A number of robust speech features have been studied in this context. The different approaches include: *i*) full-band and subband energies (Woo et al., 2000), *ii*) spectrum divergence measures between speech and background noise (Marzinzik and Kollmeier, 2002), *iii*) pitch estimation (Tucker, 1992), *iv*) zero crossing rate (Rabiner et al., 1975), and *v*) higher-order statistics (Nemer et al. 2001; Ramírez et al., 2006a; Górriz et al., 2006a; Ramírez et al., 2007). Most of the VAD methods are based on the current observation (frame) and do not consider contextual information. However, using long-term speech information (Ramírez et al., 2004a; Ramírez et al. 2005a) has shown significant benefits for detecting speech presence in high noise environments.

3.3 Formulation of the decision rule

The decision module defines the rule or method for assigning a class (speech or silence) to the feature vector **x**. Sohn et al. (Sohn et al., 1999) proposed a robust VAD algorithm based on a statistical likelihood ratio test (LRT) involving a single observation vector. (Sohn et al., 1999). The method considered a two-hypothesis test where the optimal decision rule that minimizes the error probability is the Bayes classifier. Given an observation vector to be classified, the problem is reduced to selecting the class (H_0 or H_1) with the largest posterior probability $P(H_i\,|\,\mathbf{x})$:

$$P(H_1\,|\,\mathbf{x}) \underset{H_0}{\overset{H_1}{\gtrless}} P(H_0\,|\,\mathbf{x}) \tag{5}$$

Using the Bayes rule leads to statistical likelihood ratio test:

$$\frac{P(\mathbf{x}|H_1)}{P(\mathbf{x}|H_0)} \underset{H_0}{\overset{H_1}{\gtrless}} \frac{P(H_0)}{P(H_1)} \tag{6}$$

In order to evaluate this test, the discrete Fourier transform (DFT) coefficients of the clean speech (S_j) and the noise (N_j) are assumed to be asymptotically independent Gaussian random variables:

$$\begin{aligned} p(x|H_0) &= \prod_{j=0}^{J-1} \frac{1}{\pi\lambda_N(j)} \exp\left\{ -\frac{|X_j|^2}{\lambda_N(j)} \right\} \\ p(x|H_1) &= \prod_{j=0}^{J-1} \frac{1}{\pi\left[\lambda_S(j)+\lambda_N(j)\right]} \exp\left\{ -\frac{|X_j|^2}{\lambda_S(j)+\lambda_N(j)} \right\} \end{aligned} \tag{7}$$

where X_j represents the noisy speech DFT coefficients, and $\lambda_N(j)$ and $\lambda_S(j)$ denote the variances of N_j and S_j for the j-th bin of the DFT, respectively. Thus, the decision rule is reduced to:

$$\frac{1}{J}\sum_{j=0}^{J-1}\left[\frac{\gamma_j\xi_j}{1+\xi_j} - \log(1+\xi_j)\right] \underset{H_0}{\overset{H_1}{\gtrless}} \eta \tag{8}$$

and η defines the decision threshold and J is the DFT order. ξ_j and γ_j define the *a priori* and *a posteriori* SNRs:

$$\gamma_j = \frac{|X_j|^2}{\lambda_N(j)} \qquad \xi_j = \frac{\lambda_S(j)}{\lambda_N(j)} \tag{9}$$

that are normally estimated using the Ephraim and Malah minimum mean-square error (MMSE) estimator (Ephraim and Malah, 1984).

Several methods for VAD formulate the decision rule based on distance measures like the Euclidean distance (Gorriz et al., 2006b), Itakura-Saito and Kullback-Leibler divergence (Ramírez et al., 2004b). Other techniques include fuzzy logic (Beritelli et al., 2002), support vector machines (SVM) (Ramírez et al. 2006b) and genetic algorithms (Estevez et al., 2005).

3.4 Decision smoothing

Most of the VADs that formulate the decision rule on a frame by frame basis normally use decision smoothing algorithms in order to improve the robustness against the noise. The motivations for these approaches are found in the speech production process and the reduced signal energy of word beginnings and endings. The so called hang-over algorithms extends and smooth the VAD decision in order to recover speech periods that are masked by the acoustic noise.

4. Robust VAD algorithms

This section summarizes three VAD algorithms recently reported that yield high speech/non-speech discrimination in noisy environments.

4.1 Long-term spectral divergence

The speech/non-speech detection algorithm proposed in (Ramírez et al., 2004a) assumes that the most significant information for detecting voice activity on a noisy speech signal remains on the time-varying signal spectrum magnitude. It uses a long-term speech window instead of instantaneous values of the spectrum to track the spectral envelope and is based on the estimation of the so called Long-Term Spectral Envelope (LTSE). The decision rule is then formulated in terms of the Long-Term Spectral Divergence (LTSD) between speech and noise.
Let $x(n)$ be a noisy speech signal that is segmented into overlapped frames and, $X(k,l)$ its amplitude spectrum for the k-th band at frame l. The N-order Long-Term Spectral Envelope (LTSE) is defined as:

$$LTSE_N(k,l) = \max\{X(k,l+j)\}_{j=-N}^{j=+N} \tag{9}$$

The VAD decision rule is then formulated by means of the N-order Long-Term Spectral Divergence (LTSD) between speech and noise is defined as the deviation of the LTSE respect to the average noise spectrum magnitude $N(k)$ for the k band, k= 0, 1, …, $NFFT$-1, and is given by:

$$LTSD_N(l) = 10\log_{10}\left(\frac{1}{NFFT}\sum_{k=0}^{NFFT-1}\frac{LTSE^2(k,l)}{N^2(k)}\right) \underset{H_0}{\overset{H_1}{\gtrless}} \eta \tag{9}$$

4.2 Multiple observation likelihood ratio test

An improvement over the LRT proposed by Sohn (Sohn et al., 1999) is the multiple observation LRT (MO-LRT) proposed by Ramírez (Ramírez et al., 2005b). The performance of the decision rule was improved by incorporating more observations to the statistical test. The MO-LRT is defined over the observation vectors $\{\mathbf{x}_{l-m},\ldots,\mathbf{x}_l,\ldots\mathbf{x}_{l+m}\}$ as follows:

$$\ell_{l,m} = \sum_{k=l-m}^{l+m} \ln\left(\frac{p(\mathbf{x}_k \mid H_1)}{p(\mathbf{x}_k \mid H_0)}\right) \underset{H_0}{\overset{H_1}{\gtrless}} \eta \tag{10}$$

where l denotes the frame being classified as speech (H_1) or silence (H_0). Thus, the decision rule is formulated over a sliding window consisting of observation vectors around the current frame. The so-defined decision rule reported significant improvements in speech/non-speech discrimination accuracy over existing VAD methods that are defined on a single observation and need empirically tuned hangover mechanisms.

4.3 Order statistics filters

The MO-LRT VAD takes advantage of using contextual information for the formulation of the decision rule. The same idea can be found in other existing VADs like the Li et al. (Li et al., 2002) that considers optimum edge detection linear filters on the full-band energy. Order statistics filters (OSFs) have been also evaluated for a low variance measure of the divergence between speech and silence (noise). The algorithm proposed in (Ramírez et al., 2005a) uses two OSFs for the multiband quantile (MBQ) SNR estimation. The algorithm is described as follows. Once the input speech has been de-noised by Wiener filtering, the log-energies for the l-th frame, $E(k,l)$, in K subbands (k= 0, 1, …, K-1), are computed by means of:

$$E(k,l) = \log\left(\frac{K}{NFFT}\sum_{m=m_k}^{m_{k+1}-1}|Y(m,l|^2\right) \qquad m_k = \left\lfloor \frac{NFFT}{2K}k \right\rfloor \qquad k = 0,1,\ldots,K-1 \tag{11}$$

The implementation of both OSFs is based on a sequence of log-energy values $\{E(k,l\text{-}N), \ldots, E(k,l), \ldots, E(k,l+N)\}$ around the frame to be analyzed. The r-th order statistics of this sequence, $E_{(r)}(k,l)$, is defined as the r-th largest number in algebraic order. A first OSF estimates the subband signal energy by means of

$$Q_p(k,l) = (1-f)E_{(s)}(k,l) + fE_{(s+1)}(k,l) \tag{12}$$

where $Q_p(k,l)$ is the sampling quantile, $s= \lfloor 2pN \rfloor$ and $f= 2pN\text{-}s$. Finally, the SNR in each subband is measured by:

$$QSNR(k,l) = Q_p(k,l) - E_N(k) \tag{13}$$

where $E_N(k)$ is the noise level in the k-th band that needs to be estimated. For the initialization of the algorithm, the first frames are assumed to be non-speech frames and the noise level $E_N(k)$ in the k-th band is estimated as the median of the set $\{E(0,k), E(1,k), \ldots, E(N\text{-}1,k)\}$. In order to track non-stationary noisy environments, the noise references are updated during non-speech periods by means of a second OSF (a median filter)

$$E_N(k) = \alpha E_N(k) + (1-\alpha)Q_{0.5}(k,l) \tag{14}$$

where $Q_{0.5}(k,l)$ is the output of the median filter and α= 0.97 was experimentally selected. On the other hand, the sampling quantile p= 0.9 is selected as a good estimation of the subband spectral envelope. The decision rule is then formulated in terms of the average subband SNR:

$$SNR(l) = \frac{1}{K}\sum_{k=0}^{K-1} QSNR(k,l) \underset{H_0}{\overset{H_1}{\gtrless}} \eta \tag{15}$$

Figure 7 shows the operation of the MBQ VAD on an utterance of the Spanish SpeechDat-Car (SDC) database (Moreno et al., 2000). For this example, K= 2 subbands were used while N= 8 . The optimal selection of these parameters is studied in (Ramirez et al., 2005a). It is clearly shown how the SNR in the upper and lower band yields improved speech/non-speech discrimination of fricative sounds by giving complementary information. The VAD performs an advanced detection of beginnings and delayed detection of word endings which, in part, makes a hang-over unnecessary.

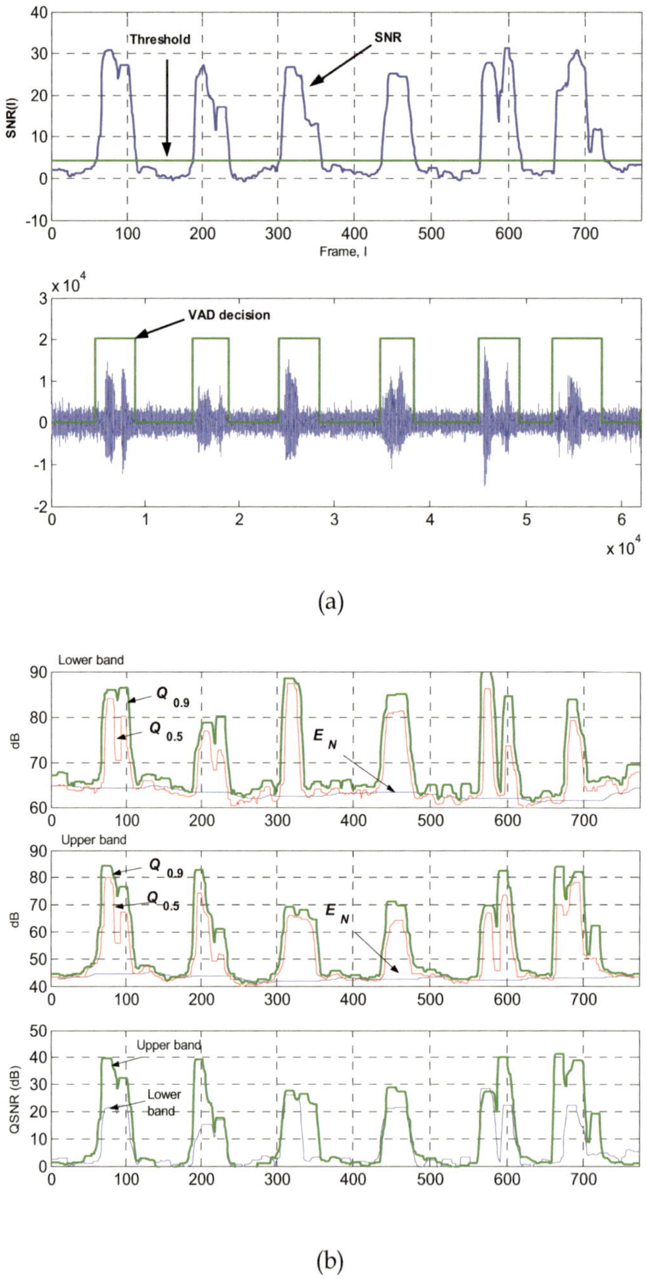

Figure 7. Operation of the VAD on an utterance of Spanish SDC database. (a) SNR and VAD decision. (b) Subband SNRs.

5. Experimental framework

Several experiments are commonly conducted to evaluate the performance of VAD algorithms. The analysis is mainly focussed on the determination of the error probabilities or classification errors at different SNR levels (Marzinzik and Kollmeier, 2002), and the influence of the VAD decision on the performance of speech processing systems (Bouquin-Jeannes and Faucon, 1995). Subjective performance tests have also been considered for the evaluation of VADs working in combination with speech coders (Benyassine et al., 1997). The experimental framework and the objective performance tests commonly conducted to evaluate VAD methods are described in this section.

5.1 Speech/non-speech discrimination analysis

VADs are widely evaluated in terms of the ability to discriminate between speech and pause periods at different SNR levels. In order to illustrate the analysis, this subsection considers the evaluation of the LTSE VAD (Ramírez et al., 2004). The original AURORA-2 database (Hirsch and Pearce, 2000) was used in this analysis since it uses the clean TIdigits database consisting of sequences of up to seven connected digits spoken by American English talkers as source speech, and a selection of eight different real-world noises that have been artificially added to the speech at SNRs of 20dB, 15dB, 10dB, 5dB, 0dB and -5dB. These noisy signals have been recorded at different places (suburban train, crowd of people (babble), car, exhibition hall, restaurant, street, airport and train station), and were selected to represent the most probable application scenarios for telecommunication terminals. In the discrimination analysis, the clean TIdigits database was used to manually label each utterance as speech or non-speech frames for reference. Detection performance as a function of the SNR was assessed in terms of the non-speech hit-rate (HR0) and the speech hit-rate (HR1) defined as the fraction of all actual pause or speech frames that are correctly detected as pause or speech frames, respectively:

$$\mathrm{HR0} = \frac{N_{0,0}}{N_0^{ref}} \qquad \mathrm{HR1} = \frac{N_{1,1}}{N_1^{ref}} \tag{15}$$

where N_0^{ref} and N_1^{ref} are the number of real non-speech and speech frames in the whole database, respectively, while $N_{0,0}$ and $N_{1,1}$ are the number of non-speech and speech frames correctly classified.

Figure 8 provides the results of this analysis and compares the proposed LTSE VAD algorithm to standard G.729, AMR and AFE (ETSI, 2002) VADs in terms of non-speech hit-rate (HR0, Fig. 8.a) and speech hit-rate (HR1, Fig. 8.b) for clean conditions and SNR levels ranging from 20 to -5 dB. Note that results for the two VADs defined in the AFE DSR standard (ETSI, 2002) for estimating the noise spectrum in the Wiener filtering stage and non-speech frame-dropping are provided. It can be concluded that LTSE achieves the best compromise among the different VADs tested; it obtains a good behavior in detecting non-speech periods as well as exhibits a slow decay in performance at unfavorable noise conditions in speech detection.

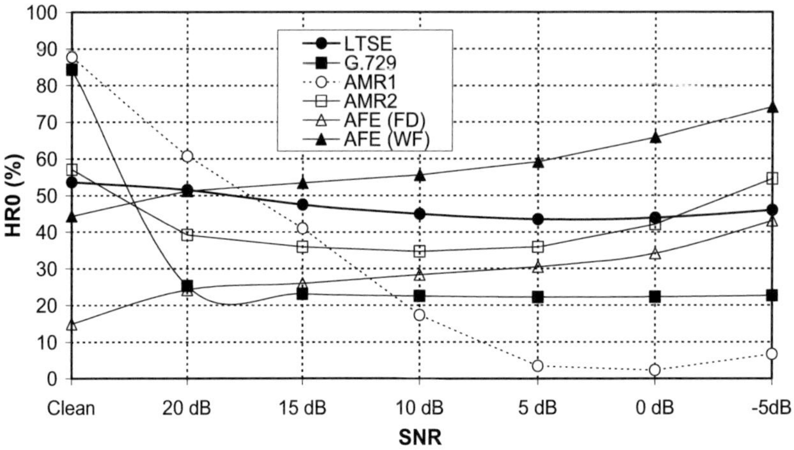

(a)

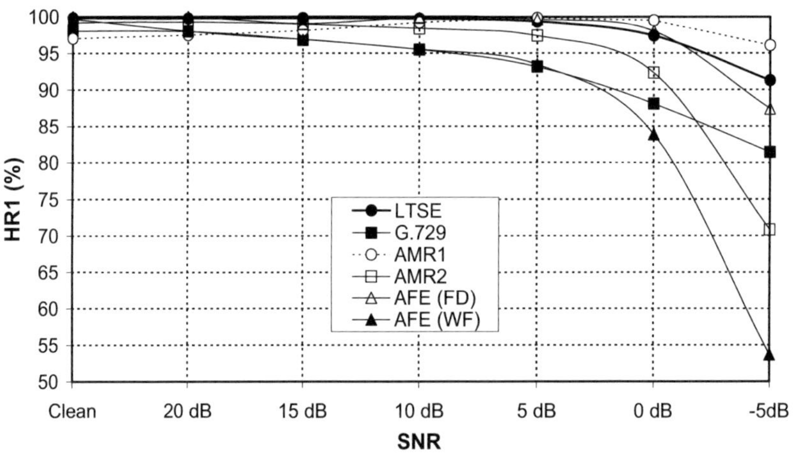

Figure 8. Speech/non-speech discrimination analysis. (a) Non-speech hit-rate (HR0). (b) Speech hit rate (HR1).

5.2 Receiver operating characteristics curves

The ROC curves are frequently used to completely describe the VAD error rate. The AURORA subset of the original Spanish SpeechDat-Car (SDC) database (Moreno et al., 2000) was used in this analysis. This database contains 4914 recordings using close-talking and distant microphones from more than 160 speakers. The files are categorized into three noisy conditions: quiet, low noisy and highly noisy conditions, which represent different driving conditions with average SNR values between 25 dB, and 5 dB. The non-speech hit rate (HR0) and the false alarm rate (FAR0= 100-HR1) were determined in each noise condition being the actual speech frames and actual speech pauses determined by hand-labeling the database on the close-talking microphone.

Figure 9 shows the ROC curves of the MO-LRT VAD (Ramírez et al., 2005b) and other frequently referred algorithms for recordings from the distant microphone in quiet and high noisy conditions. The working points of the G.729, AMR, and AFE VADs are also included. The results show improvements in detection accuracy over standard VADs and over a representative set of VAD algorithms. Thus, among all the VAD examined, our VAD yields the lowest false alarm rate for a fixed non-speech hit rate and also, the highest non-speech hit rate for a given false alarm rate. The benefits are especially important over G.729, which is used along with a speech codec for discontinuous transmission, and over the Li's algorithm, that is based on an optimum linear filter for edge detection. The proposed VAD also improves Marzinzik's VAD that tracks the power spectral envelopes, and the Sohn's VAD, that formulates the decision rule by means of a statistical likelihood ratio test.

5.3 Improvement in speech recognition systems

Performance of ASR systems working over wireless networks and noisy environments normally decreases and non efficient speech/non-speech detection appears to be an important degradation source (Karray and Martin, 2003). Although the discrimination analysis or the ROC curves are effective to evaluate a given algorithm, this section evaluates the VAD according to the goal for which it was developed by assessing the influence of the VAD over the performance of a speech recognition system.

The reference framework considered for these experiments was the ETSI AURORA project for DSR (ETSI, 2000; ETSI, 2002). The recognizer is based on the HTK (Hidden Markov Model Toolkit) software package (Young et al., 1997). The task consists of recognizing connected digits which are modeled as whole word HMMs (Hidden Markov Models) with the following parameters: 16 states per word, simple left-to-right models, mixture of three Gaussians per state (diagonal covariance matrix) while speech pause models consist of three states with a mixture of six Gaussians per state. The 39-parameter feature vector consists of 12 cepstral coefficients (without the zero-order coefficient), the logarithmic frame energy plus the corresponding delta and acceleration coefficients.

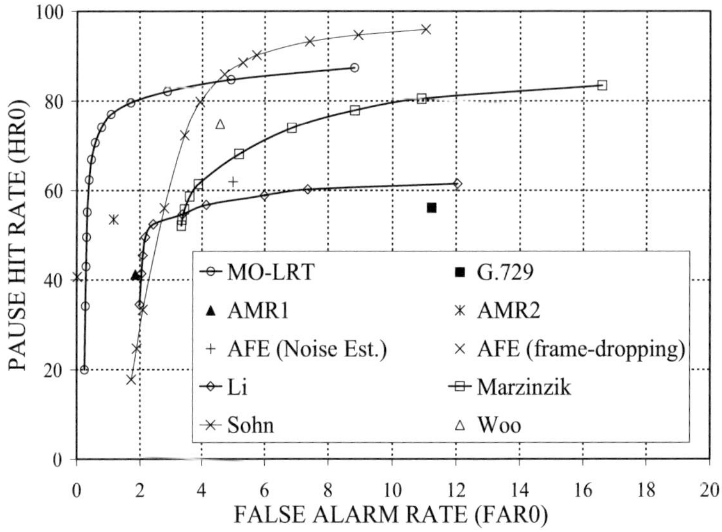

(a)

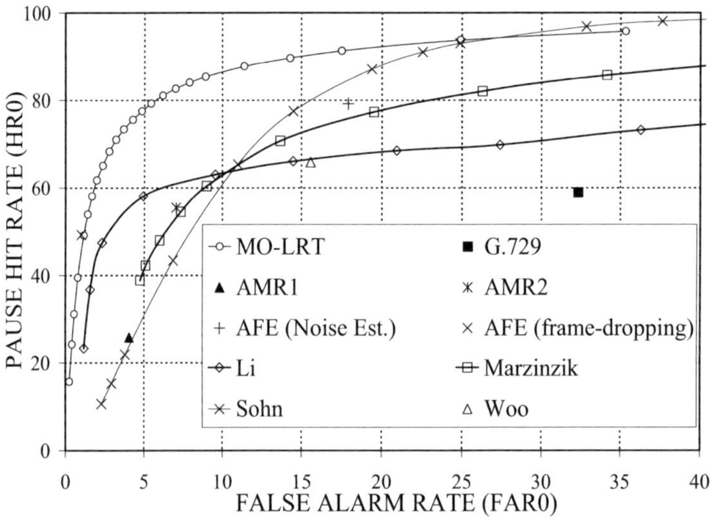

(b)

Figure 9. ROC curves. (a) Stopped Car, Motor Running. (b) High Speed, Good Road.

	G.729	AMR1	AMR2	AFE	**MBQW**

WF	66.19	74.97	83.37	81.57	**84.12**
WF+FD	70.32	74.29	82.89	83.29	**86.09**
	Woo	Li	Marzinzik	Sohn	Hand-labeled
WF	83.64	77.43	84.02	83.89	84.69
WF+FD	81.09	82.11	85.23	83.80	86.86

Table 1. Average Word Accuracy (%) for the AURORA 2 database for clean and multicondition training experiments. Results are mean values for all the noises and SNRs ranging from 20 to 0 dB.

Two training modes are defined for the experiments conducted on the AURORA-2 database: *i*) training on clean data only (Clean Training), and *ii*) training on clean and noisy data (multicondition training). For the AURORA-3 SpeechDat-Car databases, the so called well-matched (WM), medium-mismatch (MM) and high-mismatch (HM) conditions are used. These databases contain recordings from the close-talking and distant microphones. In WM condition, both close-talking and hands-free microphones are used for training and testing. In MM condition, both training and testing are performed using the hands-free microphone recordings. In HM condition, training is done using close-talking microphone material from all driving conditions while testing is done using hands-free microphone material taken for low noise and high noise driving conditions. Finally, recognition performance is assessed in terms of the word accuracy (WAcc) that considers deletion, substitution and insertion errors. An enhanced feature extraction scheme incorporating a noise reduction algorithm and non-speech frame-dropping was built on the base system (ETSI, 2000). The noise reduction algorithm has been implemented as a single Wiener filtering stage as described in the AFE standard (ETSI, 2002) but without mel-scale warping. No other mismatch reduction techniques already present in the AFE standard have been considered since they are not affected by the VAD decision and can mask the impact of the VAD precision on the overall system performance.

Table 1 shows the recognition performance achieved by the different VADs that were compared. These results are averaged over the three test sets of the AURORA-2 recognition experiments and SNRs between 20 and 0 dBs. Note that, for the recognition experiments based on the AFE VADs, the same configuration of the standard (ETSI, 2002), which considers different VADs for WF and FD, was used. The MBQW VAD outperforms G.729, AMR1, AMR2 and AFE standard VADs in both clean and multi condition training/testing experiments. When compared to recently reported VAD algorithms, it yields better results being the one that is closer to the "ideal" hand-labeled speech recognition performance.

		Base	Base + WF					Base + WF + FD				
			G.729	AMR1	AMR2	AFE	**MBQW**	G.729	AMR1	AMR2	AFE	**MBQW**
Finnish	WM	92.74	93.27	93.66	95.52	94.28	95.36	88.62	94.57	95.52	94.25	94.70
	MM	80.51	75.99	78.93	75.51	78.52	74.49	67.99	81.60	79.55	82.42	80.08
	HM	40.53	50.81	40.95	55.41	55.05	56.40	65.80	77.14	80.21	56.89	83.67
	Average	**71.26**	73.36	71.18	75.48	75.95	**75.42**	74.14	84.44	85.09	77.85	**86.15**
Spanish	WM	92.94	89.83	85.48	91.24	89.71	91.66	88.62	94.65	95.67	95.28	96.79
	MM	83.31	79.62	79.31	81.44	76.12	83.95	72.84	80.59	90.91	90.23	91.85
	HM	51.55	66.59	56.39	70.14	68.84	70.47	65.50	62.41	85.77	77.53	87.25
	Average	**75.93**	78.68	73.73	80.94	78.22	**82.03**	75.65	74.33	90.78	87.68	**91.96**
German	WM	91.20	90.60	90.20	93.13	91.48	92.87	87.20	90.36	92.79	93.03	93.73
	MM	81.04	82.94	77.67	86.02	84.11	85.58	68.52	78.48	83.87	85.43	87.40
	HM	73.17	78.40	70.40	83.07	82.01	82.56	72.48	66.23	81.77	83.16	83.49
	Average	**81.80**	83.98	79.42	87.41	85.87	**87.00**	76.07	78.36	86.14	87.21	**88.21**
Average		**76.33**	78.67	74.78	81.28	80.01	**81.48**	75.29	79.04	87.34	84.25	**88.77**

(a)

		Base	Base + WF					Base + WF + FD				
			Woo	Li	Marzinzik	Sohn	**MBQW**	Woo	Li	Marzinzik	Sohn	**MBQW**
Finnish	WM	92.74	95.25	95.15	95.39	95.21	95.36	86.81	85.60	93.73	93.84	94.70
	MM	80.51	77.70	76.74	73.94	72.16	74.49	66.62	55.63	76.47	80.10	80.08
	HM	40.53	57.74	53.85	57.28	57.24	56.40	62.54	58.34	68.37	75.34	83.67
	Average	**71.26**	76.90	75.25	75.54	74.87	**75.42**	71.99	66.52	79.52	83.09	**86.15**
Spanish	WM	92.94	90.85	91.24	91.31	91.25	91.66	95.35	91.82	94.29	96.07	96.79
	MM	83.31	81.07	84.00	82.90	82.21	83.95	89.30	77.45	89.81	91.64	91.85
	HM	51.55	61.38	64.72	65.05	69.89	70.47	83.64	78.52	79.43	84.03	87.25
	Average	**75.93**	77.77	79.99	79.75	81.12	**82.03**	89.43	82.60	87.84	90.58	**91.96**
German	WM	91.20	92.83	92.25	93.17	93.17	92.87	91.59	89.62	91.58	93.23	93.73
	MM	81.04	85.58	85.21	85.29	86.09	85.58	80.28	70.87	83.67	83.97	87.40
	HM	73.17	83.02	82.98	83.02	83.53	82.56	78.68	78.55	81.27	82.19	83.49
	Average	**81.80**	87.14	86.81	87.16	87.60	**87.00**	83.52	79.68	85.51	86.46	**88.21**
Average		**76.33**	80.60	80.68	80.82	81.20	**81.48**	81.65	76.27	84.29	86.71	**88.77**

(b)

Table 2. Average Word Accuracy for the SpeechDat-Car databases. (a) Comparison to standardized VADs. (b) Comparison to other recently reported methods.

Table 2 shows the recognition performance for the Finnish, Spanish, and German SDC databases for the different training/test mismatch conditions (HM, high mismatch, MM: medium mismatch and WM: well matched) when WF and FD are performed on the base system (ETSI, 2000). Again, MBQW VAD outperforms all the algorithms used for reference, yielding relevant improvements in speech recognition. Note that the SDC databases used in the AURORA 3 experiments have longer non-speech periods than the AURORA 2 database and then, the effectiveness of the VAD results more important for the speech recognition system. This fact can be clearly shown when comparing the performance of MBQW VAD to Marzinzik's VAD. The word accuracy of both VADs is quite similar for the AURORA 2 task. However, MBQW yields a significant performance improvement over Marzinzik's VAD for the SDC databases.

6. Conclusions

This chapter has shown an overview of the main challenges in robust speech detection and a review of the state of the art and applications. VADs are frequently used in a number of applications including speech coding, speech enhancement and speech recognition. A precise VAD extracts a set of discriminative speech features from the noisy speech and formulates the decision in terms of well defined rule. The chapter has summarized three robust VAD methods that yield high speech/non-speech discrimination accuracy and improve the performance of speech recognition systems working in noisy environments. The evaluation of these methods showed the experiments most commonly conducted to compare VADs: *i*) speech/non-speech discrimination analysis, *ii*) the receiver operating characteristic curves, and iii) speech recognition system tests.

7. Acknowledgements

This work has received research funding from the EU 6th Framework Programme, under contract number IST-2002-507943 (HIWIRE, Human Input that Works in Real Environments) and SR3-VoIP project (TEC2004-03829/TCM) from the Spanish government. The views expressed here are those of the authors only. The Community is not liable for any use that may be made of the information contained therein.

8. References

Karray, L.; Martin. A. (2003). Toward improving speech detection robustness for speech recognition in adverse environments, *Speech Communication*, no. 3, pp. 261–276.

Ramírez, J.; Segura, J.C.; Benítez, C.; de la Torre, A.; Rubio, A. (2003). A new adaptive long-term spectral estimation voice activity detector, *Proc. EUROSPEECH 2003*, Geneva, Switzerland, pp. 3041–3044.

ITU-T Recommendation G.729-Annex B. (1996). A silence compression scheme for G.729 optimized for terminals conforming to recommendation V.70.

ETSI EN 301 708 Recommendation. (1999). Voice Activity Detector (VAD) for Adaptive Multi-Rate (AMR) Speech Traffic Channels.

Sangwan, A.; Chiranth, M.C.; Jamadagni, H.S.; Sah, R.; Prasad, R.V.; Gaurav, V. (2002). VAD Techniques for Real-Time Speech Transmission on the Internet, *IEEE International Conference on High-Speed Networks and Multimedia Communications*, pp. 46-50.

Basbug, F.; Swaminathan, K.; Nandkumar, S. (2004). Noise reduction and echo cancellation front-end for speech codecs, *IEEE Trans. Speech Audio Processing*, vol. 11, no. 1, pp. 1–13.

Gustafsson, S.; Martin, R.; Jax, P.; Vary, P. (2002). A psychoacoustic approach to combined acoustic echo cancellation and noise reduction, *IEEE Trans. Speech and Audio Processing*, vol. 10, no. 5, pp. 245–256.

Sohn, J.; Kim, N.S.; Sung, W. (1999). A statistical model-based voice activity detection, *IEEE Signal Processing Letters*, vol. 16, no. 1, pp. 1–3.

Cho, Y.D.; Kondoz, A. (2001). Analysis and improvement of a statistical model-based voice activity detector, *IEEE Signal Processing Letters*, vol. 8, no. 10, pp. 276–278.

Gazor, S.; Zhang, W. (2003). A soft voice activity detector based on a Laplacian-Gaussian model, *IEEE Trans. Speech Audio Processing*, vol. 11, no. 5, pp. 498–505.

Armani, L.; Matassoni, M.; Omologo, M.; Svaizer, P. (2003). Use of a CSP-based voice activity detector for distant-talking ASR, *Proc. EUROSPEECH 2003*, Geneva, Switzerland, pp. 501–504.

Bouquin-Jeannes, R.L.; Faucon, G. (1995). Study of a voice activity detector and its influence on a noise reduction system, *Speech Communication*, vol. 16, pp. 245–254.

Woo, K.; Yang, T.; Park, K.; Lee, C. (2000). Robust voice activity detection algorithm for estimating noise spectrum, *Electronics Letters*, vol. 36, no. 2, pp. 180–181.

Li, Q.; Zheng, J.; Tsai, A.; Zhou, Q. (2002). Robust endpoint detection and energy normalization for real-time speech and speaker recognition, *IEEE Trans. Speech Audio Processing*, vol. 10, no. 3, pp. 146–157.

Marzinzik, M.; Kollmeier, B. (2002). Speech pause detection for noise spectrum estimation by tracking power envelope dynamics, *IEEE Trans. Speech Audio Processing*, vol. 10, no. 6, pp. 341-351.

Chengalvarayan, R. (1999). Robust energy normalization using speech/non-speech discriminator for German connected digit recognition, *Proc. EUROSPEECH 1999*, Budapest, Hungary, pp. 61–64.

Tucker, R. (1992). Voice activity detection using a periodicity measure, *Proc. Inst. Elect. Eng.*, vol. 139, no. 4, pp. 377–380.

Nemer, E.; Goubran, R.; Mahmoud, S. (2001). Robust voice activity detection using higher-order statistics in the lpc residual domain, *IEEE Trans. Speech Audio Processing*, vol. 9, no. 3, pp. 217–231.

Tanyer, S.G.; Özer, H. (2000). Voice activity detection in nonstationary noise, *IEEE Trans. Speech Audio Processing*, vol. 8, no. 4, pp. 478–482.

Freeman, D.K.; Cosier, G.; Southcott, C.B.; Boyd, I. (1989). The Voice Activity Detector for the PAN-European Digital Cellular Mobile Telephone Service, *International Conference on Acoustics, Speech and Signal Processing*, Vol. 1, pp. 369-372.

Itoh, K.; Mizushima, M. (1997). Environmental noise reduction based on speech/non-speech identification for hearing aids, *International Conference on Acoustics, Speech, and Signal Processing*, Vol. 1, pp. 419-422.

Benyassine, A.; Shlomot, E.; Su, H.; Massaloux, D.; Lamblin, C.; Petit, J. (1997). ITU-T Recommendation G.729 Annex B: A silence compression scheme for use with G.729 optimized for V.70 digital simultaneous voice and data applications. *IEEE Communications Magazine*, Vol. 35, No. 9, pp. 64-73.

Boll, S., F. Suppression of Acoustic Noise in Speech Using Spectral Subtraction, *IEEE Transactions on Acoustics, Speech, and Signal Processing*, vol. 27, no. 2, April 1979.

ETSI. (2002). ETSI ES 201 108 Recommendation. Speech Processing, Transmission and Quality aspects (STQ); Distributed speech recognition; Front-end feature extraction algorithm; Compression algorithms.

Ramírez, J.; Segura, J.C.; Benítez, C.; de la Torre, A.; Rubio, A. (2005a). An Effective Subband OSF-based VAD with Noise Reduction for Robust Speech Recognition, *IEEE Transactions on Speech and Audio Processing*, Vol. 13, No. 6, pp. 1119-1129.

Ramírez, J.; Górriz, J.M; Segura, J.C.; Puntonet, C.G; Rubio, A. (2006a). Speech/Non-speech Discrimination based on Contextual Information Integrated Bispectrum LRT, *IEEE Signal Processing Letters*, vol. 13, No. 8, pp. 497-500.

Górriz, J.M.; Ramírez, J.; Puntonet, C.G.; Segura, J.C. (2006a). Generalized LRT-based voice activity detector, *IEEE Signal Processing Letters*, Vol. 13, No. 10, pp. 636-639.

Ramírez, J.; Górriz, J.M.; Segura, J.C. (2007). Statistical Voice Activity Detection Based on Integrated Bispectrum Likelihood Ratio Tests, to appear in *Journal of the Acoustical Society of America*.

Ramírez, J.; Segura, J.C.; Benítez, C.; de la Torre, Á.; Rubio, A. (2004a). Efficient Voice Activity Detection Algorithms Using Long-Term Speech Information, *Speech Communication*, vol. 42, No. 3-4, pp. 271-287.

Ramírez, J.; Segura, J.C.; Benítez, C.; de la Torre, Á.; Rubio, A. (2005). An effective OSF-based VAD with Noise Suppression for Robust Speech Recognition, *IEEE Transactions on Speech and Audio Processing*, vol. 13, No. 6, pp. 1119-1129.

Ephraim Y.; Malah, D. (1984). Speech enhancement using a minimum mean-square error short-time spectral amplitude estimator, IEEE Trans. Acoustics, Speech and Signal Processing, vol. ASSP-32, no. 6, pp. 1109–1121.

Górriz, J.M.; Ramírez, J.; Segura, J.C.; Puntonet, C.G. (2006b). An effective cluster-based model for robust speech detection and speech recognition in noisy environments, *Journal of the Acoustical Society of America*, vol. 120, No. 1, pp. 470-481.

Ramírez, J.; Segura, J.C.; Benítez, C.; de la Torre, Á.; Rubio. A. (2004b). A New Kullback-Leibler VAD for Robust Speech Recognition, *IEEE Signal Processing Letters*, vol. 11, No. 2, pp. 266-269.

Beritelli, F.; Casale, S.; Rugeri, G.; Serrano, S. (2002). Performance evaluation and comparison of G.729/AMR/fuzzy voice activity detectors, *IEEE Signal Processing Letters*, Vol. 9, No. 3, pp. 85–88.

Ramírez, J.; Yélamos, P.; Górriz, J.M; Segura, J.C. (2006b). SVM-based Speech Endpoint Detection Using Contextual Speech Features, *IEE Electronics Letters*, vol. 42, No. 7.

Estevez, P.A.; Becerra-Yoma, N.; Boric, N.; Ramirez, J.A. (2005). Genetic programming-based voice activity detection, *Electronics Letters*, Vol. 41, No. 20, pp. 1141- 1142.

Ramírez, J.; Segura, J.C.; Benítez, C.; García, L.; Rubio, A. (2005b). Statistical Voice Activity Detection using a Multiple Observation Likelihood Ratio Test, *IEEE Signal Processing Letters*, vol. 12, No. 10, pp. 689-692.

Moreno, A.; Borge, L.; Christoph, D.; Gael, R.; Khalid, C.; Stephan, E.; Jeffrey, A. (2000). SpeechDat-Car: A large speech database for automotive environments, *Proc. II LREC Conf.*

Hirsch, H.G.; Pearce, D. (2000). The AURORA experimental framework for the performance evaluation of speech recognition systems under noise conditions, *ISCA ITRW ASR2000: Automatic Speech Recognition: Challenges for the Next Millennium*.

ETSI. (2002). ETSI ES 202 050 Recommend. Speech Processing, Transmission, and Quality Aspects (STQ); Distributed Speech Recognition; Advanced Front-End Feature Extraction Algorithm; Compression Algorithms.

Young, S.; Odell, J.; Ollason, D.; Valtchev, V.; Woodland, P. (1997). The HTK Book. Cambridge, U.K.: Cambridge Univ. Press.

2

Novel Approaches to Speech Detection in the Processing of Continuous Audio Streams

Janez Žibert, Boštjan Vesnicer, France Mihelič
Faculty of Electrical Engineering, University of Ljubljana
Slovenia

1. Introduction

With the increasing amount of information stored in various audio-data documents there is a growing need for the efficient and effective processing, archiving and accessing of this information. One of the largest sources of such information is spoken audio documents, including broadcast-news (BN) shows, voice mails, recorded meetings, telephone conversations, etc. In these documents the information is mainly relayed through speech, which needs to be appropriately processed and analysed by applying automatic speech and language technologies.

Spoken audio documents are produced by a wide range of people in a variety of situations, and are derived from various multimedia applications. They are usually collected as continuous audio streams and consist of multiple audio sources. These audio sources may be different speakers, music segments, types of noise, etc. For example, a BN show typically consists of speech from different speakers as well as music segments, commercials and various types of noises that are present in the background of the reports. In order to efficiently process or extract the required information from such documents the appropriate audio data need to be selected and properly prepared for further processing. In the case of speech-processing applications this means detecting just the speech parts in the audio data and delivering them as inputs in a suitable format for further speech processing. The detection of such speech segments in continuous audio streams and the segmentation of audio streams into either detected speech or non-speech data is known as the speech/non-speech (SNS) segmentation problem. In this chapter we present an overview of the existing approaches to SNS segmentation in continuous audio streams and propose a new representation of audio signals that is more suitable for robust speech detection in SNS-segmentation systems. Since speech detection is usually applied as a pre-processing step in various speech-processing applications we have also explored the impact of different SNS-segmentation approaches on a speaker-diarisation task in BN data.

This chapter is organized as follows: In Section 2 a new high-level representation of audio signals based on phoneme-recognition features is introduced. First of all we give a short overview of the existing audio representations used for speech detection and provide the basic ideas and motivations for introducing a new representation of audio signals for SNS segmentation. In the remainder of the section we define four features based on consonant-vowel pairs and the voiced-unvoiced regions of signals, which are automatically detected by a generic phoneme recognizer. We also propose the fusion of different selected representations in order to improve the speech-detection results. Section 3 describes the two SNS-segmentation approaches used in our evaluations, one of which was specially designed for the proposed feature representation. In the evaluation section we present results from a wide range of experiments on a BN audio database using different speech-processing applications. We try to assess the performance of the proposed representation using a comparison with existing approaches for two different tasks. In the first task the performance of different representations of the audio signals is assessed directly by comparing the evaluation results of speech and non-speech detection on BN audio data. The second group of experiments tries to determine the impact of SNS segmentation on the subsequent processing of the audio data. We then measure the impact of different SNS-segmentation systems when they are applied in a pre-processing step of an evaluated speaker-diarisation system that is used as a speaker-tracking tool for BN audio data.

2. Phoneme-Recognition Features

2.1 An Overview of Audio Representations for Speech Detection

As briefly mentioned in the introduction, SNS segmentation is the task of partitioning audio streams into speech and non-speech segments. While speech segments can be easily defined as regions in audio signals where somebody is speaking, non-speech segments represent everything that is not speech, and as such consist of data from various acoustical sources, e.g., music, human noises, silences, machine noises, etc.

Earlier work on the separation of audio data into speech and non-speech mainly addressed the problem of classifying known homogeneous segments as either speech or music, and not as non-speech in general. The research was focused more on developing and evaluating characteristic features for classification, and the systems were designed to work on already-segmented data.

Saunders (Saunders, 1996) designed one such system using features pointed out by (Greenberg, 1995) to successfully discriminate between speech and music in radio broadcasting. For this he used time-domain features, mostly derived from zero crossing rates. In (Samouelian et al., 1998) time-domain features, combined with two frequency measures, were also used. The features for speech/music discrimination that are closely related to the nature of human speech were investigated in (Scheirer & Slaney, 1997). The proposed measures, i.e., the spectral centroid, the spectral flux, the zero-crossing rate, the *4-Hz* modulation energy (related to the syllable rate of speech), and the percentage of low-energy frames were explored in an attempt to discriminate between speech and various types of music. The most commonly used features for discriminating between speech, music and other sound sources are the cepstrum coefficients. The mel-frequency cepstral coefficients (MFCCs) (Picone, 1993) and the perceptual linear prediction (PLP) cepstral coefficients (Hermansky, 1990) are extensively used in speaker- and speech-recognition tasks. Although these signal representations were originally designed to model the short-term spectral information of speech events, they were also successfully applied in SNS-discrimination systems (Hain et al., 1998; Beyerlein et al., 2002; Ajmera, 2004; Barras et al., 2006; Tranter & Reynolds, 2006) in combination with Gaussian mixture models (GMMs) or hidden Markov models (HMMs) for separating different audio sources and channel conditions (broadband speech, telephone speech, music, noise, silence, etc.). The use of these representations is a natural choice in speech-processing applications based on automatic speech recognition since the same feature set can be used later on for the speech recognition. An interesting approach was proposed in (Parris et al., 1999), where a combination of different feature representations of audio signals in a GMM-based fusion system was made to discriminate between speech, music and noise. They investigated energy, cepstral and pitch features.

These representations and approaches focused mainly on the acoustic properties of data that are manifested in either the time and frequency or the spectral (cepstral) domains. All the representations tend to characterize speech in comparison to other non-speech sources (mainly music). Another perspective on the speech produced and recognized by humans is to treat it as a sequence of recognizable units. Speech production can thus be considered as a state machine, where the states are phoneme classes (Ajmera et al., 2003). Since other non-speech sources do not possess such properties, features based on these characteristics can be usefully applied in an SNS classification. The first attempt in this direction was made by Greenberg (Greenberg, 1995), who proposed features based on the spectral shapes associated with the expected syllable rate in speech. Karnebäck (Karnebäck, 2002) produced low-frequency modulation features in the same way and showed that in combination with the MFCC features they constitute a robust representation for speech/music discrimination tasks. A different approach based on this idea was presented in (Williams & Ellis, 1999). They built a phoneme speech recognizer and studied its behaviour with different speech and music signals. From the behaviour of the recognizer they proposed posterior-probability-based features, i.e., *entropy and dynamism*, and used them for classifying the speech and music samples.

2.2 Basic Concepts and Motivations

The basic SNS-classification systems typically include statistical models representing speech data, music, silence, noise, etc. They are usually derived from training material, and then a partitioning method detects the speech and non-speech segments according to these models. The main problem with such systems is the non-speech data, which are produced by various acoustic sources and therefore possess different acoustic characteristics. Thus, for each type of such audio signals one needs to build a separate class (typically represented as a model) and include it in a system. This represents a serious drawback with SNS-segmentation systems, which need to be data independent and robust to different types of speech and non-speech audio sources.

On the other hand, the SNS-segmentation systems are meant to detect speech in audio data and should discard non-speech parts, regardless of their different acoustic properties. Such systems can be interpreted as two-class classifiers, where the first class represents speech samples and the second class represents everything else. In this case the speech class defines the non-speech class. Following on from this basic concept one should find and use those characteristics or features of audio signals that better emphasize and characterize speech and exhibit the expected behaviour with all other non-speech audio data.

While the most commonly used acoustic features (MFCCs, PLPs, etc.) perform well when discriminating between different speech and non-speech signals, (Logan, 2000), they still only operate on an acoustic level. Hence, the data produced by the various audio sources with different acoustic properties needs to be modelled by several different classes and represented in the training process of such systems. To avoid this, we decided to design an

audio representation that would better determine the speech and perform significantly differently on all other non-speech data.
One possible way to achieve this is to see speech as a sequence of basic speech units that convey some meaning. This rather broad definition of speech led us to examine the behaviour of a simple phoneme recognizer and analyze its performance on speech and non-speech data. In that respect we followed the idea of Williams & Ellis, (Williams & Ellis, 1999), but rather than examine the functioning of phoneme recognizers, as they did, we analyzed the output transcriptions of such recognizers in various speech and non-speech situations.

2.3 Features Derivation

Williams & Ellis, (Williams & Ellis, 1999), proposed a novel method for discriminating between speech and music. They proposed measuring the posterior probability of observations in the states of neural networks that were designed to recognise basic speech units. From the analysis of the posterior probabilities they extracted features such as the mean per-frame entropy, the average probability dynamism, the background-label ratio and the phone distribution match. The entropy and dynamism features were later successfully applied to the speech/music segmentation of audio data (Ajmera et al., 2003). In both cases they used these features for speech/music classification, but the idea could be easily extended to the detection of speech and non-speech signals, in general. The basic motivation in both cases was to obtain and use features that were more robust to different kinds of music data and at the same time perform well on speech data.
In the same manner we decided to measure the performance of a speech recognizer by inspecting the output phoneme-recognition transcriptions, when recognizing speech and non-speech samples (Žibert et al., 2006a). In this way we also examined the behaviour of a phoneme recognizer, but the functioning of the recognizer was measured at the output of the recognizer rather than in the inner states of such a recognition engine.
Typically, the input of a phoneme recognizer consists of feature vectors based on the acoustic parameterization of speech signals, and the corresponding output is the most likely sequence of pre-defined speech units and time boundaries, together with the probabilities or likelihoods of each unit in a sequence. Therefore, the output information from a recognizer can also be interpreted as a representation of a given signal. Since the phoneme recognizer is designed for recognizing speech signals it is to be expected that it will exhibit characteristic behaviour when speech signals are passed through it, and all other signals will result in uncharacteristic behaviour. This suggests that it should be possible to distinguish between speech and non-speech signals just by examining the outputs of phoneme recognizers.
In general, the output from speech recognizers depends on the language and the models included in the recognizer. To reduce these influences the output speech units should be chosen from among broader groups of phonemes that are typical for the majority of languages. Also, the corresponding speech representation should not be heavily dependent on the correct transcription produced by the recognizer. Because of these limitations and the fact that human speech can be described as concatenated syllables, we decided to examine the functioning of recognizers in terms of the consonant-vowel (CV) level (Žibert et al., 2006a) and by inspecting the voiced and unvoiced regions (VU) of recognized audio signals (Mihelič & Žibert, 2006).

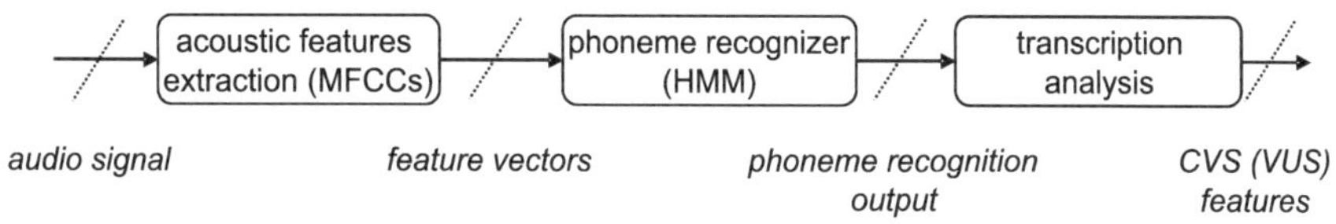

Figure 1. A block diagram showing the derivation of the phoneme-recognition features

The procedure for extracting phoneme-recognition features is shown in Figure 1. First, the acoustic representation of a given signal is produced and passed through a simple phoneme recognizer. Then, the transcription output is translated to specified phoneme classes, in the first case to the consonant (C), vowel (V) and silence (S) classes, and in the second case to the voiced (V), unvoiced (U) and silence (S) regions. At this point the output transcription is analysed, and those features that resemble the discriminative properties of speech and non-speech signals and are relatively independent of specific recognizer properties and errors are extracted. In our investigations we examined just those characteristics of the recognized outputs that are based on the *duration* and the *changing rate* of the basic units produced by the recognizer.

After a careful analysis of the functioning of several different phoneme recognizers for different speech and non-speech data conditions, we decided to extract the following features (Žibert et al., 2006a):

- **Normalized CV (VU) duration rate** of consonant-vowel (CV) or voiced-unvoiced (VU) pairs, defined in CV case as:

$$\frac{|t_C - t_V|}{t_{CVS}} + \alpha \cdot \frac{t_S}{t_{CVS}}, \tag{1}$$

where t_C is the overall time duration of all the consonants recognized in a signal window of time duration t_{CVS}, and t_V is the time duration of all the vowels in a window of duration t_{CVS}. The second term denotes the proportion of silence units (term t_S) represented in a recognized signal measured in time units. α serves as a weighting factor to emphasize the number of silence regions in a signal and has to be $0 \le \alpha \le 1$. In the VU case the above formula stays the same, whereas unvoiced phonemes replace consonants, voiced substitute vowels and silences are the same.

It is well known that speech is constructed from CV (VU) units in combination with S parts; however, we observed that speech signals exhibit relatively equal durations of C (U) and V (V) units and a rather small proportion of silences (S), which yielded small values (around 0.0) in Equation (1), measured on fixed-width speech segments. On the other hand, non-speech data were almost never recognized as a proper combination of CV or VU pairs, which is reflected in the different rates of C (U) and V (V) units, and hence the values of Equation (1) tend to be more like 1.0. In addition, when non-speech signals are recognized as silences, the values in the second term of Equation (1) follow the same trend as in the previous case.

Note that in Equation (1) we used the absolute difference between the durations, $|t_C - t_V|$, rather than the duration ratios, $\frac{t_C}{t_V}$ or $\frac{t_V}{t_C}$. This was done to reduce the effect of labelling, and not to emphasize one unit over another. The latter would result in the poor performance of this feature when using different speech recognizers.

- **Normalized average CV (VU) duration rate**, defined in the CV case as

$$\frac{|\overline{t_C} - \overline{t_V}|}{\overline{t_{CV}}}, \tag{2}$$

where $\overline{t_C}$ and $\overline{t_V}$ represent the average time durations of the C and V units in a given segment of a recognized signal, while $\overline{t_{CV}}$ is the average duration of all the recognized (C,V) units in the same segment. In the same way the normalized, average VU duration rate can be defined.
This feature was constructed to measure the difference between the average duration of the consonants (unvoiced parts) and the average duration of the vowels (voiced parts). It is well known that in speech the vowels (voiced parts) are in general longer than the consonants (unvoiced parts), and as a result this should be reflected in recognized speech. On the other hand, it was observed that non-speech signals do not exhibit such properties. Therefore, we found this feature to be sufficiently discriminative to distinguish between speech and non-speech data.
This feature correlates with the normalized time-duration rate defined in Equation (1). Note that in both cases the differences were used, instead of the ratios between the C (U) and V (V) units. This is for the same reason as in the previous case.

- **Normalized CV (VU) speaking rate**, defined in the CV case as

$$\frac{n_C + n_V}{t_{CVS}}, \tag{3}$$

where n_C and n_V are the number of C and V units recognized in the signal for the time duration t_{CVS}. The normalized VU speaking rate can be defined in the same manner. In both cases the silence units are not taken into account.
Since phoneme recognizers are trained on speech data they should detect changes when normal speech moves between phones every few tens of milliseconds. Of course, speaking rate in general depends heavily on the speaker and the speaking style. Actually, this feature is often used in systems for speaker recognition (Reynolds et al., 2003). To reduce the effect of speaking style, particularly spontaneous speech, we decided not to count the S units.
Even though the CV (VU) speaking rate in Equation (3) changes with different speakers and speaking styles, it varies less than for non-speech data. In the analyzed signals speech tended to change (in terms of the phoneme recognizer) much less frequently, but the signals varied greatly among different non-speech data types.

- **Normalized CVS (VUS) changes,** defined in the CV case as

$$\frac{c(C,V,S)}{t_{CVS}}, \tag{4}$$

where $c(C,V,S)$ counts how many times the C, V and S units exchange in the signal in the window of duration t_{CVS}. The same definition with V, U and S units can be produced in the VU case.
This feature is related to the CV (VU) speaking rate, but with one significant difference. Here, just the changes between the units that emphasize the pairs and not just the single units are taken into account. As speech consists of such CV (VU) combinations one should expect higher values when speech signals are decoded and lower values in the case of non-speech data.
This approach could be extended even further to observe higher-order combinations of the C, V, and S units to construct n-gram CVS (VUS) models (like in statistical language modelling), which could be additionally estimated from the speech and non-speech data.

As can be seen from the above definitions, all the proposed features measure the properties of recognized data on the pre-defined or automatically obtained segments of a processing signal. The segments should be large enough to provide reliable estimations of the proposed measurements. They depend on the size of the proportions of speech and non-speech data that were expected in the processing signals. We tested both possibilities of the segment sizes in our experiments. The typical segment sizes varied between 2.0 and 5.0 seconds in the fixed-segment size case. In the case of automatically derived segments the minimum duration of the segments was set to 1.5 seconds.
Another issue was how to calculate the features to be time aligned. In order to make a decision as to which proportion of the signal belongs to one or other class the time stamps between the estimation of consecutive features should be as small as possible. The natural choice would be to compute the features on moving segments between successive recognized units, but in our experiments we decided to keep a fixed frame skip, since we also used them in combination with the cepstral features.

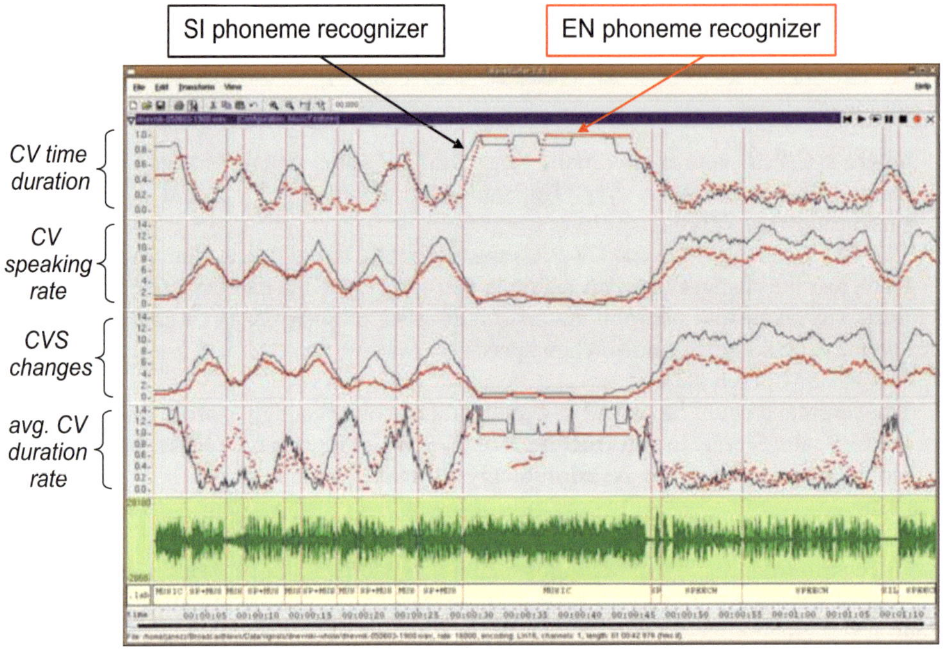

Figure 2. Estimation of the phoneme-recognition CVS features in a portion of a single broadcast news show in Slovene. The top four panes show the estimated CVS features from an audio signal that is shown in the fifth pane. The bottom pane displays the audio signal with the corresponding manual transcription. The top four panes consist of two lines. The black (darker) line represents the features obtained from a phoneme-based speech recognizer built to recognise Slovene speech, while the red (brighter) line displays the features obtained from the phoneme recognizer for English. All the data plots were produced using the *wavesurfer* tool, available at http://www.speech.kth.se/wavesurfer/.

Figure 2 shows phoneme-recognition features in action. In this example the CVS features were produced by phoneme recognizers based on two languages. One was built for Slovene (darker line in Figure 2), the other was trained on the TIMIT database (Garofolo et al., 1993) (brighter line), and was therefore used for recognizing English speech data. This example was extracted from a Slovenian BN show. The data in Figure 2 consist of different portions of speech and non-speech. The speech segments are built from clean speech, produced by different speakers in a combination with music, while the non-speech is represented by music and silent parts. As can be seen from Figure 2, each of these features has a reasonable ability to discriminate between the speech and non-speech data, which was later confirmed by our experiments. Furthermore, the features computed from the English speech recognizer, and thus in this case used on a foreign language, exhibit nearly the same behaviour as the features produced by the Slovenian phoneme decoder. This is a very positive result in terms of our objective to design features that should be language and model independent.

3. Speech Detection in Continuous Audio Streams

While there has been a lot of research done on producing appropriate representations of audio signals suitable for discriminating between speech and non-speech on already-segmented audio data, there have not been so many experiments conducted for speech detection in continuous audio streams, where the speech and non-speech parts are interleaving randomly. Such kinds of data are to be expected in most practical applications of automatic speech processing.

Most recent research in this field addresses this problem as part of large-vocabulary continuous-speech-recognition systems (LVCSRs), like BN transcription systems (Woodland, 2002; Gauvain et al., 2002; Beyerlein et al., 2002) or speaker-diarisation and speaker-tracking systems in BN data (Zhu et al., 2005; Sinha et al., 2005; Žibert et al., 2005; Istrate et al., 2005; Moraru et al., 2005; Barras et al., 2006; Tranter & Reynolds, 2006). In most of these investigations, energy and/or cepstral coefficients (mainly MFCCs) are used for the segmenting, and GMMs or HMMs are used for classifying the segments into speech and different non-speech classes. An alternative approach was investigated in (Lu et al., 2002), where the audio classification and segmentation were made by using support-vector machines. Another approach was presented in (Ajmera et al., 2003), where speech/music segmentation was achieved by incorporating GMMs into the HMM classification framework. This approach is also followed in our work and together with MFCC features it serves as a baseline SNS segmentation-classification method in our experiments.

In addition to our proposed representations, we also developed a method based on the acoustic segmentation of continuous audio streams obtained with the Bayesian information criterion (BIC) (Chen & Gopalakrishnan, 1998) and followed by the SNS classification.

In the following sections both segmentation-classification frameworks are described and compared using different audio-data representations.

3.1 Speech/Non-Speech-Segmentation Procedures

Block diagrams of the evaluated SNS-segmentation systems are shown in Figure 3.

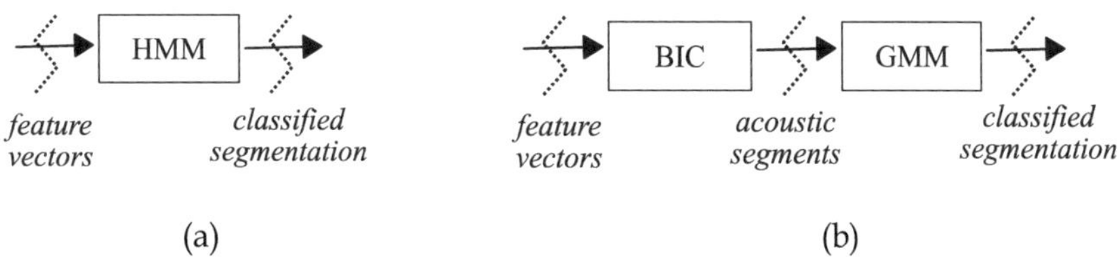

Figure 3. Block diagram of the two approaches used in the SNS segmentation. In (a) the segmentation and classification are performed simultaneously using HMM Viterbi decoding. In the second approach (b), firstly, the audio segmentation based on acoustic changes is performed by using the BIC segmentation procedure, followed by the GMM speech/non-speech classification.

The basic building blocks of both systems are GMMs. These models were trained with the EM algorithm in a supervised way (Young et al., 2004). In the first case, see Figure 3 (a), we followed the approach presented in (Ajmera, 2004), which was primarily designed for speech/music segmentation. Here, the segmentation and classification were performed simultaneously, by integrating already-trained GMMs into the HMM classification framework. We built a fully connected network consisting of N HMMs, as shown in Figure

4, where *N* represents the number of GMMs used in the speech/non-speech classification. Each HMM was constructed by simply concatenating the internal states associated with the same probability density function represented by one GMM. The number of states was fixed (*M* states in Figure 4) and set in such a way as to impose a minimum duration on each HMM. All the transitions inside each model were set manually, while the transitions between different HMMs were additionally trained on the evaluation data. In the segmentation process Viterbi decoding was used to find the best possible state sequence corresponding to speech and non-speech classes that could have produced the input-features sequence.

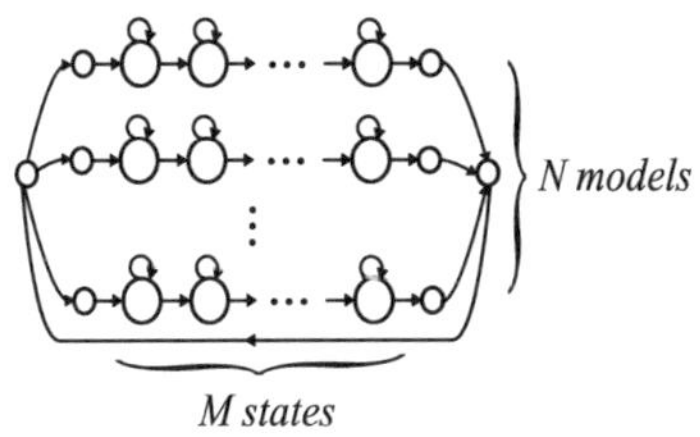

Figure 4. Topology of the HMM classification network used in the first procedure of the SNS segmentation.

In the second approach, see Figure 3 (b), the segmentation and classification were performed sequentially. The audio was segmented by applying the BIC measure to detect the acoustic-change points in the audio signals (Chen & Gopalakrishnan ,1998; Tritschler & Gopinath, 1999). Hence, in the first step of this procedure the segments based on acoustic changes were obtained, i.e., speaker, channel, background changes, different types of audio signals (music, speech), etc. In the next step these segments were classified as speech or non-speech. This classification was based on the same GMM set, which was also incorporated in the HMM classifier from the previous approach. In this way we could compare both methods using the same models. This approach is suited to the proposed CVS (VUS) features, which operate better on larger segments of signals than on smaller signal windows on a frame-by-frame basis.

In addition to both approaches, we also explored the fusion of different audio representations for SNS segmentation. The fusion of different representations was achieved at the score level in GMMs. We experimented with the fusion of the MFCC and the proposed CVS features, where each of the audio-signal representations form a separate feature stream. For each stream, separate GMMs were trained using the EM method. For SNS-segmentation purposes a similar HMM classification network to that of the non-fusion cases was built, see Figure 3 (a) and Figure 4, where in each state the fusion was made by computing the product of the weighted observation likelihoods produced by the GMMs from each stream. The product-stream weights were set empirically to optimize the performance on the evaluation dataset. In this way a fusion of the MFCC and CVS feature representations was performed by using a state-synchronous two-stream HMM (Potamianos et al., 2004).

3.3 Evaluation of Speech/Non-Speech Segmentation

We experimented with different approaches and representations of audio signals in order to find the best possible solution for the SNS discrimination in continuous audio streams.
We tested three main groups of features: acoustic features, represented by MFCCs, and the proposed CVS and VUS phoneme recognition, defined in Section 2. In addition, we combined both types of representations in one fusion SNS-segmentation system. All the representations were compared by using two SNS-segmentation approaches, presented in Section 3.1.
There were two evaluation databases: the development database, which was used to tune all the parameters of the audio representations and the SNS-segmentation systems, and the test dataset, which was composed of 12 hours of BN shows. The development dataset consisted of 6 hours of television entertainment and BN shows in different languages. A total of 4 hours of audio data were used to train the GMMs for SNS classification, the rest were used for setting the open parameters of the SNS-segmentation procedures to optimize their performances. The test database was used to compare the different audio representations and approaches in the SNS-segmentation task. This database is part of the audio database of BN shows in Slovene, which is presented in (Žibert & Mihelič, 2004).

3.3.1 Evaluation measures

The SNS-segmentation results were obtained in terms of the percentage of frame-level accuracy. We calculated three different statistics in each case: the percentage of true speech frames identified as speech, the percentage of true non-speech frames identified as non-speech, and the overall percentage of speech and non-speech frames identified correctly (the overall accuracy).
Note that in cases where one class dominates in the data (i.e., in the test-data case) the overall accuracy depends heavily on the accuracy of that class, and in such a case it cannot provide enough information on the performance of such a classification by itself. Therefore, in order to correctly assess classification methods one should provide all three statistics.

3.3.2 Evaluated SNS-segmentation systems

As a baseline system for the SNS classification we chose the MFCC features' representation in combination with the HMM classifier. We decided to use 12 MFCC features together with the normalized energy and first-order derivatives as a base representation, since no improvement was gained by introducing second-order derivatives. In that case 128-mixture GMMs for the modelling of several different speech and non-speech classes were trained. This baseline audio representation together with the HMM-based SNS segmentation is referred to as the *HMM-GMM: MFCC-E-D-26* system throughout the evaluation sections.
The above-described system was compared with different SNS approaches where phoneme-recognition features were used on their own and with the fusion system, where a combination of the MFCC and the CVS features were applied. The CVS and VUS features were obtained from two phoneme recognizers. One was built on Slovenian data, trained from three speech databases: GOPOLIS, VNTV and K211d, (Mihelič et al., 2003). It is referred as the *SI-phones* recognizer throughout the evaluation sections. The second was built from the TIMIT database, and thus was used for recognizing English speech. It is referred to as the *EN-phones* recognizer in all our experiments. Both phoneme recognizers were constructed from the HMMs of monophone units joined in a fully connected network.

Each HMM state was modelled by 32 diagonal-covariance Gaussian mixtures, built in a standard way, i.e., using 39 MFCCs, including the energy, and the first- and second-order derivatives, and setting all of the HMM parameters using the Baum-Welch re-estimation (Young et al., 2004). The phoneme sets of each language were different. In the *SI-phones* recognizer, 38 monophone base units were used, while in the TIMIT case, the base units were reduced to 48 monophones, according to (Lee & Hon, 1989). In both recognizers we used bigram phoneme language models in the recognition process. The recognizers were also tested on parts of the training databases. The *SI-phones* recognizer achieved a phoneme-recognition accuracy of about 70% on the GOPOLIS database, while the *EN-phones* recognizer had a phoneme-recognition accuracy of around 61% in a test part of the TIMIT database. Since our CVS (VUS) features were based on transcriptions of these recognizers, we also tested both recognizers on CVS recognition tasks. The *SI-phones* recognizer reached a CVS recognition accuracy of 88% on the GOPOLIS database, while for the *EN-phones* recognizer the CVS accuracy on the TIMIT database was around 75%. The same performance was achieved when recognizing the VUS units.

The CVS (VUS) features were calculated from phoneme-recognition transcriptions on the evaluation databases produced by both the *SI-phones* and *EN-phones* recognizers using the formulas defined in Section 2. The CVS (VUS) representations of the audio signal obtained from the *SI-phones* recognizer are named *SI-phones CVS (SI-phones VUS)* In the same manner, the CVS and VUS representations obtained from the *EN-phones* recognizer are marked as *EN-phones CVS (EN-phones VUS).* The models used for classifying the speech and non-speech data were 2-mixture GMMs.

In the CVS (VUS) features case we tested both segmentation procedures, which were already described in Section 3.1. The segmentation performed by the HMM classifiers, based on trained speech/non-speech GMMs is referred to as the *HMM-GMM* and the segmentation based on the BIC measure, followed by the GMM classification, is referred to as the *BICseg-GMM*. In the *HMM-GMM* case the CVS (VUS) feature vectors were produced on a frame-by-frame basis. Hence, a fixed window length of 3.0 s with a frame rate of 100 ms was used in all the experiments. In Equation (1), α was set to 0.5. In the second approach the BIC segmentation produced acoustic segments computed from 12 MFCC features, together with the energy. The BIC measure was applied by using full-covariance matrices and a lambda threshold set according to the development dataset. These segments were then classified as speech or non-speech, according to the maximum log-likelihood criteria applied to the GMMs modelled by the CVS (VUS) features.

The fusion SNS-segmentation system was designed to join the MFCC and CVS feature representations into a two-stream HMMs classification framework. The GMMs from the *MFCC-E-D-26* and *SI-phones CVS* representations were merged into HMMs, and such an SNS-segmentation system is called a *HMM-GMM: fusion MFCC+CVS* system.

In the *HMM-GMM*-segmentation case the number of states used to impose the minimum duration constraint in the HMMs was fixed. This was done according to (Ajmera et al., 2003). Since in our evaluation-data experiments speech or non-speech segments shorter than 1.4 s were not found, we set the minimum duration constraint to 1.4 s, which corresponded to a different number of states with different types of representations. All the transition probabilities (including self-loop transitions) inside the HMMs were fixed to 0.5.

The HMM classification based on the Viterbi algorithm was made with the *HTKToolkit* (Young et al., 2004), while we provided our own tools for the BIC segmentation and the GMM classification and training.

3.3.3 Development Data Evaluations

The development dataset was primarily designed to serve for determining the models and for the tuning of other open parameters of the evaluated SNS-segmentation systems. Hence, this dataset was divided into the training part (4 hours) and the evaluation part (2 hours). In this subsection experiments on the evaluation data are outlined.

The evaluation data were intended mainly for tuning the threshold probability weights to favour the speech and non-speech models in the classification systems in order to optimize the overall performance of the SNS-segmentation procedures. Such optimal models were then used in the SNS-segmentation systems on the test data.

When plotting the overall accuracy of the SNS segmentation of the evaluation data against different choices of threshold probability weights, we were able to examine the performances of the evaluated approaches in optimal and non-optimal cases. In this way the constant overall accuracy of an SNS segmentation under different choices of probability weights could indicate the more stable performance of such an SNS-segmentation system in adverse acoustic or other audio conditions. The results of such experiments are shown in Figures 5 and 6.

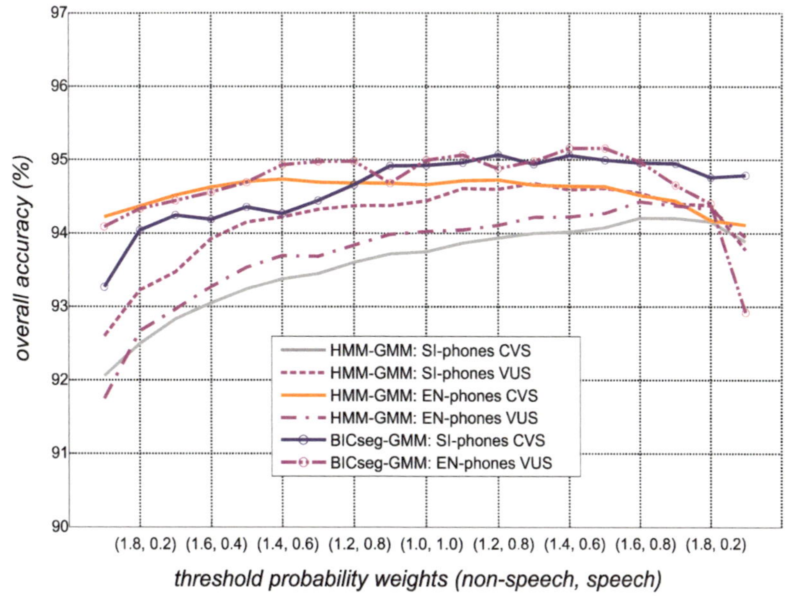

Figure 5. Determining the optimal threshold probability weights of the speech and non-speech models to maximize the overall accuracy of the CVS and VUS feature representations with different SNS-segmentation procedures.

Figure 5 shows a comparison of the different types of phoneme-recognition features with different SNS-segmentation procedures. As can be seen from Figure 5, all the segmentation methods based on both types of phoneme-recognition features are stable across the whole range of operating points of the threshold probability weights. The overall accuracy ranges between 92% and 95%. No important differences in the performance among the approaches based on the HMM classification and the BIC segmentation can be observed, even though the *BICseg-GMM* systems operated, on average, slightly better than their HMM-based counterparts. The same can be concluded when comparing CVS and VUS features computed from different phoneme recognizers. There is no significant difference in the performances when using *SI-phones* and *EN-phones* recognizers, even though the audio data in this development set are in Slovene. This proves that the phoneme-recognition features performed equally well, regardless of the spoken language that appeared in the audio data. When comparing the CVS and VUS feature types, no single conclusion can be made: the VUS features performed better than the CVS features when the *SI-phones* recognizers were used, but the opposite was the case when the CVS and VUS features derived from the *EN-phones* recognizers were applied.

In summary, the CVS and VUS features were stable and performed equally well across the whole range of threshold probability weights. They are also language independent and perform slightly better when they are derived from larger segments of data, like in the case of the *BICseg-GMM*-segmentation procedures. Therefore, we decided to use just the *SI-phones CVS* features in all the following evaluation experiments.

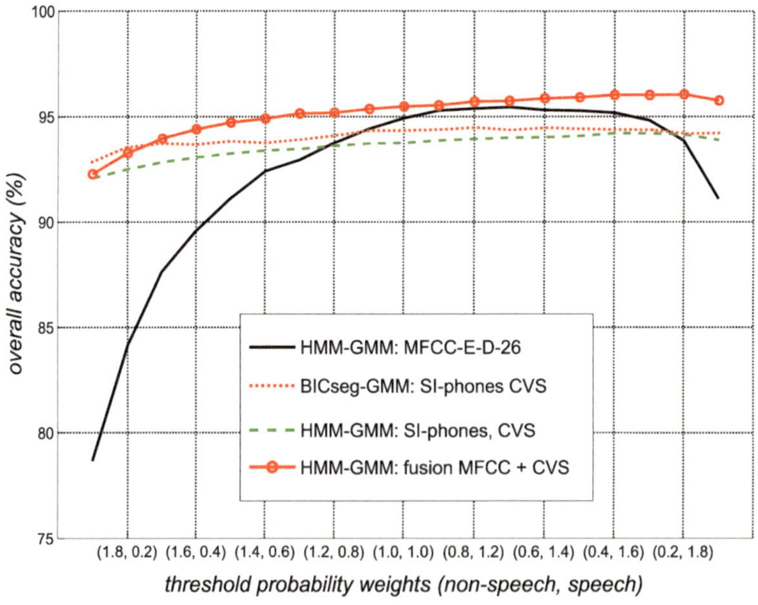

Figure 6. Determining the optimal threshold probability weights of the speech and non-speech models to maximize the overall accuracy of the different audio representations and SNS-segmentation procedures.

Figure 6 shows a comparison of the phoneme-recognition and acoustic features. The MFCC representation achieved the maximum accuracy, slightly above 95%, at the operating point (0.8,1.2). Around this point it performed better than the CVS-based segmentations, but in general the segmentation with just the MFCC features is more sensitive to the different operating points of the probability weights. The best overall performance was achieved by the fusion of both representations. The accuracy was increased to 96% (maximum values) around those operating points where the corresponding base representations achieved their own maximum performances. The fusion representation is also stable across the whole range of threshold probability weights due to the base CVS representation.

In general, it can be concluded that the CVS and VUS phoneme-recognition features were more stable than the acoustic MFCC features across the whole range of optimal and non-optimal cases. Therefore, it can be expected that they would also perform better in situations when the training and working conditions are not the same. In addition, a fusion of the phoneme and acoustic feature representations yielded the results with the highest overall accuracy.

3.3.4 Test Data Evaluations

In order to properly assess the proposed methods we performed an evaluation of the SNS-segmentation systems on 12 hours of audio data from BN shows. The results are shown in Table 1.

Classification & Features Type	*Speech Recognition (%)*	*Non-Speech Recognition (%)*	*Overall Accuracy (%)*
HMM-GMM: MFCC	97.9	58.8	95.4
HMM-GMM: *SI-phones* recognition, CVS units	98.2	91.3	97.8
BICseg-GMM: *EN-phones* recognition, CVS units	98.3	90.9	97.9
HMM-GMM: Fusion: MFCC + CVS	**99.3**	**86.4**	**98.5**

Table 1. Speech- and non-speech-segmentation results on 12 hours of audio data from BN shows.

The results in Table 1 were obtained when the optimum set of parameters was applied in all the evaluated SNS-segmentation procedures. The results on the test data reveal the same performance for the different methods as was the case in the development experiments. The results on the test set show that the proposed CVS representations of the audio signals performed better than just the acoustic MFCC representations. The advantage of using the proposed phoneme-recognition features becomes even more evident when they are compared in terms of speech and non-speech accuracies. In general, there exists a huge difference between the CVS and the MFCC representations in correctly identifying non-speech data with a relatively small loss of accuracy when correctly identifying speech data. One of the reasons for this is the stability issue discussed in the previous subsection. In all cases of the CVS features (regardless of the segmentation method) this resulted in an increased overall accuracy in comparison to the MFCC features.

When comparing the results of just the CVS representations no substantial differences in the classifications can be found. The results from the *SI-phones* and the *EN-phones* recognizers confirm that the proposed features really are independent of the phoneme recognizers trained on speech from different languages. They also suggest that there are almost no differences when using different segmentation methods, even though in the case of the BIC segmentation and the GMM classification we got slightly better results.

In the case of fusing the MFCC and CVS features we obtained the highest scores in terms of overall accuracy, and the fusion of both representations performed better than their stand-alone counterparts.

In general, the results in Table 1 and in Figures 5 and 6 speak in favour of the proposed phoneme-recognition features. This can be explained by the fact that our features were designed to discriminate between speech and non-speech, while the MFCC features were, in general, developed for speech-processing applications. Another issue concerns stability, and thus the robustness of the evaluated approaches. For the MFCC features the performance of the segmentation depends heavily on the training data and the training conditions, while the classification with the CVS features in combination with the GMMs performed reliably on the development and test datasets. Our experiments with fusion models also showed that probably the most appropriate representation for the SNS classification is a combination of acoustic- and recognition-based features.

In next section the impact of the evaluated speech-detection approaches on speech-processing applications is discussed.

4. The Impact of Speech Detection on Speech-Processing Applications

In the introduction we explained that a good segmentation of continuous audio streams into speech and non-speech has many practical applications. Such a segmentation is usually applied as a pre-processing step in real-world systems for automatic speech processing: in automatic speech recognition (Shafran & Rose, 2003), like a broadcast-news transcription (Gauvain et al., 2002; Woodland, 2002; Beyerlein et al., 2002), in automatic audio indexing and summarization (Makhoul et al., 2000; Magrin-Chagnolleau & Parlangeau-Valles, 2002), in audio and speaker diarisation (Tranter & Reynolds, 2006; Barras et al., 2006; Sinha et al., 2005; Istrate et al., 2005; Moraru et al., 2005), in speaker identification and tracking (Martin et al., 2000), and in all other applications where efficient speech detection helps to greatly reduce the computational complexity and generate more understandable and accurate outputs. Accordingly, an SNS segmentation has to be easily integrated into such systems and should not increase the overall computational load.

Therefore, we additionally explored our SNS-segmentation procedures in a speaker-diarisation application of broadcast-news audio data. We focused mainly on the impact of different SNS-segmentation approaches to the final speech (speaker) processing results. The importance of accurate speech detection in each task of the speaker diarisation is evaluated and discussed in the following section.

4.1 Evaluation of the Impact of Speech Detection in a Speaker-Diarisation System

4.1.1 Speaker Diarisation-System Framework

Speaker diarisation is the process of partitioning input audio data into homogeneous segments according to the speaker's identity. The aim of speaker diarisation is to improve the readability of an automatic transcription by structuring the audio stream into speaker turns, and in cases when used together with speaker-identification systems by providing the speaker's true identity. Such information is of interest to several speech- and audio-processing applications. For example, in automatic speech-recognition systems the information can be used for unsupervised speaker adaptation (Anastasakos et al., 1996, Matsoukas et al., 1997), which can significantly improve the performance of speech recognition in LVCSR systems (Gauvain et al., 2002; Woodland, 2002; Beyerlein et al., 2002). This information can also be applied for the indexing of multimedia documents, where homogeneous speaker or acoustic segments usually represent the basic units for indexing and searching in large archives of spoken audio documents, (Makhoul et al., 2000). The outputs of a speaker diarisation system could also be used in speaker-identification or speaker-tracking systems, (Delacourt et al., 2000; Nedic et al., 1999).

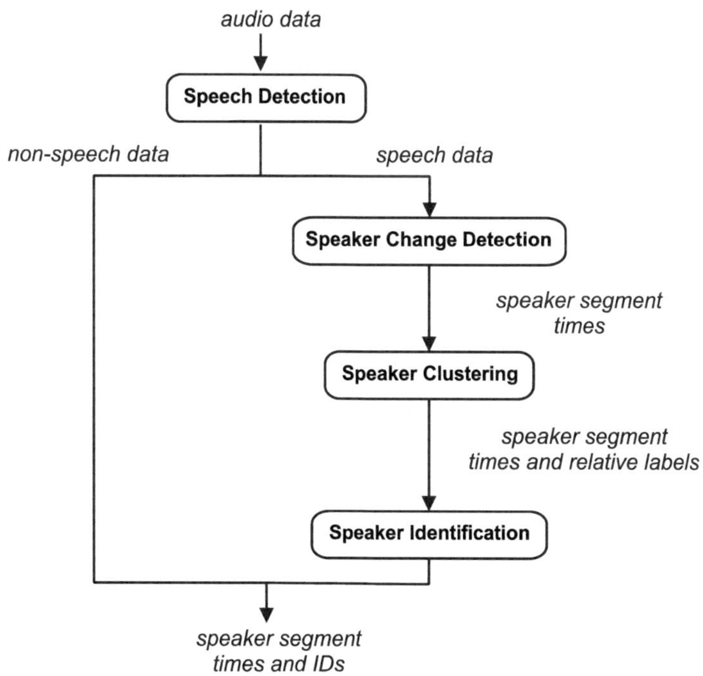

Figure 6. The main building blocks of a typical speaker-diarisation system. Most systems have components to perform speech detection, speaker or acoustic segmentation and speaker clustering, which may include components for gender detection and speaker identification.

Most speaker-diarisation systems have a similar general architecture to that shown in Figure 6. First, the audio data, which are usually derived from continuous audio streams, are segmented into speech and non-speech data. The non-speech segments are discarded and not used in further processing. The speech data are then chopped into homogeneous segments. The segment boundaries are located by finding acoustic changes in the signal, and each segment is expected to contain speech from only one speaker. The resulting segments are then clustered so that each cluster corresponds to just one speaker. At this stage, each cluster is labelled with relative speaker-identification names. Additionally, speaker identification or gender detection can be performed. In the first case, each of the speaker clusters can be given a true speaker name, or it is left unlabelled if the speech data in the cluster do not correspond to any of the target speakers. In the case of gender detection, each cluster gets an additional label to indicate to which gender it belongs. As such a speaker diarisation of continuous audio streams is a multistage process made up of four main components: speech detection, speaker audio segmentation, speaker clustering, and speaker identification. The latest overview of the approaches used in speaker-diarisation tasks can be found in (Tranter & Reynolds , 2006).

Our speaker-diarisation system, which was used for the current evaluation of speech-detection procedures, serves for speaker tracking in BN shows (Žibert, 2006b). All the components of the system were designed in such a way as to include the standard approaches from similar state-of-the-art systems. While the component for speech detection was derived from one of the SNS-segmentation procedures in each evaluation experiment, the audio segmentation, the speaker clustering and the speaker-identification procedures were the same in all experiments. The segmentation of the audio data was made using the acoustic-change detection procedure based on the Bayesian information criterion (BIC), which was proposed in (Chen & Gopalakrishnan, 1999) and improved by (Tritchler & Gopinath 1999). The applied procedure processed the audio data in a single pass, with the change-detection points found by comparing the probability models estimated from two neighbouring segments with the BIC. If the estimated BIC score was under the given threshold, a change point was detected. The threshold, which was implicitly included in the penalty term of the BIC, has to be given in advance and was in our case estimated from the training data. This procedure is widely used in most of the current audio-segmentation systems (Tranter & Reynolds, 2006; Fiscus et al., 2004; Reynolds & Torres-Carrasquillo, 2004; Zhou & Hansen, 2000; Istrate et al., 2005; Žibert et al., 2005). While the aim of an acoustic-change detection procedure is to provide the proper segmentation of the audio-data streams, the purpose of speaker clustering is to join or connect together segments that belong to the same speakers. In our system we realized this by applying a standard procedure using a bottom-up agglomerative clustering principle with the BIC as a merging criterion (Tranter & Reynolds, 2006). A speaker-identification component was adopted from a speaker-verification system, which was originally designed for the detection of speakers in conversational telephone speech (Martin et al., 2000). The speaker-verification system was based on a state-of-the-art Gaussian Mixture Model – Universal Background model (GMM-UBM) approach (Reynolds et al., 2000). The system made use of 26-dimensional feature vectors, composed of 12 MFCCs together with a log energy and their delta coefficients, computed every 10 ms and subjected to feature warping using a 3-s-long sliding window (Pelecanos & Sridharan, 2001). The log-likelihood scores produced by the system were normalized using the ZT-norm normalization technique (Auckenthaler et al., 2000).

All the open parameters and all the models used in each task of our speaker-diarisation system were estimated from the training data in such a way as to maximise the overall performance of the system.

4.1.2 Evaluation of the Impact

Since our speaker-diarisation system was constructed from four basic building blocks, we performed the evaluation of our speech-detection procedures after each processing block. Hence, the impact of the speech-detection procedures was measured, when using them as a pre-processing step of an audio-segmentation task, when using them together with an audio segmentation for speaker clustering, and in the final step, when measuring the overall speaker-tracking performance. The BN audio data used in the evaluation were the same as in the case of the evaluation of speech-detection procedures only, in Section 3.3.4. The audio-segmentation results, when using different speech-detection procedures, are shown in Table 2 and the final speaker-clustering and speaker-tracking results are shown in Figures 7 and 8, respectively.

Segmentation: baseline BIC method SNS segmentation:	*Recall* *(%)*	*Precision* *(%)*	*F-measure* *(%)*
Manual SNS segmentation	78.1	78.2	78.1
HMM-GMM: MFCC	60.0	80.7	68.8
HMM-GMM: *SI-phones* recognition, CVS	72.2	77.0	74.5
BICseg-GMM: *EN-phones* recognition, CVS	75.2	76.1	75.6
HMM-GMM: Fusion: MFCC + CVS	**75.7**	**76.8**	**76.3**

Table 2. Audio-segmentation results on BN audio data, when using different SNS-segmentation procedures.

The audio-segmentation performance in Table 2 was measured using three standard measures (Kemp et al., 2000): recall, precision and the F-measure. The recall is defined as the rate of correctly detected boundaries divided by the total number of boundaries, while the precision corresponds to the rate of correctly detected boundaries divided by the total number of hypothesized boundaries. Both measures are closely related to the well-known false-acceptance and false-rejection rates. The *F-measure* joins the recall and the precision in a single overall measure.

The overall segmentation results in Table 2 speak in favour of the proposed phoneme-recognition features (CVS), when using them as a representation of audio signals in speech-detection procedures. As has already been shown in the evaluation of speech-detection procedures alone (see Table 1), a baseline approach *HMM-GMM: MFCC* performed poorly in the detection of non-speech data. The non-speech segments were not detected, and consequently too many non-speech boundaries were not found. Therefore, the recall was too low, and regardless of the relatively high precision the overall audio-segmentation results were not as good as in the other cases. We achieved relatively good results with both CVS representations in comparison to the manual SNS segmentation (in the first row of Table 2). The best overall results were achieved with the fusion representation of the MFCC and CVS features. The corresponding audio-segmentation results are just approximately 2% worse (measured by all three measures) than in the manual SNS-segmentation case. This proves that proper speech detection is an important part of an audio-segmentation system and that a good SNS segmentation can greatly improve the overall audio-segmentation results. This fact becomes even more obvious when different speech-detection procedures were compared in a speaker-clustering task, shown in Figure 7.

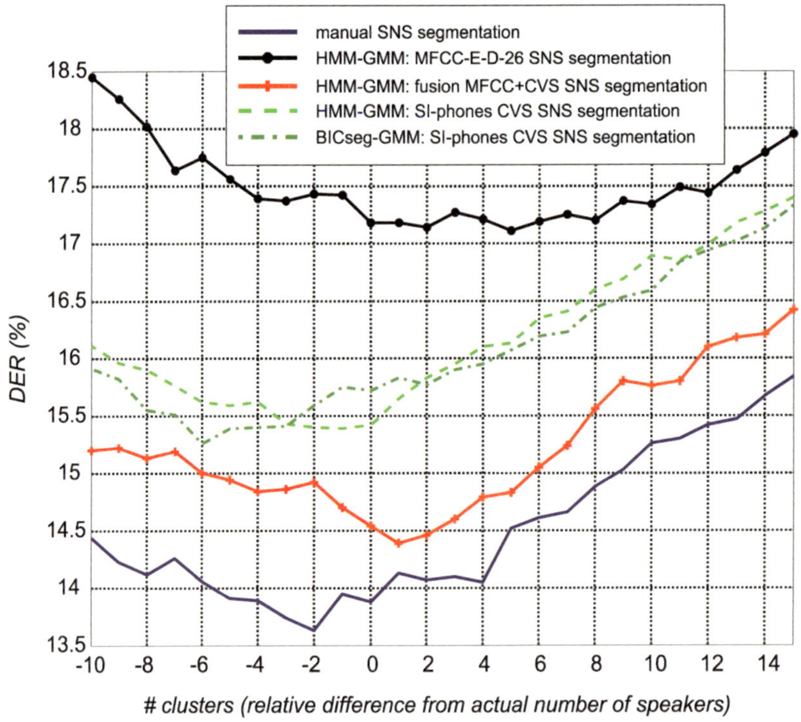

Figure 7. Speaker-clustering results when using different SNS-segmentation procedures. The lower DER values correspond to better performance.

Figure 7 shows a comparison of the four speech-detection procedures when using them together with the audio segmentation in the speaker-clustering task. The speaker clustering was evaluated by measuring the speaker-diarisation performance in terms of the diarisation error rate (DER), (Fiscus et al., 2004). The comparison was made when no stopping criteria were used in the speaker-clustering procedure. Hence, the impact of different speech-detection approaches was compared across the whole range of possible numbers of speaker clusters.

In Figure 7, the overall performance of the speaker clustering when using different SNS-segmentation procedures varies between 13.5% and 18.5%, measured using the DER. The speaker-clustering system, where the manual SNS segmentation was applied, was the best performing of all the evaluated procedures. In second place was the SNS segmentation with the fusion of the CVS and MFCC features. The DER results show on average an approximately 1% loss of performance with such speaker clustering. Speaker-clustering approaches show comparable performance, where just CVS representations of the audio signals were used in combination with different SNS-segmentation systems. A baseline speaker-clustering approach with MFCC features performed, on average, 3% worse (in absolute figures) than the best-evaluated approaches. These results also indicate the importance of speech detection in speaker-clustering procedures.

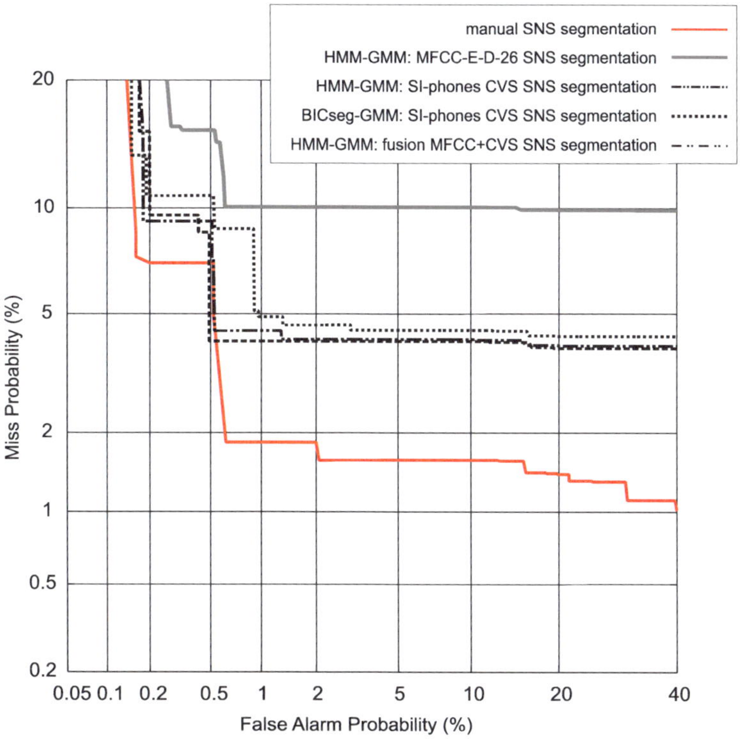

Figure 8. Overall speaker-tracking results plotted with DET curves. Lower DET values correspond to better performance.

The overall performance of the evaluated speaker-diarisation (SD) system is depicted in Figure 8, where the overall speaker-tracking results are shown. The results are presented in terms of the false-acceptance (FA) and false-rejection (FR) rates, measured at different operating points in the form of detection-error trade-off (DET) curves (Martin et al., 2000). In our case, the evaluated speaker-tracking system was capable of detecting 41 target speakers from the audio data, which included 551 different speakers. The target speakers were enrolled in the system beforehand from the training part of the evaluation BN database. The performances of the evaluated speaker-tracking systems were therefore assessed by including all 41 target speakers, with the addition of the non-speech segments, and the results were produced from the FA and FR rates measured at the time (frame) level.

Figure 8 presents the evaluation results from four tested speaker-tracking systems. In all the evaluated systems the components for the audio segmentation, the speaker clustering and the speaker identification were the same, while the speech-detection procedures were different. The overall speaker-tracking results from Figure 8 reveal the same performance for the evaluated systems as for the speaker-clustering case. The best performance was achieved when using manual SNS segmentation, while the speaker-tracking system with the baseline SNS segmentation (*HMM-GMM:MFCC*) performed worse than all the other tested systems. Our proposed SNS-segmentation approaches with CVS features produce nearly the same overall evaluation results, which are in general 3% worse (in absolute figures) than the speaker-tracking results obtained using manual SNS segmentation. Note that the fusion of the MFCC and CVS features did not improve the evaluation results in comparison to the systems when just the CVS features were used, as was the case in previous evaluations.

We can conclude that, in general, the impact of SNS segmentation on speaker-diarisation and speaker-tracking systems is direct and indirect. As shown in the evaluation of an audio segmentation, good speech detection in continuous audio streams is a necessary pre-processing step if we want to achieve good segmentation results. And since audio segmentation serves as a front-end processing component for speaker clustering and speaker tracking, an erroneous audio segmentation influences the speaker-clustering performance. Speech detection alone has a direct impact on the performance of the speaker-diarisation performance. Since speaker-clustering performance (measured using the DER) and speaker-tracking performance (measured using the DET) are expressed in terms of a miss (speaker in reference but not in hypothesis), a false alarm (speaker in hypothesis but not in reference) and speaker error (mapped reference speaker is not the same reference as the hypothesized speaker), the errors in the speech detection produce a miss, a false alarm and false rejection errors in the overall speaker-diarisation results assessed by both evaluation measures. All types of errors are consequently integrated in the DER and DET plots in Figures 7 and 8.

5. Conclusion

This chapter addresses the problem of speech detection in continuous audio streams and explores the impact of speech/non-speech segmentation on speech-processing applications. We proposed a novel approach for deriving speech-detection features based on phoneme transcriptions from generic speech-recognition systems. The proposed phoneme-recognition features were designed to be recognizer and language independent and could be applied in different speech/non-speech segmentation-classification frameworks. In our evaluation experiments two segmentation-classification frameworks were tested, one based on the Viterbi decoding of hidden Markov models, where speech/non-speech segmentation and detection were performed simultaneously, and the other framework, where segments were initially produced on the basis of acoustic information by using the Bayesian information criterion and then speech/non-speech classification was performed by applying Gaussian mixture models.

All the proposed feature representations and segmentation methods were tested and compared in the different tasks of a speaker-diarisation system, which served for speaker tracking in audio broadcast-news shows. The impact of the speech detection was measured in four different tasks of a speaker-diarisation system. The evaluation results of the audio segmentation, the speaker clustering and the speaker tracking demonstrate the importance of a good speech-detection procedure in such systems. In all tasks, our proposed phoneme-recognition features proved to be a suitable and robust representation of audio data for speech detection and were capable of reducing the error rates of the evaluated speaker-diarisation systems. At the same time the evaluation experiments showed that the speech/non-speech segmentation with the fusion of the acoustic and the phoneme features performed the best among all the systems, and was even comparable to the manual speech/non-speech segmentation systems. This confirmed our expectations that probably the most suitable representation of audio signals for the speech/non-speech segmentation of continuous audio streams is a combination of acoustic- and recognition-based features.

6. Acknowledgment

This work was supported by the Slovenian Research Agency (ARRS), development project L2-6277 (C) entitled "Broadcast news processing system based on speech technologies."

7. References

Ajmera, J.; McCowan, I. & Bourlard, H. (2003). Speech/music segmentation using entropy and dynamism features in HMM classification framework. *Speech Communication*, Vol. 40, No. 3, (May 2003), pp. 351-363.

Ajmera, J. (2004). *Robust audio segmentation, PhD thesis,* EPFL Lausanne.

Anastasakos, T.; McDonough, J.; Schwartz, R.; & Makhoul J. (1996) A Compact Model for Speaker-Adaptive Training, *Proceedings of International Conference on Spoken Language Processing (ICSLP1996),* pp. 1137-1140, Philadelphia, PA, USA, 1996.

Auckenthaler, R.; Carey, M. & Lloyd-Thomas, H. (2000). Score normalization for text-independent speaker verification system. *Digital Signal Processing,* Vol. 10, No. 1, January 2000, pp. 42-54.

Barras, C.; Zhu, X.; Meignier, S. & Gauvain, J.-L. (2006). Multistage Speaker Diarization of Broadcast News. *IEEE Transactions on Speech, Audio and Language Processing, Special Issue on Rich Transcription,* Vol. 14, No. 5, (September 2006), pp. 1505-1512.

Beyerlein, P.; Aubert, X.; Haeb-Umbach, R.; Harris, M.; Klakow, D.; Wendemuth, A.; Molau, S.; Ney, H.; Pitz, M. & Sixtus, A. (2002). Large vocabulary continuous speech recognition of Broadcast News - The Philips/RWTH approach. *Speech Communication,* Vol. 37, No. 1-2, (May 2002), pp. 109-131.

Chen, S. S. & Gopalakrishnan, P. S. (1998). Speaker, environment and channel change detection and clustering via the Bayesian information criterion, *Proceedings of the DARPA Speech Recognition Workshop,* pp. 127-132, Lansdowne, Virginia, USA, February, 1998.

Delacourt, P.; Bonastre, J.; Fredouille, C.; Merlin, T. & Wellekens, C. (2000). A Speaker Tracking System Based on Speaker Turn Detection for NIST Evaluation, *Proceedings of International Conference on Acoustics, Speech, and Signal Processing (ICASSP2000),* Istanbul, Turkey, June, 2006.

Fiscus, J. G.; Garofolo, J. S.; Le, A.; Martin, A. F.; Pallett, D. S.; Przybocki M. A. & Sanders, G. (2004). Results of the Fall 2004 STT and MDE Evaluation, *Proceedings of the Fall 2004 Rich Transcription Workshop,* Palisades, NY, USA, November, 2004.

Garofolo, J. S.; Lamel, L. F.; Fisher, W. M.; Fiscus, J. G.; Pallett, D. S. & Dahlgren, N. L. (1993). DARPA TIMIT acoustic-phonetic continuous speech corpus, *U.S. Dept. of Commerce, NIST,* Gaithersburg, MD, USA, February, 1993.

Greenberg, S. (1995). The ears have it: The auditory basis of speech perceptions, *Proceedings of International Congress of Phonetic Sciences (ICPhS 95),* pp. 34-41, Stockholm, Sweden, August , 1995.

Gauvain, J. L.; Lamel, L. & Adda, G. (2002). The LIMSI Broadcast News transcription system. *Speech Communication,* Vol. 37, No. 1-2, (May 2002), pp. 89-108.

Hermansky, H. (1990). Perceptual linear predictive (PLP) analysis of speech. *Journal of the Acoustical Society of America,* Vol. 87, No. 4, (1990), pp. 1738-1752.

Hain, T.; Johnson, S. E.; Tuerk, A.; Woodland, P. C. & Young, S. J. (1998). Segment Generation and Clustering in the HTK Broadcast News Transcription System, *Proceedings of the 1998 DARPA Broadcast News Transcription and Understanding Workshop,* pp. 133-137, Lansdowne, VA, USA, February, 1998.

Istrate, D.; Scheffer, N.; Fredouille, C. & Bonastre, J.-F. (2005). Broadcast News Speaker Tracking for ESTER 2005 Campaign, *Proceedings of Interspeech 2005 - Eurospeech,* pp. 2445-2448, Lisbon, Portugal, September, 2005.

Karnebäck, S. (2002). Expanded examinations of a low frequency modulation feature for speech/music discrimination, *Proceedings of International Conference on Spoken Language Processing (ICSLP2002 -Interspeech 2002),* pp. 2009-2012, Denver, Colorado, USA, September, 2002.

Kemp, T.; Schmidt, M.; Westphal, M. & Waibel, A. (2000). Strategies for Automatic Segmentation of Audio Data, *Proceedings of the IEEE International Conference on Acoustic Signal and Speech Processing (ICASSP 2000),* pp.1423-1426, Istanbul, Turkey, June, 2000.

Lee, K. F. & Hon, H. W. (1989). Speaker-Independent Phone Recognition Using Hidden Markov Models. *IEEE Transactions on Acoustic Speech and Signal Processing,* Vol. 37, No. 11, (1989), pp. 1641-1648.

Logan, B. (2000). Mel Frequency Cepstral Coefficients for Music Modeling, *Proceedings of the International Symposium on Music Information Retrieval,* Plymouth, Massachusetts, USA, October, 2000.

Lu, L.; Zhang, H.-J. & Li, S. Z. (2003). Content-based audio classification and segmentation by using support vector machines. *ACM Multimedia Systems Journal,* Vol. 8, No. 6, (March 2003) pp. 482-492.

Makhoul, J.; Kubala, F.; Leek, T.; Liu, D.; Nguyen, L.; Schwartz, R. & Srivastava, A. (2000). Speech and language technologies for audio indexing and retrieval. *Proceedings of the IEEE,* Vol. 88, No. 8, (2000) pp. 1338-1353.

Magrin-Chagnolleau, I. & Parlangeau-Valles, N. (2002). Audio indexing: what has been accomplished and the road ahead, *Proceedings of Joint Conference on Information Sciences, (JCIS 2002),* pp. 911-914, Durham, North Carolina, USA, March, 2002.

Martin, A.; Przybocki, M.; Doddington, G. & Reynolds, D. (2000). The NIST speaker recognition evaluation - overview, methodology, systems, results, perspectives. *Speech Communications,* Vol. 31, No. 2-3, June 2000, pp. 225-254.

Matsoukas, S.; Schwartz, R.; Jin, H. & Nguyen, L. (1997). Practical Implementations of Speaker-Adaptive Training, *Proceedings of the 1997 DARPA Speech Recognition Workshop*, Chantilly VA, USA, February, 1997.

Mihelič, F.; Žibert, J. (2006). Robust speech detection based on phoneme recognition features, *Proceedings of Text, speech and dialogue (TSD 2006)*, pp. 455-462, Brno, Czech Republic, September, 2006.

Mihelič, F.; Gros, J.; Dobrišek, S.; Žibert, J. & Pavešić, N. (2003). Spoken language resources at LUKS of the University of Ljubljana. *International Journal of Speech Technology*, Vol. 6, No. 3, (July 2003) pp. 221-232.

Moraru, D.; Ben, M. & Gravier, G. (2005). Experiments on speaker tracking and segmentation in radio broadcast news, *Proceedings of Interspeech 2005 - Eurospeech*, pp. 3049-3052, Lisbon, Portugal, September, 2005.

Nedic, B.; Gravier, G.; Kharroubi, J.; Chollet, G.; Petrovska, D.; Durou, G.; Bimbot, F.; Blouet, R.; Seck, M.; Bonastre, J.-F.; Fredouille, C.; Merlin, T.; Magrin-Chagnolleau, I.; Pigeon, S.; Verlinde, P. & Cernocky J. (1999). The Elisa'99 Speaker Recognition and Tracking Systems, *Proceedings of IEEE Workshop on Automatic Advanced Technologies*, 1999.

Parris, E. S.; Carey, M. J. & Lloyd-Thomas, H. (1999). Feature fusion for music detection, *Proceedings of EUROSPEECH 99*, pp. 2191-2194, Budapest, Hungary, September 1999.

Pelecanos, J. & Sridharan, S. (2001). Feature warping for robust speaker verification. *Proceedings of Speaker Odyssey*, pp. 213–218, Crete, Greece, June 2001.

Picone, J. W. (1993). Signal modeling techniques in speech recognition. *Proceedings of the IEEE*, Vol. 81, No. 9, (1993) pp. 1215-1247.

Potamianos, G.; Neti, C.; Luettin, J. & Matthews, I. (2004). Audio-Visual Automatic Speech Recognition: An Overview. In: *Issues in Visual and Audio-Visual Speech Processing*, Bailly, G.; Vatikiotis-Bateson; E. & Perrier, P.(Eds.), MIT Press, Cambridge.

Reynolds, D. A.; Campbell, J. P.; Campbell, W. M.; Dunn, R. B.; Gleason, T. P.; Jones, D. A.; Quatieri, T. F.; Quillen, C.B.; Sturim, D. E. & Torres-Carrasquillo, P. A. (2003). Beyond Cepstra: Exploiting High-Level Information in Speaker Recognition, *Proceedings of the Workshop on Multimodal User Authentication*, pp. 223-229, Santa Barbara, California, USA, December, 2003.

Reynolds, D. A.; Quatieri, T. F. & and R. B. Dunn, R. B. (2000). Speaker verification using adapted Gaussian mixture models. *Digital Signal Processing*, Vol. 10, No. 1, January 2000, pp. 19–41.

Reynolds, D. A. & Torres-Carrasquillo, P. (2004). The MIT Lincoln Laboratory RT-04F Diarization Systems: Applications to Broadcast Audio and Telephone Conversations, Proceedings of the Fall 2004 Rich Transcription Workshop. Palisades, NY, USA, November, 2004.

Samouelian, A.; Robert-Ribes, J. & Plumpe, M. (1998). Speech, silence, music and noise classification of TV broadcast material, *Proceedings of International Conference on Spoken Language Processing (ICSLP1998)*, pp. 1099-1102, Sydney Australia, November-December, 1998.

Saunders, J. (1996). Real-time discrimination of broadcast speech/music, *Proceedings of International Conference on Acoustics, Speech, and Signal Processing (ICASSP1996)*, pp. 993-996, Atlanta, USA, 1996.

Scheirer, E. & Slaney, M. (1997). Construction and evaluation of a robust multifeature speech/music discriminator, *Proceedings of International Conference on Acoustics, Speech, and Signal Processing (ICASSP1997)*, pp. 1331-1334, Munich, Germany, April, 1997.

Shafran, I. & Rose, R. (2003). Robust speech detection and segmentation for real-time ASR applications, *Proceedings of International Conference on Acoustics, Speech, and Signal Processing (ICASSP2003)*, pp. 432-435, Hong Kong, Hong Kong, April, 2003.

Sinha, R.; Tranter, S. E.; Gales, M. J. F. & Woodland, P. C. (1999). The Cambridge University March 2005 Speaker Diarisation System, *Proceedings of Interspeech 2005 - Eurospeech*, pp. 2437-2440, Lisbon, Portugal, September, 2005.

Tranter, S. & Reynolds, D. (2006). An Overview of Automatic Speaker Diarisation Systems. *IEEE Transactions on Speech, Audio and Language Processing, Special Issue on Rich Transcription*, Vol. 14, No. 5, (September 2006), pp. 1557-1565.

Tritschler, A. & Gopinath, R. (1999). Improved speaker segmentation and segments clustering using the Bayesian information criterion, *Proceedings of EUROSPEECH 99*, pp. 679-682, Budapest, Hungary, September, 1999.

Williams, G. & Ellis, D. P. W. (1999). Speech/music discrimination based on posterior probabilities, *Proceedings of EUROSPEECH 99*, pp. 687-690, Budapest, Hungary, September, 1999.

Woodland, P. C. (2002). The development of the HTK Broadcast News transcription system: An overview. *Speech Communication*, Vol. 37, No. 1-2, (May 2002), pp. 47-67.

Žibert, J. & Mihelič, F. (2004). Development of Slovenian Broadcast News Speech Database, *Proceedings of the International Conference on Language Resources and Evaluation (LREC 2004)*, pp. 2095-2098, Lisbon, Portugal, May 2004.

Žibert, J.; Mihelič, F.; Martens, J.-P.; Meinedo, H.; Neto, J.; Docio, L.; Garcia-Mateo, C.; David, P.; Zdansky, J.; Pleva, M.; Cizmar, A.; Žgank, A.; Kačič, Z.; Teleki, C. & Vicsi, K. (2005). The COST278 Broadcast News Segmentation and Speaker Clustering Evaluation - Overview, Methodology, Systems, Results, *Proceedings of Interspeech 2005 - Eurospeech*, pp. 629-632, Lisbon, Portugal, September, 2005.

Žibert, J.; Pavešić, N. & Mihelič, F. (2006a). Speech/Non-Speech Segmentation Based on Phoneme Recognition Features. *EURASIP Journal on Applied Signal Processing*, Vol. 2006, No. 6, Article ID 90495, pp. 1-13.

Žibert, J. (2006b).*Obdelava zvočnih posnetkov informativnih oddaj z uporabo govornih tehnologij, PhD thesis (in Slovenian language),* Faculty of Electrical Engineering, University of Ljubljana, Slovenia.

Zhu, X.; Barras, C.; Meignier, S. & Gauvain, J.-L. (2005). Combining Speaker Identification and BIC for Speaker Diarization, *Proceedings of Interspeech 2005 - Eurospeech*, pp. 2441-2444, Lisbon, Portugal, September, 2005.

Zhou, B. & Hansen, J. (2000). Unsupervised Audio Stream Segmentation and Clustering via the Bayesian Information Criterion, *Proceedings of International Conference on Spoken Language Processing (ICSLP 2000)*, pp. 714-717, Beijing, China, October, 2000.

Young, S.; Evermann, G.; Gales, M.; Hain, T.; Kershaw, D.; Moore, G.; Odell, J.; Ollason, D.; Povey, D.; Valtchev, V. & Woodland, P. C. (2004). *The HTK Book (for HTK Version 3.2),* Cambridge University Engineering Department, Cambridge, United Kingdom.

3

New Advances in Voice Activity Detection using HOS and Optimization Strategies

J.M. Górriz, J. Ramírez, C.G. Puntonet
University of Granada
Spain

1. Introduction

Nowadays, the emerging wireless communication applications require increasing levels of performance and speech processing systems working in noise adverse environments. These systems often benefit from using voice activity detectors (VADs) which are frequently used in such application scenarios for different purposes. Speech/non-speech detection is an unsolved problem in speech processing and affects numerous applications including robust speech recognition (Karray & Martin, 2003), (Ramírez et al., 2003), discontinuous transmission (ETSI, 1999), (ITU, 1996), estimation and detection of speech signals (Krasny, 2000), real-time speech transmission on the Internet (Sangwan et al., 2002) or combined noise reduction and echo cancellation schemes in the context of telephony (Basbug et al., 2003). The speech/non-speech classification task is not as trivial as it appears, and most of the VAD algorithms fail when the level of background noise increases.

During the last decade, numerous researchers have developed different strategies for detecting speech on a noisy signal (Sohn et al., 1999), (Cho & Kondoz 2001) and have evaluated the influence of the VAD effectiveness on the performance of speech processing systems (Bouquin-Jeannes & Faucon, 1995) (see also the preceding chapter about VAD). Most of them have focussed on the development of robust algorithms with special attention on the derivation and study of noise robust features and decision rules (Woo et al., 2000), (Li et al., 2002), (Marzinzik & Kollmeier, 2002), (Sohn et al., 1999). The different approaches include those based on energy thresholds (Woo et al., 2000), pitch detection (Chengalvarayan, 1999), spectrum analysis (Marzinzik & Kollmeier, 2002), zero-crossing rate (ITU, 1996), periodicity measures (Tucker, 1992) or combinations of different features (ITU, 1996), (ETSI, 1999).

In this Chapter we show three methodologies for VAD: i) statistical likelihood ratio tests (LRTs) formulated in terms of the integrated bispectrum of the noisy signal. The integrated bispectrum is defined as a cross spectrum between the signal and its square, and therefore a function of a single frequency variable. It inherits the ability of higher order statistics to detect signals in noise with many other additional advantages (Górriz, 2006a), (Ramírez et al, 2006); ii) Hard decision clustering approach where a set of prototypes is used to characterize the noisy channel. Detecting the presence of speech is enabled by a decision rule formulated in terms of an averaged distance between the observation vector and a cluster-based noise model; and iii) an effective method employing support vector machines

(SVM) , a paradigm of learning from examples based in Vapkik-Chervonenkis theory (Vapnik, 1995). The use of kernels in SVM enables to map the data, via a nonlinear transformation, into some other dot product space (called feature space) in which the classification task is settled.

2. Relevant Feature Vectors for VAD

In this section we show some standard and novel Feature Vectors (FVs) for VAD. After the framing procedure, that is processing the input signal in short time frames, these FVs are computed in the feature extraction stage. Usually, the features are extracted using overlapping frames, which results in correlation between consecutive frames, and smoothes the spectral change from frame to frame. Feature extraction attempts to present the content of the speech signal compactly, such that the characteristic information of the signal is preserved. Then, the VAD decision is made using information provided by the features in the decision-making module.

2.1 Feature Vector based on Power Spectrum

Let x(n) be a discrete zero-mean time signal. In the framing stage the input signal x(n) sampled at 8 kHz is decomposed into 25-ms overlapped frames with a 10-ms window shift. The current frame consisting of 200 samples is zero padded to 256 samples and power spectral magnitude X(ω) is computed through the discrete Fourier transform (DFT). Finally, the filterbank reduces the dimensionality of the feature vector to a suitable representation for detection including broadband spectral information. Thus, the signal is passed through a K-band filterbank which is defined by:

$$E_B(k) = \sum_{\omega=\omega_k}^{\omega_{k+1}} X(\omega); \quad \omega_k = \frac{\pi}{K}k \quad k = 0,\ldots,K-1 \tag{1}$$

This feature in combination with long term information is usually adopted as feature vector, i.e. the one used in the clustering based VAD (Górriz et al., 2006b). In addition, it also provides the definition of other feature vector, the subband SNRs (that is used in the SVM approach), which includes the environmental level of noise and can be computed as:

$$SNR(k) = 20\log_{10}\left(\frac{E_B(k)}{N_B(k)}\right); \quad k = 0,\ldots,K-1 \tag{2}$$

where N_B denotes the subband power spectral magnitude of the residual noise that is extracted from the noisy channel using the approach presented in section 3.1.

2.2 Feature Vector based on HOS

The bispectrum of a discrete-time zero-mean signal x(t) is defined as the 2-D discrete time Fourier transform:

$$B_x(\omega_1,\omega_2) = \sum_{i=-\infty}^{\infty}\sum_{k=-\infty}^{\infty} C_{3x}(i,k)\exp\{-j(\omega_1 i + \omega_2 k)\}; \tag{3}$$

where C_{3x} is the third-order cumulant of the input signal (third order moment of a zero-mean signal). Note that, from the above definition the third-order cumulant can be expressed as:

$$C_{3x}(i,k)=\left(\frac{1}{2\pi}\right)^2\int_{-\pi}^{\pi}\int_{-\pi}^{\pi}B_x(\omega_1,\omega_2)\exp\{j(\omega_1 i+\omega_2 k)\}d\omega_1 d\omega_2 \tag{4}$$

Let denote y(t)= $x^2(t)$-E{$x^2(t)$}, the cross correlation between y(t) and x(t) is defined to be:

$$r_{yx}(i,k)=E\{y(t)x(t+k)\}=E\{x^2(t)x(t+k)\}=C_{3x}(0,k) \tag{5}$$

so that its cross spectrum is given by:

$$S_{yx}(\omega)=\sum_{k=-\infty}^{\infty}C_{3x}(0,k)\exp(-j\omega k) \tag{6}$$

and the reverse transformation is also satisfied:

$$C_{3x}(0,k)=\frac{1}{2\pi}\int_{-\pi}^{\pi}S_{yx}(\omega)\exp(j\omega k)d\omega \tag{7}$$

If we compare Eq. (4) with Eq. (7) we obtain:

$$S_{yx}(\omega)=\frac{1}{2\pi}\int_{-\pi}^{\pi}B_x(\omega_1,\omega_2)d\omega_2=\frac{1}{2\pi}\int_{-\pi}^{\pi}B_x(\omega_1,\omega_2)d\omega_1 \tag{8}$$

The integrated bispectrum is defined as a cross spectrum between the signal and its square, and therefore a function of a single frequency variable. Hence, its computation as a cross spectrum leads to significant computational savings, but more important is that the variance of the estimator is of the same order as that of the power spectrum estimator. On the other hand, Gaussian processes have vanishing third order moments so that the bispectrum and integrated bispectrum functions are zero as well, preserving their detection ability. From figure 1 it can be clearly concluded that higher order statistics or polyspectra provide discriminative features for speech/non-speech classification (Górriz et. al, 2005).
Given a finite data set {x(1), x(2), ..., x(N)} the integrated bispectrum is normally estimated by splitting the data set into blocks. Thus, the data set is divided into K_B non-overlapping blocks of data each of size M_B samples so that N= $K_B M_B$. Then, the cross periodogram of the ith block of data is given by

$$\hat{S}_{yx}^{i}(\omega)=\frac{1}{M_B}X^i(\omega)\left[Y^i(\omega)\right]^* \tag{9}$$

where $X^i(\omega)$ and $Y^i(\omega)$) denote the discrete Fourier transforms of x(t) and y(t) for the ith block. Finally, the estimate is obtained by averaging K_B blocks:

$$\hat{S}_{yx}(\omega)=\frac{1}{K_B}\sum_{i=1}^{K_B}\hat{S}_{yx}^{i}(\omega) \tag{10}$$

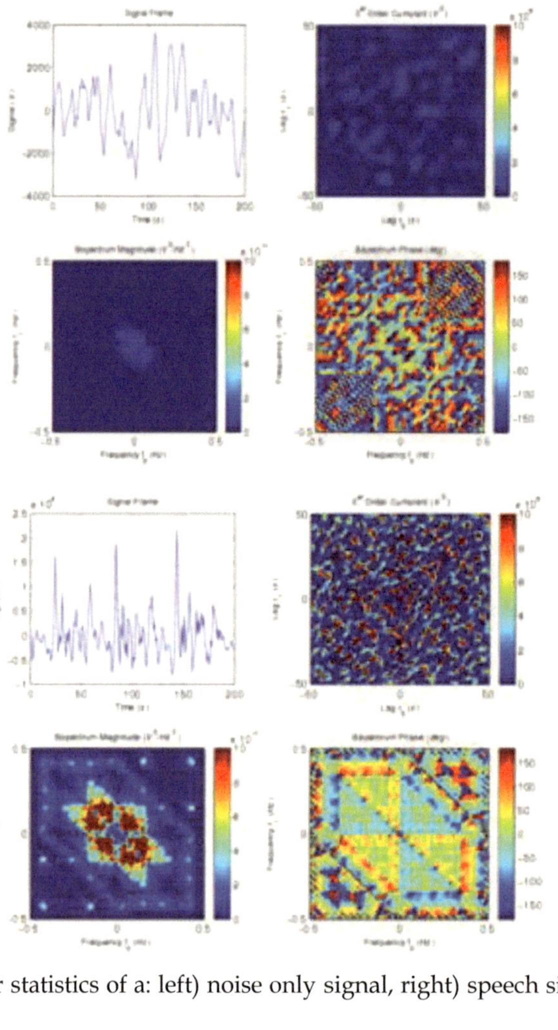

Figure 1. Third order statistics of a: left) noise only signal, right) speech signal corrupted by car noise.

3. Modelling the Noise subspace.

In the VAD problem, the background noise is usually assumed to be stationary over longer period of time than the speech signal. This enables to develop a smoothed noise model during a initialization period, and the estimation of noise statistics during non-speech periods for noise model update. Of course updating the noise parameters requires the information provided by the VAD decision in the previous frames (i.e. the non-speech periods). Then, the decision-making module can be divided to two separate parts: a primary decision, which makes the actual decision for the frame and a secondary decision, which monitors the updating of the noise parameters. These parameters or noise model are related to the feature vectors used in the VAD algorithm, the decision-making module compares them with the actual FV to detect the current speech/non-speech period.

3.1 Spectral Noise Model

Assuming that the first N overlapped frames are nonspeech frames the noise level in the kth band, $N_B(k)$ can be estimated as the median of the set $\{N_B(0, k),..., N_B(N-1,k)\}$. In order to track non stationary noisy environments, the noise spectrum $N_B(k)$ is updated during non-speech periods by means of a 1st order IIR filter on the smoothed spectrum $X_s(k)$, that is:

$$N_B(l,k) = \lambda N_B(l-1,k) + (1-\lambda)X_s(l,k); \quad \lambda \cong 0.99 \tag{11}$$

where $X_s(k)$ is obtained averaging over consecutive frames and adjacent spectral bands, i.e. two consecutive frames and two adjacent bands, l is the frame index and λ is selected empirically. This update is applied to non-speech periods exclusively where $X_s(k)$ provides the instant noise characterization.

3.2 Clustering Based Model

Recently, cluster analysis has been applied to a set of noise spectral FVs to obtain a soft model for VAD (Górriz et al., 2006b). Given an initial set of noise FVs $\{N_B(j,k)\}$ with j=1,…,N, we apply hard decision-based clustering to assign them to a prespecified number of prototypes C<N, labelled by an integer i=1,…,C. This allocation is achieved in such a way that the *similarity measure* is minimized in terms of the squared Euclidean distance between noise energy vectors:

$$d(N_B(j), N_B(j')) = \sum_{k=1}^{K} |N_B(j,k) - N_B(j',k)|^2 = \|N_B(j) - N_B(j')\|_2; \tag{12}$$

and is defined as:

$$J(\Phi) = \frac{1}{2}\sum_{i=1}^{C} \sum_{\Psi(j)=i}^{C} \left\|N_B(j) - \tilde{N}_B(i)\right\|_2 = \tag{13}$$

where $\Psi(j)=i$ denotes a many-to-one mapping, that assigns the jth observation to the ith prototype and

$$\tilde{N}_B(i) = mean(N_B(j)); \quad \forall j \,/\, \Phi(j) = i \in \{1,\ldots,C\} \tag{14}$$

is the mean vector associated with the ith prototype (the sample mean for the ith prototype. Thus, the loss function is minimized by assigning N noise spectral observations to C noise prototypes in such a way that within each prototype the average dissimilarity of the observations is minimized. Once convergence is reached, N K-dimensional pause frames are efficiently modelled by C K-dimensional noise prototype vectors (see figure 2). We call this set of clusters C-partition or noise prototypes since, in this scenario, the word "cluster" is assigned to different classes of *labelled data*, that is **K** is fixed to 2, i.e. we define two clusters: "noise" and "speech" and the cluster "noise" consists of C prototypes (Górriz et al., 2006b).

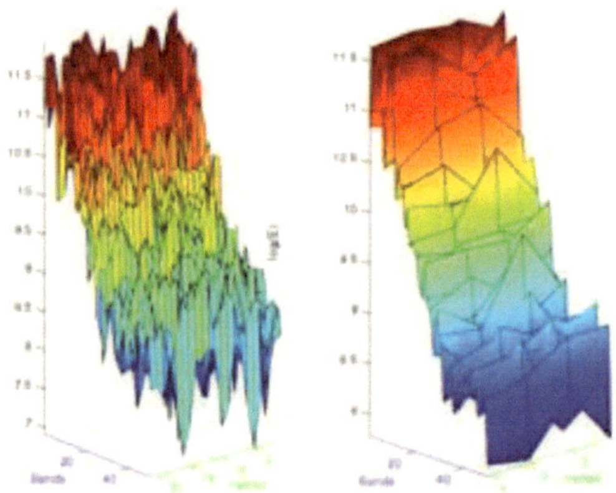

Figure 2. 20 noise log-energy frames, computed using N_{FFT}=256 and averaged over 50 subbands and clustering approach to the latter set of frames using hard decision C-means (C=4 prototypes).

4. Novel methodologies for VAD

The VAD decision is done in the decision-making module of the VAD algorithm, according to the decision rule. This section addresses the problem of voice activity detection formulated in terms of a classical binary hypothesis testing framework:

$$\begin{aligned} H_0 &: \ x(t) = n(t) \\ H_1 &: \ x(t) = s(t) + n(t) \end{aligned} \tag{15}$$

There are several ways of defining this decision rule which selects between both hypotheses, depending of the application where the VAD decision is employed. In the following, we show the most representative methodologies presented by the authors in several works over the past few years: i) multiple observation likelihood ratio tests (MO-LRT) for VAD over the integrated bispectrum (IBI) FV ii) the clustering distance based VAD using spectral FVs and iii) Support Vector Machines for solving a binary classification problem using subband SNRs as FVs.

4.1 Integrated Bispectrum based MO-LRT VAD

In a two-hypothesis test, the optimal decision rule that minimizes the error probability is the Bayes classifier. Given an observation vector **y** to be classified, the problem is reduced to selecting the class (H_0 or H_1) with the largest posterior probability $P(H_i \mid \mathbf{y})$. From the Bayes rule a statistical LRT can be defined by:

$$L(\mathbf{y}) = \frac{p_{\mathbf{y}|H_1}(\mathbf{y} \mid H_1)}{p_{\mathbf{y}|H_0}(\mathbf{y} \mid H_0)} \tag{16}$$

where the observation vector **y** is classified as H_1 if $L(\mathbf{y})$ is greater than $P(H_0)/P(H_1)$ otherwise it is classified as H_0. The LRT first proposed by Sohn (Sohn et al., 1999) for VAD, which was defined on the power spectrum, is generalized and extended to the case where successive observations. The proposed multiple-observation likelihood ratio test (MO-LRT) formulates the decision for the central frame of a (2m+1)-observation buffer $\{y_{l-m}, \ldots, y_{l-1}, y_l, y_{l+1}, \ldots, y_{l+m}\}$:

$$L_{l,m}(\mathbf{y}) = \frac{p_{\mathbf{y}_{l-m},\ldots,\mathbf{y}_{l+m}|H_1}(\mathbf{y}_{l-m},\ldots,\mathbf{y}_{l+m} \mid H_1)}{p_{\mathbf{y}_{l-m},\ldots,\mathbf{y}_{l+m}|H_0}(\mathbf{y}_{l-m},\ldots,\mathbf{y}_{l+m} \mid H_0)} \tag{17}$$

where l denotes the frame being classified as speech (H_1) or non-speech (H_0). Note that, assuming statistical independence between the successive observation vectors, the corresponding log-LRT:

$$l_{l,m}(\mathbf{y}) = \sum_{k=l-m}^{l+m} \ln\left(\frac{p_{\mathbf{y}_k|H_1}(\mathbf{y}_k \mid H_1)}{p_{\mathbf{y}_k|H_0}(\mathbf{y}_k \mid H_0)}\right) \tag{18}$$

is recursive in nature and if each term of equation (18) is defined as $\Phi(k)$ the latter equation can be recursively calculated as:

$$l_{l+1,m}(\mathbf{y}) = l_{l,m}(\mathbf{y}) - \Phi(l-m) + \Phi(l+m+1) \tag{19}$$

The so called multiple observation LRT (MO-LRT) reports significant improvements in robustness as the number of observations increases. Assuming the integrated bispectrum $\{S_{yx}(\omega): \omega\}$ as the FV **y** and to be independent zero-mean Gaussian variables in presence and absence of speech with variances λ_1 and λ_0, resp. we obtain that the ratio of likelihoods can be expressed as:

$$\Phi(\mathbf{y}_k) = \sum_{\omega} \frac{\xi_k(\omega)\gamma_k(\omega)}{1+\xi_k(\omega)}, - \log(1+\xi_k(\omega)) \tag{20}$$

where the *a priori* and *a posteriori* variance ratios are defined as:

$$\xi_k(\omega) \equiv \frac{\lambda_1^k(\omega)}{\lambda_0^k(\omega)} - 1; \quad \gamma_k(\omega) \equiv \frac{\left|S_{yx}^k(\omega)\right|}{\lambda_0^k(\omega)} \tag{21}$$

In order to evaluate the decision function the computation of variances under both hypotheses must be properly established. This is discussed further in (Ramírez et al., 2006) where a complete derivation of them is obtained in terms of the power spectrum of the noise (computed using the model presented in section 3.1) and the clean signal.
Figure 3 shows an example of the operation of the contextual MO-LRT VAD on an utterance of the Spanish SpeechDat-Car database (Moreno et al., 2000). The figure shows the decision variables for the tests defined by equation 20 and, alternatively, for the test with the second log-term in equation 20 suppressed (approximation) when compared to a fixed threshold η= 1.5. For this example, MB= 256 and m= 8. This approximation reduces the variance during non-speech periods. It can be shown that using an 8-frame window reduces the variability

of the decision variable yielding to a reduced noise variance and better speech/non-speech discrimination. On the other hand, the inherent anticipation of the VAD decision contributes to reduce the number of speech clipping errors.

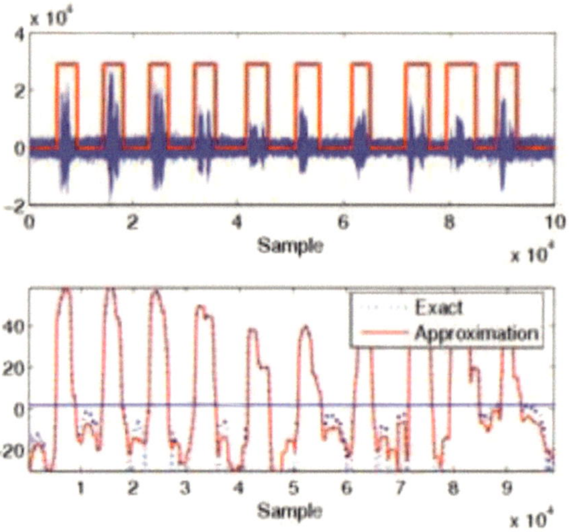

Figure 3. Operation of the MO-LRT VAD defined on the integrated bispectrum.

4.2 Long Term C-Means VAD

The speech/pause discrimination may be described as an unsupervised learning problem. Clustering is an appropriate solution for this case where the data set is divided into groups which are related ``in some sense''. Despite the simplicity of clustering algorithms, there is an increasing interest in the use of clustering methods in pattern recognition (Anderberg et al., 1973), image processing (Jain & Flynn, 1996) and information retrieval (Rasmussen, 1992). Clustering has a rich history in other disciplines such as machine learning, biology, psychiatry, psychology, archaeology, geology, geography, and marketing. Cluster analysis, also called data segmentation has a variety of goals. All of these are related to grouping or segmenting a collection of objects into subsets or "clusters" such that those within each cluster are more closely related to one another than objects assigned to different clusters. Cluster analysis is also used to form descriptive statistics to ascertain whether or not the data consists of a set of distinct subgroups, each group representing objects with substantially different properties. Consider noise model proposed in section 3.2 and let $\hat{E}(l)$ be the decision feature vector at frame l that is defined on the MO window as follows:

$$\hat{E}(l) \equiv \max\{E_B(j)\}; \quad j = l-m,\ldots,l+m \tag{22}$$

where $E_B(j)$ is defined in section 2.1 and the function *max* is applied in each frequency band *k*. The selection of this envelope feature vector, describing not only a single instantaneous frame but also a (2*m*+1) entire neighbourhood, is useful as it detects the presence of voice beforehand (pause-speech transition) and holds the detection flag, smoothing the VAD decision (as a hangover based algorithm in speech-pause transition (Marzinzik & Kollmeier, 2002), (Li et al., 2002).

In the LTCM-VAD (Górriz et al., 2006b) the presence of the second "cluster" (speech frame) is detected if the following ratio holds:

$$\eta(l) \equiv \log\left(\frac{1}{K}\sum_{k=1}^{K}\frac{\hat{E}(k,l)}{\left\langle \tilde{N}_B(i,k)\right\rangle}\right) > \gamma; \tag{23}$$

where $\langle\tilde{N}_B(i)\rangle=(1/C)\Sigma^C_{i=1}\tilde{N}_B(i)=(1/C)\Sigma^C_{i=1}\Sigma^N_{j=1}\gamma_{ij}N_B(j)$ is the averaged noise prototype center defined in terms of the noise model presented in section 3.2 and γ is the decision threshold.

In order to adapt the operation of the proposed VAD to non-stationary and noise environments, the set of noise prototypes are updated according to the VAD decision during non-speech periods (not satisfying equation 23) in a competitive manner (only the closer noise prototype $\tilde{N}_B(l)$ at time l is moved towards the current feature vector $\hat{E}(l)$):

$$\begin{aligned}\tilde{N}_B^C(l) &\equiv \arg_{\min}\left(\left\|\hat{E}(l)-\tilde{N}_B(i)\right\|_2\right) \quad i=1,\ldots,C\\ \tilde{N}_B^C(l+1) &= \alpha\tilde{N}_B^C(l)+(1-\alpha)\hat{E}(l); \quad \alpha\approx 0.9\end{aligned} \tag{24}$$

where α is a normalized constant. Its value is close to one for a soft decision function (i.e. we selected in simulation α=0.99), that is, uncorrected classified speech frames contributing to the false alarm rate will not affect the noise space model significantly.

4.3 SVM enabled VAD

SVMs have recently been proposed for pattern recognition in a wide range of applications by its ability for learning from experimental data (Vapnik, 1995). The reason is that SVMs are much more effective than other conventional parametric classifiers. In SVM-based pattern recognition, the objective is to build a function f: $R^N \rightarrow \pm 1$ using training data that is, N-dimensional patterns $\mathbf{x}_i$ and class labels y_i:

$$(\mathbf{x}_1,y_1),(\mathbf{x}_2,y_2),\ldots,(\mathbf{x}_l,y_l)\in R^N\times\{\pm 1\} \tag{25}$$

so that f will correctly classify new examples (**x**,y). The use of kernels in SVM enables to map the data into some other dot product space (called feature space) F via a nonlinear transformation Φ: $R^N \rightarrow F$ and perform the linear SVM algorithm (Vapnik, 1995) in F. The kernel is related to the Φ function by $k(\mathbf{x}_i,\mathbf{x}_j)=(\Phi(\mathbf{x}_i)\bullet\Phi(\mathbf{x}_j))$. In the input space, the hyperplane corresponds to a nonlinear decision function whose form is determined by the kernel. Thus, the decision function can be formulated in terms of a nonlinear function as:

$$f(\mathbf{x})=\mathrm{sgn}\left(\sum_{i=1}^{\ell}\upsilon_i k(\mathbf{x}_i,\mathbf{x})+b\right) \tag{26}$$

where the parameters υ_i are the solution of a quadratic programming problem that are usually determined by the well known Sequential Minimal Optimization (SMO) algorithm (Platt, 1999). Many classification problems are always separable in the feature space and are

able to obtain better results by using RBF kernels instead of linear and polynomial kernel functions (Clarkson & Moreno, 1999).
The feature vector used in the SVM approach is the subband SNR described in section 2.1 but also including long term information: the long-term spectral envelope (LTSE) (Ramírez et al., 2006b) including contextual information of the speech signal is computed by: = $\max\{X_j(\omega_m)$, where $j=l-L,\ldots,l-1, l, l+1,\ldots,l+L\}$ and its dimensionality is reduced to a wide K-band spectral representation as in section 2.1.
An optional denoising process is applied to the input signal which consist of: i) Spectrum smoothing, ii) Noise estimation., iii) Wiener Filtering (WF) design and iv) Frequency domain filtering (Ramirez et al, 2006b). Once the SVM model is trained (i.e using the LIBSVM software tool (Chang & Lin, 2001); a training set consisting of 12 utterances of the AURORA 3 Spanish SpeechDat-Car (SDC) was used), we obtain the relevant support vectors and parameters in the classification of noise and speech features which enable to build the non-linear decision function shown in equation 26. The evaluation of the latter function is computational expensive, however evaluation methods have been also proposed (Ramírez et al. 2006b) in order to speed up the VAD decision. The method is based on a off-line computation of the decision rule over an input space grid and storing it in an *N*-dimensional look-up table. Finally, given a feature vector **x** we look for the nearest point in the grid previously defined and then perform a table look-up to assign a class (speech or non-speech) to the former feature vector.
Fig. 4..left shows the training data set in the 3-band input space. It is shown that the two classes can not be separated without error in the input space. Fig. 4.right shows the SVM decision rule that is obtained after the training process. Note that, i) the non-speech and speech classes are clearly distinguished in the 3-D space, and ii) the SVM model learns how the signal is masked by the noise and automatically defines the decision rule in the input space. Fig. 4. right also suggests a fast algorithm for performing the decision rule defined by equation 26 that becomes computationally expensive when the number of support vectors and/or the dimension of the feature vector are high. Note that all the information needed for deciding the class a given feature vector **x** belongs resides in figure 4.right. Thus, the input space can be discretized over the different components of the feature vector **x**.

Figure 4. Classification rule in the input space after training a 3-band SVM model. left) Training data set, right) SVM classification rule.

5. Experimental Section.

Several experiments are commonly conducted in order to evaluate the performance of VAD algorithms. The analysis is mainly focussed on the determination of the error probabilities or classification errors at different SNR levels (Marzinzik & Kollmeier, 2002) and the influence of the VAD decision on the performance of speech processing systems (Bouquin-Jeannes & Faucon, 1995). Subjective performance tests have also been considered for the evaluation of VADs working in combination with speech coders (Benyassine et al., 1997). This section describes the experimental framework and the objective performance tests conducted in this paper to evaluate the proposed algorithms.

5.1 Receiver operating characteristics (ROC) curves

The ROC curves are frequently used to completely describe the VAD error rate. They show the tradeoff between speech and non-speech detection accuracy as the decision threshold varies. The AURORA subset of the original Spanish SpeechDat-Car database (Moreno et al., 2000) was used in this analysis. This database contains 4914 recordings using close-talking and distant microphones from more than 160 speakers. The files are categorized into three noisy conditions: quiet, low noisy and highly noisy conditions, which represent different driving conditions with average SNR values between 25dB and 5dB. The non-speech hit rate (HR0) and the false alarm rate (FAR0= 100-HR1) were determined for each noise condition being the actual speech frames and actual speech pauses determined by hand-labelling the database on the close-talking microphone.

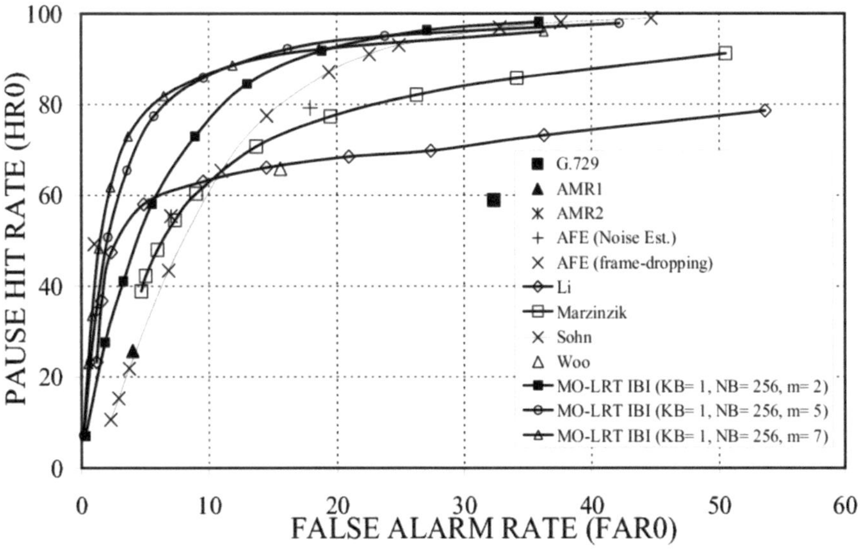

Figure 5. Classification rule in the input space after training a 3-band SVM model. left) Training data set, right) SVM classification rule.

Figure 5 shows the ROC curves of the proposed IBI-MO-LRT VAD and other frequently referred algorithms (Woo et al., 2000), (Li et al., 2002), (Marzinzik & Kollmeier, 2002), (Sohn et al., 1999) for recordings from the distant microphone in high noisy conditions. The working points of the G.729, AMR and AFE standard VADs are also included. The efficient MO-LRT IBI VAD exhibits a shift of the ROC curve when the number of observations (*m*) increases as shown in figure 5. The method shows clear improvements in detection accuracy over standardized VADs and over a representative set of recently published VAD algorithms such us (Woo et al., 2000), (Li et al., 2002), (Marzinzik & Kollmeier, 2002), (Sohn et al, 1999).

The AURORA-2 database (Hirsch & Pearce, 2000) is also an adequate database for this analysis since it is built on the clean TIdigits database that consists of sequences of up to seven connected digits spoken by American English talkers as source speech, and a selection of eight different real-world noises that have been artificially added to the speech at SNRs of 20dB, 15dB, 10dB, 5dB, 0dB and -5dB. These noisy signals have been recorded at different places (suburban train, crowd of people (babble), car, exhibition hall, restaurant, street, airport and train station), and were selected to represent the most probable application scenarios for telecommunication terminals. In the discrimination analysis, the clean TIdigits database was used to manually label each utterance as speech or non-speech on a frame by frame basis for reference. Figure 6 provide comparative results of this analysis and compare the proposed LTCM VAD to standardized algorithms including the ITU-T G.729 (ITU, 1996), ETSI AMR (ETSI, 1999) and ETSI AFE (ETSI, 2002) and recently reported (Sohn et al., 1999), (Woo et al., 2000), (Li et al., 2002), (Marzinzik & Kollmeier, 2002) VADs in terms of speech hit-rate (HR1) for clean conditions and SNR levels ranging from 20 to -5 dB. Note that results for the two VADs defined in the AFE DSR standard (ETSI, 2002) for estimating the noise spectrum in the Wiener filtering (WF) stage and non-speech frame-dropping (FD) are provided. The results shown in these figures are averaged values for the entire set of noises. Table 1 summarizes the advantages provided by LTCM VAD over the different VAD methods in terms of the average speech/non-speech hit-rates (over the entire range of SNR values). Thus, the proposed method with a mean of 97.57% HR1 and a mean of 47.81% HR0 yields the best trade-off in speech/non-speech detection.

Figure 6. right) Speech hit rates (HR1) of standard VADs as a function of the SNR for the AURORA-2 database. Left) Speech hit rates (HR1) of other VADs as a function of the SNR for the AURORA-2 database.

	G729	AMR 1	AMR2	AFE(WF)	AFE(FD)	**LTCM**
HR0(%)	31.77	31.31	42.77	57.68	28.74	**47.81**
HR1(%)	93.00	98.18	93.76	88.72	97.70	**97.57**
	Sohn	Woo	Li	Marzinzik	**LTCM**	
HR0(%)	43.66	55.40	57.03	52.69	**47.81**	
HR1(%)	94.46	88.41	83.65	93.04	**97.57**	

Table 1. Average speech/non-speech hit rates for SNRs between clean conditions and -5 dB. Comparison to standardized VADs, and other VAD methods.

Figure 7 shows the ROC curves of the proposed SVM VAD, after a training process that consists of 12 utterances of the AURORA 3 Spanish SpeechDat-Car (SDC), using for varying L and K= 4 (number of subbands). It is shown that increasing the time span up to 8 frames also leads to a shift-up and to the left of the ROC curve. The optimal parameters for the proposed VAD are then K= 4 subbands and L= 8 frames. The results show significant improvements in speech/non-speech detection accuracy over standard VADs and over a representative set of VAD algorithms. These improvements are obtained by including contextual information in the feature vector and defining a non-linear decision rule over a wide band spectral representation of the data which enables a SVM-based classifier to learn how the speech signal is masked by the acoustic noise present in the environment.

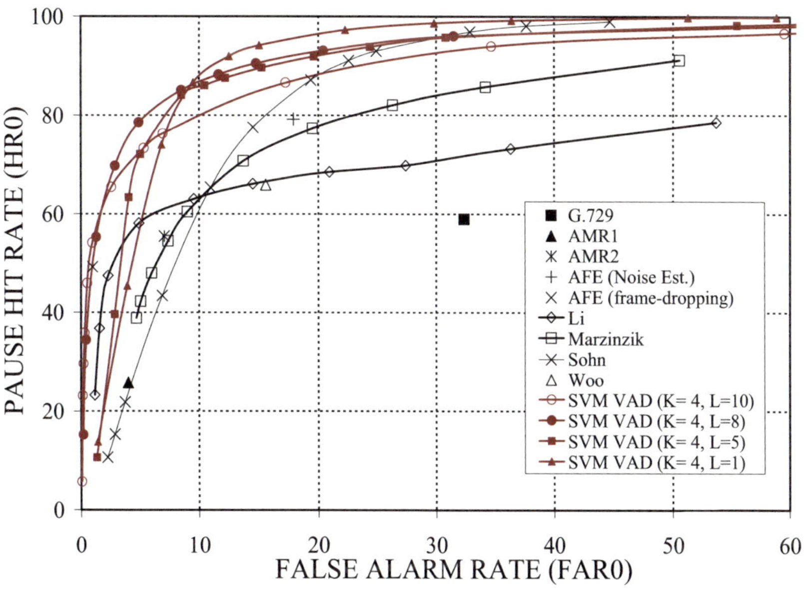

Figure 7. Influence of the time span L on the ROC curves. Comparison to standard and recently published VAD methods (High: high speed, good road, 5 dB average SNR).

5.2 Speech recognition experiments

Although the ROC curves are effective for VAD evaluation, the influence of the VAD in a speech recognition system was also studied. Many authors claim that VADs are well compared by evaluating speech recognition performance (Woo et al., 2000) since non-efficient speech/non-speech classification is an important source of the degradation of recognition performance in noisy environments (Karray & Martin, 2003). There are two clear motivations for that: i) noise parameters such as its spectrum are updated during non-speech periods being the speech enhancement system strongly influenced by the quality of the noise estimation, and ii) frame-dropping (FD), a frequently used technique in speech recognition to reduce the number of insertion errors caused by the noise, is based on the VAD decision and speech misclassification errors lead to loss of speech, thus causing irrecoverable deletion errors. This section evaluates the VAD according to the objective it was developed for, that is, by assessing the influence of the VAD in a speech recognition system.

The reference framework (base) considered for these experiments is the ETSI AURORA project for distributed speech recognition (ETSI, 2000). The recognizer is based on the HTK (Hidden Markov Model Toolkit) software package (Young et al., 1997). The task consists of recognizing connected digits which are modeled as whole word HMMs (Hidden Markov Models) with 16 states per word, simple left-to-right models and 3-gaussian mixtures per state (diagonal covariance matrix). Speech pause models consist of 3 states with a mixture of 6 Gaussians per state. The 39-parameter feature vector consists of 12 cepstral coefficients (without the zero-order coefficient), the logarithmic frame energy plus the corresponding delta and acceleration coefficients. For the AURORA-3 SpeechDat-Car databases, the so called well-matched (WM), medium-mismatch (MM) and high-mismatch (HM) conditions are used. These databases contain recordings from the close-talking and distant microphones. In WM condition, both close-talking and hands-free microphones are used for training and testing. In MM condition, both training and testing are performed using the hands-free microphone recordings. In HM condition, training is done using close-talking microphone recordings from all the driving conditions while testing is done using the hands-free microphone at low and high noise driving conditions. Finally, recognition performance is assessed in terms of the word accuracy (WAcc) that considers deletion, substitution and insertion errors.

Table 2 shows the recognition performance for the Spanish SpeechDat-Car database when WF and FD are performed on the base system (ETSI, 2000) using the IBI-MO-LRT and LTCM VADs. Our VADs outperform all the algorithms used for reference yielding relevant improvements in speech recognition. Note that, this particular database used in the AURORA 3 experiments have longer non-speech periods than the AURORA 2 database and then, the effectiveness of the VAD results more important for the speech recognition system (Ramírez et al., 2006), (Górriz et al., 2006b). This fact can be clearly shown when comparing the performance of the proposed VADs to Marzinzik VAD (Marzinzik & Kollmeier, 2002). The word accuracy of the VADs is quite similar for the AURORA 2 task. However, the proposed VADs yield a significant performance improvement over Marzinzik VAD (Marzinzik & Kollmeier, 2002) for the AURORA 3 database (Górriz et al., 2006b), (Ramírez et al., 2006).

	Base	Woo	Li	Marzinzik	Sohn	G729
WM	**92.94**	95.35	91.82	94.29	96.07	88.62
MM	**83.31**	89.30	77.45	89.81	91.64	72.84
HM	**51.55**	83.64	78.52	79.43	84.03	65.50
Ave.	**75.93**	89.43	82.60	87.84	90.58	75.65
	AMR1	AMR2	AFE	**LTCM**	**IBI-LRT**	
WM	94.65	95.67	95.28	**96.41**	**96.39**	
MM	80.59	90.91	90.23	**91.61**	**91.75**	
HM	62.41	85.77	77.53	**86.20**	**86.65**	
Ave.	74.33	90.78	87.68	**91.41**	**91.60**	

Table 1. Average speech/non-speech hit rates for SNRs between clean conditions and -5 dB. Comparison to standardized VADs, and other VAD methods.

6. Conclusion

This paper showed three different schemes for improving speech detection robustness and the performance of speech recognition systems working in noisy environments. These methods are based on: i) statistical likelihood ratio tests (LRTs) formulated in terms of the integrated bispectrum of the noisy signal. The integrated bispectrum is defined as a cross spectrum between the signal and its square, and therefore a function of a single frequency variable. It inherits the ability of higher order statistics to detect signals in noise with many other additional advantages; ii) Hard decision clustering approach where a set of prototypes is used to characterize the noisy channel. Detecting the presence of speech is enabled by a decision rule formulated in terms of an averaged distance between the observation vector and a cluster-based noise model; and iii) an effective method employing support vector machines (SVM) , a paradigm of learning from examples based in Vapkik-Chervonenkis theory. The use of kernels in SVM enables to map the data, via a nonlinear transformation, into some other dot product space (called feature space) in which the classification task is settled.

The proposed methods incorporate contextual information to the decision rule, a strategy that has reported significant improvements in speech detection accuracy and robust speech recognition applications. The optimal window size was determined by analyzing the overlap between the distributions of the decision variable and the error rate. The experimental analysis conducted on the well-known AURORA databases has reported significant improvements over standardized techniques such as ITU G.729, AMR1, AMR2 and ESTI AFE VADs, as well as over recently published VADs. The analysis assessed: i) the speech/non-speech detection accuracy by means of the ROC curves, with the proposed VADs yielding improved hit-rates and reduced false alarms when compared to all the reference algorithms, and ii) the recognition rate when the VADs are considered as part of a complete speech recognition system, showing a sustained advantage in speech recognition performance.

7. References

Karray, L. & Martin, A. (2003). Towards improving speech detection robustness for speech recognition in adverse environments, *Speech Communitation*, No. 3, (2003) (261-276), 0167-6393

Ramírez, J. ; Segura, J. C. ; Benítez, M.C.; de la Torre, A. & Rubio, A. (2003). A New Adaptive Long-Term Spectral Estimation Voice Activity Detector, *Proceedings of EUROSPEECH*, pp. 3041-3044, 1018-4074, Geneva, Switzerland, September 2003, ISCA.

ETSI, (1999). Voice Activity Detector (VAD) for Adaptive Multi-Rate (AMR) Speech Traffic Channels, 1999, ETSI EN 301 708 Recommendation.

ITU, (1996). A silence compression scheme for G.729 optimized for terminals conforming to recommendation V.70, 1996, ITU-T Recommendation G.729-Annex B

Krasny, L, (2000). Soft-decision speech signal estimation, *The Journal of the Acoustical Society of America* Vol.108 (2000), (25-75), 0001-4966.

Sangwan, A. ; Chiranth, M.C. ; Jamadagni, H.S. ; Sah, R. ; Prasad R.V. & Gaurav, V. (2002). VAD Techniques for Real-Time Speech Transmission on the Internet, *Proceedings of the IEEE International Conference on High-Speed Networks and Multimedia Communications*, pp 46-50, July 2002.

Basbug, F. ; Swaminathan, K. & Nandkumar S. (2003). Noise reduction and echo cancellation front-end for speech codecs, *IEEE Transactions on Speech and Audio Processing* Vol. 11, (2003), (1-13) , 1063-6676.

Sohn, J.; Kim, N.S. & Sung, W. (1999) A statistical model-based voice activity detection, *IEEE Signal Processing Letters*, Vol. 16, No. 1, (1-3), 1070-9908.

Cho, y.d. & Kondoz, A. (2001). Analysis and improvement of a statistical model-based voice activity detector, *IEEE Signal Processing Letters*, Vol 8, No. 10, (276-278), 1070-9908.

Bouquin-Jeannes, R.L. & Faucon G (1995). Study of a voice activity detector and its influence on a noise reduction system, *Speech Communication*, Vol 16, (1995), (245-254), 0167-6393.

Woo, K. ; Yang, T. ; Park, K. & Lee, C. (2000). Robust voice activity detection algorithm for estimating noise spectrum, Electronics Letters, Vol 36, No. 2, (2000), (180-181) 0013-5194.

Li, Q. ; Zheng, J. ; Tsai, A. &Zhou, Q. (2002). Robust endpoint detection and energy normalization for real-time speech and speaker recognition, *IEEE Transactions on Speech and Audio Processing*, Vol 10, No.3, (2002) (146-157), 1063-6676.

Marzinzik, M. & Kollmeier, B. (2002). Speech pause detection for noise spectrum estimation by tracking power envelope dynamics, *IEEE Transactions on Speech and Audio Processing*, Vol 10, No. 6, (2002), (341-351), 1063-6676.

Chengalvarayan, R. (1999). Robust energy normalization using speech/non-speech discriminator for German connected digit recognition, *Proceedings of EUROSPEECH*, pp 61-64 Budapest, Hungary, September 1999, ISCA.

Tucker, R. (1992). Voice activity detection using a periodicity measure, IEE Proceedings, Communications, Speech and Vision, Vol. 139, No. 4 (1992), (377-380). 1350-2425.

Górriz, J.M. (2006a). New Advances in Voice Activiy Detection. Ph-D., 84-338-3863-6, University of Granada, July 2006, Granada.

Ramírez, J.; Górriz J.M. & Segura J.C. (2006). Statistical Voice Activity Detection Based on Integrated Bispectrum Likelihood Ratio Tests for Robust Speech Recognition. In press *The Journal of the Acoustical Society of America,* Vol.X, No.X, (2006) (XXX-XXX), 0001-4966.

Vapnik, V.N. (1995). The Nature of Statistical Learning Theory. Springer-Verlag, 9780387945590, Berlin, (1995).

Górriz, J.M. ; Ramírez, J. ; Puntonet, C.G. & Segura, J.C (2006b). An effective cluster-based model for robust speech detection and speech recognition in noisy environments. *The Journal of Acoustical Society of America.* No. 120, Vol. 470 (2006). (470-481). 0001-4966.

Górriz, J.M. ; Ramírez, J. ; Segura, J.C. & Puntonet, C.G. (2005). Improved MO-LRT VAD based on bispectra Gaussian model, *Electronics Letters,* Vol. 41, No. 15, (2005), (877-879).

Moreno, A. ; Borge, L. ; Christoph, D. ; Gael, R. ; Khalid, C. ; Stephan, E. & Jeffrey, A. (2000). SpeechDat-Car: A Large Speech Database for Automotive Environments. *Proceedings of the II Second International Conference on Language Resources and Evaluation Conference,* May 2000, Athens.

Jain, A. & Flynn, P. (1996) Image segmentation using clustering. In Advances in Image Understanding. A Festschrift for Azriel Rosenfeld, N. Ahuja and K. Bowyer, (Ed.), (65−83) , IEEE Press, Piscataway, NJ.

Anderberg, M.R.; Odell, J. ; Ollason, D. ; Valtchev, V. & Woodland, P. (1973). Cluster Analysis for Applications. Academic Press, Inc., 0120576503. New York, NY.

Rasmussen, E. (1992). Clustering algorithms, In Information Retrieval: Data Structures and Algorithms, W. B. Frakes and R. Baeza-Yates, (Ed.). (419-442) Prentice-Hall, Inc., Upper Saddle River, NJ.

Platt, J.C. (1999). Fast Training of Support Vector Machines using Sequential Minimal Optimization In Advances in Kernel Methods - Support Vector Learning, (185-208). MIT Press.

Clarkson, P, & Moreno P.J. (1999). On the use of support vector machines for phonetic classification, *Proceedings of the IEEE International Conference on Acoustics, Speech and Signal Processing,* Vol 2, March 1999, pp 585-588. Phoenix.

Ramírez, J.; Yélamos, P.; Górriz, J.M. & Segura J.C. (2006b). SVM-based Speech Endpoint Detection Using Contextual Speech Features. *Electronic Letters* Vol 42 No.7 (65-66) 0013-5194.

Chang, C.C. & Lin, C.J. (2001), LIBSVM: a library for support vector machines, Dept. of Computer Science and Information Engineering, National Taiwan University, (2001, Software available at http://www.csie.ntu.edu.tw/~cjlin/libsvm.

Benyassine, A.; Shlomot, E.; Su, H.; Massaloux, D.; Lamblin, C. & Petit, J (1997). ITU-T Recommendation G.729 Annex B: A silence compression scheme for use with G.729 optimized for V.70 digital simultaneous voice and data applications. *IEEE Communications Magazine.* Vol 35, (64-73) .

Hirsch H. & Pearce, D. (2000). The AURORA experimental framework for the performance evaluation of speech recognition systems under noise conditions, In ISCA ITRW ASR2000 Automatic Speech Recognition: Challenges for the Next Millennium. Paris, France.

ETSI, (2002). Speech processing, transmission and quality aspects (STQ); distributed speech recognition; advanced front-end feature extraction algorithm; compression algorithms, ETSI ES 202 050 Recommendation).

ETSI, (2000). Speech processing, transmission and quality aspects (stq); distributed speech recognition; front-end feature extraction algorithm; compression algorithms, ETSI ES 201 108 Recommendation.

Young, S; Odell, J.; Ollason, D.; Valtchev, V. & Woodland, P. (1997) The HTK Book. Cambridge University.

4

Voice and Noise Detection with AdaBoost

T. Takiguchi, N. Miyake, H. Matsuda, and Y. Ariki
Kobe University
Japan

1. Introduction

Speech recognition is one of our most effective communication tools when it comes to a hands-free (human-machine) interface. Most current speech recognition systems are capable of achieving good performance in clean acoustic environments. However, these systems require the user to turn the microphone on/off to capture voices only. Also, in hands-free environments, degradation in speech recognition performance increases significantly because the speech signal may be corrupted by a wide variety of sources, including background noise and reverberation.
Sudden and short-period noises also affect the performance of a speech recognition system. Figure 1 shows a speech wave overlapped by a sudden noise (a telephone call). To recognize the speech data correctly, noise reduction or model adaptation to the sudden noise is required. However, it is difficult to remove such noises because we do not know where the noise overlapped and what the noise was. Many studies have been conducted on non-stationary noise reduction in a single channel (A. Betkowska, et al., 2006), (V. Barreaud, et al., 2003), (M. Fujimoto & S. Nakamura, 2005). But it is difficult for these methods to track sudden noises.

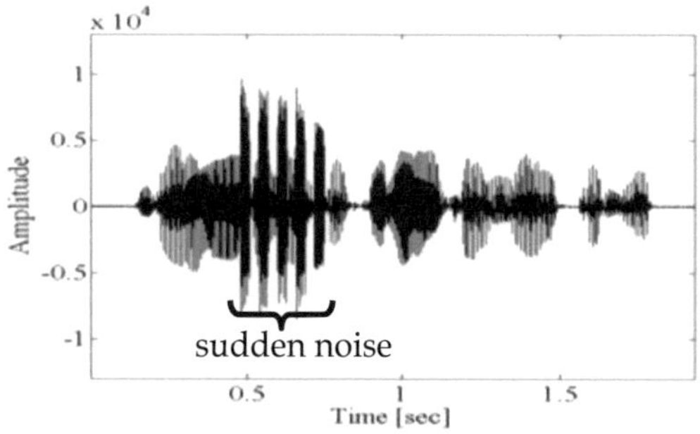

Figure 1. Speech wave overlapped by a sudden noise (telephone call)

In actual noisy environments, a speech detection algorithm plays an especially important role in noise reduction, speech recognition, and so on. In this chapter, a noise detection and classification algorithm using AdaBoost, which can achieve extremely high detection rates, is described. If a speech recognition system can detect sudden noises, it will make the system able to require the same utterance from the user again, and if clean speech data can be input, it will help prevent system operation errors. Also, if it can be determined what noise is overlapped, the noise characteristics information will be useful in noise reduction. "Boosting" is a technique in which a set of weak classifiers is combined to form one high-performance prediction rule, and AdaBoost (Y. Freund & R. E. Schapire, 1999) serves as an adaptive boosting algorithm in which the rule for combining the weak classifiers adapts to the problem and is able to yield extremely efficient classifiers. In this chapter, we discuss the AdaBoost algorithm for sudden-noise detection and classification problems. The proposed method shows an improved speech detection rate, compared to that of conventional detectors based on the GMM (Gaussian Mixture Model).

2. System Overview

Figure 2 shows the overview of the noise detection and classification system based on AdaBoost. The speech waveform is split into a small segment by a window function. Each segment is converted to the linear spectral domain by applying the discrete Fourier transform. Then the logarithm is applied to the linear power spectrum, and the feature vector (log-mel spectrum) is obtained. Next the system identifies whether or not the feature vector is a noisy speech overlapped by sudden noises using two-class AdaBoost, where the multi-class AdaBoost is not used due to the computation cost. Then the system clarifies the kind of sudden noises from only the detected noisy frame using multi-class AdaBoost.

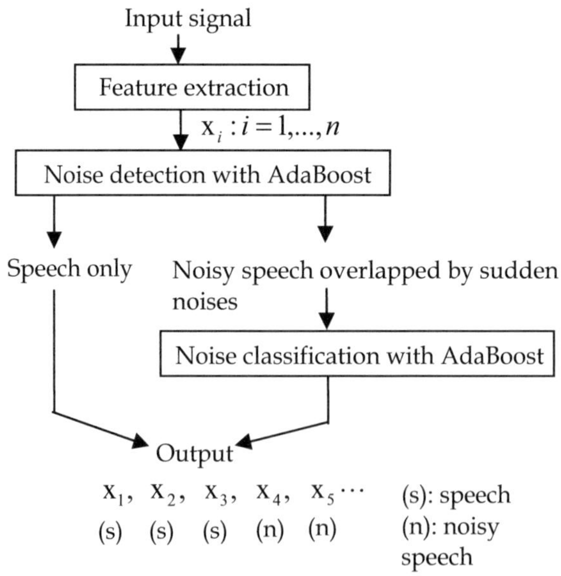

Figure 2. System overview of noise detection and classification

3. Noise Detection with AdaBoost

Boosting is a voting method by weighted weak classifier and AdaBoost is one of method of Boosting (Y. Freund & et al., 1997). The Boosting decides the weak classifiers and their weights based on the minimizing of loss function in a two-class problem. Since the Boosting is fast and has high performance, it is commonly used for face detection in images (P. Viola, et al., 2001).

Input: n examples $Z = \{(x_1, y_1), \ldots, (x_n, y_n)\}$

Initialize: $w_1(z_i) = 1/n$ for all $i = 1, \ldots, n$

Do for $t = 1, \ldots, T$

1. Train a base learner with respect to weighted example distribution w_t and obtain hypothesis $h_t : x \mapsto \{-1,1\}$.
2. Calculate the training error ε_t of h_t.

$$\varepsilon_t = \sum_{i=1}^{n} w_t(z_i) \frac{I(h_t(x_i) \neq y_i) + 1}{2}$$

3. Set

$$\alpha_t = \log \frac{1-\varepsilon_t}{\varepsilon_t}$$

4. Update example distribution.

$$w_{t+1} = \frac{w_t(z_i) \exp\{\alpha_t \cdot I(h_t(x_i) \neq y_i)\}}{\sum_{j=1}^{n} w_t(z_i) \exp\{\alpha_t \cdot I(h_t(x_i) \neq y_i)\}} \quad (1)$$

Output: final hypothesis:

$$f(x) = \frac{1}{|\alpha|} \sum_t \alpha_t \cdot h_t(x) \quad (2)$$

Figure 3. AdaBoost algorithm for noise detection

Figure 3 shows the AdaBoost learning algorithm. The AdaBoost algorithm uses a set of training data, $\{(x_1, y_1), \ldots, (x_n, y_n)\}$, where x_i is the i-th feature vector of the observed signal and y is a set of possible labels. For the noise detection, we consider just two possible labels, $Y = \{-1,1\}$, where the label, -1, means noisy speech, and the label, 1, means speech only.

As shown in Figure 3, the weak learner generates a hypothesis $h_t : x \rightarrow \{-1,1\}$ that has a small error. In this paper, single-level decision trees (also known as decision stamps) are used as the base classifiers.

$$h_t(x_i) = \begin{cases} 1, & \text{if } x_j \leq \theta_t \\ -1, & \text{else} \end{cases} \quad (3)$$

Here x_j is the *j*-dimensional feature of x and θ_t is the threshold which is decided by minimizing the error. After training the weak learner on the *t*-th iteration, the error of h_t is calculated.
Next, AdaBoost sets a parameter α_t. Intuitively, α_t measures the importance that is assigned to h_t. Then the weight w_t is updated. Equation (1) leads to the increase of the weight for the data misclassified by h_t. Therefore, the weight tends to concentrate on ``hard'' data. After the *T*-th iteration, the final hypothesis, $f(\mathrm{x})$ combines the outputs of the *T* weak hypotheses using a weighted majority vote. If $f(\mathrm{x}_i) < \eta$, AdaBoost outputs the label -1 and that means the *i*-th frame is a noisy frame overlapped by sudden noises to detect. In this paper, we set $\eta = 0$. As AdaBoost trains the weight, focusing on ``hard'' data, we can expect that it will achieve extremely high detection rates even if the power of noise to detect is low.

4. Noise Classification with Multi-Class AdaBoost

As AdaBoost is based on a two-class classifier, it is difficult to classify multi-class noises. Therefore, we use an extended multi-class AdaBoost to classify sudden noises. There are some ways to classify multi-class using a pair-wise method (such as a tree), K-pair-wise, or one-vs-rest (E. Alpaydin, 2004). In this paper, we used one-vs-rest for multi-class classification with AdaBoost. The multi-class AdaBoost algorithm is as follows:

Input: *m* examples $\{(\mathrm{x}_1, y_1), \ldots, (\mathrm{x}_m, y_m)\}$

$$y_i = \{1, \ldots, K\}$$

Do for $k = 1, \ldots, K$

1. Set labels

$$y_i^k = \begin{cases} 1, & \text{if } y_i = k \\ -1, & \text{else} \end{cases} \tag{4}$$

2. Learn *k*-th classifier $f^k(\mathrm{x})$ using AdaBoost for data set

$$Z^k = (\mathrm{x}_1, y_1^k), \ldots, (\mathrm{x}_m, y_m^k)$$

Final classifier:

$$\hat{k} = \arg\max_k f^k(\mathrm{x}) \tag{5}$$

The multi-class algorithm is applied to the detected noisy frames overlapped by sudden noises. The number of classifiers, *K*, corresponds to the noise class. The *k*-th classifier is designed to separate the class *k* and other classes (Fig. 4) using AdaBoost described in Section 3. The final classifier decides a noise class having the maximum value from all classes in (5).
The multi-class AdaBoost can be applied to the noise detection problem, too. But in this paper, due to the computation cost, the two-class AdaBoost first detects noisy speech and then the detected frame only is classified into each noise class by multi-class AdaBoost.

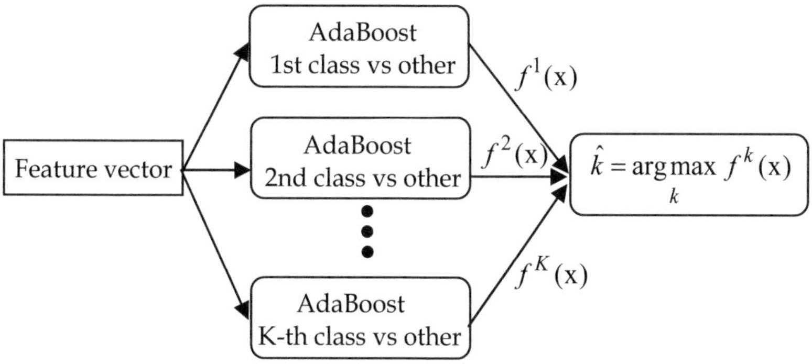

Figure 4. One-vs-rest AdaBoost for noise classification

5. GMM-Based Noise Detection and Classification

We used a conventional GMM (Gaussian mixture model) for comparing the proposed method. GMM is used widely for VAD (Voice Activity Detection) because the model is easy to train and usually powerful (A. Lee et al., 2004). In this paper, in order to detect sudden noises, we trained two GMMs, a clean speech model and a noisy speech model, where the number of mixtures is 64. Using two GMMs, the likelihood ratio is calculated by

$$L(\mathrm{x}) = \frac{\Pr(\mathrm{x} \mid \mathrm{speech\_model})}{\Pr(\mathrm{x} \mid \mathrm{noisy\_model})} \tag{6}$$

If $L(\mathrm{x}) > \theta$, **x** is detected as speech only. Otherwise **x** is detected as noisy speech.
In order to classify noise types, we need to train a noise GMM for each noise. Then, for the detected noisy speech only, we find a maximum likelihood noise from noise GMMs.

$$C(\mathrm{x}) = \arg\max_k \Pr(\mathrm{x} \mid \mathrm{noisy\_model}^{(k)}) \tag{7}$$

6. Experiments

6.1 Experimental Conditions

To evaluate the proposed method, we used six kinds of sudden noises from the RWCP corpus (S. Nakamura, et al., 2000). The following sudden noise sounds were used: spraying, telephone sounds, tearing up paper, particle-scattering, bell-ringing and horn blowing. Figure 5 shows the log-power spectrum of noises. In the database, each kind of noise has 50 data samples, which are divided into 20 data samples for training and 30 data for testing.
In order to make noisy speech corrupted by sudden noises, we added the sudden noises to clean speech in the wave domain and used 2,104 utterances of 5 men for testing and 210 utterances of 21 men for training (the total number of training data: 210 utterances $\times (6 + 1) = 1{,}470$). The speech signal was sampled at 16 kHz and windowed with a 20-msec Hamming window every 10 msec, and 24-order log-mel power spectrum and 12-order

MFCCs were used as feature vectors. The number of the training iterations, *T*, is 500, where AdaBoost is composed of 500 weak classifiers.

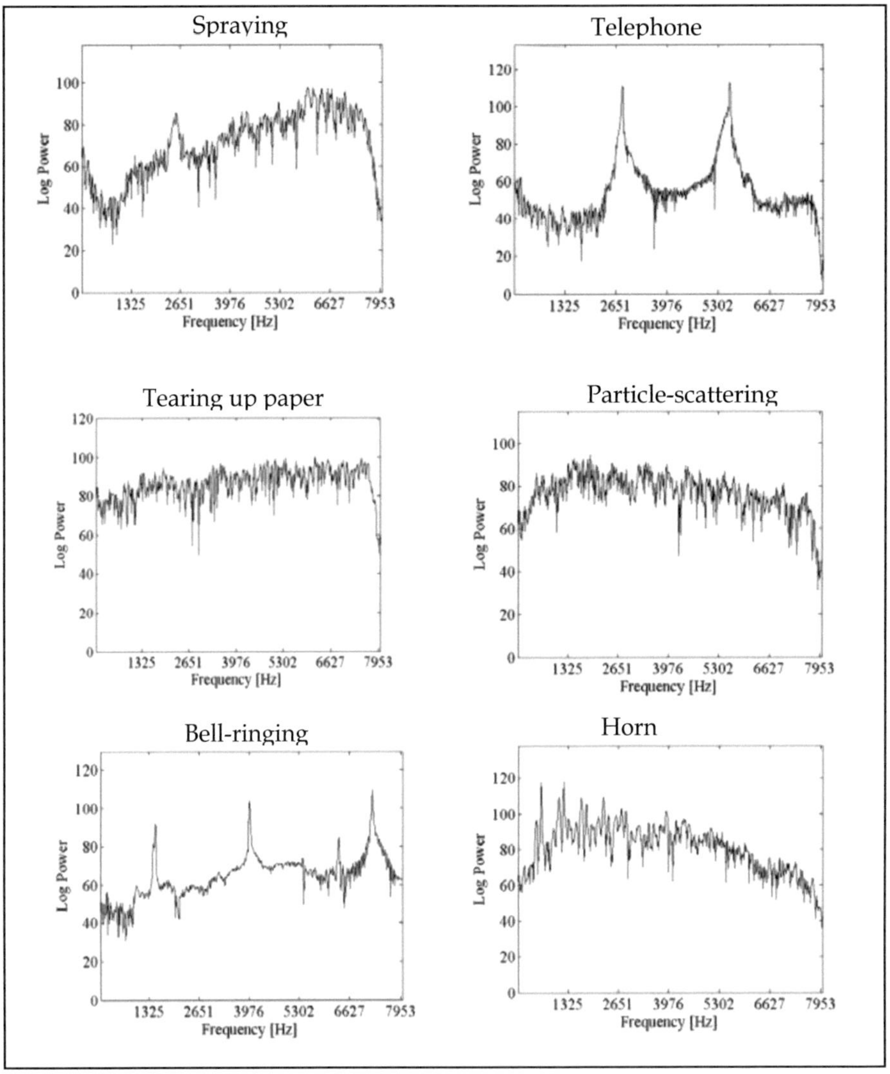

Figure 5. Log-power spectrum of noises

6.2 Experimental Results

Figure 6 and 7 show the results of the sudden-noise detection (F-measure) and classification (accuracy) at SNRs (Signal to Noise Ratio) of -5 dB, 0 dB, 5 dB and 10 dB. Here the SNR is calculated by

$$SNR = 10\log\left(\frac{E[s^2]}{E[n^2]}\right) \tag{8}$$

where $E[s^2]$ is the expectation of the power of the clean speech signal. Therefore, an increase of the SNR degrades the performance of the noise detection and classification because the noise power decreases. The F-measure used for the noise detection is given by

$$F = \frac{2 \cdot R \cdot P}{R + P}. \tag{9}$$

Here, R is recall and P is precision.
As can be seen from those figures, these results clarify the effectiveness of the AdaBoost-based method in comparison to the GMM-based method. As the SNR increases (the noise power decreases), the difference in performance is large. As the GMM-based method calculates the mean and covariance of the training data only, it may be difficult to express a complex non-linear boundary between clean speech and noisy speech (overlapped by a low-power noise). On the other hand, the AdaBoost system can obtain good performance at an SNR of 5 dB because AdaBoost can make a non-linear boundary from the training data near the boundary.

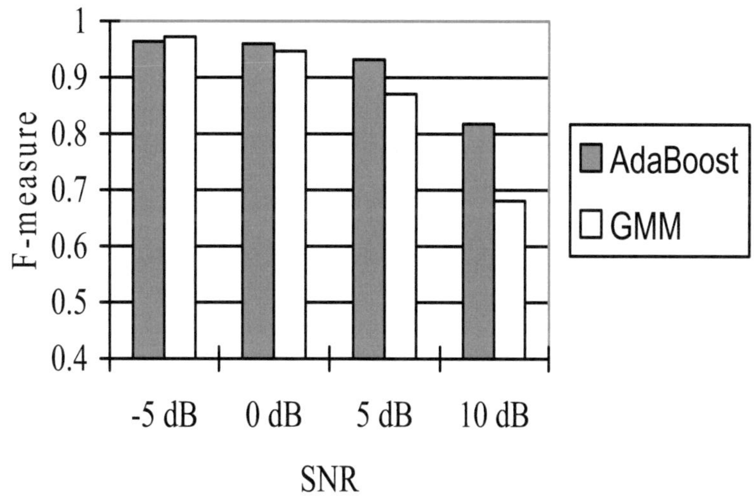

Figure 6. Results of noise detection

7. Conclusion

We proposed the sudden-noise detection and classification with Boosting. Experimental results show that the performance using AdaBoost is better than that of the conventional GMM-based method, especially at a high SNR (meaning, under low-power noise conditions). The reason is that Boosting could make a complex non-linear boundary fitting training data, while the GMM approach could not express the complex boundary because the GMM-based method calculates the mean and covariance of the training data only. Future research will include combining the noise detection and classification with noise reduction.

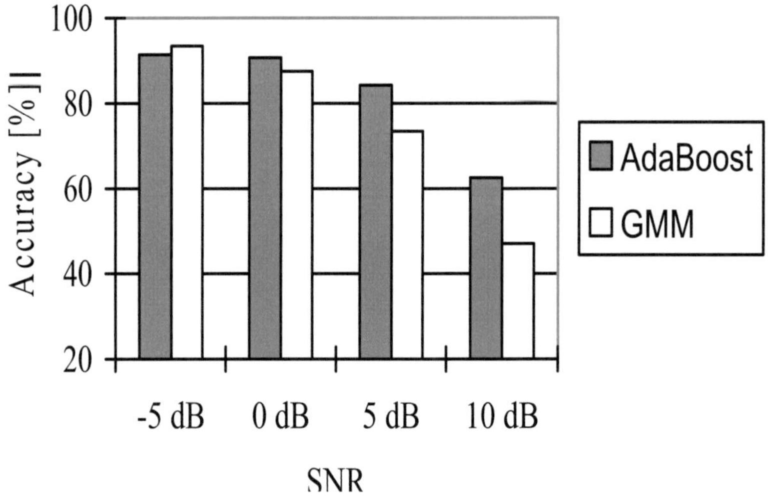

Figure 7. Results of noise classification

8. References

A. Betkowska, K. Shinoda & S. Furui (2006). FHMM for Robust Speech Recognition in Home Environment, *Proceedings of Symposium on Large-Scale Knowledge Resources,* pp. 129-132, 2006.

V. Barreaud, et al. (2003). On-Line Frame-Synchronous Compensation of Non-Stationary noise, *Proceedings of ICASSP*, pp. 652-655, 2003.

M. Fujimoto & S. Nakamura (2005). Particle Filter Based Non-stationary Noise Tracking for Robust Speech Recognition, *Proceedings of ICASSP*, pp. 257-260, 2005.

Y. Freund & R. E. Schapire (1999). A short introduction to boosting, *Journal of Japanese Society for Artificial Intelligence*, 14(5): pp. 771-780, 1999.

Y. Freund, et al. (1997). A decision-theoretic generalization of online learning and an application to boosting, *Journal of Comp. and System Sci.,* 55, pp. 119-139, 1997.

P. Viola, et al. (2001). Rapid Object Detection using a Boosted Cascade of Simple Features, *IEEE CVPR,* vol. 1, pp. 511-518, 2001.

E. Alpaydin (2004). Introduction to Machine Learning, The MIT Press, ISBN-10: 0262012111.

A. Lee et al. (2004). Noise robust real world spoken dialog system using GMM based rejection of unintended inputs, *Proceedings of ICSLP*, pp. 173-176, 2004.

S. Nakamura et al. (2000). Acoustical Sound Database in Real Environments for Sound Scene Understanding and Hands-Free Speech Recognition, *Proceedings of 2nd ICLRE*, pp. 965-968, 2000.

5

Evolutionary Speech Recognition

Anne Spalanzani
LIG Laboratory - INRIA Rhône Alpes
Grenoble, France

1. Introduction

Automatic speech recognition systems are becoming ever more common and are increasingly deployed in more variable acoustic conditions, by very different speakers. After a short adaptation, they are most of all robust to the change of speaker, to low background noise, etc. Nevertheless, using these systems in more difficult acoustic conditions (high background noise, fast changing acoustic conditions ...) still need an adapted microphone, a long time relearning, background noise computing, which make these systems fastidious to use.
The difference between learning and testing conditions is the major reason of the drop in the systems' performances. Therefore, a system that obtains good performances in a laboratory is not automatically performant in real conditions (in an office, a car, using a telephone, ...). The two main causes are the extreme acoustic variability of the conditions of use and the non exhaustive corpus faced with these multiple conditions of use. The speech signal production, the signal propagation in the acoustic environment and the way the listener perceives and interprets this signal constitute multiple sources of variability which limit the usability of these systems.
In order to ensure the adaptability of these systems to different sources of variability and in order to improve their robustness, a lot of research has been developped. Technics can operate at different levels. For example, an adaptation of the noisy signal can be done at the acoustic level by applying filters, semantic and context knowledge can be used also as well as prosodic or multimodal informations (gestures accompanying the words, lips movements, etc.)
This article presents an acoustical approache which concentrates on the adaptation of the system itself so that it recognizes noisy speech signals. It is organized as follows: section 2 presents the different sources of speech signal variability. Section 3 presents classical technics to overcome the problem of variability and a discussion on classical technics and the importance of exploring the evolutionary technics. In section 4, evolutionary algorithms and methods to combine them with neural networks are described. The application of these methods onto automatic speech recognition systems and results obtained are presented in section 5. Discussion on results and possible future directions are developped in section 6.

2. Source of speech signal variability

Speech is a dynamical acoustic signal with many sources of variation. Sources of degradation of the speech signal can be classified in 3 main categories (cf. Figure 1.) which are speaker variability, channel distortions and to room acoustic (Junqua, 2000).

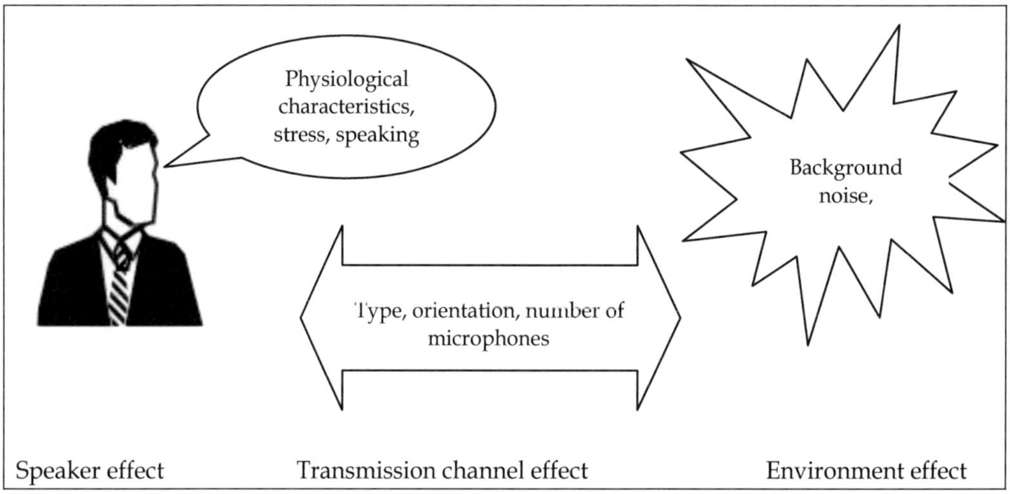

Figure 1. Schematic representation of the different sources of variability which can degrade the speech recognition system performances

The production of speech depends on many articulators that induce a lot of variability in the same linguistic message and for a unique speaker. These variations, known as speaking style, are due to factors like environment or social context. A speaker can change the quality of his voice, his speaking rate, his articulation according to some environmental factors. Stress conditions due to background noise increase the vocal effort.

The same message pronounced by two different speakers generate big variations. This is due most of all to physiological differences such as the vocal track length, male-female differences or child-adult differences.

The speech signal can be affected by the kind of microphone (or telephone) used, the number of microphones, the distance between the microphone and the speaker.

The characteristics of the environment such as the size of room, the ability of the materials used on the walls to absorb frequencies or modify the signal's properties, background noise, affect the signal quality. The characteristics of the spectrum resulting from the mix of noise and speech signal differ from the ones of a clean speech signal and the mix can be both additive (ambiant noise) or convolutive (room reverberation, microphone).

Robustness in speech recognition refers to the need to maintain good recognition accuracy even when the quality of the input speech is degraded, or when the acoustical, articulatory, or phonetic characteristics of speech in the training and testing environments differ.

The next section presents the main solutions proposed in order to deal with all these sources of degradation.

3. Classical proposed solutions in speech recognition robustness

Limiting the drop in performance due to acoustic environment changes remains a major challenge for speech recognition systems.
To overcome this problem of mismatch between a training environment and an unknown testing environment, many speech researchers have proposed different strategies which we classify in four categories:

- Speech signal processing approaches
- Model adaptation approaches
- Integration of multiple sources of information approaches
- Hybrid approaches

The first group focuses on a richer pre-processing of the input speech signal before presenting it to the model; e.g. by trying to suppress environment noises or by modifying acoustic parameters before the classification level (Bateman et al. 1992) (Mansour and Juang 1988).
In the second group, the adaptation to a new environment is achieved by changing the parameters of a speech recognition model (Das et al. 1994) (Gong 1995). For example, for a hidden markov model, this implies the modification of the number of states, of gaussians. Equivalently for a neural network, the number of units and the number of layers would be adjusted, as well as the weights' values.
The third group is increasingly addressed and corresponds to the combination of at least two sources of information to improve the robustness (Yuhas et al. 1989) (McGurk and MacDonald 1976). For example, the speaker's lips movements and their corresponding acoustic signals are processed and integrated to improve the robustness of the speech recognition systems.
The fourth group is based on the idea that hybridization should improve the robustness of systems by compensating the drawbacks of a given method with the advantages of the other (Junqua and Haton 1996). For example many contributions have focused on the combination of hidden markov models and neural networks to take advantage of the power of discrimination of neural networks while preserving the time alignment feature of hidden markov models.

3.1. Speech signal processing

3.1.1. Improving the signal-to-noise ratio

Speech enhancement techniques aim at recovering either the waveform or the parameter vectors of the clean speech embedded in noise (Gong 95). Among all the technics developped, methods working on noise filtering, spectal mapping and microphones arrays have been developped.
Different kinds of filters have been elaborated to reduce the noise. Classical filters such as Kalman or Wiener filters have been used for speech enhancement (Koo et al. 89). (Cardoso, 1989) (Jutten et al., 1991) have developped blind separation of noise and speech. These filters have shown a great capacity to reduce the noise in the spectrum but their drawback is that these methods alter also the speech signal. Bayesian methods have been developped to obtain an estimate of clean speech given noisy speech (Ephraim and Malah 1983) (Lim and Oppenheim, 1979) and the use of HMM to enhance noisy speech have been proposed in (Ephraim 92) (Seymour and Niranjan 94).

Spectral substraction is another technique which reduces the effect of added noise in speech. This method assumes that the noise and speech are uncorrelated and additive in the time domain (Gouvea and Stern, 1997) (Huerta and Stern, 1997).
The signal restoration via a mapping transformation exploits the direct correspondance between noisy and clean environments (Juang and Rabiner, 1987) (Barbier and Cholet 1991) (Gong and Haton 1994) (Guan et al. 1997) (Sagayama 1999). They propose to reduce the distance between a noisy signal and its corresponding clean signal. Unfortunalty, it requires knowing the clean speech which is not avalaible in most practical applications.
Further improvements in recognition accuracy can be obtained at lower signal-to-noise ratios by the use of multiple microphones (Silverman et al., 1997) (Seltzer, 2003).

3.1.2. Extracting robust features
Contrary to speech recognition systems, human beings are able to disregard noises to concentrate on one signal in particular. He is able to perform robust phonetical analysis which not depends on the speaker, transmissions channels or environment noises. Even if high levels are implied in the complex process of speech recognition, it seems that the auditory model has a major role.
Many ear models inspired by the human ear have been developped (Hermansky, 1990) (Allen, 1979) (Bourlard and Dupont, 1997).

3.2. Model adaptation
The noisy integration can be done by compensation that is by adapting the system to new noisy data (by restructurating the system structure and learning). Many techniques have been studied to proceed speaker adaptation (Schwartz and Kubala92) (Ström 94), channel adaptation such as telephone adaptation (Mokbel et al 93) or environment adaptation (Chiang 97). The major problem of these methods is the choice of the corpus. Very few methods propose to adapt the system on-line without knowledge on the new data to which the system should be adapted to (Kemp and Waibel 99). Practically, it is impossible to create an exhaustive corpus taking into account all the possible condition of use with all the noise characteristics. One other major problem is the systems' ability to learn correctly a huge amount of data.

3.3. Discussion
Among all these methods, very little are used in real automatic speech recognition systems. Actually, most of these methods are still at the stage of experimental research and do not provide enough convincing results to be integrated. The most common method is certainly the increase of the size of the database. As the computing power and the size of memory increase, it becomes possible to provide a good quantity of information for the training phase in order to have a powerful system in many conditions of use. However, in spite of the increase of their size, training databases are only small samples of the whole possible signal variabilities.
It is not possible to forecast all the testing conditions and it is necessary to explore new ways of search for a better comprehension of the problems involved in speech recognition (Bourlard, 1996).
We are conscious of the fragility of speech recognition. The communication between a speaker and his interlocutor is a complex mechanism. It implies acoustic signal exchanges in

a certain context (the acoustic environment) but it implies also exchanges of different kinds of signs with various levels of signification. 'Recognize' signifies for human beings 'identify' learned elements but also 'generalize' his knowledge of new elements. That is also 'recognize' missing or redondant features, 'adapt' to the environment, to the speaker or the situation. In hard conditions, the human listener takes into account the constraints offered by the linguistic code to reduce ambiguities, but he uses also information coming from the situation, redondancy, repetition. Generally, the speaker knows where he is and knows the environment's properties and limitations. He is able to take into account the semantic, pragmatic and lexical contexts (Caelen et al., 1996) and he is able to adapt his perception to the acoustic context.

Nature has created extremely complex systems with, sometimes, very simple principles. We can imagine that algorithms based on living being abilities (such as adaptation and evolution) could be able in the future to deal with all the parameters evolving during a dialogue, and reach human capacities.

The objective of the work presented in this article is to investigate innovative strategies using evolutionary algorithms inspired by Darwin. These algorithms evolve population of individuals in an environment supporting the survival and the reproduction of best suited individuals. The efficiency of this kind of algorithms is well known for the optimization of complex functions and for the resolution of the multi criteria problems. We aim at answering whether these algorithms can constitute a new approach for the adaptation of speech recognition systems to changing acoustic environments.

In order to study the possibility of incorporating evolutionary algorithms in the field of automatic speech recognition systems' robustness, we propose to remain at the acoustic level of the speech processing and more particularly at the level of the automatic speech recognition systems' adaptation with no assumption about the type of noise.

In this context, the robustness of the automatic speech recognition systems can be approached by two ways: dealing with structure or dealing with stimuli.

The first approach consists in adapting corrupted testing data so that they become close to training data (cf Figure 2.).

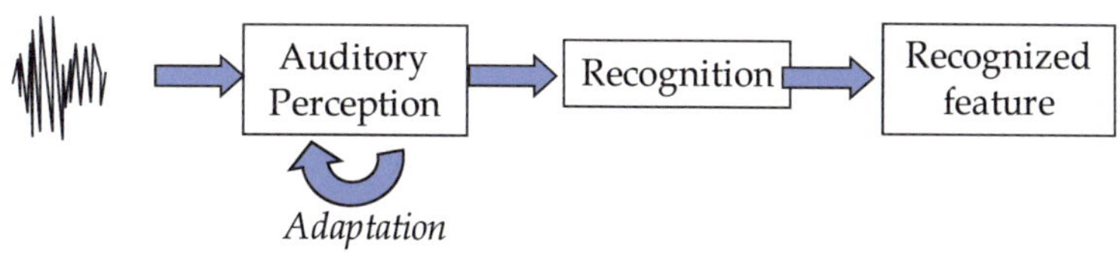

Figure 2. adaptation of the auditory perception

The speech recognition system is then able to provide good recognition rate. In this study, the system does not evolve anymore, only data do. The approach proposed first in (Spalanzani 99) processed a signal transformation via a mapping operator using a principal components analysis and evolutionary algorithms. This transformation attempted to achieve a self-adaptation of speech recognition systems under adverse conditions.

The second approach consists in adapting the speech recognition system itself (cf. Figure 3.).

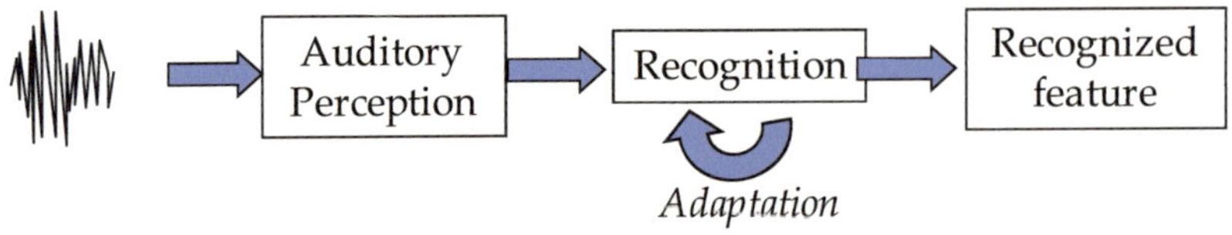

Figure 3. adaptation of the recognition system

Through the combination of evolutionary algorithms and backpropagation, a kind of relearning is operated to adapt the system to an environment different from the one in which it has been trained using the capacities of the system to adapt to changes of acoustic conditions using a local approach (by backpropagation of the gradient) and a global one (by evolution) in order to find an optimal system.
This article focuses on this second approach. Next section explains why and how combining neural networks and evolutionary algorithms.

4. Combining neural networks and evolutionary algorithms

In nature, living organisms are able to learn to adapt to the environment in order to survive and reproduce. Evolutionary algorithms are directly drawn from these principals of nature. Their principle consists of maintaining and manipulating a population of individuals (potential solutions) and implementing a "survival of the fittest" strategy (best solutions).
Neural networks are also a simplified way of simulating the ability of living organisms to adapt to their environment by learning.
It is appealing to consider hybrids of neural network learning algorithms with evolutionary search procedures, simply because Nature has so successfully done so.
The evolutionary algorithms proceed by globally sampling over the space of alternative solutions, while backpropagation proceeds by locally searching the immediate neighborhood of a current solution. This suggests that using the evolutionary algorithms to provide good initial weights sub-spaces from which backpropagation then continues to search will be effective (Belew, 1991).

4.1. Evolutionary algorithms

Evolutionary algorithms are stochastic search methods that mimic the metaphor of natural biological evolution. They operate on a population of potential solutions applying the principle of survival of the fittest to produce better and better approximations to a solution. At each generation, a new set of approximations is created by the process of selecting individuals according to their level of fitness in the problem domain and breeding them together using operators borrowed from natural genetics.
This process leads to the evolution of populations of individuals that are better suited to their environment than the individuals that they were created from, just as in natural adaptation.

4.1.1. Evolution

At the beginning of the computation a number of individuals (the population) are randomly initialized. The objective function (fitness function) is then evaluated for these individuals. The initial generation is produced.

If the optimization criteria are not met the creation of a new generation starts. Individuals are selected according to their fitness for the production of offspring. Parents are recombined to produce offspring. All offspring will be mutated with a certain probability. The fitness of the offspring is then computed. The offspring are inserted into the population replacing the parents, producing a new generation. This cycle is performed until the optimization criteria are reached.
The algorithm used to evolve to population is the following:

```
t = 0                               // time initialization
Init (P(t))                         // initial population creation
Eval (P(t))                         // population evaluation
While criteria non reached          // number of generations or good solution obtained
        P'(t) = Selection(P(t))     // mates selection
        P''(t) = Evolution (P'(t))  // mates' recombination and mutation
        Evaluation(P''(t))          // evaluation of the new population
        P(t+1) = P''(t)             // current population update
        t = t + 1                   // new generation
End While
```

Figure 4. evolutionary algorithm

4.1.2. Recombination

Recombination produces new individuals in combining the information contained in the parents. It consists in selecting a locus point and permutation the two right parts of the mates' genotypes.

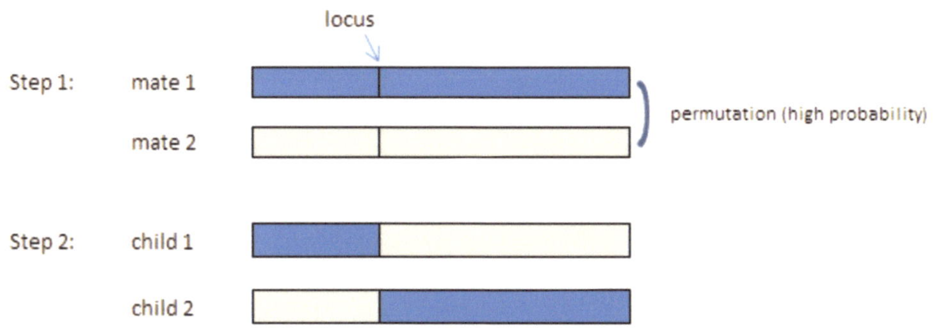

Figure 5. crossover principle

4.1.3. Mutation

After recombination, every offspring undergoes mutation. Offspring variables are mutated by small perturbations (size of the mutation step), with low probability. The representation of the genes determines the used algorithm. If the genes are binary, a bit-flip mutation is used. If the genes are real values, many possible mutations can be operated. Figure 6 shows an example of real value mutation.

Figure 6: example of mutation

Next section will explain how to evaluate the individuals based on neural networks.

4.2. Neural networks

4.2.1. Backpropagation

Neural networks are collections of units (neurons) connected by weighted links (connection weights) used to transmit signals.

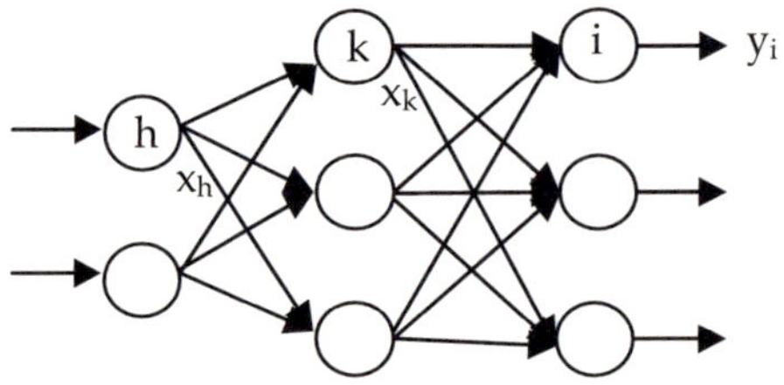

Figure 7: Extract of a multilayer neural network

The principle is based on the minimization of the quadratic error E which is function of the n desired outputs yd_i and the n outputs y_i given effectively by the network:

$$E = \sum_{i=1}^{n} (y_i - yd_i)^2 \quad (1)$$

Minimizing this error consists in modifiying the connection weights as follows:

$$\Delta W_{kh}^{(j)} = -a \cdot \delta_k^{(j)} \cdot y_h^{(j-1)} \quad (2)$$

With a the gain adaptation, $\delta_k^{(j)}$ the error of the neuron k of the jth layer and $y_h^{(j-1)}$ the output of the neuron h of the $(j\text{-}1)^{th}$ layer.
For the neuron of the last layer:

$$\delta_k^{(j)} = y_h^{(j)} - yd_k \quad (3)$$

For the neuron of the hidden layers:

$$\delta_k^{(j)} = \left[\sum_{i \in layer(j+1)} \delta_i^{(j+1)} \cdot w_{ik}^{(j+1)} \right] \cdot \sigma'(p_k^{(j)}) \quad (4)$$

with : $p_k^{(j)} = \sum_i w_{ki} \cdot x_i$ where x_i corresponds to the output of neuron i and:

$$\sigma(p_k^{(j)}) = \left[\frac{1}{1+\exp(-p_k^{(j)})} \right] \tag{5}$$

and σ' its' derivative.

4.2.2. Learning

The learning algorithm used in this work is adapted from (Schalkwyk et Fanty, 1996) which permits a fast convergence toward a good solution. The learning phase stops when the error does not decrease anymore, that is when it is not able to learn anymore. At the end of this learning phase, the algorithm gives a recognition rate which corresponds to the number of recognized features divided by the total number of features to recognize and a number of learning iterations.

4.2.3. Recognition

The recognition phase is used to evaluate the neural network based individuals. Data used for recognition are different from the one used for learning. The recognition rate given by the individuals are used as fitness function.

4.3. Hybridization

Three major approaches combining neural networks and evolutionary algorithms are presented in the literature: finding the optimal weights of the neural network (using evolution only or combined with backpropagation), finding the optimal topology of the neural network and finding optimal learning parameters (Yao, 1995) (Whitley, 1995) (Hancock 1992).

4.3.1. The topology of the neural network

The design of the network's topology is not easy. Finding the optimal number of layers as well as finding the number of neurons on each layer is usually done by empiric methods (more than based on theoric fundations).

4.3.2. The optimal weights of the neural network

The initialization of the weights before learning is crucial. It influences the convergence speed and the quality of the obtained network.

- Learning time

The learning convergence time depends on the initial and final weight space. In fact, the more initial weights are close to their final value, the faster is the convergence (Thimm, 1994) (Chan and Nutter, 1991). For example (Lee et al. 93) have shown theorically that the probability of premature saturation at the beginning epoch of learning procedure in the backpropagation algorithm derived in terms of the maximum value of initial weights, the number of nodes in each layer and the maximum slope of the sigmoidal activation function.

- Quality of the resulting network

Learning by backpropagation can be seen as a function optimization where the weights are its parameters. Its convergence toward a local minimum can be global also. If it is not the case, we can consider that the learning has not been done correctly.

4.4. Neural network encoding

The representation of a neural network in a genotype has been studied deeply in the literature (Miller et al., 1989) (Gruau and Whitley, 1993) (Mandischer, 1993). Weights manipulated by the backpropagation algorithm are real values and can be encoded by different ways as described in (Belew, 1991). In order to be efficient with the crossover operator, weights having a high interaction should be close.

Let's consider a 3 layer-network with *n* inputs, *m+1-n* hidden and *p+1-m* outputs, *wij* the connection of the neuron *i* toward the neuron *j*. Figure 8 shows the representation of this network:

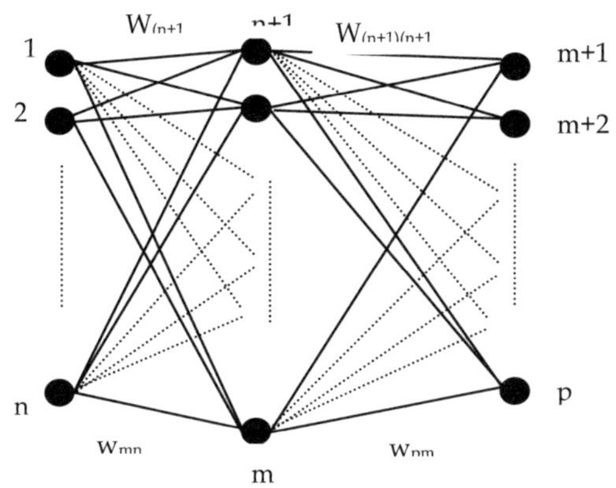

Figure 8: architecture of a neural network

The genotypic representation of this architecture is the following:

(w(n+1)1, w(n+1)2, …, w(n+1)n, w(n+2)1, w(n+2)2, …, w(n+2)n, …, w(m+1)m, …, wpm)

Figure 9. genotypic representation of the neural network architecture

4.5. Changing environment adaptation

The problem of adapting populations to changing environment is an interesting problem which gave place to a certain number of works. For example, (Nolfi and Parisi, 1997) investigated a robot adaptation in a changing environment controlled by a population of neural networks. (Cobb and Grefenstette, 1993) studied the evolution of a population tracking the optimum of complex functions (such as combination of sinusoids and gaussians) and the capacity of genetic algorithms to adapt, for example, to the translation of such functions.

Keeping diversity in the population seems to be the key for a good adaptation to environments changing quickly. (Cobb and Grefenstette, 1993) proposed a comparison of the performances of various strategies (high mutation rate (10%), triggered hypermutation and random immigrants). The high mutation rate generates a significant diversity, the triggered hypermutation varies the mutation rate according to the way the environment changes, its rate is weak when the changes are weak, high during abrupt changes, the random immigrants introduces randomness into a percentage of its population which generates diversity. It results from this work that each of these methods has advantages and disadvantages depending on the way the environment changes.
Methods based on the thermodynamic principles (Mori et al. 1996) can be found in the literature also. In addition, evolution strategy seems to be well fitted to adapt to the changes of environment (Bäck, 1996). Indeed, the integration of evolution's parameters in the genotype enables the adaptation of the mutation rates when it is necessary.

4.6. Lamarkism versus Darwinism

A certain number of works studied the influence of the heritage on the evolution of the populations (Turney et al., 1996). At the beginning of the century, two schools were confronted: The Darwinism is based on the idea that only the predisposition of the individuals to learn is transmitted to the children. Knowledge acquired by the parents is not transmitted then. Lamarckianism proposes that knowledge obtained by parents is directly transmitted to children. Hence, those parents' weights resulting from the training phase are transmitted to the following generation.
In the context of this debate, Baldwin proposed a kind of intermediary. He suggested the existence of a strong interaction between learning and evolution. The principal objective for the individuals is to integrate, by means of a neural network training, the information provided by the environment. The fittest individuals are selected for reproduction. So they transmit to their descendant their capacity to learn. If it is considered that an individual is all the more ready to integrate knowledge that the innate configuration of its neural network' weights is closed to that after training, we can consider then that knowledge is assimilated in its genes. Thus, the training time decreases. Once the individuals are able to acquire these concepts correctly, we can consider that those are comparable in the genotype.
(Nolfi et al., 1994) and (Nolfi and Spalanzani, 2000) showed that learning guides evolution (individuals having the best learning performances reproduce more often than the others), but also that evolution guides learning (the selected individuals have greater capacities to learn and these capacities are improved during generations). Thus, instinctive knowledge of the individuals is transmitted and improved during the evolution whereas, and it is the difference with the theory of Lamarck, the genotype is not affected directly by the training.
(Whitley et al., 1994) affirmed that under all the test conditions they explored, the Lamarckian evolution is much faster than that of Darwin and results are often better. Concerning the problem in which we are interested in, the adaptation to the changes of environment, (Sasaki and Tokoro, 1997) affirmed that the Darwinism is more adapted than Lamarckianism, whereas for a static environment, the opposite is noted. (Mayley 1996) proposed to penalise individuals having a long training phase. He affirmed also that knowledge assimilation can be done only if there is a neighbourhood correlation, i.e. a correlation between the distance from two genotypes and that of their associated phenotype.

5. Experimental results

5.1. Experimental plateform

Our simulations take place in EVERA (Environnement d'Etude de la Robustesse des Apprentis), our speech Artificial Life simulator which has been described in (Kabré and Spalanzani 1997). The main purpose is to provide a test-bed for the evaluation and improvement of the robustness of speech recognition systems. Two models are proposed in EVERA, a model of environment and a model of organisms (speech recognition systems) which evolve in it. In our study, the environment is a virtual acoustic environment. The virtual environment allows the simulation of the transfer function between acoustic sources (speaker and noise) and a microphone position. Thanks to Allen model of sound propagation in small rooms (Allen and Berkley 1979), by varying the reflection coefficient of walls, floor and ceiling, it is possible to control the reverberation time. This latter measures the time needed for the sound emitted in an acoustic environment to extinct. The difficulty of recognition increases with the reverberation time. The convolution between a speech signal taken from any database and the acoustic environment impulse response gives the speech signal for training the neural based speech recognition systems.
A population of speech recognition systems is built in an initial virtual acoustic environment. The creation of the initial population resorts to make a desired number of copies of a pre-trained neural network while making a random change of its weights. The environment is changed by either taking a new acoustic environment, a different speech database or a different noise (we considered different noises such as door closing, alarm, radio). The change is such that the systems are no longer well-suited to this environment. At this moment, after a period of training, an adaptation cycle starts thanks to genetic operators.

1. **Init** a population of automatic speech recognition systems.
2. **If** duration of simulation not elapsed **change** the acoustic environment **else goto** 6.
3. **Train** automatic speech recognition systems.
4. **Evaluate, Select** and **Reproduce** speech recognition systems.
5. **If** duration of adaptation elapsed **then goto** 2 **else goto** 3.
6. end.

Figure 10. Algorithm for evolving speech recognition systems so that they adapt to new virtual acoustic environments.

The acoustic environments are represented by a set of words to which noise and reverberation were added. Noises have been chosen thanks to their characteristics: PO for door closing (impulsive noise), AL for alarm and RE for alarm clock (narrow-band noises at different frequencies), FE for fire (white noise) and RA for change of radio frequency (non stationary noise).
An environment is defined by a triplet (type of noise, reverberation time, signal to noise ratio). The intelligibility of the signal is inversely proportional to the reverberation time and proportional to the signal to noise ratio. This is why a signal with a strong reverberation and a weak signal to noise ratio (for example (FE 0,7 -6)) is more difficult to recognize than a signal like (RA 0,4 20).

5.2. Comparison between Lamarckian and Darwinian evolution

First experiments determine the most effective method for our problem of adaptation to the environment. Since the opinions are divided concerning the method to use, we propose to test the performances of populations in term of quality of the individuals and in term of effectiveness. Within the framework of our experiments, this consists in studying the recognition rate of our population as well as the number of iterations necessary for each individual to optimise its training (i.e. the network converged). The objective of the individuals is to recognize a set of isolated words analysed by an acoustic analyser based on the model of the human ear (Hermansky, 1990). The vector resulting from the acoustic analysis represents the input of the networks having 7 input units, 6 hidden units and 10 output units. They are able to learn thanks to training algorithm based on backpropagation.

5.2.1 Quality of the results

On the general shape of the curves, we can also notice that results provided by the Lamarckian evolution are more stable and seem to drop less easily than those of the Darwinian population. The numerical results of the performances are presented in table 1. We can notice that the performances are quite equivalent in average. In average, the population evolving according to the method of Lamarck obtains 78% of recognition rate whereas that according to the method of Darwin obtains 76.6%. Concerning the best individual, less than 1% of improvement is noted since in average (for the 10 environments, that is to say 1000 generations), the best Darwinian individual obtains 80.1% whereas Lamarckian 80.9%.

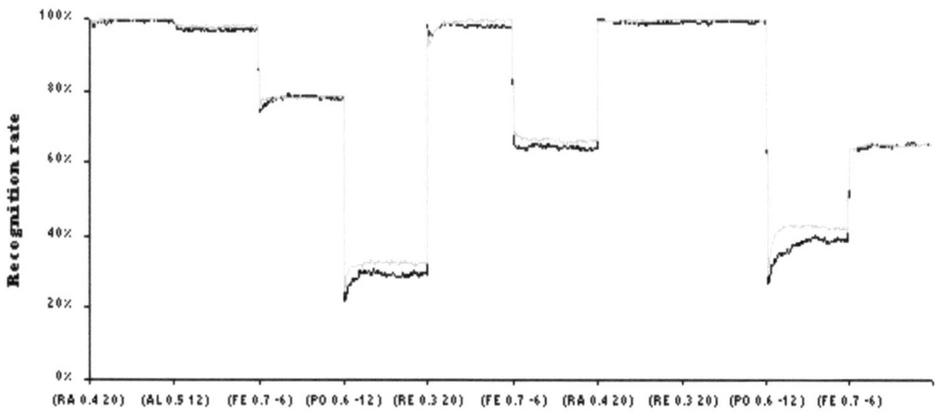

Figure 11. Recognition rates of the population of speech recognition systems evolving in a changing acoustic environment. 20 individuals evolve by genetic algorithms and neural training. Darwinian and Lamarckian heritage are compared on the average of the population.

Recognition rate	Worst	Best	Average
Lamarckian evolution	73.8 %	80.9 %	78 %
Darwinian evolution	70.5 %	80.1 %	76.6 %

Table 1. Comparison of the recognition rates between Lamarckian and Darwinian evolution.

5.2.2. Training efficiency

Concerning now the efficiency of the populations in the training phase, figures 12 shows the number of iterations necessary for a good convergence of the individuals' networks. Although, at each change of environment, the number of iterations increases in a more significant way during the evolution of Lamarck, the decrease of this number is more significant and, in average, the number of iterations is weaker. It is interesting to note that this number decreases throughout the Darwinian evolution, which can means that there is knowledge assimilation, and this without the use of penalty as proposed (Mayley 1996).

In both kinds of evolution, the number of iterations decreases during generations. Once more, we can notice that the evolution of Lamarck is more effective than that of Darwin. As indicates it table 2, Darwinian individual needs in average 91 iterations to learn correctly, whereas a Lamarckian individual need only 68.2 iterations. We can notice the differences between the best individuals (54.8 against 33.1) and worse (144 against 113.6).

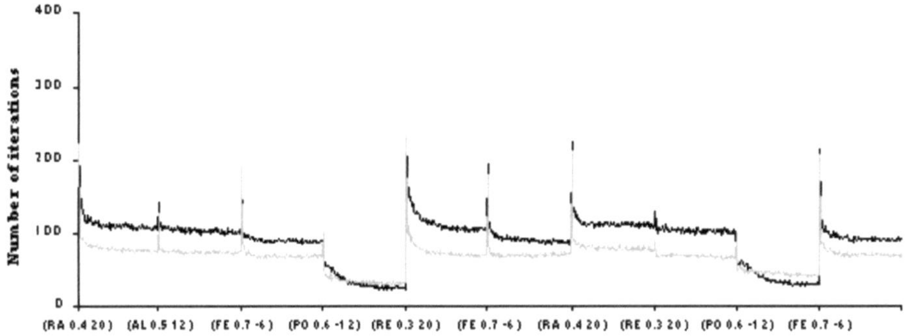

Figure 12. Learning times of ASRSs population evolving in a changing acoustic environment. 20 individuals evolve by genetic algorithms and neural training. Darwinian and Lamarckian heritage are compared on the average of the population.

Number of iterations	Worst	Best	Average
Lamarckian evolution	113.6	33.1	68.2
Darwinian evolution	144	54.8	91

Table 2. Comparison of the learning times.

5.3. Evolution during time

This experiment consists in presenting speech signals produced in several noisy environments. A sequence of several noisy environments is presented 5 times. This permits to test the systems' performances in identical acoustic conditions at different times.
Performances of 2 populations are tested. One population is made of neural networks evolving with the backpropagation algorithm only, the other is made of neural networks evolving with both backpropagation and lamarkian evolutionary algorithm. Results presented in figure 13 are the average of 9 simulations.

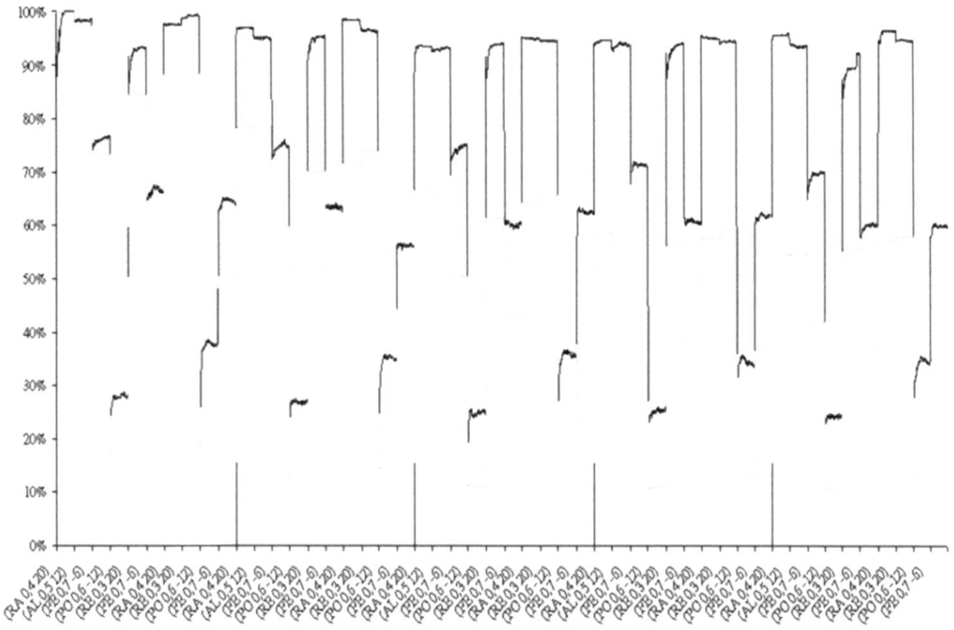

Figure 13. Evolution of the recognition rate during time while a sequence of 10 acoustic environments is presented 5 times. In gray, recognition rate of the "neural network population", in black, the recognition rate of the "evolutionary neural network population"

One can notice the regularity of the performances of the evoluted population and the constant decrease of the population using back-propagation only. Moreover, the recognition rates of the evoluted population are much higher than the ones given by the non evoluted population, whatever the acoustic environment.

6. Conclusion and perspectives

In this article, we have adapted neural networks based speech recognition systems using evolutionary algorithms in order to keep them adapted to new acoustic environments. We have compared two methods of heritage suggested by Darwin and Lamarck for the evolution of a population in changing acoustic environments. In term of speech recognition rate, both methods provide similar results. In term of learning speed, The Lamarckian

evolution seems to be more interesting in the context of changing acoustic environments. Results obtained in a long sequence of environments show that evolution provides stable results (i.e. for two identical acoustic conditions but at different times, results are similar) but systems without evolution do not.
The generic concepts presented in this article must not be limited to neural based methods. In this article, neural networks have been implemented because they are easy to controle and their convergence is quite fast. Moreover, the hybridization of neural networks and evolutionary methods have been studied deeply. But hidden markov models could be adapted also (Asselin de Beauville et al. 96) instead of neural network systems.
Moreover, (Lauri et al. 2003) have shown the efficency to combine evolutionary algorithms and Eigenvoices to adapt the system to new speakers. (Selouani and O'Shaughnessy 2003) combined hidden markov models and Karhonen-Loève transform to improve telephone speech recognition.
This work is at the frontiere between two very different fields which are automatic speech recognition and evolutionary algorithms. Work carried out comes from the idea that if the systems of recognition were able to self-modified in time, in order to adapt to the changes of acoustic environment, they could be much more robust. The idea was to take as a starting point the capacities of the alive beings to adapt to their environment to be the most powerful possible in order to survive.
Within the framework of speech recognition, we considered the automatic speech recognition systems, or filters, like individuals having to adapt to their acoustic environment changing. It appeared interesting to imagine a system able to adapt to the acoustic changes of conditions (characteristic of the speaker or the room for example) in order to remain performant whatever its conditions of use. The alive beings are able to adapt their manner of perceiving several signals while concentrating on the signal in which they are interested in. They are also able to update their knowledge of the environment when it is necessary. Considering that speech signal recognition for alive beings can be summarized in two main phases, namely perception of the signals and the attribution of entities to these signals, we have suggested to adapt one or the other independently by evolutionary technics.
We keep in mind that there is a strong interaction between these two processes but their adaptation by evolutionary algorithms in a parallel way seems, for the moment, impossible to control. Indeed, how to adapt our recognition system on data which adapt simultaneously to this one?

7. References

Allen J., B. & Berkley D. A. (1979). Image Method for efficiently simulating small-room acoustics. *JASA* 65(4):943-950.

Asselin de Beauville J-P, Slimane M., Venturini G., Laporte J-L and Narbey M. (1996). Two hybrid gradient and genetic search algorithms for learning hidden Markov models. *13th International Conference on Machine Learning*, Bari, Italy, pp.1-8.

Bäck T. (1996) *Evolutionary Algorithms in Theory and Practice*. Oxford University Press, New York.

Barbier L. et Chollet G. (1991). Robust Speech Parameters Extraction for Word Recognition in Noise Using Neural Networks. *ICASSP'91*, pp.145-148.

Bateman, D. C., Bye, D. K. & Hunt M. J. (1992). Spectral normalization and other spectral technics for speech recognition in noise. *Proceedings of the IEEE International conference. on Acoustic Speech Signal Processing,* (1)241-244. San Francisco.

Belew, R. K., McInerney, J. & Schraudolph, N. (1991). Evolving Networks : Using the Genetic Algorithm with Connectionist Learning. *In Proc. Second Artificial Life Conference,* pages 511-547, New York, Addison-Wesley.

Bourlard H. (1996). Reconnaissance Automatique de la Parole : Modélisation ou Description ? *XXIèmes Journées d'Etude sur la Parole,* Avignon, France, pp.263-272.

Bourlard H. and Dupont S. (1997). Subband-based Speech Recognition. *ICCASP'97,* pp. 1251-1254.

Caelen J., Kabré H. and Delemar O. (1996), Reconnaissance de la Parole :vers l'Utilisabilité. *XXIèmes Journées d'Etude sur la Parole,* Avignon, France, pp.325-329.

Cardoso J.F. (1989). Source separation using higher order moments. *ICASSP'89,* Glasgow, Scotland, vol. 4, pp. 2109-2112.

Chen C.L. and Nutter R.S. (1991). Improving the Training Speed of Three-Layer FeedForward Neural Nets by Optimal Estimation of the Initial Weights. *International Joint Conference on Neural Networks.*

Chiang T. (1997) Speech Recognition in Noise Using On-line HMM Adaptation. *Eurospeech'97, 5th European Conference on Speech Communication and Technology,* Rhodes, Grece.

Cobb H.G. and Grefenstette J.J. (1993). Genetic Algorithms for Tracking Changing Environments. *Fifth International Conference on Genetic Algorithms (ICGA 93),* 523-530, Morgan Kaufmann.

Das, S., Nadas, A., Nahamoo, D. & Picheny, M. (1994). Adaptation techniques for ambient noise and microphone compensation in the IBM Tangora speech recognition system. *In Proceedings of the IEEE International Conference On Acoustic Speech Signal Processing.* (1)21-23. Adelaide, Australia.

Ephraim Y. and Malah D. (1983). Speech enhancement using optimal non-linear spectral amplitude estimation. *ICASSP'83,* pp. 1118-1121.

Ephraim Y. (1992). Statistical-model-based speech enhancement systems. *Proceeding IEEE,* 80(10):1526-1555.

Gong Y. and Haton J-P. (1994). Stochastic Trajectory Modeling for Speech Recognition. *ICASSP'94,* pp. 57-60, Adelaide.

Gong, Y.: (1995) Speech recognition in noisy environments: A survey, *Journal of Speech Communication,* 16 : 261-291.

Gouvêa E.B. et Stren R.M. (1997) Speaker Normalization Through For-mant-Based Warping of the Frequency Scale. *Eurospeech'97, 5th European Conference on Speech Communication and Technology,* Rhodes, Greece.

Gruau F. et Whitley D. (1993). Adding Learning to the Cellular Development of Neural Networks : Evolution and the Baldwin Effect. *Evolutionary Computation* 1(3): 213-233.

Guan C-T., Leung S-H. et Lau W-H. (1997). A Space Transformation Approach for Robust Speech Recognition in Noisy Environments. *Eurospeech'97, 5th European Conference on Speech Communication and Technology,* Rhodes, Greece.

Hancock P.J.B. (1992). *Coding Strategies for Genetic Algorithms and NeuralNets.* Ph.D. Thesis, University of Stirling.

Hermansky, H. (1990). Perceptual Linear Predictive (PLP) Analysis of Speech, *Journal of Acoustic Society*, 87(4) 1738-1752.

Holland, H. (1975). *Adaptation in Natural and Artificial Systems.* The University of Michigan Press.

Juang B. et Rabiner L. (1987). Signal Restoration by Spectral Mapping. *ICASSP'87*, pp 2368-2371

Huerta J.M. et Stern R.M. (1997). Compensation for Environmental and speaker Variability by Normalization of Pole Locations. *Eurospeech'97, 5th European Conference on Speech Communication and Technology*, Rhodes, Greece.

Junqua J. C. (2000). *Robust Speech Recognition in Embedded Systems and PC Applications*, Kluwer Academic Publishers.

Junqua, J. C. & Haton, H. (1996). *Robustness in Automatic Speech Recognition*, Ed Kluwer Academic Publisher.

Jutten C., Hérault J., Comon P. et Sorouchyari E. (1991). Blind separation of sources. *Signal Processing*, vol. 24, pp. 1-29.

Kabré, H. & Spalanzani A. (1997). EVERA: A system for the Modeling and Simulation of Complex Systems. *In Proceedings of the First International Workshop on Frontiers in Evolutionary Algorithms, FEA'97*, 184-188. North Carolina.

Kabré, H.: (1996). On the Active Perception of Speech by Robots. *IEEE RJ/MFI (Multi-sensor Fusion and Integration for Intelligent Systems)*, 775-785. Washington D.C.

Kemp T. et Waibel A. (1999) Unsupervised Training of a Speech Recognizer: Recent Experiments. *Proceedings of the Eurospeech'99*, pp. 2725-2728, Budapest.

Koo B., Gibson J. and Gray S. (1989) Filtering of colored noise for speech enhancement and coding. *ICASSP'89*, pp. 349-352. Glasgow.

Lauri F., Illina I., Fohr D. and Korkmazsky F. (2003) Using Genetic Algorithms for Rapid Speaker Adaptation, *Eurospeech'2003*, Genève, Switzerland.

Lee Y., Oh S.-H. et Kim M.W. (1993). An Analysis of Premature Saturation in BackPropagation Learning. *Neural Networks*, vol. 6, pp. 719-728.

Lim J.S. and Oppenheim A.V. (1979). All-pole modeling of degraded speech. *IEEE Transaction on Acoustics, Speech, and Signal Processing*, 26(3):197--210, 1979.

Mandischer M. (1993). Representation and Evolution in Neural Networks. *Artificial Neural Nets and Genetic Algorithms Proceedings of the International Conference at Innsbruck*, Austria, pages 643-649.

Mansour, D. & Juang, B. H. *(1988)*. A family of distortion measures based upon projection operation for robust speech recognition. *IEEE International Acoustic Speech Signal Process*, 36-39. New York.

Mayley G. (1996). *Landscapes*, Learning Costs and Genetic Assimilation. Special *Issue of Evolutionary Computation on the Baldwin Effect*, vol. 4, n. 3.

McGurk, H., MacDonald, J. (1976). Hearing Voices and Seeing Eyes, *Nature*, 264:746-748.

Miller G.F., Todd M. et Hegde S.U. (1989). Designing Neural Networks using Genetic Algorithms. *Proceedings of the Third Conference on Genetic Algorithms*, San Mateo.

Mokbel, C., Monné, J. and Jouvet, D. (1993). On-line adaptation of a speech recognizer to variations in telephone line conditions. *EUROSPEECH'93*, 1247-1250.

Mori N., Kita H. et Nishikawa Y. (1996). Adaptation to a Changing Environment by Means of the Thermodynamical Genetic Algorithm. *4th Conference on Parallel Problem Solving from Nature*, Berlin, Allemagne.

Mühlenbein, H. & Schlierkamp-Voosen, D. (1995). Evolution as a Computational Process. *Lecture Notes in Computer Science*, 188-214, Springer, Berlin.

Nolfi S., Elman J.L. & Parisi D. (1994). Learning and evolution in neural networks. *Adaptive Behavior*, (3) 1:5-28.

Nolfi S. & Parisi D. (1997). Learning to adapt to changing environments in evolving neural networks. *Adaptive Behavior*, (5) 1:75-98,

Nolfi S. & Spalanzani A. (2000). Learning and evolution: On the effects of directional learning. Artificial Life. *Technical Report*, Institute of Psychology, Rome, Italy.

Sagayama S. (1999). Differential Approach to Acoustic Model Adaptation. *Workshop on robust Methods for Speech Recognition in Adverse Conditions*, Tampere, Finlande.

Sasaki T. and Tokoro M. (1997). Adaptation toward Changing Environments : Why Darwinian in Nature ? *Fourth European Conference on Artificial Life.*

Schalkwyk J. and Fanty M. (1996). The CSLU-C Toolkit for automatic speech recognitions. Technical Report n. CSLU-012-96.

Schwartz R. and Kubala F. (1992). Hidden Markov Models and Speaker adaptation. Speecj Recognition and Understanding. *Recent Advances, Trends and Applications.* Springer-Verlag, 1992.

Selouani S. and O'Shaughnessy D. (2003). On the Use of Evolutionary Algorithms to Improve the Robustness of Continuous Speech Recognition Systems in Adverse Conditions. *EURASIP Journal on Applied Signal Processing*, 2003:8, 814–823.

Seltzer M.L (2003). *Microphone Array Processing for Robust Speech Recognition*, Ph.D. Thesis, ECE Department, CMU.

Seymour C.W. and Niranjan M. (1994). An Hmm-Based Cepstral-Domain Speech Enhancement System, *In Proceedings ICSLP*, pages 1595—1598.

Silverman H.F., Patterson W.R., Flanagan J.L. et Rabinkin D. (1997). A Digital Processing System for Source Location and Sound Capture by Large Micro-phone Arrays. *ICASSP 97*, Volume 1, Page 251.

Spalanzani A. & Kabré H. (1998). Evolution, Learning and Speech Recognition in Changing Acoustic Environments. *5th Conference on Parallel Problem Solving from Nature*, Springer Verlag, pp. 663-671, Amsterdam, Netherland.

Spalanzani, A. (1999). *Algorithmes évolutionnaires pour l'étude de la robustesse des systèmes de reconnaissance automatique de la parole*, Ph.D. Thesis, Joseph Fourier University, Grenoble.

Spears, W.M., De Jong, K.A., Bäck, T., Fogel, D. and De Garis, H. (1993). An Overview of Evolutionary Computation. *In Proceedings of the European Conference on Machine Learning*, (667) 442-459.

Ström, N. (1994) Experiments with new algorithm for fast speaker adaptation. In *ICSLP*, pp. 459-462.

Thimm G. et Fiesler E. (1994). High Order and Multilayer Perceptron Initialization. *IDIAP technical report* 94-07.

Turney P., Whitley D. et Anderson R. (1996). Evolution, Learning, and Instinct : 100 Years of the Baldwin Effect. *Special Issue of Evolutionary Computation on the Baldwin Effect*, vol. 4, n. 3.

Wessels, L and Barnard, E. (1992). Avoiding False Local Minima by Proper Initialization of Connections. *IEEE Transactions on Neural Networks*, vol. 3, No 6.

Whitley D. (1995). Genetic Algorithms and Neural Networks. *Genetic Algorithms in Engineering and Computer Science.* Ed. J. Periaux et G. Winter.

Whitley D., Gordon S. et Mathias K. (1994). Lamarckian Evolution, the Baldwin Effect and Function Optimization. *Parallel Problem Solving from Nature* III. pp. 6-15. Springer-Verlag.

Yao X. (1995). Evolutionary Artificial Neural Networks. *Encyclopedia of Computer Science and Technology.* Ed.A. Kent et al., vol. 33, pp 137-170, Marcel Dekker Inc.

Yuhas, B.P., Goldstein, M.H. & Sejnowski, T.J. (1989). Interpretation of Acoustic and Visual Speech Signal using Neural Networks. *IEEE Common Magazine.*

6

Using Genetic Algorithm to Improve the Performance of Speech Recognition Based on Artificial Neural Network

Shing-Tai Pan[1], Chih-Chin Lai[2]
National University of Kaohsiung[1], National University of Tainan[2]
Taiwan

1. Introduction

The development for speech recognition system has been for a while. The recognition platform can be divided into three types. Dynamic Time Warping (DTW) (Sakoe, 1978), the earliest platform, uses the variation in frame's time for adjustment and further recognition. Later, Artificial Neural Network (ANN) replaced DTW. Finally, Hidden Markov Model was developed to adopt statistics for improved recognition performance.

Besides the recognition platform, the process of speech recognition also includes: recording of voice signal, point detect, pre-emphasis, speech feature capture, etc. The final step is to transfer the input sampling feature to recognition platform for matching.

In recent years, study on Genetic Algorithm can be found in many research papers (Chu, 2003a; Chen, 2003; Chu, 2003b). They demonstrated different characteristics in Genetic Algorithm than others. For example, parallel search based on random multi-points, instead of a single point, was adopted to avoid being limited to local optimum. In the operation of Genetic Algorithm, it only needs to establish the objective function without auxiliary operations, such as differential operation. Therefore, it can be used for the objective functions for all types of problems.

Because artificial neural network has better speech recognition speed and less calculation load than others, it is suitable for chips with lower computing capability. Therefore, artificial neural network was adopted in this study as speech recognition platform. Most artificial neural networks for speech recognition are back-propagation neural networks. The local optimum problem (Yeh, 1993) with Steepest Descent Method makes it fail to reach the highest recognition rate. In this study, Genetic Algorithm was used to improve the drawback.

Consequently, the mission of this chapter is the experiment of speech recognition under the recognition structure of Artificial Neural Network (ANN) which is trained by the Genetic Algorithm (GA). This chapter adopted Artificial Neural Network (ANN) to recognize Mandarin digit speech. Genetic algorithm (GA) was used to complement Steepest Descent Method (SDM) and make a global search of optimal weight in neural network. Thus, the performance of speech recognition was improved. The nonspecific speaker speech recognition was the target of this chapter. The experiment in this chapter would show that the GA can achieve near the global optimum search and a higher recognition rate would be

obtained. Moreover, two method of the computation of the characteristic value were compared for the speech recognition.
However, the drawback of GA used to train the ANN is that it will waste many training time. This is becasue that the numbers of input layer and output layer is very large when the ANN is used in recognizing speech. Hence, the parameters in the ANN is emormously increasing. Consequently, the training rate of the ANN becomes very slow. It is then necessary that other improved methods must be investigated in the future research.
The rest of this chapter is organized as follows. In section 2, the speech pre-processing is introduced. Then, in section 3 we investigate the speech recognition by ANN which is trained by genetic algorithm to attain global optimal weights. Section 4 present the experiment result of the speech recognition. Finally, in section 5, we make some conclusions about this chapter.

2. Speech pre-processing

The speech signal needs be pre-processed prior to entering the recognition platform. The speech pre-processing includes point detection, hamming windows, speech feature, etc. Each process is illustrated as follows.

2.1 Fixed-size frame and Dynamic-size frame

With fixed-size frame, the number of frame varies with speech speed due to different length of voice signal. This problem does not exist in DTW recognition system. However, this study with artificial neural network ANN has to use dynamic-size frame to obtain a fixed number of frames. There are two methods to get a fixed number of frames: (1) dynamic numbers of sample points (2) dynamic overlap rates (Chen, 2002). Either of the two methods can lead to a fixed numbers of frames, meeting the requirement by ANN recognition system.

2.2 Point Detection

A voice signal can be divided into three parts: speech segment, silence segment and background noise. How to differentiate between speech segment and silence segment is called point detection. After removal of unnecessary segments, the time frame in comparison is narrowed and the response time is shortened.
There are a number of algorithms for speech end point detection. In general, there are three types based on parameters: (1) time domain point detection method, (2) frequency domain point detection method, (3) hybrid parameters point detection method. Among the three, the time domain point detection is the simplest and the most frequently used, but has the shortcoming of lower noise resistance. On the other hand, frequency domain point detection and hybrid parameters point detection have higher noise resistance and better accuracy, but is more complicated in calculation. In this chapter, we adopted the time domain point detection method for shortening the computation time.

2.3 Hamming Window

The purpose to fetch hamming window is to prevent discontinuity in every frame and both ends of every frame. When the voice signal is multiplied by hamming window, we can reduce the effect of discontinuity (Wang, 2004).

2.4 Feature capture

In general, there are two types of features capturing of voice signal for speech recognition, time domain analysis and frequency domain analysis. Of the two, time domain analysis is more straightforward and involves less calculation, so it saves time. Frequency domain analysis needs to go through Fourier transform first, so it involves more calculation and complexity and takes more time. Common speech features capturing include Linear Predict Coding (LPC) (Chen, 1994), linear predict cepstrum coefficient (LPCC), Mel-frequency Cepstrum coefficient (MFCC) (Chu, 2003b) etc. With consideration of recognition accuracy, this study selected MFCC as the speech feature capturing method.

Using MFCC to obtain solutions involves three steps: 1. Using Fast Fourier Transform (FTT) to obtain power spectrum of the speech signal; 2. Applying a Mel-space filter-bank to the power spectrum to get logarithmic energy value; 3. We conduct the discrete cosine transform (DCT) of log filter-bank energies to obtain MFCC.

3. Speech recognition platform

BPNN is the most commonly used structure in ANN. Although ANN has fast recognition rate and fault tolerance, it is not perfect because its SDM has a problem with Local Optimum. To prevent this from happening, GA is adopted to assist in SDM for obtaining optimal weight and improved recognition performance.

3.1 Back-propagation neural network

In principle, back-propagation neural network uses Multiple-Layer Perception as system framework and SDM as training rule. Such a system is called back-propagation neural network. Multiple-layer in Multiple-Layer Perception model indicates it is composed of many layers of neurons. Besides, the signal transmittance mode between neurons in two layers is the same as that for a single layer. The study adopted three-layer structure (input layer, hidden layer, output layer) as the basic framework for speech recognition, which is depicted in Fig. 1.

3.2 Genetic algorithm

Genetic algorithm (Goldberg, 1989; Michalewicz, 1999) involves Selection, Reproduction and Mutation.

The purpose of selection is to determine the genes to retain or delete for each generation based on their degree of adaptation. There are two types of determination: (1) Roulette-Wheel Selection (2) Tournament Selection. The study adopted tournament selection. It is to follow their fitness function sequence for each gene set to determine whether they are retained. The fittest survives. Reproduction is a process to exchange chromosomes to create the next generation according to distribution rule. In general, there are one-point crossover, two-point crossover and uniform crossover, etc. The evolutionary process of GA is depicted in Fig. 2.

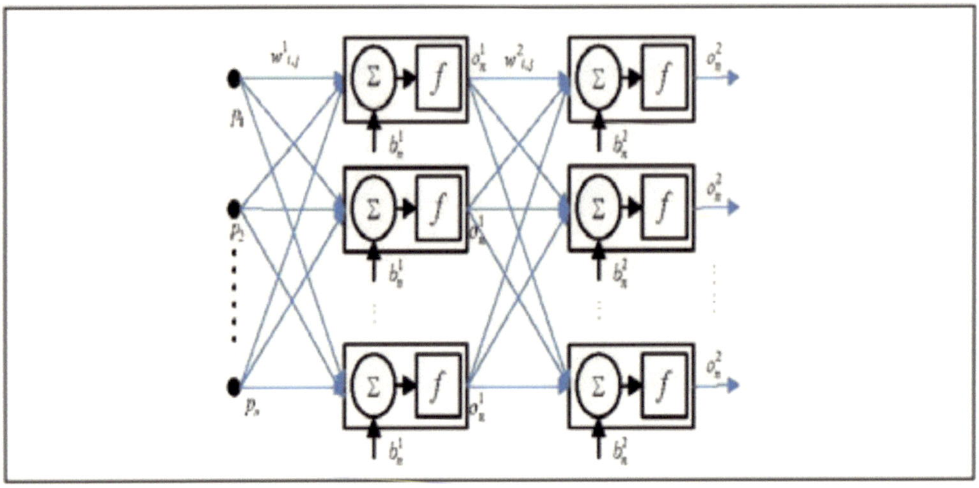

Figure 1. The three-layer structured ANN

The way of mutation is not very different from that for crossover. There are one-point mutation and two-point mutation. Mutation process depends on conditions; for example, mutation can start as adaptation function and stop changing after several generations. Mutation rate cannot be too high. Otherwise, convergence will not occur.

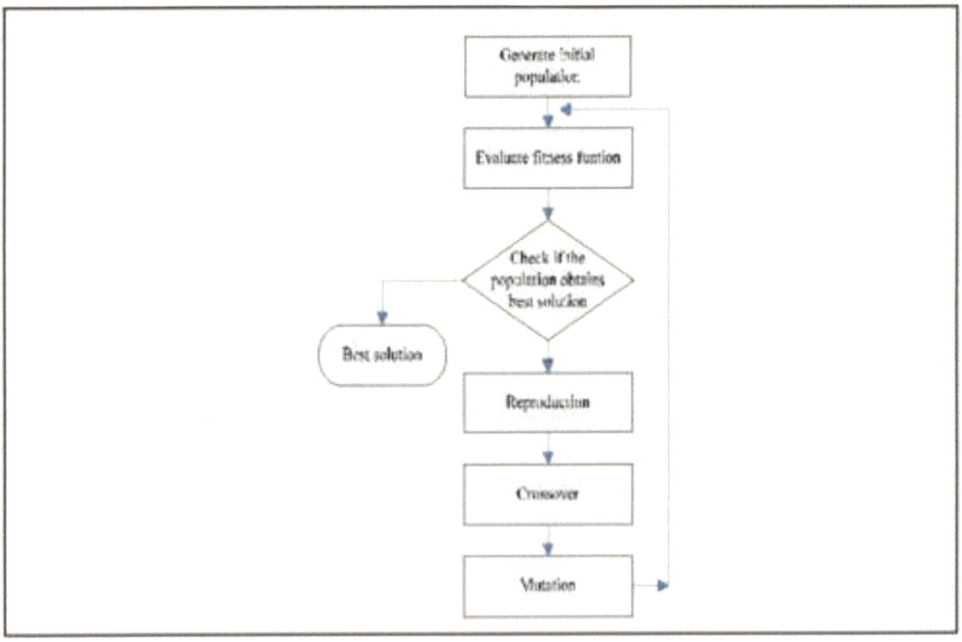

Figure 2. The evolutionary process of GA

4. Experimental results

ANN with SDM training (i.e., BPNN) was first adopted to be speech recognition platform. The result was compared to GA assisted ANN platform. Although genetic algorithm has advantages that SDM cannot provide. It has one drawback, i.e. the crossover, reproduction and mutation process needs more time to seek optimal solutions.
In the initial speech, voice files for ten people were collected. This file contains the voice of numeral 1 ~ 9. Each people recorded four sets, three of which were used for training and one of which was for test. Recording format had sampling frequency 8 kHz, mono channel 16 bit sampling point. After recording, point detection was to remove silence segment, followed by pre-emphasis. Then, speech segment was divided to 20 fixed frames. Feature parameter was extracted from each frame. One frame had 10 features. Thus, each number would have 200 features.
In the aspect of speech frame, because ANN recognition platform was adopted, speech segment needs the same number of frames regardless of its length of time. The adopted dynamic-size frame was different from the DTW fixed frame. The study also adopted dynamic sampling point (fixed overlap rate). The frame sampling point can be expressed by the following equation (1) (Chen, 2002):

$$L = \mathrm{Fix}\{\, l_s / [(N-1)(1-R)+1] \,\} \tag{1}$$

L represents the number of frame sampling points, l_s is the total signal length, N is the number of frames, R is overlap rate (%), while Fix(x) the maximum integer smaller than x. Through such function, the same number of frames can be obtained for different length of speech. Besides, the point detection in the study still adopted time-domain point detection due to the reason of less calculation load. It took the average of energies for the first few silence segments (background noise) and added it to 5%~10% of the maximum frame energy to set the threshold value for point detection, as shown in the following equation (2) (Chen, 2002):

$$Threshold = 7.5\% \times \max[E(n)] + \frac{1}{K}\sum_{i=1}^{K} E(i), \quad 1 \le n \le \tilde{N} \tag{2}$$

Threshold is the point detection threshold value. N is the number of frames prior to point detection. E(n) is the sum of energies for sampling points in the nth frame prior to point detection. K represents captured number of silence segment frames. E(i) is the sum of energies for sampling points in ith silence segment. 7.5% of the maximum frame energy was added with the average energy for five silence segment frames (K = 5) to establish point detection threshold calculation.
After completion of point detection, pre-emphasis and Hamming window were carried out to capture features. With consideration of recognition accuracy, MFCC parameter was adopted for recognition. MFCC level in this experiment was 10. After obtaining features, they were input to recognition platform to start speech recognition.

4.1 BPNN Experiment Results

In the design structure of artificial neural network, there are two output modes. One used binary coding to express output, for example, the system has 16 corresponding outputs to four output neurons. Thus, the number of output neurons was reduced. The other was one-to-one output. For example, 9 frames needed 9 outputs neurons. Although binary coding can minimize the number of neurons, it not only had low recognition rate, but difficulty in convergence after experiment comparison with one-to-one mode. Therefore, one-to-one output was adopted here. Thc entire ANN structure had 200 inputs, 30 neurons in hidden layer and 9 neurons in output layer.

In the experiment, each speech had 20 frames. Each frame had ten levels of features, indicating 200 input parameters as input layer, while 30 neurons were in the hidden layer. The number of neurons cannot be too many; otherwise, it cannot obtain convergence. If the number is too small, recognition error will be large. The number of neurons in the hidden layer (N_no) is expressed by the following equation (3) (Yeh, 1993) :

$$N\_no = (In\_number \times Out\_number)^{1/2} \tag{3}$$

In_number represents the number of input layer units, while Out_number represents the number of output layer units.

Because the number of ANN inputs is as high as 200, there will be a problem, i.e. when the input approaches a relatively large number, the output will be at the extreme condition. To solve the problem, the speech features were all downsized prior to input. It was to multiply the speech feature by 0.01 to prevent transfer function from over-saturation. From Fig. 3, it is known that once the number of training generation is over 1,500, it then fails to breakthrough and the recognition rate is 91% for the existing database. Even further training is continued, root mean square error does not progress, and recognition rate does not improve either. Under this situation, genetic algorithm is used to assist in seeking the weight.

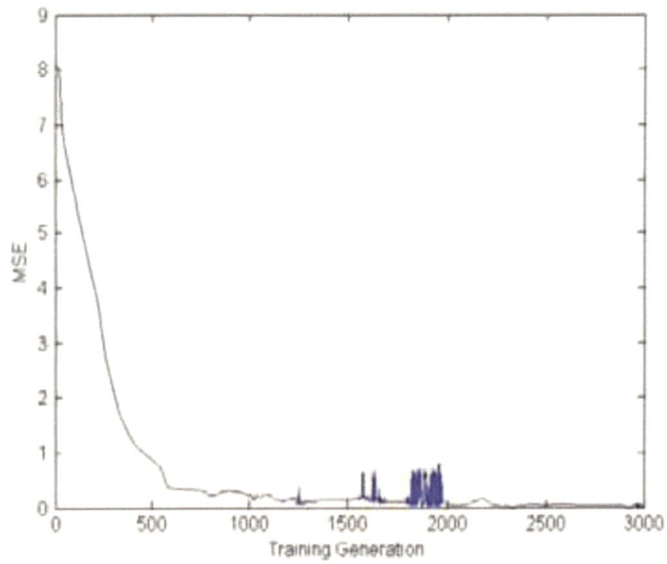

Figure 3. MSE for Output in ANN with SDM Training Process

4.2 Experiment Results with Genetic Algorithm to assist in Training

SDM in the above-mentioned artificial neural network was used to seek the weight. Back-propagation neural network tended to have problems with local optimum, so genetic algorithm was used to seek the weight for the entire domain (Chu, 2003a).

At first, the study used SDM to train ANN to obtain the weight. Then converged weight and bias were entered into genetic algorithm. It improved the initial speed and also helped SDM out of the local optimum. Fig. 4 shows the entire training structure. The experiment has shown that SDM training followed by GA training would help error break the SDM limit and greatly improve recognition rate. Fig. 5 shows the error range for SDM training followed by GA.

Through 3000 generations of GA, MSE value drops to 0.001 with recognition rate up to 95%, as shown in Table 1.

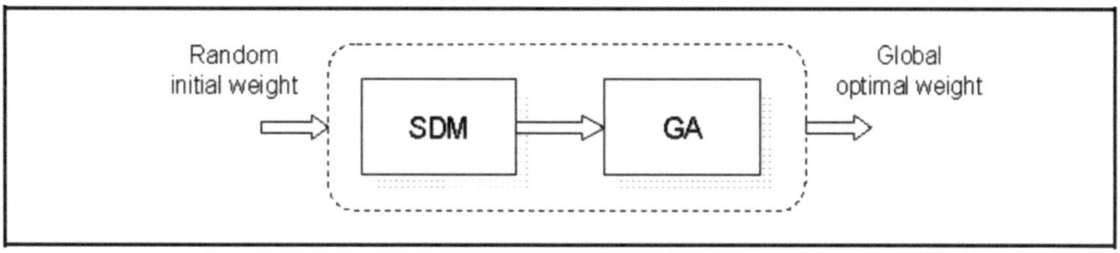

Figure 4. The Proposed ANN Training Structure

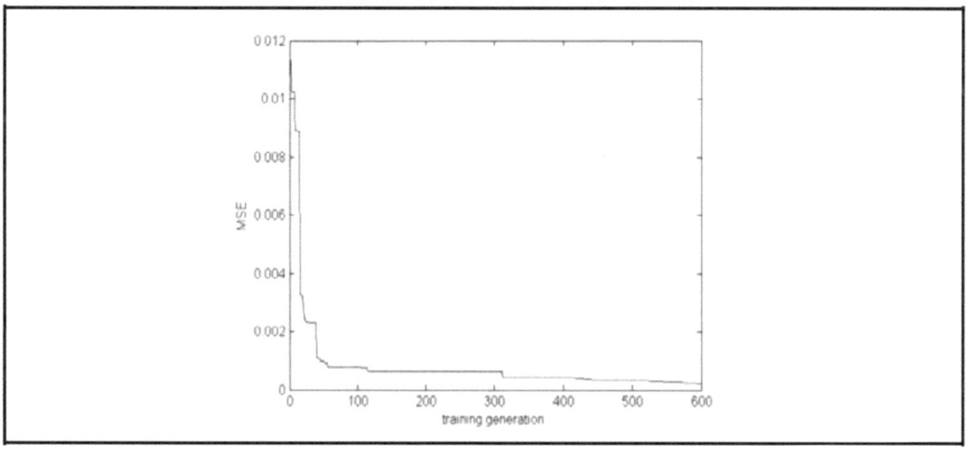

Figure 5. MSE for Output in Genetic Algorithm Training after SDM Training

5. Conclusion

In this chapter, we have seen that the recognition rate through the SDM in BPNN is up to 91% under the MFCC feature. This recognition rate is not the optimum because that the SDM can always get local optimum. To solve this problem, GA was adopted and following SDM to improve MSE. By this two stage (SDM then GA) training scheme, the recognition rate can be increasing up to 95%. However, under the condition of adopting only MFCC parameters, speech recognition rate still has room for improvement. For the future, other modes of features capturing method can be adopted, such as Cepstrum Coefficient or LPC parameter together with pitch parameter, to improve recognition rate.

Speech	Successful Recognition	Failed Recognition	Recognition Rate(%)	Total Recognition Rate(%)
1	10	0	100	
2	10	0	100	
3	7	3	70	
4	10	0	100	
5	10	0	100	95
6	9	1	90	
7	9	1	90	
8	10	0	100	
9	10	0	100	

Table 1. Speech Recognition Results after 10 sets of testing

6. References

Chen, S. C. (2003). Use of GA in CSD Coded Finite Impulse Digital Filter (FIR), Shu-Te University, MS Thesis, Taiwan.

Chen, M. Y. (1994). PC Computer Voice Operation, Chi Biao Publication, 957-717-071-4, Taiwan.

Chen, S. L. (2002). Speech Recognition based on Artificial Neural Network, National Sun Yat-Sen University, Master Thesis, Taiwan. Chu, S. H. (2003a). Combination of GA and SDM to Improve ANN Training Efficiency, Shu-Te University, MS Thesis, Taiwan. Chu, W. C. (2003b). Speech Coding Algorithms, John Wiley & Sons, 978-0-471-37312-4, USA.

Demuth, H. B., Beale, M. H., Hagan, M. T. (1996). *Neural Network Design*, Thomson Learning, 0534943322, USA. Goldberg, D. E. (1989). Genetic Algorithms in Search, Optimization, and Machine Learning, Addison-Wesley Professional, 0201157675, Reading, Massachusetts. Michalewicz, Z. (1999). Genetic Algorithms + Data Structures = Evolution Programs, Springer-Verlag, 3540606769, Berlin.

Sakoe, H. and Chiba, S. (1978). Dynamic Programming Optimization for Spoken Word Recongition, *IEEE Transactions on Signal Processing*, Vol. 26, pp 43- 49.

Wang, S. C. (2004). Voice Signal Processing, Chun Hwa Publication, 9572143840, Taiwan.

Yeh, Y. C. (1993). Implementation and Application of Artificial Neural Network, Ru Lin Publication, 957499628X, Taiwan.

7

A General Approximation-Optimization Approach to Large Margin Estimation of HMMs

Hui Jiang and Xinwei Li
York University, Toronto
Canada

1. Introduction

The most successful modeling approach to automatic speech recognition (ASR) is to use a set of hidden Markov models (HMMs) as the acoustic models for subword or whole-word speech units and to use the statistical N-gram model as language model for words and/or word classes in sentences. All the model parameters, including HMMs and N-gram models, are estimated from a large amount of training data according to certain criterion. It has been shown that success of this kind of data-driven modeling approach highly depends on the goodness of estimated models. As for HMM-based acoustic models, the dominant estimation method is the Baum-Welch algorithm which is based on the maximum likelihood (ML) criterion. As an alternative to the ML estimation, discriminative training (DT) has also been extensively studied for HMMs in ASR. It has been demonstrated that various DT techniques, such as maximum mutual information (MMI), minimum classification error (MCE) and minimum phone error (MPE), can significantly improve speech recognition performance over the conventional maximum likelihood (ML) estimation.

More recently, we have proposed the large margin estimation (LME) of HMMs for speech recognition (Li et al., 2005; Liu et al., 2005a; Li & Jiang, 2005; Jiang et al., 2006), where Gaussian mixture HMMs are estimated based on the principle of maximizing the minimum margin. From the theoretical results in machine learning (Vapnik, 1998), a large margin classifier implies a good generalization power and generally yields much lower generalization errors in new test data, as shown in support vector machine and boosting method. As in Li et al., 2005 and Li & Jiang, 2005, estimation of large margin CDHMMs turns out to be a constrained minimax optimization problem. In the past few years, several optimization methods have been proposed to solve this problem, such as *iterative localized optimization* in Li et al., 2005, *constrained joint optimization method* in Li & Jiang, 2005 and Jiang et al., 2006, and *semi-definite programming (SDP) method* in Li & Jiang, 2006a and Li & Jiang 2006b. In this paper, we present a general Approximation-optiMization (AM) approach to solve the LME problem of Gaussian mixture HMMs in ASR. Similar to the EM algorithm, each iteration of the AM method consists of two distinct steps: namely **A**-step and **M**-step. In **A**-step, the original LME problem is approximated by a simple convex optimization problem in a close proximity of initial model parameters. In **M**-step, the approximate convex optimization problem is solved by using efficient convex optimization algorithms.

This paper is structured as follows. In section 2, we present the large margin estimation formulation for HMMs in speech recognition. In section 3, we explain the proposed AM approach under a general framework. Next, as two examples, we consider to apply the AM method to solve the LME of HMMs for ASR. In section 4, we use the so-called **V-approx** for the case where competing hypotheses are given as N-Best lists. In section 5, we use **E-approx** for the case where competing hypotheses are given as word graphs. At last, some final remarks are discussed in section 6.

2. Large Margin Estimation (LME) of HMMs for ASR

In ASR, we consider a joint probability distribution between any speech utterance X and any word W, i.e. $p(X, W)$. Depending on the problem of interest, a word W may be any linguistic unit, e.g., a phoneme, a syllable, a word, a phrase, even a sentence. Given a speech utterance X, a speech recognizer will choose the word W as output based on the following plug-in MAP decision rule (Jiang et al., 1999):

$$\begin{aligned} \hat{W} &= \arg\max_W \; p(W \mid X) = \arg\max_W \; p(W) \cdot p(X \mid W) \\ &= \arg\max_W \; p(W) \cdot p(X \mid \lambda_W) = \arg\max_W \; \mathcal{F}(X \mid \lambda_W) \end{aligned} \tag{1}$$

where λ_W denotes the composite HMM representing word W and $\mathcal{F}(X|\lambda_W)$ is called discriminant function of λ_W given X, which is normally calculated in the logarithm domain as $\mathcal{F}(X|\lambda_W) = \ln\left[p(W) \cdot p(X|\lambda_W)\right] = \ln p(W) + \ln p(X|\lambda_W)$. In this work, we are only interested in estimating HMM λ_W and assume language model used to calculate $p(W)$ is fixed.

For a speech utterance X_i , assuming its true word identity as W_i, following Weston & Watkins, 1999 and Crammer & Singer, 2001 and Altun et al., 2003, the multi-class separation margin for X_i is defined as:

$$d(X_i) = \mathcal{F}(X_i|\lambda_{W_i}) - \max_{j\in\Omega \; j\neq W_i} \mathcal{F}(X_i|\lambda_j) \tag{2}$$

where Ω denotes the set of all possible words. Clearly, eq.(2) can be re-arranged as:

$$d(X_i) = \min_{j\in\Omega \; j\neq W_i} \left[\mathcal{F}(X_i|\lambda_{W_i}) - \mathcal{F}(X_i|\lambda_j)\right] \tag{3}$$

Obviously, if $d(X_i) \leq 0$, X_i will be incorrectly recognized by the current HMM set, denoted as Λ, which includes all HMMs in the recognizer. On the other hand, if $d(Xi) > 0$, X_i will be correctly recognized by the model set Λ.

Given a set of training data $\mathcal{T} = \{X_1, X_2, \cdots X_T\}$, we usually know the true word identities for all utterances in $\mathcal{T}$, denoted as $\mathcal{L} = \{W_1, W_2, \cdots W_T\}$- Thus, we can calculate the separation margin (or margin for short hereafter) for every utterance in T based on the definition in eq. (2) or (3). According to the statistical learning theory (Vapnik, 1998), the generalization error rate of a classifier in new test sets is theoretically bounded by a quantity related to its margin. A large margin classifier usually yields low error rate in new test sets and it shows more robust and better generalization capability. Motivated by the large margin principle, even for those utterances in the training set which all have positive margin, we may still want to maximize the minimum margin to build an HMM-based large margin classifier. In this paper, we will study how to estimate HMMs for speech recognition based on the principle of maximizing minimum margin. First of all, from all utterances in $\mathcal{T}$, we need to identify a subset of utterances $\mathcal{S}$ as:

$$\mathcal{S} = \{X_i \mid X_i \in \mathcal{T} \text{ and } 0 \leq d(X_i) \leq \epsilon\} \tag{4}$$

where $\epsilon > 0$ is a pre-set positive number. Analogically, we call $\mathcal{S}$ as *support vector set* and each utterance in $\mathcal{S}$ is called a support token which has relatively small positive margin among all utterances in the training set $\mathcal{T}$. In other words, all utterances in $\mathcal{S}$ are relatively close to the classification boundary even though all of them locate in the right decision regions. To achieve better generalization power, it is desirable to adjust decision boundaries, which are implicitly determined by all models, through optimizing HMM parameters Λ to make all support tokens as far from the decision boundaries as possible, which will result in a robust classifier with better generalization capability. This idea leads to estimating the HMM models Λ based on the criterion of maximizing the minimum margin of all support tokens, which is named as large margin estimation (LME) of HMMs.

$$\tilde{\Lambda} = \arg\max_{\Lambda} \min_{X_i \in \mathcal{S}} d(X_i) \tag{5}$$

The HMM models, Λ, estimated in this way, are called large margin HMMs.
Considering eq. (3), large margin estimation of HMMs can be formulated as the following *maximin* optimization problem:

$$\tilde{\Lambda} = \arg\max_{\Lambda} \min_{X_i \in \mathcal{S}\ j \in \Omega\ j \neq W_i} \left[\mathcal{F}(X_i|\lambda_{W_i}) - \mathcal{F}(X_i|\lambda_j) \right] \tag{6}$$

Note it is fine to include all training data into the support token set with a large value for *e* in eq. (4). However, this may significantly increase the computational complexity in the following optimization process and most of those data with large margin are usually inactive in the optimization towards maximizing the minimum one, especially when a gradual optimization method is used, such as gradient descent and other local optimization methods.
As shown in Li et al., 2005 and Liu et al., 2005a and Jiang et al., 2006, the above *maximin* optimization may become unsolvable for Gaussian mixture HMMs because its margin as defined in eq. (3) may become unbounded with respect to model parameters. As one possible solution to solve this problem, some additional constraints must be imposed to ensure the margin is bounded during optimization as in Li & Jiang, 2005, Jiang et al., 2006. As suggested in Li & Jiang, 2006a and Liu et al., 2007, a KL-divergence based constraint can be introduced for HMM parameters to bound the margin. The KL-divergence (KLD) is calculated between an HMM λ ($\lambda \in \Lambda$)and its initial value as follows:

$$\mathcal{D}(\Lambda \,||\, \Lambda^{(n)}) = \sum_{\lambda \in \Lambda} \mathcal{D}(\lambda \,||\, \lambda^{(n)}) \leq r^2 \tag{7}$$

or

$$\mathcal{D}(\lambda \,||\, \lambda^{(n)}) \leq r^2 \qquad (\lambda \in \Lambda) \tag{8}$$

where $\lambda^{(n)}$ denotes the initial model parameters and r^2 is a constant to control a trust region for large margin optimization which is centered at the initial models. Since the KLD constraints given in eq. (7) defines a closed and compact set, it is trivial to prove that the margin in eq. (3) is a bounded function of HMM parameters λ so that the *maximin* optimization in eq. (6) is solvable under these constraints.
Furthermore, as shown in Li, 2005 and Li & Jiang, 2006a, the *maximin* optimization problem in eq. (6) can be equivalently converted into a constrained maximization problem by introducing a new variable ρ ($\rho > 0$) as a common lower bound to represent *min* part of all terms in eq.(6) along with the constraints that every item must be larger than or equal to ρ. As the result, the *maximin* optimization in eq.(6) can be equivalently transformed into the following optimization problem:
Problem 1

$$\tilde{\Lambda} = \arg\max_{\Lambda,\,\rho} \ \rho \tag{9}$$

subject to:

$$\mathcal{F}(X_i|\lambda_{W_i}) - \mathcal{F}(X_i|\lambda_j) \geq \rho \qquad \text{for all } X_i \in \mathcal{S} \text{ and } j \in \Omega \text{ and } j \neq W_i \tag{10}$$

$$\mathcal{D}(\Lambda \,||\, \Lambda^{(n)}) = \sum_{\lambda \in \Lambda} \mathcal{D}(\lambda \,||\, \lambda^{(n)}) \leq r^2 \tag{11}$$

$$\rho \geq 0 \tag{12}$$

3. A General Approximation-optiMization (AM) Approach to Large Margin Estimation of HMMs

Obviously, we can use a gradient descent method to solve the optimization Problem 1. As in Li & Jiang, 2005 and Jiang et al., 2006, we cast all constraints in eqs.(10) to (12) as some penalty terms in the objective function so that the model parameter updating formula can be easily derived. Thus, HMM parameters can be optimized gradually by following the calculated gradient direction. The gradient descent method is easy to implement and applicable to any differentiable objective functions. However, the gradient descent method can be easily trapped into a shallow local optimum if the derived objective function is jagged and complicated in nature, especially when the gradient descent method is operated in a high-dimensionality space. Also it is very difficult to set appropriate values for some critical parameters in gradient descent, such as step size and so on. As the result, the gradient method normally can not significantly improve over the initial models in a high-dimensionality space if the initial models have been set to some reasonably good values.
In this paper, we propose a novel approach to solve the above large margin estimation problem for HMMs. The key idea behind this approach is that we first attempt to find a simpler convex function to approximate the original objective function in a close proximity of initial model parameters if the original objective function is too complicated to optimize directly. Then, the approximate function is optimized by using an efficient convex optimization algorithm. In some cases, some relaxation must be made to ensure the resultant problem is indeed an convex optimization problem. As we know, a convex optimization problem can be efficiently solved even in a very high-dimensionality space

since it never suffers from the local optimum problem in a convex optimization problem. Based on the proximity approximation, we hope the optimal solution found for this approximate convex problem will also improve the original objective function as well. Then, in next iteration, the original objective function can be similarly approximated in the close proximity of this optimal solution as another convex optimization problem based on the same approximation principle. This process repeats until convergence conditions are met for the original objective function. Analogous to the popular EM algorithm (Dempster et al., 1977 and Neal & Hinton, 1998), each iteration consists of two separate steps: i) Approximation step (**A**-step): the original objective function is approximated in a close proximity of initial model parameters; ii) optiMization step (**M**-step): the approximate function is optimized by a convex optimization algorithm (convex relaxation may be necessary for some models). Analogously, we call this method as the AM algorithm. It is clear that the AM algorithm is more general than the EM algorithm since the expectation (**E**-step) can also be viewed as a proximity approximation method as we will show later. More importantly, comparing with the EM algorithm, the AM algorithm will be able to deal with more complicated objective functions such as those arising from discriminative training of many statistical models with hidden variables.
As one particular application of the AM algorithm, we will show how to solve the large margin estimation (LME) problem of HMMs in speech recognition.

3.1 Approximation Step (A-step):

There are many different methods to approximate an objective function in a close proximity. In this section, we introduce two different methods, namely Viterbi-based approximation **(V-approx)** and Expectation-based approximation **(E-approx).**
Let us first examine the log-likelihood function of HMMs, $\ln p(X|\lambda)$. Since HMMs have hidden variables such as unobserved state sequence, denoted as **s**, and unobserved Gaussian mixture labels (for Gaussian mixture HMMs), denoted as **1**, we have the following:

$$\ln p(X|\lambda) = \ln \sum_{\mathbf{s},\mathbf{l}} p(X,\mathbf{s},\mathbf{l} \mid \lambda) \tag{13}$$

As the first way to approximate the above log-likelihood function, we can use the Viterbi approximation, i.e., we use the best Viterbi path, **s*** and **1***, to approximate the above summation instead of summing over all possible paths. And the best Viterbi path can be easily derived based on the initial models, $\lambda^{(n)}$ by the following *max* operation using the well-known Viterbi algorithm:

$$\{\mathbf{s}^*,\mathbf{l}^*\} = \arg\max_{\mathbf{s},\mathbf{l}} \; p(X,\mathbf{s},\mathbf{l} \mid \lambda^{(n)}) \tag{14}$$

Thus, the log-likelihood function can be approximated as follows:

$$\ln p(X|\lambda) \approx \mathcal{V}(\lambda) = \ln p(X,\mathbf{s}^*,\mathbf{l}^*|\lambda) \tag{15}$$

This approximation scheme is named as Viterbi approximation, i.e., **V-approx.** Obviously, for HMMs, the approximate function $\mathcal{V}(\lambda)$ is a convex function.
If we assume the language model, *p(W)*, is fixed, the discriminant function of HMM, $\mathcal{F}(\Lambda)$, in LME can be viewed as difference of log-likelihood functions. If we use the **V-approx** for both correct model $p(X_i|\lambda_{W_i})$ and incorrect competing model $p(X_i|\lambda_j)$:

$$\ln p(X_i|\lambda_{W_i}) \approx \mathcal{V}_i^+(\lambda_{W_i}) \tag{16}$$

$$\ln p(X_i|\lambda_j) \approx \mathcal{V}_i^-(\lambda_j) \tag{17}$$

Then, the constraints in eq.(10) can be approximated by difference of two convex functions as follows:

$$\mathcal{F}(X_i|\lambda_{W_i}) - \mathcal{F}(X_i|\lambda_j) \approx \mathcal{V}_{ij}(\Lambda) = \mathcal{V}_i^+(\lambda_{W_i}) - \mathcal{V}_i^-(\lambda_j) \tag{18}$$

for all possible *i* and *j*.

Now let us consider the second scheme to approximate the objective function, i.e., **E-approx.** For the log-likelihood function of HMMs, $\ln p(X|\lambda)$ in eq.(13), we consider the following auxiliary function used in the EM algorithm:

$$\begin{aligned} \mathcal{Q}(\lambda|\lambda^{(n)}) &= \mathbb{E}_{\mathbf{s},\mathbf{l}}\left[\ln p(X,\mathbf{s},\mathbf{l}\mid\lambda)\;\middle|\; X,\lambda^{(n)}\right] \\ &= \sum_{\mathbf{s}}\sum_{\mathbf{l}} \ln p(X,\mathbf{s},\mathbf{l}|\lambda)\cdot \Pr(\mathbf{s},\mathbf{l}\,|X,\lambda^{(n)}) \end{aligned} \tag{19}$$

As shown in Dempster et al., 1977 and Neal & Hinton, 1998, the above auxiliary function is related to the original log-likelihood function as follows:

$$\mathcal{Q}(\lambda|\lambda^{(n)}) \leq \ln p(X\mid\lambda) \tag{20}$$

$$\mathcal{Q}(\lambda|\lambda^{(n)})\Big|_{\lambda=\lambda^{(n)}} = \ln p(X|\lambda)\Big|_{\lambda=\lambda^{(n)}} \tag{21}$$

$$\frac{\partial\, \mathcal{Q}(\lambda|\lambda^{(n)})}{\partial\lambda}\bigg|_{\lambda=\lambda^{(n)}} = \frac{\partial\, \ln p(X|\lambda)}{\partial\lambda}\bigg|_{\lambda=\lambda^{(n)}} \tag{22}$$

From these, it is clear that $Q(\lambda|\lambda^{(n)})$ can be viewed as a close proximity approximation of log-likelihood function $\ln p(X|\lambda)$ at $\lambda^{(n)}$ with accuracy up to the first order. Under the proximity constraint in eq.(ll), it serves as a good approximation of the original log-likelihood function. Since the $\mathcal{Q}$ function is originally computed as an expectation in the EM algorithm, this approximation scheme is named as Expectation-based approximation **(E-approx).** Similarly, we use **E-approx** to approximate both correct model $p(X_i|\lambda_{W_i})$ and incorrect competing model $p(X_i|\lambda_j)$ in discriminant function as:

$$\ln p(X_i|\lambda_{W_i}) \approx \mathcal{Q}_i^+(\lambda_{W_i}|\lambda_{W_i}^{(n)}) \tag{23}$$

$$\ln p(X_i|\lambda_j) \approx \mathcal{Q}_i^-(\lambda_j|\lambda_j^{(n)}) \tag{24}$$

It can be easily shown that the $\mathcal{Q}$ function is also a convex function for HMMs. Therefore, the discriminant function can also be similarly approximated as difference of two convex functions as follows:

$$\mathcal{F}(X_i|\lambda_{W_i}) - \mathcal{F}(X_i|\lambda_j) \approx \mathcal{Q}_{ij}(\Lambda) = \mathcal{Q}_i^+(\lambda_{W_i}|\lambda_{W_i}^{(n)}) - \mathcal{Q}_i^-(\lambda_j|\lambda_j^{(n)}) \tag{25}$$

for all possible *i* and *j*.

3.2 OptiMization Step (M-step):

After the approximation, either **V-approx** or **E-approx,** the original **Problem 1** has been converted into a relatively simpler optimization problem since all constraints have been approximately represented by differences of convex functions. As we know, a difference of two convex functions is not necessarily a convex function. Thus, in some cases, we will have to make some convex relaxations to convert the problem into a convex optimization problem so that a variety of convex optimization algorithms can be applied to find the global optimum of the approximate problem under the proximity constraint in eq.(ll). Due to this proximity constraint, we expect the global optimal solution will also improve the original LME optimization problem since the approximate convex optimization problem approaches the original LME problem with sufficient accuracy under the proximity constraint.

In the remainder of this paper, we will use two examples to show how to make convex relaxations and how to perform the convex optimization for LME of Gaussian mean vectors in Gaussian mixture HMMs. In the first example, we use **V-approx** to approximate the likelihood function of HMMs and then make some convex relaxations to convert the problem into an SDP (semi-definite programming) problem. This method is suitable for both isolated word recognition and continuous speech recognition based on the string-model of N-Best lists. In the second example, we use **E-approx** to approximate likelihood function of HMMs when the competing hypotheses are represented by word graphs or lattices. Then we similarly convert the problem into an SDP problem by making the same relaxation. This method is suitable for LME in large vocabulary continuous speech recognition where competing hypotheses are encoded in word graphs or lattices.

4. LME of Gaussian Mixture HMMs based on N-Best Lists

In this section, we apply the AM algorithm to solve the large margin estimation for Gaussian mixture HMMs in speech recognition. Here, we consider to use **V-approx** in the **A-**Step of the AM algorithm. This method is applicable to isolated word recognition and continuous speech recognition using string-models based on N-Best lists.

At first, we assume each speech unit, e.g., a word W, is modeled by an N-state Gaussian mixture HMM with parameter vector $\lambda = (\pi, A, \theta)$, where λ is the initial state distribution, $A = \{a_{ij} | 1 \leq i, j \leq N\}$ is transition matrix, and θ is parameter vector composed of mixture parameters $\theta_i = \{\omega_{ik}, \boldsymbol{\mu}_{ik}, \Sigma_{ik}\}_{k=1,2,\cdots,K}$ for each state i, where K denotes number of Gaussian mixtures in each state. The state observation p.d.f. is assumed to be a mixture of multivariate Gaussian distribution:

$$\begin{aligned} p(\mathbf{x}|\theta_i) &= \sum_{k=1}^{K} \omega_{ik} \cdot \mathcal{N}(\mathbf{x}|\boldsymbol{\mu}_{ik}, \Sigma_{ik}) \\ &= \sum_{k=1}^{K} \omega_{ik} \cdot (2\pi)^{-D/2} |\Sigma_{ik}|^{-1/2} \exp\left[-\frac{1}{2}(\mathbf{x} - \boldsymbol{\mu}_{ik})^T \Sigma_{ik}^{-1} (\mathbf{x} - \boldsymbol{\mu}_{ik})\right] \end{aligned} \quad (26)$$

where D denotes dimension of feature vector $\mathbf{x}$ and mixture weights ω_{ik}'s satisfy the constraint $\sum_{k=1}^{K} \omega_{ik} = 1$. In this paper, we only consider multivariate Gaussian distribution with diagonal covariance matrix. Thus, the above state observation p.d.f. is simplified as:

$$p(\mathbf{x}|\theta_i) = \sum_{k=1}^{K} \omega_{ik}\mathcal{N}(\mathbf{x}|\boldsymbol{\mu}_{ik}, \Sigma_{ik}) = \sum_{k=1}^{K} \omega_{ik} \prod_{d=1}^{D} \sqrt{\frac{1}{2\pi\sigma_{ikd}^2}} e^{-\frac{(x_d-\mu_{ikd})^2}{2\sigma_{ikd}^2}} \tag{27}$$

We assume training data is given as $\mathcal{T} = \{X_1, X_2, \cdots, X_T\}$ along with true labels for all utterances in $\mathcal{T}$, denoted as $\mathcal{L} = \{W_1, W_2, \cdots, W_T\}$. In this section, we assume for each *Xi* in $\mathcal{T}$, its competing hypotheses are encoded as an N-Best list, Ω_i, which can be generated from an N-Best Viterbi decoding process. We also assume the correct label has been excluded from the list. Then, the LME formulation in section 2 can be easily extended to this case. The only difference is that the set of all possible words, Ω, used to define margin for each training data X_i in eq.(2), becomes different for different training data, X_i, where we denote its N-Best list as Ω_i. And each model λ_{W_i} or λ_j denotes the string model concatenated according to the true transcription or a hypothesis from N-Best lists.

4.1 A-Step: V-approx

Given any speech utterance $X_i = \{\mathbf{x}_{i1}, \mathbf{x}_{i2}, \cdots, \mathbf{x}_{iR}\}$, let $\mathbf{s} = \{s_1, s_2, \cdots, s_R\}$ be the unobserved state sequence, and $\mathbf{l} = \{l_1, l_2, \cdots, l_R\}$ be the associated sequence of the unobserved mixture component labels, if we use **V-approx,** the discriminant function, i.e., $\mathcal{F}(X_i|\lambda_j)$, can be expressed as:

$$\begin{aligned}\mathcal{F}(X_i|\lambda_j) \;\approx\; & \mathcal{V}_i(\lambda_j) = \log \pi_{s_1^*} + \sum_{t=2}^{R} \log a_{s_{t-1}^* s_t^*} + \sum_{t=1}^{R} \log \omega_{s_t^* l_t^*} \\ & - \frac{1}{2}\sum_{t=1}^{R}\sum_{d=1}^{D}\left[\log \sigma_{s_t^* l_t^* d}^2 + \frac{(x_{itd} - \mu_{s_t^* l_t^* d})^2}{\sigma_{s_t^* l_t^* d}^2}\right]\end{aligned} \tag{28}$$

where we denote the optimal Viterbi path as $\mathbf{s}^* = \{s_1^*, s_2^*, \cdots, s_R^*\}$ and the best mixture component label as $\mathbf{l}^* = \{l_1^*, l_2^*, \cdots, l_R^*\}$.

In this paper, for simplicity, we only consider to estimate Gaussian mean vectors of HMMs based on the large margin principle while keeping all other HMM parameters constant during the large margin estimation. Therefore, we have

$$\mathcal{V}_i(\lambda_j) = c_j'' - \frac{1}{2}\sum_{t=1}^{R}\sum_{d=1}^{D} \frac{(x_{itd} - \mu_{s_t^* l_t^* d})^2}{\sigma_{s_t^* l_t^* d}^2} \tag{29}$$

where c • is a constant which is independent from all Gaussian mean vectors.

Furthermore, we assume there are totally M Gaussian mixtures in the whole HMM set Λ, denoted as $\mathcal{M} = \{1, 2, \ldots, M\}$. We denote each Gaussian as $\mathcal{N}(u_k, \Sigma_k)$ where $k \in \mathcal{M}$. For notation convenience, the optimal Viterbi path **s*** and **1*** can be equivalently represented as a sequence of Gaussian mixture index, i.e., $\mathbf{j} = \{j_1, j_2, \cdots, j_R\}$, where $j_t \in \mathcal{M}$. is index of Gaussians along the optimal Viterbi path {**s***, **1***}. Therefore, we can rewrite the discriminant function in eq. (29) according to this new Gaussian index as:

$$\mathcal{V}_i(\lambda_j) = c_j'' - \frac{1}{2}\sum_{t=1}^{R}\sum_{d=1}^{D}\frac{(x_{itd} - \mu_{j_t d})^2}{\sigma_{j_t d}^2} \tag{30}$$

For $\mathcal{F}(X_i|\lambda_{W_i})$, let us assume the optimal Viterbi path is $\mathbf{i} = \{i_1, i_2, \cdots, i_R\}$, where $i_t \in \mathcal{M}$. As we are only considering to estimate mean vectors of CDHMMs, after **V-approx,** the decision margin $d_{ij}(X_i)$ can be represented as a standard diagonal quadratic form as follows:

$$\begin{aligned} d_{ij}(X_i) &= \mathcal{F}(X_i|\lambda_{W_i}) - \mathcal{F}(X_i|\lambda_j) \approx \mathcal{V}_i^+(\lambda_{W_i}) - \mathcal{V}_i^-(\lambda_j) \\ &= c_{ij} - \frac{1}{2}\sum_{t=1}^{R}\sum_{d=1}^{D}\left[\frac{(x_{itd} - \mu_{i_t d})^2}{\sigma_{i_t d}^2} - \frac{(x_{itd} - \mu_{j_t d})^2}{\sigma_{j_t d}^2}\right] \end{aligned} \tag{31}$$

where c_{ij} is another constant independent of all Gaussian means.
Furthermore, if we only estimate Gaussian mean vectors, the KL-divergence based constraint in eq.(11) can also be simplified for Gaussian mixture HMMs with diagonal covariance matrices as follows:

$$\mathcal{D}(\Lambda||\Lambda^{(n)}) = \sum_{k\in\mathcal{M}}\sum_{d=1}^{D}\frac{(\mu_{kd} - \mu_{kd}^{(n)})^2}{\sigma_{kd}^2} \leq r^2 \tag{32}$$

To convert the above optimization problem into an SDP problem, we first represent the above approximated problem in a matrix form. We first define a mean matrix U by concatenating all normalized Gaussian mean vectors in Λ as its columns as follows:

$$U = (\tilde{\boldsymbol{\mu}}_1, \tilde{\boldsymbol{\mu}}_2, \ldots, \tilde{\boldsymbol{\mu}}_M) \tag{33}$$

where each column is a normalized mean vector (column vector):

$$\tilde{\boldsymbol{\mu}}_k := (\frac{\mu_{k1}}{\sigma_{k1}}; \frac{\mu_{k2}}{\sigma_{k2}}; \ldots; \frac{\mu_{kD}}{\sigma_{kD}}) \tag{34}$$

Then we have

$$\begin{aligned} \mathcal{V}^+(\lambda_{W_i}) &= c_i' - \frac{1}{2}\sum_{t=1}^{R}\sum_{d=1}^{D}\frac{(x_{itd} - \mu_{i_t d})^2}{\sigma_{i_t d}^2} \\ &= c_i' - \frac{1}{2}\sum_{t=1}^{R}\sum_{d=1}^{D}(\tilde{x}_{itd} - \tilde{\mu}_{i_t d})^2 \\ &= c_i' - \frac{1}{2}\sum_{t=1}^{R}(\tilde{\boldsymbol{x}}_{i_t} - \tilde{\boldsymbol{\mu}}_{i_t})^T(\tilde{\boldsymbol{x}}_{i_t} - \tilde{\boldsymbol{\mu}}_{i_t}) \end{aligned} \tag{35}$$

where $\tilde{\boldsymbol{x}}_{i_t}$ denotes a normalized feature vector (column vector) as

$$\tilde{\boldsymbol{x}}_{i_t} := (\frac{x_{it1}}{\sigma_{i_t 1}}; \frac{x_{it2}}{\sigma_{i_t 2}}; \ldots; \frac{x_{itD}}{\sigma_{i_t D}}) \tag{36}$$

Since we have

$$\tilde{\boldsymbol{x}}_{i_t} - \tilde{\boldsymbol{\mu}}_{i_t} = (I_D, U)(\tilde{\boldsymbol{x}}_{i_t}; \boldsymbol{e}_{i_t})$$

$$= \left(\begin{matrix} \overbrace{\begin{matrix} 1 & \cdots & 0 \\ \vdots & \ddots & \vdots \\ 0 & \cdots & 1 \end{matrix}}^{D} & \overbrace{\begin{matrix} \tilde{\mu}_{11} & \cdots & \tilde{\mu}_{L1} \\ \vdots & \vdots & \vdots \\ \tilde{\mu}_{1D} & \vdots & \tilde{\mu}_{LD} \end{matrix}}^{L} \end{matrix} \right) \left(\begin{matrix} \left. \begin{matrix} \tilde{x}_{it1} \\ \vdots \\ \tilde{x}_{itD} \end{matrix} \right\} D \\ \left. \begin{matrix} 0 \\ \vdots \\ -1 \ (i_t) \\ \vdots \\ 0 \end{matrix} \right\} L \end{matrix} \right) \quad (37)$$

where I_D is D-dimension identity matrix and $\boldsymbol{e}_k$ is a column vector with all zeros except only one -1 in k-th location. Then, we have

$$\begin{aligned} \mathcal{V}_i^+(\lambda_{W_i}) &= c_i' - \frac{1}{2}\sum_{t=1}^{R}(\tilde{\boldsymbol{x}}_{i_t}; \boldsymbol{e}_{i_t})^T (I_D, U)^T (I_D, U)(\tilde{\boldsymbol{x}}_{i_t}; \boldsymbol{e}_{i_t}) \\ &= c_i' - \frac{1}{2}\sum_{t=1}^{R}(\tilde{\boldsymbol{x}}_{i_t}; \boldsymbol{e}_{i_t})^T Z (\tilde{\boldsymbol{x}}_{i_t}; \boldsymbol{e}_{i_t}) \\ &= c_i' - \frac{1}{2}\sum_{t=1}^{R} \mathrm{tr}\left[(\tilde{\boldsymbol{x}}_{i_t}; \boldsymbol{e}_{i_t})(\tilde{\boldsymbol{x}}_{i_t}; \boldsymbol{e}_{i_t})^T Z\right] \\ &= V_i \cdot Z + c_i' \end{aligned} \quad (38)$$

where V_i and Z are $(D + L) \times (D + L)$ dimensional symmetric matrices defined as:

$$V_i = -\frac{1}{2}\sum_{t=1}^{R}(\tilde{\boldsymbol{x}}_{i_t}; \boldsymbol{e}_{i_t})(\tilde{\boldsymbol{x}}_{i_t}; \boldsymbol{e}_{i_t})^T \quad (39)$$

$$Z = (I_D, U)^T (I_D, U) = \begin{pmatrix} I_D & U \\ U^T & Y \end{pmatrix} \quad \text{with} \quad Y = U^T U \quad (40)$$

Similarly, we can express the discriminant function, $\mathcal{V}_i^-(\lambda_j)$, as:

$$\mathcal{V}_i^-(\lambda_j) = V_j \cdot Z + c_j''$$

where V_j is a $(D + L) \times (D + L)$ dimensional symmetric matrix defined as:

$$V_j = -\frac{1}{2}\sum_{t=1}^{R}(\tilde{\boldsymbol{x}}_{j_t}; \boldsymbol{e}_{j_t})(\tilde{\boldsymbol{x}}_{j_t}; \boldsymbol{e}_{j_t})^T \quad (41)$$

Thus, it is straightforward to convert the constraint in eq. (10) into the following form:

$$\mathcal{F}(X_i|\lambda_{W_i}) - \mathcal{F}(X_i|\lambda_j) \approx \mathcal{V}_i^+(\lambda_{W_i}) - \mathcal{V}_i^-(\lambda_j) = V_{ij} \cdot Z - c_{ij} \geq \rho \quad (42)$$

where $V_{ij} = V_i - V_j$ and $c_{ij} = c''_j - c'_i$.
Following the same line, we can convert the constraint in eq. (32) into the following matrix form as well:

$$\mathcal{D}(\Lambda||\Lambda^{(n)}) = \sum_{k\in\mathcal{M}} \sum_{d=1}^{D} (\tilde{\mu}_{kd} - \tilde{\mu}_{kd}^{(n)})^2$$

$$= \sum_{k\in\mathcal{M}} (\tilde{\boldsymbol{\mu}}_k - \tilde{\boldsymbol{\mu}}_k^{(n)})^T (\tilde{\boldsymbol{\mu}}_k - \tilde{\boldsymbol{\mu}}_k^{(n)}) \quad (43)$$

$$= \sum_{k\in\mathcal{M}} (\tilde{\boldsymbol{\mu}}_k^{(n)}; \boldsymbol{e}_k)^T (I_D; U)^T (I_D; U) (\tilde{\boldsymbol{\mu}}_k^{(n)}; \boldsymbol{e}_k) \quad (44)$$

$$= \sum_{k\in\mathcal{M}} \text{tr}\left[(\tilde{\boldsymbol{\mu}}_k^{(n)}; \boldsymbol{e}_k)(\tilde{\boldsymbol{\mu}}_k^{(n)}; \boldsymbol{e}_k)^T \ Z \right]$$

$$= R \cdot Z \leq r^2 \quad (45)$$

where R is a $(D + L)$ x $(D + L)$ dimensional symmetric matrix defined as:

$$R = \sum_{k\in\mathcal{M}} (\tilde{\boldsymbol{\mu}}_k^{(n)}; \boldsymbol{e}_k)(\tilde{\boldsymbol{\mu}}_k^{(n)}; \boldsymbol{e}_k)^T \quad (46)$$

and $\tilde{\boldsymbol{\mu}}_k^{(n)}$ is normalized Gaussian mean vector in the initial model set, $\Lambda^{(n)}$ as defined in eq. (34).
In summary, after **V-approx** in the **A**-Step, the approximate optimization problem can be represented as:
Problem 2

$$\max_{Z,\rho} \quad \rho \quad (47)$$

subject to:

$$V_{ij} \cdot Z - \rho \geq c_{ij} \qquad \text{for all } X_i \in \mathcal{S} \text{ and } j \in \Omega_i \quad (48)$$

$$R \cdot Z \leq r^2 \quad (49)$$

$$Z = \begin{pmatrix} I_D & U \\ U^T & Y \end{pmatrix} \qquad \text{with} \qquad Y = U^T U \quad (50)$$

$$\rho \geq 0 \quad (51)$$

4.2 M-Step: SDP

Obviously, **Problem 2** is equivalent to the original LME optimization **Problem 1** except it is expressed in a matrix form. However, since the constraint $Y = U^T U$ is not convex, it is a non-convex optimization problem. Thus, some relaxations are necessary to convert it into a convex optimization problem. In this section, we consider to use a standard SDP (semi-definite programming) relaxation to convert **Problem 2** into an SDP problem.
As shown in Boyd et al., 1994, the following statement always holds for matrices:

$$Y - U^T U \succeq 0 \qquad \Leftrightarrow \qquad Z = \begin{pmatrix} I_D & U \\ U^T & Y \end{pmatrix} \succeq 0 \quad (52)$$

where $Z \succeq 0$ denotes Z is a positive semidefinite matrix.
Therefore, following Boyd et al., 1994, if we relax the constraint $Y = U^T U$ to $Y - U^T U \succeq 0$, we are able to make Z a positive semidefinite matrix. During the optimization, the top left corner of Z must be an identity matrix, i.e., $Z_{1:D,1:D} = I_D$, which can be easily represented as a group of linear constraints as:

$$\left[(e_k + e_l)(e_k + e_l)^T\right] \cdot Z = 2 + 2 \cdot \delta(k-l) \qquad \text{for} \qquad 1 \le k \le D,\ \ k \le l \le D \tag{53}$$

where $\delta(k-l)$ is 1 when $k = l$ and 0 otherwise. If $k = l$ (for $l \le k, l \le D$),

$$\left[(e_k + e_l)(e_k + e_l)^T\right] \cdot Z = 4z_{kk} = 4 \tag{54}$$

otherwise

$$\left[(e_k + e_l)(e_k + e_l)^T\right] \cdot Z = z_{kk} + z_{ll} + z_{kl} + z_{lk} = z_{kk} + z_{ll} + 2z_{kl} = 2 \tag{55}$$

since Z is a symmetric matrix, $z_{kl} = z_{lk}$. Obviously, the unique solution for this set of linear constraints is $z_{kk} = 1$ and $z_{kl} = z_{lk} = 0$ for all $1 \le k \le D,\ \ k \le l \le D$.
Finally, under the relaxation in eq. (52), **Problem 2** is converted into a standard SDP problem as follows:
Problem 3

$$\max_{Z,\rho}\ \rho \tag{56}$$

subject to:

$$V_{ij} \cdot Z - \rho \ge c_{ij} \qquad \text{for all } X_i \in \mathcal{S} \text{ and } j \in \Omega_i \tag{57}$$

$$R \cdot Z \le r^2 \tag{58}$$

$$Z_{1:D,1:D} = I_D \tag{59}$$

$$Z \succeq 0 \qquad \text{and} \qquad \rho \ge 0 \tag{60}$$

Problem 3 is a standard SDP problem, which can be solved efficiently by many SDP algorithms, such as interior-point methods (Boyd & Vandenberghe, 2004). In **Problem 3,** the optimization is carried out w.r.t. Z (which is constructed from all HMM Gaussian means) and ρ, and V_{ij} and c_{ij} and R are constant matrix calculated from training data and initial models, and r is a pre-set control parameter. Then, all Gaussian mean vectors are updated based on the found SDP solution Z*.
At last, the AM algorithm for LME of Gaussian mixture HMMs based on N-Best lists is summarized as follows:

Algorithm 1 The AM Algorithm for LME of HMMs based on N-Best Lists

repeat

1. Perform N-Best Viterbi decoding for all training data using models $\lambda^{(n)}$
2. Identify the support set $\mathcal{S}$ according to eq. (4).
3. **A-Step:** collect sufficient statistics including R, and V_{ij}, c_{ij} for all $X_i \in \mathcal{S}$ and $j \in \Omega_i$
4. **M-Step:** Perform SDP to solve **Problem 3** and update models.
5. $n = n + 1$.

until some convergence conditions are met.

5. LME of Gaussian mixture HMMs based on Word Graphs

As in most large vocabulary continuous speech recognition systems, competing hypotheses for training utterances are encoded in a more compact format, i.e., word graphs or word lattices. In this section, we apply the AM algorithm to LME of Gaussian mixture HMMs for speech recognition based on word graphs instead of N-Best lists. Here, we use **E-approx** in **A**-step to derive an efficient method to conduct LME for large vocabulary continuous speech recognition tasks using word graphs.

Assume we are given a training set as $\mathcal{T} = \{X_1, X_2, \cdots, X_T\}$, for each training utterance X_i, assume its true transcription is W_i and its competing hypotheses are represented as a word graph, denoted as $\mathcal{G}_i$. Ideally the true transcription Wj should be excluded from the word graph $\mathcal{G}_i$. In this case, we define the margin for X_i as follows:

$$\begin{aligned} d(X_i) &= \mathcal{F}(X_i|\lambda_{W_i}) - \mathcal{F}(X_i|\mathcal{G}_i) \\ &= \Big[\ln p(X_i|\lambda_{W_i}) + \ln p(W_i)\Big] - \ln \sum_{j \in \mathcal{G}_i} \Big[p(X_i|\lambda_j) \cdot p(W_j)\Big] \end{aligned} \quad (61)$$

where the summation is taken for all hypotheses in word graph $\mathcal{G}_i$. In this paper, we only consider to estimate acoustic models and assume language model scores $p(W_i)$ and $p(W_j)$ are constants. Then, the idea of LME in section 2 can be extended to estimate acoustic models towards maximizing the minimum margin across a selected support token set $\mathcal{S}$, as in eq.(5). In the following, we consider to solve this LME problem with the AM algorithm where **E-approx** is used in **A**-step and SDP is used to solve **M**-step. For simplicity, we only estimate Gaussian mean vectors and assume other HMM parameters are kept constant in LME. But it is quite trivial to extend to estimating all HMM parameters with the same idea.

5.1 A-Step: E-approx

Given any speech utterance $X_i = \{\mathbf{x}_{i1}, \mathbf{x}_{i2}, \cdots, \mathbf{x}_{iR}\}$, in **E-approx,** the HMM log-likelihood function $\ln p(X_i|\lambda_{W_i})$ is approximated by the following auxiliary function calculated based on expectation:

$$\begin{aligned} \mathcal{Q}_i^{+}(\Lambda|\Lambda^{(n)}) &= \sum_{\mathbf{s}} \sum_{\mathbf{l}} \ln p(X_i, \mathbf{s}, \mathbf{l} \mid \lambda_{W_i}) \cdot \Pr(\mathbf{s}, \mathbf{l} \mid X_i, \lambda_{W_i}^{(n)}) \\ &= -\frac{1}{2} \sum_{k \in \mathcal{M}} \sum_{t=1}^{R} \sum_{d=1}^{D} \frac{(x_{itd} - \mu_{kd})^2}{\sigma_{kd}^2} \cdot \gamma_i(k,t) + b_i^* \end{aligned} \quad (62)$$

where $\gamma_i(k,t)$ denotes posterior probability calculated for k-th Gaussian component in the model set ($k \in \mathcal{M}$) using the Baum- Welch algorithm conditional on the initial model $\Lambda^{(n)}$ and training utterance X_i, and b_i^* is a constant independent from all Gaussian mean vectors.

After rearranging all terms in eq. (62), we can organize $\mathcal{Q}_i^{+}(\Lambda_i|\Lambda_i^{(n)})$ as a quadratic function of all Gaussian mean vectors:

$$\mathcal{Q}_i^{+}(\Lambda|\Lambda^{(n)}) = -\frac{1}{2} \sum_{k \in \mathcal{M}} \sum_{d=1}^{D} \xi_{ik} \cdot \left(\frac{\bar{\mathbf{x}}_{ikd} - \mu_{kd}}{\sigma_{kd}}\right)^2 + b_i' \quad (63)$$

where b_i' is another constant independent of Gaussian mean vectors and

$$\xi_{ik} = \sum_{t=1}^{R} \gamma_i(k,t) \tag{64}$$

$$\bar{\mathrm{x}}_{ikd} = \frac{\sum_{t=1}^{R} \gamma_i(k,t) \cdot x_{itd}}{\sum_{t=1}^{R} \gamma_i(k,t)} \tag{65}$$

If we denote two column vectors as

$$\tilde{\boldsymbol{\mu}}_k := \left(\frac{\mu_{k1}}{\sigma_{k1}}; \frac{\mu_{k2}}{\sigma_{k2}}; \cdots; \frac{\mu_{kD}}{\sigma_{kD}} \right) \qquad (\text{for } k \in \mathcal{M}) \tag{66}$$

and

$$\tilde{\mathbf{x}}_{ik} := \left(\frac{\bar{\mathrm{x}}_{ik1}}{\sigma_{k1}}; \frac{\bar{\mathrm{x}}_{ik2}}{\sigma_{k2}}; \cdots; \frac{\bar{\mathrm{x}}_{ikD}}{\sigma_{kD}} \right) \tag{67}$$

then we have

$$\begin{aligned} \mathcal{Q}_i^+(\Lambda|\Lambda^{(n)}) &= b_i' - \frac{1}{2} \sum_{k \in \mathcal{M}} \sum_{d=1}^{D} \xi_{ik} \cdot \left(\frac{\bar{\mathrm{x}}_{ikd} - \mu_{kd}}{\sigma_{kd}} \right)^2 \\ &= b_i' - \frac{1}{2} \sum_{k \in \mathcal{M}} \xi_{ik} \cdot (\tilde{\mathbf{x}}_{ik} - \tilde{\boldsymbol{\mu}}_k)^T (\tilde{\mathbf{x}}_{ik} - \tilde{\boldsymbol{\mu}}_k) \end{aligned} \tag{68}$$

Since we have

$$\begin{aligned} \tilde{\mathbf{x}}_{ik} - \tilde{\boldsymbol{\mu}}_k &= (I_D, U)(\tilde{\mathbf{x}}_{ik};\ \boldsymbol{e}_k) \\ &= \left(\begin{array}{c} D\left\{ \begin{array}{ccc} \overbrace{\begin{array}{ccc} 1 & \cdots & 0 \\ \vdots & \ddots & \vdots \\ 0 & \cdots & 1 \end{array}}^{D} \end{array} \right. \overbrace{\begin{array}{ccc} \tilde{\mu}_{11} & \cdots & \tilde{\mu}_{L1} \\ \vdots & \vdots & \vdots \\ \tilde{\mu}_{1D} & \vdots & \tilde{\mu}_{LD} \end{array}}^{L} \end{array} \right) \left(\begin{array}{c} \left. \begin{array}{c} \tilde{x}_{ik1} \\ \vdots \\ \tilde{x}_{ikD} \end{array} \right\} D \\ \left. \begin{array}{c} 0 \\ \vdots \\ -1\ (k) \\ \vdots \\ 0 \end{array} \right\} L \end{array} \right) \end{aligned} \tag{69}$$

Then, we have

$$\begin{aligned} \mathcal{Q}_i^+(\Lambda|\Lambda^{(n)}) &= b_i' - \frac{1}{2} \sum_{k \in \mathcal{M}} \xi_{ik} \cdot (\tilde{\mathbf{x}}_{ik}; \boldsymbol{e}_k)^T (I_D, U)^T (I_D, U)(\tilde{\mathbf{x}}_{ik}; \boldsymbol{e}_k) \\ &= b_i' - \frac{1}{2} \sum_{k \in \mathcal{M}} \xi_{ik} \cdot \mathrm{tr}\left[(\tilde{\mathbf{x}}_{ik}; \boldsymbol{e}_k)(\tilde{\mathbf{x}}_{ik}; \boldsymbol{e}_k)^T Z \right] \\ &= Q_i^+ \cdot Z + b_i' \end{aligned} \tag{70}$$

where Z and Q_i^+ are (D + L) x (D + L) dimensional symmetric matrices, Z is defined as in eq.(40) and Q_i^+ is calculated as:

$$Q_i^+ = -\frac{1}{2}\sum_{k\in\mathcal{M}} \xi_{ik}\cdot(\tilde{\mathbf{x}}_{ik};\mathbf{e}_k)(\tilde{\mathbf{x}}_{ik};\mathbf{e}_k)^T \tag{71}$$

Similarly, we consider to approximate the log-likelihood function of word graph with **E-approx** as follows:

$$\begin{aligned}
\mathcal{F}(X_i|\mathcal{G}_i) &= \ln\sum_{j\in\mathcal{G}_i}\Big[p(X_i|\lambda_j)\cdot p(W_j)\Big] \approx Q_i^-(\Lambda|\Lambda^{(n)}) \\
&= \sum_{j\in\mathcal{G}_i}\sum_{\mathbf{s}}\sum_{\mathbf{l}}\Big[\ln p(X_i,\mathbf{s},\mathbf{l}\mid\lambda_j)+\ln p(W_j)\Big]\cdot\Pr(\mathbf{s},\mathbf{l}\mid X_i,\Lambda^{(n)}) \\
&= -\frac{1}{2}\sum_{j\in\mathcal{G}_i}\sum_{k\in\mathcal{M}}\sum_{t=1}^{R}\sum_{d=1}^{D}\frac{(x_{itd}-\mu_{kd})^2}{\sigma_{kd}^2}\cdot\gamma_j(k,t)+b_i^* \\
&= -\frac{1}{2}\sum_{k\in\mathcal{M}}\sum_{d=1}^{D}\xi'_{ik}\cdot\left(\frac{\bar{\mathrm{x}}'_{ikd}-\mu_{kd}}{\sigma_{kd}}\right)^2+b_i^{"}
\end{aligned} \tag{72}$$

where both b_i^* and $b_i^{"}$ are two constants independent of Gaussian mean vectors, and

$$\xi'_{ik} = \sum_{j\in\mathcal{G}_i}\sum_{t=1}^{R}\gamma_j(k,t) \tag{73}$$

$$\bar{\mathrm{x}}'_{ikd} = \frac{\sum_{j\in\mathcal{G}_i}\sum_{t=1}^{R}\gamma_j(k,t)\cdot x_{itd}}{\sum_{j\in\mathcal{G}_i}\sum_{t=1}^{R}\gamma_j(k,t)} \tag{74}$$

And ξ'_{ik} and $\bar{\mathrm{x}}'_{ikd}$ can be calculated efficiently by running the forward-backward algorithm in the word graph $\mathcal{G}_i$ as in Wessel et al., 2001.
Similarly, $\mathcal{F}(X_i|\mathcal{G}_i)$ can be expressed as the following matrix form:

$$\mathcal{F}(X_i|\mathcal{G}_i) = Q_i^-\cdot Z + b_i^{"} \tag{75}$$

where

$$Q_i^- = -\frac{1}{2}\sum_{k\in\mathcal{M}} \xi'_{ik}\cdot(\tilde{\mathbf{x}}'_{ik};\ \mathbf{e}_k)(\tilde{\mathbf{x}}'_{ik};\ \mathbf{e}_k)^T \tag{76}$$

Therefore, the margin $d(X_i)$ can be approximated as:

$$d(X_i) \approx \mathcal{Q}_i^+(\Lambda|\Lambda^{(n)}) - \mathcal{Q}_i^-(\Lambda|\Lambda^{(n)}) = Q_i^{\mathrm{d}}\cdot Z - b_i \tag{77}$$

where $Q_i^{\mathrm{d}} = Q_i^+ - Q_i^-$ and $b_i = b_i^{"} - b'_i$.
As the result, the LME problem based on the word graphs can be approximately represented as follows:

Problem 4

$$\max_{Z,\rho} \quad \rho \tag{78}$$

subject to::

$$Q_i^{\mathrm{d}} \cdot Z - \rho \geq b_i \qquad \text{for all } X_i \in \mathcal{S} \tag{79}$$

$$R \cdot Z \leq r^2 \tag{80}$$

$$Z = \begin{pmatrix} I_D & U \\ U^T & Y \end{pmatrix} \qquad \text{with} \qquad Y = U^T U \tag{81}$$

$$\rho \geq 0 \tag{82}$$

5.2 M-Step: SDP

Next, using the same relaxation in eq.(52), we convert the above optimization problem into the following SDP problem:

Problem 5

$$\max_{Z,\rho} \quad \rho \tag{83}$$

subject to::

$$Q_i^{\mathrm{d}} \cdot Z - \rho \geq b_i \qquad \text{for all } X_i \in \mathcal{S} \tag{84}$$

$$R \cdot Z \leq r^2 \tag{85}$$

$$Z_{1:D,1:D} = I_D \tag{86}$$

$$Z \succeq 0 \qquad\qquad \rho \geq 0 \tag{87}$$

The **Problem 5** can be efficiently solved using a fast SDP optimization algorithm. The found solution Z^* can be used to update all Gaussian mean vectors.

At last, the AM algorithm for LME of Gaussian mixture HMMs using **E-approx** based on word graphs is summarized as follows:

Algorithm 2 The AM Algorithm for LME of HMMs based on Word Graphs

repeat

1. Perform Viterbi decoding for all training data to generate word graphs using models $\Lambda^{(n)}$.
2. Identify the support set $\mathcal{S}$ according to eq.(4).
3. **A-Step:** collect sufficient statistics including R, and Q_i^{d}, b_i for all $X_i \in \mathcal{S}$.
4. **M-Step:** Perform SDP to solve **Problem 5** and update models.
5. $n = n+1$.

until some convergence conditions are met.

6. Final Remarks

In this paper, we have proposed a general Approximation-optiMization (AM) approach for large margin estimation (LME) of Gaussian mixture HMMs in speech recognition. Each iteration of the AM method consists of A-step and M-step. In A-step, the original LME problem is approximated by a simple convex optimization problem in a close proximity of initial model parameters. In M-step, the approximate convex optimization problem is solved by using efficient convex optimization algorithms. The AM method is a general approach which can be easily applied for discriminative training of statistical models with hidden variables. In this paper, we introduce two examples to apply the AM approach to LME of Gaussian mixture HMMs. The first method uses V-approx and is applicable for isolated word recognition and continuous speech recognition based on N-Best lists. The second method uses E-approx and can be applied to large vocabulary continuous speech recognition when competing hypotheses are given as word graphs or word lattices. Due to space limit, we can not report experimental results in this paper. Readers can refer to Li, 2005 and Li & Jiang, 2006a, Li & Jiang, 2006b for details about ASR experiments.

7. References

Altun, Y.; Tsochantaridis, I. & Hofmann, T. (2003). Hidden Markov Support Vector Machines, *Proc. of the 20th International Conference on Machine Learning (ICML-2003)*, Washington B.C..

Arenas-Garcia, J. & Perez-Cruz, F. (2003). Multi-class support vector machines: a new approach, *Proc. of IEEE International Conference on Acoustic, Speech, and Signal Processing (ICASSP'2003)*, pp.II-781-784.

Boyd, S.; Ghaoui, L. E.; Feron, E. & Balakrishnan, V. (1994). Linear matrix inequalities in system and control theory, *Society for Industrial and Applied Mathematics (SIAM)*, Philadelphia, PA.

Boyd, S & Vandenberghe, L. (2004). *Convex Optimization.* Cambridge University Press.

Crammer, K. & Singer, Y. (2001). On the algorithmic implementation of multiclass kernel-based vector machines, *Journal of Machine Learning Research*, Vol. 2, pp.265-292.

Dempster, A. P.; Laird, N. M. & Rubin, D. B. (1977). Maximum likelihood from incomplete data via the EM algorithm (with discussion), *Journal of the Royal Statistical Society B*, Vol. 39, pp. 1-38.

Jiang, EL; Hirose, K. & Huo, Q. (1999). Robust speech recognition based on Bayesian prediction approach, *IEEE Trans, on Speech and Audio Processing*, pp. 426-440, Vol. 7, No.4.

Jiang, H. (2004). Discriminative Training for Large Margin HMMs, *Technical Report CS-2004-01*, Department of Computer Science and Engineering, York University.

Jiang, H.; Soong, F. & Lee, C.-H. (2005). A dynamic in-search data selection method with its applications to acoustic modeling and utterance verification, *IEEE Trans, on Speech and Audio Processing*, pp.945-955, Vol. 13, No.5.

Jiang, H.; Li, X. & Liu, C.-J. (2006). Large Margin Hidden Markov Models for Speech Recognition, *IEEE Trans, on Audio, Speech and Language Processing*, pp.1584-1595, Vol. 14, No. 5.

Jiang, H. & Li, X. (2007). Incorporating Training Errors for Large Margin HMMs under Semi-definite Programming Framework, *Proc. of 2007 IEEE International Conference on Acoustic, Speech, and Signal Processing (ICASSP'2007),* Hawaii, USA.

Li, X.; Jiang, H. & Liu, C.-J. (2005). Large margin HMMs for speech recognition, *Proc. of 2005 IEEE International Conference on Acoustic, Speech, and Signal Processing (ICASSP'2005),* pp.V513-516, Philadelphia, Pennsylvania.

Li, X. & Jiang, H. (2005). A constrained joint optimization method for large margin HMM estimation, *Proc. of 2005 IEEE workshop on Automatic Speech Recognition and Understanding.*

Li, X. (2005). Large Margin Hidden Markov Models for Speech Recognition. *M.S. thesis,* Department of Computer Science and Engineering, York University, Canada.

Li, X. & Jiang, H. (2006a). Solving Large Margin HMM Estimation via Semi-definite Programming, *Proc. of 2006 International Conference on Spoken Language Processing (ICSLP'2006),* Pittsburgh, USA.

Li, X. & Jiang, H. (2006b). Solving Large Margin Hidden Markov Model Estimation via Semidefinite Programming, *submitted to IEEE Trans, on Audio, Speech and Language Processing.*

Liu, C.-J.; Jiang, H. & Li, X. (2005a). Discriminative training of CDHMMs for Maximum relative separation margin, *Proc. of IEEE International Conference on Acoustic, Speech, and Signal Processing (ICASSP'2005),* pp.V101-104, Philadelphia, Pennsylvania.

Liu, C.-J.; Jiang, H. & Rigazio, L. (2005b) "Maximum relative margin estimation of HMMs based on N-best string models for continuous speech recognition," *Proc. of IEEE workshop on Automatic Speech Recognition and Understanding.*

Liu, C.; Liu, P.; Jiang, H.; Soong, F. & Wang, R.-H. (2007). A Constrained Line Search Optimization For Discriminative Training in Speech Recognition, *Proc. of IEEE International Conference on Acoustic, Speech, and Signal Processing (ICASSP'2007),* Hawaii, USA.

Neal, R. & Hinton, G. E. (1998). A view of the EM algorithm that justifies incremental, sparse, and other variants, *in M. I. Jordan (Ed.), Learning in Graphical Models,* pp.355-368, Kluwer Academic Publishers.

Smola, A. J.; Bartlett, P.; Scholkopf, B. & Schuurmans, D. (ed.) (2000). *Advances in Large Margin Classifiers,* the MIT Press.

Wessel, F.; Schluter, R.; Macherey, K. & Ney, H. (2001). Confidence measures for large vocabulary continuous speech recognition. *IEEE Trans, on Speech and Audio Processing,* Vol. 9, No. 3, 288-298.

Weston, J. & Watkins, C. (1999). Support vector machines for multi-class pattern recognition, *Proc. of European Symposium on Artificial Neural Networks.*

Vapnik, V. N. (1998) *Statistical Learning Theory,* Wiley, 1998.

8

Double Layer Architectures for Automatic Speech Recognition Using HMM

Marta Casar and José A. R. Fonollosa
Dept. of Signal Theory and Communication, Universitat Politècnica de Catalunya (UPC), Barcelona, Spain

1. Introduction

Understanding continuous speech uttered by a random speaker in a random language and in a variable environment is a challenging problem for a machine. Broad knowledge of the world is needed if context is to be taken into account, and this has been the main source of difficulty in speech-related research. Automatic speech recognition has only been possible by simplifying the problem - which involves restricting the vocabulary, the speech domain, the way sentences are constructed, the number of speakers, and the language to be used-, and controlling the environmental noise.

Current speech recognition systems are usually based on the statistical modelling of the acoustic information, generally using hidden Markov models (HMM). However, these systems are subject to some restrictions regarding the incorporation of other speech-related knowledge that might have an influence on the recognition rate.

The evolution of Automatic Speech Recognition (ASR) technology over the last few years has led to the development of applications and products that are able to operate under real conditions by acknowledging the above-mentioned limitations (or simplifications). ASR applications include dialogue systems, speech-based interfaces (such as automatic access to information services) and voice-controlled systems (like voice-driven database retrieval).

Due to the number of potential ASR applications, research efforts have been focused on developing systems that can accept spontaneous speech in a wide range of environments and from a wide range of speakers. However, in the case of spontaneous speech, large vocabularies must be considered. Moreover, language must be modelled by a non-restrictive grammar, which takes into account events that are common in natural speech, such as truncated or grammatically incorrect sentences, non-speech-events and hesitation. To deal with this, and to be able to introduce all the information available into the recognition architecture, a change of paradigm from conventional speech recognition had to be proposed.

In this chapter, we will talk about different approaches to a double layer architecture using HMM for ASR, which should allow other, non-acoustic information to be incorporated and more complex modelling of the speech signal than has been possible up to now. After analyzing different approaches, the main conclusions will be summarized and possible further work in this field will be briefly discussed.

2. ASR Using HMM

2.1 Standard systems

A standard ASR system is based on a set of so-called acoustic models that link the observed features of the voice signal to the expected phonetics of the hypothesis sentence. The most typical implementation of this process is probabilistic, namely Hidden Markov Models (HMM) (Rabiner, 1989; Huang et al., 2001).

A Markov model is a stochastic model that describes a sequence of possible events in which the probability of each event only depends on the state attained in the previous event. This characteristic is defined as the Markov property. An HMM is a collection of states that fulfils the Markov property, with an output distribution for each state defined in terms of a mixture of Gaussian densities (Rabiner, 1993). These output distributions are generally made up of the direct acoustic vector plus its dynamic features (namely, its first and second derivatives), plus the energy of the spectrum. Dynamic features are the way of representing context in an HMM, but they are generally only limited to a few subsequent feature vectors and do not represent long-term variations. Frequency filtering parameterization (Nadeu et al., 2001) has become a successful alternative to cepstral coefficients.

Conventional HMM training is based on maximum likelihood estimation (MLE) criteria (Furui & Sandhi, 1992), via powerful training algorithms such as the Baum-Welch algorithm and the Viterbi algorithm. In recent years, the discriminative training method and the minimum classification error (MCE) criteria, which is based on the generalized probabilistic descent (GPD) framework, has been successful in training HMMs for speech recognition (Juang et al., 1997). For decoding, both the Viterbi and Baum-Welch algorithms have been implemented with similar results, but the former showed better computational behaviour.

The first implementations of HMMs for ASR were based on discrete HMMs (DHMMs). In a DHMM, a quantization procedure is needed to map observation vectors from the continuous space to the discrete space of the statistical models. Of course, there is a quantization error inherent to this process, which can be eliminated if continuous HMMs (CHMMs) are used.

For CHMMs, a different form of output probability function is needed. Multivariate Gaussian mixture density functions are an obvious choice, as they can approximate any continuous density function (Huan et al., 2001). However, computational complexity can become a major drawback in the maximization of the likelihood by way of re-estimation, as the M-mixture observation densities used must be accommodated.

In many implementations, the gap between the discrete and continuous mixture density HMM has been bridged under certain minor assumptions. For instance, in a tied-mixture HMM the mixture density functions are tied together across all the models to form a set of shared kernels.

Another solution is a semi-continuous HMM (SCHMM), in which a VQ codebook is used to map the continuous input feature vector **x** to o_k, as in a discrete HMM. However, in this case the output probabilities are no longer used directly (as they are in a DHMM), but rather combined with the VQ density functions. That is, the discrete model-dependent weighting coefficients are combined with the continuous codebook's probability density functions.

From another point of view, semi-continuous models are equivalent to M-mixture continuous HMMs, with all the continuous output probability density functions shared by all the Markov states. Hence, SCHMMs maintain the modelling ability of large-mixture probability density functions. In addition, the number of free parameters and the computational complexity can be reduced, because all the probability density functions are tied together, thus providing a good compromise between detailed acoustic modelling and trainability.

However, standard ASR systems still do not provide convincing results under changeable environmental conditions. Most current commercial speech recognition technologies still work using either a restricted lexicon (i.e. digits or a definite number of commands) or a semantically restricted task (i.e. database information retrieval, tourist information, flight information, hotel services, etc.). Extensions to more complex tasks and/or vocabulary still have a reputation for poor quality and are thus viewed with scepticism by both potential users and customers.

Because of the limitations of HMM-based speech recognition systems, research has had to progress in a number of different directions. Rather than adopting an overall approach to tackling problems, they have generally been dealt with individually. Regarding robust speech recognition, the spectral variability of speech signals has been studied using different methods, such as variable frame rate (VFR) search analysis of speech. Model adaptation has also been on scope or, more specifically, speaker adaptation and vocal tract normalization (VTN).

Language modelling research has played a significant role in improving recognition performance in continuous speech recognition. However, another problem that faces standard speech recognition is the dependency of the models obtained regarding to the speakers (or database) used for training. Speaker adaptation can be used to overcome this drawback, as it performs well as a solution to certain tasks. However, its benefits are not entirely clear for speaker-independent tasks, because the adaptation costs are higher.

Of all the active fields of research in speech recognition, we will focus our attention on those closest to the approach presented in this chapter.

2.2 Modelling temporal evolution using temporal and trajectory models

At the outset of speech recognition research, the application of statistical methods, i.e. Markov Models, proved to be clearly advantageous. First-order Markov Models are sufficiently flexible to accommodate variations in probability along an utterance and, at the same time, simple enough to lend themselves to mathematically rigorous optimization and the deployment of search strategies. However, as the Markov property is an artificial constraint forced upon a model of the temporal speech utterance, it was expected that some speech characteristics would not be correctly modelled.

Several approaches for modelling temporal evolution have been proposed in the past. Temporal models have been used to optimally change the duration and temporal structure of words. Experiments showed that first-order Markov chains do not model expected local duration effectively. Thus, different approaches for a more explicit modelling of duration led to an improvement in performance.

Some approaches started by directly introducing continuously variable duration into the HMM. In (Russell & Cook, 1987) and (Bonafonte et al., 1996), each HMM state is expanded to a sub-HMM (ESHMM) that shares the same emission probability density and performs the correct state duration distribution using its own topology and transition probability. To reduce the loss of efficiency introduced by the ESHMM, a post-processor duration model can be implemented (Wu et al., 2005) using the output of a Viterbi algorithm and ranking the proposed paths through the use of better models for state duration. However,

incorporating explicit duration models into the HMM also breaks up some of conventional Markov assumptions. When HMM geometric distribution is replaced with an explicitly defined one, Baum-Welch and Viterbi algorithms are no longer directly applicable.
In (Bonafonte et al., 1993), Hidden Semi-Markov models (HSMMs) are proposed as a framework for a more explicit modelling of duration. In these models, the first-order Markov hypothesis is broken in the loop transitions. The main drawback of an HSMM, however, is an increase in the computational time by a factor of D, D being the maximum time allowed in each state. Hence, the Viterbi algorithm must be modified to cope with this higher complexity and to limit the computational increase.
An alternative to this is to model the occupancy of each HMM state by means of a Markov chain (Vidal et al., 2004). This occupancy is represented using a distribution function (DF). Thus, each state of the initial HMM is expanded by the DF estimated for that state.
In another approach to overcome the limitations of standard HMM framework, alternative trajectory models have been proposed that take advantage of frame correlation. Although these models can improve the speech recognition performance, they generally require an increase in model parameters and computational complexity.
In (Tokuda et al., 2003) a trajectory model is derived by reformulating the standard HMM whose state output vector includes static and dynamic feature parameters. This involves imposing the explicit relationship between the static and dynamic features. A similar technique is based on maximizing the models' output probability under the constraints between static and dynamic features.
A smooth speech trajectory is also generated from an HMM by maximizing the likelihood subject to the constraints that exist between static and dynamic features. A parametric trajectory can be obtained using direct relationships between the vector time series for static and dynamic features, or from mixture distribution HMMs (Minami et al., 2003). This method chooses the target sequence of Gaussian distributions by selecting the best Gaussian distribution for each state during Viterbi decoding. Thus, the relationship between the cepstrum and the dynamic coefficients is now taken into account in the recognition phase, unlike in previous approaches.

2.3 Second-order models (HMM2)

HMM-based speech modelling assumes that the input signal can be split into segments, which are modelled as states of an underlying Markov chain, and that the waveform of each segment is a stationary random process. As previously mentioned, the sequence of states in an HMM is assumed to be a first-order Markov chain. This assumption is motivated by the existence of efficient, tractable algorithms for model estimation and recognition.
To overcome the drawbacks of regular HMMs regarding segment duration modelling and trajectory (frame correlation) modelling, some authors have proposed a new class of models in which the underlying state sequence is a second-order Markov chain (HMM2) (Mari et al., 1997). These models show better state occupancy modelling, at the cost of higher computational complexity. To overcome this disadvantage, an appropriate implementation of the re-estimation formulation is needed. Algorithms that yield an HMM only N_i times slower than an HMM1 can be obtained, N_i being the average input branching factor of the model.
Another approach to a second-order HMM is a mixture of temporal and frequency models (Weber et al., 2003). This solution consists of a primary (conventional) HMM that models the

temporal properties of the signal, and a secondary HMM that models the speech signal's frequency properties. That is, while the primary HMM is performing the usual time warping and integration, the secondary HMM is responsible for extracting/modelling the possible feature dependencies, while also performing time warping and integration.
In these models, the emission probabilities of the temporal (primary) HMM are estimated through a secondary, state-specific HMM that works in the acoustic feature space. Such models present a more flexible modelling of the time/frequency structure of the speech signal, which results in better performance. Moreover, when such systems are working with spectral features, they are able to perform non-linear spectral warping by implementing a form of non-linear vocal-tract normalization.
To solve the increase in computational complexity associated with this solution, the Viterbi algorithm must be modified, which leads to a considerable computational increase.
The differences in performance between an HMM and HMM2 are not particularly remarkable when a post-processor step is introduced. In this post-processor step, durational constraints based on state occupancy are incorporated into conventional HMM-based recognition. However, in this case HMM2s are computationally better, while the complexity increase is similar in both cases.

2.4 Layered speech recognition

With regard to the integration of different information into the ASR architecture, and going one step further from the HMM2, several authors have proposed using layered HMM-based architectures (Demuynck et al., 2003).
Layered ASR systems fit all the knowledge levels commonly used in automatic speech recognition (acoustic, lexical and language information) in a final model. From these architectures, a modular framework can be suggested that allows a two-step (or multi-step) search process. The usual acoustic-phonetic modelling is divided into two (or more) different layers, one of which is closer to the voice signal for modelling acoustic and physical characteristics, whilst the other is closer to the phonetics of the sentence. The modelling accuracy and the ease with which acoustic and phonetic variability can be managed are thus expected to increase.
By splitting the recognition scheme into an acoustic lower layer and a language-based upper layer, the introduction of new functionalities may be consigned to the second layer. The goal is to develop models that are not limited by acoustic constraints (such as left-to-right restrictions). This also provides an open field for the introduction of new (and high-level) information with no loss of efficiency. Moreover, layered architectures can increase speaker independence if the upper layer is trained with a different set of recordings to that used for the acoustic layer, which approaches conditions similar to those faced in the recognition of unknown speakers.
In the following sections, two approaches for a double-layer architecture are presented and justified. Thanks to the advantages mentioned above, layered architectures are expected to bring standard HMM-based ASR systems up to date.

3. HMM State Scores Evolution Modelling

3.1 Justification

In standard HMM-based modelling, feature vectors only depend on the states that generated them. Dynamic features (generally first and second derivatives of the cepstral coefficients and derivatives of the energy) are used to represent context in HMM. However, they only consider a few subsequent vectors and do not represent long-term variations. Moreover, first-order Markov chains do not effectively model expected local duration. Furthermore, as seen above, incorporating explicit state duration models into the HMM breaks up some of conventional Markov assumptions. An alternative way of incorporating context into an HMM lies in taking a similar approach to the evolution of state scores as that used for well-known trajectory models. However, in this case a double-layer architecture is used.

In (Casar & Fonollosa, 2006a), a method is presented for incorporating context into an HMM by considering the state scores obtained by a phonetic-unit recognizer. These state scores are obtained from a Viterbi grammar-free decoding step that is added to the original HMM, which yields a new set of "expanded" HMMs. A similar approach was used by (Stemmer et al., 2003), who integrated the state scores of a phone recognizer into the HMM of a word recognizer, using state-dependent weighting factors.

3.2 Mathematical formalism

To better understand the method for implementing HMM state scores evolution modelling presented in (Casar & Fonollosa, 2006a), the formulation on which it relies must be introduced.

In a standard SCHMM, the density function $b_i(x_t)$ for the output of a feature vector x_t by state i at time t is computed as a sum over all codebook classes $m \in M$ (the number of mixture components):

$$b_i(x_t) = \sum_m c_{i,m} \cdot p(x_t \mid m,i) \approx \sum_m c_{i,m} \cdot p(x_t \mid m) \quad (1)$$

where $p(x_t \mid m) = \mathcal{N}(x_t, \mu_m, \Sigma_m)$ denotes the Gaussian density function shared across all Markov models and $c_{i,m}$ are the weights for the kth codeword that satisfy $\sum c_{i,m} = 1$.

As in (Stemmer et al., 2003) probability density functions can be considered that make it possible to integrate a large context $x_1^{t-1} = x_1, \ldots x_{t-1}$ of feature vectors observed thus far into the HMM output densities.

If we tried to directly integrate this context into b_i, this would result in a large increase of computational effort. Therefore, a new hidden random variable l (henceforth called *class label*) is introduced, which is a discrete representation of the feature vectors x_1^{t-1}. These class labels l can correspond to the units whose context is to be modelled, for instance phone symbols.

From now on, each state i not only chooses between the codebook classes $m \in M$ but also takes an independent decision for the class label l. The integration of l into the output density makes b_i dependent on the history x_1^{t-1}.

Thus, Equation (1) is expanded by defining the new output probability and integrating the context, as in (Stemmer et al., 2003):

$$b_i(x_t \mid x_1^{t-1}) = \sum_{m,l} p(x_t \mid l,m) \cdot P(l,m \mid i, x_1^{t-1}) \tag{2}$$

Moreover, as x_1^{t-1} is the same for all states i at time t there is no increase in the computational complexity of the algorithms for training and decoding.
However, the representation of $b_i(x_t \mid x_1^{t-1})$ needs additional simplifications if the number of parameters to be estimated is to be reduced.
Since the decisions of l and m are independent, we can use the following approximation:

$$P(l,m \mid i, x_1^{t-1}) = P(l \mid i, x_1^{t-1}) \cdot P(m \mid i, x_1^{t-1}) \tag{3}$$

and as m does not depend on x_1^{t-1}, $P(m \mid i, x_1^{t-1}) = P(m \mid i) = c_{i,m}$.
Thus, Equation (3) can be reformulated as:

$$P(l,m \mid i, x_1^{t-1}) = c_{i,m} \cdot P(l \mid i, x_1^{t-1}) \tag{4}$$

We can also split the second term $P(l \mid i, x_1^{t-1})$ into two parts in which i is considered separately from x_1^{t-1} and by applying Bayes' rule:

$$P(l \mid i, x_1^{t-1}) = C_{l,i} \cdot P(l \mid x_1^{t-1}) \tag{5}$$

where $C_{l,i}$ is related to $P(l \mid i)$ by means of a variable proportionality term.
To summarize, we can express Equation (2) by splitting the separately considered contributions of m and l, thus:

$$b_i(x_t \mid x_1^{t-1}) \approx \left[\sum_m c_{i,m} \cdot p(x_t \mid m)\right] \cdot \left[\sum_l C_{l,i} \cdot P(l \mid x_1^{t-1}) p(x_t \mid l)\right] \tag{6}$$

where the first term corresponds to Equation (1).
In this case, we do not want to introduce the modelling of the context for each feature vector into the HMM output densities, but to create a new feature by modelling the context. A new probability term is defined:

$$b_i'(x_t) = \sum_l C_{l,i} \cdot P(l \mid x_1^{t-1}) p(x_t \mid l) \tag{7}$$

Thus, when a regular $b_i(x_t)$ for each spectral feature and a $b_i'(x_t)$ for the phonetic-unit feature are combined, the joint output densities of the expanded set of models are equivalent to Equation (6).
We can express $P(l \mid x_1^t) = P(l \mid x_t, x_1^{t-1})$, and applying Bayes' rule to the second term of this expression:

$$P(l \mid x_1^t) = \frac{p(x_t \mid l, x_1^{t-1}) P(l \mid x_1^{t-1})}{p(x_t, x_1^{t-1})} \tag{8}$$

Given that class l is itself a discrete representation of feature vectors x_1^{t-1}, we can approximate $p(x_t \mid l, x_1^{t-1}) \approx p(x_t \mid l)$.

Likewise, $p(x_t,x_1^{t-1})$ is a constant in its evaluation across the different phonetic units so we can simplify Equation (8) to $P(l\,|\,x_1^{\,t}) = K\,p(x_t\,|\,l)\;P(l\,|\,x_1^{t-1})$ (with K as a constant).
Finally,

$$b_i^{'}(x_t) = \sum_l C_{l,i}^{'} \cdot P(l\,|\,x_1^t) \tag{9}$$

The new terms in Equation (9) are obtained as follows: $C'_{l,i}$ is estimated during the Baum-Welch training of the expanded set of models, whilst $P(l\,|\,x_1^{t})$ corresponds to the state scores output obtained by the Viterbi grammar-free decoding step. Thus, the output probability distribution of the models in the second layer can be estimated through a regular second training process.

3.3 Recognition system

The double-layer architecture proposed (Figure 1) divides the modelling process into two levels and trains a set of HMMs for each level. For the lower layer, a standard HMM-based scheme is used, which yields a set of regular acoustic models. From these models, a phonetic-unit recognizer performs a Viterbi grammar-free decoding step, which provides (at each instant t) the current most likely last state score for each unit.

This process can also be seen as a probabilistic segmentation of the speech signal, for which only the last state scores associated with the unit with the highest accumulated probability are kept.

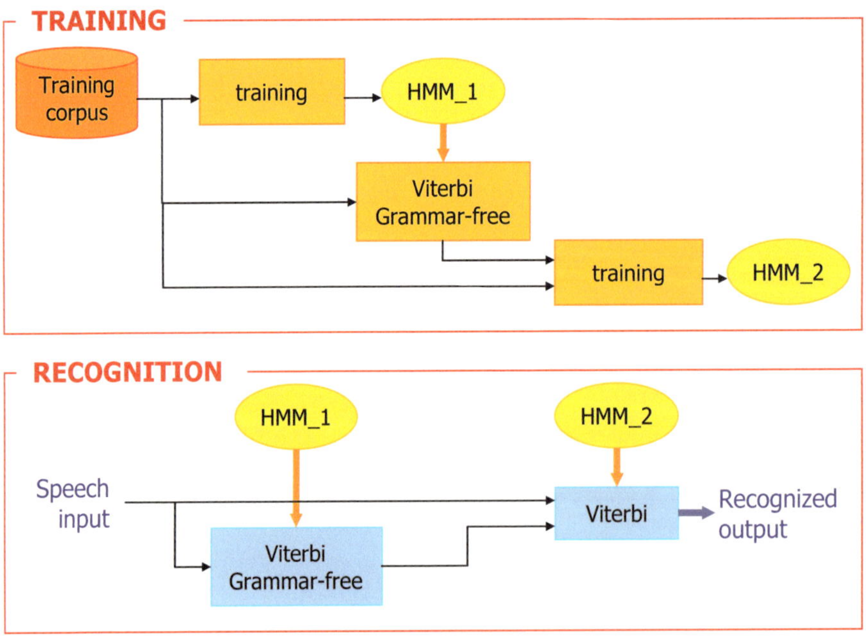

Figure 1. Double-layer ASR system with HMM state scores modelling

Let us consider, for instance, semidigit acoustic models for the first layer. In this case, labels l in the second layer represent the last states of each semidigit model. Thus, the output density value for each unit can be computed as the probability that the current state s_t of a semidigit model is equal to l:

$$P(l \mid x_1^t) := P(s_t = l \mid x_1^t) \quad (10)$$

where $P(s_t = l \mid x_1^t)$ is calculated from the forward score:

$$P(s_t = l \mid x_1^t) = \frac{P(s_t = l, x_1^t)}{\sum_j P(s_t = j, x_1^t)} \quad (11)$$

The last state scores probability will be the new parameter to be added to the original set of features (spectral parameters). Henceforth, five features are considered for further training the joint output densities of the expanded set of HMM parameters. However, they are not independent features as the phonetic-unit feature models the evolution of the other features. A weighting factor w is also introduced, as in (Stemmer et al., 2003) to control the influence of the new parameter regarding the spectral features. A global, non-state-dependent weighting factor will be used.
In Table 1, digit chain recognition results obtained using this architecture are compared with the baseline results obtained using the regular RAMSES SCHMM system (Bonafonte et al., 1998). Results show a significant improvement in both sentence and word recognition rates.

Configuration		**Sentence recognition rate**	**Word recognition rate**	**Relative reduction in WER**
System	**w**			
Baseline	-	93.304 %	98.73 %	-
Layered	0.5	93.605 %	98.80 %	5.51 %
	0.2	93.699 %	98.81 %	6.3 %

Table 1. Recognition rates using expanded state-scores based HMM.

The relevance of choosing a suitable weighting factor w is reflected in the results. Different strategies can be followed for selecting w. In this case, as in Stemmer et al. (2003), an experimental weighting factor is selected and its performance verified using an independent database.

4. Path-based Layered Architectures

4.1 Justification

HMM-based speech recognition systems rely on the modelling of a set of states and transitions using the probability of the observations associated with each state. As these probabilities are considered independent in SCHMMs, the sequence of states leading to each recognized output remains unknown. Thus, another interesting approach for implementing the second layer of a double-layer architecture consists in training the appearance pattern instead of modelling the temporal evolution of the states scores.
In (Casar & Fonollosa, 2003b) the "path" followed by the signal is modelled; each final active state is taken as a step. Recognition is then associated with decoding the best

matching path. This aids the recognition of acoustic units regardless of the fact that they may vary when they are uttered in different environments or by different speakers, or if they are affected by background noise.

Let us examine an example using phoneme HMMs, with three states each, which allows a maximum leap of 2 for intra-model state transitions, as in Figure 2.

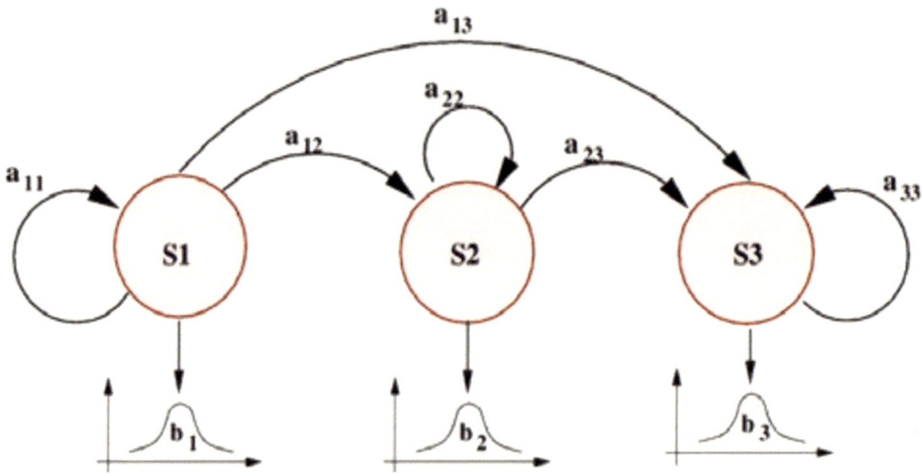

Figure 2. A three-state HMM with a maximum leap of 2 for intra-model state transitions

Thus, when a word is uttered, for example "zero", the speech signal is able to go through the different states of the models associated with each of the word's phonemes. The graph in Figure 3 represents the different "paths" that the speech signal can follow through these states at the decoding stage.

As the intra-model and inter-model state transitions allowed are also represented, by modelling this path we are also modelling the different durations of the utterance as local modifications of the path.

In a double-layer framework, the recognition architecture is broken down into two levels and performs a conventional acoustic modelling step in the first layer. The second layer is consigned to model the evolution followed by the speech signal. This evolution is defined as the path through the different states of the sub-word acoustic models defined in the first layer.

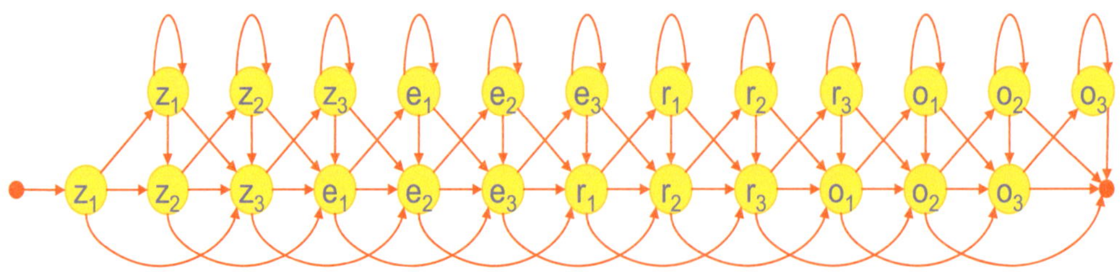

Figure 3. Example of paths that can be followed when the word "zero" is uttered

To model this path without taking into account the causal relationships between neighbour states, we can implement a transparent second layer. This is because we are doing a direct mapping of the acoustic probabilities of the activated states. However, while in traditional acoustic HMMs the Gaussian densities model the probability with which a state generates certain spectral parameters (acoustic or physical information), the new HMM generated in this second layer will give the probability of being at a certain point of the path followed by the speech signal.

If we take it one step further, the context of each state will be considered in the process of modelling the path. As shown in Figure 5, the speech signal will now be modelled by means of the different paths through the activated states, in which each path has its own associated probability. Thus, each state will be allowed to be part of different paths and to have different contexts. This increases the variability of the path and helps to model different utterances of the same speech symbol.

4.2 Mathematical formalism

In a semi-continuous HMM, a VQ codebook is used to map the continuous input feature vector x to o_k (the kth codeword) by means of the distribution function $f(x \mid o_k)$. Therefore, we can use a discrete output probability distribution function (PDF) $b_j(k)$ for state j:

$$b_j(x) = \sum_{k=1}^{M} b_j(k) f(x \mid o_k) \tag{12}$$

If Equation (12) is taken as the output density function of the models from the first layer, the input into the HMM of the second layer will be the vector of state probabilities given by the acoustic models of the first layer. Hence, a new set of semi-continuous output PDFs $b'_j(k)$ is defined for the second layer:

$$b'_j(x) = \sum_{k=1}^{M} b'_j(k) b_k(x) \tag{13}$$

This equation can also be expressed in terms of a new distribution function $f'(x \mid b_k)$, where the output probability vectors b_k play the role usually carried out by o_k in the first level. In fact, by doing this we are defining a new codebook that covers the sub-word state-probability space by means of the distribution function $f'(x \mid b_k) = b_k(x)$.

The new weights $b'(x)$ will be obtained through a new Baum-Welch estimation in a second modelling step. New observation distributions for the second-layer HMM are trained using the same stochastic matrix as that of the original acoustic HMM.

In practice, as M and M' are large, Equations (12) and (13) are simplified using the most significant values of I and I'. Thus, it is possible to avoid certain recognition paths from being activated, and this can result in a different decoding when $I \neq I'$. This simplification also means that the preceding and following states to be activated for each state are pruned.

In the previous formulation, we model the path followed by the signal, taking each final active state as a step, but without studying the possible causal relationships between adjacent states. When context-dependent path-based modelling is implemented, the mapping of the models will be undertaken using windows centred in each state and that embrace one or more adjacent states, that is, the states that are most likely to have been visited before the current state and those that will most probably become future ones. Therefore, instead of taking the output probability vectors b_k of the first layer as o_k for the new distribution function $f'(x\,|\,b_k)$, we will work with a combination between the output probabilities of the adjacent states considered.

4.3 Path-based double-layer architectures

The main aims of the path-based double-layer architecture developed are twofold: firstly, to achieve a better modelling of speech units as regards their variation when they are uttered in a changeable environment, and secondly, to improve speaker independence by taking advantage of the double layer.

Two implementations are possible for the second layer, namely, the state context in the definition of the path can either be taken into account or ignored. The two schemes are presented below. Firstly, in the one-state width path-based modelling scheme, the state context is not considered, that is, the path followed by the signal is considered without taking into account the causal relationships between adjacent states. This context is subsequently introduced in the L-state width path-based modelling scheme. In this case, L-1 is the number of adjacent states considered as the significant context for each state of the path.

Path-based modelling without context

In Figure 4, a basic diagram of the proposal for a double-layer architecture that implements path-based modelling without context in the second layer is shown.

The first layer of both the training and recognition schemes is equivalent to a regular acoustic HMM-based system. The second layer consists in mapping the acoustic models obtained in the first layer into a state-probability-based HMM. In addition, a new codebook that covers the probability space is defined. This means that we are no longer working with spectral parameter distributions but with the probabilities for the whole set of possible states. Thus, we have moved from the signal space (covered by the spectrum) to the probability space (defined by the probability values of each of the states).

In traditional HMMs, Gaussian densities model the probability with which a state generates certain spectral parameters (acoustic information). The new HMMs generated by this second layer will give the probability of being at a certain point of the path followed by the speech signal.

In practice, this means that in acoustic HMMs the probability of reaching a certain state s_i of model m_i depends on the parameterization value of the four spectral features, which depend on physical and acoustic characteristics. For instance, the "z" in "zero" may vary considerably when it is uttered by two different speakers (in terms of acoustic and physical parameters). It is the task of the HMM parameter to achieve a correct modelling of these variations. However, if a very flexible model is trained to accept a wide range of different utterances in the acoustic segment, the power of discrimination between units will be lost.

When we are working with path-based HMM, we are directly modelling the probability of reaching state s_i of model m_i regardless of the acoustic features' values. We use the new codebook to map the spectral feature to the new probability space. Thus, we decode the path followed by the speech signal in terms of the probabilities of each active state.

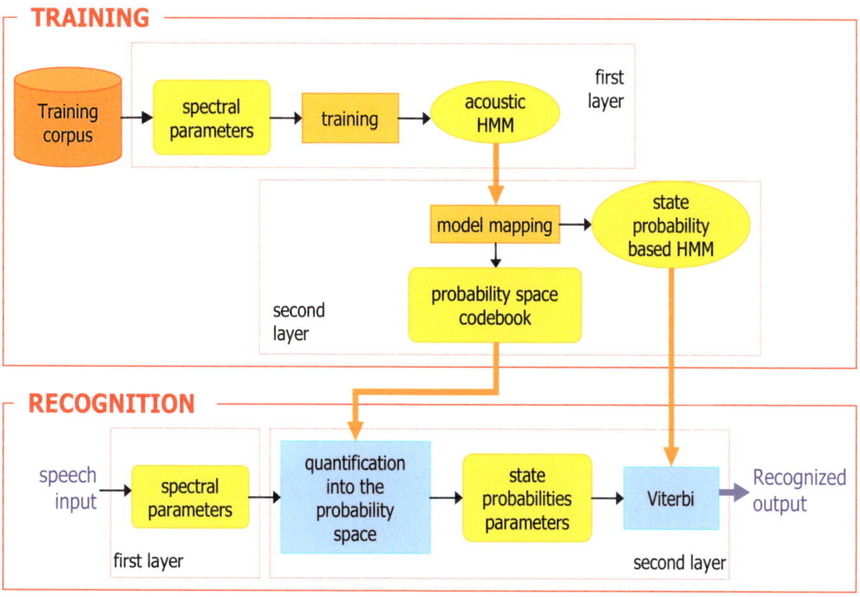

Figure 4. Basic diagram of a one-state width path-based double-layer ASR system

As the models are mapped to a space of dimension N (the total number of HMM states from the first layer), some pruning can be implemented by keeping only the N/2 most significant values (see Equation (13)). We are therefore constraining the possible states preceding and following each active state, which prevents some recognition paths from being activated. This solution will increase speed, and an improvement in recognition performance is also expected.

In fact, this can be seen as a similar strategy to CHMM Gaussian mixture pruning, in which each state is modelled using a mixture of private Gaussians and only the most likely mixtures are considered.

L-states width path-based modelling

From a mathematical point of view, speech signals can be characterized as a succession of Markov states, in which transitions between states and models are restricted by the topology of the models and the grammar. Hence, each state of every model is unique, even though the topology can allow multiple repetitions.

Thus, speech can be modelled by means of different *state successions* (or *paths*). Each path has its own associated probability, which allows one state to be part of different paths (see Figure 5). Furthermore, the context of each state becomes relevant, which brings about a higher variability in the possible paths that make up an utterance.

However, the maximum likelihood estimation criteria still apply. Thus, the path with maximum likelihood will be that configured by the succession of states that maximizes the joint probability (defined by the product of probabilities of each state in the path).

Theoretically, each path should be defined as the complete succession of states. However, as can be seen in Figure 5, the number of paths to consider can become too high (close to infinite) if the total number of previous and following states is considered for each state context.

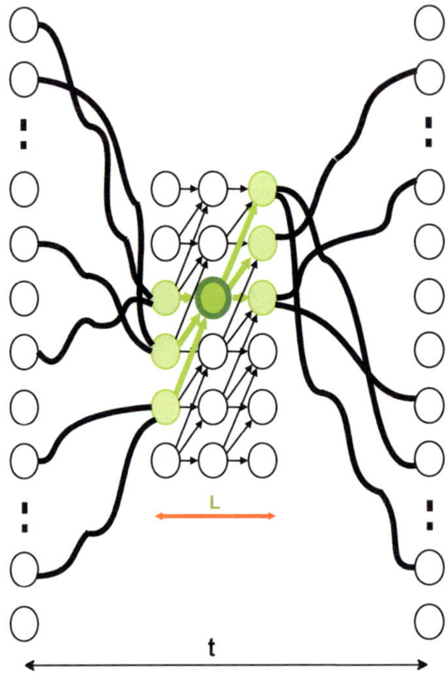

Figure 5. Different paths go into a certain state. Only those enclosed in a window of length L will be considered.

In practice, each state context is limited to a window of length L in order to allow generalization and to make implementation computationally feasible. That is, we will not deal with the whole path followed by the signal in the successive states defining a certain speech utterance. Instead, for each state that defines the path only the possible previous and subsequent L/2-1 states will be considered. Grammatical (phonetic) concordance along the path will likewise be verified.

By stretching this simplification to its limit, if a window of length L=1 were used we would be directly mapping the acoustic models into state-probability models in the same way as in the previous proposal (path-based modelling without context). This means that this second proposal can be seen as an extension of the previous one.

The training and recognition schemes for this architecture, in which L-states width path-based modelling in the second layer are implemented, is very similar to the previous one (for path-based modelling without context, see Figure 4). Only some modifications to the second layer of the training scheme are needed to take the L-states with context into account.

In this case, by mapping the acoustic models obtained in the first layer, a new codebook that covers the probability space is built. Furthermore, a table with all the possible state combinations is defined, which takes the aforementioned restrictions into account. If all state combinations are considered, the input speech is statistically defined and a new set of parameters is obtained. These parameters represent the probabilities of each sequence of states. A new set of state-probability-based models is built, which makes it possible to decode the path followed by the speech signal that uses the state probability parameters.

4.4 Results

If working with the first implementation, without considering the context for the path-based modelling in the second layer, it is assumed that there is a "transparent" second layer, as it is equivalent to a direct mapping of the acoustic probabilities. Performance would be expected to be equivalent to that of a baseline system (without the second layer being implemented). However, due to (and thanks to) the pruning implemented by keeping only the most significant N/2 values of the total number of HMM states (N), it is possible to prevent some recognition paths from being activated.

For the L-states width path-based modelling, the total number of possible state combinations represented in the new codebook is a result of considering the characteristics of the acoustic models in the lower layer (number of models and number of states) and the window length. Again, for the new representation of the input signal that uses the probability space codebook, only the most significant N/2 values will be kept.

In Table 2, digit recognition results obtained with these two architectures are compared against the baseline results obtained with a regular RAMSES SCHMM system (Bonafonte et al., 1998). Using one-width path-based modelling for the second layer, there is an improvement in the sentence and word recognition rate. This is achieved thanks to a positive weighting of the states with higher likelihood (implicit in the solution proposed) and the pruning of the preceding and following states to be activated for each state.

The results for the L-states width path-based modelling show a noticeable improvement in sentence and word recognition, but lower than that resulting from the first approach. This responds to the growth of the information to be modelled and the pruning performed, which induces a loss of information.

However, the general performance of the L-states width path-based implementation for the second layer is good and the flexibility of this approach would allow added value information to be introduced into the recognition. Recognition speed, which is slightly higher than with the first implementation, is also a point in its favour.

The gain obtained by these two approaches is also shown by means of the word error rate (WER). As the original recognition error rate of the baseline is low for the task under consideration, the perceptual relative reduction of the WER achieved is a good measure of the goodness of these solutions. Therefore, what would initially seem to be just a slight improvement in the (word/sentence) recognition rates can actually be considered a substantial gain in terms of perceptual error rate reduction.

Recognition system	**Sentence recognition rate**	**Word recognition rate**	**Relative reduction in WER**
Baseline	93.304 %	98.73 %	-
One-state width path-based double-layer	94.677 %	99.10 %	29.1%
L-states width path-based double-layer	93.717 %	98.98 %	19.7%

Table 2. Recognition rates using path-based double-layer recognition architectures

5. Discussion

The future of speech-related technologies is connected to the improvement of speech recognition quality. Until recently, speech recognition technologies and applications had assumed that there were certain limitations regarding vocabulary length, speaker independence, and environmental noise or acoustic events. In the future, however, ASR must deal with these restrictions and it must also be able to introduce other speech-related non-acoustic information that is available in speech signals.

Furthermore, HMM-based statistical modelling—the standard state-of-the-art ASR—has several time-domain limitations that are known to affect recognition performance. Context is usually represented by means of spectral dynamic features (namely, its first and second derivatives). However, they are generally limited to a few subsequent feature vectors and do not represent long-term variations.

To overcome all these drawbacks and to achieve a qualitative improvement in speech recognition, a change of paradigm from conventional speech recognizers has been proposed by several authors. Although some authors propose a move away from HMM-based recognition (or, at the very least, introducing hybrid solutions), we are adhering to Markov-based acoustic modelling as we believe its approach is still unbeatable. However, to overcome HMM-related limitations certain innovative solutions are required.

Throughout this chapter we have pointed out different approaches for improving standard HMM-based ASR systems. The main solutions for modelling temporal evolution and speech trajectory have been introduced, together with some ideas on how second-order HMMs deal with the same problems. These models provide an improvement in most cases, but they also require major modifications in the decoding of algorithms. Generally, there is also a considerable increase in complexity, even if this is compensated for by a moderate gain.

Layered architectures have been presented, and special attention has been paid to the implementation of the second layer using extended HMMs. Two implementations for this second layer have been described in detail. The first relies on modelling the temporal evolution of acoustic HMM state scores. In the second one, the evolution of the acoustic HMM is modelled by the speech utterance as a new way of modelling state transitions. This can be done in two ways, namely, by taking into account or ignoring the context of each active state while the "path" followed by the speech signal through the HMM states is being modelled. Again, speech recognition performance improves that of a conventional HMM-based speech recognition system, but at the cost of increased complexity.

Although current research solutions should not be unduly concerned by the computational cost (due to the constant increase in the processing capacity of computers), it is important to keep their implementation in commercial applications in mind. Therefore, a great deal of work remains if layered architectures are to be generalized for large vocabulary applications that keep complexity down to a moderate level.

Efforts should be made in the field of research for defining and testing innovative approaches to implementing layered architectures. Although keeping an HMM-based scheme for the different layers reduces the overall complexity, a change in paradigm may help to bring about significant improvements.

6. References

Bonafonte, A.; Ros, X. & Mariño, J.B. (1993). An efficient algorithm to find the best state sequence in HSMM. *Proceedings of the 3th European Conference on Speech Communication and Technology (EUROSPEECH93)*, 1993.

Bonafonte, A.; Vidal, J. & Nogueiras, A. (1996). Duration modelling with Expanded HMM Applied to Speech Recognition. *Proceedings of International Conference in Spoken Language Processing (ICSLP96)*, Volume2, pp:1097-1100, ISBN:0-7803-3555-4. Philadelphia (USA), October, 1996.

Bonafonte, A.; Mariño, J.B.; Nogueiras, A. & Fonollosa, J.A.R. (1998). RAMSES: el sistema de reconocimiento del habla continua y gran vocabulario desarrollado por la UPC. *VIII Jornadas de Telecom I+D (TELECOM I+D'98)*, Madrid, Spain, 1998.

Casar, M. & Fonollosa, J.A.R. (2006a). Analysis of HMM temporal evolution for ASR Utterance verification. *Proceedings of the Ninth International Conference on Spoken Language Processing (Interspeech2006-ICSLP)*, pp:613-616, ISSN:1990-9772. Pittsburgh, USA, September 2006.

Casar, M. & Fonollosa, J.A.R. (2006b). A path-based layered architecture using HMM for automatic speech recognition. *Proceedings of the 14th European Signal Processing Conference (EUSIPCO2006)*. Firenze, Italia. September 2006.

Demuynck, K.; Kaureys, T., Van Compernolle, D. & Van Hamme, H. (2003). FLAVOR: a flexible architecture for LVCSR. *Proceedings of the 8th European Conference on Speech Communication and Technology (EUROSPEECH2003)*, pp:1973-1976. Genova, 2003.

Furui, S. & Sandhi, M. (1992). *Advances in Speech Signal Processing*, Marcel Dekker, Inc. ISBN 0-8247-8540-1, 1st edition, 1992, New York (USA).

Huang, X.; Acero, A. & Hon, H.W. (2001). *Spoken Language Processing*, Prentice Hall PTR, ISBN 0-13-022616-5, 1st edition, 2001, New Jersey (USA).

Juang, B.H.; Chou, W. & Lee, C.H. (1997). Minimum Classification Error rate methods for speech recognition, *IEEE Transaction on Speech and Audio Processing*, Vol. 5, No. 3, (May, 1997) pp: 257-265, ISSN: 1063-6676.

Mari, J.-F.; Haton, J.-P. & Kriouile, A. (1997). Automatic word recognition based on Second-Order Hidden Markov Models, *IEEE Transaction on Speech and Audio Processing*, Vol. 5, No. 1, (January, 1997) pp: 22-25, ISSN:1063-6676.

Nadeu, C.; Macho, D. & Hernando, J. (2001). Time and frequency filtering of filter-bank energies for robust HMM speech recognition. *Speech Communication*, Vol. 34, Issues 1-2 (April, 2001) pp: 93-114, ISSN:0167-6393.

Rabiner, L.R. (1989). A tutorial on Hidden Markov Models and selected applications in speech recognition. *Proceedings of the IEEE*, No. 2, Vol. 77, (March, 1989), pp: 257-289, ISSN:0018-9219.

Rabiner, L. & Juang, B.H. (1993). *Fundamentals of Speech Recognition*, Prentice Hall PTR, ISBN:0-13-015157-2. NY, USA, 1993.

Russell, M.J. & Cook, A.E. (1987). Explicit modelling of state occupancy in Hidden Markov Models for automatic speech recognition. *Proceedings of IEEE International Conference on Acoustics, Speech and Signal Processing (ICASSP'85)*, Volume 10, pp:5-8. April, 1987.

Stemmer, G.; Zeissler, V.; Hacker,C.; Nöth, E. & Niemann,H. (2003). Context-dependent output densities for Hidden Markov Models in speech recognition. *Proceedings of the 8th European Conference on Speech Communication and Technology (EUROSPEECH2003)*, pp:969-972. Genova, 2003.

Tokuda, K.; Zen, H. & Kitamura,T. (2003). Trajectory modelling based on HMMs with the explicit relationship between static and dynamic features. *Proceedings of the 8th European Conference on Speech Communication and Technology (EUROSPEECH2003)*, pp:865-868. Genova, 2003.

Vidal,J.; Bonafonte, A. & Fernández,N. (2004) Rational characteristic functions and Markov Chains: application to modelling probability density functions, *Signal Processing*, No. 12, Vol. 84 (December, 2004) pp: 2287-2296, ISSN: 0165-1684.

Weber, K.; Ikbal, S.; Bengio, S. & Bourlard, H. (2003). Robust speech recognition and feature extraction using HMM2. *Computer, Speech and Language*, Vol. 17, Issues 2-3 (April-July 2003) pp: 195-211, ISSN:0885-2308.

Wu,Y.-J.; Kawai,H.; Ni,J. & Wang,R.-H. (2005) Discriminative training and explicit duration modelling for HMM-based automatic segmentation, *Speech Communication*, Vol. 47, Issue 4 (December, 2005) pp: 397-410, ISSN: 0167-6393.

9

Audio Visual Speech Recognition and Segmentation Based on DBN Models

Dongmei Jiang[1,2], Guoyun Lv[1], Ilse Ravyse[2], Xiaoyue Jiang[1], Yanning Zhang[1], Hichem Sahli[2,3] and Rongchun Zhao[1]
Joint NPU-VUB Research Group on Audio Visual Signal Processing (AVSP)
[1] Northwestern Polytechnical University (NPU), School of computer Science, 127 Youyi Xilu, Xi'an 710072, P.R.China
[2] Vrije Universiteit Brussel (VUB), Electronics & Informatics Dept., VUB-ETRO, Pleinlaan 2, 1050 Brussels, Belgium
[3] IMEC, Kapeldreef 75, 3001 Leuven, Belgium

1. Introduction

Automatic speech recognition is of great importance in human-machine interfaces. Despite extensive effort over decades, acoustic-based recognition systems remain too inaccurate for the vast majority of real applications, especially those in noisy environments, e.g. crowed environment. The use of visual features in audio-visual speech recognition is motivated by the speech formation mechanism and the natural speech ability of humans to reduce audio ambiguities using visual cues. Moreover, the visual information provides complementary cues that cannot be corrupted by the acoustic noise of the environment. However, problems such as the selection of the optimal set of visual features, and the optimal models for audio-visual integration remain challenging research topics. In recent years, the most common model fusion methods for audio visual speech recognition are Multi-stream Hidden Markov Models (MSHMMs) such as product HMM and coupled HMM. In these models, audio and visual features are imported to two or more parallel HMMs with different topology structures. These MSHMMs describe the correlation of audio and visual speech to some extent, and allow asynchrony within speech units. Compared with the single stream HMM, system performance is improved especially in noisy speech environment. But at the same time, problems remain due to the inherent limitation of the HMM structure, that is, on some nodes, such as phones, syllables or words, constraints are imposed to limit the asynchrony between audio stream and visual stream to phone (or syllable, word) level. Since for large vocabulary continuous speech recognition task, phones are the basic modeling units, audio stream and visual stream are forced to be synchronized at the timing boundaries of phones, which is not coherent with the fact that the visual activity often precedes the audio signal even by 120 ms.

Besides the audio visual speech recognition to improve the word recognition rate in noisy environments, the task of audio visual speech units (such as phones or visemes) segmentation also requires a more reasonable speech model which describes the inherent correlation and asynchrony of audio and visual speech.

Dynamic Bayesian Network (DBN) is a good speech model due to its strong description ability and flexible structure. DBN is a statistic model that can represent multiple collections of random variables as they evolve over time. Coupled HMM and product HMM are special cases of much more general DBN models. In fact, many DBN models have been proposed in recent years for speech recognition. For example, in [Zweig 1998], a baseline DBN model was designed to implement a standard HMM, while in [Bilmes 2001], a single stream DBN model with whole-word-state structure, i.e a fixed number of states are assigned to one word to assemble the HMM of the word, was designed for small vocabulary speech recognition. Experimental results show that it obtains high word recognition performance and robustness to noise. But the DBN model with whole-word-state structure, does not allow to make a speech subunit segmentation. [Zhang 2003] extended the single stream whole-word-state DBN model to multi-stream inputs with different audio features such as Mel filterbank cepstrum coefficients (MFCC) and perceptual linear prediction (PLP) features, and built two multi-stream DBN (MSDBN) models: i) a synchronous MSDBN model which assumes that multiple streams are strictly synchronized at the lowest state level, namely, all the different types of feature vectors on the same time frame are tied to one state variable; ii) an asynchronous MSDBN model which allows for limited asynchrony between streams at the state level, forcing the two streams to be synchronized at the word level by resetting the state variables of both streams to their initial value when a word transition occurs. [Gowdy 2004] combined the merit of the synchronous and asynchronous MSDBN models on a mixed type MSDBN model, and extended the speech recognition experiments on an audio visual digit speech database. In the mixed type MSDBN model, on each time slice, all the audio features share one state variable, while the visual stream and the composite audio stream each depend on different state variables which introduces the asynchrony between them. [Bilmes 2005] introduced a new asynchronous MSDBN model structure in which the word transition probability is determined by the state transitions and the state positions both in the audio stream and in the visual stream. Actually this structure assumes the same relationship between word transition and states with the asynchronous MSDBN model in [Zhang 2003], but describes it by different conditional probability distributions. Despite their novelties in breaking through the limitation of MSHMMs by allowing the asynchrony between streams to exceed the timing boundaries of states in a word, all the MSDBN models above build the whole-word-state model for a word i.e emulate the HMM that a word is composed of a fixed number of states, and therefore, the relationships between words and their corresponding subword units (for example phones) are not described. As a consequence, no subword unit level recognition and segmentation output can be obtained from these synchronous and asynchronous MSDBN models.

[Bilmes 2005] also presented a single stream bigram DBN model, in which the composing relationship between words and their corresponding phone units are defined by conditional probability distributions. This model emulates another type of word HMM in which a word is composed of its corresponding phone units instead of fixed number of states, by associating each phone unit with the observation feature vector, one set of Gaussian Mixture Model (GMM) parameters are trained. This model gives the opportunity to output the phone units with their timing boundaries, but to our best knowledge, no experiments have been done yet on evaluating its recognition and segmentation performance of the phone units (or viseme units in visual speech). Further more, it has not been extended to a synchronous or asynchronous multi-stream DBN model to emulate the word composition of its subword units simultaneously in audio speech and visual speech.

In our work, the new contributions to the speech modeling are: 1) the single stream DBN (SDBN) model in [Bilmes 2005] is implemented, speech recognition and segmentation experiments are done on audio speech and visual speech respectively. Besides the word recognition results, phone recognition and segmentation outputs are also obtained for both audio and visual speech. 2) a novel multi-stream asynchronous DBN (MSADBN) model is designed, in which the composition of a word with its phone units in audio stream and visual stream is explicitly described by the phone transitions and phone positions in each stream, as well as the word transition probabilities decided by both streams. In this MSADBN model, the asynchrony of audio speech and visual speech exceeds the timing boundaries of phone units but is restricted to word level. 3) for evaluating the performance of the single stream and multi-stream asynchronous DBN models, besides the word recognition rate, recognition and segmentation accuracy of the phone units with their timing boundaries in the audio stream is compared to the results from the well trained triphone HMMs, segmentation of visemes in the visual stream is compared to the manually labeled references, and the asynchrony between the segmented phone and viseme units is also analyzed.

The sections are organized as follows. Section 2.1 discusses the visual features extraction, starting from the detection and tracking of the speaker's head in the image sequence, followed by the detailed extraction of mouth motion, and section 2.2 lists the audio features. The structures of the single stream DBN model and the designed multi-stream asynchronous DBN model, as well as the definitions of the conditional probability distributions, are addressed in section 3. While section 4 analyzes the speech recognition and phone segmentation results in the audio and visual stream obtained by the SDBN and the MSADBN model, concluding remarks and future plans are outlined in section 5.

2. Audio-Visual Features Extraction

2.1 Visual Feature Extraction

Robust location of the speaker's face and the facial features, specifically the mouth region, and the extraction of a discriminant set of visual observation vectors are key elements in an audio-video speech recognition system. The cascade algorithm for visual feature extraction used in our system consists of the following steps: face detection and tracking, mouth region detection and lip contour extraction for 2D feature estimation. In the following we describe in details each of these steps.

Head Detection and Tracking The first step of the analysis is the detection and tracking of the speaker's face in the video stream. For this purpose we use a previously developed head detection and tracking method [Ravyse 2006]. The head detection consists of a two-step process: (a) face candidates selection, carried out here by iteratively clustering the pixel values in the YC_rC_b color space and producing labeled skin-colored regions $\{R_i\}_{i=1}^{N}$ and their best fit ellipse $E_i = (x_i, y_i | a_i, b_i, \theta)$ being the center coordinates, the major and minor axes length, and the orientation respectively, and (b) the face verification that selects the best face candidate. In the verification step a global face cue measure M_i, combining gray-tone cues and ellipse shape cues, is estimated for each face candidate region R_i. Combining shape and facial feature cues ensures an adequate detection of the face. The face candidate that has the maximal measure M_i localizes the head region in the image.

The tracking of the detected head in the subsequent image frames is performed via a kernel-based method wherein a joint spatial-color probability density characterizes the head region [Ravyse 2005].

Fig. 1 illustrates the tracking method. Samples are taken from the initial ellipse region in the first image, called *model target*, to evaluate the model target joint spatial-color kernel-based probability density function (p.d.f.). A hypothesis is made that the true target will be represented as a transformation of this model target by using a motion and illumination change model. The hypothesized target is in fact the modeled new look in the current image frame of the initially detected object. A *hypothesized target* is therefore represented by the *hypothesized p.d.f.* which is the transformed model p.d.f. To verify this hypothesis, samples of the next image are taken within the transformed model target boundary to create the *candidate target* and the joint spatial-color distribution of these samples is compared to the *hypothesized p.d.f.* using a distance-measure. A new set of transformation parameters is selected by minimizing the distance-measure. The parameter estimation or tracking algorithm lets the target's region converge to the true object's region via changes in the parameter set.

This kernel-based approach is proved to be robust, and moreover, incorporating an illumination model into the tracking equations enables us to cope with potentially distracting illumination changes.

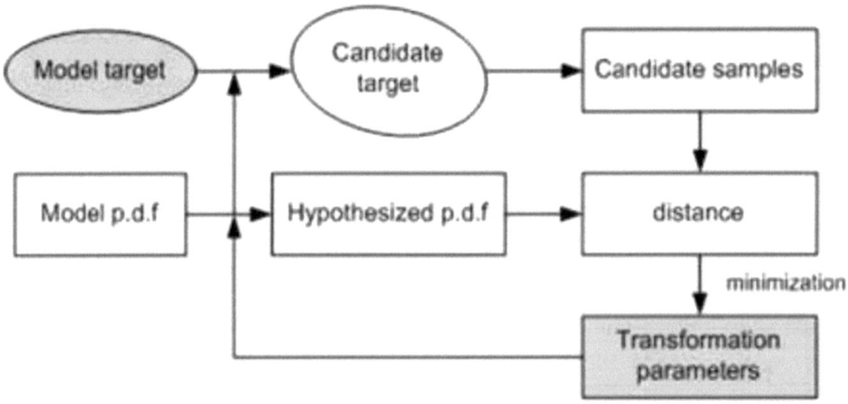

Figure 1. Tracking algorithm

2D Lip Contour Extraction The contour of the lips is obtained through the Bayesian Tangent Shape Model (BTSM) [Zhou 2003]. Fig. 2 shows several successful results of the lip contour extraction.

The lip contour is used to estimate a visual feature vector consisting of the mouth opening measures shown in Fig. 3. In total, 42 mouth features have been identified based on the automatically labeled landmark feature points: 5 vertical distances between the outer contour feature points; 1 horizontal distance between the outer lip corners; 4 angles; 3 vertical distances between the inner contour feature points; 1 horizontal distance between the inner lip corners; and the first order and second order regression coefficient (delta and acceleration in the image frames at 25 fps) of the previous measures.

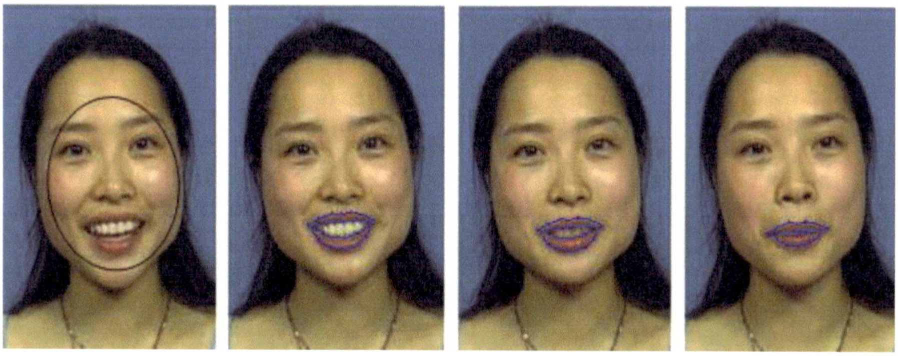

Figure 2. Face detection/tracking and lip contour extraction

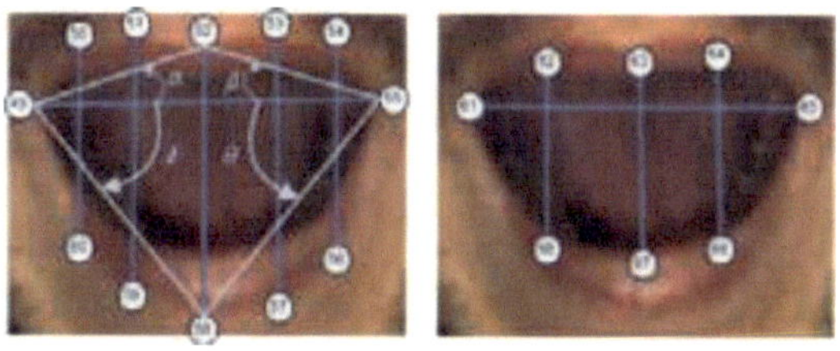

(a) (b)

Figure 3. Vertical and horizontal opening distances and angle features of the mouth: (a) outer contour features; (b) inner contour features

2.2 Audio Feature Extraction

The acoustic features are computed with a frame rate of 100frames/s. In our experiments, two different types of acoustic features are extracted: (i) 39 MFCC features: 12 MFCCs [Steven 1980], energy, together with their differential and acceleration coefficients; (ii) 39 dimension PLP features: 12 PLP coefficients [Hermansky 1990], energy, together with their differential and acceleration coefficients.

3. Single Stream DBN Model and Multi-Stream Asynchronous DBN Model

3.1 Single Stream DBN Model (SDBN)

In our framework, we first implement the single-stream DBN model following the idea of the bigram DBN model in [Bilmes 2005], and adopt it to the segmentation of phone units and viseme units both in the audio speech and in the visual speech respectively. The training data consists of the audio and video features extracted from word labeled speech sentences.

The DBN models in Fig. 4 represent the unflattened and hierarchical structures for a speech recognition system. (a) is the training model and (b) the decoding model. They consist of an initialization with a *Prologue* part, a *Chunk* part that is repeated every time frame (t), and a closure of a sentence with an *Epilogue* part. Every horizontal row of nodes in Fig. 4 depicts a separate temporal layer of random variables. The arcs between the nodes are either deterministic (straight lines) or random (dotted lines) relationships between the random variables, expressed as conditional probability distributions (CPD).

In the training model, the random variables *Word Counter* (WC) and *Skip Silence* (SS), denote the position of the current word or silence in the sentence, respectively. The other random variables in Fig. 4 are: (I) the word identity (W); (II) the occurrence of a *transition to another word* (WT), with *WT* = 1 denoting the start of a new word, and *WT* = 0 denoting the continuation of the current word; (III) the position of the current phone in the current word (PP); (iv) the occurrence of a *transition to another phone* (PT), defined similarly as WT; and (v) the *phone identification* (P), e.g. 'f' is the first phone in the word 'four'.

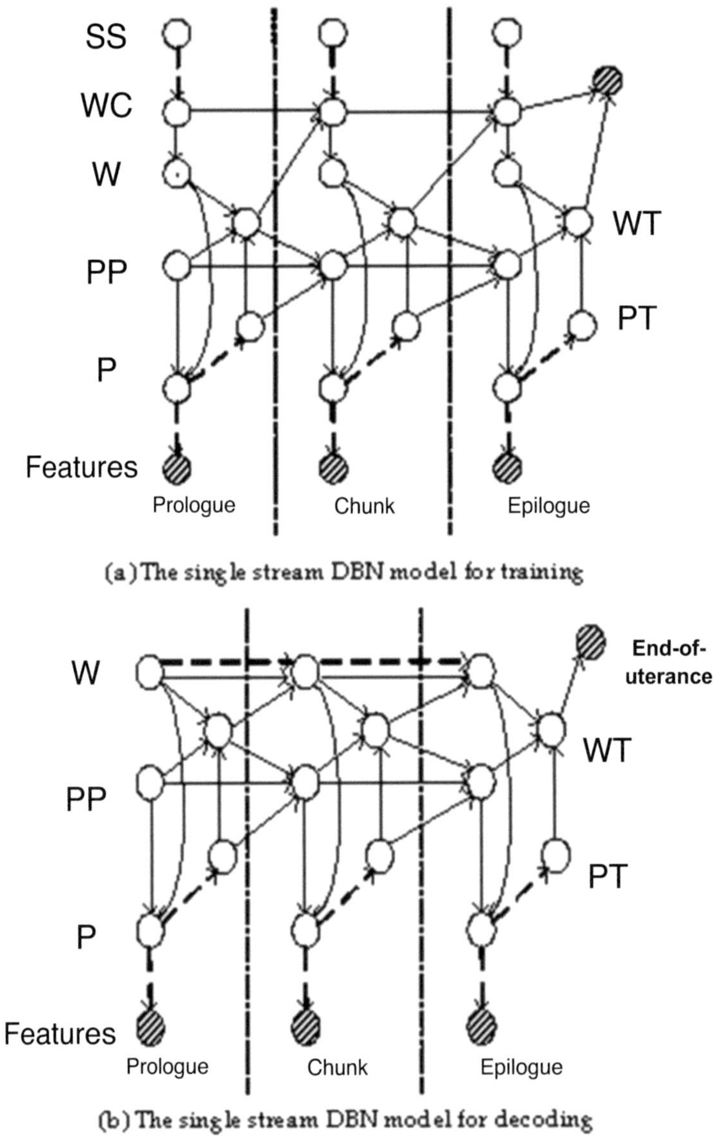

Figure 4. The single stream DBN model

Suppose the input speech contains T frames of features, for the decoding model of SDBN as shown in Fig.4, the set of the all the hidden nodes is denoted as $H_{1:T}=(W_{1:T},WT_{1:T},PP_{1:T},PT_{1:T},P_{1:T})$, then the probability of observations can be computed as

$$P(O_{1:T})=\sum_{H_{1:T}}P(H_{1:T},O_{1:T})$$

The graph thus specifies the following factorization for the joint probability distribution as:

$$\begin{aligned}P(H_{1:T},O_{1:T})&=P(W_{1:T},WT_{1:T},PP_{1:T},PT_{1:T},P_{1:T},O_{1:T})=\\ &\prod_{t=1}^{T}P(O_t|P_t)\cdot P(P_t|PP_t,W_t)\cdot P(PT_t|P_t)\cdot P(PP_t|PT_{t-1},PP_{t-1},WT_{t-1})\\ &\cdot P(WT_t|W_t,PP_t,PT_t)\cdot P(W_t|W_{t-1},WT_{t-1})\end{aligned} \tag{1}$$

The different conditional probability distributions (CPD) are defined as follows.

- Feature O. The observation feature O_t is a random function of the phone P_t in the CPD $P(O_t|P_t)$, which is denoted by a Gaussian Mixture Model as

$$b_{P_t}(O_t)=P(O_t|P_t)=\sum_{k=1}^{M}\omega_{P_tk}N(O_t,\mu_{P_tk},\sigma_{P_tk}) \tag{2}$$

  where $N(O_t,\mu_{P_tk},\sigma_{P_tk})$ is the normal distribution with mean μ_{P_tk} and covariance σ_{P_tk}, and ω_{P_tk} is the weight of the probability from the kth mixture.

- Phone node P. The CPD $P(P_t|PP_t,W_t)$ is a deterministic function of its parents nodes phone position PP and word W :

$$P(P_t=j|W_t=i,PP_t=m)=\begin{cases}1 & \text{if } j \text{ is the } m-th \text{ phone of the word } i\\ 0 & \text{otherwise}\end{cases} \tag{5}$$

  This means that, given the current word W and the phone position PP, the phone P is known with certainty. For example, given the phone position PP as 2 in the word "five", we can know exactly the corresponding phone unit "ay".

- Phone transition probability PT which describes the probability of the transition from the current phone to the next phone. The CPD $P(PT_t|P_t)$ is a random distribution since each phone has a nonzero probability for staying at the current phone of a word or moving to the next phone.

- Phone position PP. It has three possible behaviors. (i) It might not change if the phone unit is not allowed to transit ($PT_{t-1}=0$); (ii) It might increment by 1 if there is a phone transition ($PT_{t-1}=1$) while the phone doesn't reach the last phone of the current word, i.e. the word unit doesn't transit ($WT_{t-1}=0$); (iii) It might be reset to 0 if the word transition occurs ($WT_{t-1}=1$).

$$P(PP_t = j \mid PP_{t-1} = i, WT_{t-1} = m, PT_{t-1} = n) = \begin{cases} 1 & m = 1, j = 0 \\ 1 & m = 0, n = 1, j = i+1 \\ 1 & \mathrm{m} = 0, n = 0, j = i \\ 0 & otherwise \end{cases} \tag{7}$$

- Word transition probability *WT*. In this model, each word is composed of its corresponding phones. The CPD $P(WT_t | W_t, PP_t, PT_t)$ is given by:

$$P(WT_t = j | W_t = a, PP_t = b, PT_t = m) = \begin{cases} 1 & j = 1, m = 1, b = lastphone\,(a) \\ 1 & j = 0, m = 1, b =\sim lastphone\,(a) \\ 0 & otherwise \end{cases} \tag{8}$$

The condition $b = lastphone(a)$ means that *b* corresponds to the last phone of the word *a*, where *b* is the current position of the phone in the word. Equation (8) means that when the phone unit reaches the last phone of the current word, and phone transition is allowed, the word transition occurs with $WT_t = 1$.

- Word node *W*. In the training model, the word units are known from the transcriptions of the training sentences. In the decoding model, the word variable W_t uses the switching parent functionality, where the existence or implementation of an edge can depend on the value of some other variable(s) in the network, referred to as the switching parent(s). In this case, the switching parent is the word transition variable. When the word transition is zero ($WT_{t-1} = 0$), it causes the word variable to copy its previous value, i.e., $W_t = W_{t-1}$ with probability one. When a word transition occurs, $WT_{t-1} = 1$, however, it switches the implementation of the word-to-word edge to use bigram language model probability i.e. *bigram* which means the probability of one word transiting to another word whose value comes from the statistics of the training script sentences. The CPD $P(W_t = j \mid W_{t-1} = i, WT_t = m)$ is:

$$P(W_t = j \mid W_{t-1} = i, WT_t = m) = \begin{cases} bigram(i, j) & if \quad m = 1 \\ 1 & if \quad m = 0, \quad i = j \\ 0 & otherwise \end{cases} \tag{9}$$

- In the training DBN model, the Word Counter (*WC*) node is incremented according to the following CPD:

$$p(WC_t = i \mid WC_{t-1} = j, WT_{t-1} = k, SS = l) = \begin{cases} 1 & i = j \quad and \quad k = 0 \\ 1 & i = j \quad and \quad bound(w,j) \quad and \quad k = 1 \\ 1 & i = j+1 \quad and \quad \sim bound(w,j) \quad and \quad l = 0 \quad and \quad k = 1 \\ 1 & i = j+2 \quad and \quad \sim bound(w,j) \quad and \quad realword(w) \quad and \quad l = 1 \quad and \quad k = 1 \\ 1 & i = j+1 \quad and \quad \sim bound(w,j) \quad and \quad l = 1 \quad and \quad \sim realword(w) \quad and \ k = 1 \\ 0 & otherwise \end{cases} \tag{10}$$

where $bound(w, j)$ is a binary indicator specifying if the position j of the current word w exceeds the boundary of the training sentence, if so, $bound(w, j) = 1$. $realword(w) = 1$ means that the coming word w after silence is a word with real meaning. If there is no word transition, $WC_t = WC_{t-1}$. On the contrary, if the word transits, the word number counts in different ways depending if the position of the word exceeds the boundary of the sentence: (i) if it does, word counter keeps the same as $WC_t = WC_{t-1}$; (ii) otherwise, it needs to check further the coming word, if there is no Skip Silence (SS) before the coming word, the word counter increments by one; If there is a SS, then check if the coming word has a real meaning, the word counter increments by 2 for the answer "yes" , and 1 for the answer "no".

3.2 Multi-Stream Asynchronous DBN Model (MSADBN)

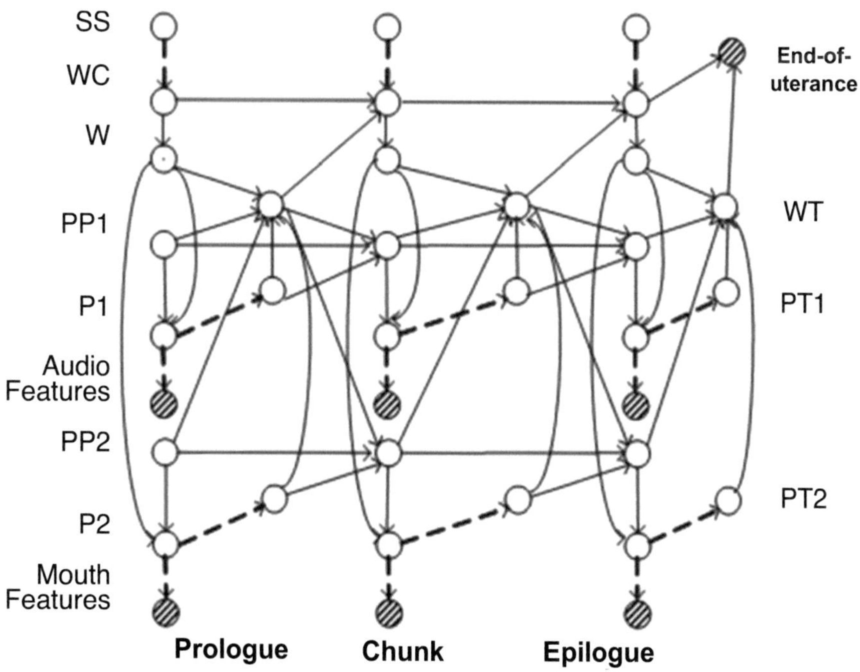

Figure 7. the audio visual asynchronous DBN model for training

For the audio visual speech unit segmentation, a multi-stream asynchronous DBN model is designed as shown in Fig.7. Audio features and visual features are imported into two independent graphical models in the same structure as the single stream DBN model of Fig.6, but are forced to be synchronized at the timing boundaries of words, by sharing one word variable *W* and word transition variable *WT*. In order to represent in the best way how the audio and visual speech are composed, between the succeeding word variables, the graphical topology of the audio stream with the phone variable *P1* is also allowed to be different with that of the visual stream with another phone variable *P2*. In other words, for each stream an independent phone variable is assigned, and its transition depends only on the phone instances inside the stream. This makes sure that the phone units in the audio stream and the visual stream may vary asynchronously. But at the same time, this asynchrony is limited inside the word by the word transition variable *WT*. The transition between words has to consider the cues from both the audio stream and the visual stream. Vice versa, it will affect the variations of both the phone positions *PP1* in the audio stream, and *PP2* in the visual stream: when and only when both the phone units in the two streams arrive the last phone position of a word, and both the phones are allowed to transit, the word transition occurs with the probability of 1. On the other hand, when a word transits to another word, it will reset the phone positions in the audio and in the visual stream to their initial values 0, in order to count the phone positions in the new word.
For the node variables that are not shared by the audio stream and visual stream as *W* and *WT*, the definitions of their conditional probability distributions are kept the same as that in the single stream DBN model. However, in this multi-stream DBN model, *WT* has five parent nodes: word *W*, phone position *PP1* and phone transition *PT1* in the audio stream, phone position *PP2* and phone transition *PT2* in the visual stream. As is explained above, the conditional probability distribution of *WT* can be defined as

$$\begin{aligned} & p(WT_t = j \mid W_t = a, PP1_t = b, PP2_t = c, PT1_t = m, PT2_t = n) \\ & = \begin{cases} 1 & j = 1, m = 1, n = 1, b = lastphone\,1(a), c = lastphone\,2(a) \\ 0 & otherwise \end{cases} \end{aligned} \tag{11}$$

where $b = lastphone1(a)$ and $c = lastphone2(a)$ mean that the phone position b in the audio stream, and the phone position c in the visual stream correspond to the last phone of the word "a".

4. Experiments on Audio and Visual Speech

GMTK [Bilmes 2002] has been used for the inference and learning of the DBN models. In the experiments, we recorded our own audiovisual speech database with the scripts of the Aurora 3.0 audio database containing connected digits sequence from telephone dialing[Bilmes 2001]. 100 recorded sentences are selected as training data, and another 50 sentences as testing data. White noise with signal to noise ratio (SNR) ranging from 0dB to 30dB has been added to obtain noisy speech.

$$SNR = 10\log(E_s / E_N) \tag{12}$$

with E_s denoting the average energy of the speech sentence, and E_N the mean energy of white noise.

In the training process of the SDBN model, we first extract a word-to-phone dictionary from the standard TIMITDIC dictionary [Garofolo 1993] for the 11 digits. Actually, only 24 phone units--22 phones for the 11 digits together with the silence and short pause 'sp', are used due to the small size of the vocabulary. Associating each of the 22 phones with the observation features, the conditional probability distribution is modelled by 1 Gaussian mixture. Together with the silence model, and the short pause model which ties its state with the middle state of the silence model, a total parameter set of 25 Gaussian mixtures need to be trained.

For the MSADBN model, phone units are adopted in both graphical structures corresponding with audio and visual input. For each individual stream, the setup of the parameters is the same as that in the SDBN model. Therefore, for the 11 digits, 25 Gaussian mixtures are trained for the audio speech, and another 25 Gaussian mixtures for the visual speech.

To evaluate the speech recognition and phone segmentation performance of the SDBN and the MSADBN model, experiments are also done on the tied-state triphone HMMs with 8 Gaussian mixtures trained by the HMM toolkit HTK [Young 2006].

4.1 Speech Recognition Results

For the SDBN, Table 1 summarizes the word recognition rates (WRR) using acoustic features MFCC or PLP with white noise at different SNRs. Compared to the trained triphone HMMs, one can notice that with the SDBN model we obtain equivalent results in case of 'clean' signal and better results with strong noise. Over all (SNR=0dB to 30dB), SDBN with MFCC features shows an average improvement of 5.33%, and even 23.59% with PLP features in word accuracies over the triphone HMMs. Another interesting aspect of these results is that the improvement in word accuracies is more pronounced in cases of low SNRs.

Setup	0db	5db	10db	15db	20db	30db	Clean	0-30db
SDBN (MFCC_D_A)	42.94	66.10	71.75	77.97	81.36	96.61	97.74	72.79
SDBN (PLP_D_A)	76.27	88.70	92.09	93.79	97.18	98.31	98.87	91.05
Triphone HMM (MFCC_D_A)	27.55	42.76	58.67	83.85	93.82	98.10	98.34	67.46

Table 1. Speech recognition rate from audio stream (%)

For the speech recognition on the visual stream with SDBN, the word recognition rate is 67.26 percent for all SNR levels, which is also higher than 64.2% from the triphone HMMs.

Setup	0db	5db	10db	15db	20db	30db	Clean	0-30db
MSADBN (MFCC_D_A +GF)	53.94	70.61	86.06	89.39	93.03	95.76	97.27	81.46
MSADBN (PLP_D_A+GF)	90.96	94.92	96.05	96.61	97.19	98.87	98.31	95.76
MSHMM (MFCC_D_A +GF)	42.73	54.24	67.88	77.27	85.15	91.21	92.73	69.74

Table 2. Audio visual speech recognition rate (%)

Table 2 shows the word recognition rates from the audio visual multi-stream models. Comparing with the recognition results in Table 1 from only the audio stream, one can notice that in noisy environment, visual speech information, such as geographical features (GF) of lip, helps to improve the perception of speech. For the MSHMM, the MSADBN with MFCC features and MSADBN with PLP features, the average WRR improvements of 2.28%, 8.67% and 4.71% are obtained respectively for SNR=0dB to 30dB. Comparing the results from MSADBN and MSHMM with the same MFCC and geographical features, it can be seen that the designed MSADBN model outperforms MSHMM in modelling the dynamics of words in the two streams.

4.2 Phone Segmentation Results in the Audio Stream

Besides the word recognition results, the novelty of our work lies in the fact that we also obtain the phone segmentation sequence from the SDBN model, and further more, the asynchronous phone segmentation results in both audio and visual stream simultaneously from the MSADBN model.

Here we first evaluate the phone segmentation accuracies in the audio stream. An objective evaluation criterion, the phone segmentation accuracy (PSA) is proposed as follows: the phone segmentation results of the testing speech from the triphone HMMs are used as references. We convert the timing format of all the phone sequences obtained from the triphone HMM, the SDBN model and the MSADBN model with 10ms as frame rate, and then compare the phone units frame by frame. For each frame, if the segmented phone result from the SDBN (or MSADBN) model is the same as that in the reference, the score A is incremented. For the phone sequence of a speech sentence with C frames, the PSA is defined as

$$PSA = A / C \tag{11}$$

This evaluation criterion is very strict since it takes into account both phone recognition results together with their timing boundary information.

The average *PSA* values for the 50 testing sentences from the SDBN model and the MSADBN model with different features are shown in Table 3. One can notice that the SDBN model, either with MFCC features or with PLP features, gives phone segmentation results very close to those of the triphone HMMs, the standard continuous speech recognition

models. While for the MSADBN model, the phone segmentations in the audio stream with timing boundaries differ even more to those from the triphone HMMs. This is reasonable because in the MSADBN model, it takes into account the phone units in the audio and in the visual streams simultaneously, and forces them to be synchronized on the timing boundaries of words.
As for the segmented timing boundaries of phones in the audio stream, whether the results from the single stream DBN model, or the results from the MSADBN model which also considers the visual features are more reasonable, will be discussed further in section 4.4.

Setup	0dB	5dB	10dB	15dB	20dB	30dB	Clean
SDBN (MFCC_D_A)	33.1	41.3	45.5	53.2	60.2	79.6	81.5
SDBN (PLP_D_A)	55.1	61.8	64.2	71.5	78.5	79.7	81.7
MSADBN (MFCC_D_A + GF)	25.4	26.9	28.2	31.4	33.3	38.4	40.4
MSADBN (PLP_D_A+GF)	35.2	36.0	39.2	40.8	42.1	45.6	46.4

Table 3. Phone segmentation accuracy in the audio stream (%)

4.3 Viseme Segmentation Results in the Visual Stream

To evaluate the phone segmentation results in the visual stream, the phone sequences are mapped to viseme sequences with a phone-to-viseme mapping table containing 16 viseme units that we previously proposed[Xie 2003]. The reference viseme sequences for the 50 testing sentences are obtained by manually labelling the image sequences, while also listening to the accompanying audio.
Viseme Segmentation Accuracy Firstly, the average viseme segmentation accuracies (VSA) for the 50 testing sentences from SDBN and MSADBN, calculated in the same way as PSA, are obtained as shown in Table 4. One can notice that MSADBN gets the improvement of 17.6% over SDBN for clean speech, with the consideration of audio cues. So by combining the audio and visual information together, we obtain more correct and accurate viseme segmentation in the visual speech.

Setup	0dB	5dB	10dB	15dB	20dB	30dB	Clean
SDBN (MFCC_D_A)	50.7	50.7	50.7	50.7	50.7	50.7	50.7
MSADBN (MFCC_D_A +GF)	51.5	52.9	56.2	58.5	59.8	62.5	68.3

Table 4. Viseme segmentation accuracy (%)

Relative Viseme Segmentation Accuracy (RVSA) VSA is a very strict criterion for evaluating the viseme segmentation results in the visual stream: only when the corresponding viseme units are correctly recognized, and the segmented timing boundaries are the same with the references, the score can be incremented. On the other hand, in our task, the purpose of segmenting the viseme sequence is for constructing a mouth animation in the future: suppose for each viseme, one representative mouth image is built, a mouth animation can be constructed by concatenating the mouth images corresponding to the viseme sequence. So from the speech intelligibility point of view, it is also acceptable if a viseme is recognized as another viseme unit with very similar mouth shape. RVSA is thus a measurement to evaluate the global similarity between the mouth animation constructed from the reference viseme sequence, and the one constructed from the segmented viseme sequence.

The RVSA is calculated as follows:

For two gray level images I_{ref} and I with the same size, their difference can be measured by Mean Square Error

$$MSE(I_{ref}, I) = \frac{1}{M}\sum_{u}\sum_{v}(I_{ref}(u,v) - I(u,v))^2 \tag{12}$$

with M the number of pixels, $I(u,v)$ the gray level of the pixel on the coordinate (u,v). The difference of an arbitrary viseme representative image pair (vis_m, vis_n) can be measured by eq. (12) and then be normalized to a viseme similarity weight (VSW) which shows their similarity contrariwise.

$$VSW(vis_m, vis_n) = 1 - \frac{MSE(vis_m, vis_n)}{MAX_{i,j=1,2,\ldots N}\left(MSE(vis_i, vis_j)\right)} \tag{13}$$

The lower the difference is, the higher the VSW is. If two visemes are totally the same, the VSW is 1.

Therefore, for the whole viseme image sequence of N frames, the RVSA can be calculated by the VSW between the resulting and reference visemes on each image frame t.

$$RVSA = \frac{1}{N}\sum_{t} VSW_t \tag{14}$$

Table 5 shows the average RVSA values of the viseme sequences for the 50 testing sentences, obtained from the SDBN model and from the MSADBN respectively. One can notice that in relative clean environment with SNR higher than 20dB, the MSADBN model creates more close mouth shape animations to the reference animations. While with the increasing of noise, the viseme segmentations from MSADBN will get worse.

Setup	0dB	5dB	10dB	15dB	20dB	30dB	Clean
SDBN	75.1	75.1	75.1	75.1	75.1	75.1	75.1
MSADBN (MFCC_D_A+GF)	71.8	73.1	73.8	74.3	75.6	77.6	82.6

Table 5. Relative viseme segmentation accuracy based on image (%)

4.3 Asynchronous Segmentation Timing Boundaries

The asynchronous timing boundaries of phone segmentation in the audio stream, and the viseme segmentation in the visual stream can be obtained, either by performing the SDBN for two times (with audio features and with visual features respectively), or by inputting the audio and visual features into the MSADBN simultaneously. As an example to illustrate the segmentation results, we adopt a simple audio-video speech corresponding to the sentence "two nine". Table 6 shows the segmentation results in both audio and visual streams, together with the manually labeled phone and viseme timing boundaries as references. To see clearly the asynchrony between the phones and visemes obtained from the SDBN model and the MSADBN model, the results are also expressed in Fig.8, together with the temporal changes of audio and visual features. The mapping relationships between visemes and phones are: viseme 'vm' corresponds to the mouth shape of the phone 't', 'vg' to phone 'uw', 'vp' to phone 'n', and 'vc' to phone 'ay'.

setup	t (vm)	uw (vg)	n (vp)	ay (vc)	n (vp)
Reference (audio)	0.43-0.56	0.56-0.83	0.83-0.98	0.98-1.23	1.23-1.39
Reference(visual)	0.36-0.44	0.45-0.76	0.77-0.88	0.89-1.20	1.21-1.36
SDBN(audio)	0.43-0.54	0.55-0.84	0.85-0.97	0.98-1.20	1.21-1.34
SDBN(visual)	0.36-0.40	0.41-0.67	0.68-0.71	0.72-1.18	1.19-1.24
MSADBN(audio)	0.42-0.50	0.51-0.76	0.77-0.99	1.00-1.29	1.30-1.36
MSADBN(visual)	0.42-0.45	0.46-0.76	0.77-0.87	0.88-0.97	0.98-1.36

Table 6. The phone and viseme segmentation timing boundaries (s)

From Fig.8, one can notice that for the single stream segmentation from SDBN, without considering the mutual effect of the other accompanying cue, the asynchronies between the phones and the corresponding visemes are quite large. For example, the first viseme "vm" in the visual stream ends at 0.54s, preceding about 140ms than the corresponding phone unit "t" in the audio stream. And for the viseme "vp" (phone "n") at the beginning of the word "nine", the ending time in the visual stream is even 260ms earlier than that in the audio stream.

Considering the asynchronous segmentation from the MSADBN model, one can notice that by integrating the audio features and visual features in one model, and forcing them to be aligned at the timing boundaries of words, that for most of the segmented timing boundaries in the two streams, they seem to attract each other to be closer. Now the distance of the ending times in the visual stream and in the audio stream, becomes 50ms for the first viseme "vm" (phone "t"), and 120ms for the first viseme "vp" (phone "n") of "nine". But this behavior is not always this case, for example, an exception occurs with the ending times of the viseme "vc" (phone "ay"). From the MSADBN model, the distance between the timing boundaries in visual and in audio stream is 220ms, which is longer than 20ms obtained from the SDBN model. Comparing the asynchronous audio visual phone (viseme) segmentation results from the SDBN model and the MDBN model with the reference timing boundaries, we can see that in most cases, the asynchrony obtained from the MSADBN model is more reasonable.

5. Discussion

In this chapter, we first implement an audio or visual single stream DBN model proposed in [Bilmes 2005], which we demonstrate that it can break through the limitation of the state-of-the-art 'whole-word-state DBN' models and output phone (viseme) segmentation results. Then we expand this model to an audio-visual multi-stream asynchronous DBN (MSADBN) model. In this MSADBN model, the asynchrony between audio and visual speech is allowed to exceed the timing boundaries of phones/visemes, in opposite to the multi-stream hidden markov models (MSHMM) or product HMM (PHMM) which constrain the audio stream and visual stream to be synchronized at the phone/viseme boundaries.

In order to evaluate the performances of the proposed DBN models on word recognition and subunit segmentation, besides the word recognition rate (WRR) criterion, the timing boundaries of the segmented phones in the audio stream are compared to those obtained from the well trained triphone HMMs using HTK. The viseme timing boundaries are compared to manually labeled timing boundaries in the visual stream. Furthermore, suppose for each viseme, one representative image is built and hence a mouth animation is constructed using the segmented viseme sequence, the relative viseme segmentation accuracy (RVSA) is evaluated from the speech intelligibility aspect, by the global image sequence similarity between the mouth animations obtained from the segmented and the reference viseme sequences. Finally, the asynchrony between the segmented audio and visual subunits is also analyzed. Experiment results show: 1) the SDBN model for audio or visual speech recognition has higher word recognition performance than the triphone HMM, and with the increasing noise in the audio stream, the SDBN model shows more robust tendency; 2) in a noisy environment, the MSADBN model has higher WRR than the SDBN model, showing that the visual information increases the intelligibility of speech. 3) compared with the segmentation results by running the SDBN model on audio features and on visual features respectively, the MSADBN model, by integrating the audio features and visual features in one scheme and forcing them to be synchronized on the timing boundaries of words, in most cases, gets more reasonable asynchronous relationship between the speech units in the audio and visual streams.

In our future work, we will expand the MSADBN model to the subunits segmentation task of a large vocabulary audio visual continuous speech database, and test its performance in speech recognition, as well as analyze its ability of finding the inherent asynchrony between audio and visual speech.

6. Acknowledgement

This research has been conducted within the "Audio Visual Speech Recognition and Synthesis: Bimodal Approach" project funded in the framework of the Bilateral Scientific and Technological Collaboration between Flanders, Belgium(BILO4/CN/02A) and the Ministry of Science and Technology (MOST), China([2004]487), and the fund of 'The Developing Program for Outstanding Persons' in NPU—DPOP: NO. 04XD0102.

7. References

Bilmes, J. & Zweig, G. (2001). *Discriminatively structured dynamic graphical models for speech recognition*. Technical report, JHU 2001 Summer Workshop, 2001.

Bilmes, J., Zweig, G.: The graphical models toolkit: an open source software system for speech and time-series processing. *Proceedings of the IEEE Int. Conf. on Acoustic Speech and Signal Processing(ICASSP)*. Vol. 4(2002), pp. 3916-3919.

Bilmes,J. & Bartels, C. (2005). Graphical Model Architectures for Speech Recognition. *IEEE Signal Processing Magazine*, vol.22, pp. 89-100, 2005.

Eisert, P. (2000). *Very low bit-rate video coding using 3-d models*. PhD thesis, Universitat Erlangen, Shaker Verlag, Aachen, Germany (2000) , ISBN 3-8265-8308-6.

Garofolo, J.S.; Lamel, L.F & Fisher, W.M. et al (1993). TIMIT Acoustic-Phonetic Continuous Speech Corpus, *Linguistic Data Consortium*, Philadelphia. http://www.ldc.upenn.edu/Catalog/CatalogEntry.jsp?catalogId=LDC93S1.

Gowdy, J.; Subramanya, A.; Bartels, C. & Bilmes, J. (2004). DBN-based multistream models for audio-visual speech recognition. *Proc. IEEE Int. Conf. Acoustics, Speech, and Signal Processing*, pp. 993–996, May 2004.

Hermansky, H. (1990). Perceptual linear predictive (PLP) analysis of speech. *The Journal of the Acoustical Society of America*. Vol. 87, Issue 4 (1990), pp. 1738-1752.

Lee, Y.; Terzopoulos, D. & Waters, K. (1993). Constructing physics based facial models of individuals. *Proceedings of the Graphics Interface '93 Conference*, Toronto, Canada. (1993), pp. 1-8.

Ravyse, I. (2006). *Facial Analysis and Synthesis*. PhD thesis, Vrije Universiteit Brussel, Dept. Electronics and Informatics, Belgium. online: www.etro.vub.ac.be/Personal/icravyse/RavysePhDThesis.pdf.

Ravyse, I.; Enescu, V. & Sahli, H. (2005). Kernel-based head tracker for videophony. *The IEEE international Conference on Image Processing 2005 (ICIP2005)*, Vol. 3, pp.1068-1071, Genoa, Italy, 11-14/09/2005.

Steven, B.D.& P.M. (1980). Comparison of parametric representation for monosyllable word recognition in continuously spoken sentences. IEEE Transactions on Acoustics, Speech, and Signal Processing. Vol. 28, (1980) pp. 357-366.

Vedula, S. & Baker, S. et al (2005). Three-dimensional scene flow. *IEEE transactions on Pattern Analysis and Machine Intelligence*. Vol. 27, (2005), pp. 137-154.

Xie, L. & Jiang, D.M.et al (2003). Context dependent viseme models for voice driven animation. *4th EURASIP Conference focused on Video/Image Processing and Multimedia Communications, EC-VIP-MC 2003*, Vol.2 (2003), pp. 649-654, Zagreb, Croatia, July, 2003.

Young, S.J.; Kershaw, D.; Odell, J. & Woodland, P. (2006). The HTK Book (for HTK Version 3.4). http://htk.eng.cam.ac.uk/docs/docs.shtml.

Zhang, Y.; Diao, Q., & Huang, S. et al (2003). DBN based multi-stream models for speech. *Proc. IEEE Int. Conf. Acoustics, Speech, and Signal Processing*, pp. 836–839, Hong Kong, China, Apr. 2003.

Zhou, Y.; Gu, L. & Zhang, H.J. (2003). Bayesian tangent shape model: Estimating shape and pose parameters via bayesian inference. *Proceedings of the IEEE Conference on Computer Vision and Pattern Recognition(CVPR2003)*. Vol. 1. pp. 109-118, 2003.

Zweig, G. (1998). *Speech recognition with dynamic Bayesian networks*, Ph.D. dissertation, Univ. California, Berkeley,1998.

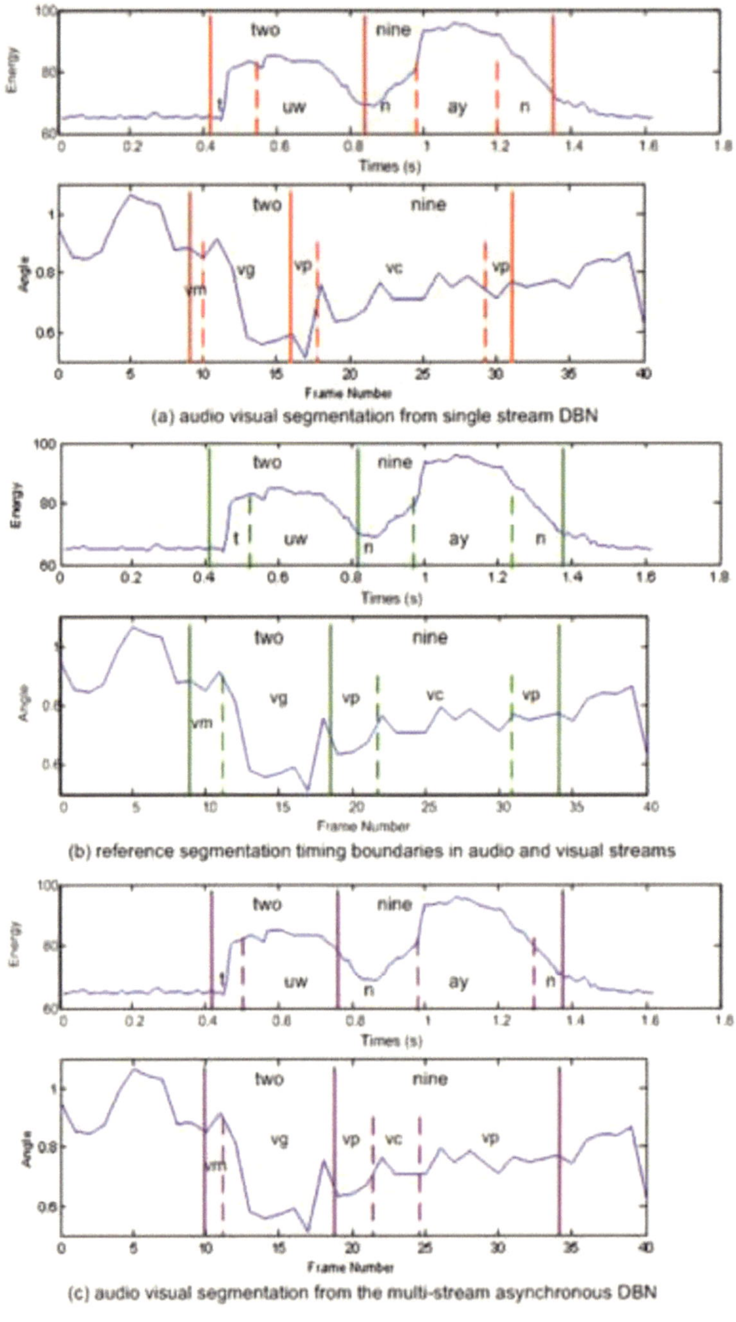

Figure 8. Audio visual asynchronous phone/viseme segmentation results

10

Discrete-Mixture HMMs-based Approach for Noisy Speech Recognition

Tetsuo Kosaka, Masaharu Katoh and Masaki Kohda
Yamagata University
Japan

1. Introduction

It is well known that the application of hidden Markov models (HMMs) has led to a dramatic increase of the performance of automatic speech recognition in the 1980s and from that time onwards. In particular, large vocabulary continuous speech recognition (LVCSR) could be realized by using a recognition unit such as phones. A variety of speech characteristics can be modelled by using HMMs effectively. The HMM represents the transition of statistical characteristics by using the state sequence of a Markov chain. Each state of the chain is composed by either a discrete output probability or a continuous output probability distribution. In 1980s, discrete HMM was mainly used as an acoustic model of speech recognition. The SPHINX speech recognition system was developed by K.-F. Lee in the late 1980s (Lee & Hon, 1988). The system was a speaker-independent, continuous speech recognition system based on discrete HMMs. It was evaluated on the 997-word resource management task and obtained a word accuracy of 93% with a bigram language model. After that, comparative investigation between discrete HMM and continuous HMM had been made and then it was concluded that the performance of continuous-mixture HMM overcame that of discrete HMM. Then almost all of recent speech recognition systems use continuous-mixture HMMs (CHMMs) as acoustic models.

The parameters of CHMMs can be estimated efficiently under assumption of normal distribution. Meanwhile, the discrete Hidden Markov Models (DHMMs) based on vector quantization (VQ) have a problem that they are effected by quantization distortion. However, CHMMs may unfit to recognize noisy speech because of false assumption of normal distribution. The DHMMs can represent more complicated shapes and they are expected to be useful for noisy speech.

This chapter introduces new methods of noise robust speech recognition using discrete-mixture HMMs (DMHMMs) based on maximum *a posteriori* (MAP) estimation. The aim of this work is to develop robust speech recognition for adverse conditions which contain both stationary and non-stationary noise. Especially, we focus on the issue of impulsive noise which is a major problem in practical speech recognition system.

DMHMM is one type of DHMM frameworks. The method of DMHMM was originally proposed to reduce computation costs in decoding process (Takahashi et al., 1997).

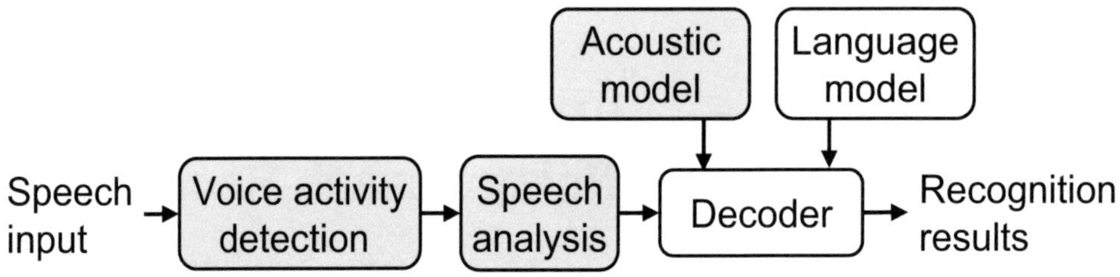

Figure 1. Block diagram of speech recognition system

DMHMM has more advantages of recognition performance than original DHMM. Nevertheless, the performance of DMHMM was lower than that of CHMM. In our work, we propose some new methods to improve the performance of DMHMM and demonstrate that the performance of DMHMM overcome that of CHMM in noisy conditions. We describe the characteristics of DMHMM and indicate the effectiveness and impact of the DMHMM for noisy speech recognition.

2. Noise Robust Speech Recognition

2.1 Basic approach of speech recognition under noisy conditions

Many efforts have been made for the issue of noise robust speech recognition over the years. For example, Parallel Model Combination (PMC) (Gales & Young, 1993), and Spectral Subtraction (SS) (Boll, 1979) are well known as effective methods of noisy speech recognition. And many other methods of noise robust speech recognition have been proposed. They are organized by some category. Fig. 1 is the block diagram of speech recognition system. Here, categorized methods of noise robust recognition are explained by using this figure. The noise robust methods can be roughly categorized into three groups: voice activity detection (VAD), speech analysis and acoustic modeling.

First, input speech is processed in voice activity detector. In this module, the presence or absence of speech is determined in noisy environment. If the speech detection fails, it is difficult to recognize input speech accurately. In recent years, the investigation on noise robust VAD has become active.

After a speech segment is detected, the speech signal is analyzed to extract the useful information for speech recognition. A cepstral analysis is a popular method for feature extraction in speech recognition. In particular, mel-scale frequency cepstrum coefficients (MFCC) are widely used as speech parameter in recent speech recognition system. Some noise reduction algorithms have been proposed to remove noise in speech waveform. The spectral subtraction method we mentioned above is one of those algorithms. One of the working groups in the European Telecommunication Standards Institute has approved the front-end (feature extraction module) for distributed speech recognition (ETSI, 2002). In this front-end, a noise reduction algorithm based on Wiener filter theory is employed. It is well known that this front-end is effective for various kinds of noise conditions and it is used as the baseline of the evaluation of proposed noise robust technique. Some new feature

extraction methods have been also proposed. Relative-Spectral Perceptual linear prediction (RASTA-PLP) method is one of the extraction methods and was reported that it was effective for noisy speech recognition (Hermansky et al., 1992).
Analysed speech is recognized in decoding process. In the decoder, a search algorithm is carried out with acoustic and language models. Those acoustic models are basically trained by clean data in which training utterances are recorded in quiet condition. However, models trained in clean condition cause a mismatch between models and input features in noisy condition. In order to eliminate it, many methods have been proposed. Multi-condition training is direct way to eliminate the mismatch condition (Pearce & Hirsch, 2000). In this training method, several types of noises are artificially added to the 'clean speech' data at several SNRs. The obtained noisy data were used for creating acoustic models. It was reported that this training method was effective, even if the noise conditions between training data and test data were different. Parallel Model Combination we mentioned above is also the one of the effective methods in this category. In this method, noisy speech model can be derived by combining the noise model and the clean speech model. Due to the assumption that the speech signal is affected by the additive noise in the linear spectral domain, cepstral parameters of the models are transformed to liner spectral domain for the combination. After the model combination, combined parameters are re-transformed to cepstral domain again.

2.2 Problem to be solved in this work

We categorized the previous works in the field of noise robust speech recognition and introduced some proposed methods in section 2.1. All the three approaches are important and many methods have been proposed. Most of these researches are, however, focused on stationary noise in which spectrum of noise signal is stationary in time domain. In contrast, speech recognition in non-stationary noise environments remains as a major problem. In practical speech recognition systems, the speech signals can be corrupted by transient noises created by tongue clicking, phone rings, door slams, or other environmental sources. These noises have a large variety of spectral features, onset time and amplitude, and a modeling of those features is difficult. Here, we call them 'impulsive noise'. The aim of this work is to develop robust speech recognition technology for adverse conditions which contain both stationary and non-stationary noise. In particular, we focus on the issue of impulsive noise.

2.3 Two types of approaches for noisy speech recognition

In order to solve the problem as shown in Section 2.2, we employ DMHMM as acoustic model. While three approaches are introduced in Fig. 1, the proposed method is categorized into the model-based approach. For model-based approach of robust speech recognition, we propose two different strategies.
In the first strategy, adverse conditions are represented by acoustic model. In this case, a large amount of training data and accurate acoustic models are required to present a variety of acoustic environments. This strategy is suitable for recognition in stationary or slow-varying noise conditions, because modeling of stationary noise is easier than that of non-stationary noise. In recent years, large speech corpora which contain much amount of training data are available. For ASR in stationary or slow-varying noise conditions, the effectiveness of multi-condition training has been reported (Pearce & Hirsch, 2000). For the

multi-condition training, a scheme of accurate modeling is needed because a large amount of noisy data created artificially is available.
In contrast, such training method is inadequate to recognize speech under impulsive noise. As mentioned above, impulsive noise has a large variety of features. However hard you may try to collect speech data in impulsive noise conditions, accurate modeling is very difficult. Then the second strategy is based on the idea that the corrupted frames are either neglected or treated carefully to reduce the adverse effect.
In order to achieve robust speech recognition in both stationary and impulsive noise conditions, we employ both strategies in this work. The concrete methods to realize both strategies are described in the next section. They are based on DMHMM framework which is one type of discrete HMM (DHMM). The method of DMHMM was originally proposed to reduce computation costs in decoding process. Two types of DMHMM systems have been proposed in recent years. One is subvector based quantization (Tsakalidis et al., 1999) and the other is scalar based quantization (Takahashi et al., 1997). In the former method, feature vectors are partitioned into subvectors, and then the subvectors are quantized by using separate codebooks. In the latter, each dimension of feature vectors is scalar-quantized. The quantization size can be reduced largely by partitioning feature vectors. For example, quantization size was reported as 2 to 5 bits in the former, and in the latter method, it was 4 to 6 bits. Because the quantization size is small, the DMHMM system has superior trainability in acoustic modeling.

2.4 MAP estimation and model compensation in DMHMM approach

As we mentioned in the previous sub-section, two kinds of strategies are employed to achieve robust speech recognition in both stationary and non-stationary noise conditions. In order to realize the first strategy, we propose a new modeling scheme of DMHMMs based on maximum *a posteriori* (MAP) estimate. For the second strategy, a method of compensating the observation probabilities of DMHMMs is proposed.
First, a new method of the MAP estimated DMHMMs for the first strategy is described below. In recent speech recognition systems, continuous-mixture HMMs (CHMMs) are generally used as acoustic models. It is well known that the CHMM system has an advantage in recognition performance over discrete HMM system. The parameters of CHMMs can be estimated efficiently under assumption of Gaussian distribution. However, CHMMs may unfit to recognize noisy speech because of false assumption of Gaussian distribution.
Fig. 2 shows an example of the discrete probability in DMHMM estimated by the method which is described below. The xy-plane represents the cepstrum (c1- c2) space and the z-axis represents the probability. The estimation was performed on noisy speech. It is obviously found that the shape of the distribution is not similar to that of the Gaussian distribution. As just described, discrete HMM can represent more complicated shapes and they are expected to be useful for noisy speech.
Considering the use of DHMMs, the insufficient performance is the major problem. The main reason why DHMMs show worse performance than CHMMs is because the accuracy of quantization in DHMM is insufficient. There is a trade off between quantization size and trainability. It is well known that reduction of quantization size of DHMMs leads to increase of quantization distortions, conversely, increase of quantization size leads to a lack of training data and poor estimation of parameters. As described above, the DMHMMs require

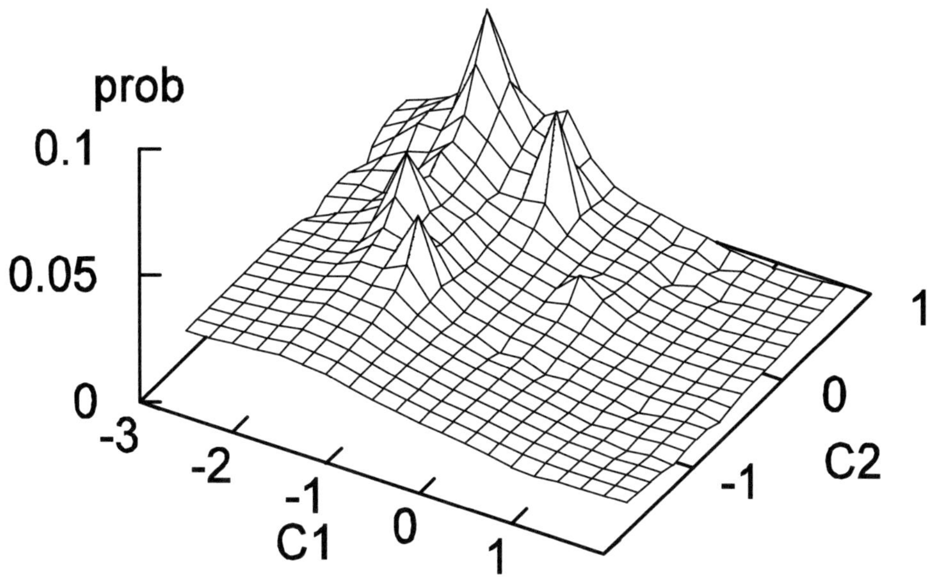

Figure 2. An example of discrete-mixture output distribution taken from the triphone 'a-a+a'.

a smaller amount of training data than ordinary discrete HMMs. Nevertheless, they still require larger amount of training data than CHMMs. In order to reduce the amount of training data and improve trainability further, we propose a new method for MAP estimation of DMHMM parameters. The MAP estimation is successfully used for adaptation of CHMM parameters (Lee & Gauvain, 1993). It uses information of an initial model as *a priori* knowledge to complement the training data.

In order to achieve the second strategy, we propose a method of compensating the observation probabilities of DMHMMs. Observation probabilities of impulsive noise tend to be much smaller than those of normal speech. The motivation in this approach is that flooring the observation probability reduces the adverse effect caused by impulsive noise. The method is based on missing feature theory (MFT) (Cooke et al., 1997) to reduce the effect of impulsive noise, so that the decoding process may become insensitive to distortions. In the MFT framework, input frames are partitioned into two disjoint parts, one having reliable frames and the other having unreliable frames which are corrupted by noise. Two different approaches are explored in the MFT framework: marginalization and imputation. In the marginalization approach, unreliable data are either ignored or treated carefully. The motivation of this approach is that unreliable components carry no information or even wrong information. In the imputation approach, values for the unreliable regions are estimated by knowledge of the reliable regions. The proposed compensation method is based on the first approach. Applying the MFT framework to speech recognition, it is difficult to determine reliable and unreliable regions. The proposed method does not require any determination of two regions in advance.

3. MAP Estimation of DMHMM Parameters

3.1 Discrete-Mixture HMMs

Before explaining MAP estimation of DMHMM parameters, the DMHMM proposed by Tskalidis (Tsakalidis et al., 1999) is briefly introduced here. As mentioned in Section 2, there are two types of DMHMM systems. In this paper, subvector based DMHMMs are employed. The feature vector is partitioned into S subvectors, $\boldsymbol{o}_t = [\boldsymbol{o}_{1t}, \cdots, \boldsymbol{o}_{st}, \cdots, \boldsymbol{o}_{St}]$. VQ codebooks are provided for each subvector, and then the feature vector $\boldsymbol{o}_t$ is quantized as follows:

$$q(\boldsymbol{o}_t) = [q_1(\boldsymbol{o}_{1t}), \cdots, q_s(\boldsymbol{o}_{st}), \cdots, q_S(\boldsymbol{o}_{St})]. \tag{1}$$

where $q_s(\boldsymbol{o}_{st})$ is the discrete symbol for the s-th subvector. The output distribution of DMHMM $b_i(\boldsymbol{o}_t)$ is given by:

$$b_i(\boldsymbol{o}_t) = \sum_m w_{im} \prod_s \hat{p}_{sim}(q_s(\boldsymbol{o}_{st})) \tag{2}$$

$$\sum_m w_{im} = 1.0 \tag{3}$$

where w_{im} is the mixture coefficient for the m-th mixture in state i, and $\hat{p}_{sim}$ is the probability of the discrete symbol for the s-th subvector. In this equation, it is assumed that the different subvectors are conditionally independent in the given state and mixture index.

3.2 MAP Estimation

For creating HMMs from training data, maximum likelihood (ML) estimation is generally used as a parameter estimation method. MAP estimation is successfully used for adaptation of CHMM parameters (Lee & Gauvain, 1993). MAP estimation uses information from an initial model as *a priori* knowledge to complement the training data. This *a priori* knowledge is statistically combined with *a posteriori* knowledge derived from the training data. When the amount of training data is small, the estimates are tightly constrained by the *a priori* knowledge, and the estimation error is reduced. On the other hand, the availability of a large amount of training data decreases the constraints of the *a priori* knowledge, thus preventing loss of the *a posteriori* knowledge. Accordingly, MAP estimation tends to achieve better performance than ML estimation, if the amount of training data is small. The amount of training data tends to lack of the parameter estimation of DMHMMs, because the number of parameters in DMHMMs is larger than that in CHMMs.

In order to improve trainability further, we propose an estimation method of DMHMM parameters based on MAP. The ML estimate of discrete probability $p_{sim}(k)$ is calculated in the following form:

$$p_{sim}(k) = \frac{\sum_{t=1}^{T} \gamma_{imt} \delta(q_s(\boldsymbol{o}_{st}), k)}{\sum_{t=1}^{T} \gamma_{imt}} \tag{4}$$

$$\delta(q_s(\boldsymbol{o}_{st}), k) = \begin{cases} 1 & \text{if} \quad q_s(\boldsymbol{o}_{st}) = k \\ 0 & \text{otherwise} \end{cases} \tag{5}$$

where k is the index of subvector codebook and γ_{imt} is the probability of being in state i at time t with the m-th mixture component. Assume that the prior distribution is represented by Dirichlet distribution. The MAP estimate of DMHMM $\hat{p}_{sim}(k)$ is given by:

$$\hat{p}_{sim}(k) = \frac{(v_{simk} - 1) + n_{im} \cdot p_{sim}(k)}{\sum_{k=1}^{K} (v_{simk} - 1) + n_{im}} \tag{6}$$

where v_{simk} is the parameter of the prior distribution. And n_{im} is given as follows:

$$n_{im} = \sum_{t=1}^{T} \gamma_{imt} \tag{7}$$

In order to simplify the calculation, some constraints were added on the prior parameters. Assume that v_{simk} is given by:

$$v_{simk} = \tau \cdot p_{sim}^{0}(k) + 1 \tag{8}$$

$$\sum_{k=1}^{K} p_{sim}^{0}(k) = 1 \tag{9}$$

where $p_{sim}^{0}(k)$ is the constrained prior parameter. Applying Eq. (8) to Eq. (6), the MAP estimate $\hat{p}_{sim}(k)$ can be calculated by:

$$\hat{p}_{sim}(k) = \frac{\tau \cdot p_{sim}^{0}(k) + n_{im} \cdot p_{sim}(k)}{\tau + n_{im}} \tag{10}$$

where τ indicates the relative balance between the corresponding prior parameter and the observed data. In our experiments, τ was set to 10.0. Although both mixture coefficient and transition probability can be estimated by MAP, only output probability is estimated by MAP in this work.

3.3 Prior Distribution

The specification of the parameters of prior distributions is one of the key issues of MAP estimation. In this work, it is assumed that the prior distributions can be represented by models which are converted from CHMMs to DMHMMs. The conversion method is described below.

First, input vector $\boldsymbol{o}_t$ is divided into S subvectors, $\boldsymbol{o}_t = [o_{1t}, \cdots, o_{st}, \cdots, o_{St}]$. The probability density of CHMMs in subvector s, state i and the m-th mixture component is given by:

$$b'_{sim}(\boldsymbol{o}_{st}) = \frac{1}{(2\pi)^{\frac{d}{2}} |\boldsymbol{\Sigma}_{sim}|^{\frac{1}{2}}} \cdot \exp\left[-\frac{1}{2} (\boldsymbol{o}_{st} - \boldsymbol{\mu}_{sim})' \boldsymbol{\Sigma}_{sim}^{-1} (\boldsymbol{o}_{st} - \boldsymbol{\mu}_{sim}) \right] \tag{11}$$

where $\boldsymbol{\mu}_{sim}$ is mean vector, $\boldsymbol{\Sigma}_{sim}$ is covariance matrix and d is the number of dimension for subvector s. In the case of $d = 2$, $\boldsymbol{o}_{st}$, $\boldsymbol{\mu}_{sim}$ and $\boldsymbol{\Sigma}_{sim}$ are given by:

$$\boldsymbol{o}_{st} = \begin{bmatrix} o_{s_1 t} \\ o_{s_2 t} \end{bmatrix} \tag{12}$$

$$\boldsymbol{\mu}_{sim} = \begin{bmatrix} \mu_{s_1 im} \\ \mu_{s_2 im} \end{bmatrix} \tag{13}$$

$$\boldsymbol{\Sigma}_{sim} = \begin{bmatrix} \sigma^2_{s_1 im} & 0 \\ 0 & \sigma^2_{s_2 im} \end{bmatrix} \tag{14}$$

where s_1 and s_2 represent 1st and 2nd dimensions respectively. An output probability $b_i^{'}(\boldsymbol{o}_t)$ is calculated by:

$$b_i^{'}(\boldsymbol{o}_t) = \sum_m w_{im}^{'} \prod_s b_{sim}^{'}(\boldsymbol{o}_{st}) \tag{15}$$

where $w_{im}^{'}$ is the weighting coefficient of mixture component m. In order to obtain discrete parameters, the probability density for each centroid is calculated and normalized. As a result, parameters of the prior distribution $p_{sim}^{0}(k)$ are solved by:

$$p_{sim}^{0}(k) = \frac{b_{sim}^{'}(\boldsymbol{v}_s(k))}{\sum_k b_{sim}^{'}(\boldsymbol{v}_s(k))} \tag{16}$$

where $\boldsymbol{v}_s(k)$ is the centroid for each subvector s. While $p_{sim}^{0}(k)$ has a constraint of a normal distribution, $\hat{p}_{sim}(k)$ in Eq. (10) does not have such constraint. Thus it is expected that $\hat{p}_{sim}(k)$ will be updated to represent more complicated shapes in training session.

Some experimental results on MAP estimation are shown in Table 1 where word error rates (WERs) are indicated. 'DMHMM-ML' means ML estimated DMHMM and 'DMHMM-MAP' means MAP estimated DMHMM. MAP and ML estimation methods were compared at $SNR = \infty$ dB and $SNR = 5$ dB. The maximum number of training samples is 15,732. It is apparent that the performance of MAP is superior to that of ML. Then it can be concluded that the trainability of DMHMMs is improved by using MAP estimation.

SNR	model\number of samples	1000	5000	10000	15732
∞ dB	DMHMM-ML	100.0	54.66	27.54	18.63
	DMHMM-MAP	22.26	13.56	11.18	9.42
5dB	DMHMM-ML	99.0	45.01	31.99	29.45
	DMHMM-MAP	58.26	36.31	30.82	27.92

Table 1. Word error rate (%) results of the comparison between ML and MAP

4. Compensation of Discrete Distributions

In this section, a method of compensating the observation probabilities of DMHMMs is described to achieve robust speech recognition in noisy conditions. In particular, this method is effective for impulsive noise. The proposed method is based on the idea that the corrupted frames are either neglected or treated carefully to reduce the adverse effect. In other words, the decoding process becomes insensitive to distortions in the method. It is more likely that significant degradation of output probability appears in the case of mismatch conditions caused by unknown noise. Since the effect of impulsive noise is not considered in model training process, it is treated as unknown noise. If one of the subvector probabilities, $\hat{p}_{sim}(q_s(\boldsymbol{o}_{st}))$, is close to 0 in Eq. (2), the value of output probability, $b_i(\boldsymbol{o}_t)$, is also close to 0. It causes adverse effects in decoding process, even if the length of noise segment is short. Since an acoustic outlier such as impulsive noise is just unknown signal for acoustic model, difference in log likelihoods between outliers doesn't make sense for speech recognition. However, small difference between features of outliers causes large difference between log likelihoods, and it leads to changing the order of hypothesis in some situations.

In the proposed method, flooring the observation probability by threshold is employed. Since no difference in log likelihoods between outliers is shown in this method, it can reduce a negative effect in decoding process. Suppose that unreliable part can be found by using the value of discrete probability. In the proposed method, threshold for discrete probability is set, and negative effect is reduced in decoding process. Especially the method is effective for short duration noise. It is expected that pruning the correct candidate caused by impulsive noise is avoided.

For CHMM system, some compensation methods have been proposed with the same motivation. For example, Veth et al. proposed acoustic backing-off (Veth et al., 2001) where unreliable information is either neglected or treated carefully. Also the similar method was proposed in (Yamamoto et al., 2002). In those methods, the Gaussian distribution was compensated by threshold value. In our method, threshold can be set directly by value of probability. In other words, each threshold is given in the same way based on a probabilistic criterion. In contrast, it requires a kind of complicated way in CHMM system, because observation probabilities are given by probability density functions.

In the method proposed by Yamamoto (Yamamoto et al., 2002), single threshold was given for all Gussian distributions. In this case, since each shape of distribution is different, magnitude of the effect of threshold is also different. In the acoustic backing-off method, compensation values are different in each distribution. However, the compensation values depend on training data in the method. Comparison experiments with the acoustic backing-off are shown in Section 5.8.

Three types of compensation processing are proposed as follows:

Compensation at subvector level

A compensation is done at subvector level. In Eq. (2), $\hat{p}_{sim}(q_s(\boldsymbol{o}_{st}))$ is compensated by the threshold for subvector, *dth*.

$$\hat{p}'_{sim}(q_s(\boldsymbol{o}_{st})) = \begin{cases} \hat{p}_{sim}(q_s(\boldsymbol{o}_{st})) & if \;\; \hat{p}_{sim}(q_s(\boldsymbol{o}_{st})) \geq dth \\ dth & otherwise \end{cases} \tag{17}$$

where $\hat{p}'_{sim}(q_s(\boldsymbol{o}_{st}))$ is the compensated discrete probability of $\boldsymbol{o}_{st}$. This threshold is especially effective in the case that specific subvector is corrupted.

Compensation at mixture level

A compensation is done at mixture level. In Eq. (2), $\prod_s \hat{p}_{sim}(q_s(\boldsymbol{o}_{st}))$ is compensated by the threshold for mixture component, *mth*.

$$\prod_s \hat{p}'_{sim}(q_s(\boldsymbol{o}_{st})) = \begin{cases} \prod_s \hat{p}_{sim}(q_s(\boldsymbol{o}_{st})) & \textit{if } \prod_s \hat{p}_{sim}(q_s(\boldsymbol{o}_{st})) \geq mth \\ mth & \textit{otherwise} \end{cases} \tag{18}$$

where $\prod_s \hat{p}'_{sim}(q_s(\boldsymbol{o}_{st}))$ is the compensated discrete probability of $\boldsymbol{o}_{st}$ at mixture level. This threshold is useful in the case that corruption affects a wide range of subvectors.

Compensation at both levels

Effectiveness of the above compensation methods depends on noise types. Thus, a combination of both compensation methods is expected to be effective for various types of noises.

Three types of compensation methods were compared in noisy speech recognition. The result of comparison in average error rate reduction among three was mixture level < subvector level < combination at both levels, and the reduction rate was 30.1%, 48.2% and 48.5%, respectively. The combination method obtained the best performance. From the viewpoint of the calculation cost, however, the compensation at subvector is not bad because the performance is similar. In the subvector method, the best performance can be obtained by the threshold from 2.0×10^{-3} to 5.0×10^{-3}. In the case that threshold is set to 5.0×10^{-3}, 68.6% of probability values in discrete distributions are floored. It turns out that a large proportion of probability values are useless for speech recognition.

5. Overview of Speech Recognition System Using DMHMMs

5.1 System Configuration

An experimental system of speech recognition for the study of DMHMMs has been developed. In this section, we describe the overview of the system. The recognition system makes use of a statistical speech recognition approach that uses DMHMM as the acoustic model and statistical language models such as word bigrams. This type of recognition system is called a large vocabulary continuous speech recognition (LVCSR) system. It can recognize more than several thousands of different words. Fig. 3 shows a block diagram of the system. It employs a time-synchronous beam search. The recognition results indicated in the previous sessions were obtained by this system.

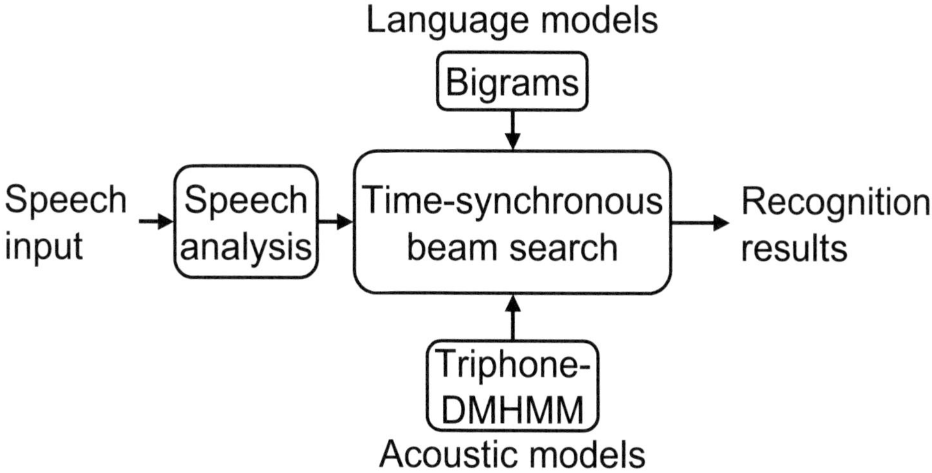

Figure 3. Speech recognition system

5.2 Speech Analysis

In the speech analysis module, a speech signal is digitized at a sampling frequency of 16kHz and at a quantization size of 16bits with the Hamming window. The length of the analysis frame is 32ms and the frame period is set to 8ms. The 13-dimensional feature (12-dimensional MFCC and log power) is derived from the digitized samples for each frame. Additionally, the delta and delta-delta features are calculated from MFCC feature and log power. Then the total number of dimensions is 39. The 39-dimentional parameters are normalized by the cepstral mean normalization (CMN) method (Furui, 1974) which can reduce the adverse effect of channel distortion.

5.3 Decoder

For a large vocabulary continuous speech recognition (LVCSR), search space is very large and an expensive computation cost is required. A language model, which represents linguistic knowledge, is used to reduce search space. The detail of the language model is described in the next sub-section. In our system, one-pass frame-synchronous search algorithm with beam searching has been adopted. The searching algorithm calculates acoustic and language likelihood to obtain word sequence candidates. These word sequence candidates are pruned according to their likelihood values to reduce the calculation cost. Triphone models and word bigrams are used as acoustic and language models, respectively.

5.4 Language Model

A bigram is an occurrence probability of a pair of words that directly follow each other in text and is used as a linguistic constraint to reduce a calculation cost and improve recognition performance. The set of the probabilities are calculated with a large amount of text data. In this system, the bigrams have a 5000-vocabulary and are trained from 45 months' worth of issues of the Mainichi newspaper. Those data are in the database of 'JNAS: Japanese Newspaper Article Sentences'. It contains speech recordings and their orthographic transcriptions. Text sets for reading were extracted from the articles of newspaper. The Mainichi Newspaper is one of the major nation-wide newspapers in Japan.

5.5 Acoustic Model

In recent years, context dependent models are widely used as acoustic models for speech recognition, since allophones or co-articulations can be modeled more accurately than context independent ones. Triphone model is one of the context dependent models and both the left and the right context are taken into consideration. It is well known that triphone is the effective model for continuous speech recognition. However, there is a problem when model parameters of triphone are estimated. The number of models exponentially increases depending on the number of contextual factors ant it causes the decrease of estimation accuracy. Then state sharing technique is widely used for context dependent models. In our system, shard-state triphone DMHMMs are uses as acoustic models. The topology of shard-state DMHMMs is represented by a hidden Markov network (HM-Net) which has been proposed by Takami (Takami & Sagayama, 1992). The HM-Net is a network efficiently representing context dependent left-to-right HMMs which have various state lengths and share their states each other. Each node of the network is corresponding to an HMM state and has following information:

- state number,
- acceptable context class,
- lists of preceding states and succeeding states,
- parameters of the output probability density distribution,
- state transition probabilities.

When the HM-Net is given, a model corresponding to a context can be derived by concatenating states which can accept the context from the starting node to the ending node.

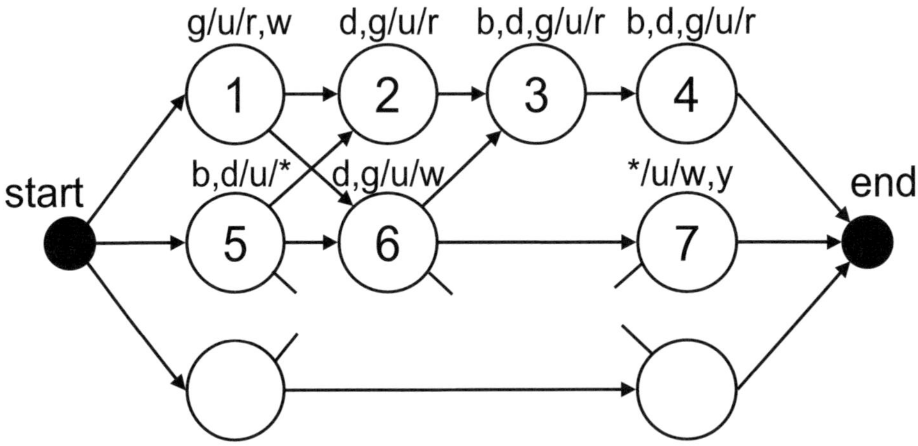

Figure 4. Example of the HM-Net

Fig. 4 shows an example of the HM-Net. In this figure, A/B/C stands for the acceptable context class, where A, B and C are the acceptable preceding, base and succeeding phone classes respectively. And the asterisk represents a class consisted of all phones. For example, the model for a context g/u/w is derived from a string of the states 1, 6 and 7. The extracted model is equivalent to general left-to-right HMMs. The structure of HM-Net we used in this work is determined by the state clustering-based method proposed by Hori (Hori et al., 1998). Although the output probability distribution of a HMM state is represented by Gaussian mixture density in original HM-Net, discrete mixture density is used in this system. The acoustic model we used is 2000-state HM-Net, and the number of mixture components was 4, 8 and 16, respectively. The 2000-state continuous mixture HM-Net is also prepared, and it is used for comparative experiments. As a comparative experiments in various number of mixture components, 16-mixture HM-Net shows the best result with either DMHMMs or CHMMs.

5.6 Codebook design of DMHMM

The codebook design in our experiments was determined in reference to the results in the paper written by Tsakalidis (Tsakalidis et al., 1999) and the split vector quantizer in the DSR front-end (ETSI, 2002). Tsakalidis has reported that DMHMMs with from 9 to 24 subvectors showed better performance. The feature vector is partitioned into subvectors that contain two consecutive coefficients. The consecutive coefficients that comprise subvector are expected to be correlated more closely. It was also reported that subvectors that contained consecutive coefficients performed well. Table 2 shows subvector allocation and codebook size. In the table, although delta and delta-delta parameters are omitted, those codebooks are designed in the same manner. The total number of codebooks is 21. The LBG algorithm was utilized for creating the codebook. Two types of codebooks were generated: 1) Clean codebook: A codebook derived from clean data. 2) Noisy codebook: A codebook derived from multi-condition data. Fig. 5 shows the examples of two codebooks. One represents c1-c2 plane, and the other is $\Delta c1 - \Delta c2$ plane. Each point represents the codebook centroid and its number is 64 on c1-c2 or $\Delta c1 - \Delta c2$ plane. Both clean codebook and noisy codebook are shown. As the experiment results, the performance of the DHMMs with noisy codebooks overcame that with clean codebooks for noisy speech recognition.

5.7 Training Data for Acoustic modeling

There are two sets of training data. They are on JNAS database. One is used for clean training, and the other is used for multi-condition training. The training data set consists of 15,732 Japanese sentences uttered by 102 male speakers. For clean training, no noise was added to the data. For multi-condition training, those utterances were divided into 20 subsets. No noise was added to 4 subsets. In the rest of the data, noise was artificially added.

parameter	logP, c0	c1,c2	c3,c4	c5,c6	c7,c8	c9,c10	c11,c12
codebook size	256	64	64	64	64	64	64

Table 2. Codebook design

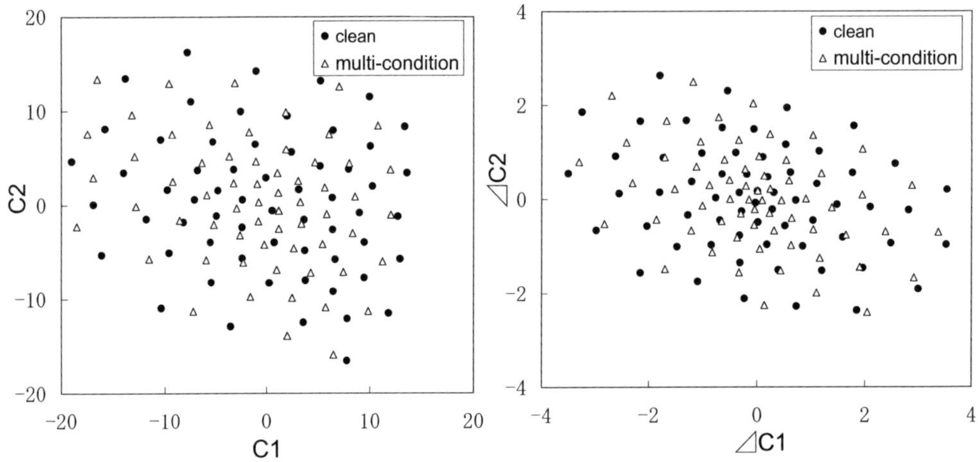

Figure 5. Examples of the codebooks (left figure: $c1-c2$ plane, right figure: $\Delta c1-\Delta c2$ plane)

Four types of noise (train, crowd, car and exhibition hall) were selected, and those were added to the utterances at SNRs of 20, 15, 10 and 5dB. The set of clean training data was used for parameter estimation of initial CHMMs and also used for clean codebook creation. The set of multi-condition training data was used for parameter re-estimation of both CHMMs and DMHMMs, and that was also used for creation of noisy codebook.

The procedures of acoustic model training are described as follows: First, initial CHMMs were trained by using clean speech data. Then the CHMMs were converted into DMHMMs using Eq. (16). The parameters of the DMHMMs derived here were used as the prior parameters of MAP estimation. After that, MAP estimation of DMHMMs was carried out by using multi-condition data.

5.8 Comparative experiments with other methods

Comparative experiments with other methods were conducted in adverse conditions that contain both stationary and impulsive noises. Noise signals from two test sets were mixed artificially to make new testset. Twelve types of noises (4 noise types (train, crowd, car and exhibition hall) times 3 SNR conditions) were prepared as stationary or slow-varying noise. These noises were mixed with 3 impulsive noises which were selected from RWCP database (Nakamura et al., 2000). Thus 36 types of noises were used for evaluation. Three types of impulsive noise were as follows:

- whistle3 blowing a whistle
- claps1 handclaps
- bank hitting a coin bank

The impulsive noises were added at intervals of 1-sec into speech data at SNR of 0 dB.

In the experiments, DMHMMs were compared with conventional CHMMs and CHMMs with acoustic backing-off method which is introduced in Section 4. As we described in the previous section, the compensation of discrete distributions is effective for noisy speech recognition. The acoustic backing-off is a similar method for CHMMs. In this method, likelihood is calculated by using robust mixture distribution which consists of distribution $p(y)$ and 'outlier' distribution $p_o(y)$. Log likelihood $\log(p_{ab}(y))$ is given by

$$\log(p_{ab}(y)) = \log\{(1-\varepsilon)p(y) + \varepsilon \cdot p_o(y)\} \tag{19}$$

$$p_o(y) = (R_{\max} - R_{\min})^{-1} \tag{20}$$

where ε is the backing-off parameter, $R_{\max}$ and $R_{\min}$ are the maximum and minimum values for each component as observed in the training data.

Comparative experiments between acoustic backing-off and the proposed method were carried out. In the paper by Veth (Veth et al., 2001), $R_{\max}$ and $R_{\min}$ are given the maximum and minimum values of training data respectively. To avoid the dependence on training data, $R_{\max}$ and $R_{\min}$ are set to

$$R_{\max} = \mu + r \cdot \sigma^2 \tag{21}$$

and

$$R_{\min} = \mu - r \cdot \sigma^2 \tag{22}$$

where σ^2 is a variance of training data. Both r and ε were varied to find the best performance. As a result, r and ε were set to 3.0 and 5.0×10^{-5}, respectively.

The results of the comparison among DMHMMs, CHMMs and CHMMs with the acoustic backing-off are shown in Table 3. The threshold value of compensation for subvector and mixture component were set to 5.0×10^{-3} and 1.0×10^{-40}, respectively.

The proposed method shows the best performance among three methods. In the table, 'improvement' means the average error rate reduction from CHMM. It was 28.1% with the proposed method. In contrast, it was only 5.5% with the acoustic backing-off method. For DMHMMs, various thresholds for subvector were applied. The best performance was obtained by the threshold of 2.0×10^{-3}. More detailed results can be shown in the paper by Kosaka (Kosaka et al., 2005).

The results of CHMMs were too bad. It has been generally believed that the recognition error rates of DHMM were much higher than those of CHMM until now. Our experiments showed that the DMHMM framework performed better than conventional CHMM in noisy condition. In contrast, it was found that CHMM system showed similar or even better performance at high SNR in our experiments. In clean condition, the WER of DMHMMs was 6.7% and that of CHMMs with the acoustic backing-off was 6.6%. Recognition in clean conditions remains as an issue to be solved in the DMHMM system.

6. Conclusions

This chapter introduced a new method of robust speech recognition using discrete-mixture HMMs (DMHMMs) based on maximum *a posteriori* (MAP) estimation. The aim of this work was to develop robust speech recognition for adverse conditions which contain both stationary and non-stationary noise. In order to achieve the goal, we proposed two methods.

First, an estimation method of DMHMM parameters based on MAP was proposed. The second was a method of compensating the observation probabilities of DMHMMs to reduce adverse effect of outlier values. Experimental evaluations were done on Japanese speech recognition for read newspaper task. Compared with conventional CHMMs and CHMMs using the acoustic backing-off method, MAP estimated DMHMMs performed better in noisy conditions than those systems. The average error rate reduction from CHMMs was 28.1% with the proposed method. It has been generally believed that the recognition error rates of DHMM were much higher than those of CHMM until now. However, our experiments showed that the DMHMM framework performed better in noisy conditions than conventional CHMM framework.

method\noise		WER(%)			improvement(%)
		whistle3	claps1	bank	
CHMM		65.9	43.9	37.5	-
CHMM-AB		65.2	39.5	36.8	5.5
DMHMM	5.0×10^{-4}	51.5	34.9	31.2	22.7
	2.0×10^{-3}	46.8	32.9	30.5	28.1
	5.0×10^{-3}	46.5	35.2	31.2	24.7

Table 3. The WER results of the comparison among three methods in mixed noise conditions

Although, the proposed method is effective in noisy conditions, its performance is insufficient in clean conditions. What we are aiming for as a future work is to improve trainability and recognition performance in clean conditions further.

7. Future prospects

We are now conducting the evaluation of the method on more difficult task. In Japan, a large-scale spontaneous speech database 'Corpus of Spontaneous Japanese (CSJ)" has been used as the common evaluation database for spontaneous speech now (Furui et al., 2005). This corpus consists of roughly 7M words with a total speech length of 650 h. In the corpus, monologues such as academic presentations and extemporaneous presentations have been recorded. The recordings were carried out by a headset microphone with relatively little background noise. It is well known that the recognition of this task is too difficult because those presentations are real and the spontaneity is high. For example, 25.3% of word error rate was reported by Furui (Furui et al., 2005). In our experiments, 20.72% of word error rate has been obtained with 6000-state 16-mixture DMHMMs and the trigram model of 47,099 word-pronunciation entries (Yamamoto et al., 2006). It shows that DMHMM system has a high performance even if in low noise conditions. The DMHMM-based system has much more potential for speech recognition, because it needs no assumption of Gaussian distribution. For example, model adaptation in which the shape of distribution of HMM is modified intricately cannot be carried out in CHMM framework, but could be done in DMHMM. We plan to develop DMHMM-related technologies further for improving speech recognition performance.

8. References

Boll, S. (1979), Suppression of acoustic noise in speech using spectral subtraction, *IEEE Trans. on Acoustics, Speech and Signal Processing,* Vol. ASSP-27, No. 2, Apr. 1979, pp.113-120

Cooke, M. P.; Morris, A. & Green, P. D. (1997), Missing data techniques for robust speech recognition, *Proceedings of ICASSP97,* pp.863-866, Munich, Germany, Apr. 1997, IEEE

ETSI, (2002), ETSI ES 202 050 V1.1.1, *STQ; Distributed speech recognition; advanced front-end feature extraction algorithm; compression algorithms,* European Telecommunications Standards Institute, France

Furui, S. (1974), Cepstral analysis technique for automatic speaker verification, *Journal of Acoustical Society of America,* Vol. 55, Jun. 1974, pp. 1204-1312

Furui, S.; Nakamura, M.; Ichiba, T. & Iwano, K. (2005), Analysis and recognition of spontaneous speech using corpus of spontaneous Japanese, *Speech Communication,* Vol. 47, Sept. 2005, pp. 208-219, ISSN 0167-6393

Gales, M & Young, S. (1993). HMM recognition in noise using parallel model combination, *Proceedings of Eurospeech 93,* pp. 837-840, Berlin, Germany, Sept. 1993, ESCA

Hermansky, H.; Morgan, N.; Baya, A. & Kohn, P. (1992), RASTA-PLP speech analysis technique", *Proceedings of ICASSP92,* pp. 121-124, Sam Francisco, USA, Mar. 1992, IEEE

Hori, T.; Katoh, M.; Ito, A. & Kohda M. (1998), A study on a state clustering-based topology design method for HM-Nets, *IEICE Transactions (Japanese),* Vol. J81-D-II, No. 10, Oct. 1998, pp. 2239-2248

Kosaka, T.; Katoh, M. & Kohda M. (2005), Robust speech recognition using discrete-mixture HMMs, *IEICE Transactions,* Vol. E88-D, No. 12, Dec. 2005, pp. 2811-2818

Lee, C.-H. & Gauvain, J.-L. (1993), Speaker adaptation based on MAP estimation of HMM parameters, *Proceedings of ICASSP93,* pp. 558-561, Minneapolis, USA, Apr. 1993, IEEE

Lee, K.-F. & Hon, H.-W. (1988), Large-vocabulary speaker-independent continuous speech recognition using HMM, *Proceedings of ICASSP88,* pp. 123-126, New York, USA, Apr. 1988, IEEE

Nakamura, S.; Hiyane, K.; Asano, F.; Nishimura, T. & Yamada, T. (2000), Acoustical sound database in real environments for sound scene understanding and hands-free speech recognition, *Proceedings of LREC2000,* pp. 965-968, Athens, Greece, May. 2000

Pearce, D & Hirsch, H.-G. (2000). The AURORA experimental framework for the performance evaluation of speech recognition systems under noisy conditions, *Proceedings of ICSLP2000,* Vol.4, pp.29-32, Beijing, China, Oct. 2000

Takahashi, S.; Aikawa K. & Sagayama S. (1997). Discrete mixture HMM, *Proceedings of ICASSP97,* pp.971-974, Munich, Germany, Apr. 1997, IEEE

Takami, J. & Sagayama S. (1992). A successive state splitting algorithm for efficient allophone modeling, *Proceedings of ICASSP92*, pp. 573-576, San Francisco, USA, Mar. 1992, IEEE

Tsakalidis, S.; Digalakis, V. & Newmeyer, L. (1999). Efficient speech recognition using subvector quantization and discrete-mixture HMMs, *Proceedings of ICASSP99*, pp.569-572, Phoenix, USA, Mar. 1999, IEEE

Veth, J.; Cranen, B. & Boves, L. (2001), Acoustic backing-off as an implementation of missing feature theory, *Speech Communication*, Vol. 34, No. 3, Jun. 2001, pp. 247-265, ISSN0167-6393

Yamamoto, A.; Kumakura, T.; Katoh, M.; Kosaka, T. & Kohda, M. (2006), Lecture speech recognition by using codebook adaptation of discrete-mixture HMMs, *Proceedings of ASJ Autumn Meeting (Japanese)*, pp. 69-70, Kanazawa, Japan, Sept. 2006, ASJ

Yamamoto, H.; Shinoda, K. & Sagayama, S. (2002), Compensated Gaussian distribution for robust speech recognition against non-stationary noise, *Technical Report of IEICE (Japanese)*, SP2002-45, pp.19-24, Sendai, Japan, Jun. 2002, IEICE

11

Speech Recognition in Unknown Noisy Conditions

Ji Ming[1] and Baochun Hou[2]
[1]*Queen's University Belfast*
[2]*University of Hertfordshire*
United Kingdom

1. Introduction

This chapter describes our recent advances in automatic speech recognition, with a focus on improving the robustness against environmental noise. In particular, we investigate a new approach for performing recognition using noisy speech samples without assuming prior information about the noise. The research is motivated in part by the increasing deployment of speech recognition technologies on handheld devices or the Internet. Due to the mobile nature of such systems, the acoustic environments and hence the noise sources can be highly time-varying and potentially unknown. This raises the requirement for noise robustness in the absence of information about the noise. Traditional approaches for noisy speech recognition include noise filtering or noise compensation. Noise filtering aims to remove the noise from the speech signal. Typical techniques include spectral subtraction (Boll, 1979), Wiener filtering (Macho et al., 2002) and RASTA filtering (Hermansky & Morgan, 1994), each assuming *a priori* knowledge of the noise spectra. Noise compensation aims to construct a new acoustic model to match the noisy environment thereby reducing the mismatch between the training and testing data. Typical approaches include parallel model combination (PMC) (Gales & Young, 1993), multicondition training (Lippmann et al., 1987; Pearce & Hirsch, 2000), and SPLICE (Deng et al., 2001). PMC composes a noisy acoustic model from a clean model by incorporating a statistical model of the noise; multicondition training constructs acoustic models suitable for a number of noisy environments through the use of training data from each of the environments; SPLICE improves noise robustness by assuming that stereo training data exist for estimating the corruption characteristics. More recent studies are focused on the approaches requiring less information about the noise, since this information can be difficult to obtain in mobile environments subject to time-varying, unpredictable noise. For example, recent studies on missing-feature theory suggest that, when knowledge of the noise is insufficient for cleaning up the speech features, one may alternatively ignore the severely corrupted features and focus the recognition only on the features with little or no contamination. This can effectively reduce the influence of noise while requiring less knowledge than usually needed for noise filtering or compensation (e.g., Lippmann & Carlson, 1997; Raj et al., 1998; Cooke et al., 2001; Ming et al., 2002). However, missing-feature theory is only effective given partial feature corruption, i.e., the noise only affects part of the speech representation and the remaining part not severely affected by noise can thus be exploited for recognition. This assumption is not realistic for many real-world applications in which the noise will affect all time-frequency components of the speech signal, i.e., we face a full feature corruption problem.

In this chapter, we investigate speech recognition in noisy environments assuming a highly unfavourable scenario: an accurate estimation of the nature and characteristics of the noise is difficult, if not impossible. As such, traditional techniques for noise removal or compensation, which usually assume a prior knowledge of the noise, become inapplicable. We describe a new noise compensation approach, namely *universal compensation*, as a solution to the problem. The new approach combines subband modeling, multicondition model training and missing-feature theory as a means of minimizing the requirement for the information of the noise, while allowing any corruption type, including full feature corruption, to be modelled. Subband features are used instead of conventional fullband features to isolate noisy frequency bands from usable frequency bands; multicondition training provides compensations for expected or generic noise; and missing-feature theory is applied to deal with the remaining training and testing mismatch, by ignoring the mismatched subbands from scoring.

The rest of the chapter is organized as follows. Section 2 introduces the universal compensation approach and the algorithms for incorporating the approach into a hidden Markov model for speech recognition. Section 3 describes experimental evaluation on the Aurora 2 and 3 tasks for speech recognition involving a variety of simulated and realistic noises, including new noise types not seen in the original databases. Section 4 presents a summary along with the on-going work for further developing the technique.

2. Universal Compensation

2.1 The model

Let Φ_0 denote the training data set, containing *clean* speech data, and let $p(X \mid s, \Phi_0)$ represent the likelihood function of frame feature vector X associated with speech state s trained on data set Φ_0. In this study, we assume that each frame vector X consists of N subband features: $X=(x_1, x_2, ..., x_N)$, where x_n represents the feature for the n'th subband. We obtain X by dividing the whole speech frequency-band into N subbands, and then calculating the feature coefficients for each subband independently of the other subbands. Two different methods have been used to create the subband features. The first method produces the subband MFCC (Mel-frequency cepstral coefficients), obtained by first grouping the Mel-warped filter bank uniformly into subbands, and then performing a separate DCT (discrete cosine transformation) within each subband to obtain the MFCC for that subband (Ming et al., 2002). It is assumed that the separation of the DCT among the subbands helps to prevent the effect of a band-limited noise from being spread over the entire feature vector, as usually occurs within the traditional fullband MFCC. The second method uses the decorrelated log filter-bank energies as the subband features, which are obtained by filtering the log filter-bank energies using a high-pass filter (Ming, 2006). The subband feature framework allows the isolation of noisy bands and selection of the optimal subbands for recognition, thereby improving the robustness against band-selective noise.

The universal compensation approach comprises two steps. The first step is to simulate the effect of noise corruption. This is done by adding noise into the clean training data Φ_0. We have primarily added white noise at variable signal-to-noise ratios (SNRs) to simulate the variation of noise, but different types of noises could be used depending on the expected environments. Assume that this leads to multiple training sets Φ_0, Φ_1, ..., Φ_K, where Φ_k denotes the k'th training set derived from Φ_0 with the addition of a specific level of corruption. Then a new likelihood function for the test frame vector can be formed by combining the likelihood functions trained on the individual training sets:

$$p(X \mid s) = \sum_{k=0}^{K} p(X \mid s, \Phi_k) P(\Phi_k \mid s) \tag{1}$$

where $p(X \mid s, \Phi_k)$ is the likelihood function of frame vector X associated with state s trained on data set Φ_k, and $P(\Phi_k \mid s)$ is the prior probability for the occurrence of the corruption condition Φ_k at state s. Eq. (1) is a multicondition model. A recognition system based on Eq. (1) should have improved robustness to the noise conditions seen in the training sets $\{\Phi_k\}$, as compared to a system based on $p(X \mid s, \Phi_0)$.

The second step of the approach is to make Eq. (1) robust to noise conditions not fully matched by the training sets $\{\Phi_k\}$ without assuming extra information about the noise. One way to achieve this is to ignore the heavily mismatched subbands and focus the score only on the matching subbands. Let $X=(x_1, x_2, ..., x_N)$ be a test frame vector and X_k be a specific subset of features in X which are corrupted at noise condition Φ_k. Then, using X_k in place of X as the test vector for each training noise condition Φ_k, Eq. (1) can be modified as

$$p(X \mid s) = \sum_{k=0}^{K} p(X_k \mid s, \Phi_k) P(\Phi_k \mid s) \tag{2}$$

where $p(X_k \mid s, \Phi_k)$ is the marginal likelihood of the matching feature subset X_k, derived from $p(X \mid s, \Phi_k)$ with the mismatched subband features ignored to improve mismatch robustness between the test frame X and the training noise condition Φ_k. For simplicity, assume independence between the subband features. So the marginal likelihood $p(X_{sub} \mid s, \Phi_k)$ for any subset X_{sub} in X can be written as

$$p(X_{sub} \mid s, \Phi_k) = \prod_{x_n \in X_{sub}} p(x_n \mid s, \Phi_k) \tag{3}$$

where $p(x_n \mid s, \Phi_k)$ is the likelihood function of the n'th subband feature at state s trained under noise condition Φ_k.

Multicondition or multi-style model training (e.g., Eq. (1)) has been a common method used in speech recognition to account for varying noise sources or speaking styles. The universal compensation model expressed in Eq. (2) is novel in that it combines multicondition model training with missing-feature theory, to ignore noise variations outside the given training conditions. This combination makes it possible to account for a wide variety of testing conditions based on limited training conditions (i.e., Φ_0 through Φ_K), as will be demonstrated later in the experiments.

Missing-feature theory is applied in Eq. (2) for ignoring the mismatched subbands. However, it should be noted that the approach in Eq. (2) extends beyond traditional missing-feature approaches. Traditional approaches assess the usability of a feature against its clean data, while the new approach assesses this against the data containing variable degrees of corruption, modelled by the different training conditions Φ_0 through Φ_K. This allows the model to use noisy features, close to or matched by the noisy training conditions,

for recognition. These noisy features, however, may become less usable or unusable with traditional missing-feature approaches due to their mismatch against the clean data.
Given a test frame X, the matching feature subset X_k for each training noise Φ_K may be defined as the subset in X that gains maximum likelihood over the appropriate noise condition. Such an estimate for X_k is not directly obtainable from Eq. (3). This is because the values of $p(X_{sub} | s, \Phi_k)$ for different sized subsets X_{sub} are of a different order of magnitude and are thus not directly comparable. One way around this is to select the matching feature subset X_k for noise condition Φ_k that produces maximum likelihood ratio for noise condition Φ_k as compared to all other noise conditions $\Phi_j \neq \Phi_k$. This effectively leads to a posterior probability formulation of Eq. (2). Define the posterior probability of state s and noise condition Φ_k given test subset X_{sub} as

$$P(s, \Phi_k | X_{sub}) = \frac{p(X_{sub} | s, \Phi_k) P(s, \Phi_k)}{\sum_{\varsigma, j} p(X_{sub} | \varsigma, \Phi_j) P(\varsigma, \Phi_j)} \tag{4}$$

On the right, Eq. (4) performs a normalization for $p(X_{sub} | s, \Phi_k)$ using the average likelihood of subset X_{sub} calculated over all states and training noise conditions, with $P(s, \Phi_k) = P(\Phi_k | s)P(s)$ being a prior probability of state s and noise condition Φ_k. The normalization makes it possible to compare the probabilities associated with different feature subsets X_{sub} and to obtain an estimate for X_k based on the comparison. Specifically, we can obtain an estimate for X_k by maximizing the posterior probability $P(s, \Phi_k | X_{sub})$ with respect to X_{sub}. Dividing the numerator and denominator of Eq. (4) by $p(X_{sub} | s, \Phi_k)$ gives

$$P(s, \Phi_k | X_{sub}) = \frac{P(s, \Phi_k)}{P(s, \Phi_k) + \sum_{\varsigma, j \neq s, k} P(\varsigma, \Phi_j) p(X_{sub} | \varsigma, \Phi_j) / p(X_{sub} | s, \Phi_k)} \tag{5}$$

Therefore maximizing posterior probability $P(s, \Phi_k | X_{sub})$ with respect to X_{sub} is equivalent to the maximization of likelihood ratios $p(X_{sub} | s, \Phi_k)/p(X_{sub} | \varsigma, \Phi_j)$, for all $(\varsigma, \Phi_j) \neq (s, \Phi_k)$, by choosing X_{sub}. The universal compensation model, Eq. (2), can be expressed in terms of the posterior probabilities $P(s, \Phi_k | X_{sub})$ as follows (the expression will be derived later)

$$p(X | s) \propto \sum_{k=0}^{K} \max_{X_{sub} \subset X} p(s, \Phi_k | X_{sub}) \tag{6}$$

where the maximization at each noise condition Φ_k accounts for the selection of the optimal set of subband features for that noise condition.

2.2 Incorporation into a hidden Markov model (HMM)

Assume a speech signal represented by a time sequence of T frames $X_{1\sim T}=(X(1), X(2), \ldots, X(T))$, and assume that the signal is modelled by an HMM with parameter set λ. Based on the HMM formulation, the likelihood function of $X_{1\sim T}$, given the state sequence $S_{1\sim T}$=(s(1), s(2), …, s(T)), where s(t) is the state for frame X(t), can be written as

$$p(X_{1\sim T} \mid S_{1\sim T}, \lambda) = \prod_{t=1}^{T} p(X(t) \mid s(t)) \tag{7}$$

where p(X | s) is the state-based observation probability density function with the HMM. To incorporate the above universal compensation approach into the HMM, we first express the state-based observation density p(X | s) in terms of P(s, Φ_k | X), i.e., the posterior probabilities of state s and noise condition Φ_k given frame vector X. Using Bayes's rules it follows

$$\begin{aligned} p(X \mid s) &= \frac{P(s \mid X) p(X)}{P(s)} \\ &= \frac{\sum_{k=0}^{K} P(s, \Phi_k \mid X)}{P(s)} p(X) \end{aligned} \tag{8}$$

The last term in Eq. (8), p(X), is not a function of the state index and thus has no effect in recognition. Substituting Eq. (8) into Eq. (7), replacing each P(s, Φ_k | X) with the maximized posterior probability for selecting the optimal set of subbands and assuming an equal prior probability P(s) for all the states, we obtain a modified HMM which incorporates the universal compensation approach

$$p(X_{1\sim T} \mid S_{1\sim T}, \lambda) \propto \prod_{t=1}^{T} \sum_{k=0}^{K} \max_{X_{sub} \subset X(t)} P(s(t), \Phi_k \mid X_{sub}) \tag{9}$$

where P(s, Φ_k | X_{sub}) is defined in Eq. (4) with P(s, Φ_k) replaced by P(Φ_k | s) due to the assumption of a uniform prior P(s). In our experiments, we further assume a uniform prior P(Φ_k | s) for noise conditions Φ_k, to account for the lack of prior knowledge about the noise.

2.3 Algorithm for implementation

The search in Eq. (9) for the matching feature subset can be computationally expensive for frame vectors with a large number of subbands (i.e., N). We can simplify the computation by approximating each p(X_{sub} | s, Φ_k) in Eq. (4) using the probability for the union of all subsets of the same size as X_{sub}. As such, p(X_{sub} | s, Φ_k) can be written, with the size of X_{sub} indicated in brackets, as (Ming et al. 2002)

$$p(X_{sub}(M) \mid s, \Phi_k) \propto \sum_{\text{all } X'_{sub}(M) \subset X} p(X'_{sub}(M) \mid s, \Phi_k) \tag{10}$$

where X_{sub}(M) represents a subset in X with M subband features (M≤N). Since the sum in Eq. (10) includes all feature subsets, it includes the matching feature subset that can be assumed to dominate the sum due to the best data-model match. Therefore Eq. (4) can be rewritten, by replacing p(X_{sub} | s, Φ_k) with p(X_{sub}(M) | s, Φ_k), as

$$P(s, \Phi_k \mid X_{sub}(M)) = \frac{p(X_{sub}(M) \mid s, \Phi_k) P(s, \Phi_k)}{\sum_{\varsigma, j} p(X_{sub}(M) \mid \varsigma, \Phi_j) P(\varsigma, \Phi_j)} \tag{11}$$

Note that Eq. (11) is not a function of the identity of X_{sub} but only a function of the size of X_{sub} (i.e., M). Using $P(s, \Phi_k \mid X_{sub}(M))$ in place of $P(s, \Phi_k \mid X_{sub})$ in Eq. (9), we therefore effectively turn the maximization for the exact matching feature subset, of a complexity of $O(2^N)$, to the maximization for the size of the matching feature subset, with a lower complexity of O(N). The sum in Eq. (10) over all $p(X_{sub}(M) \mid s, \Phi_k)$ for a given number of M features, for $0<M\leq N$, can be computed efficiently using a recursive algorithm assuming independence between the subbands (i.e., Eq. (3)). We call Eq. (11) the *posterior union model*, which has been studied previously (e.g., Ming et al., 2006) as a missing-feature approach without requiring identity of the noisy data. The universal compensation model Eq. (9) is reduced to a posterior union model with single, clean condition training (i.e., K=0).

3. Experimental Evaluation

The following describes the experimental evaluation of the universal compensation model on the Aurora 2 and 3 databases, involving a variety of simulated and realistic noises, including additional noise types not seen in the original databases. In all the experiments, the universal compensation system assumed no prior information about the noise.

3.1 Experiments on Aurora 2

Aurora 2 (Pearce & Hirsch, 2000) is designed for speaker independent recognition of digit sequences in noisy conditions. Aurora 2 involves nine different environments (eight noisy and one noise-free) and two different channel characteristics. The eight environmental noises include: subway, bubble, car, exhibition hall, restaurant, street, airport and train station. The two channel characteristics are G712 and MIRS. Aurora 2 has been divided into three test sets, each corresponding to a different set of noise conditions and/or channel characteristics. These are: 1) test set A - including clean data and noisy data corrupted by four different noises: subway, babble, car and exhibition hall, each at six different SNRs: 20 dbB, 15 dB, 10 dB, 5 dB, 0 dB and -5 dB, filtered with a G712 characteristic; 2) test set B - including data corrupted by four different noises: restaurant, street, airport and train station, each at the same range of SNRs as in test set A, filtered with a G712 characteristic; and 3) test set C - including data corrupted by two different noises: subway and street, each at the same range of SNRs as in test set A, filtered with an MIRS characteristic.

Aurora 2 offers two training sets, for two different training modes: 1) clean training set, consisting of only clean training data filtered with a G712 characteristic; and 2) multicondition training set, consisting of both clean data and multicondition noisy data involving the same four types of noise as in test set A, each at four different SNRs: 20 dB, 15 dB, 10 dB, 5 dB, and filtered with a G712 characteristic - also the same as for test set A. As such, it is usually assumed that the multicondition training set matches test set A more closely than it matches test set B. However, as noted in (Pearce & Hirsch, 2000), the noises in test set A seem to cover the spectral characteristics of the noises in test set B, and therefore no significant differences in performance have been found between test set A and test set B based on the model trained on the multicondition data. Mismatches exist between the multicondition training data and test set C, because of the different channel characteristics (i.e., G712 versus MIRS).

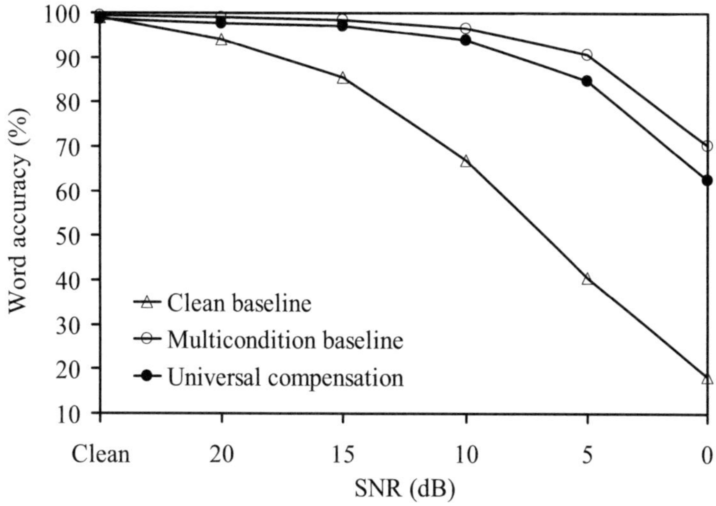

Figure 1. Word accuracy on the Aurora 2 database

The universal compensation model was compared with two baseline systems. The first baseline system was trained on the clean training set and the second was trained on the multicondition training set. The universal compensation model was trained using only the clean training set. This clean training set was expanded by adding computer-generated wide-band noise to each of the training utterances at ten different SNR levels, starting with SNR = 20 dB, reducing 2 dB every level, until SNR = 2 dB. This gives a total of eleven corruption levels (including the no corruption condition) for training the universal compensation model. The wide-band noise used in the training was computer-generated white noise filtered by a low-pass filter with a 3-dB bandwidth of 3.5 kHz. In modelling the digit words, the same HMM topology was adopted for all the three models: each word being modelled with 16 states, and each state being modelled with Gaussian mixture densities. Thirty two mixtures were used in each state for the universal compensation model and the multicondition baseline model, while 3 mixtures were used in each state for the clean baseline model trained only on the clean data. The speech signal, sampled at 8 kHz, was divided into frames of 25 ms at a frame period of 10 ms. The universal compensation model used subband features, consisting of 6 subbands derived from the decorrelated log filter-bank energies, as the feature set for each frame. The baseline systems used fullband MFCC as the feature set. Both models included the first- and second-order time differences as dynamic features. More details of the implementation can be found in (Ming, 2006).

Fig. 1 shows the word accuracy rates for the three systems: clean baseline, multicondition baseline and universal compensation, as a function of SNR averaged over all the noise conditions in test set A, B and C. As indicated in Fig. 1, the universal compensation model significantly improved over the clean baseline model, and achieved an average performance close to that obtained by the multicondition baseline model trained on the Aurora noisy training data. Note that the universal compensation model achieved this based only on the clean training data and simulated noisy training data, without having assumed any knowledge about the actual test noise.

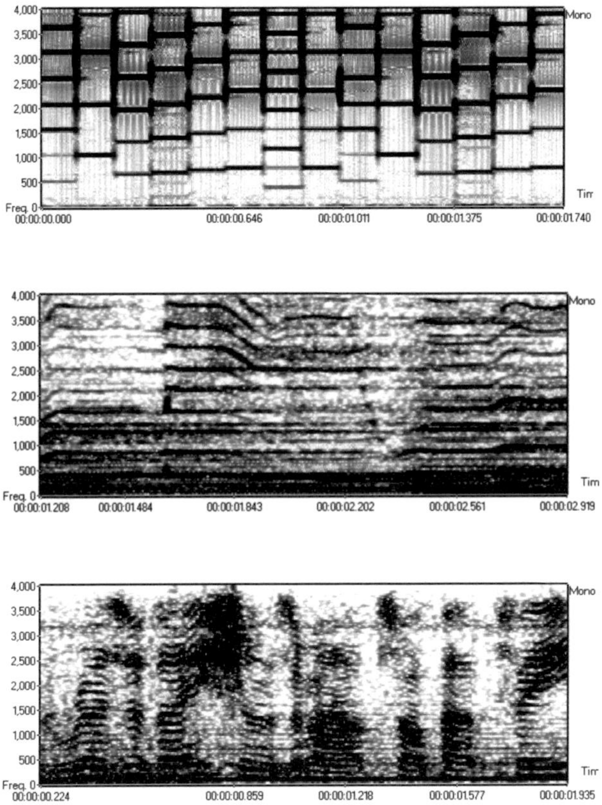

Figure 2. Spectrograms of three new noises unseen in Aurora 2. From top to bottom: mobile phone ring, pop song, broadcast news

To further investigate the capability of the universal compensation model to offer robustness for a wide variety of noises, three new noise conditions unseen in the Aurora 2 database were added in the test. The three new noises are: 1) a polyphonic mobile phone ring, 2) a pop song segment with a mixture of background music and the voice of a female singer, and 3) a broadcast news segment from a male speaker. Fig. 2 shows the spectral characteristics of the three new noises. Fig. 3 shows a comparison between the universal compensation model and the multicondition baseline model across the Aurora 2 noise conditions and the new noise conditions. As expected, the multicondition baseline trained using the Aurora data performed better than the universal compensation model under the Aurora 2 noise conditions. However, the multicondition baseline performed poorer than the universal compensation model for all the unseen noises, due to the mismatched conditions between the training and testing. The universal compensation model achieved a better average performance across all the noise conditions, indicating improved robustness for dealing with unknown/mismatched noises.

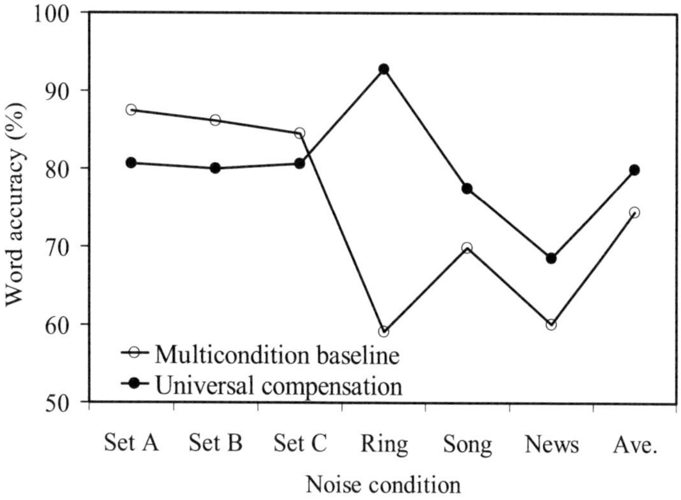

Figure 3. Word accuracy in different noise conditions within and outside the Aurora 2 database (averaged over SNRs between 0-10 dB)

The universal compensation approach involves a combination of multicondition model training and missing-feature theory. The importance of the combination, in terms of improved recognition performance, is studied. We first considered a system which was built on the same simulated noisy training data as used for the universal compensation model, but did not apply missing-feature theory to optimally select the subbands for scoring. The system thus used the full set of subbands for recognition. Comparisons were conducted for all the Aurora 2 noises and the three new noises as described above. Fig. 4 shows the absolute improvement in word accuracy obtained by the universal compensation model over the system without optimal subband selection. The results indicate that the optimal subband selection in the universal compensation model has led to improved accuracy in all tested noisy conditions. As expected, the improvement is more significant for those noises with a spectral structure significantly different from the wide-band noise spectral structure as used in the universal compensation model for noise compensation. In our experiments, these noises include, for example, the mobile phone ring, pop song, broadcast news and airport noises. Fig. 4 also indicates that the absolute improvement from the optimal subband selection is more significant in low SNR conditions (except for the exhibition-hall noise).

The above experimental results indicate the importance of the missing-feature component in the universal compensation model, for achieving robustness to mismatched training and testing. Likewise, the multicondition training component in the model plays an equally important role, particularly for dealing with broad-band noise corruption for which the conventional missing-feature methods usually fail to function. To show this, we considered a system which performed optimal subband selection as the universal compensation model, but was not trained using the simulated multicondition noisy data. Rather, it was trained using only the clean training data. Comparisons were conducted on test set A of the Aurora 2 database. Fig. 5 shows the absolute improvement in word accuracy obtained by the universal compensation model over the system with the missing-feature component but without being trained on the multicondition data. This missing-feature system performed better than the clean baseline model (i.e., the baseline model trained on the clean training data), due to the optimal selection of the subbands, but worse than the universal compensation model. The broad-band nature of the noises in test set A causes the poor performance for this missing-feature system.

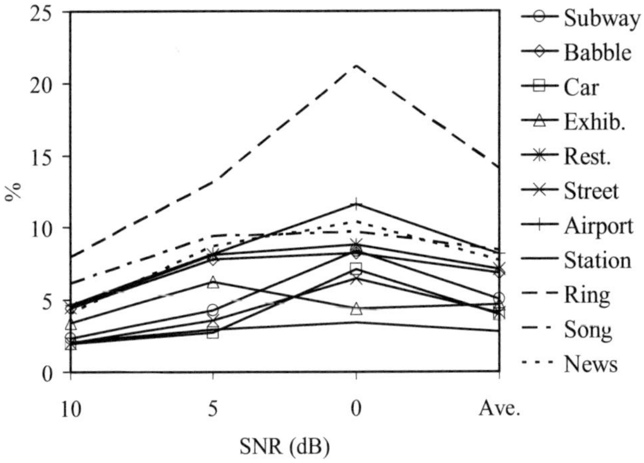

Figure 4. Absolute improvement in word accuracy obtained by optimal subband selection

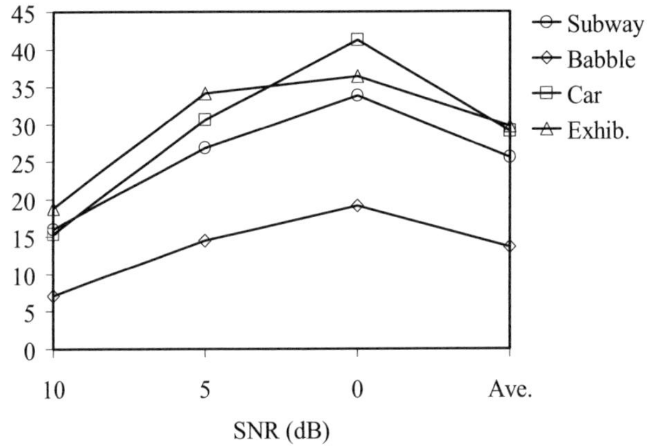

Figure 5. Absolute improvement in word accuracy obtained by multicondition training

3.2 Experiments on Aurora 3

Unlike Aurora 2, the Aurora 3 database consists of digit sequences (in four languages - Danish, Finnish, German and Spanish) recorded in real-world in-car environments, with realistic noise and channel effects. Speech data were recorded in three different noisy (driving) conditions - quite, low noise and high noise, and each utterance was recorded simultaneously by using two microphones, a close-talk microphone and a hand-free microphone. Three experimental conditions are defined in Aurora 3: 1) well-matched condition in which the training and testing data sets contain well-matched data for both the microphones and noise conditions; 2) moderately-mismatched condition in which the training and testing data are both from the hand-free microphone but differ in noise levels - quite and low-noise data for training and high-noise data for testing; 3) highly-mismatched condition in which the training and testing sets differ in both the microphone and noise levels - the data collected using the close-talk microphone in all the three conditions are used for training and the data collected using the hand-free microphone in the low-noise and high-noise conditions are used for testing. The hand-free microphone picked up more noise than the close-talk microphone from the background. In our experiments, the universal compensation model was trained using the training data for the highly-mismatched condition, by treating the close-talk data as "clean" data. The close-talk training data were expended by adding simulated wide-band noise at ten different SNRs between 2 - 20 dB. These simulated noisy speech data were used to train the universal compensation model, which used the same subband feature structure as for Aurora 2.

Training vs. Testing	Danish	Finnish	German	Spanish	Average
Well matched	12.7	7.3	8.8	7.1	8.9
Moderately mismatched	32.7	19.5	18.9	16.7	21.9
Highly mismatched	60.6	59.5	26.8	48.5	48.9
Average	35.3	28.8	18.2	24.1	26.6

Table 1. Word error rates on the Aurora 3 database, by the ETSI baseline system

Training vs. Testing	Danish	Finnish	German	Spanish	Average
Well matched	11.2	6.1	7.5	6.7	7.9
Moderately mismatched	26.8	17.2	16.3	15.5	18.9
Highly mismatched	19.9	12.5	13.7	12.2	14.6
Average	19.3	11.9	12.5	11.5	13.8

Table 2. Word error rates on the Aurora 3 database, by the universal compensation model

Table 1 shows the word error rates produced by the ETSI (European Telecommunications Standards Institute) baseline system, included for comparison. Table 2 shows the word error rates produced by the universal compensation model. As indicated in Tables 1 and 2, the universal compensation model performed equally well as the baseline system trained and tested in the well-matched conditions. The universal compensation model outperformed the baseline system when there were mismatches between the training and testing conditions. The average error reduction is 70.1%, 13.7% and 11.2%, respectively, for the highly-mismatched, moderately-mismatched and well-matched conditions.

4. Conclusion

This chapter investigated the problem of speech recognition in noisy conditions assuming absence of prior information about the noise. A method, namely universal compensation, was described, which combines multicondition model training and missing-feature theory to model noises with unknown temporal-spectral characteristics. Multicondition training can be conducted using simulated noisy data, to provide a coarse compensation for the noise, and missing-feature theory is applied to refine the compensation by ignoring noise variations outside the given training conditions, thereby accommodating mismatches between the training and testing conditions. Experiments on the noisy speech databases Aurora 2 and 3 were described. The results demonstrate that the new approach offered improved robustness over baseline systems without assuming knowledge about the noise. Currently we are considering an extension of the principle of universal compensation to model new forms of signal distortion, e.g., handset variability, room reverberation, and distant/moving speaking. To make the task tractable, these factors can be "quantized" as we did for the SNR. Missing-feature approaches will be used to deemphasize the mismatches while exploiting the matches arising from the quantized data.

5. References

Boll, S. (1979). Suppression of acoustic noise in speech using spectral subtraction. *IEEE Transactions on Acoustics, Speech and Signal Processing*, Vol. 27, Apr 1979, pp. 113-120.

Cooke, M.; Green, P.; Josifovski, L. & Vizinho, A. (2001) Robust automatic speech recognition with missing and unreliable acoustic data. *Speech Communication*, Vol. 34, 2001, pp. 267-285.

Deng, L.; Acero, A.; Jiang, L.; Droppo, J. & Hunag, X.-D. (2001). High-perfromance robust speech recognition using stereo training data, *Proceedings of ICASSP*, pp. 301-304, Salt Lake City, Utah, USA, 2001.

Gales, M. J. F. & Young, S. (1993). HMM recognition in noise using parallel model combination, *Proceedings of Eurospeech'93*, pp. 837-840, Berlin, Germany, 1993.

Hermansky, H. & Morgan, N. (1994). RASTA processing of speech. *IEEE Transactions on Speech and Audio Processing*, Vol. 4, Oct 1994, pp. 578-589.

Lippmann, R. P.; Martin, E. A. & Paul, D. B. (1987). Multi-style training for robust isolated-word speech recognition, *Proceedings of ICASSP*, pp. 705-708, Dallas, TX, USA, 1987.

Lippmann, R. P. & Carlson, B. A. (1997). Using missing feature theory to actively select features for robust speech recognition with interruptions, filtering and noise, *Proceedings of Eurospeech*, pp. 37-40, Rhodes, Greece, 1997.

Macho, D.; Mauuary, L.; Noe, B.; Cheng, Y. M.; Ealey, D.; Jouver, D.; Kelleher, H.; Pearce, D. & Saadoun, F. (2002). Evaluation of a noise-robust DSR front-end on Aurora databases, *Proceedings of ICSLP*, pp. 17-20, Denver, CO, USA, 2002.

Ming, J.; Jancovic, P. & Smith, F. J. (2002). Robust speech recognition using probabilistic union models. *IEEE Transactions on Speech and Audio Processing*, Vol. 10, Sep 2002, pp. 403-414.

Ming, J.; Lin, J. & Smith, F. J. (2006). A posterior union model with applications to robust speech and speaker recognition. *EURASIP Journal on Applied Signal Processing*, Vol. 2006, 2006, Article ID 75390.

Ming, J. (2006). Noise compensation for speech recognition with arbitrary additive noise. *IEEE Transactions on Speech and Audio Processing*, Vol. 14, May 2006, pp. 833-844.

Pearce, D. & Hirsch, H.-G. (2000). The Aurora experimental framework for the performance evaluation of speech recognition systems under noisy conditions, *Proceedings of ISCA ITRW ASR*, Paris, France, 2000.

Raj, B.; Singh, R. & Stern, R. M. (1998). Inference of missing spectrographic features for robust speech recognition, *Proceedings of ICSLP*, pp. 1491-1494, Sydney, Australia, 1998.

12

Uncertainty in Signal Estimation and Stochastic Weighted Viterbi Algorithm: A Unified Framework to Address Robustness in Speech Recognition and Speaker Verification

N. Becerra Yoma, C. Molina, C. Garreton and F. Huenupan
Speech Processing and Transmission Laboratory
Department of Electrical Engineering
Universidad de Chile
Chile

1. Introduction

Robustness to noise and low-bit rate coding distortion is one of the main problems faced by automatic speech recognition (ASR) and speaker verification (SV) systems in real applications. Usually, ASR and SV models are trained with speech signals recorded in conditions that are different from testing environments. This mismatch between training and testing can lead to unacceptable error rates. Noise and low-bit rate coding distortion are probably the most important sources of this mismatch. Noise can be classified into additive or convolutional if it corresponds, respectively, to an additive process in the linear domain or to the insertion of a linear transmission channel function. On the other hand, low-bit rate coding distortion is produced by coding - decoding schemes employed in cellular systems and VoIP/ToIP. A popular approach to tackle these problems attempts to estimate the original speech signal before the distortion is introduced. However, the original signal cannot be recovered with 100% accuracy and there will be always an uncertainty in noise canceling.

Due to its simplicity, spectral subtraction (SS) (Berouti et al., 1979; Vaseghi & Milner, 1997) has widely been used to reduce the effect of additive noise in speaker recognition (Barger & Sridharan, 1997; Drygajlo & El-Maliki, 1998; Ortega & Gonzalez, 1997), despite the fact that SS loses accuracy at low segmental SNR. Parallel Model Combination (PMC) (Gales & Young,1993) was applied under noisy conditions in (Rose et. al.,1994) where high improvements with additive noise were reported. Nevertheless, PMC requires an accurate knowledge about the additive corrupting signal, whose model is estimated using appreciable amounts of noise data which in turn imposes restrictions on noise stationarity, and about the convolutional distortion that needs to be estimated a priori (Gales, 1997). Rasta filtering (Hermansky et al., 1991) and Cepstral Mean Normalization (CMN) can be very useful to cancel convolutional distortion (Furui, 1982; Reynolds, 1994; van Vuuren, 1996) but, if the speech signal is also corrupted by additive noise, these techniques lose

effectiveness and need to be applied in combination with methods such as SS (Hardt & Fellbaum, 1997).
The idea of uncertainty in noise removal was initially proposed by the first author of this chapter in (Yoma et al., 1995; 1996-A; 1996-B; 1997-A; 1997-B; 1998-A; 1998-B; 1998-C; 1999) to address the problem of additive noise. The main idea was to estimate the uncertainty in noise canceling using an additive noise model and to weight the information provided by the signal according to the local SNR. As a consequence, Weighted DTW and Viterbi algorithms were proposed. Then, it was shown that convolutional noise could also be addressed in the framework of weighted matching algorithms. In (Yoma & Villar, 2001), the uncertainty in noise or distortion removal was modeled from the stochastic point of view. As a result, in the context of HMM, the original signal was modeled as a stochastic variable with normal distribution, which in turn leads to consider the expected value of the observation probability. If the observation probability is a Gaussian mixture, it is proved that its expected value is also a Gaussian mixture. This result, known as Stochastic Weighted Viterbi (SWV) algorithm, makes possible to address the problems of additive/convolutional (Yoma & Villar, 2001; 2002; Yoma et al., 2003-B), noise and low-bit rate coding distortion (Yoma et al., 2003-A; 2004; 2005; Yoma & Molina, 2006) in ASR and SV in a unified framework.
It is worth highlighting that SWV allows the interaction between the language and acoustic models in ASR just like in human perception: the language model has a higher weight in those frames with low SNR or low reliability (Yoma et al., 2003-B). Finally, the concept of uncertainty in noise canceling and weighted recognition algorithms (Yoma et al., 1995; 1996-A; 1996-B; 1997-A; 1997-B; 1998-A; 1998-B; 1998-C; 1999) have also widely been employed elsewhere in the fields of ASR and SV in later publications (Acero et al, 2006-A; 2006-B; Arrowood & Clements, 2004; Bernard & Alwan, 2002; Breton, 2005; Chan & Siu, 2004; Cho et al., 2002; Delaney, 2005; Deng, et al., 2005; Erzin et al., 2005; Gomez et al., 2006; Hung et al., 1998; Keung et al., 2000; Kitaoka & Nakagawa, 2002; Li, 2003; Liao & Gales, 2005 ; Pfitzinger, 2000; Pitsikalis et al., 2006; Tan et al., 2005; Vildjiounaite et al., 2006; Wu & Chen, 2001).

2. The model for additive noise

Given that $s(i)$, $n(i)$ and $x(i)$ are the clean speech, the noise and the resulting noisy signal, respectively, the additiveness condition in the temporal domain is expressed as:

$$x(i) = s(i) + n(i) \tag{1}$$

In the results discussed here, the signals were processed by 20 DFT mel filters. If inside each one of these DFT filters the phase difference between $s(i)$ and $n(i)$, and the energy of both signals are considered constant, the energy of the noisy signal at the output of the filter m, $\overline{x_m^2}$, can be modeled as (Yoma et al., 1998-B):

$$\overline{x_m^2} = \overline{s_m^2} + \overline{n_m^2} + 2 \cdot \sqrt{c_m} \sqrt{\overline{s_m^2}} \cdot \sqrt{\overline{n_m^2}} \cdot \cos(\phi) \tag{2}$$

where $\overline{s_m^2}$ and $\overline{n_m^2}$ are the energy of the clean speech and noise signals at the output of the filter m, respectively; ϕ is the phase difference, which is also considered constant inside each one of the DFT mel filters, between the clean and noise signals; and c_m is a constant that was included due to the fact that these assumptions are not perfectly accurate in practice (Yoma et al., 1998-B); the filters are not highly selective, which reduces the validity of the assumption of low variation of these parameters inside the filters; and, a few discontinuities in the phase difference may occur, although many of them are unlikely in a short term analysis (i.e. a 25 ms frame). Nevertheless, this model shows the fact that there is a variance in the short term analysis and defines the relation between this variance and the clean and noise signal levels. Due to the approximations the variance predicted by the model is higher than the true variance for the same frame length, and the correction c_m had to be included. In (Yoma et al., 1998-B), this coefficient c_m was estimated with clean speech and noise-only frames. However, employing clean speech is not very interesting from the practical application point of view and in (Yoma & Villar, 2002) a different approach was followed by observing the error rate for a range of values of c_m. Solving (2), $\overline{s_m^2}$ can be written as:

$$\overline{s_m^2}(\phi,\overline{n_m^2},\overline{x_m^2}) = 2\cdot A_m^2 \cdot \cos^2(\phi) + B_m - 2\cdot A_m \cdot \cos(\phi)\cdot\sqrt{A_m^2 \cdot \cos^2(\phi) + B_m} \tag{3}$$

where $A_m = \sqrt{\overline{n_m^2}\cdot c_m}$ and $B_m = \overline{x_m^2} - \overline{n_m^2}$. Notice that $\overline{n_m^2}$ can be replaced with an estimate of the noise energy made in non-speech intervals, $E\left[\overline{n_m^2}\right]$, $\overline{x_m^2}$ is the observed noisy signal energy and ϕ can be considered as a random variable. If $f_\phi(\phi)$, the probability density function of ϕ, is considered as being uniformly distributed between $-\pi$ and π, it can be shown that:

$$E\left[\log(\overline{s_m^2}(\phi))\right] = \int_{-\pi}^{\pi} \log(\overline{s_m^2}(\phi))\cdot f_\phi(\phi)\cdot d(\phi) \cong \log(E[B_m]) \tag{4}$$

where $E[B_m] = \overline{x_m^2} - E\left[\overline{n_m^2}\right]$. To simplify the notation, $\overline{n_m^2}$ and $\overline{x_m^2}$ are withdrawn as arguments of the function $\overline{s_m^2}(\ )$ defined in (3). It is important to emphasize that $\overline{x_m^2} - E\left[\overline{n_m^2}\right]$ can be seen as the spectral subtraction (SS) estimation of the clean signal.

In (Yoma et al., 1998-A; 1998-B) the uncertainty in noise canceling was modeled as being the variance:

$$Var\left[\log(\overline{s_m^2}(\phi))\right] = E\left[\log^2(\overline{s_m^2}(\phi))\right] - E^2\left[\log(\overline{s_m^2}(\phi))\right] \tag{5}$$

where $E\left[\log^2(\overline{s_m^2}(\phi))\right]$ was computed by means of numerical integration.

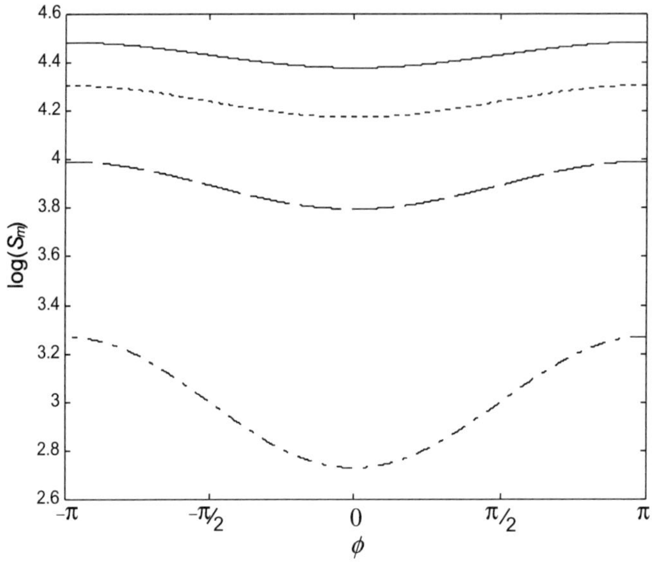

Figure 1. The log energy at filter m, $\log(S_m) = \log(\overline{s_m^2}(\phi))$, vs. ϕ, where $\overline{s_m^2}(\phi)$ is defined according to (5), for $\overline{x_m^2} / \overline{n_m^2}$ equal to 28 (——), 18 (- - - -), 8 (— — ·) and 2 (— · —). $\overline{n_m^2}$ was made equal to 1000 and c_m to 0.1.

2.1 Approximated expressions for the additive noise model

Figure 1 shows the function $\log\left(\overline{s_m^2}(\phi)\right)$, when $\overline{s_m^2}(\phi)$ is given by (3), for several values of the ratio $\overline{x_m^2} / \overline{n_m^2}$. As suggested in Fig.1, and easily verified in (3), the function $\log\left(\overline{s_m^2}(\phi)\right)$ is even and its minimum and maximum values are, respectively, $\log\left(\overline{s_m^2}(0)\right)$ and $\log\left(\overline{s_m^2}(\pi)\right)$ or $\log\left(\overline{s_m^2}(-\pi)\right)$. Employing $\log(1+x) \cong x$ for $x \ll 1$ and considering $B_m >> A_m^2$, which is easily satisfied at moderate SNR (greater or equal than 6dB), it is possible to show that (see appendix):

$$\log\left(\overline{s_m^2}(\phi)\right) \cong -\frac{2 \cdot A_m}{\sqrt{B_m}} \cos(\phi) + E\left[\log(\overline{s_m^2}(\phi))\right] \cong -\frac{2 \cdot A_m}{\sqrt{B_m}} \cos(\phi) + \log\left(E[B_m]\right) \quad (6)$$

Using (6), it can be shown that the uncertainty variance defined in (5) can be estimated with:

$$Var\left[\log\left(\overline{s_m^2}(\phi)\right)\right] \cong \frac{2E\left[A_m^2\right]}{E[B_m]} \quad (7)$$

where $E\left[A_m^2\right] = c_m \cdot E\left[\overline{n_m^2}\right]$ and $E[B_m]$ is defined above. Due to the fact that (6) and (7) are derived considering that $B_m >> A_m^2$, this condition imposes a domain where these expressions can be used. Assuming that B needs to be greater or equal than $10 \cdot A_m^2$, to satisfy the condition above, means that (7) is valid when $\overline{x_m^2} - E\left[\overline{n_m^2}\right] \geq 10 \cdot c_m \cdot E\left[\overline{n_m^2}\right]$. When $\overline{x_m^2} - E\left[\overline{n_m^2}\right] < 10 \cdot c_m \cdot E\left[\overline{n_m^2}\right]$ a linear extrapolation could be used and (7) is modified to:

$$Var\left[\log\left(\overline{s_m^2}(\phi)\right)\right] = \begin{cases} \dfrac{2 \cdot c_m \cdot E\left[\overline{n_m^2}\right]}{\overline{x_m^2} - E\left[\overline{n_m^2}\right]} & \text{if } \overline{x_m^2} - E\left[\overline{n_m^2}\right] \geq 10 \cdot c_m \cdot E\left[\overline{n_m^2}\right] \\ -\dfrac{\overline{x_m^2} - E\left[\overline{n_m^2}\right]}{50 \cdot c_m \cdot E\left[\overline{n_m^2}\right]} + 0.4 & \text{if } \overline{x_m^2} - E\left[\overline{n_m^2}\right] < 10 \cdot c_m \cdot E\left[\overline{n_m^2}\right] \end{cases} \quad (8)$$

2.2 Spectral subtraction

As mentioned above, (4) could be considered as a definition for SS (spectral subtraction). However, (4) presents the same problems at low SNR when the additive noise model loses accuracy and $E[B_m] = \overline{x_m^2} - E\left[\overline{n_m^2}\right]$ can be negative, which in turn is incompatible with the log operator. In (Yoma & Villar, 2003) the clean signal was estimated using the SS defined as:

$$SSE_m = \max\left\{\overline{x_m^2} - E\left[\overline{n_m^2}\right] \; ; \; \beta \cdot \overline{x_m^2}\right\} \quad (9)$$

which corresponds to a simplified version of an SS defined in (Vaseghi & Milner, 1997). SSE_m denotes the estimation of the clean signal energy by means of SS.

In order to improve the applicability at low segmental SNR of the additive noise model discussed here, some modifications would be necessary: first, the domain of ϕ requires to be modified, affecting the integral in (4), to satisfy the condition $\overline{s_m^2}(\phi) \geq 0$; second, the noise energy $\overline{n_m^2}$ should also be treated as a random variable at low SNR, but the estimation of its distribution may require long non-speech intervals, which imposes restrictions on the dynamics of the corrupting additive process; third, a more accurate model should also take into consideration an a priori distribution of the clean speech energy. Consequently, employing the SS defined as in (9) is an interesting compromise between the applicability of the approach proposed here and the theoretical model for the addition of noise discussed in section 2. The SS as in (9) reduces the distortion at low SNR by setting a lower threshold proportional to the noisy signal energy.

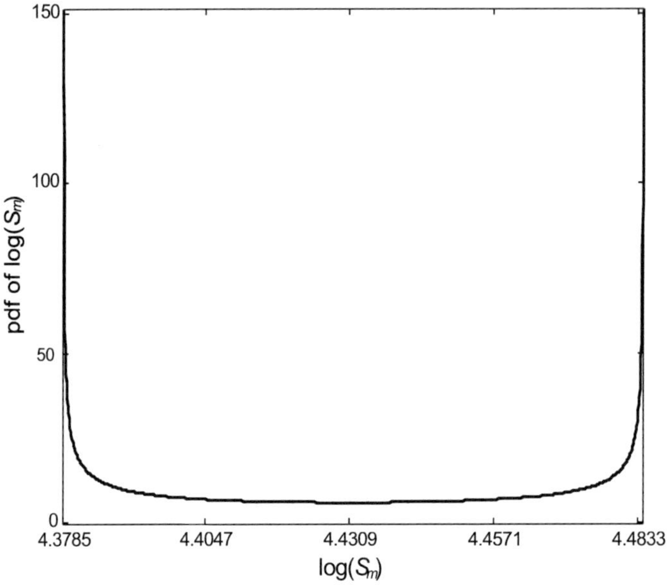

Figure 2. Probability density function of $\log(S_m) = \log(\overline{s_m^2(\phi)})$ assuming that ϕ is a random variable uniformly distributed between $-\pi$ and π. $\overline{x_m^2}/\overline{n_m^2}$ was made equal to 28, $\overline{n_m^2}$ to 1000 and c_m to 0.1. The p.d.f. curve of $\log(S_m)$ was estimated using the following theorem (Papoulis, 1991): to find $f_y(y)$ for a specific y, the equation $y = g(x)$ is solved; if its real roots are denoted by x_n, then $f_y(y) = f_x(x_1)/|g'(x_1)| + \cdots + f_x(x_n)/|g'(x_n)|$ where $g'(x)$ is the derivative of $g(x)$. In this case $y = \log(\overline{s_m^2(\phi)})$ and $x = \phi$.

2.3 Uncertainty variance in the cepstral domain

Most speech recognizers and speaker verification systems compute cepstral coefficients from the filter log energies. The static cepstral coefficient C_n is defined as:

$$C_n = \sum_{m=1}^{M} \log\left(\overline{s_m^2(\phi)}\right) \cos\left(\frac{\pi \cdot n}{M} \cdot (m - 0.5)\right) \tag{10}$$

where M is the number of DFT filters. Observing that (10) is a sum and assuming that $\log\left(\overline{s_m^2(\phi)}\right)$ with $1 \le m \le M$ are independent random variables, C_n tends to a random variable with Gaussian distribution according to the Central Limit Theorem (Papoulis, 1991). The independence hypothesis is strong but substantially simplifies the mapping between the log and cepstral domain for the uncertainty variance. Consequently, the variance of C_n is given by (Yoma et al., 1998-A; Yoma & Villar, 2002):

$$Var[C_n] = \sum_{m=1}^{M} Var\left[\log\left(\overline{s_m^2}(\phi)\right)\right]\cos^2\left(\frac{\pi \cdot n}{M}\cdot(m-0.5)\right). \quad (11)$$

In order to counteract the limitation discussed in section 2.2, $E\left[\log\left(\overline{s_m^2}(\phi)\right)\right]$ was replaced with $\log(SSE_m)$, where SSE_m is defined according to (9), to estimate $E[C_n]$:

$$E[C_n] = \sum_{m=1}^{M} \log(SSE_m)\cos\left(\frac{\pi \cdot n}{M}\cdot(m-0.5)\right). \quad (12)$$

The probability density functions (p.d.f.) of $\log\left(\overline{s_m^2}(\phi)\right)$ and C_n are shown in Figs.2 and 3. As can be seen in Fig.3, approximating the distribution of C_n with a Gaussian seems a reasonable approach.

Considering the variables $\log\left(\overline{s_m^2}(\phi)\right)$ as being independent should be interpreted as a hypothesis that is inaccurate for contiguous filters but more realistic when the separation between filters increases. This assumption is able to simplify the formulation of the approach proposed here and to lead to significant improvements in the system performance as shown later. Assuming $\log\left(\overline{s_m^2}(\phi)\right)$ is correlated requires a more complex analysis to estimate the uncertainty variance in the cepstral domain and the distribution of the cepstral coefficients of the hidden clean signal. This analysis, which would incorporate further knowledge about the speech signal in the spectral domain but also would make the estimation of the expected value of the output probability in section 3 more difficult, is not addressed in (Yoma & Villar, 2002) although could still lead to some improvements when compared with the current model.

In speech recognition and speaker verification systems delta cepstral coefficients are used in combination with the static parameters. The delta cepstral coefficient in frame t, $\delta C_{t,n}$ is defined as:

$$\delta C_{t,n} = \frac{C_{t+1,n} - C_{t-1,n}}{2}. \quad (13)$$

where $C_{t+1,n}$ and $C_{t-1,n}$ are the static cepstral features in frames $t+1$ and $t-1$. If the frames are supposed uncorrelated, the same assumption made by HMM, the uncertainty mean and variance of $\delta C_{t,n}$ are, respectively, given by:

$$E\left[\delta C_{t,n}\right] = \frac{E\left[C_{t+1,n}\right] - E\left[C_{t-1,n}\right]}{2}. \quad (14)$$

$$Var\left[\delta C_{t,n}\right] = \frac{Var\left[C_{t+1,n}\right] + Var\left[C_{t-1,n}\right]}{4}. \quad (15)$$

Concluding, the cepstral coefficients could be treated as random variables with normal distribution whose mean and variance are given by (12) (11) and (14) (15). As a result, the HMM output probability needs to be modified to represent the fact that the spectral features should not be considered as being constants in noisy speech.

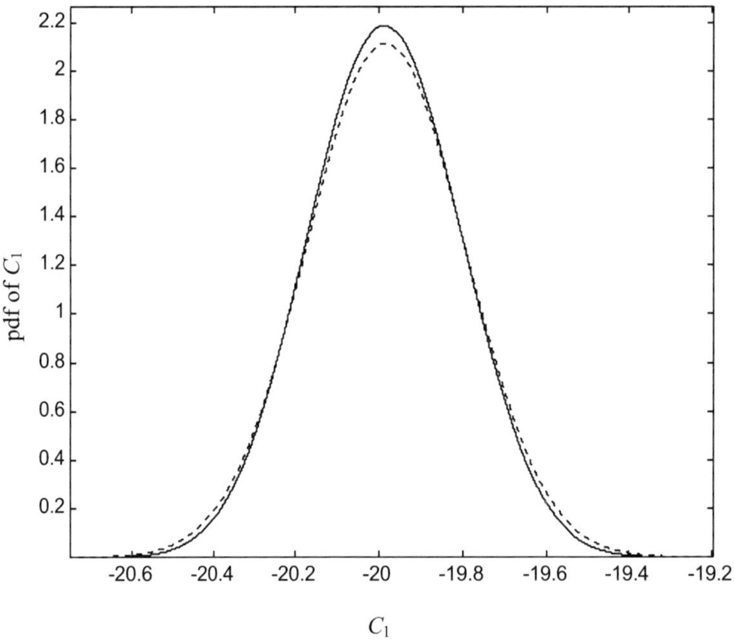

Figure 3. Probability density function of the static cepstral coefficient C_1 computed with 20 log energies $\log(\overline{s_m^2}(\phi))$. As a consequence, this density function corresponds to the convolution (——) of 20 p.d.f.´s similar to the one shown in Fig. 2. The theoretic Normal p.d.f. with the same mean and variance is represented with (- - - -).

3. Modelling low-bit rate coding-decoding distortion

As discussed in (Yoma et al., 2006), to model the distortion caused by coding algorithms, samples of clean speech were coded and decoded with the following coding schemes: 8 kbps CS-CELP (ITU-T, 1996) 13 kbps GSM (ETSI, 1992), 5.3 kbps G723.1 (ITU-T, 1996-B), 4.8 kbps FS-1016 (Campbell et al, 1991) and 32 kbps ADPCM (ITU-T, 1990). After that, the original and coded-decoded speech signals, which were sampled at a rate of 8000 samples/second, were divided in 25ms frames with 12.5ms overlapping. Each frame was processed with a Hamming window, the band from 300 to 3400 Hz was covered with 14 Mel DFT filters, at the output of each channel the energy was computed and the log of the energy was estimated. The frame energy plus ten static cepstral coefficients, and their first and second time derivatives were estimated. Then, the parameterized original and coded-decoded utterances were linearly aligned to generate Figs. 4-9.

It is worth mentioning that the estimation and compensation of the coding-decoding distortion proposed in (Yoma et al., 2006) was tested with SI continuous speech recognition experiments using LATINO-40 database (LDC, 1995). The training utterances were 4500 uncoded sentences provided by 36 speakers and context-dependent phoneme HMMs were employed. The vocabulary is composed of almost 6000 words. The testing database was composed of 500 utterances provided by 4 testing speakers (two females and two males). Each context-dependent phoneme was modeled with a 3-state left-to-right topology without skip transition, with eight multivariate Gaussian densities per state and diagonal covariance matrices. Trigram language model was employed during recognition.

The points (O_n^o, O_n^d), where O_n^o and O_n^d are the cepstral coefficient n estimated with the original and coded-decoded signals, respectively, are symmetrically distributed with respect to the diagonal axis in the 8 kbps CS-CELP (Fig. 4a) and in the 32 kbps ADPCM (Fig. 4b). This suggests that the coding-decoding distortion, defined as $D_n = O_n^o - O_n^d$, presents a reasonably constant dispersion around the mean that seems to be close to zero. As a consequence, the distribution of the coding–decoding distortion does not show a strong dependence on O_n^o in those cases. However, the same behavior is not observed in the 13 kbps GSM coder (Fig. 5) where the pairs (O_n^o, O_n^d) seems to be symmetrically distributed around a center near (0, 0).

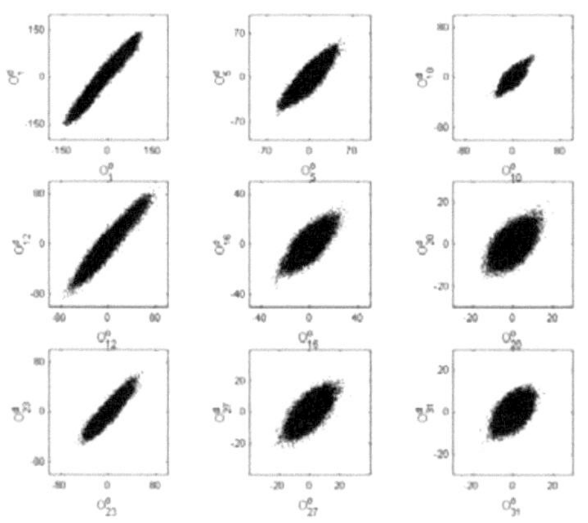

(a) 8 kbps CS-CELP

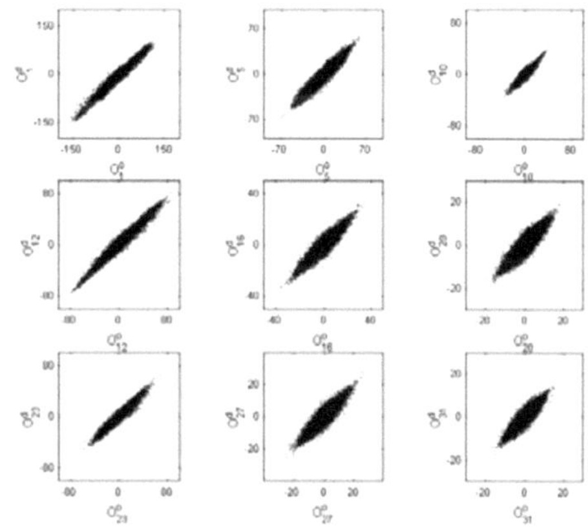

(b) 32 kbps ADPCM

Figure 4. Cepstral coefficients from uncoded (O^o) vs. coded-decoded (O^d) speech signals. The coders correspond to a) the 8 kbps CS-CELP from the ITU-T standard G.729, and b) the 32 kbps ADPCM from the ITU-T standard G.726 The parameters employed in the figures correspond to static (1, 5, 10), delta (12, 16, 20) and delta-delta (23, 27, 31) cepstral coefficients. The pairs (O^o, O^d) were generated by linearly aligning uncoded with coded-decoded speech.

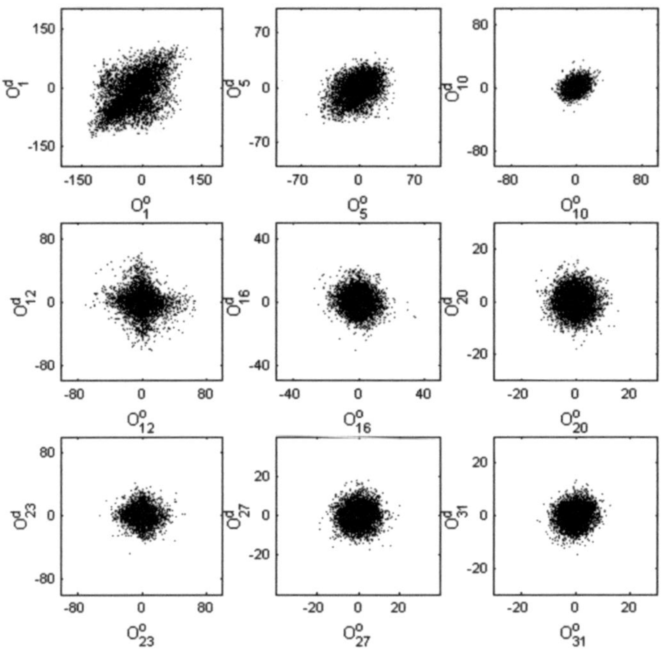

Figure 5. Cepstral coefficients from uncoded (O^o) vs. coded-decoded (O^d) speech signals. The coder is the 13 kbps GSM from the ETSI GSM-06.10 Full Rate Speech Transcoding. The parameters employed in the figures correspond to static (1, 5, 10), delta (12, 16, 20) and delta-delta (23, 27, 31) cepstral coeffcients. The pairs (O^o,O^d) were generated by linearly aligning uncoded with coded-decoded speech.

The histograms presented in Fig. 6 (8 kbps CS-CELP) and Fig. 7 (5.3 kbps G723.1) strongly suggest that the coding-decoding distortion could be modeled as a Gaussian p.d.f., although the 5.3 kbps G723.1 coder provides (O_n^o,O_n^d) patterns similar to those observed with the 13 kbps GSM coder (Yoma et al., 2006). The expected value, normalized with respect to the range of the observed O_n^o, of the coding-decoding distortion vs. O_n^o is shown in Fig. 8. Notice that the dependence of the expected value on O_n^o is weak for the 8 kbps CS-CELP and the 32 kbps ADPCM. Nevertheless, in the case of the 13 kbps GSM scheme this dependence is more significant, although the expected value is low compared to O_n^o itself and displays an odd symmetry. It is interesting to emphasize that the fuzzy circular-like (O_n^o,O_n^d) patterns observed with the 13 kbps GSM (Fig. 5) and the 5.3 kbps G723.1 coders are the result of this odd symmetry presented by the expected value of the distortion. The variance of the coding-decoding distortion vs. O_n^o is shown in Fig. 9. According to Fig. 9, the assumption related to the independence of the variance with respect O_n^o does not seem to be unrealistic. Moreover, this assumption is strengthen by the fact that the distribution of O_n^o tends to be concentrated around $O_n^o = 0$.

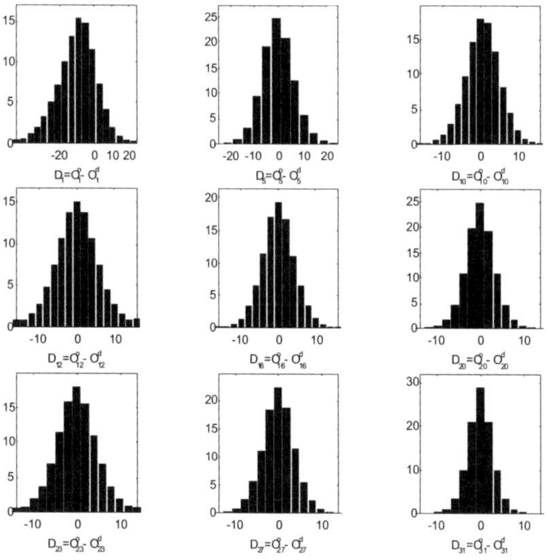

Figure 6. Distribution of coding distortion ($O^o - O^d$) with signals processed by 8 kbps CS-CELP from the ITU-T standard G.729. The parameters employed in the figures correspond to static (1, 5, 10), delta (12, 16, 20) and delta-delta (23, 27, 31) cepstral coefficients. The histograms were generated with the same data employed in Fig. 4.

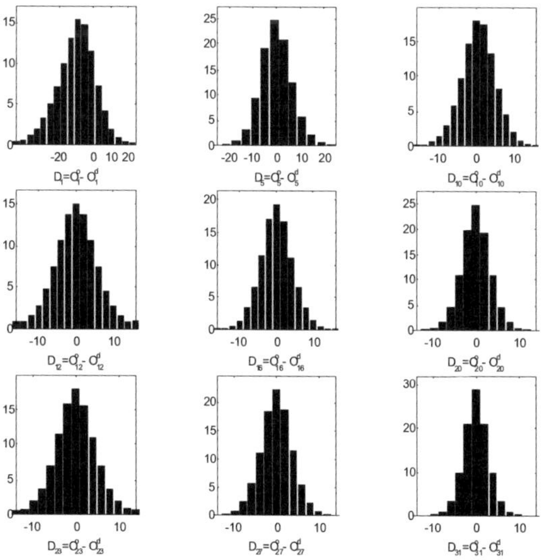

Figure 7. Distribution of coding distortion ($O^o - O^d$) with signals processed by 5.3 kbps G723-1 from the ITU-T standard G.723.1. The parameters employed in the figures correspond to static (1, 5, 10), delta (12, 16, 20) and delta-delta (23, 27, 31) cepstral coefficients. The histograms were generated with the same data employed in Fig. 4.

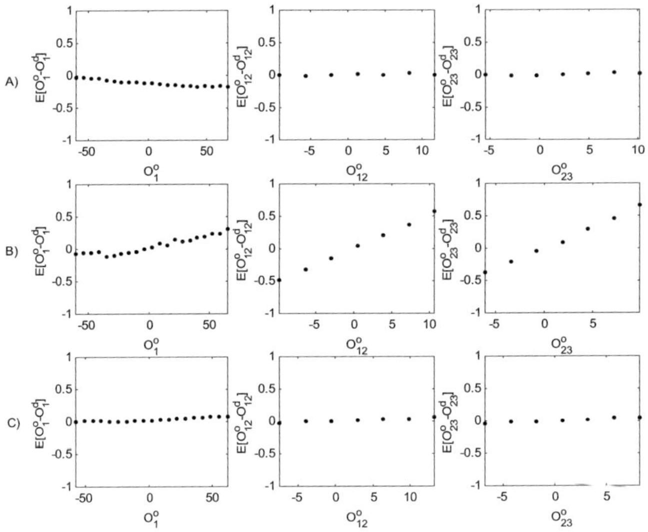

Figure 8. Expected value of the coding-decoding error, $E[O^o_n - O^d_n] = m^d_n$, vs. O^o. The expected value is normalized with respect to the range of observed O^o. The following coders are analyzed: A) 8 kbps CS-CELP; B) 13 kbps GSM; and, C) 32 kbps ADPCM . The cepstral coefficients correspond to a static (1), a delta (12) and a delta-delta (23).

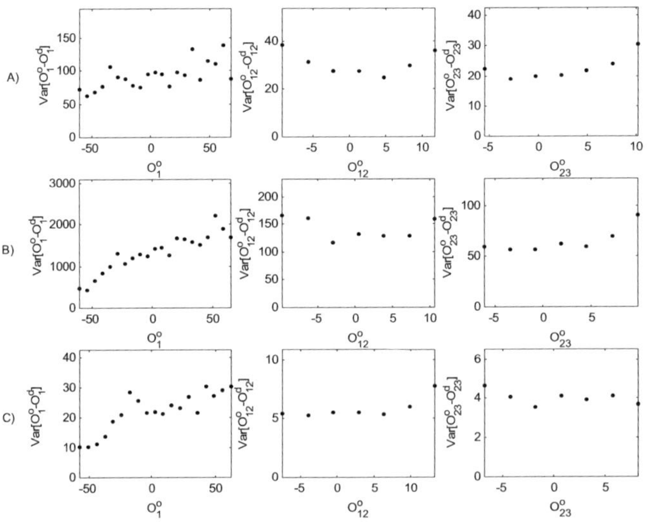

Figure 9. Variance of the coding-decoding error, $Var[O^o_n - O^d_n] = v^d_n$, vs. O^o. The following coders are analyzed: A) 8 kbps CS-CELP; B) 13 kbps GSM; and, C) 32 kbps ADPCM . The cepstral coefficients correspond to a static (1), a delta (12) and a delta-delta (23).

From the previous analysis based on empirical observations and comparisons of the uncoded and coded-decoded speech signals, it is possible to suggest that the cepstral coefficient n in frame t of the original signal, $O^o_{t,n}$, could be given by (Yoma et al., 2006):

$$O^o_{t,n} = O^d_{t,n} + D_n \tag{16}$$

where $O^d_{t,n}$ is the cepstral coefficient corresponding to the coded-decoded speech signal; D_n is the distortion caused by the coding-decoding process with p.d.f. $f_{D_n}(D_n) = N(m^d_n, v^d_n)$ that does not depend on the value of the cepstral coefficient n, and therefore the phonetic class; $N(m^d_n, v^d_n)$ is a Gaussian distribution with mean m^d_n and variance v^d_n. The assumption related to the independence of D_n with respect to the value of a cepstral coefficient or the phonetic class is rather strong but seems to be a realistic model in several cases, despite the odd symmetry shown by the expected value of the coding-decoding distortion with some coders. Notice that this analysis takes place in the log-cepstral domain that is not linear. Moreover, as discussed later, this model is able to lead to dramatic improvements in WER with all the coding schemes considered in (Yoma et al., 2006).

In a real situation, $O^d_{t,n}$ is the observed cepstral parameter and $O^o_{t,n}$ is the hidden information of the original speech signal. From (16), the expected value of $O^o_{t,n}$ is given by:

$$E\left[O^o_{t,n}\right] = O^d_{t,n} + m^d_n \tag{17}$$

Concluding, according to the model discussed in this section, the distortion caused by the coding-decoding scheme is represented by the mean vector $M^d = \left[m^d_1, m^d_2, m^d_3, \ldots m^d_n, \ldots, m^d_N\right]$ and the variance vector $V^d = \left[v^d_1, v^d_2, v^d_3, \ldots v^d_n, \ldots, v^d_N\right]$. Moreover, this distortion could be considered independent of the phonetic class and is consistent with the analysis presented in (Huerta, 2000).

4. Estimation of coding-decoding distortion

In this section the coding-decoding distortion as modeled in section 3 is evaluated employing the maximum likelihood criteria. Estimating the coding distortion in the HMM acoustic modeling is equivalent to find the vectors M^d and V^d defined above. In (Yoma et al., 2006) these parameters are estimated with the Expectation-Maximization (EM) algorithm using a code-book, where every code-word corresponds to a multivariate Gaussian, built with uncoded speech signals. The use of a code-book to represent the p.d.f. of the features of the clean speech is due to the fact that M^d and V^d are considered independent of the phonetic class. Inside each code-word cw_j the mean $\mu^o_j = \left[\mu^o_{j,1}, \mu^o_{j,2}, \ldots, \mu^o_{j,N}\right]$ and variance $(\sigma^o_j)^2 = \left[(\sigma^o_{j,1})^2, (\sigma^o_{j,2})^2, \ldots, (\sigma^o_{j,N})^2\right]$ are computed, and the distribution of frames in the cells is supposed to be Gaussian:

$$f(O^o_t / \phi^o_j) = \frac{1}{(2\pi)^{\frac{N}{2}} \left|\Sigma^o_j\right|^{\frac{1}{2}}} \cdot e^{-\frac{1}{2}\cdot\left(O^o_t - \mu^o_j\right)^t \left(\Sigma^o_j\right)^{-1} \left(O^o_t - \mu^o_j\right)} \tag{18}$$

where N is the number of cepstral coefficients and also the dimension of the code-book; Σ_j^o is the N-by-N covariance matrix that is supposed diagonal; and, $\phi_j^o = \left(\mu_j^o, \Sigma_j^o\right)$. In this case the speech model is composed of J code-words. Consequently, the p.d.f. associated to the frame O_t^o given the uncoded speech signal model is:

$$f(O_t^o / \Phi^o) = \sum_{j=1}^{J} f(O_t^o \mid \phi_j^o) \cdot \Pr(cw_j) \tag{19}$$

where $\Phi^o = \left\{\phi_j^o \;\middle|\; 1 \le j \le J\right\}$ denotes all the means and variances of the code-book. Equation (19) is equivalent to modeling the speech signal with a Gaussian mixture with J components. If the coded-decoded distortion is independent of the code-word or class, it is possible to show that the coded-decoded speech signal is represented by the model whose parameters are denoted by $\Phi^d = \left\{\phi_j^d \middle| 1 \le j \le J\right\}$, where $\phi_j^d = \left(\mu_j^d, \Sigma_j^d\right)$ and,

$$\mu_j^d = \mu_j^o - M^d \tag{20}$$

$$(\sigma_{j,n}^d)^2 = (\sigma_{j,n}^o)^2 + v_n^d \tag{21}$$

Consequently, the code-book that corresponds to the coded-decoded speech signal can be estimated from the original code-book by means of adding the vectors $-M^d$ and V^d, which model the compression distortion, to the mean and variance vectors, respectively, within each code-word.

In (Yoma et al., 2006) M^d and V^d are estimated with the maximum likelihood (ML) criterion using adaptation utterances. Due to the fact that the maximization of the likelihood does not lead to analytical solutions, the EM algorithm (Huang et al., 1990; Moon, 1996) was employed. Given an adaptation utterance O^d distorted by a coding-decoding scheme and composed of T frames,

$$O^d = \left[O_1^d,\ O_2^d,\ O_3^d,\ \ldots, O_t^d, \ldots,\ O_T^d\right]$$

O^d is also called observable data. In the problem addressed here, the unobserved data is represented by:

$$Y^d = \left[y_1^d,\ y_2^d,\ y_3^d,\ \ldots, y_t^d, \ldots,\ y_T^d\right]$$

where y_t^d is the hidden number that refers to the code-word or density of the observed frame O_t^d. The function $Q(\Phi, \hat{\Phi})$ is expressed as:

$$Q(\Phi, \hat{\Phi}) = E\left[\log\left(f(O^d, Y^d / \hat{\Phi})\right) \middle| O^d, \Phi\right] \tag{22}$$

where $\hat{\Phi} = \left\{\hat{\phi}_j \middle| 1 \le j \le J\right\}$, where $\hat{\phi}_j = \left(\mu_j^d, \Sigma_j^d\right)$ denotes the parameters that are estimated in an iteration by maximizing $Q(\Phi, \hat{\Phi})$. It can be shown that (22) can be decomposed in two terms:

$$A = \sum_{t=1}^{T}\sum_{j=1}^{J} \Pr(cw_j \mid O_t^d, \hat{\Phi}) \cdot \log\left(\hat{\Pr}(cw_j)\right) \tag{23}$$

and

$$B = \sum_{t=1}^{T}\sum_{j=1}^{J} \Pr(cw_j \mid O_t^d, \Phi_j) \cdot \log\left(f(O_t^d \mid cw_j, \hat{\Phi}_j)\right) \tag{24}$$

the probabilities $\hat{\Pr}(cw_j)$ are estimated by means of maximizing A with the Lagrange method:

$$\hat{\Pr}\left(cw_j\right) = \frac{1}{T}\sum_{t=1}^{T} \Pr\left(cw_j \mid O_t^d, \phi_j\right) \tag{25}$$

The distortion parameters defined in (16) could be estimated by applying to B the gradient operator with respect to M^d and V^d, and setting the partial derivatives equal to zero. However, this procedure does not lead to an analytical solution for V^d. In order to overcome this problem, the following algorithm is proposed:

1. Start with $\Phi = \Phi^o$, where $\Phi = \left\{\phi_j \middle| 1 \le j \le J\right\}$ and $\phi_j = \left(\mu_j, \Sigma_j\right)$.
2. Compute $\Pr(cw_j | O_t^d, \phi_j)$

$$\Pr(cw_j | O_t^d, \phi_j) = \frac{f(O_t^d \mid \phi_j) \cdot \Pr(cw_j)}{\sum_{k=1}^{J} f(O_t^d \mid \phi_k) \cdot \Pr(cw_k)} \tag{26}$$

3. Estimate $\hat{\Pr}(cw_j)$ with (25)
4. Estimate $\Delta\mu_n$ with

$$\Delta\mu_n = \frac{\sum_{t=1}^{T}\sum_{j=1}^{J}\left(\hat{\Pr}(cw_j \mid O_t^d, \phi_j) \cdot \frac{\left(O_{t,n}^d - \mu_{j,n}\right)}{\sigma_{j,n}^2}\right)}{\sum_{t=1}^{T}\sum_{j=1}^{J}\left(\frac{\hat{\Pr}(cw_j \mid O_t^d, \phi_j)}{\sigma_{j,n}^2}\right)} \tag{27}$$

5. Estimate $\hat{\mu}_{j,n}$, $1 < j < J$ and $1 < n < N$

$$\hat{\mu}_{j,n} = \mu_{j,n} + \Delta\mu_n \tag{28}$$

6. Estimate $\hat{\sigma}_{j,n}^2$ for each code-book

$$\hat{\sigma}_{j,n}^2 = \frac{\sum_{t=1}^{T} \hat{\Pr}(cw_j \mid O_t^d, \phi_j) \cdot \left(O_{t,n}^d - \hat{\mu}_{j,n}\right)^2}{\sum_{t=1}^{T} \hat{\Pr}(cw_j \mid O_t^d, \phi_j)} \tag{29}$$

7. Estimate likelihood of the adaptation utterance O^d with the re-estimated parameters:

$$f(O^d / \hat{\Phi}) = \sum_{t=1}^{T}\sum_{j=1}^{J} f(O_t^d \mid \hat{\phi}_j) \cdot \hat{\Pr}(cw_j) \tag{30}$$

8. Update parameters:

$$\Phi = \hat{\Phi}$$

$$\Pr(cw_j) = \hat{\Pr}(cw_j)$$

9. If convergence was reached, stop iteration; otherwise, go to step 2.
10. Estimate M^d and V^d :

$$m_n^d = -\ (\mu_{j,n} - \mu_{j,n}^o) \tag{31}$$

for any $1 < j < J$, and

$$v_n^d = \frac{\sum_{j=1}^{J}\left[\sigma_{j,n}^2 - (\sigma_{j,n}^o)^2\right] \cdot \Pr(\mathrm{cw_j})}{\sum_{j=1}^{J}\Pr(\mathrm{cw_j})} \tag{32}$$

where $1 < n < N$. If $v_n^d < 0$, v_n^d is made equal to 0.

It is worth observing that (27) was derived with $\frac{\partial B}{\partial(\Delta\mu_n)} = 0$, where B is defined in (24), $\hat{\mu}_{j,n} = \mu_{j,n} + \Delta\mu_n$ corresponds to the re-estimated code-word mean in an iteration. Expression (29) was derived by $\frac{\partial B}{\partial \hat{\sigma}_{j,n}^2} = 0$. Moreover, expressions (31) and (32) assume that the coding-distorting is independent of the code-word or class, and (32) attempts to weight the information provided by code-words according to the a priori probability $\Pr(cw_j)$.

The EM algorithm is a maximum likelihood estimation method based on a gradient ascent algorithm and considers the parameters M^d and V^d as being fixed but unknown. In contrast, maximum a posteriori (MAP) estimation (Gauvain & Lee, 1994) would assume the parameters M^d and V^d to be random vectors with a given prior distribution. MAP estimation usually requires less adaptation data, but the results presented in (Yoma et al., 2006) show that the proposed EM algorithm can lead to dramatic improvements with as few as one adapting utterance. Nevertheless, the proper use of an a priori distribution of M^d and V^d could lead to reductions in the computational load required by the coding-decoding distortion evaluation. When compared to MLLR (Gales, 1998), the proposed computation of the coding-decoding distortion requires fewer parameters to estimate, although it should still lead to high improvements in word accuracy as a speaker adaptation method. Finally, the method discussed in this section to estimate the coding-decoding distortion is similar to the techniques employed in (Acero and Stern, 1990; Moreno et al., 1995; Raj et al., 1996) to compensate additive/convolutional noise and estimate the unobserved clean signal. In those papers the p.d.f. for the features of clean speech is also modeled as a summation of multivariate Gaussian distributions, and the EM algorithm is applied to estimate the mismatch between training and testing conditions. However, (Yoma et. al, 2006) proposes a model of the low bit rate coding-decoding distortion that is different from the model of the additive and convolutional noise, although they are similar to some extent. The mean and variance compensation is code-word dependent in (Acero & Stern, 1990; Moreno et al., 1995; Raj et al., 1996). In contrast, M^d and V^d are considered independent of the code-word in (Yoma et. al, 2006). This assumption is very important because it dramatically reduces the number of parameters to estimate and the amount of adaptation data required. Despite the fact that (27) to estimate M^d is the same expression employed to estimate convolutional distortion (Acero & Stern, 1990) if additive noise is not present (Yoma, 1998-B), the methods in (Acero & Stern, 1990; Moreno et al., 1995; Raj et al., 1996) do not compensate the HMMs. Notice that the effect of the transfer function that represents a linear channel is supposed to be an additive constant in the log-cepstral domain. On the other hand, additive noise corrupts the speech signal according to the local SNR (Yoma & Villar, 2002), which leads to a variance compensation that clearly depends on the phonetic class and code-word.

5. The expected value of the observation probability: The Stochastic Weighted Viterbi algorithm

In the ordinary HMM topology the output probability of observing the frame O_t at state s, $b_s(O_t)$, is computed, either in the training or in the testing algorithms, considering O_t as being a vector of constants. As can be seen in (Yoma & Villar; 2002; Yoma et al., 2006) the observation vector is composed of static, delta and delta-delta cepstral coefficients, and according to sections 2 and 3 these parameters should be considered as being random variables with normal distributions when the speech signal is corrupted by additive noise and coding-decoding distortion. Therefore, to counteract this incompatibility (Yoma & Villar; 2002) proposes to replace, in the Viterbi algorithm, $b_s(O_t)$ with $E[b_s(O_t)]$ that denotes the expected value of the output probability. This new output probability, which takes into consideration the additive noise model, can be compared an empiric weighting function previously proposed in (Yoma et al., 1998-B).

5.1 An empiric weighting function

The uncertainty in noise canceling variance was estimated in each one of the DFT mel filters and employed to compute a coefficient $w(t)$ to weight the information provided by the frame t (Yoma et al., 1998-B). This weighting coefficient was included in the Viterbi algorithm by means of raising the output probability of observing the frame O_t at state s, $b_s(O_t)$, to the power of $w(t)$. The weighting parameter was equal to 0 for noise-only signal and equal to 1 for clean speech. As a consequence, if $w(t)$=0, $[b_s(O_t)]^{w(t)} = 1$ that means that the frame does not give any reliable information. This weighted Viterbi algorithm was able to show reductions in the error as high as 80 or 90% in isolated word speech recognition experiments. However, the approach presented some drawbacks: first, the function to estimate the weighting coefficient from the uncertainty variance was empiric, although coherent; second, the variance in (5) was estimated using numeric approximations which resulted in a high computational load. It is worth highlighting that the same weighting $[b_s(O_t)]^{w(t)}$ has been used later by other authors. For instance, in (Bernard & Alwan, 2002; Tan, Dalsgaard, & Lindberg, 2005) this weighting function was used to address the problem of speech recognition in packet based and wireless communication. Notice that a lost packet would corresponds to reliability in signal estimation equal to zero.

5.2 The expected value of the output probability

In most HMM systems the output probability is modeled with a mixture of Gaussians with diagonal covariance matrices (Huang et al., 1990):

$$b_s(O_t) = \sum_{g=1}^{G} p_g \cdot \prod_{n=1}^{N} (2\cdot\pi)^{-0.5} \cdot \left(Var_{s,g,n}\right)^{-0.5} \cdot e^{-\frac{1}{2}\cdot\frac{\left(O_{t,n}-E_{s,g,n}\right)^2}{Var_{s,g,n}}} \tag{33}$$

where s, g, n are the indices for the states, the Gaussian components and the coefficients, respectively; p_g is a weighting parameter; $O_t = \left[O_{t,1},\ O_{t,2},\ \ldots,\ O_{t,N}\right]$ is the observation vector composed of N coefficients (static, delta and delta-delta cepstral parameters); and, $E_{s,g,n}$ and $Var_{s,g,n}$ are the HMM mean and variance, respectively. Assuming that the coefficients $O_{t,n}$ are uncorrelated, which in turn results in the diagonal covariance matrices, the expected value of $b_s(O_t)$ is given by:

$$E\left[b_s(O_t)\right] = \sum_{g=1}^{G} p_g \cdot \prod_{n=1}^{N} E\left[\frac{1}{\sqrt{2\cdot\pi\cdot Var_{s,g,n}}} \cdot e^{-\frac{1}{2}\cdot\frac{\left(O_{t,n}-E_{s,g,n}\right)^2}{Var_{s,g,n}}}\right] \tag{34}$$

where

$$E\left[\frac{1}{\sqrt{2\cdot\pi\cdot Var_{s,g,n}}} \cdot e^{-\frac{1}{2}\cdot\frac{\left(O_{t,n}-E_{s,g,n}\right)^2}{Var_{s,g,n}}}\right] = \int_{-\infty}^{\infty} \frac{1}{\sqrt{2\cdot\pi\cdot Var_{s,g,n}}} \cdot e^{-\frac{1}{2}\cdot\frac{\left(O_{t,n}-E_{s,g,n}\right)^2}{Var_{s,g,n}}} \cdot G\left(O_{t,n}; E(O_{t,n}); Var(O_{t,n})\right) \cdot dO_{t,n} \tag{35}$$

and, according to sections 2 and 3, $G\left(O_{t,n}; E(O_{t,n}); Var(O_{t,n})\right)$ is the Gaussian distribution of $O_{t,n}$. When the speech signal is corrupted with addittive noise, the mean, $E(O_{t,n})$, and variance, $Var(O_{t,n})$, are estimated with (11) (12) and (14) (15) for the static and delta cepstral coefficients, respectively. The delta-delta cepstral parameters can be computed using the same strategy employed in (14) (15). When the speech signal is affected by coding-decoding distortion, $E(O_t) = M^d$ and $Var(O_t) = V^d$, as discussed in section 3. As a consequence, it is possible to show that:

$$E\left[\frac{1}{\sqrt{2\cdot\pi\cdot Var_{s,g,n}}}\cdot e^{-\frac{1}{2}\cdot\frac{\left(O_{t,n}-E_{s,g,n}\right)^2}{Var_{s,g,n}}}\right]=\frac{1}{\sqrt{2\cdot\pi\cdot Vtot_{s,g,n,t}}}\cdot e^{-\frac{1}{2}\cdot\frac{\left(E\left[O_{t,n}\right]-E_{s,g,n}\right)^2}{Vtot_{s,g,n,t}}} \tag{36}$$

where $Vtot_{s,g,n,t}=Var_{s,g,n}+Var(O_{t,n})$. Therefore, (34) can be written as:

$$E\left[b_s(O_t)\right]=\sum_{g=1}^{G}p_g\cdot\prod_{n=1}^{N}\frac{1}{\sqrt{2\cdot\pi\cdot Vtot_{s,g,n,t}}}\cdot e^{-\frac{1}{2}\cdot\frac{\left(E\left[O_{t,n}\right]-E_{s,g,n}\right)^2}{Vtot_{s,g,n,t}}} \tag{37}$$

This is an elegant and generic result, and deserves some comments. Firstly, the expression (37) means that the expected value of the output probability is also represented by a sum of Gaussian functions. Secondly, if $Var(O_{t,n})\rightarrow 0$ (i.e. high SNR) $O_{t,n}$ can be considered as a constant and (37) is reduced to the ordinary output probability because $E\left[O_{t,n}\right]=O_{t,n}$. Finally, if $Var(O_{t,n})$ is high (i.e. low SNR) the expected value given by (37) tends to zero independently of $E\left[O_{t,n}\right]$, and of the HMM parameters $E_{s,g,n}$ and $Var_{s,g,n}$, which means that the information provided by a noisy observation vector is not useful and has a low weight in the final decision procedure of accepting or rejecting a speaker. The weighting mechanism could be defined by the fact that the original output probability is mapped to the same value (1 in the empirical weighting function, and 0 in (37)) when the segmental SNR is very low. As a consequence, the expression (37) is consistent with the weighting function mentioned in section 6.1 and can define a stochastic version of the weighted Viterbi algorithm, which in turn was proposed to take into consideration the segmental SNR.

5.3 SWV applied to speaker verification with additive noise

As shown in (Yoma & Villar; 2002), experiments with speech signal corrupted by car noise show that the expected value of the output probability using the additive noise model combined with SS led to reductions of 10%, 34%, 35% and 31% in the EER_{SD} at SNR=18dB, 12dB, 6dB and 0dB, respectively, when compared with the ordinary Viterbi algorithm also with SS. In the same conditions, the reductions in the EER_{SI} were 26%, 41%, 43% and 30% at, respectively, SNR=18dB, 12dB, 6dB and 0dB as shown in Table 1. Although an optimum might be considered around $c_m=0.25$, according to Figs. 10 and 11 the EER_{SD} and the EER_{SI} did not present a high variation with c_m, which confirms the stability of the approach proposed. Preliminary experiments showed that the lower the reduction due to spectral subtraction, the higher the improvement due to the weighted Viterbi algorithm. The effectiveness of spectral subtraction is closely related to how low SNR frames are processed. According to the experiments presented in (Yoma & Villar; 2002) and Table 1 the weighted Viterbi algorithm defined by the expected observation probability in (37) can improve the accuracy of the speaker verification system even if SS is not employed. For instance, the average reduction in EER_{SD} and EER_{SI} without SS is 11%. As can be seen in (Yoma & Villar; 2002) shown in Table 2 and in Fig. 12, the expected value of the output probability using the additive noise model substantially reduced the variability of $TEER_{SD}$ and $TEER_{SI}$ with and without SS. According to Table 2, the differences $TEER_{SD}$(18dB) - $TEER_{SD}$ (0dB) and $TEER_{SI}$(18dB) - $TEER_{SI}$(0dB) with SS are, respectively, 53% and 55% lower with the weighted

Viterbi algorithm than with the ordinary one. This must be due to the fact that, when the segmental SNR decreases, $Var(O_{t,n})$ increases and the output probability according to (37) tends to 0 for both the client and global HMM in the normalized log likelihood (log $L(O)$) (Furui, 1997)::

$$\log L(O) = \log P(O \mid \lambda_i) - \log P(O \mid \lambda_g) \tag{38}$$

where $P(O \mid \lambda_i)$ is the likelihood related to the speaker *i;* and $P(O \mid \lambda_g)$ is the likelihood related to the global HMMs.

The results presented in (Yoma & Villar; 2002) with speech noise basically confirmed the tests with car noise. The expected observation probability in (37) led to average reductions in EER_{SD} and in EER_{SI} equal to 23% and 30%, respectively, with SS. Significance analysis with the McNamar´s testing (Gillik & Cox, 1989) shows that this improvement due to the expected value of the output probability using the additive noise model combined with SS, when compared with the ordinary Viterbi algorithm also with SS, are significant ($p<0.1$ at SNR=18dB and $p<0.001$ at SNR=12, 6 and 0dB). Also, the differences $TEER_{SD}$(18dB) - $TEER_{SD}$ (0dB) and $TEER_{SI}$(18dB) - $TEER_{SI}$(0dB) were dramatically improved by the weighted Viterbi algorithm in combination with the additive noise model.

Finally, it is worth mentioning that the performance of SS is highly dependent on the parameters related to the thresholds (Berouti et al., 1979; Vaseghi & Milner, 1997) that are defined to make the technique work properly. In the case of the SS as defined in (9), parameter β, which defines the lower bound for the estimated signal energy, was not optimized for each SNR although its optimum values is case dependent. For instance, Table 3 shows that the expected observation probability led to a reduction of 26% in the EER_{SI} at SNR=18dB although SS alone did not give any improvement. This result suggests that the weighted Viterbi algorithm also improves the robustness of SS by means of giving a lower weight to those frames with low segmental SNR, where in turn SS is not reliable.

SNR	18dB	12dB	6dB	0dB
Vit-Nss	2.50	5.11	14.70	32.94
Vit-SS	2.59	4.71	11.14	26.73
SWVit-NSS	2.26	4.40	12.22	31.35
SWVit-SS	1.92	2.79	6.40	18.85

Table 1. EER_{SI} (speaker-independent Equal Error Rate) % with speech corrupted by additive noise (car noise). The correction coefficient c_m was made equal to 0.25.

	Vit-NSS	Vit-SS	SWVit-NSS	SWVit-SS
$TEER_{SD}$	1.72	1.93	1.01	0.90
$TEER_{SI}$	1.62	1.88	0.93	0.84

Table 2. Difference in the threshold of equal error rate at 18dB and 0dB, TEER(18dB)-TEER(0dB), with speech corrupted by additive noise (car noise). The correction coefficient c_m was made equal to 0.25.

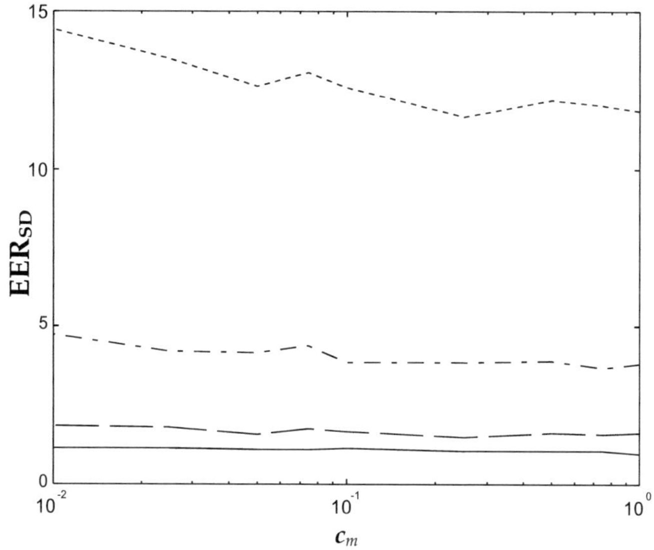

Figure 10. EER_{SD} vs. c_m with speech corrupted by additive noise (car noise): 18dB (——), 12dB (— —), 6dB (— · —) and 0dB (- - -).

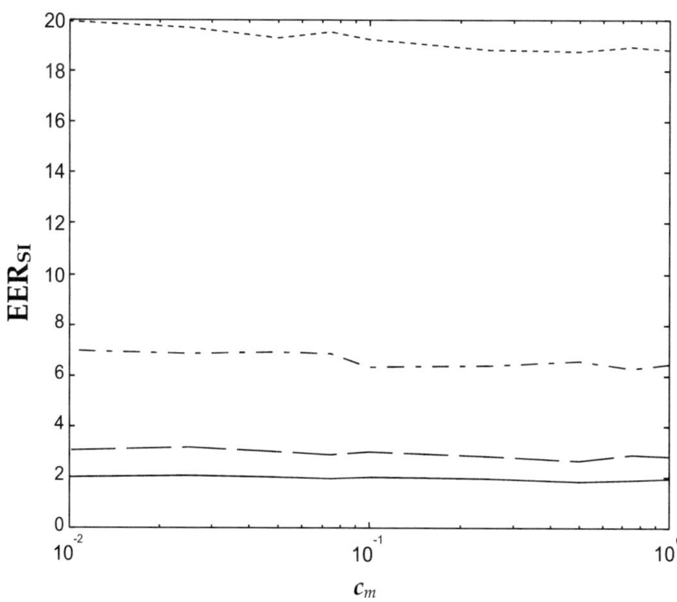

Figure 11. EER_{SI} vs. c_m with speech corrupted by additive noise (car noise): 18dB (——), 12dB (— —), 6dB (— · —) and 0dB (- - -).

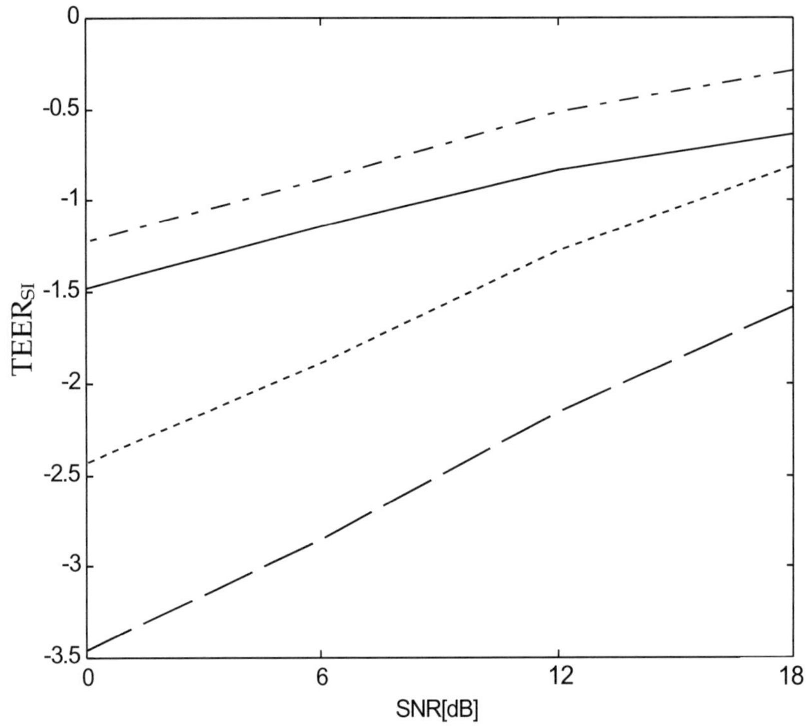

Figure 12. Speaker-independent threshold of equal error rate ($TEER_{SI}$) vs. SNR with speech corrupted by additive noise (car noise): *WVit-SS* (———); *Vit-SS* (— —); *WVit-NSS* (— · —) and *Vit-NSS* (- - -). The correction coefficient c_m was made equal to 0.25.

5.4 SWV applied to low-bit rate coding-decoding distortion compensation

The code-book to model the non-distorted speech process was composed of 256 code-words and was generated with the uncoded training utterances. The techniques are indicated as follows: *HMM-Comp*, with HMM compensation where M^d and V^d are estimated with the training utterances by directly aligning original and coded-decoded speech signals; and, *HMM-Comp-EM*, with HMM compensation where M^d and V^d are estimated according to the EM-based algorithm explained in section 4. Observe that *Baseline* indicates that no HMM compensation was applied. The baseline system with non-distorted speech and without any compensation gave a WER equal to 5.9%.

According to the results presented in (Yoma et. al., 2006) and shown in Table 3, the ADPCM, GSM, CS-CELP, G723-1 and FS-1016 coders increased the error rate from 5.9% (baseline system) to 6.2%, 6.9%, 11.2%, 11.9% and 15.2%, respectively. Also in Table 3, it is possible to observe that the HMM compensation led to a reduction as high as 37% or 71% in the error rate introduced by the coding schemes when the average coding-decoding distortion was estimated by directly aligning the training uncoded and coded-decoded speech, *HMM-*

Comp. This result clearly shows the validity of the method to model the coding distortion and to compensate the HMMs. However, it is worth mentioning that in *HMM-Comp* all the training speakers were employed to compute the average M^d and V^d. Notice that *HMM-Comp* gave a WER lower than the one achieved by the baseline system with uncoded speech (i.e. 5.9%) in some cases. This result could suggest that the HMMs are slightly under trained, so V^d could also tend to compensate this effect.

Coder	Bit rate	Baseline WER(%)	HMM-Comp. WER(%)	HMM-Comp-EM WER(%).
ADPCM	32 kbps	6.2	3.9	2.8
GSM	13 kbps	6.9	3.8	3.3
CS-CELP	8 kbps	11.2	3.3	2.6
G723-1	5.3 kbps	11.9	5.8	2.6
FS-1016	4.8 kbps	15.2	7.4	3.6

Table 3. WER (%) with signal processed with the following coders: 32 kbps ADPCM, 13 kbps GSM, 8kbps CS-CELP, 5.3 kbps G723-1 and 4.8 kbps FS-1016. The baseline system without any compensation gives a WER equal to 5.9% with uncoded utterances.

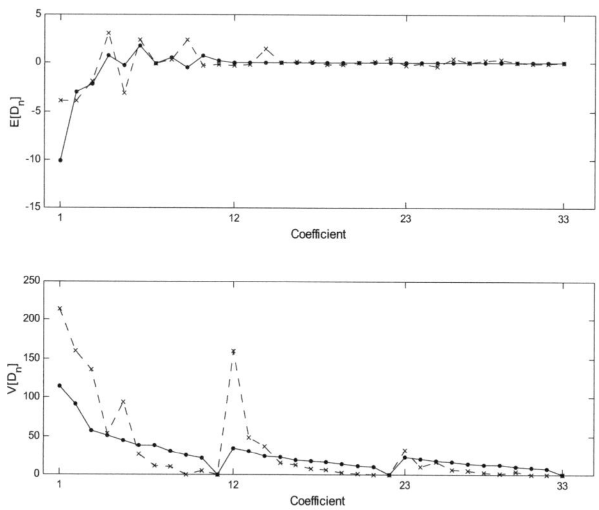

Figure 13. M^d (top) and V^d (bottom) estimated with the EM based algorithm (--×--) and computed with the training database by directly aligning uncoded and coded-decoded speech samples (——). The signals were processed by the 8 kbps CS-CELP from the ITU-T standard G.729.

According to Fig. 13, the EM algorithm described here can lead to a reasonable approximation of M^d and V^d when compared to the average coding-decoding distortion computed with the training database. The difference between the EM estimation and the average M^d and V^d (Fig. 13) could be due to fact that the coding-decoding distortion depends on the speaker. As can be seen in Table 3, the EM estimation of M^d and V^d with only one adaptation utterance dramatically reduced the effect of the ADPCM, GSM, CS-CELP, G723-1 and FS-1016 coding distortion, and gave a WER lower than *HMM-Comp* and than the one achieved by the baseline system with uncoded speech. A reasonable hypothesis could be the fact that the approaches described in sections 3 and 4 also provides an adaptation to testing condition beyond the type of codification because the estimation of the vectors M^d and V^d may also account for a speaker adaptation effect. Actually, the results presented in (Yoma et. al., 2006), show that the EM estimation algorithm applied to uncoded signal reduces in 56% the WER when compared to the baseline system. In fact, this result would be consistent with (Zhao, 1994), where additive bias compensation in the cepstral domain for speaker adaptation was studied. Also according to Table 3, it is possible to observe that the reduction in WER compared to the baseline system is as high as 52% or 78%, which in turn suggests that the approach proposed here is effective to model, estimate and compensate the coding-decoding distortion. It is worth emphasizing the fact that the reduction in WER increases when the bit-rate decreases. Finally, when compared to the baseline system, *HMM-Comp-EM* reduces the averaged difference between WER with distorted speech and clean signal from 4.4% to 0.4%.

The training database was composed of utterances from just 36 speakers. Consequently, the fact that the EM compensation method also introduces a speaker adaptation effect would be consistent with the size of the database. Most of the compensation methods for HMMs attempt to adapt means or variances of the observation probability density functions. Moreover, it is to be expected that a canceling/compensation technique proposed to address a given distortion also helps to reduce the error introduced by another type of distortion. For instance, RASTA filtering was initially proposed to cancel convolutional noise but it also reduces the effect of additive noise. It is also hard to believe that a speaker adaptation scheme could not compensate or reduce convolutional noise. Finally, as was shown in (Yoma et. al., 2006), a speaker adaptation should also be useful for diminishing coding-decoding distortion, although this reduction would depend on the model adopted to estimate the means and variances. However, in additional speaker-dependent (SD) experiments with all the coders tested here, *HMM-Comp-EM* was able to lead to an average reduction in WER as high as 54% when compared to the baseline system. Those SD experiments were done by training the HMMs with both the training and testing databases. Consequently, the mismatch was restricted to the coding decoding distortion. This result strongly suggests that: first, the speaker adaptation effect in *HMM-Comp-EM*, if there is any, is not the most important mechanism in the reduction of WER provided by the *HMM-Comp-EM* technique; and second, the improvement in word accuracy given by the method presented in (Yoma et. al., 2006) is not due to under trained conditions.

The EM adaptation method is unsupervised and requires only one adaptation utterance. In (Yoma et. al., 2006), RATZ (Moreno et. al., 1995), without variance compensation and supervised ML estimation (Afify et. al., 1998), based on forced Viterbi alignment was compared with *HMM-Comp-EM* algorithm. According to (Moreno et. al., 1995), blind RATZ jointly compensates for additive and convolutional noise by employing the EM algorithm and a summation of multivariate Gaussian distributions to model the p.d.f. for the features of clean speech. Notice that blind RATZ is an unsupervised method. Word accuracy given by RATZ strongly depends on the number of adapting utterances employed to compute $O^{o}_{t,n}$. When compared to the baseline system, RATZ could provide an improvement in WER if the number of adapting utterances is higher than 4 or 10. If the method employs only one adaptation utterance, it always gave a WER even higher than the one achieved with the baseline system. It is worth highlighting that *HMM-Comp-EM* provides higher recognition accuracy even when the whole testing data was employed by RATZ. Supervised ML, *Superv-ML,* estimation evaluated in (Yoma et al., 2006) is similar to the one presented in (Afify et. al., 1998) except for the fact that the Forward-Backward procedure was replaced with the Viterbi algorithm. The improvement in WER given by *Superv-ML* also depends on the number of adapting utterances. The stochastic model employed by the proposed EM unsupervised algorithm is more robust than the one provided by the *Superv-ML* method, which in turn is composed of only the HMMs corresponding to the adapting utterances. Consequently, the requirement with respect to the amount of adaptation data to achieve the highest reduction in WER is more severe in *Superv-ML.* When the number of adapting utterances is equal to 500, *Superv-ML* could give improvements in WER worse than *HMM-Comp-EM* with GSM and ADPCM, despite the fact that the proposed EM unsupervised estimation algorithm employed only one adaptation utterance and *Superv-ML* made use of the whole testing database.

5.5. SWV to address the problem of joint compensation of additive noise and low-bit rate coding-decoding distortion

As can be seen in Fig. 14 (Yoma et. al., 2003), the problem of additive noise and low-bit rate coding-decoding distortion corresponds to a clean signal *s(t)* firstly corrupted by an additive noise in the temporal domain, *x(t)*, and then coded and decoded, $x^D(t)$. The observation parameter vectors of the signals *s(t)*, *x(t)* and $x^D(t)$. are $O_t^{S,U}$, $O_t^{X,U}$ and $O_t^{S,D}$, respectively. *S* and *X* denote the clean and noisy signal, respectively; *U* and *D* correspond to the signals before (uncoded) and after (distorted) the coding-decoding process.

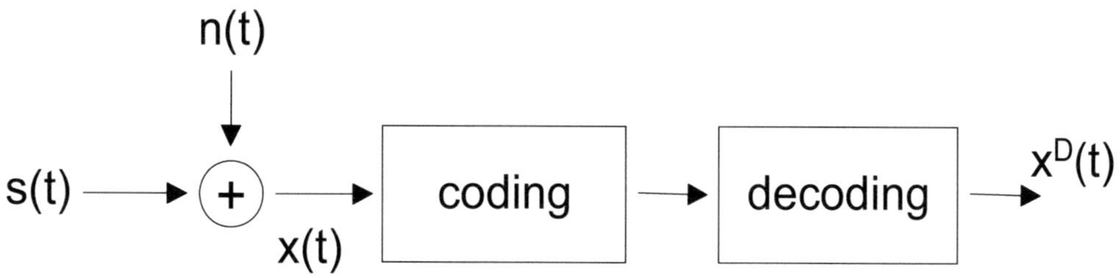

Figure 14. Additive noise and coding distortion.

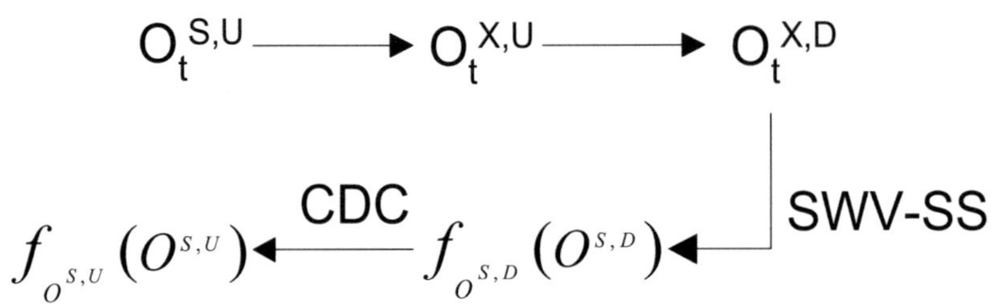

Figure 15. Join compensation of additive noise and coding distortion: $f_{O^{S,D}}(O^{S,D})$ denotes the p.d.f. of the distorted by coding clean signal; $f_{O^{S,U}}(O^{S,U})$ corresponds to the p.d.f. of the uncoded clean signal.

As is shown in Fig. 15, the method proposed in (Yoma et. al., 2003) firstly compensates the presence of additive noise by applying SS and estimating the uncertainty variance in noise canceling as in section 2 using $x^D(t)$. As a result, the p.d.f. of the distorted by coding clean speech, $f_{O^{S,D}}(O^{S,D})$, is generated. Then, as discussed in section 3, $f_{O^{S,U}}(O^{S,U})$ is estimated by adding M^d and V^d to the mean and variance, respectively, of $f_{O^{S,D}}(O^{S,D})$. Finally, by taking the expected value of the output p.d.f., the compensation of the additive noise and of the coding distortion are incorporated in the Viterbi decoding as in (37).

As can be seen in Tables 4 and 5 (Yoma et al., 2003), the additive noise and the coder dramatically degraded the WAC at SNR equal to 18dB and 12dB. SWV and SS substantially reduced the WER, but the highest improvement was achieved when coding-decoding compensation was also applied. Reductions as high as 50% or 60% in WER were observed at 18dB and 12dB. Nevertheless, the degradation of the system at 12dB is still too severe. According to Tables 4 and 5, the additive noise has probably a more significant effect on rising the WER than the coding-decoding distortion. As a result, improving the accuracy of the additive noise model (Yoma et. al., 1998-B) at low SNR should certainly increase the effectiveness of the approach proposed here.

SNR	18dB	12dB
Baseline	27.4	38.5
SWV-SS	11.9	18.3
SWV-SS-CDC	10.2	16.9

Table 4. WER (%) with signal corrupted with additive noise (car noise) and coded by 8kbps CS-CELP.

SNR	18dB	12dB
Baseline	26.2	37.9
SWV-SS	11.7	17.5
SWV-SS-CDC	10.0	15.3

Table 5. WER (%) with signal corrupted with additive noise (speech noise) and coded by 8kbps CS-CELP.

6. Language model accuracy and uncertainty in noise canceling in SWV

No significant improvements were observed when the SWV algorithm in combination with the additive noise model proposed in (Yoma et al, 1998-B) and SS was applied to the connected digit task. This result must be due to fact that the SWV algorithm makes the HMM observation p.d.f. lose discrimination ability at noisy frames. This hypothesis means that the Viterbi decoding should be guided by the information from higher layers, such as language modeling, in those intervals with low SNR. In contrast, the connected digit task employs a flat language model. In (Yoma et al, 2003-B), the SWV algorithm was applied to a continuous speech, medium vocabulary, speaker independent (SI) task opening a new paradigm in speech recognition where the noise canceling could interact with the information from higher layers in the same way the human perceptions works. Bigram and trigram language models were tested and, in combination with spectral subtraction, the SWV algorithm coul lead to reductions as high as 20% or 45% in word error rate (WER) using a rough estimation of the additive noise made in a short non-speech interval. Also, the results presented in (Yoma et al, 2003-B) suggest that the higher the language model accuracy, the higher the improvement due to SWV. Consequently, the problem of noise robustness in speech recognition should be classified in two different contexts: firstly, at the acoustic-phonetic level only, as in small vocabulary tasks with flat language model; and, by integrating noise canceling with the information from higher layers.

7. Conclusions

The Stochastic Weighted Viterbi algorithm offers a unified framework to reduce the effect of additive/convolutional noise and low-bit rate coding-decoding distortion. SWV started a new paradigm in speech processing by considering the original speech signal information as a stochastic variable. Consequently, the ordinary HMM observation probability needs to be replaced with its expected value. SWV is interesting from the theoretic and applied points of view: first, it is based on stochastic models of additive noise and low-bit rate coding-decoding distortion; and second, it assumes reasonable hypotheses such as a rough estimation of additive noise and a low number of adaptation utterances. It is worth emphasizing that SWV allows the interaction between the higher layers of language modeling (semantic, syntactic, etc...) and acoustic models in ASR just like in human perception: the higher layer of the linguistic information should have a higher weight in those frames with low SNR or low reliability. Finally, the concepts of uncertainty in noise canceling and weighted recognition algorithms, which were firstly proposed by the first author of this chapter, have also widely been employed elsewhere in the fields of ASR and SV in later publications.

8. Acknowledgement

This research described here was funded by Conicyt - Chile under grants Fondecyt N° 1030956, Fondecyt N° 1000934, and Fondef N° D02I-1089.

9. References

Acero, A. & Stern, R. (1990). Environmental robustness in automatic speech recognition. *Proceedings of IEEE International Conference on Acoustics, Speech and Signal Processing ICASSP'90*,pp. 849-852.

Acero, A., Deng, L. & Droppo, J. G. (2006-A). Method of iterative noise estimation in a recursive framework. *United States Patent 7139703.*

Acero, A.; Deng, L. & Droppo, J. G. (2006-B). Non-linear observation model for removing noise from corrupted signals. *United States Patent 7047047.*

Afify, M.; Gong, Y. & Haton, J. (1998). A General Joint Additive and Convolutive Bias Compensation Approach Applied to Noise Lombard Speech Recognition *IEEE Transactions on Speech and Audio Processing*, Vol. 6, No. 6, pp. 524-538.

Arrowood, J.A. & Clements, M.A. (2004). Extended cluster information vector quantization (ECIVQ) for robust classification, *Proceedings of IEEE International Conference on Acoustics, Speech and Signal Processing ICASSP 2004*, pp. I889-I892.

Barger, P. and Sridharan, S. (1997). Robust speaker identification using multi-microphone systems. *Proceedings of TENCON '97*, pp. 261 –264.

Bernard, A. & Alwan, A. (2002). Low-bitrate distributed speech recognition for packet-based and wireless communication. *IEEE Transactions on Speech and Audio Processing*, Vol. 10, No. 8, pp. 570-579.

Berouti, M.; Schwartz, R. & Makhoul, J. (1979). Enhancement of speech corrupted by acoustic noise. *Proceedings of IEEE International Conference on Acoustics, Speech and Signal Processing ICASSP'79*. pp.208-211.

Breton, P. A. (2005). Method and device for voice recognition in environments with fluctuating noise levels. *United States Patent 6859773.*

Campbell, J. P.; Tremain, T. E. & Welch, V. C. (1991). The federal standard 1016 4800 bps CELP voice coder. *Digital Signal Processing*, Vol. 1, No. 3, pp. 145--155,.

Chan, S.M. & Siu, M.H. (2004). Discrimination power weighted subword-based speaker verification. *Proceedings of IEEE International Conference on Acoustics, Speech and Signal Processing ICASSP 2004*, pp. I45-I4.

Cho, H.Y.; Kim, L.Y. & Oh, Y.H. (2002). Segmental reliability weighting for robust recognition of partly corrupted speech. *IEE Electronics Letters*, Vol. 38, No. 12, pp. 611-612.

Delaney, B. (2005). Increased robustness against bit errors for distributed speech recognition in wireless environments. *Proceedings of IEEE International Conference on Acoustics, Speech and Signal Processing ICASSP 2005*, pp. I313-I316.

Deng, L.; Droppo, J. & Acero, A. (2005). Dynamic compensation of HMM variances using the feature enhancement uncertainty computed from a parametric model of speech distortion. *IEEE Transactions on Speech and Audio Processing*, Vol. 13, No. 3, pp. 412-421.

Drygajlo, A. & El-Maliki, M. (1998). Speaker verification in noisy environments with combined spectral subtraction and missing feature theory. *Proceedings of IEEE International Conference on Acoustics, Speech and Signal Processing ICASSP´98*, pp. 121 -124.

Erzin, E.; Yemez, Y. & Tekalp, A.M. (2005). Multimodal speaker identification using an adaptive classifier cascade based on modality reliability. *IEEE Transactions on Multimedia*, Vol. 7, No. 5, pp. 840-852.

ETSI (1992). GSM-06.10 Full Rate Speech Transcoding. RPE-LTP (Regular Pulse Excitation, Long Term Predictor), *ETSI, France.*

Furui, S. (1982). Cepstral analysis technique for automatic speaker verication. *IEEE Transactions on Speech and Audio Processing*, Vol. 29, No.2, pp.254-272.

Furui, S. (1997). Recent advances in speaker recognition. *Pattern Recognition Letters*, Vol. 18, pp. 859-872.

Gales M.J.F. (1998). Maximum likelihood linear transformations for HMM-based speech recognition. *Computer Speech and Language*, Vol. 12, no. 2, pp. 75-98.

Gales, M.J.F. & Young, S.J. (1993). HMM recognition in noise using parallel model combination. *Proceedings of. Eurospeech'93*, pp. 837-840.

Gales, M.J.F. (1997). "Nice" model-based compensation schemes for robust speech recognition. *Proceedings of. Esca-Nato Workshop on robust speech recognition for unknown channels*. pp. 55-64.

Gauvain J. & Lee, C-H (1994). Maximum a posteriori estimation for multivariate Gaussian Mixture Observation of Markov Chains, *IEEE Transactions on Speech and Audio Processing*, Vol. 2, No. 2, pp. 291-298.

Gillik, L. & Cox, S.J. (1989). Some statistical issues in the comparison of speech recognition algorithms. *Proceedings of IEEE International Conference on Acoustics, Speech and Signal Processing ICASSP´98*, pp.532-535.

Gomez, A. M.; Peinado, A. M. & Sanchez, V. (2006). Combining media-specific FEC and error concealment for robust distributed speech recognition over loss-prone packet channels. *IEEE Transactions on Multimedia*, Vol. 8, No. 6, pp. 1228-1238.

Hardt, D. & Fellbaum, K. (1997). Spectral subtraction and RASTA-filtering in text-dependent HMM-based speaker verification. *Proceedings of IEEE International Conference on Acoustics, Speech and Signal Processing ICASSP´97.*, pp. 867 -870.

Hermansky, H. et al. (1991). Compensation for the effect of the communication channel in auditory-like analysis of speech (RASTA-PLP). *Procedings of Eurospeech' 91*, pp.1367-1370.

Huang, X.D.; Ariki, Y. & Jack, M. (1990). Hidden Markov Models for speech recognition. Edinburgh University Press.

Huerta , J.M. (2000). Speech Recognition in Mobile Environments. *Ph.D thesis*, Department of Electrical and Computer Engineering, Carnegie Mellon University, Pittsburgh, PA, USA.

Hung, J.; Shen, J. & Lee, L. (1998). Improved robustness for speech recognition under noisy conditions using correlated Parallel Model Combination. *Proceedings of IEEE International Conference on Acoustics, Speech and Signal Processing ICASSP'98*, Vol. 1, pp. 549-552 .

ITU-T (1990). Recommendation G.726, 40-,32-,24-, and 16-Kb/s adaptive differential pulse code modulation.

ITU-T (1996). Recommendation G.729-Coding of speech at 8 kbit/s using conjugate-structure algebraic-code-excited linear-prediction (CS-CELP).

ITU-T (1996-B). Recommendation G.723.1 Dual Rate Speech Coder for Multimedia Communications Transmitting at 5.3 and 6.3 kbps, Marzo 1996.

Keung, C. L.; Au, O. C.; Yim, C. H. & Fung, C. C. (2000). Probabilistic Compensation of Unreliable Feature Components for Robust Speech Recognition, *Proceedings of International Conference of Spoken Language Processing ICSLP 2000*, pp. 1085-1087.

Kitaoka, N. & Nakagawa, S. (2002). Evaluation of spectral subtraction with smoothing of time direction on the aurora 2 task. *Proceedings of International Conference on Spoken Language Processing ICSLP 2002*, pp. 1085-1087.

LDC (1995). Latino database provided by Linguistic Data Consortium (LDC), University of Pennsylvania: http://www.ldc.upenn.edu/Catalog/LDC95S28.html.

Li, S. C. (2003). Applying eigenvoice model adaptation for user verbal information verification. *M.Sc. Thesis in Computer Science and Information Engineering*, National Chen Kung University, Tainan, Taiwan, R.O.C.

Liao, H. & Gales, M.J.F. (2005). Joint Uncertainty Decoding for Noise Robust Speech Recognition. *Proceedings of Interspeech 2005*, pp. 3129-3132.

Moon, T.K. (1996). The Expectation-Maximization Algorithm. *IEEE Signal Processing Magazine*, Vol. 13, No.6, pp.47-60.

Moreno P. J., Raj B., Govea E. and Stern R. M. (1995). Multivariate Gaussian Based Cepstral Normalization for Robust Speech Recognition. *Proceedings of IEEE International Conference on Acoustics, Speech and Signal Processing ICASSP'95*, pp. 137-140.

Ortega-Garcia, J. & Gonzalez-Rodriguez, J. (1997). Providing single and multi-channel acoustical robustness to speaker identification systems. *Proceedings of IEEE International Conference on Acoustics, Speech and Signal Processing ICASSP´97*, pp. 1107-1110.

Papoulis, A. (1991). Probability, random variables, and stochastic processes. McGraw-Hill International Editions.

Pfitzinger, H.R. (2000). Removing Hum from Spoken Language Recources. *Proceedings of International Conference of Spoken Language Processing ICSLP 2000*, pp. 618-621.

Pitsikalis, V.; Katsamanis, A.; Papandreou, G. & Maragos. P. (2006). Adaptive Multimodal Fusion by Uncertainty Compensation. *Proceedings of International Conference of Spoken Language Processing ICSLP 2006*, pp. 2458-2461.

Raj, B.; Gouvea, E. B.; Moreno, P. J. & Stern, R. M. (1996). Cepstral compensation by polynomial approximation for environment-independent speech recognition. *Proceedings of International Conference of Spoken Language Processing ICSLP'96*, Vol 4, pp. 2340-2343.

Reynolds, D.A. (1994). Experimental evaluation of features for robust speaker identification. *IEEE Transactions on Speech and Audio Processing*, Vol. 2, No.4, pp. 639-643.

Rose, R.C. ; Hofstetter, E.M. & Reynolds D.A. (1994). Integrated models of signal and background with application to speaker identification in noise. *IEEE Transactions on Speech and Audio Processing*, Vol. 2, No.2 , pp. 245-257.

Tan, Z. H.; Dalsgaard, P. & Lindberg, B. (2005). Automatic speech recognition over error-prone wireless networks, *Speech Communication*, Vol. 47, No. 1-2, pp. 220-242.

van Vuuren, S. (1996). Comparison of text-independent speaker recognition methods on telephone speech with acoustic mismatch. *Proceedings of International Conference of Spoken Language Processing ICSLP'96*, pp. 1788 -1791.

Vaseghi, S.V. & Milner, B.P. (1997). Noise compensation methods for Hidden Markov Model speech recognition in adverse environments. *IEEE Transactions on Speech and Audio Processing*, Vol. 5, No. 1, pp. 11-21.

Vildjiounaite, E.; Makela, S.M.; Lindholm, M.; Riihimaki, R.; Kyllonen, V.; Mantyjarvi, J. & Ailisto, H. H. (2006). Unobtrusive multimodal biometrics for ensuring privacy and information security with personal devices. *Lecture Notes in Computer Science*, No. 3968, pp. 187-201.

Wu, C. H. & Chen, Y. J. (2001). Multi-keyword spotting of telephone speech using a fuzzy search algorithm and keyword-driven two-level CBSM, *Speech Communication*. Vol. 33, No. 3, pp. 197-212.

Yoma, N.B.; McInnes, F. & Jack, M. (1995). Improved Algorithms for Speech Recognition in Noise using Lateral Inhibition and SNR Weighting. *Proceedings of Eurospeech'95*, pp.461-464

Yoma, N.B.; McInnes, F. & Jack, M. (1996-A). Lateral inhibition net and weighted matching algorithm for speech recognition in noise. *IEE Proceedings of Vision, Image and Signal Processing*, Vol. 143, No. 5, pp. 324-330.

Yoma, N.B.; McInnes, F. & Jack, M. (1996-B). Use of a Reliability coefficient in noise canceling by Neural Net and Weighted Matching Algorithms. *Proceedings of International Conference of Spoken Language Processing ICSLP'96*, pp. 2297-2300.

Yoma, N.B.; McInnes, F. & Jack, J. (1997-A). Weighted Matching Algorithms and Reliability in Noise Canceling by Spectral Subtraction. *Proceedings of IEEE International Conference on Acoustics, Speech and Signal Processing ICASSP'97*, Vol.2, pp. 1171-1174.

Yoma, N.B.; McInnes, F. & Jack, J. (1997-B). Spectral Subtraction and Mean Normalization in the context of Weighted Matching Algorithms. *Proceedings of Eurospeech'97*, pp. 1411-1414.

Yoma, N.B.; McInnes, F. & Jack, J. (1998-A). Weighted Viterbi Algorithm and State Duration Modeling for Speech Recognition in Noise. *Proceedings of IEEE International Conference on Acoustics, Speech and Signal Processing ICASSP'98*, pp. 709-712.

Yoma, N.B.; McInnes, F. & Jack, J. (1998-B). Improving Performance of Spectral Subtraction in speech recognition using a model for additive noise. *IEEE Transactions on Speech and Audio Processing*, Vol. 6, No. 6, pp. 579-582.

Yoma, N.B. (1998-C). Speech recognition in noise using weighted matching algorithms. *Ph.D. Thesis*, University of Edinburgh, UK.

Yoma, N. B.; Ling, L. L.& Dotto, S. (1999). Robust connected word speech recognition using weighted Viterbi algorithm and context-dependent temporal constraints. *Proceedings of Eurospeech'99*, pp. 2869-2872.

Yoma, N. B. & Villar, M. (2001). Additive and convolutional noise canceling in speaker verification using a stochastic weighted Viterbi algorithm". *Proceedings of Eurospeech 2001*, pp. 2845-2848.

Yoma, N. B. & Villar, M. (2002). Speaker Verification in noise using a stochastic version of the weighted Viterbi algorithm". *IEEE Transactions on Speech and Audio Processing*, Vol. 10, No 3, pp. 158-166.

Yoma, N. B.; Silva, J.; Busso, C. & Brito, I. (2003-A). On compensating additive noise and CS-CELP distortion in speech recognition using the stochastic weighted Viterbi algorithm. *IEE Electronics Letters*, Vol 39, No. 4, pp. 409-411.

Yoma, N. B.; Brito, I. & Silva, J. (2003-B). Language Model Accuracy and Uncertainty in Noise Canceling in the Stochastic Weighted Viterbi Algorithm. *In Proceedings of Eurospeech 2003*, pp. 2193-2196.

Yoma, N. B.; Brito, I. & Molina, C. (2004). The stochastic weighted Viterbi algorithm: a framework to compensate additive noise and low bit rate coding distortion. *Proceedings of International Conference of Spoken Language Processing ICSLP 2004*, pp. 2821-2824.

Yoma, N. B.; Molina, C.; Silva, J. & Busso, C. (2005). Modelling, estimating and compensating low-bit rate coding distortion in speech recognition. *IEEE Transactions on Speech and Audio Processing*, Vol. 14, No.1, pp. 246-255.

Yoma, N. B.; Molina, C. (2006). Feature-dependent compensation of coders in speech recognition. *Signal Processing (Elsevier)*, Vol. 86, No. 1, pp. 38-49.

Zhao, Y. (1994). An acoustic-phonetic based speaker adaptation technique for improving speaker independent continuous speech recognition. *IEEE Transactions on Speech and Audio Processing*, Vol. 2, pp. 380-394.

13

The Research of Noise-Robust Speech Recognition Based on Frequency Warping Wavelet

Xueying Zhang and Wenjun Meng
Taiyuan University of Technology, Taiyuan University of Science & Technology
China

1. Introduction

The main task of speech recognition is to enable computer to understand human languages (Lawrence, 1999; Jingwei et al., 2006). This makes it possible that machine can communicate with human. Usually, speech recognition includes three parts: pre-processing, feature extraction and training (recognition) network. In this paper, the speech recognition system is described as Fig. 1. It consists of filter bank, feature extraction and training (recognition) network. The function of filter bank is dividing speech signal into different frequency band to be good for extraction feature. The good feature can improve the system recognition rate. The training (recognition) network trains (recognizes) the feature vectors according to feature mode and outputs recognition results.
The research on noise-robust capability of speech recognition system is a difficult problem that has been limiting the practical application of the speech recognition system (Tianbing et al., 2001). Because human ear has strong noise-robust capability, it is very important to abstract the features of fitting auditory characters of human ear for improving system noise-robust performance. The warping wavelet overcomes the disadvantage that the common wavelet divides frequency band in octave band and it is more suitable to the auditory characters of human ear. Bark wavelet is a warping wavelet that divides frequency band according to critical band (Qiang et al., 2000). At the same time, MFCC (Mel Frequency Cepstrum Coefficients) (Lawrence, 1999) and ZCPA (Zero-Crossing with Peak Amplitude) (Doh-suk et al., 1999) features themselves have noise-robust performance. HMM is classical recognition network, and wavelet neural network is also popular recognition network (Tianbing et al., 2001). So considering above three parts of speech recognition system, the paper used the two kinds of filters: FIR filter and Bark wavelet filter; two kinds of features:

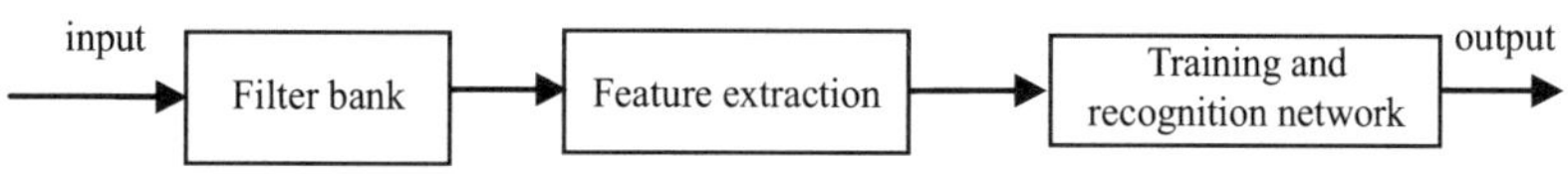

Figure 1. The speech recognition system

MFCC and ZCPA; two kinds of recognition networks: HMM and WNN (Wavelet Neural Network). Limited by article length, the paper selected a few of composite modes, described their principles and presented experimental results. The three parts of Fig.1 have effect on one another. Their different combination can get different results. In practical application we can select optimum combination mode. The combination modes selected in the research are listed in Table 1.The article includes five sections: the first section is introduction; the second section describes the principle of ZCPA and implementation method of combination mode 1 and 2 in Table 1; and the third section describes the principle of Bark wavelet and implementation method of combination mode 3 and 4 in Table 1; the fourth section is the experimental results and discussion; the fifth section is conclusions.

Combination modes index	Filter	Feature	Training and recognition network
1	FIR	ZCPA	HMM
2	FIR	ZCPA	WNN
3	Bark wavelet	ZCPA	HMM
4	Bark wavelet	MFCC	HMM

Table 1. The combination modes of speech recognition system in the paper

2. The Principle of ZCPA and Implementation Methods of Combination Mode 1 and 2

2.1 The principle of ZCPA

The human auditory system consists of outer ear, middle ear and inner ear. Speech signals are transformed into mechanical vibrations of the eardrum at the outer ear, and then are transmitted to the cochlea of the inner ear through the middle ear. The role of the middle ear is known as impedance matching between the outer ear and the inner ear. The speech signals are mainly processed in the inner ear, especially in the cochlear of the inner ear. The basilar membrane of the cochlear has the function of frequency choice and tune. Speech signals transmitted through the oval window at the base of the cochlear are converted into travelling waves of the basilar membrane. The site of maximum excursion of the travelling wave on the basilar membrane is dependent on frequency. High frequencies show maximum excursion near the base while low frequencies near the apex. Frequencies are distributed according to logarithm relationship along the basilar membrane over 800Hz. The frequency-position relationship can be expressed as Equation (1) (Doh-suk et al., 1999):

$$F = A(10^{ax} - 1) \tag{1}$$

Where F is frequency in Hz, and x is the normalized distance along the basilar membrane with a value of from zero to one. A and a are the constants. A=165.4 and a=2.1.

The cochlear takes a very important role in the auditory system, which can apperceive and transmit the speech signals. In fact, with the function of series-parallel conversion, it corresponds to a bank of parallel band-pass filters. Signals imported by series are decomposed and exported by parallel. Then it provides evidence to some extent for cochlear filter model.

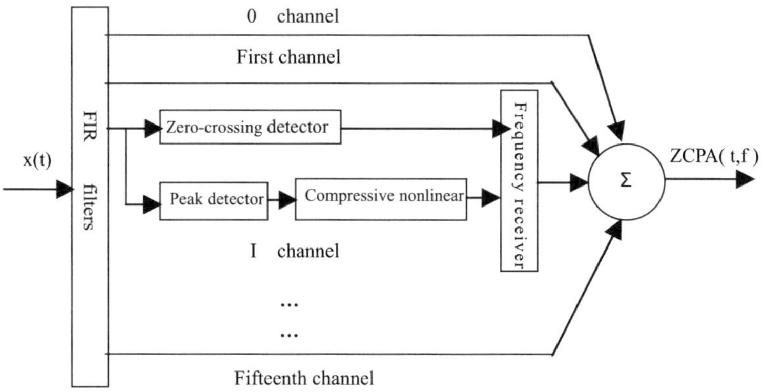

Figure 2. ZCPA feature extraction scheme

Fig. 2 shows the feature extraction block scheme of ZCPA (Doh-suk et al., 1999). This system consists of a bank of band-pass filters, zero-crossing detector, peak detector, nonlinear compression and frequency receiver. The filter bank consists of 16 FIR band-pass filters that are designed to simulate the basilar membrane of cochlear. And zero-crossing detector, peak detector and nonlinear compression simulate the auditory nerve fibers. The frequency information is obtained by computing the zero-crossing intervals of speech signal from zero-crossing detector. And the intensity information is obtained by detecting peak amplitudes between the intervals and making nonlinear amplitude compression from peak detector and the nonlinear compression. The frequency receiver combines the frequency with the peak information. Finally, this information is compounded to form the feature output of speech signals.

2.1.1 The design of the filters

Because the basilar membrane of cochlear corresponds to a bank of parallel band-pass filters, we can choose 16 points along the basilar membrane and get 16 FIR filters, whose frequencies change from 200Hz to 4000Hz. The centre frequency of every filter can be obtained from the Equation (1). And bandwidths are set to be proportional to the equivalent rectangular bandwidth (ERB) (Oded, 1992; Doh-suk et al., 1999).

$$ERB = 6.23F^2 + 93.39F + 28.52 \quad (2)$$

Where F is the centre frequency of each filter in Hz. Table 2 shows the centre frequencies and the bandwidths of each FIR filter, f_i is the centre frequency, Δf_i is the bandwidth.

Filter No.	0	1	2	3	4	5	6	7	8	9	10	11	12	13	14	15
f_i(Hz)	200	264	340	429	534	657	802	1011	1172	1408	1685	2011	2395	2845	3376	4000
Δf_i(Hz)	46	53	61	71	82	95	111	129	151	176	206	241	283	331	389	456

Table 2. The relationship between centre frequency and bandwidth of FIR filters

2.1.2 The theory of the zero-crossing

When the two adjacent samples have the different sign, we name this phenomenon as zero-crossing. And the up-going zero-crossing is that the current sample value is bigger than zero and the former sample value is smaller than zero. Because the number of the zero-crossing is different for different frequency's signals, that is to say, high frequency signals have more zero-crossings than low frequency signals. So the up-going zero-crossing rates can reflect the frequency information of the speech signals.

2.1.3 Extraction of the intensity information

To simulate the relation between the phase-locking degree of the auditory nerve fibers and the intensity of the stimulus, the maximal peak value between the two adjacent zero-crossing samples need be detected. This relation can be described by a monotonic function. That is expressed as Equation (3) :

$$g(x) = \lg(1.0+20x) \tag{3}$$

Where x is the maximal peak value, and g(x) is the result of the nonlinear compression.

2.1.4 Frequency receiver

The frequency band of speech signal is mainly between 200Hz and 4000Hz. For obtaining low dimension and high effect feature parameters, we used ERB-rate (Oded, 1992) scale to divide the frequency band into 16 bands. And each band is named as a frequency bin. By computing the up-going zero-crossing number of the signal duration, it can be known that the signal duration belong to some frequency bins. The frequency information included in the speech signals can be reflected consequently.The frequency information and the intensity information across all channels are combined to obtain the frequency histograms (i.e. frequency bins) by the frequency receiver (Oded, 1994). The course can be described by Equation (4).

$$zcpa(m,\ i) = \sum_{k=1}^{N_{ch}} \sum_{l=1}^{Z_k - 1} \delta_{ij_l} g(p_{kl}),\ 1 \le i \le N \tag{4}$$

Where, zcpa(m, i) are output features , m is frame index , i is the index of frequency bin. And N is the number of frequency bin, which is equal to 16. N_{ch} is the number of FIR filters , here N_{ch}=16. Each of filters is a signal processing channel and k is its index. Z_k denotes the number of the up-going zero-crossings at frame m and channel k. l is the index of up-going zero-crossings, l = 1, 2, …, Z_k-1. And p_{kl} denotes the peak amplitude between the l-th and (l+1)-th up-going zero-crossings. δ_{ij_l} is the Kronecker delta (When i= j_l, δ_{ij_l} =1; When i ≠ j_l, δ_{ij_l} =0). j_l is the frequency bin index mapped by the interval between the l-th and(l+1)-th up-going zero-crossings , $1 \le j_l \le N$.

2.1.5 Time and amplitude normalization

The feature form obtained is zcpa(m, i). In most case, because m is of different values, the number of feature vectors obtained is also different. Thus, it is necessary to normalize time. In the paper, the dimension of feature vectors is 64×16 after time normalization. The time normalization method used is Non-Linear Partition method (Zhiping et al., 2005). It is also necessary to normalize amplitude for latter processing convenience.

2.2 The implementation method of combination mode 1: FIR+ZCPA+HMM

2.2.1 The experimental principle

An isolated word speech recognition system with FIR filter, ZCPA feature and discrete HMM is implemented on Windows operating system in C++ language in this paper. The system diagram is shown in Fig. 3. In the experiment, speech data with different SNRs of 50 words 16 persons is used (including data of 15dB, 20dB, 25dB, 30dB and clean). Each person says each word 3 times. The model is trained by speech data (a certain SNR) of 9 persons and the recognition is carried out by speech data (under the same SNR) of other 7 persons, so the recognition result is obtained under this SNR. The parameters of HMM for each word is trained by 27 samples (9 persons×3 times), and the number of test data file depends on the number of word using in the experiment.

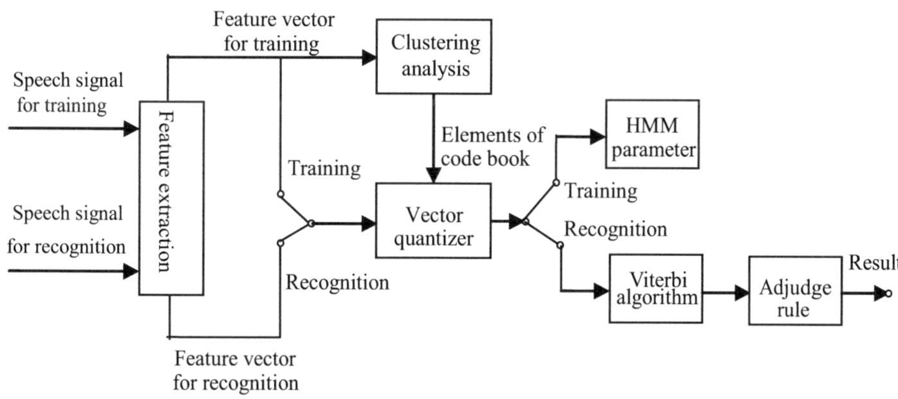

Figure 3. Isolated word speech recognition diagram based on HMM

2.2.2 The experimental step

Step 1: Feature extraction.

Two problems commonly need to be solved: one is to extract representative appropriate feature parameters from speech signal; the other is to compress properly data. The feature parameter of speech is extracted once each frame, and each frame feature parameter commonly constitutes a vector, so speech feature is a vector sequence. At the front end of the system, sampling rate of speech signal is 11.025 kHz, frame length is 10ms, sampling point number is 110, and frame shift is 5ms. Uniform 64×16 (or 1024) dimensional feature vector sequence is obtained through time and amplitude normalizing.

Step 2: Vector quantization.

The extracted feature need be quantized in vector way to satisfy the demands of discrete HMM adopted as recognition network. Vector quantization is an effective data compressing technology, and the codebook is obtained by LBG clustering method in this article. The feature extracted from speech signal becomes speech pattern after data compressing. Obviously, that speech pattern is of representative is one of the main factors to improve speech recognition rate.

Firstly, all the features of training words form a large set of speech feature vectors (for example, the number of vectors of 50 words is 50×27× (1024/4)), which is used to train codebook. In the system, the size of the codebook is 128, and the dimension of the code word is 4. These vectors are distributed to 128 classes, and each class has a tab (from 1 to 128). Secondly, 1024 feature values of each word can form 256 feature vectors with 4 dimensions to enter vector quantizer that has been trained. According to the nearest neighbourhood rule, 256 vectors are quantized and each vector is represented by the tab of class which the vector belongs to. Finally, the tab of codeword replaces former vector and becomes speech pattern of each word as input signal for the next processing.

Step 3: Training HMM.

After above processing, the feature tab of the word is obtained as the input sequence $\{O=O_1, O_2, \ldots, O_T\}$ of discrete HMM. For discrete HMM, each word is represented by a HMM ($\lambda = (A, B, \pi)$) (Lawrence, 1999), and is trained by 27 sampling sequences. The HMM is from left to right mode without span, and each word model has 5 states (shown in Fig.4). After trained, the state transfer matrix of a certain word is shown in Fig.5. Because the size of codebook is 128, the number of observation sign is M=128.

About the assumption of initial value, three parameters in this system are set as equal probability values. Training method is classical Baum-Welch algorithm, and training terminate condition is that according to the logarithm of probability for one pronunciation, the absolute value changing before and after the revaluation of the parameter is less than a certain threshold value (in the experiment the threshold is 0.01).

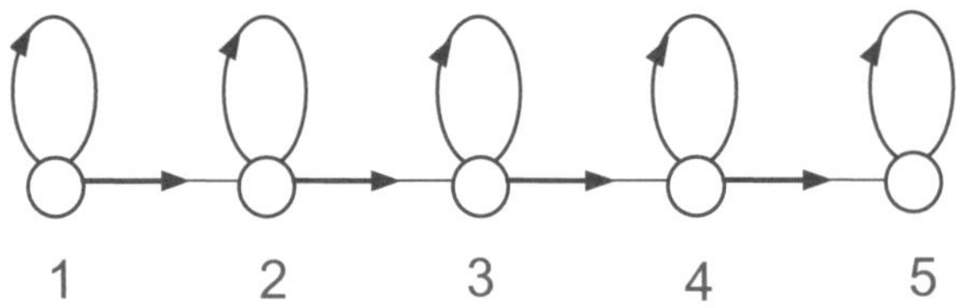

Figure 4. From left to right model without span

$$A = \begin{bmatrix} 0.97922 & 0.02078 & 0 & 0 & 0 \\ 0 & 0.985461 & 0.014539 & 0 & 0 \\ 0 & 0 & 0.97241 & 0.02759 & 0 \\ 0 & 0 & 0 & 0.969138 & 0.030862 \\ 0 & 0 & 0 & 0 & 1 \end{bmatrix}$$

Figure 5. State transfer matrix

Step 4: The recognition of word.
After previous training, each word has its own model parameter. It is similar to quantization of training data set that feature vector used in test (speech data of another 7 persons in a certain SNR) enters vector quantizer formed in step 2. Thus, each word is quantized into a codeword tab sequence, which is used in computing probability through all the parameters for HMM of all the words, and Viterbi algorithm is used in this process. The criterion in this algorithm is searching the single best state sequence, in other words, making condition probability P (Q | O, λ) maximum, which also equals to making P (Q, O| λ) maximum (Shuyan et al., 2005). Therefore, the model corresponding to the maximum probability is the recognition result. The recognition rate is the ratio between the number of correctly recognized words and the number of all the test words.
Table 5 shows the recognition results of different words using the combination of FIR+ZCPA+HMM under different SNRs.

2.3 The implementation method of combination mode 2: FIR+ZCPA+WNN

2.3.1 The structure of WNN

In the structure of FIR+ZCPA+WNN, the training and recognition network uses WNN instead of HMM , other condition is unchanged, as shown in Fig. 6. The theory base of wavelet neural network is the reconstructing theory of wavelet function. It ensures the continuous wavelet basis has the ability of approximating any function, so we can take place the Sigmoid or Gaussian function of neural network by wavelet basis to construct a new feed-forward neural network. This system constructed the WNN according to the wavelet basis fitting. It is known to us that a signal function f(t) can be fitted via linear combination of selected wavelet basis (Zhigang et al., 2003):

$$\widehat{f}(t)=\sum_{k=1}^{K} w_k \phi\left(\frac{t-b_k}{a_k}\right) \tag{5}$$

Where b_k is position factor, a_k is scale factor and k is the number of basis function. The network topology can refer to Fig. 7.

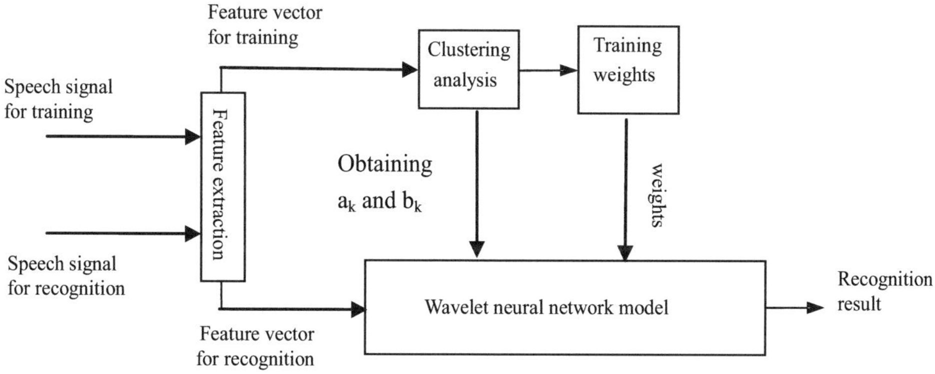

Figure 6. Diagram of speech recognition based on wavelet neural network

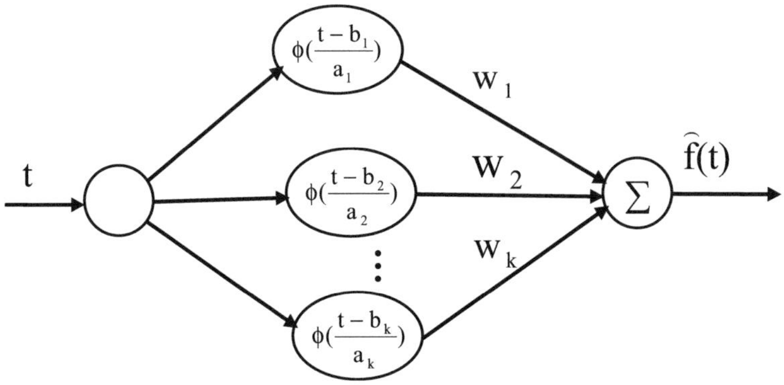

Figure 7. Wavelet neural network topology with single input and single output

Where, a_k and b_k are variables, only w_k acts as the weight between the hidden and output layer, and $\phi\left(\frac{t-b_k}{a_k}\right)$ can be regarded as the output value of input nodes. The network structure is similar to the traditional forward multi-layer perceptron; the key difference depends on the hidden layer function. The system this paper presented is a three-layer neural network with multi-input and multi-output. The inputs are the feature parameters of every word, and their dimension is 1024, so the number of input nodes is 1024. The number of hidden nodes depends on words number recognized. Here, 10 nodes for 10 words and 50 nodes for 50 words.

It is a total connection with weight value 1 between input layer and hidden layer, and the same as that between hidden layer and output layer, while they have weights. The nodes of output layer equal to the classification number of words. So this system has same nodes in hidden and output layer. The form of the basis function of every hidden node is uniform, while the scale and position parameters vary with nodes. Strictly speaking, this network is not based on the wavelet mathematical analysis; in fact, it was used to approximate function in wavelet combination of certain form. In this system, it was for word recognition. As for the selecting method of wavelet basis function, there are no uniform rules in theories (Johnstone, 1999). Generally, it can be determined by experience and practical application. Here, Mexican Hat wavelet was selected. The experiment showed that Mexican Hat wavelet certainly has excellent characteristics in recognition.

2.3.2 The determining of WNN parameters

The parameters to be determined in the system are number of hidden nodes, scale factor a_k, position factor b_k and connection weights w_k between all hidden and output nodes. Estimation of the number of hidden nodes also has no uniform rules in theories. In this paper, the hidden nodes number equal to that of the output layer, i.e. the word classification number. Otherwise, a bias should be added to hidden layer, it has fixed value of 1. This bias factor also should be connected to all the output nodes in order to estimate weight values.

Several methods can be used to estimate the three parameters of wavelet network, such as BP network training method and orthogonal least square which optimized these three parameters simultaneously. The network topology of this paper makes it possible that the training of scale and position can be separated from the weights training. One of common methods of estimating a_k and b_k is clustering. The clustering algorithm just assigns the given vectors into several finite classes according to certain distortion measure. However, this method does not take full advantage of the information of training samples. The clustering algorithm of K-Means has been used in this experiment to estimate the parameters, but the recognition results are not satisfying.

Because the given training samples have involved the corresponding classification information of every training feature, this information can be used to estimate the position parameter b_k. The hidden exciting function of wavelet network is a local function; it has strong approximation ability for the function with big difference in localness. The same as the feature with big difference, they can be classified properly. In recognition network, we hope the output of all training samples corresponding to a certain word via the hidden node which is determined by its position factor can get the biggest value. In other words, the more adjacent to position factor b_k, the bigger the output of the k-th node will be. Hence, for all the training samples corresponding to a certain word, their centroid can be calculated to be a position factor. Once a position factor has been estimated, there will be a scale factor under the condition of corresponding to it. Here Equation (6) was used to calculate scale factor knowing position factor (Musavi et al., 1992):

$$a_k = \sqrt{\frac{1}{1+\sqrt{2}} \sum_{k=1}^{K} \left\| x_k - b_k \right\|^2} \tag{6}$$

Where x_k is feature vector, b_k and x_k have same dimension.

LMS method was adopted to train the weights between hidden and output layer in this paper. Training weight by LMS only needs to compute several matrix multiplications, so it need less time to train. And the hidden nodes can be added to meet the practical requirement. The added nodes will not have an obvious effect on the training time. In this system, the number of input nodes is 1024. Generally, wavelet network with high dimension will lead to a "dimension disaster", which means with the increasing of dimension of input and training sample, the network converge speed will descend severely. In this paper, the calculating of position and scale factor was separated from weights training, so it will avoid effectively the "dimension disaster" because of high dimension.

2.3.3 The experimental steps

Step 1: ZCPA feature extraction.

After pre-processing speech signal we obtained ZCPA feature with 1024 dimension of every word. It can be directly inputted to following wavelet network.

Step 2: Confirming network structure.

The node number of input layer equals feature vector dimension, or 1024. The node number of hide layer or output layer equals classification words number. Hidden layer sets a bias node which output value is 1. It was also connected to all nodes of output layer to take part in weight training.

Step 3: Confirming position factor and scale factor.

Input features were divided into N classes by using clustering method supervised. Where, N is the classification number of words. For each classification, the position factor was obtained by calculating the centroids of all training samples of classification. And corresponding scale factor was calculated by Equation (6).

Step 4: Calculating weight values.

Using LMS method to calculate the weight values from hidden layer to output. Because LMS method has not the course of iterative operation, its convergence speed is very fast and it fits to real-time speech recogintion system.
Table 5 shows also the recognition results of different words using the combination of FIR+ZCPA+WNN under different SNRs.

3. The Principle of Bark Wavelet and Implementation Methods of Combination mode 3 and 4

3.1 The principle of Bark wavelet

The binary wavelet used commonly divides frequency band in octave band way (Gowdy et al., 2000). This does not fit entirely to the auditory character of human ear to speech. Bark wavelet was put forward on the basis of hearing perception, so it should have better function than binary wavelet.
The basilar membrane of the cochlear has the function of the frequency choice and tune. For different centre frequencies, the signals of corresponding critical frequencies band can arouse the different place librations of the basilar membrane. So from 20Hz to 16kHz, these frequencies can divide into 24 bands. The different frequency speech signals of the same place of the basilar membrane are added to evaluate, that is to say, the perception of the human auditory system to speech frequency is a nonlinear mapping relation with actual frequency. So this introduces the conception of the Bark scale, Traunmular (Zhiping et al., 2005) presents the relation of the linear frequency and Bark frequency. That is:

$$b = 13\arctan(0.76f) + 3.5\arctan(f/7.5)^2 \tag{7}$$

Where b is Bark frequency, and f is the linear frequency in Hz.
The basic thought of constructing Bark wavelet is: firstly, because of the same importance of the time and frequency information in the speech analysis, wavelet mother function selected should satisfy time and bandwidth product least; secondly, for being consistent with conception of the frequency group, mother wavelet should has the equal bandwidth in the Bark domain; furthermore, their bandwidth are the unit bandwidthes, namely 1 Bark (Qiang et al., 2000).
According to the above analysis, the formation of wavelet function selected is Equation (8) in the Bark domain.

$$W(b) = e^{-c_1 b^2} \tag{8}$$

Furthermore, when the bandwidth is the 3dB, the constant c_1 is selected 4ln2. It is easy to prove that

$$\int_{-\infty}^{\infty} \frac{\left|e^{-c_1 b^2}\right|^2}{b} db < \infty \tag{9}$$

Simultaneously, since the Equation (7) is a monotonic function, the transformation from the Bark frequency to linear frequency do not influence the Equation (8). Therefore Bark wavelet satisfies "admissible condition", that is to say, Bark wavelet transform can perfectly reconstruction.

Supposing the speech signals analyzed is s(t), whose linear frequency bandwidth satisfies $|f| \in [f_1, f_2]$, and corresponding Bark frequency bandwidth is $[b_1, b_2]$. Thus wavelet function in Bark domain can be defined as:

$$W_k(b)=W(b-b_1-k\Delta b),\ k=0, 1, 2, \ldots, K-1 \qquad (10)$$

Where , Δb is the translation step-length and k is the scale parameter. According to the equal bandwidth principia, there has $\Delta b = \frac{(b_2 - b_1)}{K-1}$.

Then substitute Equation (8) into (10) , we can get

$$W_k(b) = e^{-4\ln 2(b-b_1-k\Delta b)^2} = 2^{-4(b-b_1-k\Delta b)^2},\ k = 0,1,2\cdots\cdots K-1 \qquad (11)$$

Then substitute Equation (7) into (11), so in the linear frequency the Bark wavelet function can be described as:

$$W_k(f) = c_2 \cdot 2^{-4[13\arctan(0.76f)+3.5\arctan(f/7.5)^2-(b_1+k\Delta b)]^2} \qquad (12)$$

In the Equation (12), c_2 is the normalization factor, and c_2 can be obtained through Equation

$$c_2\sum_{k=0}^{K-1} W_k(b) = 1,\ 0 < b_1 \le b \le b_2 \qquad (13)$$

From Equation (12), in the frequency domain Bark wavelet transform can be expressed as:

$$s_k(t) = \int_{-\infty}^{\infty} S(f)\cdot W_k(f)\cdot e^{j2\pi f}df \qquad (14)$$

Where, S(f) is the spectrum of speech signal s(t) analyzed, $s_k(t)$ is the signal of the k-th channel, which had been transformed by Bark wavelet.

Notice that the Equation (13) is also correct for linear frequencies, so there has

$$\sum_{k=0}^{K-1} s_k(t) = \sum_{k=0}^{K-1}\int_{-\infty}^{\infty} W_k(f)\cdot S(f)\cdot e^{j2\pi ft}df = \int_{-\infty}^{\infty}\sum_{k=0}^{K-1} W_k(f)\cdot S(f)\cdot e^{j2\pi ft}df \qquad (15)$$

In Equation (13), let c_2=1, we get

$$\int_{-\infty}^{\infty} S(f)\cdot e^{j2\pi ft}df = s(t) \qquad (16)$$

Therefore, the Equation (16) is called as the engineering perfect reconstruction condition of the Bark wavelet.

3.2 The realization method of combination mode 3：Bark+ZCPA+HMM

3.2.1 The design of Bark wavelet filter

The sub-section uses Bark wavelet filter to replace FIR filter forming the mode: Bark+ZCPA+HMM. Fig.8 shows the use method of Bark wavelet filter in preprocessing of

ZCPA feature extraction. Where, S(f) is the spectrum of s(t) and W(f) is Bark wavelet function. They meet the relations as S(f)=FFT[s(t)], Y(f)=S(f)W(f) and $\hat{s}(t) = \text{IFFT}[Y(f)]$.

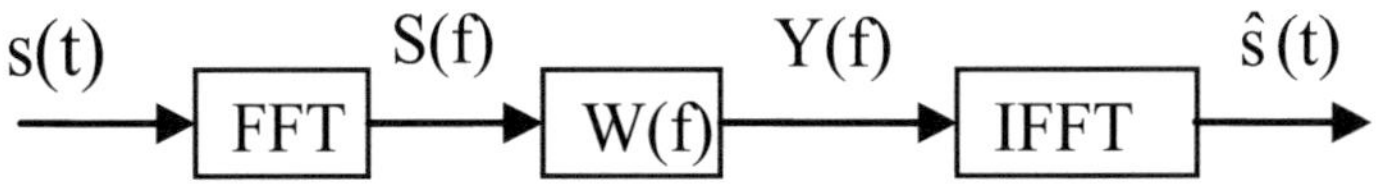

Figure 8. The scheme of the Bark wavelet filters used in preprocessing

Bark scale can be seen as the mapping from linear frequency field to perception frequency field. By using Equation (7) the mapping relation may be realized. This builds the base of critical band filter bank analysis technology. The frequency between 20Hz~16kHz can be divided into 24 fields(or frequency groups).Their pass band bandwidth are equal to the critical band of corresponding frequency, that have become the standard in fact (See Table 3).

Bark No	Low (Hz)	High (Hz)	Bandwidth (Hz)	Bark No.	Low (Hz)	High (Hz)	Bandwidth (Hz)
1	20	100	80	13	1720	2000	280
2	100	200	100	14	2000	2320	320
3	200	300	100	15	2320	2700	380
4	300	400	100	16	2700	3150	450
5	400	510	110	17	3150	3700	550
6	510	630	120	18	3700	4400	700
7	630	770	140	19	4400	5300	900
8	770	920	150	20	5300	6400	1100
9	920	1080	160	21	6400	7700	1300
10	1080	1270	190	22	7700	9500	1800
11	1270	1480	210	23	9500	12000	2500
12	1480	1720	240	24	12000	15500	3500

Table 3. The allocation about 24 critical frequency bands

The critical bandwidth changes with its centre frequency f. The higher f is, the wider the critical bandwidth is. Their relation is as Equation (17).

$$BW_{critical} = 25 + 75 \times [1 + 1.4(\frac{f}{1000})^2]^{0.69} \text{ (Hz)} \tag{17}$$

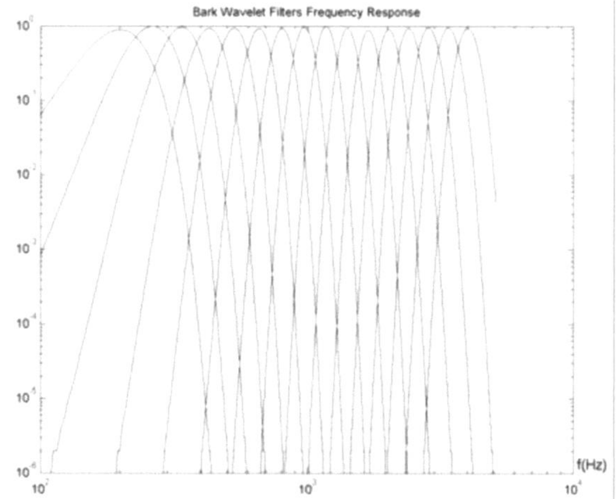

Figure 9. The frequency responses of the 16 Bark wavelet filters

From Table 4, we can see that in Bark field each filter bandwidth follows the equal bandwidth principle, or 3 Bark. During the course of experiment, 1 Bark and 2 Bark bandwidth were seleted, but the results were not good. The parameter k was seleted such as followings. From Equation (1) the centre frequencies of 16 Bark wavelet filters were calculated and from Equation (12) the maxmium responses at centre frequencies can be got, so k values can be determined. From Equation (17) the bandwidthes of all filters can be determined.Having the parameters of Table 4, Bark wavelet filters can be realized.

b_1	b_2	k	Bandwidth (Hz)	b_1	b_2	k	Bandwidth (Hz)
1	4	7	100	9	12	4	180
2	5	5	100	10	13	6	210
3	6	2	100	11	14	7	250
4	7	1	110	12	15	9	300
5	8	0	120	13	16	10	360
6	9	1	130	14	17	10	450
7	10	1	140	15	18	10	550
8	11	4	160	16	19	10	680

Table 4. Confirmation about all the Bark wavelet parameters

3.2.2 The calculation steps of the Bark wavelet filters

Step 1: Read the original speech datum, and estimate the speech data length.

Step 2: Frame the speech data, so that we can obtain the time domain signals of the every frame. Use the 20ms as the frame length, and 10ms as the frame shift.

Step 3: Then go along the FFT transform to obtain the spectrum information of the speech signals, and the width of the window is 256.

Step 4: Initialize the Bark wavelet different parameters.
Step 5: Begin the Bark wavelet transform. Because we used the computer to simulate this transform, there need the discrete Bark wavelet transform. It can be described as:

$$W_k(N-i) = W_k(i-1) = W_k(i \cdot \frac{f_s}{N}),\ i = 1 \cdots, \frac{N}{2} \tag{18}$$

Where N is the last speech data and f_s is sampling frequency.
Step 6: The transform to the input speech signals of the every filter with Bark wavelet should also adopt the discrete Equation (19). As follows:

$$s_k(n) = \sum_{l=0}^{N-1} S(l) W_k(l) e^{\frac{j2\pi nl}{N}} \tag{19}$$

Step 7: Then continue to operate the next frame speech signal as above. Finally we can obtain all the values through Bark wavelet transform.
Through the above steps, we can obtain the results of signal passing Bark wavelet filters, and then we can use the ZCPA theory to extract the features.
Table 7 shows the recognition rates comparison of different words using the ZCPA and BWZCPA (Bark Wavelet ZCPA) features in different SNRs.

3.3 The realization method of combination mode 4：Bark+MFCC+HMM

3.3.1 The principle of the MFCC feature extraction

MFCC feature extraction flow chart is showed as Fig. 10. The working process is:
1. Pre-emphasis of the speech signal, frame, adding window, then make the FFT to obtain the frequency information.
2. Pass the signal through the Mel frequency coordinate triangle filter bank to mimic the human hearing mechanism and the human hearing sensibility to different speech spectrum.
3. Calculate the logarithm value of the signal through the Mel filters to obtain the logarithmic spectrum.
4. Make the discrete cosine transform to the signal and obtain the MFCC feature. In the MFCC algorithm, we use the FFT to calculate the frequency spectrum of the signal in the front-end, while in the back-end we use DCT to further reduce the speech signal's

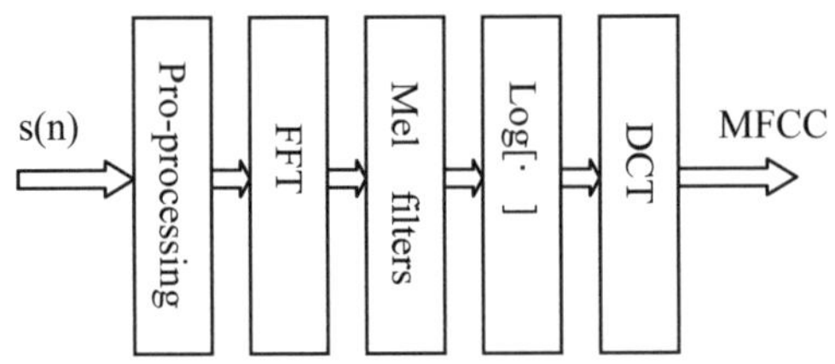

Figure 10. The feature extraction of the MFCC

redundant information, and reach the aim of normalizing speech feature coefficients with small dimensions. The analysis method is based on the assumption that the speech signal is short time stationary signal, so using the fixed window's Fourier transform, we can get the local time-frequency information. As to the any speech segment, the time-frequency resolution is fixed. Based on the uncertainty principle we can find that the time-frequency resolution can't be both high simultaneously. This will make the speech signal details fuzzy, especially to those speech segments with non-stationary, like the explodent sound and spirant, it will definitely lose significant information.

DCT is the FFT with zero valued imaginary part. The feature vectors based on the DCT cover all the frequency band, if only one frequency segment is destroyed by noise interference, then all of MFCC coefficients will be strongly interfered. A speech frame may include two adjacent phonemes, suppose one is sonant and the other is surd, this will definitely blur the two phonemes' information and reduce the speech recognition rate. But if the speech spectrum can be divided into several sub-frequency bands, the situation will be different. Fixed window DFT feature vectors in the time domain and frequency domain all have the same resolutions, and unable to meet requirement of the variant time-frequency resolution which is needed by the feature vectors. Therefore, the FFT and DCT algorithm is unsuitable for the usage in non-stationary speech signal analysis.

3.3.2 The extraction of Bark wavelet MFCC feature

Having analysed the drawbacks of the MFCC, we presented the improving method using Bark wavelet, just as the Fig.11. After the signal is pre-processed and before making FFT, Bark wavelet filtering is inserted. Because the wavelet has the property of multi-resolution, it can divide the signal into some parts with different time-frequency resolution that is suitable to speech signal processing. Here, the front-end Bark wavelet divides signal frequency into 25 sub-bands and we calculate the FFT of each band. Then the spectrum combination, Mel filter processing and the logarithmic energy calculating are performed. Finally the DCT of the former algorithm is replaced by Bark wavelet transform and we obtain the BWMFCC features.

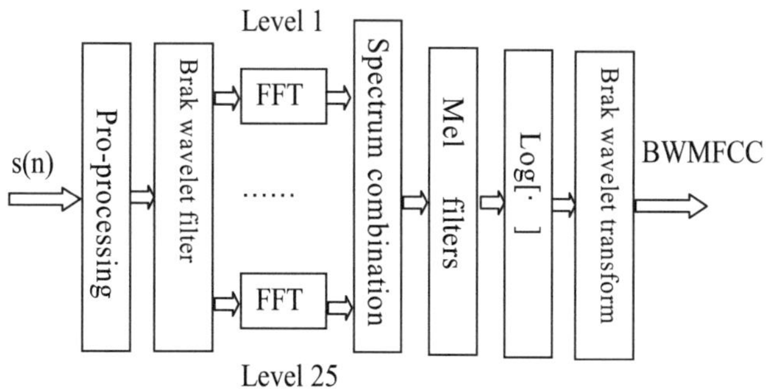

Figure 11. The feature extraction of the Bark wavelet MFCC

The calculation process is as follows:

1. Making pre-emphasis, framing and window adding processes to the original speech data file s(n).
2. Making the Bark wavelet filtering to each frame signal, by using Equation (20).

$$S_k(n) = W_k(n) \cdot S(n),\ 0 \le k \le K-1 \qquad (20)$$

Where, $W_k(n)$ is the discrete form of Equation (12), S(n) is the speech signal frequency spectrum, $S_k(n)$ is the k-th sub-band's speech spectrum.

3. The spectrum combination is performed by using Equation (21) to obtain:

$$S'(n) = \sum_{k=0}^{K-1} S_k(n) \qquad (21)$$

4. Passing the $S'(n)$ signal through Mel filter bank. The Mel filter bank can smooth the frequency spectrum, and reduce the harmonic, and emphasis the original formant of the speech signal. Therefore, the tone and the pitch of the sound will not appear in the feature coefficients, the speech signal recognition will not be interfered by the different pitch of the input signal.
5. Using the Equation (22) computing the logarithmic energy D(n).

$$D(n) = \log\left(\sum_{k=0}^{N-1} |S'(k)|^2 H_n(k)\right), (0 \le n < N) \qquad (22)$$

6. Finally, passing the D(n) through Bark filter to get the final speech features BWMFCC(m) by using Equation (23) .

$$BWMFCC(m) = \sum_{n=0}^{N-1} W_m(n) \cdot D(n) \quad (0 \le m \le M-1,\ 0 \le n \le N) \qquad (23)$$

Where, N is the number of Mel filters. $H_n(k)$ is Mel frequency filter. In our experiment, N=26, M is the sub-band's number of back-end Bark wavelet, here M=16.

Table 8 shows the recognition rates comparison of different words using the MFCC and BWMFCC features in different SNRs.

4. Results and Analysis

The section will present the experimental results and discussion of the second section and the third section. The exprimental condition and the database used are same. The ZCPA or MFCC feature of every word is normalized into speech feature vector sequence of 64X16 demension. In the experiments, speech data with different SNRs of 50 words 16 persons is used (including data of 15dB, 20dB, 25dB, 30dB and clean). Each person says each word 3 times. The model is trained by speech data (a certain SNR) of 9 persons and the recognition is carried out by speech data (under the same SNR) of other 7 persons, so the recognition result is obtained under this SNR.

4.1 The combination mode 1: FIR+ZCPA+HMM and mode 2: FIR+ZCPA+WNN

Table 5 shows the recognition rates of different words using the combination of FIR+ZCPA+HMM or FIR+ZCPA+WNN under different SNRs. We analysis these experimental results in the tables as follows.

1. HMM is the statistical model based on the time sequence structure of speech signal, and it can simulate reasonably speech time changing process, and describe the whole non-stationary and local stationary of speech well. But a shortcoming of HMM is that

distinguish ability is not strong enough. HMM is influenced by the number of training samples, along with the increase in number of samples, the recognition rate will be improved greatly (see Table 6). Table 6 is the recognition rates using FIR+ZCPA+HMM after adding training samples from 9 to 16, but test samples are unchanged.

2. Wavelet neural network (WNN).
   This network has great advantages in recognition. Not only the structure is simple, algorithm is easy to be implemented and the recognition rate is high, but also linear least square method is used to train weight value, the convergence speed is fast, and training time is only a few minutes. From the table we can see that, along with the increase in the number of words, the number of hidden nodes of network increases, and the recognition rate rises gradually. When reaching a certain number of words, the recognition rate descends but descends little. Although the number of hidden nodes increases, training time is not obviously influenced. Besides, under noisy environment, the recognition rate of the system decreases little, for the speech under the SNR of 15dB, the recognition rate of 50 words is near 90%. It is sufficiently showed that the system combined of ZCPA feature parameter with WNN has good robust performance, so this recognition system can fulfill the task of large number of words, non-special person, real time speech recognition and has wide application foreground.

Noumber of words	SNR / Feature	15dB	20dB	25dB	30dB	Clean
10	HMM	85.7	84.7	86.2	85.7	89.1
	WNN	87.1	90.5	90.5	91.4	92.9
20	HMM	76.6	81.2	82.4	81.7	85.7
	WNN	89.5	92.1	93.3	93.1	94.5
30	HMM	77.1	81.9	83.1	82.9	83.5
	WNN	92.1	93.2	93.3	94.3	94.0
40	HMM	76.6	79.0	81.3	82.6	83.0
	WNN	91.9	93.3	94.3	94.1	94.4
50	HMM	72.1	74.5	80.1	79.0	81.7
	WNN	89.7	91.7	93.3	93.4	94.3

Table 5. The recognition rates using FIR+ZCPA+HMM or FIR+ZCPA+WNN mode (%)

SNR / Number of words	15 dB	20 dB	25 dB	30 dB	Clean
10	88.0	88.7	90.7	91.3	92.0
20	86.0	87.7	90.3	89.3	91.7
30	84.2	87.3	89.1	89.6	90.4
40	82.8	87.7	88.7	90.7	90.8
50	81.7	85.6	87.7	86.7	89.3

Table 6. The recognition rates using FIR+ZCPA+HMM after adding training samples (%)

4.2 The combination mode 3: Bark+ZCPA+HMM and mode 4: Bark+MFCC+HMM

4.2.1 The combination mode 3 : Bark+ZCPA+HMM

As showed in Table 7, ZCPA means the recognition results of using FIR as preprocessing and BWZCPA means the recognition results of using Bark wavelet as preprocessing.

From Table 7 we can see that the recogntion results with Bark wavelet filter are better than the ones with FIR filter in bigger words and higher noise environment. Especially, the system function was improved with increasing of words number. This illustrated Bark wavelet more closer to the hearing perception of human ear than common wavelet.

Noumber of words	SNR / Feature	15dB	20dB	25dB	30dB	Clean
10	ZCPA	85.71	84.76	86.19	85.71	89.05
	BWZCPA	84.00	87.14	90.00	90.48	90.00
20	ZCPA	76.6	81.19	82.38	81.67	85.71
	BWZCPA	77.14	83.57	87.56	84.29	88.20
30	ZCPA	77.14	81.90	83.17	82.86	83.49
	BWZCPA	78.42	83.31	85.71	85.56	87.98
40	ZCPA	76.55	78.26	81.31	82.62	82.98
	BWZCPA	77.50	81.48	84.76	85.00	87.14
50	ZCPA	72.10	74.48	80.09	78.95	81.71
	BWZCPA	73.14	78.20	83.71	85.52	85.24

Table 7. The recognition rates using ZCPA and BWZCPA features in different SNRs (%)

4.2.2 The combination mode 4: Bark+MFCC+HMM

Table 8 shows the recognition rates comparison using MFCC and BWMFCC features in different SNRs. From the table, we can see the recognition rates are significantly increased by using the BWMFCC. The analysis reasons are as follows.

1. By using the wavelet transform in front-end MFCC, we can extract and separate the speech in different transform scales. These in the frequency domain are similar to the frequency segmental processing, and make the subsequent speech analysis to be of natural local property. Thus, the analysis is more delicate.
2. By using wavelet instead of DCT, we overcome the shortage of the DCT. If some frequency segment is destroyed, it only interferes fewer coefficients not all coefficients. We can remove these destroyed coefficients so as to not making strong influence to the speech recognition system.
3. The Bark wavelet transform is designed especially for the speech signal processing. The changing of analysis scale is based on the concept of critical band, and makes wavelet band of each scale be a frequency group. By using the method, we obtain a model which is more close to the human hearing mechanism. The method based on wavelet transform has better robust feature. The result shows that BWMFCC feature can remain high recognition rate under low SNR and large vocabulary conditions. It makes the practical speech recognition system become possible.

Noumber of words	SNR / Feature	15dB	20dB	25dB	30dB	Clean
10	MFCC	86.67	91.90	92.86	93.33	95.24
	BWMFCC	95.72	97.14	96.19	97.14	99.05
20	MFCC	83.80	88.57	90.47	91.47	93.57
	BWMFCC	93.33	94.52	96.19	96.19	96.67
30	MFCC	83.33	87.73	90.32	90.48	93.74
	BWMFCC	94.76	96.19	97.14	97.30	96.35
40	MFCC	82.76	87.57	90.00	91.47	93.57
	BWMFCC	93.69	94.88	95.71	96.07	96.31
50	MFCC	81.19	86.66	89.90	92.28	92.85
	BWMFCC	92.29	93.43	94.19	94.67	94.29

Table 8. The recognition rates using MFCC and BWMFCC features in different SNRs (%)

5. Conclusion

The later conculsions can be obtained from the experimental results of the fourth section.

1. The three parts of speech recognition are conjunct one another and exist the relation restricted among themselves. Bark wavelet was used in improving the feature of ZCPA and MFCC , the latter effect is obviously better than the former.It illustrates that Bark wavelet and the speech character described by MFCC feature are more closer than Bark wavelet and the speech character described by ZCPA feature. The fact is also as such. Bark wavelet is constructed directly according to the hearing perception of human ear, and MFCC is the cepstrum coefficents on the basis of Mel frequency. While Mel frequency is just the hearing frequency of human ear. Though the frequency bins of ZCPA are divided according to the hearing perception, the zero-crossing rate and peak amplitude are time-domain parameters , which are transformed nonlinearly mapping to frequency bin. This kind of nonlinear transform may affect the consistency of ZCPA and hearing frequency, that results in decreasing in function.
2. If the selection of training or recognition network is different, they have different effect on the results. Furthermore, the function of recogntion network has direct relationship with front-end filter and feature extracted. This point can be seen from the experimental results of combination mode1 (FIR+ZCPA+HMM) and mode 2 (FIR+ZCPA+WNN) . Comparing the two modes, the former two parts are same and the third part is different from using HMM or WNN , the results obtained have much more different.The wavelet neural network has bright foreground for speech recognition.Its training speed is fast, which is good for implementation in real time. Further,it has also good recognition rates under no noise or noise environment and the number of recogintion words is larger.
3. The paper researched some kinds combination modes aiming to the three parts of speech recognition system in Fig. 1. For other combination modes, such as Bark+MFCC+WNN , Bark+ZCPA+WNN and so on, we will research them in later work. Which of combination ever is optimal? This needs considering practical application case. We hope the research can be refered by interesting researcher and get to the purpose of communication mutually and progress.

6. Acknowledgements

The project is sponsored by the Natural Science Foundation of China (No. 60472094), Shanxi Province Scientific Research Foundation for Returned Overseas Chinese Scholars (No. 2006-28), Shanxi Province Scientific Research Foundation for University Young Scholars ([2004] No.13), Shanxi Province Natural Science Foundation.(No. 20051039), Shanxi Province Natural Science Foundation (No. 2006011064) and Ph.D. Start-up Fund of TYUST, China. The authors gratefully acknowledge them.

7. References

Doh-suk, Kim , Soo-Young, Lee & Rhee M., Kil. (1999). Auditory Processing of Speech Signal for Robust Speech Recognition in Real-World Noisy Environments. *IEEE Transactions on speech and audio processing,* Vol.7, No.1, (Jan. 1999) 55-68, 1063-6676

Gowdy J., N; Tufekci Z. (2000). Mel-Scaled Discrete Wavelet Coefficients for Speech Recognition, *Proceedings of IEEE ICASSP'2000,* pp.1351-1354, 0-7803-6293-4, Turkey, Jun. 2000, Publisher, Istanbul

Jingwei, Liu ; Xi, Xiao. (2006). Research and Prospect on Robustness Technology in Real-environment Speech Recognition. *Computer Engineering and Applications,* Vol.42 No.24 , (Aug. 2006) 7-12, 1002-8331

Lawrence, Rabiner. (1999). *Fundamentals of Speech Recognition,* Tsinghua University Press, 7302036403, Beijing, China

Lain M., Johnstone. (1999). Wavelets and the Theory of Non-parametric Function Estimation. *Philosophical Transactions: Mathematical, Physical and Engineering Sciences,* Vol.357, No.1760, (Sept. 1999) 2475-2493, Phil.Trans. R. Soc. Lond. A, 1364503X

Musavi, M.; et al. (1992). On the Training of Radial Basis Function Classifiers. *Neural Networks e,* Vol.5, No.4, (July 1992) 595-603, 0893-6080

Oded, Ghitza. (1992). Auditory Nerve Representation as a Basis for Speech Processing, In: *Advances in speech signal processing, S. Furui and M. M. Sondhi,* 453-485, Marcel Dekker, New York

Oded, Ghitza. (1994). Auditory Models and Human Performance in Tasks Related to Speech Coding and Speech Recognition. *IEEE Transactions on Speech and Audio Processing,* Vol.2, No.1, (Jan. 1994) 113-131, 1063-6676

Qiang, Fu; Kechu, Yi. (2000). Bark Wavelet Transform of Speech and its Application in Speech Recognition. *Journal of Electronics,* Vol.28, No.10, (Oct. 2000) 102-105, 0372-2112

Shuyan,Zhao; et al. (2005). A Speech Recognition System of Isolated Words Based on ZCPA and DHMM, Vol.36, No.3, (May 2005) 246-249, 1007-9432

Tianbing,Yao; Tianren, Yao & Tao, Han. (2001). Development and Prospect of Robust Speech Recognition. *Signal Processing,* Vol.17, No.6, (Dec. 2001) 484-497, 1003-0530

Zhiping, Jiao; et al. (2005).A Noise-Robust Feature Extration Method Based on Auditory Model in Speech Recognition, Vol.36, No.1, (Jan. 2005) 13-15, 1007-9432

Zhigang, Liu; Xiaoru, Wang & Qingquan, Qian. (2003). A Review of Wavelet Networks and Their Applications. *Automation of Electric Power Systems,* Vol.27, No.6, (Mar. 2003) 73-79, 1000-1026

14

Autocorrelation-based Methods for Noise-Robust Speech Recognition

Gholamreza Farahani, Mohammad Ahadi and
Mohammad Mehdi Homayounpour
Amirkabir University of Technology
Iran

1. Introduction

One major concern in the design of speech recognition systems is their performance in real environments. In such conditions, different sources could exist which may interfere with the speech signal. The effects of such sources could generally be classified as additive noise and channel distortion. As the names imply, noise is usually considered as additive in spectral domain while channel distortion is multiplicative and therefore appears as an additive part in logarithmic spectrum. These could both result in severe performance degradations in *automatic speech recognition* (ASR) systems. Thus, in recent years, a substantial amount of research has been devoted to improving the performance of Automatic Speech Recognition (ASR) Systems in such environments.

The main approaches taken to improve the performance of ASR systems could be roughly divided into three main categories, namely, robust speech feature extraction; speech enhancement and model-based compensation for noise.

The main goal of the robust speech feature extraction techniques is to find a set of parameters, to represent speech signal in the ASR system, that are robust against the variations in the speech signal due to noise or channel distortions. Extensive research has resulted in such well-known techniques as RASTA filtering (Hermansky & Morgan, 1994), *cepstral mean normalization* (CMN) (Kermorvant, 1999), use of dynamic spectral features (Furui, 1986), *short-time modified coherence* (SMC) (Mansour & Juang, 1989a) and also *one-sided autocorrelation LPC* (OSALPC) (Hernando & Nadeu, 1997), *differential power spectrum* (DPS) (Chen et al., 2003) and *relative autocorrelation sequence* (RAS) (Yuo & Wang, 1998, 1999).

In the case of speech enhancement, some initial information about speech and noise is needed to allow the estimation of noise and clean up of the noisy speech. Widely used methods in this category include *spectral subtraction* (SS) (Beh & Ko, 2003; Boll, 1979) and Wiener filtering (Lee et al., 1996).

In the framework of model-based compensation, statistical models such as Hidden Markov Models (HMMs) are usually considered. The compensation techniques try to remove the mismatch between the trained models and the noisy speech to improve the performance of ASR systems. Methods such as *parallel model combination* (PMC) (Gales & Young, 1995, 1996), *vector Taylor series* (VTS) (Acero et al., 2000; Kim et al., 1998; Moreno, 1996; Moreno et al.,

1996; Shen et al., 1998) and *weighted projection measure* (WPM) (Mansour & Juang, 1989b) can be classified into this category.

From another point of view, methods can be categorized according to the type of distortion they deal with. Methods used to suppress the effect of additive noise such as SS, lin-log RASTA, PMC, DPS, *minimum variance distortion-less response* (MVDR) (Yapanel & Dharanipragada, 2003; Yapanel and Hansen, 2003) and RAS can be placed in one category while those trying to remove channel distortion such as CMN, logarithmic-RASTA, *blind equalization* (BE) (Mauuary, 1996, 1998) and *weighted Viterbi recognition* (WVR) (Cui et al., 2003) are placed in the other category.

Although all the aforementioned efforts had a certain level of success in speech recognition tasks, it is still necessary to investigate new algorithms to further improve the performance of ASR systems. Extracting appropriate speech features is crucial in obtaining good performance in ASR systems since all of the succeeding processes in such systems are highly dependent on the quality of the extracted features. Therefore, robust feature extraction has attracted much attention in the field. Use of the autocorrelation domain in speech feature extraction has recently proved to be successful for robust speech recognition. A number of feature extraction algorithms have been devised using this domain as the initial domain of choice. These algorithms were initiated with the introduction of SMC (Mansour & Juang, 1989a) and OSALPC (Hernando & Nadeu, 1997). Recently, further improvements in this field have been reported (Yuo & Wang, 1998, 1999; Shannon and Paliwal, 2004).

Pole preserving is an important property of the autocorrelation domain, i.e. if the original signal can be modelled by an all-pole sequence which has been excited by an impulse train and a white noise, the poles of the autocorrelation sequence would be the same as the poles of the original signal (McGinn & Johnson, 1989). This means that the features extracted from the autocorrelation sequence could replace the features extracted from the original speech signal. Another property of autocorrelation sequence is that for many typical noise types, noise autocorrelation sequence is more significant in lower lags. Therefore, noise-robust spectral estimation is possible with algorithms that focus on the higher lag autocorrelation coefficients such as *autocorrelation mel-frequency cepstral coefficient* (AMFCC) method (Shannon & Paliwal, 2004). Moreover, as the autocorrelation of noise could in many cases be considered relatively constant over time, a high pass filtering of the autocorrelation sequence, as is done in RAS, could lead to substantial reduction of the noise effect.

Furthermore, it has been shown that preserving spectral peaks is very important in obtaining a robust set of features for ASR (Padmanabhan, 2000; Strope & Alwan, 1998; Sujatha et al., 2003). Methods such as *peak-to-valley ratio locking* (Zhu, 2001) and *peak isolation* (PKISO) (Strope & Alwan, 1997) have been found very useful in speech recognition error rate reduction. In DPS, as an example, differentiation in the spectral domain is used to preserve the spectral peaks while the flat parts of the spectrum, that are believed to be more vulnerable to noise, are almost removed.

Each of the above-mentioned autocorrelation-based methods has its own disadvantages. RAS, while working well in low SNRs, does not perform as well in higher SNRs and clean condition. The main reason is that while filtering the lower frequency parts of noisy autocorrelation sequence can lead to the suppression of noise in low SNR conditions (large noise energies), it in fact filters out parts of the signal autocorrelation sequence in high SNRs. However, the removal of the lower lags of the sequence leads to a good performance in high SNRs in comparison to high-pass filtering.

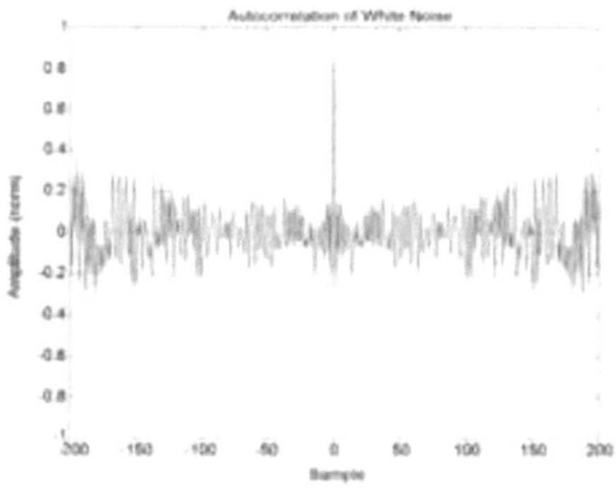

(a)

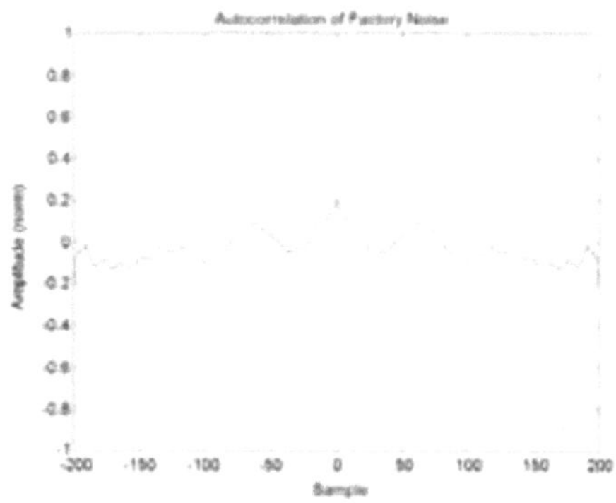

(b)

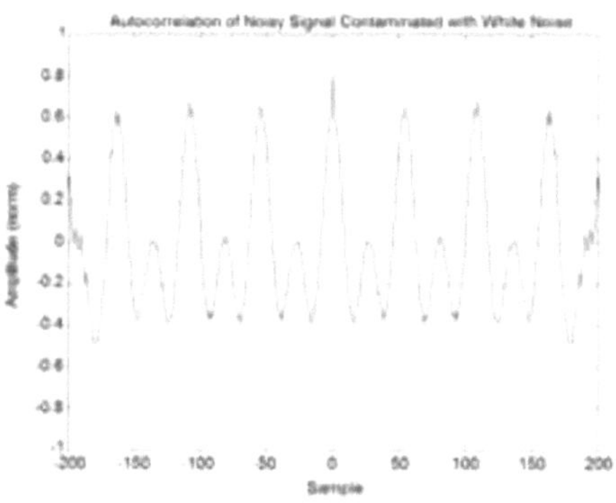

(c)

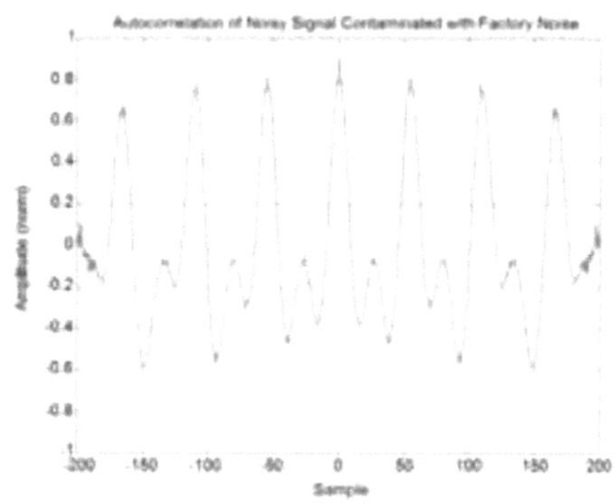

(d)

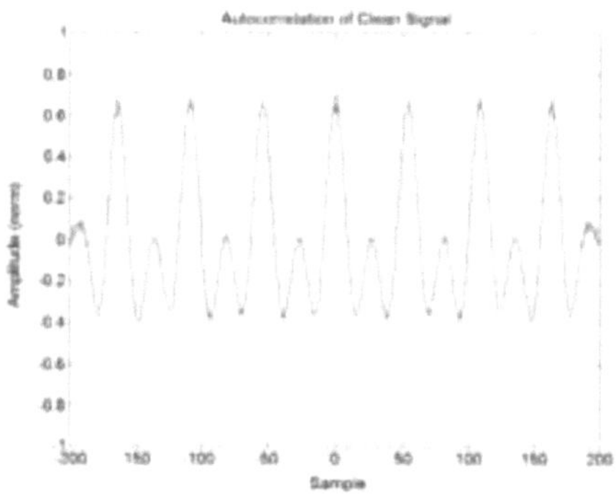

(e)

Figure 1. (a) Autocorrelation sequence of white noise, (b) Autocorrelation sequence of factory noise, (c) Autocorrelation sequence for one frame of speech signal contaminated with white noise at 10 dB SNR, (d) Autocorrelation sequence for one frame of speech signal contaminated with factory noise at 10 dB SNR, (e) Autocorrelation of clean speech signal (vowel).

According to (Shannon & Paliwal, 2004), AMFCC works well for car and subway noises of the Aurora 2 task, but in babble and exhibition noises does not work as well. This is attributed to high similarities between the properties of the latter two and speech.

Fig. 1 displays examples of white and factory noise autocorrelation sequences (a and b), together with sequences for a speech signal (vowel) contaminated with those noises. Apparently, the lower lags of white noise are more important in comparison to those of factory noise that features a more spread out sequence.

Also we can classify autocorrelation-based robust feature extraction methods, from another point of view, into two major fields, i.e. magnitude and phase domains. Some examples of the methods that work in the magnitude domain are RAS, AMFCC, SS, RASTA filtering etc. On the other hand, an example for a phase domain method is *phase autocorrelation* (PAC) (Ikbal et al., 2003). However, recent studies on speech perception have revealed the importance of the phase of speech signal (Paliwal & Alsteris, 2003; Bozkurt et al., 2004; Bozkurt & Couvreur, 2005). The above-mentioned findings in the phase domain have persuaded further work using signal phase information in the feature vector.

In this chapter, we discuss some of the newest robust feature extraction approaches.

2. Autocorrelation-based Feature Extraction Background

While different methods have used different approaches to autocorrelation-based feature extraction, these methods could roughly be divided into two sub-categories: those that use the amplitude and those that use the phase. We will discuss these two groups of methods separately.

2.1. Autocorrelation amplitude-based approaches

2.1.1. Calculation of the autocorrelation for noisy signal

If we assume $v(m,n)$ to be the additive noise, $x(m,n)$ noise-free speech signal and $h(n)$ impulse response of the channel, then the noisy speech signal $y(m,n)$ can be written as

$$y(m,n) = x(m,n) * h(n) + v(m,n) \qquad 0 \le m \le M-1, \quad 0 \le n \le N-1, \tag{1}$$

where * denotes the convolution operation, N is the frame length, n is the discrete time index in a frame, m is the frame index and M is the number of frames. If $x(m,n)$, $v(m,n)$ and $h(n)$ are considered uncorrelated, the autocorrelation of the noisy speech can be expressed as

$$r_{yy}(m,k) = r_{xx}(m,k) * h(k) * h(k) + r_{vv}(m,k) \qquad 0 \le m \le M-1, \quad 0 \le k \le N-1, \tag{2}$$

where $r_{yy}(m,k)$, $r_{xx}(m,k)$ and $r_{vv}(m,k)$ are the short-time autocorrelation sequences of the noisy speech, clean speech and noise respectively and k is the autocorrelation sequence index within each frame. Since additive noise is assumed to be stationary, its autocorrelation sequence can be considered the same for all frames. Therefore, the frame index, m, can be omitted from the additive noise part in (2) leading to

$$r_{yy}(m,k) = r_{xx}(m,k) * h(k) * h(k) + r_{vv}(k) \quad 0 \le m \le M-1, \quad 0 \le k \le N-1. \tag{3}$$

The one-sided autocorrelation sequence of each frame can then be calculated using an unbiased estimator. However, alternatively, one may use a biased estimator for its calculation. The unbiased and biased estimators for the calculation of one-sided autocorrelation sequence are given in (4) and (5) respectively (Yuo & Wang, 1998, 1999).

$$r_{yy}(m,k)=\frac{1}{N-K}\sum_{i=0}^{N-1-K} y(m,i)y(m,i+k) \tag{4}$$

$$r_{yy}(m,k)=\sum_{i=0}^{N-1-K} y(m,i)y(m,i+k) \tag{5}$$

2.1.2. Filtering of one-sided autocorrelation sequence

As our target in this chapter is to remove, or reduce, the effect of additive noise from noisy speech signal, the channel effect, *h(k)*, may be removed at this point from (3). We will then have

$$r_{yy}(m,k)=r_{xx}(m,k)+r_{vv}(k) \qquad 0\le m\le M-1\,,\quad 0\le k\le N-1\,. \tag{6}$$

In order to reduce the effect of channel distortion, one may add a simple approach, such as cepstral mean normalization, to the final cepstral coefficients, as we will mention later.
Considering the noise autocorrelation to be constant over the frames of concern, differentiating both sides of equation (6) with respect to *m*, will remove the noise autocorrelation and yields (Yuo & Wang, 1999)

$$\frac{\partial r_{yy}(m,k)}{\partial m}=\frac{\partial r_{xx}(m,k)}{\partial m}+\frac{\partial r_{vv}(k)}{\partial m}\cong\frac{\partial r_{xx}(m,k)}{\partial m}=\frac{\sum_{t=-L}^{L} t.r_{yy}(m+t,k)}{\sum_{t=-L}^{L} t^2}$$

$$0\le m\le M-1,\ 0\le k\le N-1\,. \tag{7}$$

Equation (7) is equal to a filtering process on the temporal one-sided autocorrelation trajectory by a *FIR* filter where L is the length of the filter. This filtering process can be written in z domain as

$$H(z)=\frac{\sum_{t=-L}^{L} t.z^{t}}{\sum_{t=-L}^{L} t^2}=\frac{-L.z^{-L}+(-L+1).z^{(-L+1)}+...+(-2).z^{-2}+(-1).z^{-1}+z+2.z^{2}+...+(L-1).z^{L-1}+L.z^{L}}{2.(1+2^2+...+(L-1)^2+L^2)} \tag{8}$$

2.1.3. Lower lag elimination

As we mentioned before, the main effects of noise autocorrelation on the clean speech signal autocorrelation is on its lower lags. Therefore eliminating the lower lags of the noisy speech signal autocorrelation should lead to removal of the main noise components. The maximum autocorrelation index to be removed is usually found experimentally. The resulting sequence would be

$$\hat{r}_{yy}(m,k) = r_{yy}(m,k), \qquad D < m \le M-1, \quad 0 < k \le K-1$$

$$\hat{r}_{yy}(m,k) = 0, \qquad 0 \le m \le D, \qquad 0 \le k \le K-1, \tag{9}$$

where D is the elimination threshold.

2.2. Autocorrelation phase-based approaches

As mentioned earlier, feature extraction from magnitude spectrum will be obtained by applying DFT on the frame samples. DFT assumes each frame, $y(m,n)$, is a part of periodic signal, $\tilde{y}(m,n)$, which is defined as :

$$\tilde{y}(m,n) = \sum_{k=-\infty}^{+\infty} y(m,n+kN) \qquad 0 \le m \le M-1, \quad 0 \le n \le N-1. \tag{10}$$

The estimator for the calculation of autocorrelation sequence is then given as:

$$\tilde{r}_{yy}(m,k) = \sum_{i=0}^{N-1} \tilde{y}(m,i)\tilde{y}(m,i+k) \quad 0 \le m \le M-1, \; 0 \le k \le N-1. \tag{11}$$

Another view to equation (11) is that $\tilde{r}_{yy}(m,k)$ gives the correlation between the samples spaced at interval k, which is computed as dot product of two vectors in N-dimensional domain, i.e.

$$Y_0 = \{\tilde{y}(m,0), \tilde{y}(m,1), \ldots, \tilde{y}(m,N-1)\}$$

$$Y_k = \{\tilde{y}(m,k), \ldots, \tilde{y}(m,N-1), \tilde{y}(m,0), \ldots, \tilde{y}(m,k-1)\}$$

$$\tilde{r}_{yy}(m,k) = Y_0^{\,T} Y_k. \tag{12}$$

If we carry out these steps for clean speech, $x(n,m)$, we would have

$$X_0 = \{\tilde{x}(m,0), \tilde{x}(m,1), \ldots, \tilde{x}(m,N-1)\}$$

$$X_k = \{\tilde{x}(m,k), \ldots, \tilde{x}(m,N-1), \tilde{x}(m,0), \ldots, \tilde{x}(m,k-1)\}$$

$$\tilde{r}_{xx}(m,k) = X_0^{\,T} X_k \tag{13}$$

where $\tilde{x}(m,n)$ is the periodic signal obtained from $x(m,n)$.

Clearly, the autocorrelation sequences for clean and noisy signals are different. Therefore, features extracted from autocorrelation sequences would be sensitive to noise. From (12), the magnitudes of two vectors Y_0 and Y_k are the same. If we assume $|Y(m)|$ to be the magnitude of vectors and $\theta_y(m,k)$ the angle between them, then the relationship between the autocorrelation, $\tilde{r}_{yy}(m,k)$, magnitude of the vectors and the angle between them would be

$$\tilde{r}_{yy}(m,k) = |Y(m)|^2 \cos\theta_y(m,k), \qquad 0 \le m \le M-1, \quad 0 \le k \le N-1. \tag{14}$$

Now the angle $\theta_y(m,k)$ between the two vectors will be calculated as:

$$\theta_y(m,k) = \cos^{-1}\left(\frac{\tilde{r}_{yy}(m,k)}{|Y(m)|^2}\right) \qquad 0 \le m \le M-1,\ 0 \le k \le N-1. \tag{15}$$

3. Autocorrelation-based robust feature extraction

In this section we will describe several autocorrelation-based approaches developed by the authors to deal with the problem of robust feature extraction. These methods use either amplitude or phase in the autocorrelation domain, as discussed above. Performance of these methods in various noisy speech recognition tasks will be discussed in a later section.

3.1. Differentiated autocorrelation sequence (DAS)

In this section first we present the calculation of differential power spectrum and then describe DAS method.

3.1.1. Calculating differential power spectrum (DPS)

Although not necessarily an autocorrelation-based approach, we discuss DPS here as it will be used in the following discussions. If the noise and clean speech signals are assumed mutually uncorrelated, by applying short-time DFT to both sides of equation (6), we can calculate the relationship between autocorrelation power spectrums of noisy speech signal, clean speech signal and noise as follows:

$$Y(\omega) = FT\{r_{yy}(m,k)\} \approx FT\{r_{xx}(m,k)\} + FT\{r_{vv}(k)\} = X(\omega) + V(\omega), \tag{16}$$

where $FT[.]$ denotes the Fourier Transform and ω indicates radian frequency. The differential power spectrum will then be defined as

$$Diff_Y(\omega) = Y'(\omega) = \frac{dY(\omega)}{d\omega}, \tag{17}$$

where $\frac{d}{d\omega}$ or prime represent differentiation with respect to ω.

Therefore, by applying differentiation to both sides of equation (16) we have:

$$Diff_Y(\omega) = \frac{dY(\omega)}{d\omega} = \frac{dX(\omega)}{d\omega} + \frac{dV(\omega)}{d\omega} = Diff_X(\omega) + Diff_V(\omega), \tag{18}$$

where $Diff_X(\omega)$ and $Diff_V(\omega)$ are differential autocorrelation power spectrums of clean speech signal and noise respectively.

In discrete domain, the definition of DPS can be approximated by the following equation

$$Diff_Y(k) = Diff_X(k) + Diff_V(k) \approx \sum_{l=-Q}^{P} a_l Y(k+l) \cong \sum_{l=-Q}^{P} a_l [X(k+l) + V(k+l)], \quad 0 \le k \le K-1 \tag{19}$$

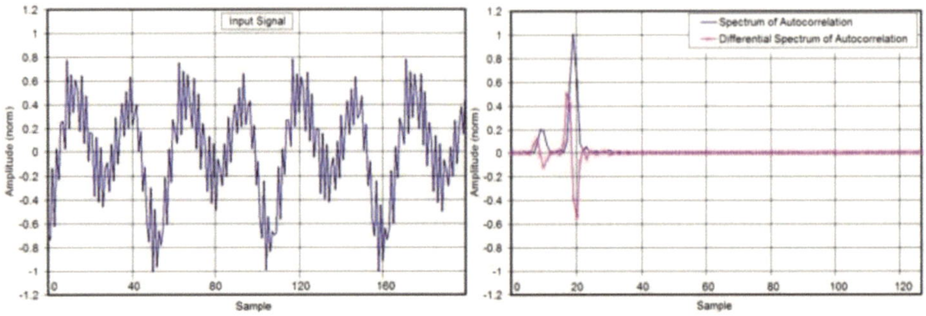

(a) (b)

Figure 2. (a) A sample speech signal, and (b) the autocorrelation spectrum magnitude and the differentiated autocorrelation spectrum magnitude of the same signal with a 512-point FFT. Only 128 points of the spectrum are shown for clarity. The sample signal is one frame of phone /iy/ (Farahani et al., 2007).

where P and Q are the orders of the difference equation, a_l are real-valued weighting coefficients and K is the length of FFT. The absolute value of the differentiation indicates the peak points of the spectrum.

3.1.2. DAS algorithm

This approach combines the advantages of RAS and DPS. In this algorithm (Farahani & Ahadi, 2005; Farahani et al., 2007), splitting the speech signal into frames and applying a pre-emphasis filter, the autocorrelation sequence of the frame signal is obtained using either an unbiased or a biased estimator, as shown in (4) and (5). A *FIR* filter is then applied to the noisy speech signal autocorrelation sequence. Hamming windowing and short-time Fourier transform constitute the next stages. Then, the differential power spectrum of the filtered signal is calculated. By differentiation of the spectrum, we preserve the peaks, except that each peak is split into two, one positive and one negative, and the flat part of the power spectrum is approximated to zero.

Fig. 2 depicts a sample speech signal, its short-time autocorrelation spectrum and the differentiated short-time autocorrelation spectrum. This sample signal is one frame of phone /iy/. In order to simplify the representation, only the significant lower-frequency parts of the spectrum have been shown and the non-significant parts omitted.

As shown in Fig. 2 and mentioned above, the flat parts of the spectrum have been transformed to zero by differentiation and each peak of it split into two positive and negative parts. Since the spectral peaks convey the most important information in speech signal, this fact that the differential power spectrum retains spectral peaks means that we will not lose the important information of the speech signal (Chen et al., 2003). Furthermore, since noise spectrum is often flat and the differentiation either reduces or omits the relatively flat parts of the spectrum, it will lead to suppression of the noise effect on the spectrum. A set of cepstral coefficients can then be derived by applying a conventional mel-frequency filter-bank to the resultant spectrum and finally passing the logarithm of bin outputs to the DCT block. Fig. 3 displays the overall front-end diagram of this method. We call these new features Differentiated Autocorrelation Sequence (DAS).

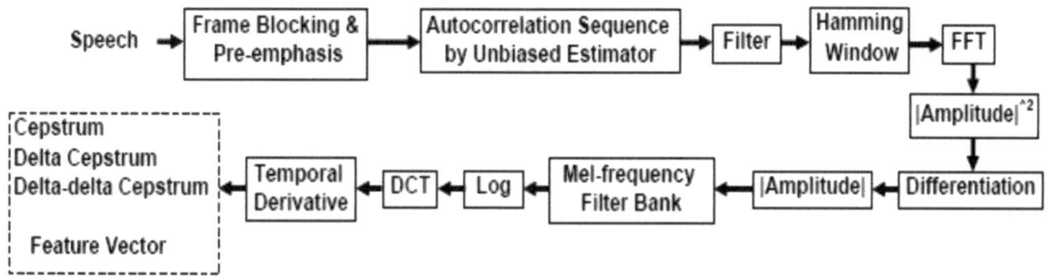

Figure 3. Block diagram of DAS front-end for robust feature extraction.

3.1.3. Experiments

If the process of feature extraction does not include the extraction of autocorrelation spectral peaks, as mentioned in (Yuo & Wang, 1999), using 5 frames of speech for filtering can lead to the best results. Therefore, in order to be able to compare our results to the best results of RAS, the same filter length (L=2) is used. Thus, equation (8) will be simplified as

$$H(z) = \frac{\sum_{t=-2}^{2} t.z^t}{\sum_{t=-2}^{2} t^2} = \frac{-2z^{-2} - 1z^{-1} + z + 2z^2}{10} . \tag{20}$$

Furthermore, as discussed in (Chen et al., 2003), the best results for spectral differentiation was obtained using the following equation

$$Diff(k) = Y(k) - Y(k+1) , \tag{21}$$

i.e. a simple difference.

The above-mentioned parameter and formula were used in the implementation of RAS, DPS, DAS, SPFH, ACP, ACPAF and APP methods on different mentioned tasks, unless otherwise specified. All model creation, training and tests in all our experiments have been carried out using the HMM toolkit (HTK, 2002).

3.1.3.1. Database

Three speech corpora have been used throughout the experiments reported in this chapter. These include an isolated-word Farsi task, a continuous Farsi task and Aurora 2, a noisy English connected digits task.

The Isolated-word Farsi task is a set of isolated-word Farsi (Persian) speech data collected from 65 male and female adult speakers uttering the names of 10 Iranian cities. The data was collected in normal office conditions with SNRs of 25dB or higher and a sampling rate of 16 kHz. Each speaker uttered 5 repetitions of words, some of which were removed from the corpus due to problems that occurred during the recordings. A total of 2665 utterances from 55 speakers were used for HMM model training. The test set contained 10 speakers (5 male

& 5 female) that were not included in the training set. The noise was then added to their speech in different SNRs. The noise data was extracted from the NATO RSG-10 corpus (SPIB, 1995). We have considered babble, car, factory and white noises and added them to the clean signal at 20, 15, 10, 5, 0 and -5 dB SNRs.

The Continuous Farsi task is a speaker-independent medium-vocabulary continuous speech Farsi (Persian) corpus. FARSDAT speech corpus was used for this set of experiments (Bijankhan et al., 1994; FARSDAT). This corpus was originally collected from 300 male and female adult speakers uttering 20 Persian sentences in two sessions. The sentences uttered by each speaker were randomly selected from a set of around 400 sentences. Some of the speakers were removed from the corpus due to their accent or problems occurred during the recordings. The data was originally collected in quiet environment with SNRs of 25dB or higher and a sampling rate of 44.1 kHz. The sampling rate was later reduced to 16 kHz. A total of 1814 utterances from 91 speakers were used for HMM model training in these experiments. The test set contained 46 speakers that were not included in the training set. A total of 889 utterances were used as the test set. The noise was then added to the speech in different SNRs. As with the isolated-word experiments, the noise data was extracted from the NATO RSG-10 corpus and included babble, car, factory and F16 noises added to the clean signal at 20, 15, 10, 5, 0 and -5 dB SNRs.

Aurora 2 (Hirsch & Pearce, 2000) is a noisy connected-digit recognition task. It includes two training modes, training on clean data only (clean-condition training) and training on clean and noisy data (multi-condition training). In clean-condition training, 8440 utterances from TIDigits speech corpus (Leonard, 1984) containing those of 55 male and 55 female adults are used. For multi-condition mode, 8440 utterances from TIDigits training part are split equally into 20 subsets with 422 utterances in each subset. Suburban train, babble, car and exhibition hall noises are added to these 20 subsets at SNRs of 20, 15, 10, 5, 0 and -5 dB.

Three test sets are defined in Aurora 2, named A, B and C. 4004 utterances from TIDigits test data are divided into four subsets with 1001 utterances in each. One noise is added to each subset at different SNRs.

In test set A, suburban train, babble, car and exhibition noises are added to the above mentioned four subsets, leading to a total of $4 \times 7 \times 1001$ utterances. Test set B is created similar to test set A, but with four different noises, namely, restaurant, street, airport and train station. Finally, test set C contains two of four subsets with speech and noise filtered using different filter characteristics in comparison to the data used in test sets A and B. The noises used in this set are suburban train and street.

3.1.3.2. Results on the isolated-word Farsi task

The experiments were carried out using MFCC (for comparison purposes), MFCC applied to the signal enhanced by spectral subtraction, RAS-MFCC, cepstral coefficients derived using DPS and DAS. In all cases, 25 msec. frames with 10 msec. of frame shifts and a pre-emphasis coefficient of 0.97 were used. Also, for each speech frame, a 24-channel mel-scale filter-bank was used. Here, each word was modelled by an 8-state left-right HMM and each state was represented by a single-Gaussian PDF. The feature vectors were composed of 12 cepstral and log-energy parameters, together with their first and second order derivatives (39 coefficients in total). Fig. 4 depicts the results of the implementation.

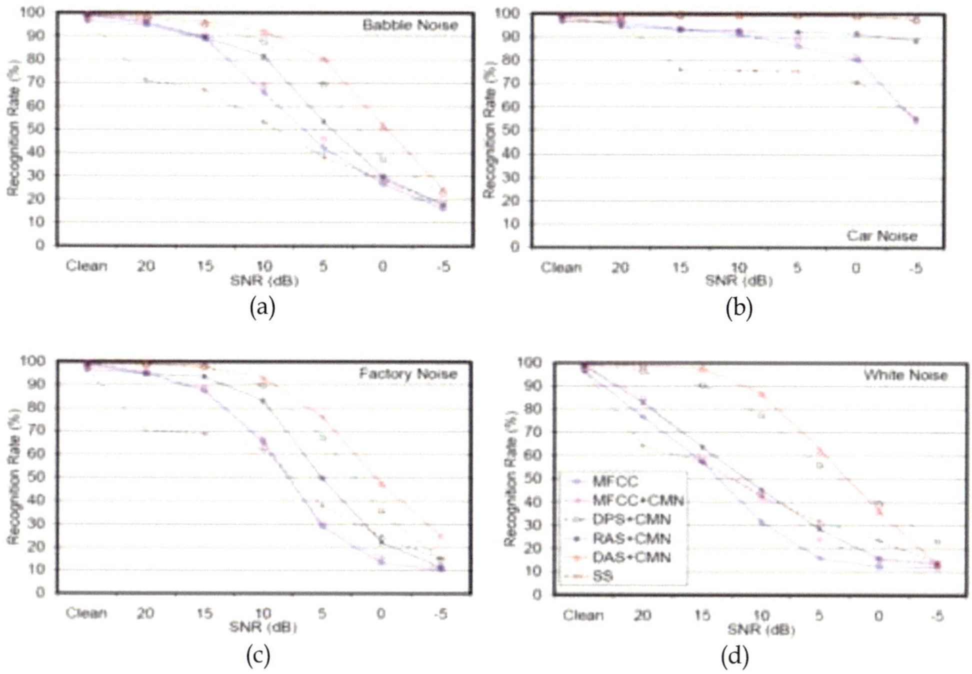

Figure 4. Isolated-word recognition results for speech signal contaminated with (a) babble, (b) car, (c) factory and (d) white noises in different SNRs. The results correspond to MFCC, MFCC+CMN, DPS+CMN, RAS+CMN, DAS+CMN and SS methods for isolated-word task with 1 mixture component per state.

Also, in Tables 1 and 2, the clean recognition results and the average noisy speech recognition results are included for comparison purposes. The average values mentioned in Table 2 were calculated over the results obtained from 0 dB to 20 dB SNRs, omitting the clean and -5 dB results. This is in accordance with average result calculations in Aurora 2 task.

Note that, all the reported results are for clean-trained models and no matched condition or multi-conditioned noisy training was carried out. Furthermore, also for comparison purposes, the results of an implementation of cepstral mean normalization, as a feature post-processing enhancement method, applied after standard MFCC, DPS and DAS parameter extractions, are included. These are denoted by CMN. Note that, for better comparison, the results of an implementation of spectral subtraction as an initial enhancement method, applied before standard MFCC parameter extraction, are also included. These are denoted by SS and the algorithm was applied as explained in (Junqua & Haton, 1996). As can be seen in Fig. 4, DAS outperforms all other methods in almost all noise types and SNRs. The average results on different SNRs, as shown in Table 2, are again considerably better for DAS in comparison to the other feature extraction techniques, except for the case of car noise, where it is very close to DPS results. As an example, DAS has about 29% reduction on the average word error rate for babble noise, compared to DPS, which performs the best among the others. Similar conclusions can be made from this table for factory and white noises.

Feature type	Recognition Rate (%)
MFCC	96.60
SS	96.60
MFCC+CMN	99.20
DPS+CMN	99.20
RAS+CMN	98.80
DAS+CMN	99.20

Table 1. Comparison of baseline isolated-word recognition rates for various feature types.

Feature type	Average Recognition Rate (%)			
	Babble	Car	Factory	White
MFCC (Baseline)	63.60	89.44	57.92	38.68
SS	51.60	78.88	52.72	43.88
MFCC+CMN	66.00	91.00	59.24	45.08
DPS+CMN	77.28	99.24	77.84	71.84
RAS+CMN	70.00	92.88	68.72	47.24
DAS+CMN	83.88	99.12	82.80	76.36

Table 2. Comparison of average isolated-word recognition rates for various feature types with babble, car, factory and white noises.

3.1.3.3. Results on continuous Farsi task

The feature parameters were extracted similar to the isolated-word recognition case. The modeling was carried out using 30 context-independent models for the basic Farsi phonemes plus silence and pause models. These, except the pause model, consisted of 3 states per model, while the pause model included one state only. The number of mixture components per state was 6 and no grammar was used during the recognition process to enable us better evaluate our acoustic models under noisy conditions. The size of the recognition lexicon was around 1200.

Figures 5 and 6 display the results of our FARSI CSR experiments. These results were obtained using a set of parameters similar to the isolated-word experiments parameters.

According to Fig. 5, DAS outperforms all other front-ends such as RAS, DPS and MFCC in almost all cases. While RAS performance is acceptable in low SNRs, it performs inferior to other front-ends in SNRs over 10dB. DPS performs slightly better than MFCC except in car noise.

Fig. 6 depicts the results obtained when CMN is applied alongside the above front-ends. Here again, the DAS front-end outperforms the others in almost all cases.

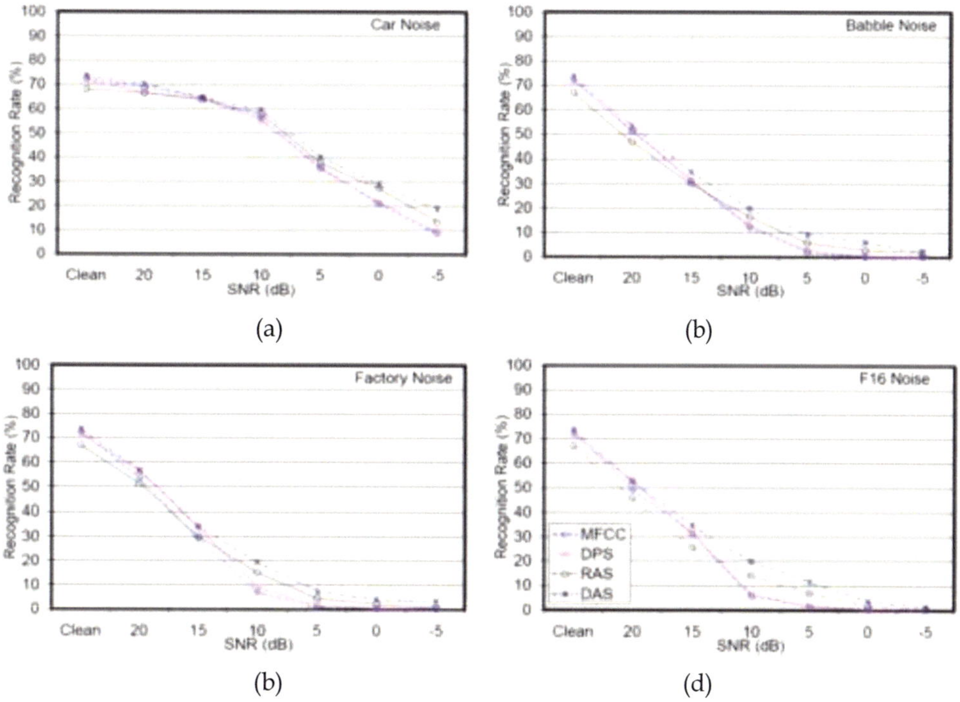

Figure 5. Continuous speech recognition accuracies for speech signal contaminated with (a) babble, (b) car, (c) factory and (d) F16 noises in different SNRs. The results correspond to MFCC, DPS, RAS and DAS front-ends and 6 mixture components per state, without CMN.

Table 3 summarizes recognition rates for various front-ends with/without CMN and contaminated with babble, car, factory and f16 noises with six mixture components per state. According to this table, DAS with/without CMN outperforms the other methods in average, proving its effectiveness in noisy speech recognition.

3.1.3.4. Results on Aurora 2 task

The features in this case were computed using 25 msec. frames with 10 msec. of frame shifts. Pre-emphasis coefficient was set to 0.97. For each speech frame, a 23-channel mel-scale filter-bank was used. The feature vectors were composed of 12 cepstral and log-energy parameters, together with their first and second order derivatives (39 coefficients in total). MFCC feature extraction and all model creation, training and tests were carried out using the HMM toolkit.

Fig. 7 shows the results obtained using MFCC, DPS, RAS and DAS front-ends with CMN on models created using the clean-condition training section of Aurora 2 task. Once again, the DAS front-end leads to better recognition rates in comparison to other methods. Also, Fig. 8 depicts the recognition rates of different methods obtained using the multi-condition training set of Aurora 2 task. The multi-condition results of different front-ends show very close performances. However, DAS still performs slightly better compared to the others.

3.1.3.5. Adjusting the Parameters

For parameter setting in DAS, the length of the FIR filter (filter type is same as (8)) and the order of differentiation was taken into consideration. A set of preliminary experiments were carried out to find the most appropriate filtering and differentiation parameters. These experiments were performed on the continuous Farsi task as explained in section 3.1.3.1. Here, the length of the filter was changed from L=1 (three frames) to L=5 (eleven frames) in steps. Also, biased and unbiased estimators were used for calculating the one-sided autocorrelation sequence. Table 4 summarize the results by displaying the average recognition accuracies on the test set with various noises (babble, car, factory and F16) and in various SNRs, with two different autocorrelation estimators. At this step, for computing the autocorrelation spectral peaks the differentiation defined in (21) was considered.

As can be seen in Table 4, the best average recognition results using DAS features were obtained using the filter length L=3. Furthermore, the unbiased estimator led to better results compared to the biased one.

In order to find the best differentiation methods, the following differentiation formulas were used.

$$Diff(k) = Y(k) - Y(k+2), \tag{22}$$

$$Diff(k) = Y(k-2) + Y(k-1) - Y(k+1) - Y(k+2), \tag{23}$$

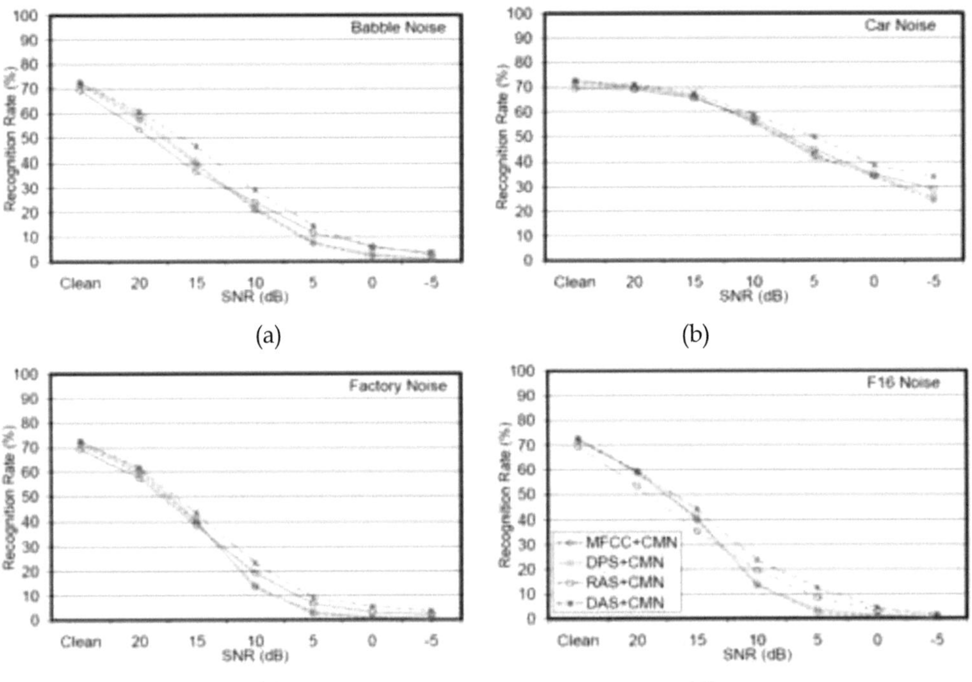

Figure 6. Continuous speech recognition accuracies for speech signal contaminated with (a) babble, (b) car, (c) factory and (d) f16 noises in different SNRs. The results correspond to MFCC, DPS, RAS and DAS front-ends with CMN and 6 mixture components per state.

Recognition Rate (%) - 6 mix per state				
Noise Type	Babble	Car	Factory	F16
MFCC (Baseline)	19.23	49.39	18.23	17.64
MFCC+CMN	25.39	53.69	23.22	23.24
DPS	19.90	48.06	20.32	18.42
DPS+CMN	26.43	53.62	23.80	23.54
RAS	20.32	50.67	20.70	21.84
RAS+CMN	26.44	54.21	25.05	24.03
DAS	24.72	52.78	26.22	26.42
DAS+CMN	31.31	57.09	28.67	28.84

Table 3. Comparison of average continuous speech recognition accuracies for various feature types in babble, car, factory and f16 noises with different SNRs. Recognition was carried out using 6 mixture components per state.

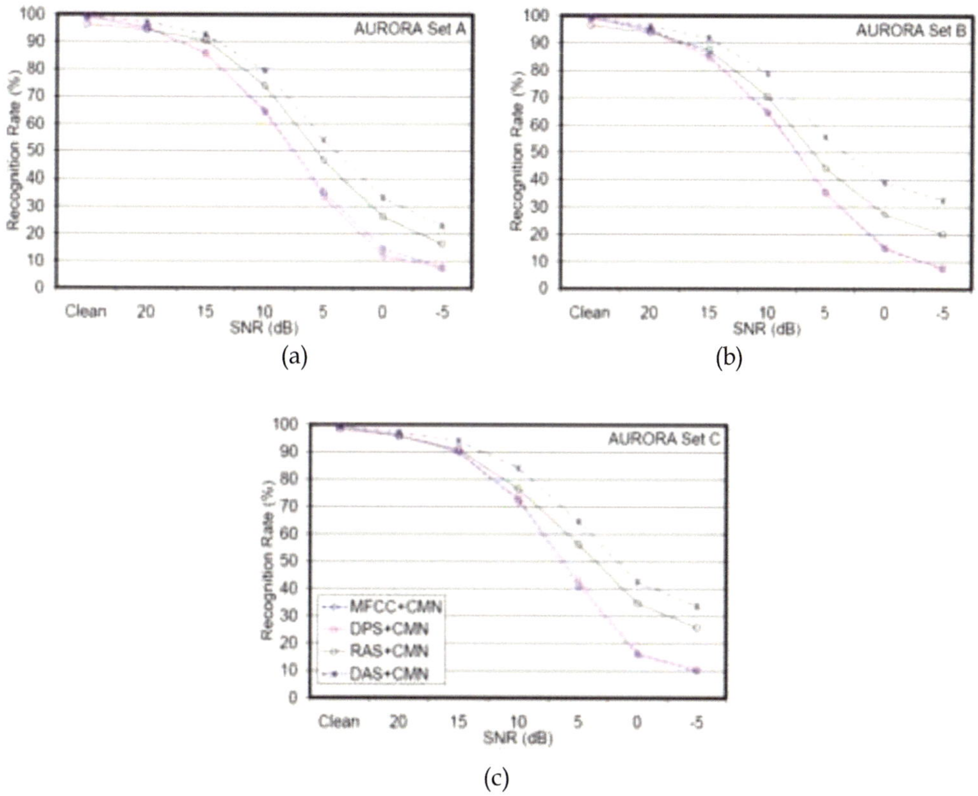

Figure 7. Average recognition accuracies for clean-condition on AURORA2.0 (a) set A, (b) set B and (c) set C. The results correspond to MFCC, DPS, RAS and DAS front-ends with CMN.

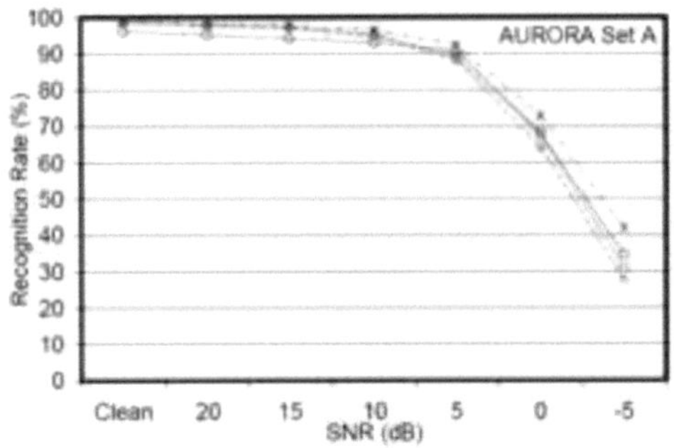

(a)

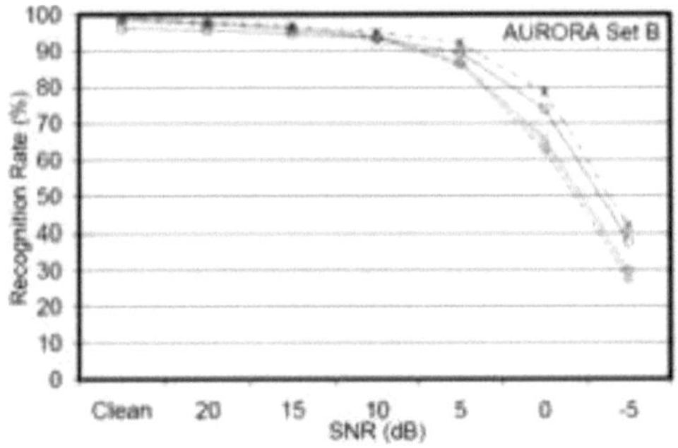

(b)

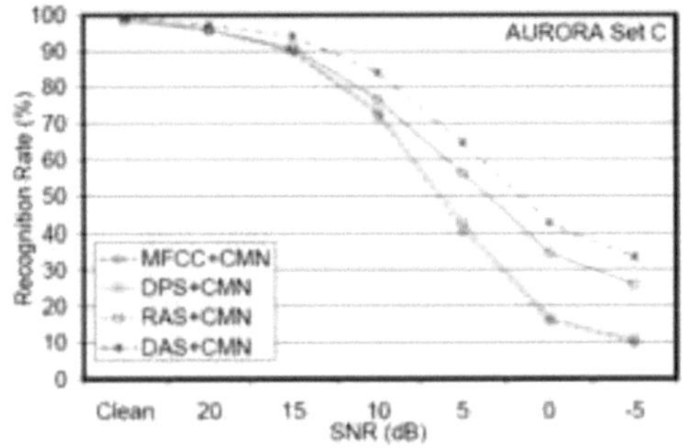

(c)

Figure 8. Average recognition accuracies for AURORA 2 multi-condition training. (a) set A, (b) set B and (c) set C. The results correspond to MFCC, DPS, RAS and DAS front-ends with CMN.

Since the filter with length L=3, using unbiased estimator, had led to better results in noisy speech recognition, this type of filter and estimator have been tested together with the difference equations given in (21), (22) and (23). The results are reported in Table 5.
According to this table, the one sample difference equation, (21), has led to better overall results, compared to (22) and (23).

	Biased Estimator				Unbiased Estimator			
Filter Lenght	Babble	Car	Factory	F16	Babble	Car	Factory	F16
L=1 3 frames	22.07	49.06	22.59	21.72	24.08	51.80	23.77	23.25
L=2 5 frames	22.97	50.00	23.24	22.95	24.72	52.78	24.43	24.53
L=3 7 frames	24.69	51.34	24.41	24.42	26.00	53.24	26.49	25.38
L=4 9 frames	23.82	50.89	23.76	23.15	25.31	53.06	25.61	23.78
L=5 11 frames	23.07	49.91	23.35	22.89	25.09	52.59	25.41	23.76

Table 4. The average continuous speech recognition rates using DAS for various noise and SNRs with different filter lengths. Biased and Unbiased estimator was used for one-sided autocorrelation sequence calculation and the models featured 6 mixture components per state.

3.2. Spectral Peaks of filtered higher-lag autocorrelation sequence (SPFH)

In this method, after splitting the speech signal into frames and pre-emphasizing, the autocorrelation sequence of the frame signal was obtained using an unbiased estimator (equation (4)). The lower lags of the autocorrelation sequence were then removed according

Noise Type	Recognition Rate (%) equation (21)	Recognition Rate (%) equation (22)	Recognition Rate (%) equation (23)
Babble	26.00	24.83	25.19
Car	53.24	51.56	52.35
Factory	26.49	25.17	25.82
F16	25.38	23.71	24.25

Table 5. CSR averaged accuracies over various SNRs with different noise types, filter length L=3 and unbiased estimator for one-sided autocorrelation sequence obtained using equations (21), (22) and (23).

to the criterion discussed in section 3.2.2. A *FIR* high-pass filter similar to section 3.1.2 was then applied to the signal autocorrelation sequence to further suppress the effect of noise. Hamming windowing and short-time Fourier transform were the next stages. In the next step, the differential power spectrum of the filtered signal was found using (19). This has an effect similar to what discussed in 3.1.2, leading to even further suppression of the effect of noise. The steps of this algorithm are shown in Fig. 9. The resultant feature set was called *spectral peaks of filtered higher-lag autocorrelation sequence* (SPFH) (Farahani et al., 2006b).

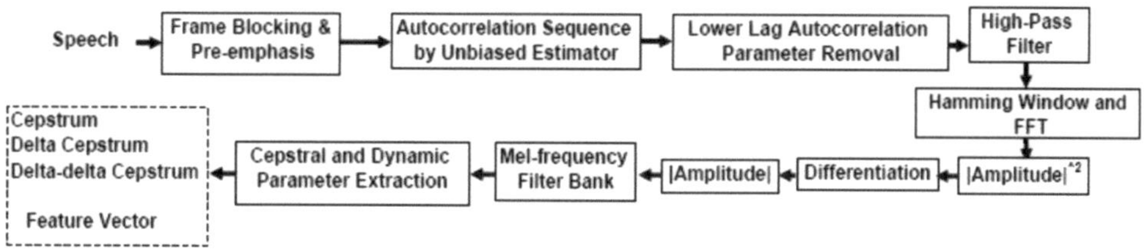

Figure 9. Front-end diagram for SPFH feature extraction

3.2.1. SPFH results on Aurora 2 task

The discussed approach was implemented on Aurora 2 task. Fig. 10 depicts the results obtained using MFCC, RAS, AMFCC, DAS and SPFH front-ends. According to this figure, SPFH has led to better recognition rates in comparison to other methods for all test sets. Also, in Table 6, average recognition rates obtained for each test set of Aurora 2 are shown. As shown in Fig. 10, the recognition rates using MFCC are seriously degraded in lower SNRs, while, AMFCC, RAS, DAS and SPFH are more robust to different noises with SPFH outperforming all the others.

3.2.2. Adjusting the parameters

In our experiments we have used a filter length of L=2. Furthermore, the best results for spectral differentiation were obtained using a simple difference equation (21). Therefore we

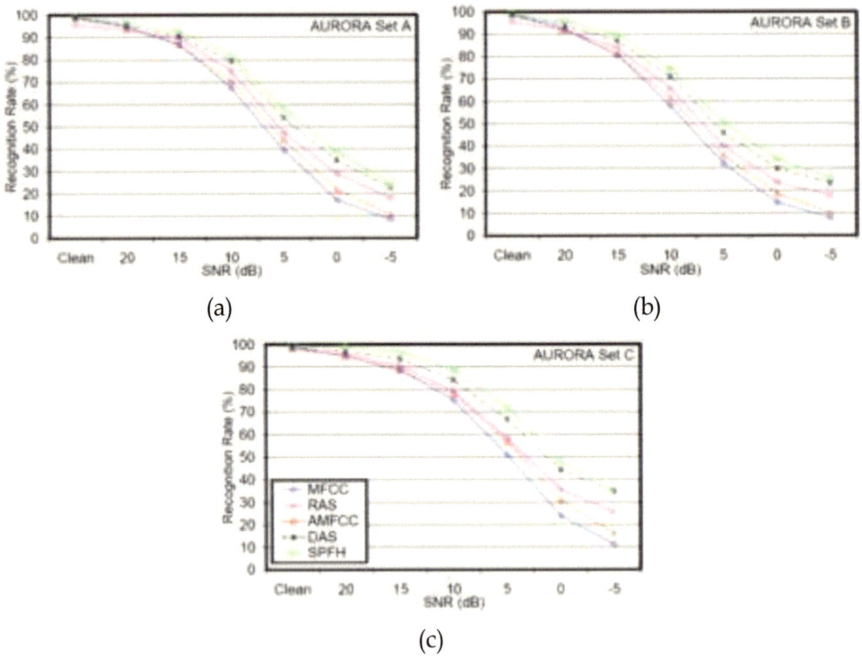

Figure 10. Average recognition rates on Aurora 2 task. (a) Test set a, (b) Test set b, (c) Test set c. The results correspond to MFCC, RAS, AMFCC, DAS and SPFH methods.

Feature type	Average Recognition Rate (%)		
	Set A	Set B	Set C
MFCC	61.13	55.57	66.68
RAS	66.77	60.94	71.81
AMFCC	63.41	57.67	69.72
DAS	70.90	65.57	77.17
SPFH	73.61	68.98	80.89

Table 6. Comparison of Average recognition rates for various feature types on Aurora 2 test sets.

used (21) in our experiments. In order to find the most suitable autocorrelation lag for discarding, we have tested several different lag values. The results are reported in Fig. 11. According to this figure, the best results were obtained when lags of lower than 2.5 ms (20 samples) were discarded. Hence, this value was used as the discarding threshold in our experiments. The same value was also used with AMFCC.

3.3. Autocorrelation peaks after filtering (ACPAF) and autocorrelation peaks (ACP) methods

In this section, first we explain the extraction of the frequency locations of peaks. Then we explain ACPAF and ACP methods and finally report the results of their implementation.

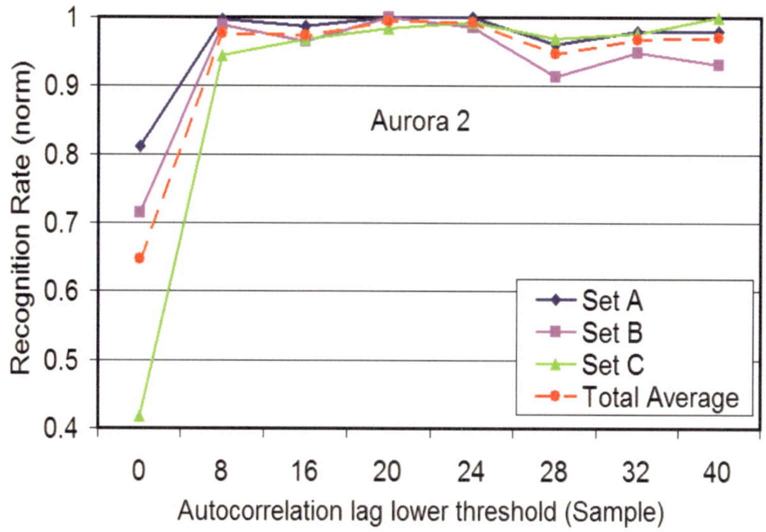

Figure 11. Average normalized recognition rates for each of the three test sets of Aurora 2 and their total average versus autocorrelation lag threshold.

3.3.1. Peak frequency location

For peak calculations, we used the *peak threading* method that is rather accurate in finding the location of peak frequencies in spectral domain (Strope & Alwan, 1998). For this, we first applied a set of triangular filters to the signal. These filters had bandwidths of 100 Hz for centre frequencies below 1 kHz and bandwidths of one tenth the centre frequency for the frequencies above 1 kHz. Then, an AGC (Automatic Gain Control) was applied to the filter outputs. In our implementation, we used a typical AGC that slowly adapts the output level, so that its value is maintained near that of the target level when the levels of input change. Therefore, the inputs below 30 dB are amplified linearly by 20dB and inputs above 30 dB are amplified increasingly less. After finding the isolated peaks, the peaks were threaded together and smoothed. Then three peak frequencies and two peak derivatives were found and added to the feature vector.

3.3.2. Algorithm implementation

Due to the importance of spectral peaks and also the effectiveness of autocorrelation function, the autocorrelation domain has also been used for extracting frequencies of the first three peaks and two derivatives of them. Fig. 12 depicts the block diagram of this feature extraction approach. Once again, feature extraction starts with frame blocking, pre-emphasis and unbiased autocorrelation calculation. Then, the first three spectral peak locations and their derivatives are calculated using the signal autocorrelation, to be later added to the feature vector. Furthermore, the front-end diagram continues with/without filtering, as pointed out in (8). Hamming windowing, FFT and the rest of blocks normally used in MFCC calculations constitute the remainder of feature extraction procedure. If the filter is used after the autocorrelation of the signal, a cleaner signal, compared to the original noisy signal, could result.

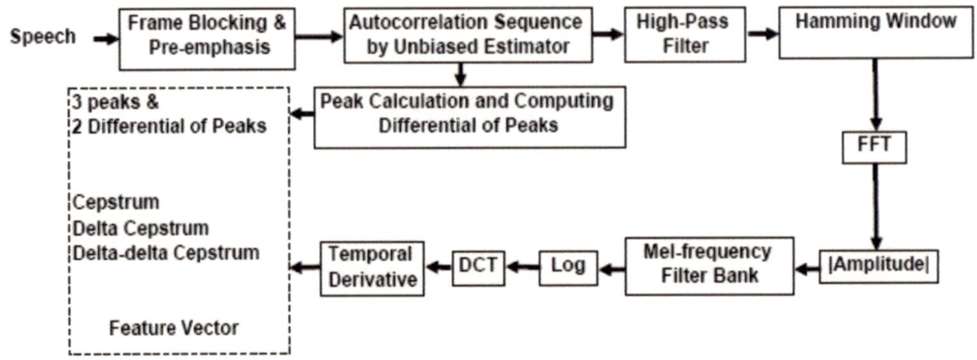

Figure 12. Front-end diagram to extract ACPAF features in autocorrelation domain.

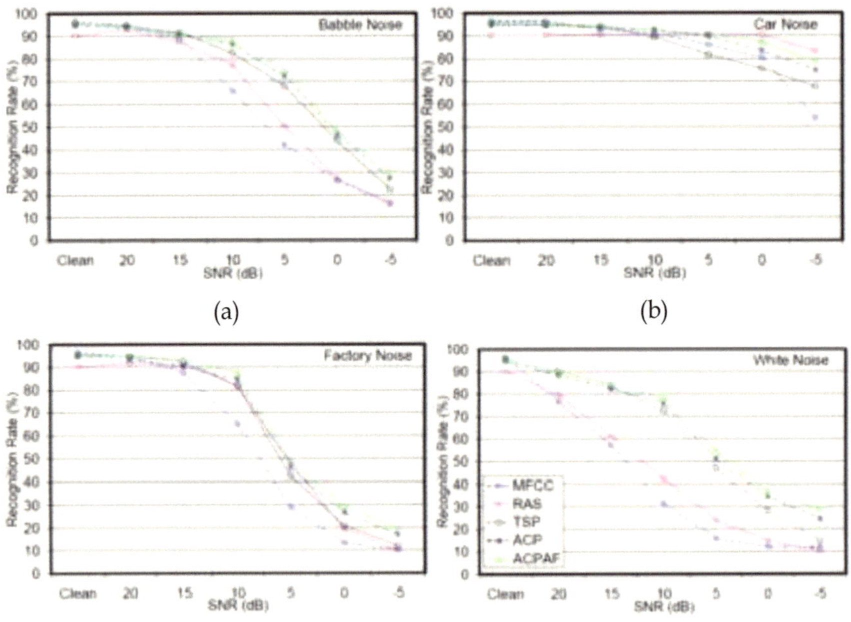

(a) (b)

(c) (d)

Figure 13. Recognition Rates for different noises on isolated-word Farsi corpus. (a) babble, (b) car, (c) factory and (d) white noises in different SNRs. The results correspond to MFCC, RAS, TSP, ACP and ACPAF.

In Fig. 12, the box named "peak calculation and computing differential of peaks" displays how the peak threading method can be integrated in this front-end. Since after the application of autocorrelation function, the spectral peaks become clearer, we expect the resultant feature vectors to be more robust to noise.

As mentioned in (Strope & Alwan, 1998; Farahani et al., 2006a), the peaks of the speech spectrum are important for speech recognition. Hence, we decided to add three peak frequencies and two peak derivatives to the feature vector. The spectral peaks obtained using unfiltered signal autocorrelation, as depicted in the front-end diagram, are called ACP (autocorrelation peaks) and those obtained using filtered signal autocorrelation, ACPAF (autocorrelation peaks after filtering). For comparison purposes, we have also implemented a feature extraction procedure similar to (Strope & Alwan, 1998), except that a different AGC was used, as explained above. This will be called *threaded spectral peaks* (TSP).

3.3.3. Experiments

The speech corpus used in these experiments is the speaker-independent isolated-word Farsi (Persian) corpus. Our experiments were carried out using MFCC (for comparison purposes), RAS, GDF, TSP and our three new methods, ACP and ACPAF. The feature vectors for both proposed methods were composed of 12 cepstral and a log-energy parameter, together with their first and second derivatives and five extra components of which three are for the first three formants and the other two for the frequency peak derivatives. Therefore, our feature vectors were of size 44. For implementation of these methods, we have used a filter length of L=2. Also unbiased autocorrelation sequence is used for feature extraction.

Fig. 13 depicts the results of the implementations. Also the averages of the results are reported in Table 7. Once again, the average values mentioned in this table are calculated over the results obtained from 0 dB to 20 dB SNRs, omitting the clean and -5 dB results. As is clear, the recognition rates using MFCC features are seriously degraded by different noises, while RAS method exhibits more robustness. Adding the frequencies of peaks approved the effectiveness of autocorrelation domain for peak tracking. As the results indicate, while ACP achieves a noticeable improvement in the baseline performance in noise, the combination of ACP with FIR filter works better than ACP alone, outperforming other methods in noisy conditions. The results obtained can be listed in brief as:

1. The ACPAF outperforms other methods.
2. The improvements for car noise are very slight, as most of the feature extraction techniques perform almost similar in that case.
3. Appending frequency peaks to the feature vector can further improve the results obtained using autocorrelation based features.

3.4. Autocorrelation peaks and phase features (APP)

In this section, feature extraction in phase domain plus the extraction of extra feature parameters in autocorrelation domain will be discussed (Farahani et al., 2006c). Due to the effectiveness of autocorrelation function in preserving peaks, we will also report the results of using the autocorrelation domain for extracting the first 3 formants of the speech signal (Strope & Alwan, 1998; Farahani et al., 2006a).

In Fig. 14 we have shown the procedure followed to extract feature parameters in autocorrelation phase parameters. Most of the diagram is similar to previously discussed methods with the exception of the calculation of the phase angle, $\theta_y(m,k)$, as mentioned in (15). As it is clear from (15), these features are related only to the phase variations, in contrast to the features based on the magnitude, such as MFCC, that are related to both $|Y(m)|$ and $\theta_y(m,k)$ (Ikbal et al., 2003).

Feature type	Average Recognition Rate (%)			
	Babble	Car	Factory	White
MFCC	63.60	89.44	57.92	38.68
RAS	67.04	90.56	66.40	44.44
TSP	76.16	87.20	66.44	64.36
ACP	77.92	90.76	68.16	66.44
ACPAF	79.28	92.12	70.76	68.64

Table 7. Comparison of average recognition rates for various feature types with babble, car, factory and white noises.

Here again, the first three spectral peak locations and their derivatives are also calculated using the signal autocorrelation spectrum, as explained in 3.3.1 and later added to the feature vector in phase domain. The new coefficients were named *Autocorrelation Peaks and Phase features* (APP).

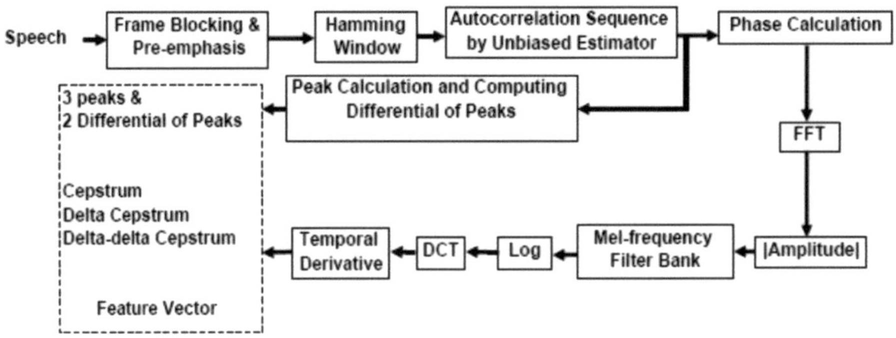

Figure 14. Front-end diagram to extract features in phase domain along with autocorrelation function.

3.4.1. Experiments

This method was implemented on Aurora 2 task. The feature vectors were composed of 12 cepstral and one log-energy parameters, together with their first and second derivatives and five extra components of which three were for the first three formants and the other two for the frequency peak derivatives. Therefore, the overall feature vector size was 44. In this method, we have used a filter length of L=2.

Fig. 15 displays the results obtained using MFCC, PAC (*phase autocorrelation*) and APP. Also, for comparison purposes, we have included the results of adding spectral peaks to feature vectors calculated using magnitude spectrum and called it TSP (*threaded spectral peaks*) (Strope & Alwan, 1998) and ACP (*autocorrelation peaks*) (Farahani et al., 2006a). According to Fig. 15, APP has led to better recognition rates in comparison to most of the other methods and outperformed other methods for all test sets. This result shows that the autocorrelation domain is more appropriate for peak isolation in phase domain.

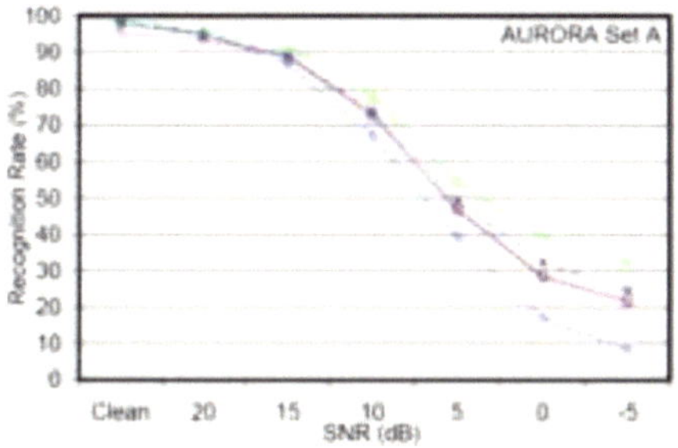

(a)

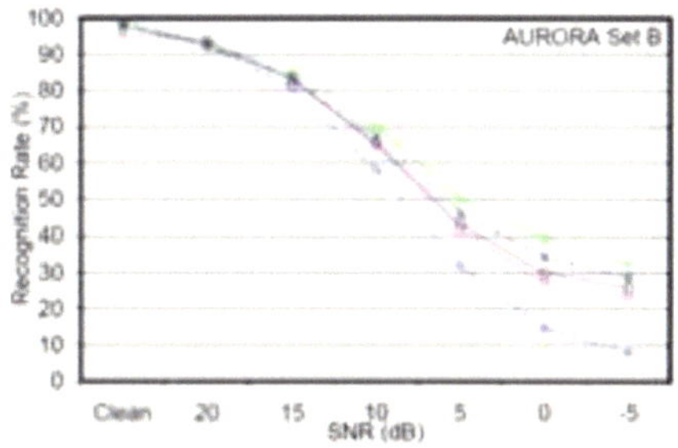

(b)

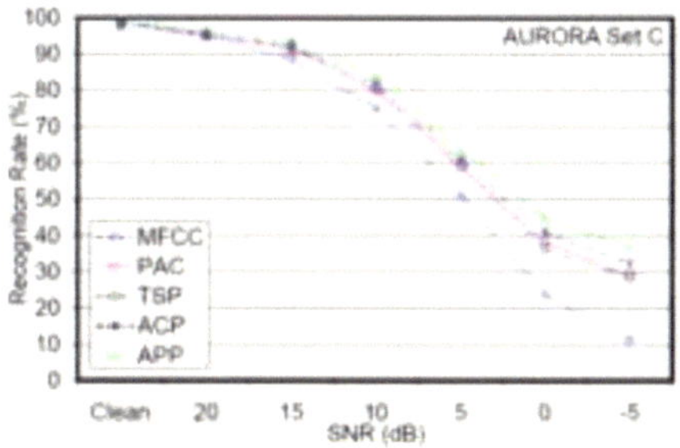

(c)

Figure 15. Average recognition rates on Aurora 2 database. (a) Test set a, (b) test set b and (c) test set c. The results correspond to MFCC, PAC, TSP, ACP, and APP methods.

In Table 8, we have summarized the average recognition rates obtained for each test set of Aurora 2. As can be seen, average recognition rates for features extracted using the autocorrelation domain with phase features (APP) tops all other results obtained.

Feature type	Average Recognition Rate (%)		
	Set A	Set B	Set C
MFCC	61.13	55.57	66.68
PAC	66.02	62.25	72.60
TSP	66.31	62.86	72.89
ACP	68.03	64.86	74.46
APP	71.83	67.69	76.53

Table 8. Comparison of Average recognition rates for various feature types on three test sets of Aurora 2 task.

4. Conclusion

In this chapter, the importance of autocorrelation domain in robust feature extraction for speech recognition was discussed. To prove the effectiveness of this domain, some recently proposed methods for robust feature extraction against additive noise were discussed. These methods resulted in cepstral feature sets derived from the autocorrelation spectral domain. The DAS algorithm used the differentiated filtered autocorrelation spectrum of the noisy signal to extract cepstral parameters. We noted that similar to RAS and DPS, DAS can better preserve speech spectral information for recognition. Experimental results were used to verify the improvements obtained using DAS feature set in comparison to MFCC, RAS and DPS. Its superior performance in comparison to both RAS and DPS is an indication of the rather independent effectiveness of the two steps in reducing the effect of noise. Its combination with CMN has also been found effective. The impact of filter length and type of differentiation on recognition results were also examined.

Also, the performance of DAS and RAS have further been improved by SPFH where the effect of noise has further been suppressed using an extra step of discarding the lower lags of the autocorrelation sequence. The experiments showed the better performance of this new approach in comparison to the previous autocorrelation-based robust speech recognition front-ends.

Techniques based on the above methods and the use of spectral peaks were also discussed in this chapter. The proposed front-end diagrams in autocorrelation domain, ACP and ACPAF, were evaluated together with several different robust feature extraction methods. The usefulness of these techniques was shown and the results indicated that the spectral peaks inherently convey robust information for speech recognition, especially in autocorrelation domain. Better parameter optimization for these two methods can be a basis for the future work as it is believed to have important influence on the system performance.

As discussed, the features extracted in magnitude domain are more sensitive to the background noise in comparison to the phase domain. Appending the frequencies of spectral peaks and their derivatives to feature parameters extracted in phase domain, similar to what was done in magnitude domain, led to even better results in comparison to the parameters extracted using the magnitude spectrum. Once again, the autocorrelation domain was used here for spectral peak extraction.

5. References

Acero, A.; Deng, L.; Kristjansson, T. & Zhang, J. (2000). HMM adaptation using vector Taylor series for noisy speech recognition. *Proc. ICSLP*, 3, 869-872.

Beh, J. & Ko, H. (2003). A novel spectral subtraction scheme for robust speech recognition: spectral subtraction using spectral harmonics of speech. *Proc. ICASSP*, I (648-651).

Bijankhan, M. et al. (1994). FARSDAT-The Speech Database of Farsi Spoken Language. *Proc. 5th Australian International Conference on Speech Science and Technology (SST'94).*

Boll, S.F. (1979). Suppression of acoustic noise in speech using spectral subtraction. *IEEE Trans. on Acoustic, Speech and Signal Processing*. 27 (2), 113-120.

Bozkurt, B. & Couvreur, L. (2005). On the use of phase information for speech recognition. *Proc. EUSIPCO*, Antalya, Turkey.

Bozkurt, B.; Doval, B.; D'Alessandro, C. & Dutoit, T. (2004). Improved differential phase spectrum processing for formant tracking. *Proc. ICSLP*, Jeju, Korea.

Chen, J.; Paliwal, K.K. & Nakamura, S. (2003). Cepstrum derived from differentiated power spectrum for robust speech recognition. *Speech Communication*. 41 (2-3), 469-484.

Cui, X.; Bernard, A. & Alwan, A. (2003). A noise robust ASR back-end technique based on weighted Viterbi recognition. *Proc. Eurospeech*, 2169-2172.

Farahani, G. & Ahadi, S.M. (2005). Robust features for noisy speech recognition based on filtering and spectral peaks in autocorrelation domain. *Proc. EUSIPCO*, Antalya, Turkey.

Farahani, G.; Ahadi, S. M. & Homayounpoor, M. M. (2006a). Use of spectral peaks in autocorrelation and group delay domains for robust speech recognition. *Proc. ICASSP*, Toulouse, France.

Farahani, G.; Ahadi, S. M. & Homayounpoor, M. M. (2006b). Robust feature extraction using spectral peaks of the filtered higher lag autocorrelation sequence of the speech signal. *Proc. ISSPIT*, Vancouver, Canada.

Farahani, G.; Ahadi, S. M. & Homayounpour, M. M. (2006c). Robust Feature Extraction based on Spectral Peaks of Group Delay and Autocorrelation Function and Phase Domain Analysis. *Proc. ICSLP*, Pittsburgh PA, USA.

Farahani, G.; Ahadi S. M. & Homayounpour, M. M. (2007). Features based on filtering and spectral peaks in autocorrelation domain for robust speech recognition. *Computer. Speech and Language*, 21, 187-205.

FARSDAT. FARSDAT Persian speech database. Available from http://www.elda.org/catalogue/en/speech/ S0112.html.

Furui, S. (1986). Speaker-independent isolated word recognition using dynamic features of speech spectrum. *IEEE Trans. on Acoustics, Speech and Signal Processing*. 34 (1), 52-59.

Gales, M.J.F. & Young, S.J. (1995). Robust speech recognition in additive and convolutional noise using parallel model combination. *Computer Speech and Language*. 9, 289-307.

Gales, M.J.F. & Young, S.J. (1996). Robust Continuous Speech Recognition Using Parallel Model Combination. *IEEE Trans. Speech Audio Processing*. 4 (5), 352-359.

Hermansky, H. & Morgan, N. (1994). RASTA processing of speech. *IEEE Trans. Speech Audio Processing*. 2 (4), 578-589.

Hernando, J. & Nadeu, C. (1997). Linear prediction of the one-sided autocorrelation sequence for noisy speech recognition. *IEEE Trans. Speech Audio Processing*. 5 (1), 80-84.

Hirsch, H.G. & Pearce, D. (2000). The Aurora experimental framework for the performance evaluation of speech recognition systems under noisy conditions. *Proc. ISCA ITRW ASR*.

HTK. (2002). The hidden Markov model toolkit. Available from http://htk.eng.cam.ac.uk.

Ikbal, S.; Misra, H. & Bourlard, H. (2003). Phase autocorrelation (PAC) derived robust speech features. *Proc. ICASSP*, 133-136, Hong Kong.

Junqua, J-C. & Haton, J-P. (1996). *Robustness in Automatic Speech Recognition: Fundamentals and Applications*, Kluwer Academic Press, Norwell.

Kermorvant, C. (1999). A comparison of noise reduction techniques for robust speech *recognition*. IDIAP-RR99-10.

Kim, D.Y.; Un, C.K. & Kim, N.S. (1998). Speech recognition in noisy environments using first-order vector Taylor series. *Speech Communication*. 24 (1), 39-49.

Lee, C.-H.; Soong, F.K. & Paliwal, K.K. (1996). *Automatic speech and speaker recognition*. Kluwer Academic Publishers.

Leonard, R. (1984). A database for speaker-independent digit recognition. *Proc. ICASSP*, 328-331.

Mansour, D. & Juang, B.-H. (1989a). The short-time modified coherence representation and noisy speech recognition. *IEEE Trans. on Acoustics and Signal Processing*. 37 (6), 795-804.

Mansour, D. & Juang, B.H. (1989b). A Family of Distortion Measures Based Upon Projection Operation for Robust Speech Recognition. *IEEE Trans. on Speech and Audio Processing*. 37 (11), 1659-1671.

Mauuary, L. (1996). Blind equalization for robust telephone based speech recognition. *In: Proceedings of the European Signal Processing Conference*.

Mauuary, L. (1998). Blind equalization in the cepstral domain for robust telephone based speech recognition. *In Proceedings of the European Signal Processing Conference*.

McGinn, D.P. & Johnson, D.H. (1989). Estimation of all-pole model parameters from noise-corrupted sequence. *IEEE Trans. on Acoustics, Speech and Signal Processing*. 37 (3), 433-436.

Moreno, P.J. (1996). *Speech recognition in noisy environments*. PhD Thesis, Carnegie-Mellon University.

Moreno, P.J.; Raj, B. & Stern, R.M. (1996). A vector Taylor series approach for environment-independent speech recognition. *Proc. ICASSP*, 733-736.

Padmanabhan, M. (2000). Spectral peak tracking and its use in speech recognition. *Proc. ICSLP*.

Paliwal, K. K. & Alsteris, L. D. (2003). Usefulness of phase spectrum in human speech perception. *Proc. Eurospeech*, Geneva, Switzerland.

Shannon, B.J. & Paliwal, K.K. (2004). MFCC Computation from Magnitude Spectrum of higher lag autocorrelation coefficients for robust speech recognition. *Proc. ICSLP*, 129-132.

Shen, J.-L.; Hung, J.-W. & Lee, L.-S. (1998). Improved robust speech recognition considering signal correlation approximated by Taylor series. *Proc. ICSLP*.

SPIB. (1995). SPIB noise data. Available from http://spib.rice.edu/spib/select_noise.html.

Strope, B. & Alwan, A. (1997). A model of dynamic auditory perception and its application to robust word recognition. *IEEE Trans. on Speech and Audio Processing*. 5 (5), 451-464.

Strope, B. & Alwan, A. (1998). Robust word recognition using threaded spectral peaks. *Proc. ICASSP*, 625-628, Washington, USA.

Sujatha, J.; Prasanna Kumar, K.R.; Ramakrishnan, K.R. & Balakrishnan, N. (2003). Spectral maxima representation for robust automatic speech recognition. *Proc. Eurospeech*, 3077-3080.

Yapanel, U.H. & Dharanipragada, S. (2003). Perceptual MVDR-based cepstral coefficients (PMCCs) for noise robust speech recognition. *Proc. ICASSP*, 644-647.

Yapanel, U.H. & Hansen, J.H.L. (2003). A New Perspective on feature extraction for robust in-vehicle speech recognition. *Proc. Eurospeech*, 1281-1284.

Yuo, K.-H. & Wang, H.-C. (1998). Robust features derived from temporal trajectory filtering for speech recognition under the corruption of additive and convolutional noises. *Proc. ICASSP*, 577-580.

Yuo, K.-H. & Wang, H.-C. (1999). Robust features for noisy speech recognition based on temporal trajectory filtering of short-time autocorrelation sequences. *Speech Communication*. 28, 13-24.

Zhu, Q.; Iseli, M.; Cui, X. & Alwan, A. (2001). Noise robust feature extraction for ASR using the AURORA2 database. *Proc. Eurospeech*.

15

Bimodal Emotion Recognition using Speech and Physiological Changes

Jonghwa Kim
Institute of Computer Science, University of Augsburg
Germany

1. Introduction

With exponentially evolving technology it is no exaggeration to say that any interface for human-robot interaction (HRI) that disregards human affective states and fails to pertinently react to the states can never inspire a user's confidence, but they perceive it as cold, untrustworthy, and socially inept. Indeed, there is evidence that HRI is more likely to be accepted by the user if it is sensitive towards the user's affective states, as expression and understanding of emotions facilitate to complete the mutual sympathy in human communication. To approach the affective human-robot interface, one of the most important prerequisites is a reliable emotion recognition system which guarantees acceptable recognition accuracy, robustness against any artifacts, and adaptability to practical applications.

Emotion recognition is an extremely challenging task in several respects. One of the main difficulties is that it is very hard to uniquely correlate signal patterns with a certain emotional state because even it is difficult to define what emotion means in a precise way. Moreover, it is the fact that emotion-relevant signal patterns may widely differ from person to person and from situation to situation. Gathering "ground-truth" dataset is also problematical to build a generalized emotion recognition system. Therefore, a number of assumptions are generally required for engineering approach to emotion recognition.

Most research on emotion recognition so far has focused on the analysis of a single modality, such as speech and facial expression (see (Cowie et al., 2001) for a comprehensive overview). Recently some works on emotion recognition by combining multiple modalities are reported, mostly by fusing features extracted from audiovisual modalities such as facial expression and speech. We humans use several modalities jointly to interpret emotional states in human communication, since emotion affects almost all modes, audiovisual (facial expression, voice, gesture, posture, etc.), physiological (respiration, skin temperature etc.), and contextual (goal, preference, environment, social situation, etc.) states. Hence, one can expect higher recognition rates through the integration of multiple modalities for emotion recognition. On the other hand, however, more complex classification and fusion problems arise.

In this chapter, we concentrate on the integration of speech signals and physiological measures (biosignals) for emotion recognition based on a short-term observation. Several advantages can be expected when combining biosensor feedback with affective speech. First of all, biosensors allow us to continuously gather information on the users' affective state while the analysis of emotions from speech should only be triggered when the microphone receives speech signals from the user. Secondly, it is much harder for the user to deliberately manipulate biofeedback than external channels of expression which allows us to largely circumvent the artifact of social masking. Finally, an integrated analysis of biosignals and speech may help to resolve ambiguities and compensate for errors.

When combining multiple modalities, the following questions arise: (1) How to handle conflicting cases between the single modalities? For instance, a user may consciously or unconsciously conceal his/her real emotions by external channels of expression, but still reveal them by internal channels of expression. (2) At which level of abstraction should the single modalities be fused in order to increase the accuracy of the recognition results? (3) How should the window sizes of different modalities be synchronized when same emotional cues in the modalities occur with a time discrepancy?

In the next section, we discuss selected previous work. Section 3 reports on the dataset we used and describes the features we extracted from speech signal 5-channel biosignal. Several fusion methods are presented including feature-level fusion, decision-level fusion, and a hybrid fusion scheme. In Section 4, we analyze the classification results with respect to the effect of bimodal integration. We conclude this work with a short outlook on future work.

2. Related Work

2.1 Modeling of discrete emotions

As people display the emotional expressions of others to their various degrees individually, it is not an easy task to judge or to model human emotions. The researchers often use two different methods to model emotions. One approach is to label the emotions in discrete categories, i.e. human judges have to choose from a prescribed list of word labels, e.g. joy, sadness, surprise, anger, love, fear, etc. One problem with this method is that the stimuli may contain blended emotions that can not adequately be expressed in words since the choice of words may be too restrictive and culturally dependent. Another way is to have multiple dimension or scales to categorize emotions. Instead of choosing discrete labels or words, observers can indicate their impression of each stimulus on several continuous scales, for example, pleasant-unpleasant, attention-rejection, simple-complicated, etc. Two common scales are valence and arousal. Valence represents the pleasantness of stimuli, with positive (or pleasant) on the end, and negative (or unpleasant) on the other. For example, happiness has a positive valence, while disgust has a negative valence. Another dimension is arousal (activation level). For example, sadness has low arousal, whereas surprise has high arousal level. The different emotional labels could be plotted at various positions on a two-dimensional plane spanned by these two axes to construct a 2D emotion model (Lang, 1995) (see Fig. 1.(a)).

Recently, the low consistency of physiological configurations supported the hypothesis that ANS activation during emotions indicates the demands of a specific action tendency and action disposition, instead of reflecting emotions per se (Tooby & Cosmides, 1990; Lazarus, 1991; Davidson, 1993). (Scholsberg, 1954) suggested a three-dimensional model in which he had attention-rejection in addition to the 2D model. Researchers have summarized these associated action tendencies as "stance" in three-dimensional emotion model, i.e., arousal, valence, and stance (Fig. 1.(b)).

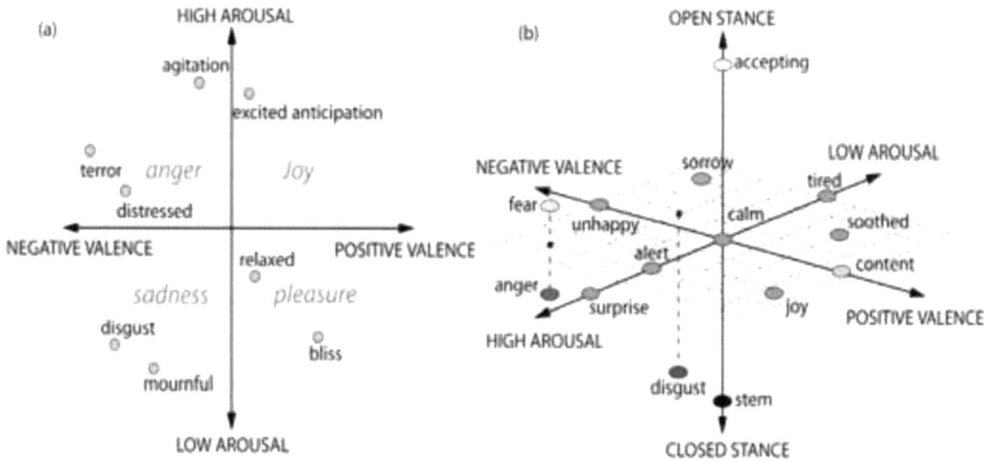

Figure 1. Emotion models: (a) Two-dimensional model by valence and arousal, (b) Three-dimensional model by valence, arousal, and stance

For example, fear is associated with the action pattern of "flight", anger calls to mind the urge to "fight", and so on. However, it is not immediately obvious what elemental problem happiness solves and what action pattern or motor program is associated with this emotion. Thus such positive emotions seem to be characterized by a lack of autonomic activation, and this might be one reason why research on positive emotions has been behind negative emotions so far. Interestingly, (Fredricson & Levenson, 1998) reported "undoing" effect of positive emotions that certain positive emotions speed recovery from the cardiovascular sequelae of negative emotions1. It is a useful finding to support symmetry process of emotion system, that the negative emotions act to help the organism escape from homeostasis and the positive emotions such as contentment and amusement catalyze a more rapid return to homeostatic levels.

2.2 Automatic emotion recognition using speech and biosignals

There is a vast body of literature on the automatic recognition of emotions. With labelled data collected from different modalities, most studies rely on supervised pattern classification approaches to automatic emotion recognition.

Following the long tradition of speech analysis in signal processing, many efforts were taken to recognize affective states from vocal information. As emotion-specific contents in speech, supra-segmental prosodic features including intensity, pitch, and duration of utterance have been widely used in recognition systems. To exploit the dynamic variation along an utterance, Mel-frequency cepstral coefficients (MFCC) are extensively employed. For example, (New et al., 2001) achieved an average accuracy of 66% for six emotions acted by two speakers using 12 MFCC features as input to a discrete hidden Markov model (HMM). A rule-based method for emotion recognition was proposed by (Chen, 2000). The data used in this work contained two foreign languages (Spanish and Sinhala) for the judges who did not comprehend either language and were therefore able to make their judgment based on vocal expression without being influenced by linguistic/semantic content. (Batliner et al., 2003) achieved about 40% for a 4-class problem with elicited emotions in spontaneous speech.

Relatively little attention has been paid so far to physiological signals for emotion recognition compared to other channels of expression. A significant series of work has been conducted by Picard and colleagues at MIT Lab. For example, they showed that certain affective states may be recognized by using physiological measures including heart rate, skin conductivity, temperature, muscle activity, and respiration velocity (Picard et al., 2001). Eight emotions deliberately elicited from a subject in multiple weeks were classified with an overall accuracy of 81%. (Nasoz et al., 2003) used movie clips to elicit target emotions from 29 subjects and achieved the best recognition accuracy (83%) by applying the Marquardt Backpropagation algorithm. More recently, (Wagner et al., 2005) presented an approach to the recognition of emotions elicited by music using 4-channel biosignals which were recorded while the subject was listening to music songs, and reached an overall recognition accuracy of 92% for a 4-class problem.

In order to improve the recognition accuracy obtained from unimodal recognition systems, many studies attempted to exploit the advantage of using multimodal information, especially by fusing audio-visual information. For example, (De Silva & Ng, 2000) proposed a rule-based singular classification of audio-visual data recorded from two subjects into six emotion categories. Moreover, they observed that some emotions are easier to identify with audio, such as sadness and fear, and others with video, such as anger and happiness. Using decision-level fusion in bimodal recognition system, a recognition rate of 72% has been reported. A set of singular classification methods was proposed by (Chen & Huang, 2000), in which audio-visual data collected from five subjects was classified into the Ekman's six basic emotions (happiness, sadness, disgust, fear, anger, and surprise). They could improve the performance of decision-level fusion by considering the dominant modality, determined by empirical studies, in case significant discrepancy between the outputs of each unimodal classifier has been observed. Recently, a large-scale audio-visual dataset was collected by (Zeng et al., 2004), which contains five HCI-related affective responses (confusion, interest, boredom, and frustration) in addition to seven affects (the six basic emotions + neutral). To classify the 11 emotions subject-dependently, they used the SNoW (Sparse Network of Winnow) classifier with Naive Bayes as the update rule and achieved a recognition accuracy of almost 90% through bimodal fusion while the unimodal classifiers yielded only 45-56%. Most previous studies have shown that the performance of emotion recognition systems can be improved by the use of audio-visual information. However, it should be noted that the achieved recognition rates depend rather on the type of the underlying dataset, whether the emotions were from acted, elicited or real-life situation, than the used algorithms and classification methods. Moreover, apart from our previous work (Kim et al., 2005), work on the integration of biosignals and speech is rare. In this paper, we will investigate in how far the robustness of an emotion recognition system can be increased by integrating both vocal and physiological cues. We evaluate two fusion methods that combine bimodal information at different levels of abstraction as well as a hybrid integration scheme. Particularly we focus on shorter observations compared to or earlier work.

3. Methodology

3.1 Dataset

We use the same Quiz dataset as in our prior work (Kim et al., 2005). The dataset contains speech (using microphone by 48 KHz/16Bit), physiological (using 6-channel biosensors), and visual information (using video camera) from three male German-speaking subjects in their twenties.

To acquire a corpus of spontaneous vocal and physiological emotions, we used a slightly modified version of the quiz "Who wants to be a millionaire?". Questions along with options for answers were presented on a graphical display whose design was inspired by the corresponding quiz shows on German TV. In order to make sure that we got a sufficient amount of speech data, the subjects were not offered any letters as abbreviations for the single options (as very common in quiz shows on TV), but were forced to produce longer utterances. Furthermore, the users current score was indicated as well as the amount of money s/he may win or loose depending on whether his/er answer is correct or not. Each of the session took about 45 minutes to complete. The subjects were equipped with a directed microphone to interact with a virtual quiz master via spoken natural language utterances. The virtual quiz master was represented by a disembodied voice using the AT&T Natural Voices speech synthesizer. While the users interacted with the system, their bio and speech signals as well as the interaction with the quiz master were recorded.

The quiz experiment was designed in a Wizard-Of-Oz fashion where the quiz agent who presents the quiz is controlled by a human quiz master who guides the actual course of the quiz, following a working script to evoke situations that lead to a certain emotional response. The wizard was allowed to freely type utterances, but also had access to a set of macros that contain pre-defined questions or comments which made it easier for the human wizard to follow the script and to get reproducible situations (see Fig. 2).

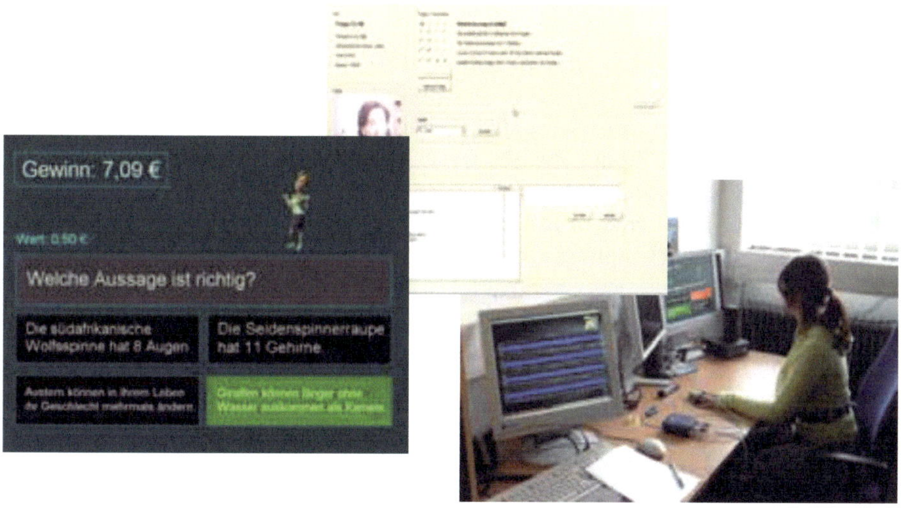

Figure 2. Interface for the user (left) and for the wizard (middle)

The wizards working script can be roughly divided into four situations which serve to induce certain emotional states in the user. We make use of a dimensional emotion model which characterizes emotions in terms of the two continuous dimensions of arousal and valence (see (Lang, 1995)). Arousal refers to the intensity of an emotional response. Valence determines whether an emotion is positive or negative and to what degree. Apart from the ease of describing emotional states that cannot be distributed into clear-cut fixed categories, the two dimensions valence and arousal are well suited for emotion recognition. The four phases of the experiment correspond to four quadrants the 2-D emotion model in Fig. 1.(a): (1) low arousal, positive valence, (2) high arousal, positive valence, (3) low arousal, negative valence and (4) high arousal, negative valence.
First, the users are offered a set of very easy questions every user is supposed to know to achieve equal conditions for all of them. This phase is characterized by a slight increase of the score and gentle appraisal of the agent and serves to induce an emotional state of positive valence and low arousal in the user. In phase 2, the user is confronted with extremely difficult questions nobody is supposed to know. Whatever option the user chooses, the agent pretends the users answer is correct so that the user gets the feeling that s/he hits the right option just by chance. In order to evoke high arousal and positive valence, this phase leads to a high gain of money. During the third phase, we try to stress the user by a mix of solvable and difficult questions that lead, however, not to a drastic loss of money. Furthermore, the agent provides boring information related to the topics addressed in the questions. Thus, the phase should lead to negative valence and low arousal. Finally, the user gets frustrated by unsolvable questions. Whatever option the user chooses, the agent always pretends the answer is wrong resulting in a high loss of money. Furthermore, we include simple questions for which we offer similar-sounding options. The user is supposed to choose the right option, but we make him/er believe that the speech recognizer is not working properly and deliberately select the wrong option. This phase is intended to evoke high arousal and negative valence.

3.2 Used biosensors

The physiological signals are measured by using the Procomp[1] Infiniti™ with the 6-channel biosensors: electromyogram (EMG), skin conductivity (SC), electrocardiogram (ECG), blood volume pulse (BVP), temperature (Temp), and respiration (RSP). The sampling rates are 32 Hz for EMG, SC, RSP, and Temp, 256 Hz for ECG and BVP. The positions and typical waveforms of the biosensors we used are illustrated in Fig. 3.
Electrocardiogram (ECG): we used a pre-amplified electrocardiograph sensor (bandwidth: 0.05Hz-1 KHz) connected with pre-gelled single Ag/AgCl electrodes. We cannot measure individual action potentials direct in the heart. We can however measure the average action potential on the skin. The mean movement of the action potential is along the ``electrical axis'' of the heart. The action potential starts high in the right atrium, moves to the centre of the heart, then down towards the apex of the heart. Therefore the main electrical signal from heart is flowing away from the upper right of the body, and towards the lower left of the body.

[1] This is an 8 channel multi-modal Biofeedback system with 14 bit resolution and a fiber optic cable connection to the computer. www.MindMedia.nl

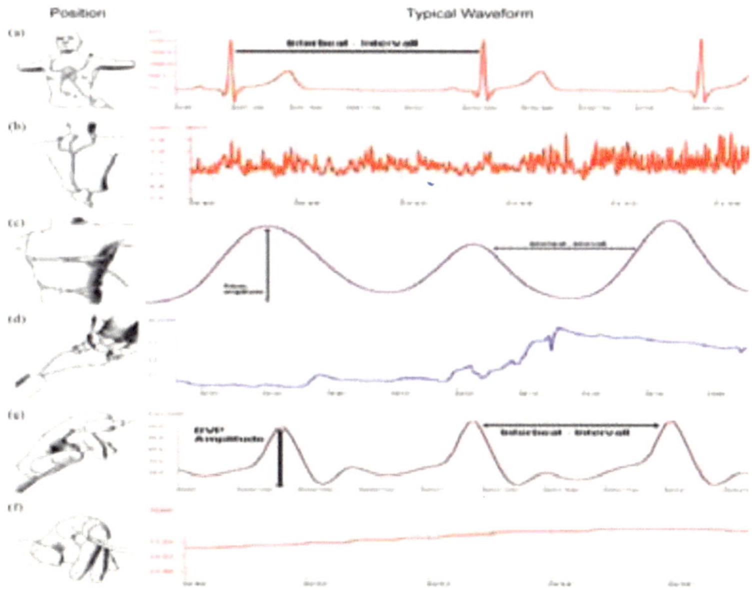

Figure 3. Position and typical waveforms of the biosensors: (a) ECG, (b) EMG, (c) RSP, (d) SC, (e) BVP, (f) Temp.

Electromyogram (EMG): we used Myoscan-Pro™ sensor with active range 20-500Hz and pre-gelled single Ag/AgCl electrodes. It can record EMG signals of up to 1600 micro volt. We positioned the sensor at the nape of the neck of the subjects. Electromyography measures muscle activity by detecting surface voltages that occur when a muscle is contracted. Therefore the best readings are obtained when the sensor is placed on the muscle belly and its positive and negative electrodes are parallel to the muscle fibers. Since the number of muscle fibers that are recruited during any given contraction depends on the force required to perform the movement, the intensity (amplitude) of the resulting electrical signal is proportional to the strength of contraction. Particularly, the EMG signal required additional pre-processing, such as deep smoothing because of the nature of the signal that all the muscle fibers within the recording area of the sensor contract at different rates.

Respiration (RSP): a stretch sensor using latex rubber band fixed with velcro respiration belt is used to capture breathing activity of the subjects. It can be worn either thoracically or abdominally, over clothing. The amount of stretch in the elastic is measured as a voltage change and recorded. Rate of respiration and depth of breath are the most common measures of respiration. Although respiration rate generally decreases with relaxation, startle events and tense situations may result in momentary respiration cessation. Negative emotions generally cause irregularity in the respiration pattern.

Skin Conductivity (SC): skin conductivity is one of the mostly used measurements to capture the affective state of users, especially for arousal difference in emotion. SC sensor measures skin's ability to conduct electricity. A small voltage is applied to the skin and the skin's current conduction or resistance is measured. Therefore, skin conductance is considered to be a function of the activity of the eccrine sweat glands (located in palms of the hands and soles of the feet) and the skin's pore size. We used Ag/AgCl electrodes fixed with two finger band and positioned at the index and ring finger of the non-dominant hand.

Temperature (Temp): Temp is a highly sensitive temperature sensor and can monitor skin temperature changes smaller than 0.0001 (1/10000th) degree between 10°C – 45°C (50°F - 115°F). The sensor can be applied on the finger, hands, or other parts of the body.

Blood Volume Pulse (BVP): BVP sensor measures the relative blood flow in the hands (fingers) with near infrared light, using the method known as photoplethysmography. The sensor housed in a small finger worn package can be used to monitor HR, HRV (heart rate variability), bloodflow and pulse.

3.3 Synchronized segmentation of the bimodal signals

In the previous work (Kim et al., 2005), we segmented and labelled the data based on the four experimental phases taking into account that the agreement between coders annotating material of everyday emotions is usually not very high (Douglas-Cowie et al., 2005). All speech and physiological signals that may be interpreted as a response to the same question have been segmented into one chunk and labelled with the emotion corresponding to the experimental phase in which they occurred

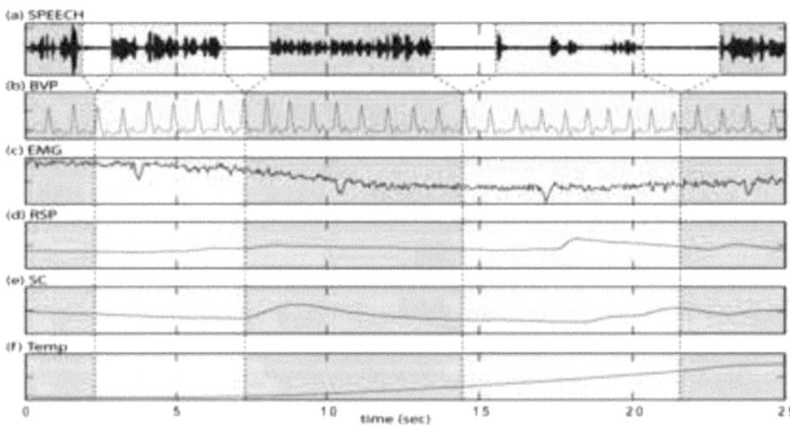

Figure 4. Segmentation of bimodal signals based on verbal phrases: (a) speech, (b) BVP, (c) EMG, (d) RSP, (e) SC, (f) Temp.

For the analysis described in this paper, the segmentation and labelling was refined by two expert labellers considering the situative context as well as the audio-visual expression of the subjects. In this way, we tried to handle cases where we did not succeed in eliciting the intended emotion. To segment speech and physiological data, we started from verbal phrases. The borders of the segments for both modalities were chosen to lie in the middle of two verbal phrases so that they cover the same time span. For the analysis of speech, we only consider the part of the segment when the verbal phrase occurs while for the analysis of physiological data the complete segment is taken. As a consequence, the observations for speech are usually shorter than the observations for the physiological data, but the length of the corresponding segments is the same which facilitates the later fusion process.

In total, we got 343 samples for classification (343 x 6 channels = 2058 segments in total) from the dataset. Based on the four phases of the experiments, our labellers relied on dimensional rating (i.e. labelling within the 4 quadrants of the 2D emotion model). Disagreements between the ratings of the two labellers were discussed and resolved after the annotation process.

Fig. 4 shows sample segmentation for data from the used channels. The length of the observations varies from 2 to 6 seconds for the speech and from 3 to 15 seconds for the biosignals. That is the observations are rather short-term compared to previous studies that start from a segment length between 50 and 300 seconds (Kim et al., 2004).

3.4 Feature extraction

An essential step in pattern classification is to extract class-relevant features (preferably in a compressed form) from the raw signal. Moreover the classification of short-term observations requires more reasonable treatments in signal processing stages, e.g. extracting spectral features in biosignals (containing very low frequencies) within limited bandwidth due to the very short window size.

From the speech signal: for all segments, the conventional statistics in time domain are calculated, such as mean, absolute extremum, root mean square, standard deviation, energy/power, intensity in dB etc. In frequency domain, three spectrum contents are obtained using the STFT; pitches using a window length of 40 ms, energy spectrum, and formant object using a window length of 25 ms. In addition, 10 MFCCs from each segment are calculated using a window length of 15 ms. From pitch and energy spectrum, also the series of the minima and maxima, and of the distances, magnitudes and steepness between adjacent extrema were obtained. For the MFCCs, we first exponentiated the cepstral coefficients to obtain non-negative values and calculated the spectral entropy as in the case of the biosignal in order to capture the distribution of cepstral energy. From each feature content above, we tried to extract single features (i.e., mean, standard deviation, mean of first and second derivative) representing characteristics (i.e., variance and slop) of each time series vector of spectrum, instead of taking all feature vectors. As a result, we obtained a total of 61 features from the speech segments.

From physiological data: differing from (Kim et al., 2005), we employ the BVP signal instead of the ECG signal and use the Temp signal as an additional channel from the dataset.[2] To remove noisy signals, all segments of the 5- channel biosignals (BVP, EMG, SC, RSP, and Temp) are lowpass-filtered using pertinent cut-off frequencies that are empirically determined for each biosensor channel. Different types of artifacts were observed such as transient noise due to movement of the subjects during the recording, mostly at the begin and end of the each recording. Particularly to the EMG signal, we needed to pay closer attention because the signal contains artifacts generated by respiration and heart beat (Fig. 5). We found that it was due to the position of EMG sensor at the nape of the neck.

---

[2] Generally the ECG is measured by using electrodes which do need a firm skin contact, whereas the BVP is measured by using a photoplethysmograph. Hence, using the BVP signal has some advantages such as robustness against motion artifacts during recording process and stable baseline in the signal flow.

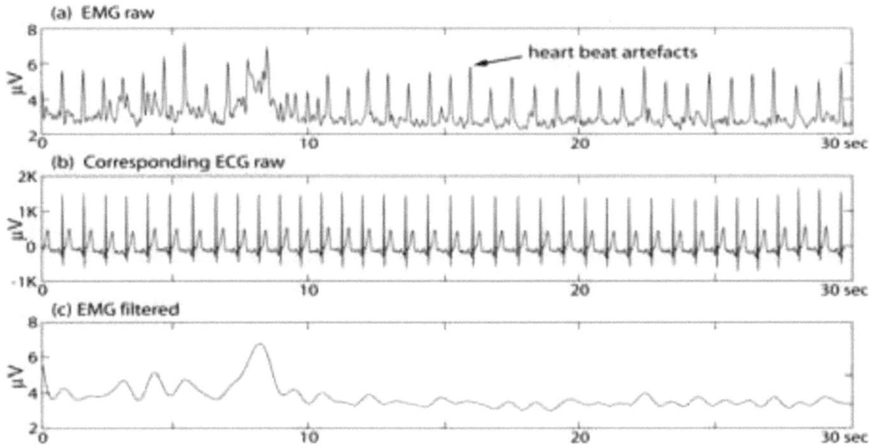

Figure 5. Example of EMG signal with heart beat artifacts and denoised signal

From the raw BVP signal, we first calculated the 8 subband spectral powers using the conventional 512 points short-time Fourier transform (STFT). To capture the irregularity and the local spectral distribution, the spectral entropy is calculated from each subband by converting the spectrum into a PMF-like (Probability Mass Function) form. Heart rate variability (HRV) is the most frequently used characteristic of the heart activity in biomedical engineering to assess cardiac health. Using the QRS detection algorithm of (Pan & Tompkins, 1985), the HRV like time series (we refer to as PRV)[3] is obtained and typical statistics (mean value, standard deviation, slope, etc.) are calculated from the time series. By calculating the standard deviations in different distances of pulse-pulse interbeats, we also added the Poincaré geometry in the feature set to capture the nature of pulse interval fluctuations. Figure 6 shows an example plot of the geometry.

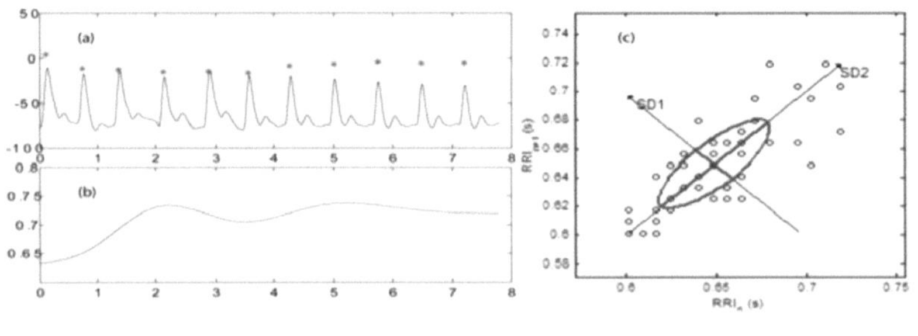

Figure 6. Example of BVP Analysis: (a) detected pulse interbeats, (b) interpolated PRV like series, (c) Poincaré plot of the PRV

[3] Strictly speaking, it is the pulse rate variability (PRV) when relying on the BVP, not on the ECG signal, because in BVP signal one can not observe the clear QRS waveform, which enables a fine analysis of HRV.

Lastly from the spectrum of the PRV time series, power spectrum densities (PSD) from three subbands are calculated from the ranges of VLF (0-0.04Hz), LF (0.05-0.15 Hz), and HF (0.16-0.4 Hz), respectively and the ratio of LF/HF. Since the RSP signal is quasi periodic we calculated similar types of features like the BVP features including the typical statistics, except for the geometric features and the PSDs. After appropriate detrending the signals using mean value and lowpass filter, we calculated the BRV (time series of the breathing rates) by detecting the peaks using the maxima ranks within zero-crossing.

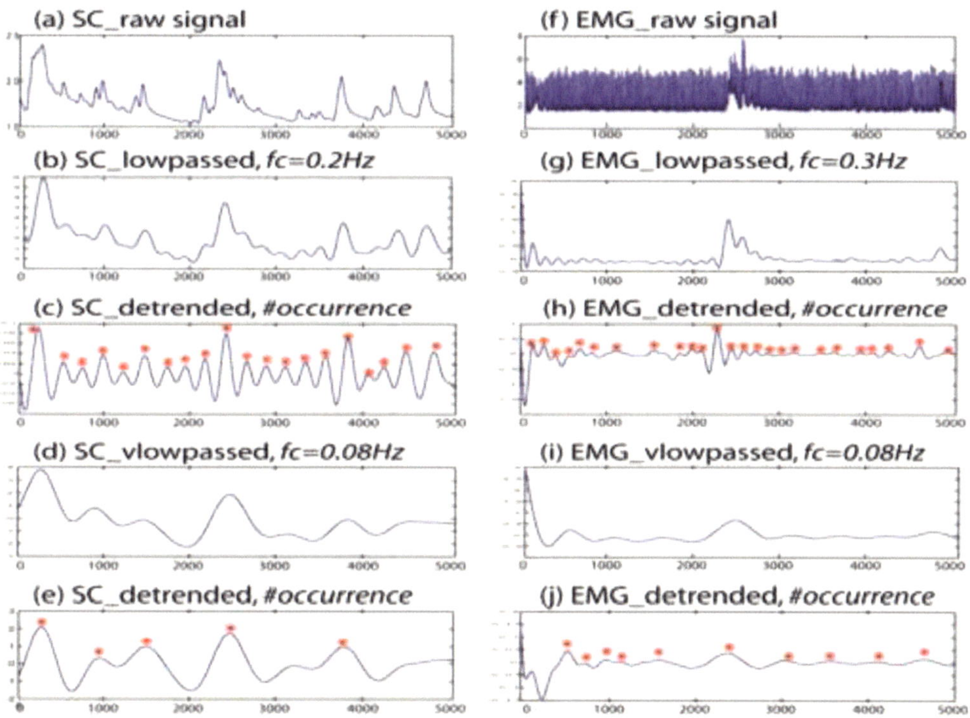

Figure 7. Analysis examples of SC and EMG signals

From the SC and EMG signal respectively we calculated 10 features including the mean value, standard deviation, and mean values of first and second derivations. The number of transient changes (occurrences) within 4 seconds in SC and EMG signals are calculated from two low-passed signals, very low-passed (SC: 0.08 Hz, EMG: 0.3 Hz) and low-passed signals (SC: 0.2 Hz, EMG: 0.8 Hz) respectively (see Fig. 7). From the Temp signals, three statistical features are calculated: mean value, standard deviation, and ratio of max/min. Finally, we obtained a total of 77 features from the 5-channel biosignals.

3.5 Feature selection and classification

As the next step, we tried to determine which features are most relevant to differentiate each affective state. Reducing the dimension of the feature space has two advantages. First of all, the computational costs are lowered and secondly the removal of noisy information may lead to a better separation of the classes. In all cases, we achieved indeed considerably higher accuracy rates (an increase of about 30 %) when applying sequential backward selection (SBS) to reduce the set of features. Of course, the success of the selection process heavily depends on the employed classifier. Several features were selected by SBS for all three subjects, e.g., the subband spectral entropy from BVP, the number of occurrences in SC and EMG, and the mean values of the MFCCs in the speech features. However, due to the small number of subjects, these findings should not be generalized.

After testing several classification schemes, such as kNN (k-nearest neighbour), MLP (multilayer perception), and LDA (Linear discriminant analysis), we have chosen the LDA classifier which gave the highest accuracy in our case and which we already used for emotion recognition from physiological data in (Wagner et al., 2005). However it should be noted that there is no single best classification algorithm and the choice of the best classification method strongly depends on characteristics of dataset to be classified. In work (King et al., 1995), for example, this conclusion has been supported by wide comparative studies of about 20 different machine learning algorithms, including symbolic learning, neural networks, and statistical approaches, evaluated on 12 different real-world datasets.

To combine the two modalities, we need to decide at which level the single modalities should be fused. A straightforward approach is to simply merge the features calculated from each modality (feature-level). An alternative would be to fuse the recognition results at the decision-level based on the outputs of separate unimodal classifiers (decision-level). Finally, we may combine both methods by applying a hybrid integration scheme (see Figure 8).

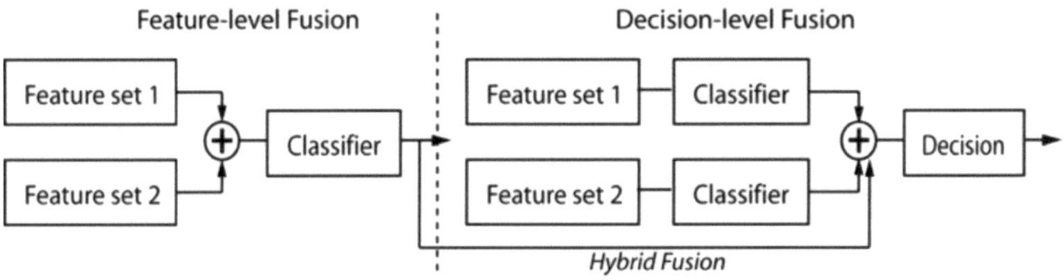

Figure 8. Considered fusion schemes for integrating bimodal information

We performed both feature-level fusion and decision-level fusion using LDA in combination with SBS. Feature-level fusion is performed by merging the calculated features from each modality into one cumulative structure, selecting the relevant features using SBS, and feeding them to the LDA classifier. Decision-level fusion caters for integrating asynchronous, but temporally correlated modalities. Each modality is first classified independently by the LDA classifier, and the final decision is obtained by fusing the output from the modality-specific classification processes. Three criteria, maximum, average, and product (Busso et al., 2004) were applied to evaluate the posterior probabilities of the unimodal classifiers at the decision stage. As a further variation of decision-level fusion, we employed a new hybrid scheme of the two fusion methods in which the output of feature-level fusion is also fed as an auxiliary input to the decision-level fusion stage.

In Table 1, the best results are summarized that we achieved by the classification schemes described above. We classified the bimodal data subject-dependently (Subject A, B, and C)

and subject-independently (All) since this gave us a deeper insight on what terms the multimodal systems could improve the results of unimodal emotion recognition.

System	high/pos	high/neg	low/neg	low/pos	*Average*
		Subject A			
Biosignal	0.95	0.92	0.86	0.85	0.90
Speech signal	0.64	0.75	0.67	0.78	0.71
Feature Fusion	0.91	0.92	1.00	0.85	**0.92**
Decision Fusion	0.64	0.54	0.76	0.67	0.65
Hybrid Fusion	0.86	0.54	0.57	0.59	0.64
		Subject B			
Biosignal	0.50	0.79	0.71	0.45	0.61
Speech Single	0.76	0.56	0.74	0.72	0.70
Feature Fusion	0.71	0.56	0.94	0.79	**0.75**
Decision Fusion	0.59	0.68	0.82	0.69	0.70
Hybrid Fusion	0.65	0.64	0.82	0.83	0.73
		Subject C			
Bio Single	0.52	0.79	0.70	0.52	0.63
Speech Single	0.55	0.77	0.66	0.71	0.67
Feature Fusion	0.50	0.67	0.84	0.74	**0.69**
Decision Fusion	0.32	0.77	0.74	0.64	0.62
Hybrid Fusion	0.40	0.73	0.86	0.71	0.68
		All: Subject-independent			
Bio Single	0.43	0.53	0.54	0.52	0.51
Speech Single	0.40	0.53	0.70	0.53	0.54
Feature Fusion	0.46	0.57	0.63	0.56	**0.55**
Decision Fusion	0.34	0.50	0.70	0.54	0.52
Hybrid Fusion	0.41	0.51	0.70	0.55	0.54

Table 1. Recognition results in rates (1.0=100% accuracy) achieved by using SBS, LDA, and leave-one-out cross validation.

4. Analysis of results

As shown in Table 1, the performance of the unimodal systems varies not only from subject to subject, but also for the single modalities. During our experiment, we could observe individual differences in the physiological and vocal expressions of the three test subjects and it is well revealed in the recognition results. The emotions of subject A were more accurately recognized by using biosignals (90 %) than by his voice (71 %) whereas it is the case of inverse for subject B and C (70 % and 67 % for voice and 61 % and 63 % for biosignals). In particular, for subject A, the difference between the accuracies of the two modalities is sizable. However, no suggestively dominant modality could be observed in the results of subject-dependent classification in general, which may be used as a decision criterion in the decision-level fusion process to improve the recognition accuracy.

Different accuracy rates were also obtained by using the single fusion methods. Overall, we obtained the best results from feature-level fusion. Generally, feature-level fusion is more appropriate for combining modalities with analogous characteristics. For instance, we got an acceptable recognition accuracy of 92 % for subject A when using feature-level fusion which considerably went down, however, when using decision-level or hybrid fusion.

As our data show, a high accuracy obtained from one modality may be declined by a relatively low accuracy from another modality when fusing data at the decision level. This observation may indicate the limitations of the decision-level fusion scheme we used, which is based on to a pure arithmetic evaluation of the posterior probabilities at the decision stage rather than a parametric assessment process. Actually, the design of optimal strategies for decision-level fusion, such as the integration of a parametric refinement stage, is still an open research issue.

As expected, the accuracy rates for subject-independent classification were not comparable to those obtained for subject-dependent classification. Figure 9 illustrates examples of Fisher projection which is often used to preview the distribution of the features. Obviously, merging the features of all subjects does not refine the information related to target emotions, but rather leads to scattered class boundaries.

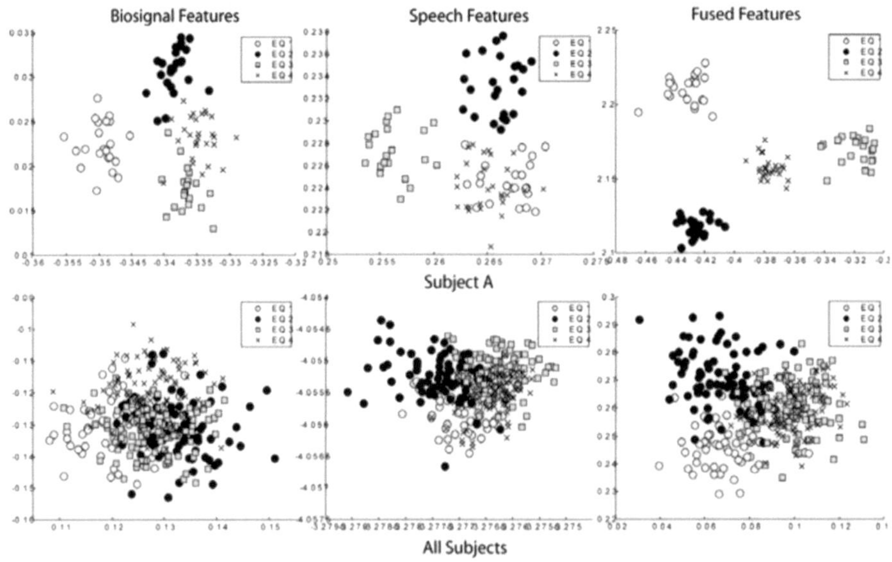

Figure 9. Fisher projection examples for Subject A and all subjects (person-independent).

5. Conclusion

In this paper, we treated all stages of emotion analysis, from data collection to classification using short-term observations, and evaluated several fusion methods as well as a hybrid decision scheme. We also compared the results from multimodal classification with the unimodal results. As in our earlier work (Kim et al. 2005) where we relied on longer observation phases and a different set of features, the best results were obtained by feature-level fusion method in combination with feature selection stage. In this case, not only user-dependent, but also user-independent emotion classification could be improved compared to the unimodal methods.

We did not achieve the same high gains that were achieved for audio-visual data which seems to indicate that speech and physiological data contain less complementary information. Furthermore, in a natural setting like ours, we cannot exclude that the subjects are inconsistent in their emotional expression. Inconsistencies are less likely to occur in scenarios where actors are asked to deliberately express emotions via speech and mimics. In this case, it might be the reason why fusion algorithms lead to a greater increase of the recognition rate. Ambiguities in emotional expressions are also reflected by work on corpus annotation. For instance, (Cowie et al., 2005) noticed that the agreement between human coders labeling multimodal corpora of everyday emotions was lower when considering both audio and video than when relying on a single modality.

Furthermore some important problems are pointed out, such as the use of posterior probabilities when fusing information with high disparity in accuracy. Most of the existing classifiers used in the literature are generalized methods based on statistics or estimating linear regression of given data. Such classifiers may not be able to capture emotion-specific features and to apply self-adapting decision rules that consider contextual information, for instance. Therefore, the design of an emotion-specific classification scheme is one of the most important issues for the future, and this issue becomes even more critical when classifying combined multimodal observations. To overcome these problems, we need to develop a multilayer fusion scheme with parametric refinement stages in each decision layer.

More important issue in future work would be how to *complementarily* combine the multiple modalities, since it is obvious that combining modalities by equally weighting them does not always guarantee improving recognition accuracy. Toward the human-like analysis and finer resolution of recognizable emotion classes, an essential step would be therefore to find innate priority among the modalities to be preferred for each emotional state. A considerable scheme might be to decompose an emotion recognition problem into several refining processes using additional modalities, for example, arousal recognition through physiological channels, valence recognition by using audiovisual channels, and then resolving subtle uncertainty between adjacent emotion classes, or predicting even the "stance" in 3D emotion model, by cumulative analysis of user's context information.

6. References

Batliner, A.; Zeissler, V.; Frank, C.; Adelhardt, J.; Shi, R. P. & Nöth, E. (2003). We are not amused-but how do you know? user states in a multi-modal dialogue system, In *EUROSPEECH'03*, Geneva, pp. 733–736.

Busso, C.; Deng, Z.; Yildirim, S.; Bulut, M.; Lee, C. H.; Kazemzaden, A.; Lee, S.; Neumann, U. & Narayanan, S. (2004). Analysis of emotion recognition using facial expression, speech and multimodal information, in *ICMI'04*, State College, Pennsylvania, USA, pp. 205–211

Chen, L. S.; & Huang, T. S. (2000). Emotional expressions in audiovisual human computer interaction," in *ICME-2000*, pp. 423–426

Chen, L. S. (2000). Joint processing of audio-visual information for the recognition of emotional expression in human-computer interaction, *Ph.D. dissertation*, University of Illinois at Urbana-Champaign, Dept. of Electrical Engineering

Cowie, R.; Douglas-Cowie, E.; Tsapatsoulis, N.; Votsis, G.; Kollias, S.; Fellenz, W. & Taylor, J. G. (2001). Emotion recognition in human-computer interaction, *IEEE Signal Processing Mag.*, vol. 18, pp. 32–80

Davidson, R. J. (1993). Parsing affective space: Perspectives from neuropsychology and psychophysiology, *Neuropsychology*, vol. 7, no. 4, pp. 464–475

De Silva, L. C. & Ng, P. C. (2000). Bimodal emotion recognition, In: *IEEE International Conf. on Automatic Face and Gesture Recognition*, pp. 332–335

Douglas-Cowie, E.; Devillers, L.; Martin, J.-C.; Cowie, R.; Savvidou, S.; Abrilian, S. & Cox, C. (2005). Multimodal Databases of Everyday Emotion: Facing up to Complexity," in *InterSpeech*, Lisbon

Fredricson, B. L. & Levenson, R. W. (1998). Positive emotions speed recovery from the cardiovascular sequelae of negative emotions, *Cognition and Emotion*, vol. 12, no. 2, pp. 191–220

Kim, J.; André, E.; Rehm, M.; Vogt, T. & Wagner, J. (2005). Integrating information from speech and physiological signals to achieve emotional sensitivity, in *INTERSPEECH-2005*, Lisbon, Portugal, pp. 809–812

Kim, K. H.; Bang, S. W. & Kim, S. R. (2004). Emotion recognition system using short-term monitoring of physiological signals. *Med. Biol. Eng. Comput*, vol. 42, no. 3, pp. 419–427

King, R. D.; Feng, C. & Shutherland, A. (1995). StatLog: Comparison of Classification Algorithms on Large Real-world Problems, *Applied Artificial Intelligence*, vol. 9(3), pp. 259-287

Lang, P. (1995). The emotion probe: Studies of motivation and attention, *American Psychologist*, vol. 50(5), pp. 372–385

Lazarus, R. S. (1991) Emotion and adaptation. Cambridge UK: Cambridge University Press

Nasoz, F.; Alvarez, K.; Lisetti, C. & Finkelstein, N. (2003). Emotion recognition from physiological signals for presence technologies, *International Journal of Cognition, Technology, and Work - Special Issue on Presence*, vol. 6(1)

Nwe, T. L.; Wei, F. S. & Silva, L. C. D. (2001). Speech based emotion classification, In *IEEE Region 10 International Conference on Electrical Electronic Technology*, vol. 1, pp. 297–301

Pan, J. & Tompkins, W. (1985). A real-time qrs detection algorithm, *IEEE Trans. Biomed. Eng.*, vol. 32, no. 3

Picard, R.; Vyzas, E. & Healy, J. (2001). Toward machine emotional intelligence: Analysis of affective physiological state, *IEEE Trans. Pattern Anal. and Machine Intell.*, vol. 23, no. 10, pp. 1175–1191

Scholsberg, H. (1954). Three dimensions of emotion, *Psychological Review*, vol. 61, pp. 81–88

Tooby, J. & Cosmides, L. (1990). The past explains the present: Emotional adaptations and the structure of ancestral environments, *Ethology and Sociobiology*, vol. 11, pp. 375–424

Wagner, J.; Kim, J. & Andr´e, E. (2005). From physiological signals to emotions: Implementing and comparing selected methods for feature extraction and classification, In: ICME'05, Amsterdam

Zeng, Z.; Tu, J.; Liu, M.; Zhang, T.; Rizzolo, N.; Zhang, Z.; Huang, T. S.; Roth, D. & Levinson, S. (2004). Bimodal HCI-related affect recognition, *in ICMI 2004*

16

Emotion Estimation in Speech Using a 3D Emotion Space Concept

Michael Grimm and Kristian Kroschel
Universität Karlsruhe (TH)
Germany

1. Introduction

Automated recognition of emotions conveyed in the speech is an important research topic that has emerged in recent years with a number of possible applications (Picard, 1997). The most important one is probably the improvement of the man-machine interface, knowing that human communication contains a large amount of emotional messages which should be recognized by machines such as robot assistants in the household, computer tutors, or automatic speech recognition (ASR) units in call-centers.

Most research on recognizing emotions in the speech focuses on a small number of emotion categories (Dellaert et al., 1996; Lee et al., 2001; Yu et al., 2004; Vidrascu & Devillers, 2005; Schuller et al., 2005). However, such categorization is a strong restriction if we think of the continuum in the expression of human emotions. In particular, if we want to resolve moderate emotions in spontaneous utterances in addition to the stereotype portrayal of exaggerated emotions, several questions must be asked:

- How can we estimate the emotion conveyed in the speech signal more detailed than in the state-of-the-art categorization?
- How many features are necessary for such estimation, and which method is suitable for selection?
- Which estimation methods are suitable, and what are the pros and the cons of each method?

In this contribution we intend to give some answers to these questions, building upon our previous work reported in (Grimm et al., 2007a; 2007b). We propose a generalized framework using a continuous-valued, three-dimensional emotion space method. This method defines emotions as points in a three-dimensional emotion space spanned by the three basic attributes ("primitives") *valence* (positive-negative axis), *activation* (calm-excited axis), and *dominance* (weak-strong axis) (see Kehrein, 2002). Figure 1 shows a schematic sketch of this emotion space. *Anger,* e.g., would be represented by negative *valence,* high excitation level on the *activation* axis, and strong *dominance*. Such real-valued notion was shown to be transferable to emotion categories, if desired (Grimm et al., 2006). At the same time, it lends itself to a gradual description of emotion which is helpful to describe intensity changes over time or speaker-dependent emotion expression behaviors, for example.

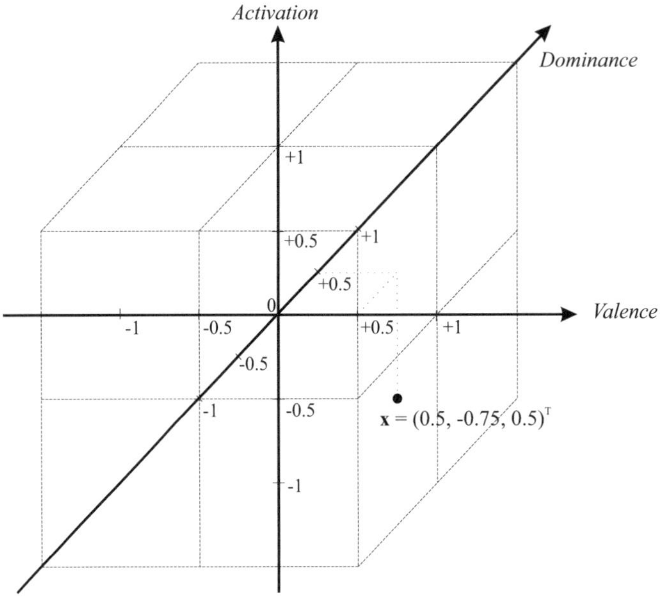

Figure 1. Three-dimensional emotion space, spanned by the primitives *valence, activation,* and *dominance,* with a sample emotion vector added for illustration of the component concept.

While emotion space concepts have been named as an alternative to emotion categories in many studies (see Cowie, et al., 2001 or Cowie & Cornelius, 2003 for a comprehensive overview), they have so far only been used for emotional speech synthesis (Schröder, 2003), and hardly for emotion recognition. In the few other studies on detecting emotions in speech using an emotion space concept, first the emotion space is subdivided into 2 or 3 subregions and then these emotion space regions are classified just as emotion categories (Fragopanagos & Taylor, 2005; Vidrascu & Devillers, 2005). Thus, we consider the direct, continuous-valued estimation of these emotion primitives in this contribution.

Based on a German speech database containing authentic emotional expressions from a TV talk-show, the automatic estimation of these three emotion primitives was studied. The reference was built by a human listener test using the text-free method of Self Assessment Manikins (see Section 2.2). The speech signal was segmented into utterances for this study yielding 893 samples of 47 speakers. For the automatic estimation of the emotion in these utterances, a feature vector was built containing the statistics of the fundamental frequency, energy and the MFCCs, such as mean value, standard deviation, minimum, maximum, range, and quartiles. Two different techniques to reduce the feature vector size were studied. As an automatic emotion estimation method we used Support Vector Regression (SVR), which provides a kernel-based, non-linear estimation of the three emotion primitives. This method showed promising results and a moderate to high correlation with the human listeners' ratings in a preliminary study. It is now compared to KNN and Fuzzy Logic both with respect to the estimation error and the learning curve properties (see Sections 5.1 and 5.2, respectively).

The rest of the paper is organized as follows. Section 2 briefly introduces the data we used, and it also describes the emotion evaluation by human listeners. Section 3 describes the pre-processing steps of feature extraction and feature selection. Section 4 presents the different classifiers used for continuous-valued emotion primitive estimation. Section 5 describes the results and discusses the different estimator outcomes. Section 6 contains the conclusion and directions for future work.

The term "emotion" is very difficult to define. It refers to a very complex inner state of a person including a wide range of cognitive and physical events (Scherer, 1990). In addition to the truly felt affective state, the expression of emotions is superimposed by the display rules of the situation. In the scope of this chapter we understand the term "emotion" only as the visible part of this inner state that is transmitted through the speech signal and thus observable by a human receiver. Also, the conclusions drawn from the automatic estimation have to be seen in the context of the situation. Analyzing additional channels, such as the mimics, gestures, or physiological signals, might improve the understanding of the situation and thus help identify the emotional state of a person more precisely.

2. Data

2.1 Data acquisition

To study the emotion recognition on authentic emotions in speech we extracted dialogue episodes from a talk-show on TV. In this talk-show, two or three persons discuss problems such as fatherhood questions, friendship issues, or difficulties in the family. Due to the spontaneous and unscripted manner of the episodes, the emotional expressions can be considered authentic. Due to the topics, the data contains many negative emotions and few positive ones.

This data was first introduced as *VAM corpus*[1] in (Grimm & Kroschel, 2005b). All signals were sampled at 16 kHz and 16 bit resolution. In total the corpus contains 893 sentences from 47 speakers (11m/36f).

The emotion in each utterance was evaluated in a listener test (c.f. Section 2.2). Based on such a human evaluation, Figure 2 shows the histogram of the emotions contained in the database. The attested emotion was taken as the reference for the automatic recognition, since assessment by the speakers themselves was not available.

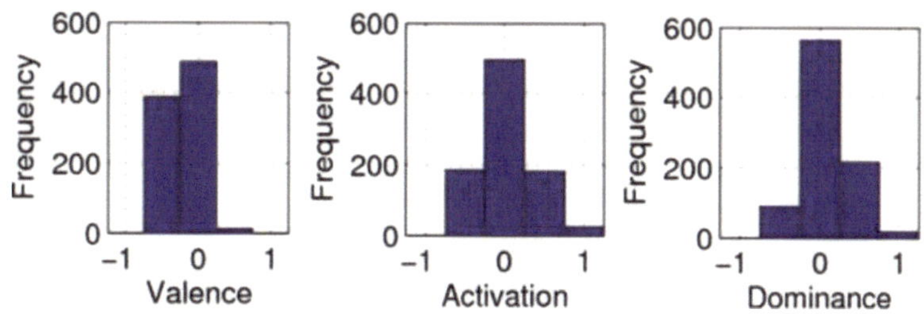

Figure 2. Distribution of the emotions present in the VAM corpus.

[1] The acronym VAM resides from the title of the talk-show, "Vera am Mittag" (German: Vera at Noon).

2.2. Emotion evaluation

For evaluation we used a listener test. A group of evaluators listened to the emotional sentences and assessed the emotional content. For this human evaluation we used the Self Assessment Manikins (Fischer, et al., 2002; Grimm & Kroschel, 2005a). In this method five images were offered per emotion primitive. For each sentence, an evaluator listened to the speech signal. Then he/she was asked to select the best describing image for each primitive. This evaluation method yields one reference value $x_n^{(i)} \in \{-1, -0.5, 0, 0.5, 1\}$ for each primitive $i \in$ {*valence, activation, dominance*} and each utterance n. The individual listener ratings were averaged using confidence scores as described in (Grimm & Kroschel, 2005a).

One half of the database was evaluated by 17 listeners, the other by 6 listeners, which was due to the fact that the second half of the database was recorded and evaluated later, when only a smaller number of evaluators was available. In comparison with other studies on emotion recognition which included 2 to 5 independent evaluations (Vidrascu & Devillers, 2005; Yu et al., 2004), we used a much higher number of evaluators to gain statistical confidence.

The average standard deviation in the evaluation was 0.29, 0.34, and 0.31 for *valence*, *activation*, and *dominance*, respectively. Thus, the average human deviation in the evaluation test was slightly above one half of the distance between two images, which was notably low for such a difficult task. The mean correlation between the evaluators was 0.49, 0.72, and 0.61, respectively (Grimm et al., 2007a), measured by Pearson's empirical correlation coefficient. Thus, *valence* was significantly more difficult to evaluate than *activation* or *dominance*. However, this result might also be an artifact of the correlation coefficient including the variance of the distribution, which is also smaller for *valence*.

3. Pre-processing

3.1. Feature extraction

The speaker's emotion is conveyed through a number of different channels. The most apparent correlates are found in the prosody of the speech. An overview on the acoustic expression of emotions can be found in (Murray & Arnott, 1993; Cowie & Cornelius, 2003). Analyzing the linguistic content provided by ASR in addition to the prosody might improve the estimation of the emotion (Lee & Narayanan, 2005). However, it has to be kept in mind that the performance of the ASR degrades remarkably in the case of emotional speech. Therefore, we concentrate on the non-linguistic information in the speech signal in this study.

In accordance with other research on automatic emotion recognition, we extracted prosodic features from the fundamental frequency (pitch) and the energy contours of the speech signals. The first and the second derivatives were also used. For pitch extraction, the autocorrelation method was used. For each of these 6 signals (pitch, energy x 0th, 1st, 2nd derivative) we calculated the following 9 statistical parameters:

- mean value
- standard deviation
- median
- minimum (not for energy)
- maximum
- 25% quantile

- 75% quantile
- difference between maximum and minimum
- difference between the quartiles

In addition we used 6 temporal characteristics:

- pause-to-speech ratio
- speech duration mean
- speech duration standard deviation
- pause duration mean
- pause duration standard deviation
- speaking rate

Finally, the spectral characteristics were added to the feature set. The Mel Frequency Cepstral Coefficients (MFCCs) were calculated in 13 subbands. The increased bandwidth with increasing center frequency of the individual subbands thereby reflects the hearing characteristics of the human ear (O'Shaughnessy, 1999). The mean value and the standard deviation of each of the 39 MFCC trajectories (13 subbands x 0th, 1st, 2nd derivative) were added to the feature set.

Thus, in total 137 acoustic features were extracted: 53 features derived from pitch and energy, 6 temporal characteristics, and 78 features to describe the spectral variability in the cause of the utterance. They were normalized to the range [0, 1].

3.2. Feature selection

To reduce the large amount of acoustic features, we used two different methods: Sequential Forward Selection (SFS) and Principal Component Analysis (PCA).

In the Sequential Forward Selection (SFS) technique for feature selection (Kittler, 1978), the feature set is increased sequentially. In each iteration, the one feature is added to the set which minimizes the classification error. Listing 1 contains the pseudo-code for this procedure.

```
current_best_feature_set := { }
remaining_features := {feat1, ..., feat137}
for num_features = 1 to 137
  error := { }
  for new_feature in remaining_features
    current_feature_set := current_best_feature_set ∪ {new_feature}
    error(new_feature):= classific_test(current_feature_set)
  end
  best_feature := arg min error
  current_best_feature_set := current_best_feature_set ∪ {best_feature}
  remaining_features := remaining_features \ {best_feature}
end
feature_ranking : = current_best_feature_set
```

Listing 1: Pseudo-code for the Sequential Forward Feature Selection method.

Figure 3 shows the classification error as a function of the feature set size. For this procedure the Support Vector Regression estimation method was applied, which is introduced in

Section 4.1. With an increasing number of features the classification error shrinks rapidly. However, for large feature sets, the error increases again, though only marginally. This effect might be caused by the fact that some features bear contradictory information concerning the emotion that is being conveyed. Thus, we found that, for each of the primitives and each of the classifiers, using 20 features was sufficient. Adding more features did not improve the results. The variance of the error was almost constant for feature sets of 10 or more features with a value of $\sigma^2 \approx 0.015$.

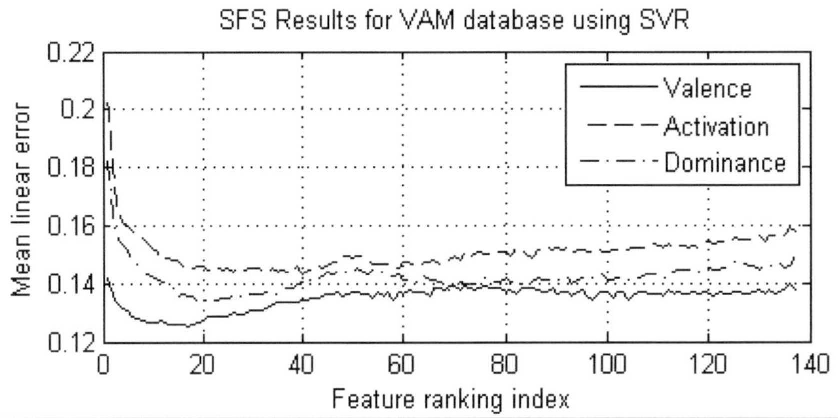

Figure 3. Classification error as a function of the feature set.

The SFS method was compared to Principal Component Analysis (PCA). While SFS includes the classifier in the selection routine, the PCA does not use the classification result as a feedback. It is based only on the N = 893 observations of the M = 137 features,

$$\mathbf{v}_n = (v_{n,1}, \dots, v_{n,M})^{\mathrm{T}}, \quad n = 1, \dots, N, \tag{1}$$

which are combined in the observation matrix

$$\mathbf{V} = (\mathbf{v}_1, \dots, \mathbf{v}_N). \tag{2}$$

Note that the features have to be zero-mean, which can be achieved by subtracting the estimated mean value $\bar{v}_m = \frac{1}{N}\sum_{n=1}^{N} v_{n,m}$ for each feature $m = 1,\dots,M$. The $M \times M$ covariance matrix of the features can thus be stated as $\mathbf{C_{VV}} = \mathbf{VV^T}$. According to (Kroschel, 2004), the features can be decorrelated by transforming them to a orthonormal basis $\mathbf{\Phi} = (\boldsymbol{\varphi}_1, \dots, \boldsymbol{\varphi}_M)$, where the basis vectors $\boldsymbol{\varphi}_m$, $m = 1,\dots,M$, are determined by solving the deterministic equation

$$\mathbf{C_{VV}} \cdot \boldsymbol{\varphi}_m = \lambda_m \cdot \boldsymbol{\varphi}_m. \tag{3}$$

Thus, the basis vectors are the eigenvectors of the covariance matrix $\mathbf{C_{VV}}$. The transformed, uncorrelated features $\mathbf{u}_n$ can be calculated by

$$\mathbf{u}_n = \mathbf{\Phi}^* \mathbf{v}_n, \quad (4)$$

where $\mathbf{\Phi}^*$ denotes the complex conjugate transpose of $\mathbf{\Phi}$. In the PCA, now the eigenvectors are sorted in decreasing order of the eigenvalues, and only those eigenvectors are kept as new basis vectors whose eigenvalue exceeds a threshold of, in our case, 1% of the maximum eigenvalue:

$$\tilde{\mathbf{u}}_n = \tilde{\mathbf{\Phi}}^* \mathbf{v}_n, \quad (5)$$

with

$$\tilde{\mathbf{\Phi}} = (\boldsymbol{\varphi}_1, \ldots, \boldsymbol{\varphi}_{\tilde{M}}), \quad \tilde{M} < M. \quad (6)$$

Figure 4 shows the eigenvalues of the covariance matrix based on our observations of acoustic features derived from emotional speech. It can be seen that the eigenvalues decrease quickly with increasing index. Thus, the first ten components carry already a large amount of the information. However, to include 90% of the total eigenvalue sum, at least $\tilde{M} = 61$ components must be included in the uncorrelated feature set; to include 99%, $\tilde{M} = 96$ components are required.

Since such a large number of features is not desirable for the classifier, we preferred the SFS method to the PCA method in order to reduce the size of the feature set. Note that SFS also reduces the computational demand since only a smaller number of features have to be calculated in contrast to PCA where still all features would be necessary to apply Equation (5).

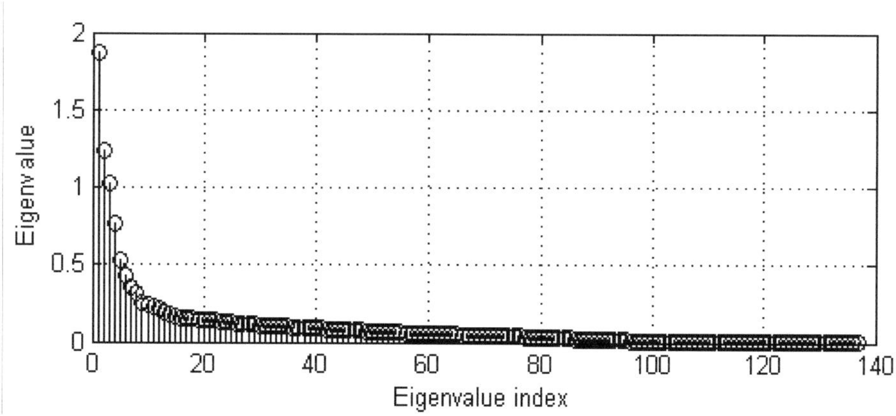

Figure 4. Eigenvalues of the covariance matrix derived from 893 observations of 137 acoustic features extracted from emotional speech.

4. Emotion primitives estimation

The task of the emotion estimator is to map the acoustic features to the real-valued emotion primitives. We analyzed several classifiers: Support Vector Regression, Fuzzy *k*-Nearest Neighbor classifiers, and a rule-based Fuzzy Logic inference method. In the following subsections we briefly describe the individual estimators. The desired output is not a classification into one of a finite set of categories but an estimation of continuous-valued emotion parameters, the primitives $x_n^{(i)} \in [-1,+1] \subset \mathbb{R}$, $i \in$ {*valence, activation, dominance*}. The results of these three estimators are discussed in Section 5.

4.1. Support Vector Regression

Support Vector Regression (SVR) is a regression method based on Support Vector Machines (Vapnik, 1995; Campbell, 2001; Schölkopf & Smola, 2001). Support Vector Machines are applied to a wide range of classification tasks (Abe, 2005). Based on a solid theoretical framework, they were shown to not only minimize the empirical training error but, more general, the structural risk. The decision function in SVMs is found by the hyperplane which maximizes the margin between two classes. Non-linear classification can be applied very efficiently by using the so-called *kernel trick*, i.e., by replacing the inner products that appear in the calculation of the decision function by (optionally) non-linear kernel functions. This kernel trick replaces a transformation of the features into a higher-dimensional space, linear classification in this higher-dimensional space, and re-transformation into the original space. In Support Vector Regression the role of the separation margin is inverted, i.e., the aim is to find the optimal regression hyperplane so that most training samples lie *within* an ε-margin around this hyperplane. Figure 5 shows a schematic sketch for SVR in which the non-linear regression curve was found using the kernel trick. The technical terms included in the figure will be described below. First results of using SVR for emotion primitives estimation were reported in (Grimm et al., 2007b).

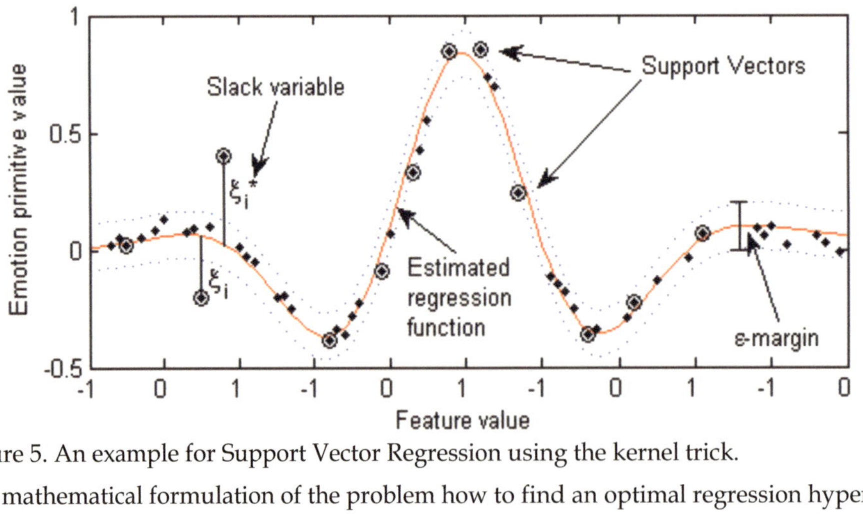

Figure 5. An example for Support Vector Regression using the kernel trick.

The mathematical formulation of the problem how to find an optimal regression hyperplane using a finite set of training samples can be found in (Vapnik, 1995; Schölkopf & Smola, 2001). Here we give only a short summary.

The goal is to find a function $f^{(i)}$ which maps the m acoustic features $\mathbf{v} = (v_1, \dots, v_m)^{\mathrm{T}} \in \mathbb{R}^m$ to the emotion primitive value $x^{(i)} \in \mathbb{R}$,

$$\hat{x}^{(i)} = f^{(i)}(\mathbf{v}). \tag{7}$$

We need three SVR functions to estimate the three emotion primitives separately: $i \in$ {*valence, activation, dominance*}. For improved readability we omit the notion of the index (i) in the following.

The easiest solution is a linear function, i.e., a hyperplane in $\mathbb{R}^m$,

$$f(\mathbf{v}) = \langle \mathbf{w}, \mathbf{v} \rangle + b, \tag{8}$$

where $\mathbf{w} \in \mathbb{R}^m$ and $b \in \mathbb{R}$ are the parameters of the hyperplane and $\langle \cdot \rangle$ denotes the inner product. To determine the parameters we need a set of N learning samples $(\mathbf{v}_n;\ x_n), n = 1, \dots, N,$ and a loss function $l(\eta)$ to penalize the distance between the function's output $\hat{x}_n$ and the (for the training samples well-known) true x_n,

$$l(\eta) = l(\hat{x}_n - x_n). \tag{9}$$

We chose the ε-insensitive loss function

$$l_\varepsilon(\eta) = \begin{cases} -\eta - \varepsilon & \text{for} \quad \eta < -\varepsilon \\ 0 & \text{for} \quad -\varepsilon \le \eta \le \varepsilon, \\ \eta - \varepsilon & \text{for} \quad \eta > \varepsilon \end{cases} \tag{10}$$

which assigns zero loss within a margin of width ε around the true value and linear loss for larger deviations. This loss function allows for the neglection of a large amount of training samples in the calculation of the hyperplane (Smola, 1996). The remaining samples are called *Support Vectors* (see Figure 5).

Since the structural risk is minimized for the function f with the least complexity, the problem can be formulated as

$$\begin{aligned} &\text{minimize } \frac{1}{2}\|\mathbf{w}\|^2 \\ &\text{subject to } \begin{cases} x_n - (\langle \mathbf{w}, \mathbf{v}_n \rangle + b) \le \varepsilon \\ (\langle \mathbf{w}, \mathbf{v}_n \rangle + b) - x_n \le \varepsilon \end{cases} \quad \text{for n} = 1,\dots,\text{N} \end{aligned} \tag{11}$$

It is common and in our applications absolutely necessary to allow some outliers. This can be achieved by introducing *slack variables* ξ_n, ξ_n^* (see Figure 5) and a *soft margin parameter C*, which yields the following problem:

$$\text{minimize } \frac{1}{2}\|\mathbf{w}\|^2 + C\sum_{n=1}^{N}(\xi_n + \xi_n^*)$$

$$\text{subject to} \begin{cases} x_n - (\langle \mathbf{w}, \mathbf{v}_n \rangle + b) \leq \varepsilon + \xi_n^* \\ (\langle \mathbf{w}, \mathbf{v}_n \rangle + b) - x_n \leq \varepsilon + \xi_n \\ \xi_n, \xi_n^* \geq 0 \end{cases}$$

$$\text{for n} = 1, \ldots, \text{N}. \tag{12}$$

This problem can be reformulated using the dual Lagrange function involving the Lagrange multipliers α_n, α_n^* as functions of the slack variables,

$$\text{maximize } -\frac{1}{2}\sum_{n,l=1}^{N}(\alpha_n^* - \alpha_n)(\alpha_l^* - \alpha_l)\langle \mathbf{v}_n, \mathbf{v}_l \rangle - \varepsilon\sum_{n=1}^{N}(\alpha_n^* + \alpha_n) + \sum_{n=1}^{N} x_n(\alpha_n^* - \alpha_n)$$

$$\text{subject to} \begin{cases} \sum_{n=1}^{N}(\alpha_n^* - \alpha_n) = 0 \\ \alpha_n, \alpha_n^* \in \left[0, \frac{C}{N}\right]. \end{cases} \tag{13}$$

In this maximization task the training samples $\mathbf{v}_n$ only occur as inner products. Since one of the Lagrange conditions requires

$$\mathbf{w} = \sum_{n=1}^{N}(\alpha_n^* - \alpha_n)\mathbf{v}_n, \tag{14}$$

which means that **w** can completely be expressed as a linear combination of the feature vectors (*Support Vector Expansion*), the target function f can be stated as

$$f(\mathbf{v}) = \sum_{n=1}^{N}(\alpha_n^* - \alpha_n)\langle \mathbf{v}_n, \mathbf{v} \rangle + b. \tag{15}$$

While (15) is a functional formulation, it is easily applied to any query feature vector $\mathbf{v}_0$ with unknown emotion primitive values $x^{(i)}$ by evaluating $f(\mathbf{v} = \mathbf{v}_0)$.
It is obvious that both in (13) and (15) the feature vectors only occur as inner products. These inner products can be replaced by a (non-linear) kernel function:

$$\langle \mathbf{v}_n, \mathbf{v}_l \rangle \rightarrow K(\mathbf{v}_n, \mathbf{v}_l). \tag{16}$$

This replacement expresses the kernel trick mathematically. It allows non-linear regression in an efficient way.
We used the following kernel functions:

- Radial basis function (SVR-RBF):

$$K(\mathbf{v}_n, \mathbf{v}_l) = \exp\{-\|\mathbf{v}_n - \mathbf{v}_l\|^2/(2\sigma^2)\} \tag{17}$$

- Polynomial kernel (SVR-Poly):

$$K(\mathbf{v}_n, \mathbf{v}_l) = (\langle \mathbf{v}_n, \mathbf{v}_l \rangle + 1)^d \tag{18}$$

Both, the choice of the kernel function and the kernel parameter, is important. If σ in SVR-RBF is small, the regression function will follow closely the training samples. For $\sigma = 0.01$, e.g., we can observe clear overfitting. The larger σ, the flatter gets the target curve; therefore it cannot be chosen too big. We tested for the range of $\sigma \in [10^{-4}, 10^4]$ and found that $\sigma \in [2.5, 10]$ gives good results. We finally chose $\sigma = 3.5$.
In the polynomial kernel the parameter d determines the order of the polynomial. The higher d, the more complex gets the regression curve. However, we found that, on a search interval of $d \in [1, 10]$, the best results can be achieved with $d = 1$. This choice results in a polynomial of order 1, i.e., a linear function.
In addition to the choice of the kernel function, the parameters of the SVR, C and ε, have to be set. We used a first, grid-based search on a logarithmic scale and a second, fine-grained search in the best region to find those parameters that give the lowest error (Chudoba, 2006). The soft margin parameter C has an influence on how many sample vectors are finally used for the calculation of the regression curve. The higher C, the more outliers are allowed, and the more sample vectors are included as support vectors. Our search region was $C \in [10^{-4}, 10^4]$, and the best results were achieved for $C \in [0.1, 50]$. Since this parameter has to be regarded jointly with the kernel function parameter, we chose $C = 10$ for SVR-RBF and $C = 0.1$ for SVR-Poly, respectively.
The parameter ε defines the width of the margin around the regression curve. This parameter essentially influences the number of support vectors used. Since, in general, those feature vectors are used as support vectors which are lying outside or at least close to the margin border, a larger margin yields less support vectors. The number of support vectors is computationally relevant because the summation in (15) in practice reduces to the summation of the support vectors only. Testing on the range of $\varepsilon \in [0,1]$, we decided to choose $\varepsilon = 0.2$ for all kernels.
For all experiments, the *libsvm* implementation was used (Chang & Lin, 2001).

4.2. Fuzzy k-Nearest Neighbor estimator

As an alternative to SVM, the *k*-Nearest Neighbor method was studied. This method was shown to give comparable results on related problems, namely the discrete categorization of emotion stereotypes (Yacoub et al., 2003; Dellaert et al., 1996). The *k*-Nearest Neighbor (KNN) method is a distance-based approach. It determines the *k* closest neighbors of a query $\mathbf{v} = \mathbf{v}_0$ in the feature space and assigns the properties of these neighbors to the query

(Kroschel, 2004). Such method can be regarded as spanning a hypersphere S around the feature vector $\mathbf{v}_0$,

$$S = \{\mathbf{v} \in V \,|\, \|\mathbf{v} - \mathbf{v}_0\|_p \leq r\}, \tag{19}$$

where

$$V = \{\mathbf{v}_1, \ldots, \mathbf{v}_N\} \subset \mathbb{R}^M \tag{20}$$

is the set of all sample vecors $\mathbf{v}_n$, $n = 1,\ldots,N$, and the radius r is chosen to have exactly k sample feature vectors lie within this hypersphere,

$$|S| = k. \tag{21}$$

Thus, without loss of generality, S can be stated as

$$S = \{\mathbf{v}_{n_1}, \ldots, \mathbf{v}_{n_k}\}, \tag{22}$$

with the indices $n_1, \ldots, n_k \in [1, \ldots, N]$.

In our case, the properties of the neighbors are the emotion primitive values $x_{n_1}^{(i)}, \ldots, x_{n_k}^{(i)}$. These values are averaged to get the final emotion estimate $\hat{x}^{(i)}$ for a query feature vector $\mathbf{v}_0$,

$$\hat{x}^{(i)} = \frac{1}{k} \sum_{\kappa=1}^{k} x_{n_\kappa}^{(i)}. \tag{23}$$

Due to this average, all k neighbors have an influence on the estimate. This led us to calling the method *Fuzzy KNN*.

The parameters to choose are p of the L_p distance in (19) and k, the number of neighbors considered. According to (Kroschel, 2004), the vector distance $\|\cdot\|_p$ in (19) is defined as

$$\|\mathbf{v} - \mathbf{v}_0\|_p = \left(\sum_{m=1}^{M} |v_m - v_{0,m}|^p \right)^{\frac{1}{p}}. \tag{24}$$

We tested $p \in \{1, 1.5, \ldots, 4\}$ and found that the results were almost independent of the distance norm. Thus, we finally chose $p = 2$ (Euclidean distance).

The second design parameter, k, had a greater impact on the results. We tested $k \in \{1, 3, \ldots, 15\}$ and found that the error decreased rapidly with increasing k. The error remained at a relatively constant level for values of $k \geq 9$. Thus, we decided for $k = 11$ for our experiments.

4.3. Rule-based Fuzzy Logic estimator

A rule-based Fuzzy Logic (FL) estimator has previously been used for automatic emotion primitive estimation (Grimm & Kroschel, 2005b; Grimm et al., 2007a). Therefore, it will be described very briefly here. This method can be regarded as the state-of-the art in emotion primitive estimation.

The fuzzy logic captures well the nature of emotions, which in general is fuzzy in description and notation. This fuzzy description is reflected in the number of linguistic terms which are used to describe feelings, moods, and affective attitudes.

A fuzzy logic estimator consists of three major elements (Kroschel, 2004):

- Fuzzification
- Inference
- Defuzzification

The fuzzification step transforms the crisp variables, which are the acoustic features in our case, into fuzzy, linguistic variables. We transformed each feature into three linguistic variables, *low, medium,* and *high,* respectively. We assigned membership grades to each of these fuzzy variables according to the relative position of the crisp feature value within the range between the 10% and the 90% quantiles of the overall feature value distribution observed in the training samples.

The rules in the inference system can be derived from expert knowledge. However, we decided to derive them automatically by analysis of the relation between the acoustic features and the desired emotion primitives. We used a set of three linguistic, fuzzy variables for each primitive: *negative, neutral,* and *positive* for *valence*; *calm, neutral,* and *excited* for *activation*; and *weak, neutral,* and *strong* for *dominance.* Thus, each fuzzy variable of the acoustic features was related to each fuzzy variable of the emotion primitives.

The individual steps of the inference part are the following (Kroschel, 2004; Grimm et al., 2007a): First, all features were aggregated using maximum aggregation method. Then, inference was performed using the product method; this process determines the conclusion drawn from the fuzzy acoustic features onto the fuzzy emotion values. Finally, accumulation of the three fuzzy membership contours for each primitive was achieved using the maximum method. The result was the fusion of *negative, neutral,* and *positive* contours into one membership function for *valence,* etc.

In the last step, the fuzzy emotion values were defuzzified to yield crisp emotion primitive values. We used the centroid method for this task.

5. Results

This section reports the results of our experiments on estimating the emotion primitives conveyed in spontaneous speech. First, the results are compared with respect to the different estimators. While these results were already presented very briefly in (Grimm et al., 2007b), we provide a more elaborate discussion of these results here. Second, we present the learning curves of the different estimators to show the dependence on the data size that is necessary for training.

5.1 Comparison of the emotion estimation results

All experiments were performed using a 10-fold cross-validation. To assess the estimation results we used two different measures:

- The mean linear error between the emotion estimates $\hat{x}_n^{(i)}$ and the reference annotated manually by the human evaluators, $x_n^{(i)}$,

$$e^{(i)} = \sum_{n=1}^{N} \left| \hat{x}_n^{(i)} - x_n^{(i)} \right| \tag{25}$$

- The empirical correlation coefficient between the emotion estimates and the reference,

$$r^{(i)} = \frac{\sum_{n=1}^{N} \left(\hat{x}_n^{(i)} - \bar{\hat{x}}^{(i)} \right) \left(x_n^{(i)} - \bar{x}^{(i)} \right)}{\sqrt{\sum_{n=1}^{N} \left(\hat{x}_n^{(i)} - \bar{\hat{x}}^{(i)} \right)^2 \sum_{n=1}^{N} \left(x_n^{(i)} - \bar{x}^{(i)} \right)^2}} \tag{26}$$

Table 1. summarizes (a) the mean linear error for each estimator, for each emotion primitive separately, and (b) the correlation coefficient to measure the tendency in the emotion estimates.

The results in Table 1(a) indicate that all primitives can be estimated with a small error in the range of 0.13 to 0.18. There was only one exception when *valence* was estimated using the FL estimator (0.27). Considering the range of values, which was [-1,+1], it can be stated that the emotion primitives are mostly estimated in the correct region, and, e.g., a very excited utterance might get estimated as moderately excited to very excited, but not as very calm.

	(a) Mean Error			(b) Correlation Coefficient		
	Valence	*Activation*	*Dominance*	*Valence*	*Activation*	*Dominance*
SVR-RBF	0.13	0.15	0.14	0.46	0.82	0.79
SVR-Pol	0.14	0.16	0.15	0.39	0.80	0.77
FL	0.27	0.17	0.18	0.28	0.75	0.72
KNN	0.13	0.16	0.14	0.46	0.80	0.78

Table 1. Mean error and correlation with reference of the emotion primitive estimation.

The error is thus even better than the human evaluation, which showed on average a standard deviation of 0.31 (c.f. Section 2.2). However, it has to be noted that this standard deviation also includes the quantization error of the emotion axes due to the finite set of values offered to the evaluators. Also the automatic estimation might benefit from the relatively large amount of neutral and moderate emotions that yielded better individual results than the extreme emotions.

The correlation between the estimates and the reference was significantly different for the individual emotion primitives, as shown in Table 1(b). The correlation for *valence* was between 0.28 and 0.46 for the different estimators, and it was between 0.72 and 0.82 for *activation* and *dominance*. It has to be noted that the correlation coefficients for *valence* are only moderately significant at $p > 10^{-3}$, while all other correlation coefficients are statistically significant at $p < 10^{-5}$. These different significance levels reflect the fact that the distribution in the values for *valence* was much narrower than for *activation* or *dominance*. Thus the results imply very good recognition results for *activation* and *dominance*, and moderate recognition results for *valence*.

Comparing the individual estimation methods, we can say that the best results were achieved using the SVR-RBF estimator with errors of 0.13, 0.15, and 0.14, and correlation coefficients of 0.46, 0.82, and 0.79 for *valence*, *activation*, and *dominance*, respectively. The Fuzzy KNN estimator performed almost as well as the SVR-RBF. The SVR-Poly estimator gave worse results for *valence* in comparison to almost as good results for *activation* and *dominance*. Similarly, the FL estimator gave even worse results for *valence* but still very good ones for *activation* and *dominance*.

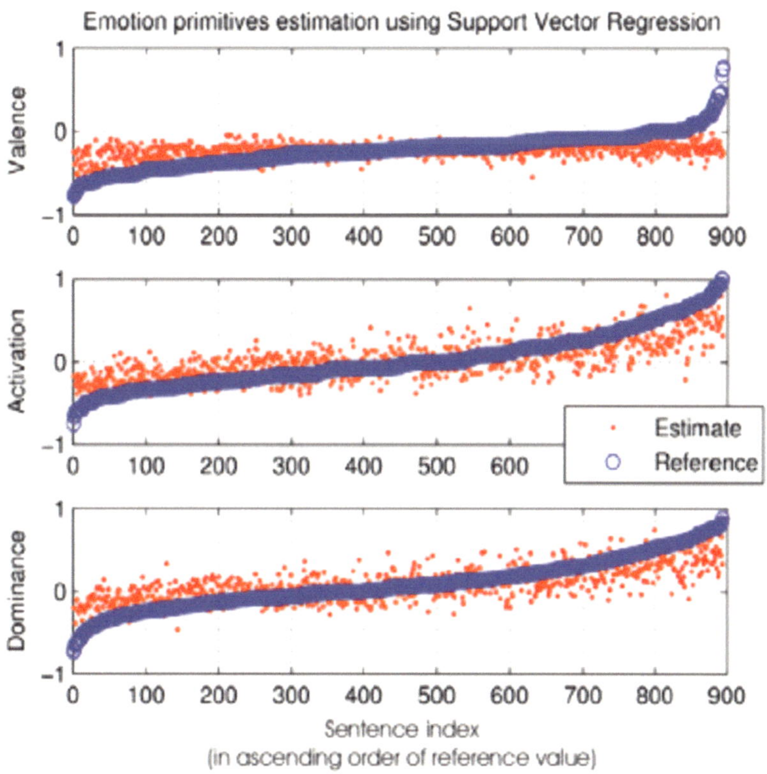

Figure 6. Emotion primitives estimation: results in comparison with manually labeled human reference.

Thus, the kernel-based method outperformed all other methods only marginally, apart from the FL method which seems to be clearly the last choice. These differences are probably caused by the complexity in the representation of the relation between the acoustic features and the emotion primitives. While Fuzzy Logic only uses the rules derived from the correlation coefficients, which is a rather coarse generalization, the SVR method provides a more complex, nonlinear relation in form of the regression curve in a high-dimensional feature space. KNN does not provide such sophisticated abstraction, but uses a huge amount of comparison options to choose the neighbors from.

Thus, on deciding between SVR and KNN, the focus must be set on the computational demand: If we have enough computational power to calculate all the distances necessary in the KNN method, this might be the choice due to the simplicity in the setup of the classifier. Alternatively, if we are forced to have low computational demands at runtime, we might decide for SVR-RBF and provide the computational power only once, which is at the instant of generating the regression hyperplane.

As a summary of the results, Figure 6 shows the estimation results using the SVR-RBF estimator. In this graph, the emotion primitive values are arranged in ascending order. This order is in contrast to the experiment, where we provided random order, but helps in grasping the benefits and the limits of the presented method, in particular with respect to the mentioned difficulty of having relatively few positive emotions but a wide range of *activation* and *dominance* values.

Figure 6 reveals some information about the nature of the errors. Most of the estimates are located within a small margin around the references. However, a small number of very high or very low primitive values was occasionally underestimated.

5.2 Learning curves

In addition to the direct comparison of the estimator results, it is interesting to see the amount of training data that is necessary to achieve such results. We analyzed a wide range of 50% to 98% of the data to be available for training and compared the estimation results for these individual conditions. Figure 7 shows these learning curves for (a) SVR-RBF, (b) FL, and (c) KNN.

It can be seen that the error curves are very different. For the FL estimator, the error curves are almost constant over the total range. This result is very interesting since it shows that although the FL absolute error was higher than the one using alternative estimators, it is more robust considering the necessary amount of training data. Therefore this method might be worth using for applications in which few training data is available.

If we compare the SVR-RBF and the KNN learning curves, we can observe that the error for KNN depends more on the training data size than the respective error using SVR. This difference can be explained by the nature of learning in these two methods. SVR uses a generalizing method that yields a more abstract representation of the training data in form of the regression curve parameters. In contrast, KNN uses only an explicit representation of a set of training features. Thus, providing a smaller number of training samples directly reduces the options for comparison when trying to find the most appropriate neighbors.

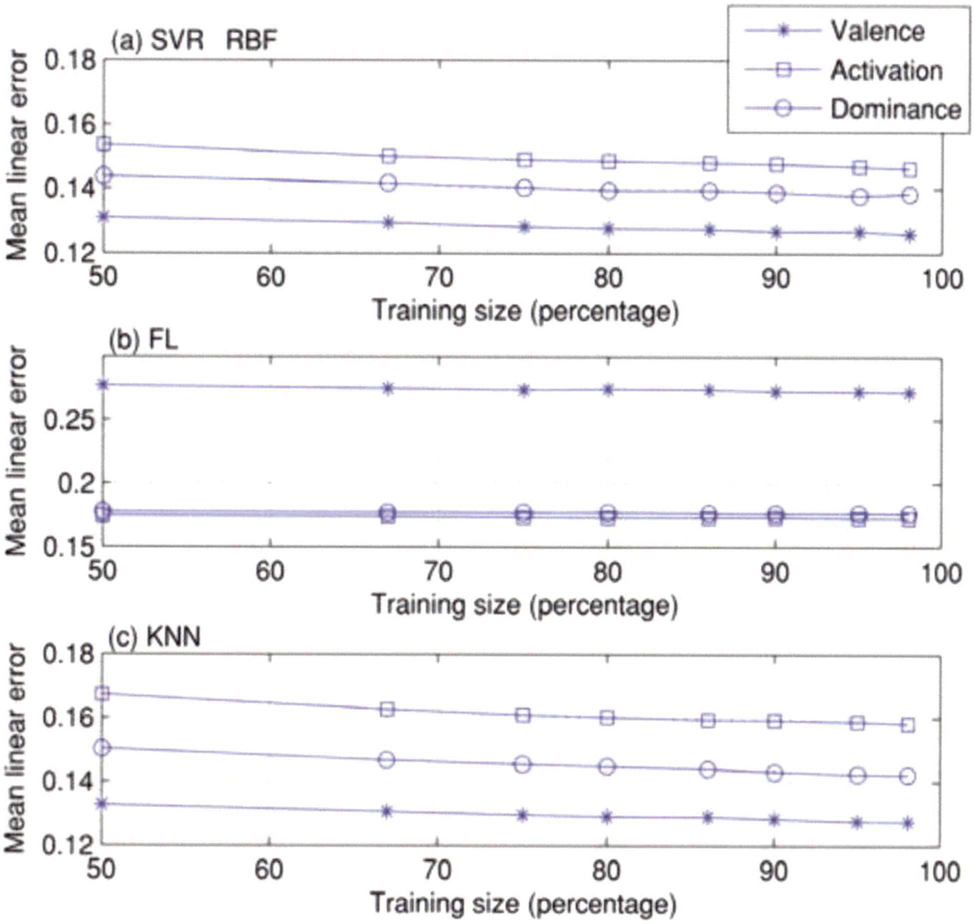

Figure 7. Learning curves of different estimators for emotion primitive estimation, based on the VAM corpus.

6. Conclusion

In this chapter we discussed the recognition of emotions in spontaneous speech. We used a general framework motivated by emotion psychology to describe emotions by means of three emotion "primitives" (attributes), namely *valence, activation*, and *dominance*. With these emotion primitives, we proposed a real-valued three-dimensional emotion space concept to overcome the limitations in the state-of-the-art emotion categorization. We tested the method on the basis of 893 spontaneous emotional utterances recorded on a German TV talk-show.

For the acoustic representation of the emotion conveyed in the speech signal, we extracted 137 features. These reflected the prosody and the spectral characteristics of the speech. We tested two methods to reduce the problem of large feature sets, Principal Component Analysis and Sequential Feature Selection. Thus, we selected the 20 most relevant acoustic features that yielded the best recognition results.

For the estimation of the emotion primitives, Support Vector Regression, Fuzzy Logic, and Fuzzy k-Nearest Neighbor methods were used. We found that the emotion primitives could be estimated with a small error of 0.13 to 0.15, where the range of values was [-1,+1]. The correlation between the reference annotated manually by the evaluators and the automatically calculated estimates was moderate (0.46, *valence*) to high (0.82/0.79, *activation/dominance*). In comparison to the Fuzzy Logic estimator, which was the baseline, the error for *valence, activation* and *dominance* estimation could be reduced by 52%, 12% and 22%, respectively.

Thus, Support Vector Regression gave the best estimation results, however, closely followed by KNN. Note that while SVR is computationally much more demanding for initialization (finding the regression hyperplane), the KNN method requires more computational power at the actual estimation step due to the distance matrix that has to be calculated. The rule-based FL algorithm is computationally less demanding but gives clearly inferior results, at least for *valence*. However, when regarding the learning curves of the three estimators, i.e., assessing the estimation error as a function of the training data size, it was shown that the Fuzzy Logic method gave the most robust results. Thus, in the case of very few training data available, the FL method might be an appropriate choice again.

In our future work we will study the fusion of the emotion primitive estimation with the automated speech recognition (ASR). While the emotion recognition might be used to parameterize or personalize the ASR unit, the phoneme estimates of the ASR, on return, might be used to improve the emotion recognition. Future work will also investigate the design of a real-time system using the algorithms that were reported here. The advantage of continuous-valued estimates of the emotional state of a person could be used to build an adaptive emotion tracking system. Such a system might be capable to adapt to individual personalities and long-term moods, and thus finally provide indeed humanoid man-machine interfaces.

7. Acknowledgment

This work was supported by grants of the Collaborative Research Center (SFB) 588 "Humanoid Robots - Learning and Cooperating Multimodal Robots" of the Deutsche Forschungsgemeinschaft (DFG). We thank Robert Chudoba who contributed a relevant part to this research in his Master Thesis.

8. References

Abe, S. (2005). Support Vector Machines for Pattern Recognition. Berlin, Germany: Springer.

Campbell, C. (2001). An Introduction to Kernel Methods. In R. Howlett, & L. Jain (Eds.), Radial Basis Function Networks 1 (pp. 155-192). Heidelberg, Germany: Physica-Verlag.

Chang, C.-C., & Lin, C.-J. (2001). LIBSVM: A Library for Support Vector Machines. Retrieved from http://www.csie.ntu.edu.tw/~cjlin/libsvm.

Chudoba, R. (2006). Klassifikation von Emotionen mit Support Vector Machines. Karlsruhe, Germany: Universität Karlsruhe (TH): Diploma Thesis.

Cowie, R., Douglas-Cowie, E., Tsapatsoulis, N., Votsis, G., Kollias, S., Fellenz, W., et al. (2001). Emotion recognition in human-computer interaction. IEEE Signal Processing Magazine , 18 (1), pp. 32-80.

Cowie, R., & Cornelius, R. (2003). Describing the Emotional States That Are Expressed in Speech. Speech Communication , 40, pp. 5-32.
Dellaert, F., Polzin, T., & Waibel, A. (1996). Recognizing Emotion in Speech. Proc. International Conference on Spoken Language Processing, 3, pp. 1970-1973. Philadelphia, PA, USA.
Fischer, L., Brauns, D., & Belschak, F. (2002). Zur Messung von Emotionen in der angewandten Forschung. Lengerich, Germany: Pabst Science Publishers.
Fragopanagos, N., & Taylor, J. (2005). Emotion Recognition in Human-Computer Interaction. Neural Networks , 18 (4), pp. 389-405.
Grimm, M., & Kroschel, K. (2005a). Evaluation of Natural Emotions Using Self Assessment Manikins. Proc. ASRU, (pp. 381-385).
Grimm, M., & Kroschel, K. (2005b). Rule-Based Emotion Classification Using Acoustic Features. Proc. Int. Conf. on Telemedicine and Multimedia Communication.
Grimm, M., Mower, E., Kroschel, K., & Narayanan, S. (2006). Combining Categorical and Primitives-Based Emotion Recognition. Proceedings European Signal Processing Conference (Eusipco). Florence, Italy.
Grimm, M., Mower, E., Kroschel, K., & Narayanan, S. (2007a). Primitives-Based Evaluation and Estimation of Emotions in Speech. Speech Communication .
Grimm, M., Kroschel, K., & Narayanan, S. (2007b). Support Vector Regression for Automatic Recognition of Spontaneous Emotions in Speech. Proc. International Conference on Acoustics, Speech, and Signal Processing (ICASSP). Honolulu, HI, USA: Accepted for Publication.
Kehrein, R. (2002). The prosody of authentic emotions. Proc. Speech Prosody Conf., (pp. 423-426).
Kittler, J. (1978). Feature Set Search Algorithms. Pattern Recognition and Signal Processing , pp. 41-60.
Kroschel, K. (2004). Statistische Informationstheorie (4. ed.). Berlin, Germany: Springer.
Lee, C. M., Narayanan, S., & Pieraccini, R. (2001). Recognition of Negative Emotions from the Speech Signal. Proc. IEEE Automatic Speech Recognition and Understanding Wsh. (ASRU).
Lee, C. M., & Narayanan, S. (2005). Toward Detecting Emotions in Spoken Dialogs. IEEE Transactions on Speech and Audio Processing , 13 (2), pp. 293-303.
Murray, I., & Arnott, J. (1993). Toward the Simulation of Emotion in Synthetic Speech: A Review of the Literature on Human Vocal Emotion. Journal of the Acoustic Society of America , 93 (2), pp. 1097-1108.
O'Shaughnessy, D. (1999). Speech Communications: Human and Machine (2. ed.). John Wiley & Sons Inc.
Picard, R. (1997). Affective Computing. Cambridge, MA, USA: MIT Press.
Scherer, K. (1990). Psychologie der Emotion. Göttingen, Germany: Hogrefe.
Schölkopf, B., & Smola, A. (2001). Learning with Kernels: Support Vector Machines, Regularization, Optimization, and Beyond. Cambridge, MA, USA: The MIT Press.
Schröder, M. (2003). Speech and Emotion Research: An Overview of Research Frameworks and a Dimensional Approach to Emotional Speech Synthesis. Universität des Saarlandes, Germany: Ph.D. Thesis.

Schuller, B., Reiter, S., Muller, R., Al-Hames, M., Lang, M., & Rigoll, G. (2005). Speaker Independent Speech Emotion Recognition by Ensemble Classification. Proc. Int. Conf. on Multimedia and Expo, (pp. 864-867).

Smola, A. (1996). Regression Estimation with Support Vector Learning Machines. Master Thesis: Technische Universität München.

Vapnik, V. (1995). The Nature of Statistical Learning Theory. New York: Springer.

Vidrascu, L., & Devillers, L. (2005). Real-Life Emotion Representation and Detection in Call Centers Data. Proc. Int. Conf. on Affective Computing and Intelligent Interaction, (pp. 739-746).

Yacoub, S., Simske, S., Lin, X., & Burns, J. (2003). Recognition of Emotions in Interactive Voice Response Systems. Palo Alto, USA: HP Laboratories .

Yu, C., Aoki, P., & Woodruff, A. (2004). Detecting User Engagement in Everyday Conversations. Proc. Int. Conf. Spoken Lang. Processing, (pp. 1329-1332).

17

Linearly Interpolated Hierarchical N-gram Language Models for Speech Recognition Engines

Imed Zitouni[1] and Qiru Zhou[2]
[1]*IBM T.J. Watson Research Center, NY*, [2]*Bell Labs Alcatel-Lucent, NJ*
USA

1. Introduction

Language modeling is a crucial component in natural language continuous speech recognition, due to the difficulty involved by continuous speech [1], [2]. Language modeling attempts to capture regularities in natural language for the purpose of improving the recognition performance. Many studies have shown that the word error rate of automatic speech recognition (ASR) systems decreases significantly when using statistical language models [3], [4], [5]. The purpose of language models (LMs) is to compute the probability $P(w_1^I)$ of a sequence of words $w_1^I = w_1, \ldots w_I$. The probability $P(w_1^I)$ can be expressed as: $P(w_1^I) = \prod_{i=1}^{I} P(w_i|h_i)$, where $h_i = w_1, \ldots, w_{i-1}$ is the history or the context of word w_i. The probability $P(w_1^I)$ becomes difficult to estimate as the number of words in h_i increases. To overcome this problem, we can introduce equivalent classes on the histories h_i in order to reduce their cardinality. The n-gram language models approximate the dependence of each word (regardless of i) to the $n - 1$ words preceding it: $h_i \approx w_{i-n+1} \ldots w_{i-1}$. The probability $P(w_1^I)$ can then be expressed as:

$$P(w_1^I) = \prod_{i=1}^{I} P(w_i|w_{i-n+1} \ldots w_{i-1})$$

The n-gram approximation is based on the formal assumption that language is generated by a time-invariant Markov process [6].
Word n-gram LMs (mainly 2-gram and 3-gram LMs) are the most commonly used approach in language modeling. When enough data is available, word n-gram LMs have proved extremely useful in estimating the likelihood of frequently occurring n-grams, $(w_1, \ldots w_n)$. When using this approach, estimating the probability of low-frequency and unseen n-grams is still inherently difficult. The problem becomes more acute as the vocabulary size increases since the number of low-frequency and unseen n-grams events increases considerably.
Automatic continuous speech recognition systems still make errors especially on unseen and rare events. Because of the Zipf's law [7], we will always expect unseen and rare events during recognition. Hence, the data sparseness constitutes a crucial point to take into account when building language models.

Many approaches have been reported to overcome the probability estimation problem of low-frequency n-grams. One of them is the class n-gram language models [1], [8]. Using this approach, words are partitioned into equivalence classes, and the inter-word transition probability is assumed to depend only on the word classes. Class n-gram language models are more compact and generalize better on unseen n-grams compared to standard word-based language models. Nevertheless, for large training corpora, word n-gram language models are still better than class-based language models in capturing collocational relations between words.

A better approach is to build a language model that is general enough to better model unseen events, but specific enough to capture the ambiguous nature of words. Our solution is to hierarchically cluster the vocabulary words, building a word tree. The leaves represent individual words, while the nodes define clusters, or word classes: a node contains all the words of its descendant nodes. The closer a node is to the leaves, the more specific the corresponding class is. At the top of the tree, the root cluster contains all the words in the vocabulary. The tree is used to balance generalization ability and word specificity when estimating the probability of n-gram events. Then, we build a hierarchical n-gram language models that take benefit of the different information in every node of the tree to estimate the probability $P(w_i|w_{i-n+1}\cdots w_{i-1})$ of a word w_i given its context $w_{i-n+1}\cdots w_{i-1}$. This approach allows us to take advantage of both the power of word n-grams for frequent events and the predictive power of class n-grams for unseen or rare events.

One way to benefit from the word class hierarchy is to use the backoff hierarchical class n-gram language models (HCLMs) that we introduced recently [9], [10], [11], [12]. The backoff hierarchical class n-gram language models estimate the probability of an unseen event using the most specific class of the tree that guarantees a minimum number of occurrences of this event, hence allowing accurate estimation of the probability. This approach is a generalization of the well known backoff word n-gram language modeling technique [13]. The backoff word n-gram language modeling technique estimates the probability of an unseen n-gram (w_{i-n+1}^{i}) using a more general context, which is the (n-l)-gram (w_{i-n+2}^{i}). However, when using the backoff hierarchical class n-gram language models, the probability of an unseen n-gram (w_{i-n+1}^{i}) is computed according to a more specific context than the (n-l)-gram: we use the class of the most distant word w_{i-n+1} followed by the other words: $F(w_{i-n+1}), w_{i-n+2}^{i-1}$. The function $F(x)$ represents the class (parent) of x within the hierarchical word tree, where x can be a class itself, or a single word, depending on its location in the class hierarchy.

In this chapter we introduce a novel language modeling technique named linearly interpolated hierarchical n-gram language models. This approach combine the power of word n-grams for frequent events and the predictive power of class n-grams for unseen or rare events. It linearly interpolate different n-gram LMs each one of them is trained on one level of the class hierarchy. The model trained on the leaves level (level 0) is the standard word n-gram language models. Those language models trained on a level in the class hierarchy greater than 0 are in fact the class n-gram language models. The higher the number of levels in the class hierarchy is, the more compact and general the class n-gram language models become.

In the next section we briefly describe previously published related works. In section III we introduce the linearly interpolated hierarchical n-gram language models (LIHLMs). We study the properties and parameters defining this model to show how it leads to better estimate the probability of *n*-gram events. Section IV describes the backoff hierarchical class *n*-gram language modeling approach (HCLMs). The goal is to compute its performance to the performance of LIHLMs reported in section III. Section V presents the technique we use in building the class hierarchy. Section VI reports the data we used for training and evaluation and section VII describes the conducted experiments where we confirm the effectiveness of our approach to estimate the likelihood of n-gram events. Section VIII concludes the chapter.

2. Previous works

The idea of using classes to estimate the probability of unseen events in a backoff word *n*-gram model was proposed by several scientists [14], [15]. The basic principle of these approaches is to estimate the likelihood of unseen *n*-grams based on the class *n*-gram model and then, if needed, the (n-l)-grams. The originality of our approach is to use a hierarchical representation of the classes rather than an unstructured set of classes.
L. Bahl *et al.* proposed a tree-based statistical language model [16] where a linear interpolation is used to smooth the relative frequency at each node of the tree. L. Bahl *et al.* use information theoretic measures to construct equivalence classes of the context to cope with data sparseness. Using the approach of L. Bahl *et al.*, the likelihood of an *n*-grams $(wi,... w_n)$ is computed as the linear interpolation of several word class language models extracted from the word class tree. P. Heeman investigated a similar hierarchical language modeling approach where POS tags, word identities, and a decision tree technique are used to estimate the probability distribution allowing generalization between POS tags and words [17]. Their tree-building strategy is based on the approach of L. Bahl *et al.* [16], and uses Breiman's decision tree learning algorithm [18] to partition the context into equivalence classes. P. Heeman uses a *binary* tree where at each node the clustering algorithm find a question about the POS tags and left context word identities in order to partition the node into 2 leaves. The approaches proposed by L. Bahl *et al.* in [16] and P. Heeman in [17] have some similarity with the technique of LIHLMs we propose. The main difference between LIHLMs and the approaches proposed by L. Bahl *et al.* in [16] and P. Heeman in [17] is in the technique we use for the interpolation scheme, the way we select active nodes, and the approach we use to build the class hierarchy. Also, the LIHLMs don't use POS information.
In 2003, one year after we introduced the hierarchical class n-gram approach [19], J. Bilmes and K. Kirchhoff published a hierarchical language model [20] where the likelihood of a word given its context is computed based on a vector of factors, instead of the word history. Factors may represent morphological classes, stems, etc. In the approach we propose, we do not use syntactic and morphological features. One advantage of our approach compared to those cited before is the use of a data-driven method to build the class hierarchy, which eliminate the costly *decision* tree build step.
P. Dupont and R. Rosenfeld proposed a multi-dimensional lattice approach where the likelihood of a word given a history is estimated based on multi-dimensional hierarchies. The strength of their approach lies in its generality and in the dynamic selection of a small subset of predictor contexts. An interpolation between these predictor contexts is then used to estimate the likelihood of a word given a history. However, the selection of these predictor nodes is still an open problem, which makes their approach difficult to use in real ASR applications. As stated by P. Dupont and R. Rosenfeld in [21], the reported results are preliminary and are based on perplexity only. The HCLMs we proposed in [9] shares some

similarities with the two-dimensional lattice technique of P. Dupont and R. Rosenfeld [21], where the first dimension is the length of the history equivalence class and the second dimension is the position in a word class hierarchy. Compared to P. Dupont and R. Rosenfeld, HCLMs do not need to select a subset of predictor contexts. Instead, HCLMs use the backoff technique and the most specific class to balances generalization ability and word specificity when estimating the likelihood of a word given a history. This makes HCLMs less complex and easy to integrate in real-time ASR applications.
Recently, another tree-based language modeling approach is proposed by P. Xu and F. Jelinek [22]. It explores the use of Random Forests in the structured language model, which uses rich syntactic information in predicting the next word based on words already seen. The goal is to construct Random Forests by randomly growing decision trees using syntactic information. Random Forests are a combination of decision tree classifiers originally developed for classification purposes.

3. Linearly interpolated hierarchical n-gram language models

The conditional probability of a word w given a history h, $P(w|h)$, is in general obtained by combining two components: a discounting model and a redistribution model. Discounting is related to the zero-frequency estimation problem [23]. The idea behind discounting is that a probability for all the words never observed after the history h must be estimated by discounting the n-gram relative frequency:

$$fr(w|h) = \frac{N(hw)}{N(h)} \tag{1}$$

where $N(.)$ denotes the frequency of the argument in the training data. By definition $N(h) = 0$ implies $fr(w|h) = 0$. Discounting produces a discounted conditional frequency $fr^*(w|h)$, such that:

$$0 \leq fr^*(w|h) \leq fr(w|h) \tag{2}$$

The zero-frequency probability $\lambda(h)$ is then defined as follows:

$$\lambda(h) = 1 - fr^*(w|h) \tag{3}$$

The zero-frequency probability $\lambda(h)$ is redistributed among the set of words never observed in the context h. Redistribution of the probability $\lambda(h)$ is performed proportionally to a more general distribution $P(w|h')$, where h' denotes a more general context.
Using the linear interpolation smoothing technique [24], [2], the conditional probability of a word w given a history h, $p(w|h)$, is estimated as follows:

$$P(w|h) = (1 - \lambda(h))\ fr(w|h) + \lambda(h)P(w|h') \tag{4}$$

where the same scheme applies to the lower-order distribution $P(w|h')$. The $\lambda(h)$ are such that $0 < \lambda(h) \leq 1$ if $N(h) > 0$, and $\lambda(h) = 1$ otherwize. The interpolation parameter is estimated using the expectation maximization algorithm [25].

When using classical linearly interpolated word n-gram models, typically the more general (n-l)-gram distribution is used to estimate the n-gram distribution. We recursively estimate the (n-k)-gram distribution using (n-k-l)-gram distribution until we reach the uniform distribution. Linear interpolation can be seen as a general smoothing approach that allows the combination of an arbitrary number of distribution or even language models. The most known and original version of the linear interpolated trigram (3-gram) language model [1] was not defined recursively as described in equation 4. It was presented as a linear combination of all order empirical distributions:

$$P(w_i|h) = P(w_i|w_{i-2}, w_{i-1}) =$$

$$\lambda_1(w_{i-2}, w_{i-1})\ fr(w_i|w_{i-2}, w_{i-1})\ +\ \lambda_2(w_{i-2}, w_{i-1})\ fr(w_i|w_{i-1}) + \tag{5}$$

$$\lambda_3(w_{i-2}, w_{i-1})\ fr(w_i)\ +\ \lambda_4(w_{i-2}, w_{i-1})$$

where $\lambda_i(h) \geq 0$ (i = 1, 2, 3, 4) and $\sum_i \lambda_i(h) = 1$.
Hence, using a recursive representation, the classical linearly interpolated word n-gram language models estimate the conditional probability of a word w given a history h, $P(w|h)$, according to the (n-l)-gram distribution:

$$P(w_i|h) = P(w_i|w_{i-n+1}^{i-1}) =$$

$$(1 - \lambda(w_{i-n+1}^{i-1}))fr(w_i|w_{i-n+1}^{i-1}) + \lambda(w_{i-n+1}^{i-1})P(w_i|w_{i-n+2}^{i-1}) \tag{6}$$

To better explore the power of word n-grams for frequent events and the predictive power of class n-grams for unseen or rare events, we propose the linearly interpolated hierarchical n-gram language models (LIHLMs). LIHLMs combine discounting and redistribution according to the linear interpolation smoothing technique [24], [2]. These models estimate the conditional probability of an n-gram (w_{i-n+1}^{i}), $P(w_i|w_{i-n+1}^{i-1})$ according to more general distribution extracted from the class hierarchy: we use the class of the most distant word w_{i-n+1} followed by the other words:

$$F(w_{i-n+1}), w_{i-n+2}^{i-1}$$

The function $F(x)$ represents the class (parent) of x within the hierarchical word tree, where x can be a class itself, or a single word, depending on its location in the tree (cf. Section V). Let F_i^j denote the jth parent of word w_i:

$$F_i^j = F^{(j)}(w_i)$$

The probability $P(w_i|w_{i-n+1}^{i-1})$ is estimated as follows:

$$P(w_i|w_{i-n+1}^{i-1}) =$$

$$(1 - \lambda(w_{i-n+1}^{i-1}))fr(w_i|w_{i-n+1}^{i-1}) + \lambda(w_{i-n+1}^{i-1})P(w_i|F_{i-n+1}^1, w_{i-n+2}^{i-1}) \tag{7}$$

where $P(w_i|F^j_{i-n+1}, w^{i-1}_{i-n+2})$ is recursively estimated according to more general distribution by going up one level at a time in the hierarchical word clustering tree:

$$P(w_i|F^j_{i-n+1}, w^{i-1}_{i-n+2}) = \begin{cases} (1-\lambda(F^j_{i-n+1}, w^{i-1}_{i-n+2}))fr(w_i|F^j_{i-n+1}, w^{i-1}_{i-n+2})+ \\ \lambda(F^j_{i-n+1}, w^{i-1}_{i-n+2})P(w_i|w^{i-1}_{i-n+2}) \\ \qquad\qquad\qquad\qquad \textbf{if } F^{j+1}_{i-n+1} \textbf{ is the root} \\ (1-\lambda(F^j_{i-n+1}, w^{i-1}_{i-n+2}))fr(w_i|F^j_{i-n+1}, w^{i-1}_{i-n+2})+ \\ \lambda(F^j_{i-n+1}, w^{i-1}_{i-n+2})P(w_i|F^{j+1}_{i-n+1}, w^{i-1}_{i-n+2}) \\ \qquad\qquad\qquad\qquad\qquad \textbf{otherwise} \end{cases} \tag{8}$$

As a result, the whole procedure provides a consistent way to compute the probability of any n-gram event by exploring the classes that are in the hierarchical word tree. If the parent of the class F^j_{i-n+1} (respectively, the word w_{i-n+1}) is the class root, the context becomes the last (n-2) words, which is similar to the traditional linearly interpolated word n-gram models as described in equation 6.

Based on this definition, the linearly interpolated hierarchical n-gram approach is a generalization of the classical linearly interpolated word n-gram language models: word n-gram language models can be seen as linearly interpolated hierarchical n-gram language models with a single level (leaves) in the hierarchical word tree.

4. Backoff hierarchical class n-gram language models

The backoff hierarchical class n-gram models are introduced in [9]. The goal of this section is to briefly describe this approach in order to compare its performance to the performance of the linearly interpolated hierarchical n-gram language models.

When using the backoff hierarchical class n-gram models, the conditional probability of an unseen n-gram $P(w_i|w^{i-1}_{i-n+1})$ is estimated according to a more specific context than the (n-l)-gram $P(w_i|w^{i-1}_{i-n+2})$ We use as context the class of the most distant word w_{i-n+1} followed by the other words:

$$F(w_{i-n+1}), w^{i-1}_{i-n+2}$$

We remind that *F(x)* denotes the class (parent) of *x* within the hierarchical word tree.

The probability $P(w_i|w^{i-1}_{i-n+1})$ is estimated as follows:

$$P(w_i|w_{i-n+1}^{i-1}) = \begin{cases} \tilde{P}(w_i|w_{i-n+1}^{i-1}) & \textbf{if } N(w_{i-n+1}^{i}) > 0 \\ \alpha'(w_{i-n+1}^{i-1})P(w_i|F_{i-n+1}^{1}, w_{i-n+2}^{i-1}) & \textbf{otherwise} \end{cases} \tag{9}$$

where F_i^j as stated before denotes the jth parent of word w_i, $N(.)$ denotes the frequency of the argument in the training data and $\alpha'(w_{i-n+1}^{i-1})$ is a normalizing constant guaranteeing that all probabilities sum to 1 [13]:

$$\alpha'(w_{i-n+1}^{i-1}) = \frac{1 - \sum_{w_i:N(w_{i-n+1}^{i})>0} P(w_i|w_{i-n+1}^{i-1})}{1 - \sum_{w_i:N(w_{i-n+1}^{i})>0} P(w_i|F(w_{i-n+1}), w_{i-n+2}^{i-1})} \tag{10}$$

The $\tilde{P}(.)$ in equation 9 is estimated as follows:

$$\tilde{P}(w_i|w_{i-n+1}^{i-1}) = d_{N(w_{i-n+1}^{i})} \frac{N(w_{i-n+1}^{i})}{N(w_{i-n+1}^{i-1})} \tag{11}$$

where the term $d_{N(.)}$ denotes the Turing's discounting coefficient [13].
If the event $F_{i-n+1}^{j}, w_{i-n+2}^{i}$ is not found in the training data ($N(F_{i-n+1}^{j}, w_{i-n+2}^{i}) = 0$), we recursively use a more general context by going up one level at a time in the hierarchical word clustering tree. This context is obtained by taking the parent of the first class in the hierarchy, followed by the $n-2$ last words:

$$P(w_i|F_{i-n+1}^{j}, w_{i-n+2}^{i-1}) = \begin{cases} \tilde{P}(w_i|F_{i-n+1}^{j}, w_{i-n+2}^{i-1}) & \textbf{if } N(F_{i-n+1}^{j}, w_{i-n+2}^{i}) > 0 \\ \alpha'(F_{i-n+1}^{j}, w_{i-n+2}^{i-1})P(w_i|w_{i-n+2}^{i-1}) & \textbf{if } F_{i-n+1}^{j+1} \textbf{ is the root} \\ \alpha'(F_{i-n+1}^{j}, w_{i-n+2}^{i-1})P(w_i|F_{i-n+1}^{j+1}, w_{i-n+2}^{i-1}) & \textbf{otherwise} \end{cases} \tag{12}$$

where the normalizing constant $\alpha'(F_{i-n+1}^{j}, w_{i-n+2}^{i-1})$ is computed as follows to guarantee that all probabilities sum to 1:

$$\alpha'(F_{i-n+1}^{j}, w_{i-n+2}^{i-1}) = \begin{cases} \dfrac{1-\sum_{w_i:N(F_{i-n+1}^{j}, w_{i-n+2}^{i})>0} P(w_i|F_{i-n+1}^{j}, w_{i-n+2}^{i-1})}{1-\sum_{w_i:N(F_{i-n+1}^{j}, w_{i-n+2}^{i})>0} P(w_i|w_{i-n+2}^{i-1})} & \textbf{if } F_{i-n+1}^{j+1} \textbf{ is the root} \\ \dfrac{1-\sum_{w_i:N(F_{i-n+1}^{j}, w_{i-n+2}^{i})>0} P(w_i|F_{i-n+1}^{j}, w_{i-n+2}^{i-1})}{1-\sum_{w_i:N(F_{i-n+1}^{j}, w_{i-n+2}^{i})>0} P(w_i|F_{i-n+1}^{j+1}, w_{i-n+2}^{i-1})} & \textbf{otherwise} \end{cases} \quad (13)$$

The procedure provides a consistent way to compute the probability of rare or unseen n-grams by backing-off along the classes that are defined in the hierarchical word tree. If the parent of the class F_{i-n+1}^{j} (respectively, the word w_{i-n+1}) is the class root, the context becomes the last $n - 2$ words, which is similar to the traditional back-off word n-gram model [13]. Word n-gram language models are the backoff hierarchical class n-gram language models with a single level in the hierarchical word tree.

5. Hierarchical word clustering algorithm

The hierarchical approaches we propose relies on the design of a classifier that allows finding a parent (class) for a word w. It is important to note that the two hierarchical n-gram languages describes in the two previous sections are able to integrate any classification approach. A better classifier will lead to a more accurate hierarchical model. The Maximum Mutual Information (MMI) clustering algorithm proposed by P. Brown *et al.* in [26] and by F. Jelinek in [1] has been widely adopted. Using the MMI approach, the computation required to obtain a language model with C classes using a vocabulary of V words is in the order of V^3. A greedy merge method is also used, based on the MMI theory, and requires an order of V^2C operations. Several iterations of the algorithm can be performed to improve performance. However, when using large vocabularies, this becomes quickly intractable given the computational complexity [27]. On the other hand, the minimum discriminative information (MDI) clustering approach proposed by S. Bai *et al.* gives similar results as the MMI method, while dramatically reducing the computation [27], as it only involves computing less than V^2 logarithms; for comparison results between MDI and MMI approaches, readers may refer to [27]. Consequently, in our approach we adopted the clustering technique of S. Bai *et al.*, which is based on minimum discriminative information.
The hierarchical word clustering algorithm proceeds in a top-down manner to cluster a vocabulary word set V, and is controlled by two parameters: (1) the maximum number of descendant nodes (clusters) C allowed at each node, (2) the minimum number of words K in one class O_c: $(N(O_c) \geq K)$. In our case, K is set to 2. Starting at the root node, which contains a single cluster representing the whole vocabulary, we compute the centroid o_i, of the entire space (word set). An initial codebook is then built by assigning the C closest words to o_i, into C clusters, which define the immediate child nodes of the root node [9]. The

process is continued recursively on each descendant node to grow the tree. The algorithm stops when a predefined number of levels (depth) is reached or when the number of proposed clusters for one node O_c is equal to 1 [10]. Each word in the vocabulary constitutes a leaf in the tree, words are clustered into classes, and classes are recursively clustered into more general sets of classes, until the root. At the top of the tree, the root node is a class containing all the words in the vocabulary. A summary of the minimum discriminative information methods is presented in the next section, followed by a detailed description of the word clustering algorithm.

A. Minimum Discriminative Information

The left and right contexts are used to cluster a word set, meaning that words occurring frequently in similar contexts should be assigned to the same class. The contextual information of a word w, $p_d\{w\}$, is estimated by the probability of w given its d left and right neighboring words. Given a set of V words, in the case of $d = 1$, we have:

$$p_1\{w\} = \{p_1 l\{w\}, p_1 r\{w\}\} \tag{14}$$

The terms $p_1 l\{w\}$ and $p_1 r\{w\}$ denote respectively the left-bigram and right-bigram contextual information of word w, given a vocabulary of V words $\{w_v\}_{v=1}^{V}$:

$$p_1 l\{w\} = \{pl(w_1|w), \ldots pl(w_V|w)\} \tag{15}$$

and

$$p_1 r\{w\} = \{pr(w_1|w), \ldots pr(w_V|w)\} \tag{16}$$

The clustering algorithm is based on two principles: (1) words with similar contexts are merged into the same cluster; (2) a word cluster is built according to the cluster of its neighboring words (contextual information). The contextual information of word w, $p\{w\}$, is represented by the probability of w given its right and left context bigrams. The problem is then to define the similarity of two words in terms of their contextual information. To define the similarity of two words w_1 and w_2 in terms of their contextual information, we use the Kullback-Leibler distortion measure $D(w_1, w_2\}$ [6]:

$$\begin{aligned} D(w_1, w_2) &= \sum_{v=1}^{V} pl(w_v|w_1)\ log \frac{pl(w_v|w_1)}{pl(w_v|w_2)} \\ &+ \sum_{v=1}^{V} pr(w_v|w_1)\ log \frac{pr(w_v|w_1)}{pr(w_v|w_2)} \end{aligned} \tag{17}$$

which is also known as relative entropy. The objective of partitioning the vocabulary is to find a set of centroids $\{o_c\}$ for clusters $\{O_c\}$, $c = 1, \ldots C$ that leads to the minimum global discriminative information:

$$
\begin{aligned}
GDI &= \sum_{c=1}^{C} \sum_{i \in O_c} D(w_i, o_c) \\
&= \sum_{i=1}^{V} \sum_{v=1}^{V} pl(w_v|w_i)\ \ log\ pl(w_v|w_i) \\
&+ \sum_{i=1}^{V} \sum_{v=1}^{V} pr(w_v|w_i)\ \ log\ pr(w_v|w_i) \\
&- \sum_{c=1}^{C} \sum_{i \in O_c} \sum_{v=1}^{V} pl(w_v|w_i)\ \ log\ pl(w_v|o_c) \\
&- \sum_{c=1}^{C} \sum_{i \in O_c} \sum_{v=1}^{V} pr(w_v|w_i)\ \ log\ pr(w_v|o_c) \\
&= B(w) - R(w).
\end{aligned} \tag{18}
$$

The term $B(w)$ is a constant independent of the partitioning. Hence, $R(w)$ is maximized when the global discriminative information is minimized. Each cluster O_c is represented by a centroid o_c. According to equation 14, $p_1\{w\}$ is defined as a vector of dimension $2 \bullet V$, whose first V components are based on the left-context bigrams, and last V components are based on the last V right-context bigrams. For simplicity, let us drop the left/right indices, and represent $p_1\{w\}$ as follows:

$$p_1\{w\} = \{p(k|w),\ k = 1, \ldots 2V\} \tag{19}$$

Given equation 19, the centroid of the class $O_c = \{wi, i = 1 \ldots v_c\}$ is estimated as follows [28], [29]:

$$o_c = \{o(k|o_c),\ k = 1, \ldots 2V\}$$

where $o(k|o_c)$ is approximated by [27]:

$$o(k|o_c) = \frac{1}{v_c} \sum_{i=1}^{v_c} p(k|w_i) \tag{20}$$

B. Word Clustering Algorithm

We present in this section how to classify a word set into C classes, under the constraint that at least K words should appear in each class O_c. Our approach is based on the **K**-means clustering technique [30], [31], where we define centroids and distances specific to words.

We start at the root note by computing the centroid o_i, of the entire space (word set). An initial codebook is then built by assigning the C closest words to o_i, into C clusters. The centroids of each cluster are then re-computed, and the process is iterated until the average distortion GDI converges. This process is then recursively applied. The pseudo-code of the algorithm is as follows:

- step 1: start with an initial codebook;
- step 2: for each w_i, $i = 1, \ldots V$,

- find the closest class O to w_i using Kullback-Leibler distortion measure and add w_i to it [19].
- step 3: update the codebook using the minimum distance or nearest neighbor rule [9], [28];
- step 4: **if** *GDI* > *t* **then** go to step 2
    - where *t* is an experimentally tuned threshold controlling the convergence of the process; the current set of clusters may leads to the minimum global discriminative information (cf. equation 18).
- step 5: **if** $\exists\ O_c\ /\ N(O_c) < K$ **then** $(C \leftarrow C - 1)$ and go to 1, **otherwise** stop.

Step 5 is necessary since it is used to control the number of words in a class: if there are too few words in a class *($N(O_C) < K$)*, that class is merged with another one. In practice, only a few iterations of the algorithm are required to achieve fairly good results [27]. Since each word is characterized by the contextual statistical vector $p_d\{w\}$, the centroid of each class is easily found using equation 20. The advantage of this algorithm is its simplicity in finding centroids; the cost of merging words or classes becomes less expensive. Once C classes have been defined, the algorithm is recursively applied within each class to grow the tree.

6. Corpus

Experiments are performed on the Wall Street Journal 94-96 text corpus. This database is divided into training, development and test sets. For language modeling purposes, the training set contains 56 million words, and the test set contains approximately 6 million words. A development set of 5 million words is also used to tune the different parameters of the model, including the depth of the clustering tree. Two vocabulary sizes are used: a first one containing 5,000 words *(5K)* and a second one including 20,000 words *(20K)*. Note that the *5K* vocabulary leads to about 2% of out-of-vocabulary words on the test data, and in that regard differs substantially from the official WSJ *5K* lexicon that was designed for a closed-set evaluation (no OOV words). The *20K* vocabulary has a 1.1% out-of-vocabulary rate on the test data. In our experiments, we use *open* vocabulary where the unknown word is part of the model [1].

7. Experiments

Our objective is to show that the use of word class hierarchy in language modeling better handle the likelihood estimation of n-gram events. We show in this section the performance of linearly interpolated hierarchical n-gram language models as well as the performance of the backoff hierarchical class n-gram language models. We compare the performance of these two techniques to the performance of commonly used methods such as the linearly interpolated n-gram language models (LILMs) and the backoff n-gram language models.

Performance is evaluated in terms of test perplexity and word error rate (WER) using Bell Labs' speech recognizer [32]. Both HCLMs and the backoff word n-gram LMs use the backing-off smoothing technique to estimate the likelihood of unseen events [13]. Also, both LIHLMs and LILMs combine discounting and redistribution according to the linear interpolation smoothing technique [24], [2].

As a reminder, HCLMs and LIHLMs with a number of levels in the class hierarchy equal to 0 are in fact the classical backoff word n-gram LMs and LILMs respectively. Hence, we believe that it is fair to consider both backoff word n-gram LMs and LILMs as baselines for comparison purpose. We also report in this section comparison results with word class n-gram (n-class) LMs as well as a linear interpolation between word n-gram and n-class LMs [1]. In addition, we investigate how the number of levels defined in the class hierarchy impacts the performance of our approach.

A. Perplexity Experiments

Perplexity is typically used to measure the performance of language models. It is therefore interesting to look at the perplexity obtained by the two hierarchical n-gram models for different number of levels in the hierarchy. The number of levels in the hierarchy L represents the depth of the word class tree. The maximum number of direct descendant of a class is fixed to $C = 6$ (cf. section 5). Experiments carried out with different values of C led to similar results [9]. The *maximum* number of classes generated when building the class tree is $\sum_{l=1}^{L} C^l$: e.g., for a word class tree of two levels, the root node is split into a maximum of C classes and each class is split into C other classes, leading to a maximum of C^2 clusters at the second level. This number is optimized at each level of the hierarchy by the classification algorithm in order to converge to an optimum (cf. section 5-B).

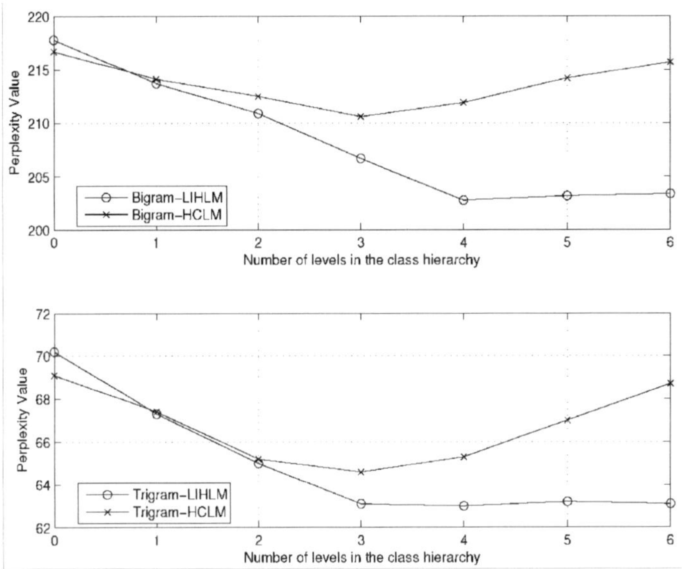

Figure 1. Trigram and bigram test perplexity on WSJ using 5K vocabulary with different number of levels in the class hierarchy

Figure 1 presents the performance of LIHLMs, HCLMs, LILMs and backoff word n-gram LMs when the 5K vocabulary is used. We remind that LILMs and backoff word n-gram LMs are respectively the LIHLMs and HCLMs with a number of levels in the class hierarchy equal to 0. Experimental results show that we do not need a large number of levels in the class hierarchy to improve upon the baseline: three or four levels are enough to achieve a good performance compare to baseline models. When using the *5K* vocabulary, trigram LIHLM improves the baseline backoff word trigram language model by 10% (63.0 vs. 69.1). However, a very slight improvement of 3% in terms of perplexity is obtained by the trigram LIHLM when compared to trigram HCLM (63.0 vs. 64.6). A similar behavior is obtained for bigram events: a 6% improvement of the test perplexity on the whole test set is observed

(97.2 for bigram LIHLM vs. 103.0 for backoff word bigram model). A very small improvement of 3% is also obtained by the bigram LIHLM when compared to bigram HCLM (97.2 vs. 100.3).

Performance in terms of perplexity when using the *20K* vocabulary is presented in Figure 2. Results in Figure 2 again show the effectiveness of the LIHLMs in improving the perplexity value of the backoff word n-gram LMs: 7% improvement for bigrams (202.8 vs. 216.7) and 10% improvement for trigrams (127.5 vs. 140.8). The LIHLMs also effectively improves the performance of HCLMs by 4% for both bigrams (202.8 vs. 210.6) and trigrams (127.5 vs. 132.2).

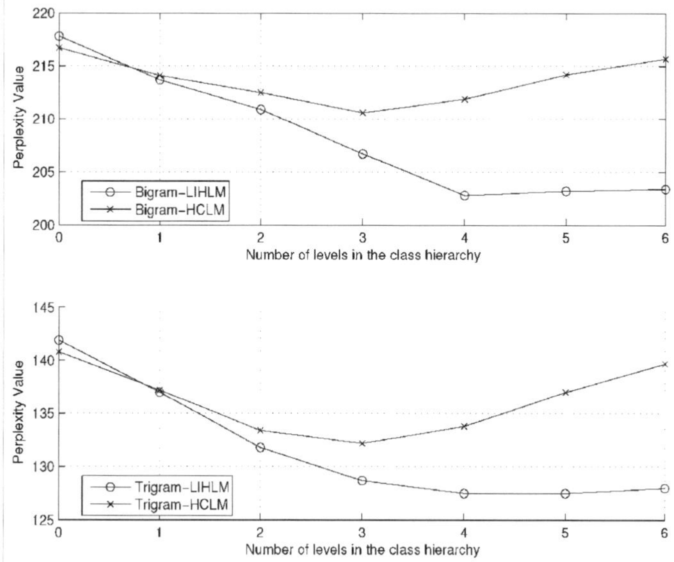

Figure 2. Trigram and bigram test perplexity on WSJ using 20K vocabulary with different number of levels in the class hierarchy

For both the *5K* and *20K* vocabularies, we notice that backoff word n-gram LMs are doing slightly better that classic linearly interpolated LMs. We believe that the difference is statistically insignificant, which will not allow us to draw any conclusion. Another important point to mention is that in both the *5K* and *20K* vocabularies, the perplexity value of the HCLMs decreased for the first three levels in the class hierarchy and then it starts to increase. This observation is not true for the LIHLMs, where the perplexity value achieves its optimum with four levels in the class hierarchy and doesn't increase afterward. One may conclude that, compared to HCLMs, LIHLMs are less sensitive to the depth of the tree (number of levels in the class hierarchy).

Results reported in Figure 1 and Figure 2 are computed on the test data. We observed the same behavior on the development set: with (C = 6, the best performance in terms of perplexity on the entire development set is obtained with a maximum level in the class hierarchy set to L = 3. On 20K vocabulary, trigram perplexity of HCLMs decreased from 142.4 for L = 0 (i.e., baseline backoff word n-gram LMs) to 134.6 for L = 3 and then it starts to increase. The same behavior is observed on the 5K vocabulary: trigram perplexity of HCLMs decreased from 71.0 for L = 0 to 66.7 for L = 3 and then starts to increase.

B. Comparison with Word Class n-gram Language Models

As stated in the introduction, one of the approaches that can overcome the probability estimation problem of unseen n-grams event is the class n-gram language models [1], [8]. For sparse data, class n-gram language models usually generalize better on unseen n-grams than standard word-based language models. Nevertheless, for large training corpus, word n-gram LMs are still better in capturing collocational relations between words. To confirm this point, we built word class n-gram (n-class) LMs and compared their performance to the baseline n-gram models as well as the hierarchical approaches. We also investigate a comparison results with linear interpolation of word n-gram and n-class LMs. In the backoff n-class models, the conditional probability of the n-gram $w_{i-n+1}^{i} = w_{i-n+1}, \ldots w_i$, is estimated as follows:

$$P(w_i|w_{i-n+1}^{i-1}) = P(w_i|F(w_{i-n+1}), \ldots F(w_{i-1})) \quad (21)$$

where the function $F(x)$ represents the class of x. As stated by J. Goodman in [33], equation 21 showed to give stronger class model than estimating the conditional probability as follows:

$$P(w_i|w_{i-n+1}^{i-1}) = P(w_i|F(w_i)) \;\; P(F(w_i)|F(w_{i-n+1}), \ldots F(w_{i-1})) \quad (22)$$

Notice that the hierarchical class n-gram LMs is able to integrate any classification approach for building the class hierarchy. In order to make a fair comparison between the proposed hierarchical approach and the backoff n-class LMs, we *should* use the same classification technique. Hence, to build the class set, we use the MDI approach (cf. section 5-B) that assigns each word to a unique class. We initialize the MDI classifier with a maximum number of classes equal to 1200 assuming that one class should contains at least 5 words. We present in table I, the perplexity values obtained by the different LMs on the entire test set. The hierarchical approach uses a maximum number of direct descendant of a class fixed to C = 6 and a number of levels in the hierarchy set to L = 3; both values are tuned on the development set (cf. section 7- A).

	5K-WSJ	**20K-WSJ**
Bigram LMs		
Class	115.2	228.9
Word (Baseline)	103.0	216.7
LI (Word + Class)	102.2	215.8
HCLM	100.3	210.6
LIHLM	97.2	202.8
Trigram LMs		
Class	76.5	154.0
Word (Baseline)	69.1	140.8
LI (Word + Class)	68.2	138.6
HCLM	64.6	132.2
LIHLM	63.0	127.5

Table 1. Perplexity on WSJ of world class n-gram LMs (class), word n-gram LMs (word), linear interpolation of word n-gram and n-class LMS (LI), hierarchical class n-gram LMS (HCLM), and linearly interpolated hierarchical n-gram LMs (LIHLM)

As expected, the perplexity of the baseline word n-gram LMs is better than the class word n-gram LMs: 216.7 vs. 228.9 for the bigram model and 140.8 vs. 154.0 for the trigram model with the 20K vocabulary (similar behavior was observed with the 5K vocabulary). Also, compared to the baseline word n-gram LMs, we notice that a linear interpolation of word n-gram LMs and n-class LMs doesn't led to a considerable improvement (215.8 vs. 216.7 for bigram and 138.6 vs. 140.8 for trigram on 20K vocabulary). On both bigram and trigram, results show that the proposed hierarchical LMs outperform the other approaches.

C. Speech Recognition Experiments

For ASR experiments, the word error rate (WER) on the 5K WSJ has been evaluated on the 330 sentences of the si_et_05 evaluation set. The 333 sentences of the si_et_20 evaluation set were used for the 20K ASR experiment. We used tied-state triphone acoustic models built on the WSJ SI-84 database. The speech recognition experiments were performed using the Bell Labs ASR system [32]. The ASR system is based on a Viterbi algorithm, where at each node in the search the acoustic score is interpolated with the language modeling score. Hence, we do not need to modify the decoder structure in order to integrate LIHLMs and HCLMs: we only replaced the language modeling score, initially estimated using the trigram language model, with the score estimated using LIHLMs and HCLMs respectively. Once the language model is integrated to the ASR system, the pruning parameters are re-computed to boost its accuracy. We gave equivalent setting to the pruning parameters to make sure that the decoder search doesn't favor one model over another.

Recall that the *5K* vocabulary differs from the official WSJ *5K* lexicon which was designed for a closed-set evaluation. Results presented in Table II show that there is no significant improvement in performance between the baseline backoff bigram model, bigram HCLM, and bigram LIHLM. These results can be explained by the small number of unseen bigrams in this experimental setup and therefore the lack of room for any significant improvement: unseen bigrams constitute 4% and 8% of the total bigrams for the *5K* and *20K* vocabularies respectively. However, when the trigram model is used, the number of unseen events increases to 27% for the *5K* vocabulary and to 34% for the 20K vocabulary, leading to 12% and 10% reduction of the WER, respectively. We also note that HCLMs and LIHLMs have the same ASR performance. Compared to the recognizer using linear interpolation between word and class trigram model, the use of hierarchical approaches improves performance by 6% (11.1% vs. 12.0%) and by 8% (6.7% vs. 7.3%) relative for WSJ-20K and WSJ-5K respectively.

	5K		20K	
	bigram	trigram	bigram	trigram
Baseline	9.3%	7.6%	14.2%	12.4%
LI (word + class)	9.2%	7.3%	14.1%	12.0%
HCLM	9.0%	6.7%	13.9%	11.2%
LIHLM	9.0%	6.7%	13.8%	11.1%

Table 2. **WER** on *5K* and *20K* vocabularies using word n-gram (baseline), linear interpolation between word and class n-gram (LI), hierarchical class n-gram (HCLM), and linearly interpolated hierarchical n-gram LMS (LIHLM) respectively

We think that the effectiveness of our approach may also depend on the quality of the acoustic model and the domain on which the recognizer is employed. For instance, if the language model has very low perplexity on unseen events and if the acoustic model is able to well discriminate words under these unseen context, then a big portion of the errors made by the recognizer are more likely to be accumulated on frequent context. The opposite is also true: if the language model has low perplexity on frequent events and the acoustic model is able to discriminate words under these frequent events, then errors are more likely to be accumulated on low acoustic certainty. Hence, similarly to [9], [10], we would like to raise the fact that we may not need to improve the perplexity on the whole data in order to reduce the word error rate of ASR systems. It may be sufficient to reduce the perplexity of unseen events rather than the frequently seen events, since ASR systems are more sensitive to unseen events.

8. Conclusion

We have investigated a new language modeling approach called linearly interpolated *n*-gram language models. We showed in this chapter the effectiveness of this approach to estimate the likelihood of *n*-gram events: the linearly interpolated *n*-gram language models outperform the performance of both linearly interpolated *n*-gram language models and backoff *n*-gram language models in terms of perplexity and also in terms word error rate when intergrated into a speech recognizer engine. Compared to traditional backoff and linearly interpolated LMs, the originality of this approach is in the use of a class hierarchy that leads to a better estimation of the likelihood of *n*-gram events. Experiments on the WSJ database show that the linearly interpolated *n*-gram language models improve the test perplexity over the standard language modeling approaches: 7% improvement when estimating the likelihood of bigram events, and 10% improvement when estimating the likelihood of trigram events.

Speech recognition results show to be sensitive to the number of unseen events: up to 12% reduction of the WER is obtained when using the linearly interpolated hierarchical approach, due to the large number of unseen events in the ASR test set. The magnitude of the WER reduction is larger than what we would have expected given the observed reduction of the language model perplexity; this leads us to an interesting assumption that the reduction of unseen event perplexity is more effective for improving ASR accuracy than the perplexity associated with seen events. The probability model for frequently seen events may already be appropriate for the ASR system so that improving the likelihood of such events does not correct any additional ASR errors (although the total perplexity may decrease.) Thus, it may be that similar reductions of the perplexity are not equivalent in terms of WER improvement. The improvement in word accuracy also depends on the errors the recognizer makes: if the acoustic model alone is able to discriminate words under unseen linguistic contexts, then improving the LM probability for those events may not improve the overall WER.

Compared to hierarchical class *n*-gram LMs, we observed that the new hierarchical approach is not sensitive to the depth of the hierarchy. As future work, we may explore this approach with a more accurate technique in building the class word hierarchy.

9. References

F. Jelinek, Self-organized language modeling for speech recognition, *Readings in Speech Recognition, A. Waibel and K-F. Lee editors,* pp. 450-506, Morgan Kaufmann, San Mateo, Calif., 1990. [1]

Renato DeMori, Ed., *Spoken Dialogues with Computers,* Academic Press, 1998. [2]

V. Gupta, M. Lenning, and P. Mermelstein, A language model for very large vocabulary speech recognition, *Computer Speech and Language,* pp. 331-344, 1992. [3]

J. Bellegarda, Exploiting latent semantic information in statistical language modeling, *Proceedings of the IEEE,* vol. 88, no. 8, August 2000. [4]

R. Rosenfeld, Two decades of statistical language modeling: Where do we go from here?, *Proceedings of the IEEE,* vol. 88, no. 8, 2000. [5]

T.M. Cover and J.A. Thomas, *Elements of Information Theory,* Wiley and Sons, 1991. [6]

Z. Bi, C. Faloutsos, and F. Korn, The 'DGX distribution for mining massive, skewed data, in *Conference on Knowledge Discovery and Data Mining,* 2001. [7]

B. Suhm and W. Waibel, Towards better language models for spontaneous speech, in *Proc. ICSLP-1994,* 1994. [8]

I. Zitouni, Backoff hierarchical class n-gram language models: Effectiveness to model unseen events in speech recognition, *Journal of Computer Speech and Language, Academic Press,* vol. 21, no. 1, pp. 88-104, 2007. [9]

I. Zitouni, O. Siohan, and C-H. Lee, Hierarchical class n-gram language models: Towards better estimation of unseen events in speech recognition, in *Proc. Eurospeech-2003,* Geneva, Switzerland, 2003. [10]

I. Zitouni, Q. Zhou, and Q.P. Li, A hierarchical approach for better estimation of unseen event likelihood in speech recognition, in *Proc. IEEE NLPKE-2003,* Beijing, China, 2003. [11]

I. Zitouni and H.J. Kuo, Effectiveness of the backoff hierarchical class n-gram language models to model unseen events in speech recognition, in *Proc. IEEE ASRU-2003,* St. Thomas, US Virgin Islands, 2003. [12]

S.M. Katz, Estimation of probabilities from sparse data for the language model component of a speech recognizer, *IEEE Transactions on Acoustic, Speech, and Signal Processing,* vol. 35, no. 3, 1987. [13]

J.W. Miller and F. Alleva, Evaluation of a language model using a clustered model backoff, in *Proc. ICSLP-1996,* 1996. [14]

C. Samuelsson and W. Reichl, A class-based language model for large-vocabulary speech recognition extracted from part-of-speech statistics, in *Proc. ICASSP-1999,* 1999. [15]

L. Bahl, P. Brown, P. de Souza, and R. Mercer, A tree-based statistical language model for natural language speech recognition, in *IEEE Transaction on Acoustics, Speech and Signal Processing,* July 1987, vol. 37, pp. 1001-1008. [16]

P.A. Heeman, Pos tags and decision trees for language modeling, in *Joint SIGDAT Conference on Empirical Methods in Natural Language Processing and Very Large Corpora,* College Park, Maryland, June 1999, pp. 129-137. [17]

L. Breiman, J. Friedman, R. Olshen, and C. Stone, *Classification and Regression Trees,* Wadsworth & Brooks, 1984. [18]

I. Zitouni, O. Siohan, H-K.J. Kuo, and C-H. Lee, Backoff hierarchical class n-gram language modelling for automatic speech recognition systems, in *Proc. ICSLP-2002,* Denver, USA, 2002. [19]

J.A. Bilmes and K. Kirchhoff, Factored language models and generalized parallel backoff, in *Proceeding of HLT/NAACL,* Canada, May 2003. [20]

P. Dupont and R. Rosenfeld, Lattice based language models, Tech. Rep. CMU-CS-97-173, Carnegie Mellon University, 1997. [21]

P. Xu and F. Jelinek, Random forests in language modeling, in *Conference on Empirical Methods in Natural Language Processing,* 2004. [22]

I.H. Witten and T.C. Bell, The zero-frequency problem: estimating the probabilities of novel events in adaptive text compression, *IEEE Transactions on Information Theory,* vol. 37, no. 4, pp. 1085-1094, 1991. [23]

F. Jelinek and R.L. Mercer, Interpolated estimation of markov source parameters from sparse data, in *Pattern Recognition in Practice,* Amsterdam, Holland, 1980, pp. 381-397. [24]

A.P. Dempster, N.M. Laird, and D.B. Rubin, Maximum likelihood from incomplete data via the em algorithm, *Journal of the Royal Statistical Society ser B,* vol. 39, pp. 1-38, 1977. [25]

P.P. Brown, V.J. DellaPietra, P.V. DeSouza, J.C. Lai, and R.L. Mercer, Class-based n-gram models of natural language, *Computational Linguistics,* vol. 18, no. 4, pp. 467-479, 1992. [26]

S. Bai, H. Li, Z. Lin, and B. Yuan, Building class-based language models with contextual statistics, in *Proc. ICASSP-1998,* 1998. [27]

H. Li, J.P Haton, J. Su, and Y. Gong, Speaker recognition with temporal transition models, in *Eurospeech-95,* Madrid, Spain, 1995. [28]

T.M. Cover and P.E. Hart, Nearest neighbor pattern classification, *IEEE Transaction on Information Theory,* vol. 13, no. 1, pp. 21-27, 1967. [29]

J. MacQueen, Some methods for classification and analysis of multi-variate observations, in *Proc. of the Fifth Berkeley Symp. on Math., Statistics and Probability, LeCam, L.M., and Neyman, J., (eds.), Berkeley: U. California Press, 281,* 1967. [30]

C. Darken and J. Moody, Fast adaptive k-means clustering: Some empirical results, in *Int. Joint Conf. on Neural Networks,* 1990, vol. 2, pp. 233-238. [31]

Q. Zhou and W. Chou, An approach to continuous speech recognition based on self-adjusting decoding graph, in *Proc. ICASSP-1997,* 1997, pp. 1779-1782. [32]

J. Goodman, A bit of progress in language modeling, *Computer Speech and Language,* pp. 403-434, October 2001. [33]

18

A Factored Language Model for Prosody Dependent Speech Recognition

Ken Chen, Mark A. Hasegawa-Johnson and Jennifer S. Cole
University of Illinois at Urbana-Champaign
U.S.A.

1. Introduction

Prosody refers to the suprasegmental features of natural speech (such as rhythm and intonation) that are used to convey linguistic and paralinguistic information (such as emphasis, intention, attitude, and emotion). Humans listening to natural prosody, as opposed to monotone or foreign prosody, are able to understand the content with lower cognitive load and higher accuracy (Hahn, 1999). In automatic speech understanding systems, prosody has been previously used to disambiguate syntactically distinct sentences with identical phoneme strings (Price et al., 1991), infer punctuation of a recognized text (Kim & Woodland, 2001), segment speech into sentences and topics (Shriberg et al., 2000), recognize the dialog act labels (Taylor et al., 1997), and detect speech disfluencies (Nakatani and Hirschberg, 1994). None of these applications use prosody for the purpose of improving word recognition (i.e., the word recognition module in these applications does not utilize any prosody information). Chen et al. (Chen et al., 2003) proposed a prosody dependent speech recognizer that uses prosody for the purpose of improving word recognition accuracy. In their approach, the task of speech recognition is to find the sequence of word labels $W=(w_1,\ldots,w_M)$ that maximizes the recognition probability:

$$\begin{aligned}[\hat{W}] &= \arg\max p(O \mid W,P)p(W,P) \\ &= \arg\max p(O \mid Q,H)p(Q,H \mid W,P)p(W,P),\end{aligned} \tag{1}$$

where $P=(p_1,\ldots,p_M)$ is a sequence of prosody labels, one associated with each word, $O=(o_1,\ldots,o_T)$ is a sequence of observed acoustic feature vectors, $Q=(q_1,\ldots,q_L)$ is a sequence of sub-word units, typically allophones dependent on phonetic context, and $H=(h_1,\ldots,h_L)$ is a sequence of discrete ``hidden mode'' vectors describing the prosodic states of each allophone. The combination $[w_m,p_m]$ is called a prosody-dependent word label, the combination $[q_l,h_l]$ is called a prosody-dependent allophone label, $p(O \mid Q,H)$ is a prosody-dependent acoustic model, $p(Q,H \mid W,P)$ is a prosody-dependent pronunciation model, and $p(W,P)$ is a prosody-dependent language model. In this framework, word and prosody are conditioned on each other and are recognized at the same time. The system described in equation (1) has the advantage that both the acoustic model and the language model can be potentially improved through their dependence on prosody.

In (Chen et al. 2006), the prosody variable p_m takes 8 possible values composed by 2 discrete prosodic variables: a variable a that marks a word as either ``a'' (pitch-accented) or ``u'' (pitch-unaccented), and a variable b that marks a word as ``i,m,f,o'' (phrase-initial, phrase-medial, phrase-final, one-word phrase) according to its position in an intonational phrase. Thus, in this scheme, a prosody-dependent word transcription may contain prosody-dependent word tokens of the form $w_{ab}$. For example, the sentence ``well, what's next,'' uttered as two intonational phrases with two accented words, might be transcribed as ``well$_{ao}$ what's$_{ui}$ next$_{af}$.''

A prosody dependent language model $p(W,P)$ that models the joint probability distribution of concurrent word and prosody sequences, is different from a standard prosody independent language model $p(W)$ in the sense that not only word context but also prosody context affect the prediction of the next possible word and its prosody. This model is useful in at least two respects. First, it can be used to effectively reduce the search space of possible word hypotheses. (Kompe, 1997) have shown that a prosody dependent language model can be used to speed up the word recognition process without sacrificing accuracy. Second, it is potentially useful in improving word recognition accuracy. Waibel (Waibel, 1988) reports that prosodic knowledge sources, when added to a phonetic speaker-independent word hypothesizer, are able to reduce the average rank of the correct word hypothesis by a factor of 3. Arnfield (Arnfield, 1994) gives an example in his dissertation: the words ``witch'' and ``which'', having identical acoustic observations, can be distinguished prosodically (``witch'' is more likely to be accented than is ``which'' because it is a content word while ``which'' is a function word). The word to be predicted is more likely to be ``witch'' instead of ``which'' if an accent is predicted from the current word-prosody context. In the results reported by (Chen et al., 2006), a prosody dependent language model can significantly improve word recognition accuracy over a prosody independent language model, given the same acoustic model.

N-gram models can be conveniently used for prosody dependent language modeling. The n-gram probabilities are estimated from their maximum likelihood estimators (the relative frequency count of the n-grams). For example, the bigram probability $p(w_j,p_j \mid w_i,p_i)$ (the probability of observing token $[w_j,p_j]$ given token $[w_i,p_i]$) can be estimated using the following equation:

$$p(w_j,p_j \mid w_i,p_i)=\frac{n(w_j,p_j,w_i,p_i)}{n(w_i,p_i)}, \tag{2}$$

where $n(\cdot)$ is the number of the n-grams observed in the training set. Equation (2) treats each prosody dependent word token $[w_j,p_j]$ as a distinct unit, resulting in a recognizer that has $|p|$ times larger vocabulary size than does a standard prosody independent recognizer (where $|p|$ is the number of options for tag p_i). If any word-prosody combination can occur in English, the number of prosody dependent n-grams is equal to $|p|^n$ times the number of prosody independent n-grams. In practice, the number of possible prosody dependent n-grams increases by far less than $|p|^n$ times, because a considerable amount of prosody dependent n-grams never occur in natural English. Nevertheless, the number of possible prosody dependent n-grams still greatly increases as $|p|$ increases due to the prosody variation induced by high level contextual information and by different speaking styles. Hence, robust estimation of prosody dependent language modeling using equation (2) requires an increasingly large amount of prosodically labeled data which are normally expensive to acquire. When the size of training text is limited, increasing $|p|$ decreases the trainability of the n-gram models and reduces the consistency between the training and test text: the accuracy of the estimated probability mass functions (PMFs) decreases due to the prosody induced data sparseness and the number of possible unseen prosody dependent n-grams increases.

In this chapter, we propose to improve the robustness of prosody dependent language modeling by utilizing the dependence between prosody and syntax. There is evidence indicating that syntax is a strong conditioning factor for prosody. For example, conjunctions (e.g., ``but",``so") occur more frequently at phrase initial positions than at phrase medial or final positions in fluent speech; content words (e.g., nouns) have much higher probability of being accented than function words (e.g., prepositions, articles). In a corpus based study, Arnfield (Arnfield, 1994) proved empirically that although differing prosodies are possible for a fixed syntax, the syntax of an utterance can be used to generate an underlying ``baseline" prosody regardless of actual words, semantics or context. The bigram models developed by Arnfield were able to predict prosody from parts-of-speech with a high accuracy (91% for stress presence prediction). The experiments conducted by (Hirschberg, 1993) and (Chen et al., 2004) also indicate that parts-of-speech can predict the presence of pitch accent with accuracies of around 82%-85% on the Radio New Corpus.

This chapter is organized as following: Section 2 reviews previous research on factored language models and provides a Bayesian network view of spoken language that further explains our motivation, Section 3 describes our methods for creating prosody dependent factored language models, Section 4 reports our experiments on the Radio News Corpus and discusses results, and conclusions are given in Section 5.

2.Background: Factored Language Models

2.1 Previous work

The objective of a statistical language model is to accurately predict the next word w_j from current history $h_j = [w_0, \dots w_{j-1}]$. In the past two decades, enormous efforts have been reported in the literature to find the factors in h_j that best predict w_j (Rosenfeld, 2000) including the use of syntactic and semantic information extracted from h_j (Khudanpur & Wu, 2000; Bellegarda, 2000). Language modeling for speech recognition has been shown to be a difficult task due to the many sources of variability existing in spoken language including disfluency, sentence fragments, dialect, and stylistic and colloquial language use. The existence of these intrinsic properties of spoken language (which are quit different from written language) have forced researchers to expand the space h_j to include additional streams of knowledge.

One example is the system proposed by Heeman and Allen (Heeman and Allen, 1999), in which the word sequences and parts-of-speech (POS) sequences are modeled jointly and recognized simultaneously in a unified framework:

$$\begin{aligned}[\tilde{W}, \tilde{S}] &= \arg\max p(O \mid W, S) p(W, S) \\ &\approx \arg\max p(O \mid W) p(W, S).\end{aligned} \quad (3)$$

The language model $p(w_j, s_j | W_{0,j-1}, S_{0,j-1})$ can be factored into two component language models, which makes it possible to utilize the syntactic knowledge encoded in the joint history of word and POS to improve the predictability of the next word (and its POS):

$$\begin{aligned} & p(w_j, s_j | W_{0,j-1}, S_{0,j-1}) \\ & = p(w_j | W_{0,j-1}, S_{0,j-1}, s_j) p(s_j | W_{0,j-1}, S_{0,j-1}), \end{aligned} \tag{4}$$

where s_j is the POS of w_j, $W_{0,j-1}$ is the word history up to w_{j-1}, and $S_{0,j-1}$ is the POS history up to s_{j-1}. Heeman used decision trees to cluster the word and POS history into equivalence classes. This multi-stream POS-based language model $p(W,S)$ achieved a 7% reduction of word perplexity over the single stream word-based n-gram language model $p(W)$ and improved the prediction of word and POS simultaneously. Heeman further extended this multi-stream language modeling frame work to include more knowledge sources (e.g., intonational phrase boundaries, speech repairs, discourse markers) and found that the inter-dependence among these knowledge sources can further improve the quality of the language model for the modeling of conversational spoken language.

In a different context, Kirchhoff (Kirchhoff et al., 2003) applied the idea of multi-stream language modeling to handle the morphological complexity in Arabic text, where she modeled multiple streams of word features such as the morphological class (m_i), patterns (p_i) and roots (r_i) in place of the single stream of words. For example, represent $w_i = (r_i, p_i, m_i)$,

$$\begin{aligned} & p(w_i | w_{i-1}, w_{i-2}) \\ & = p(r_i, p_i, m_i | r_{i-1}, p_{i-1}, m_{i-1}, r_{i-2}, p_{i-2}, m_{i-2}) \\ & = p(r_i | p_i, m_i, r_{i-1}, p_{i-1}, m_{i-1}, r_{i-2}, p_{i-2}, m_{i-2}) \\ & \quad p(p_i | m_i, r_{i-1}, p_{i-1}, m_{i-1}, r_{i-2}, p_{i-2}, m_{i-2}) \\ & \quad p(m_i | r_{i-1}, p_{i-1}, m_{i-1}, r_{i-2}, p_{i-2}, m_{i-2}). \end{aligned} \tag{5}$$

The three factored probability functions in equation (5) can be modeled individually using n-grams or other modeling techniques. Since each word feature has much smaller cardinality than the word vocabulary, and is less fractured by the nuances of morphological variation, this factored language model can effectively help reduce the data sparseness in dialectal Arabic.

The language models we are proposing can be viewed as an extension to these previous works. Rather than modeling POS explicitly in the language model, we propose to model prosody explicitly while using POS implicitly to reduce the data sparseness induced by prosody. We argue that this method of modeling prosody makes the acoustic models and language models fuse more tightly through their interaction with prosody and brings the potential of improving both word recognition and prosody recognition performance.

2.2 A Bayesian Network View for Spoken Language

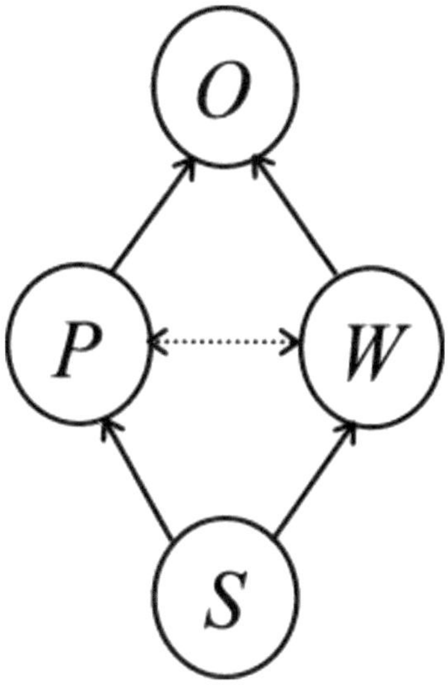

Figure 1. A Bayesian network representing the complex relationship among the acoustic observation sequence (O), word sequence (W), prosody sequence (P) and syntax sequence (S) of an utterance.

To better understand our reasoning behind the idea of prosody dependent speech recognition, we plot in Fig. 1 the complex relationship among the sequences of acoustic observations O, words W, prosody P and syntax S for an arbitrary utterance in terms of a Bayesian Network. The dependence of O over P is well defined because it is well known that prosody affects the acoustic realization of words in systematic ways. For example, unaccented vowels tend to be centralized and reduced in a function word, accented vowels tend to be longer and less subject to coarticulatory variation (Cho, 2001); accented consonants are produced with greater closure duration (DeJong, 1995), greater linguopalatal contact (Fougeron & Keating, 1997), longer voice onset time, and greater burst amplitude (Cole et al., 2007). Conditioning O over both P and W brings us a framework in which prosody induced acoustic variations can be accurately modeled. The dependence of W over S is well-established and has been used to build various types of POS-based language models. The dependence of P over S is supported by the experiments of Arnfield and others, described at the end of Section 1. The inter-dependence between P and W has been depicted by a dashed arrow to express the fact that P can be assumed to be independent of W given S with no knowledge about the pragmatic context (i.e., there is no reason to believe that one noun is more likely to be accented than any other given no pragmatic context). This assumption is useful in our later derivation in Section 3.

Modeling W and P jointly in this prosody dependent framework creates a new search space in which the candidate word sequences are weighted in terms of their conformability with natural prosody. An information-theoretic analysis in (Chen & Hasegawa-Johnson, 2004; Hasegawa-Johnson et al, 2005; Chen et al., 2006) showed that it is possible for a prosody-dependent speech recognizer to improve word recognition accuracy even if the acoustic model and the language model do not separately lead to improvements. Even if prosody does not improve the recognition of words in isolation, the likelihood of the correct sentence-level transcription may be improved by a language model that correctly predicts prosody from the word string, and an acoustic model that correctly predicts the acoustic observations from the prosody. In their experiments on the Radio News Corpus (Chen et al., 2006), as large as 11% word recognition accuracy improvement over a prosody independent speech recognizer was achieved by a prosody dependent recognizer that has comparable total parameter count.

3. Method

In this section, we propose an approach that creates prosody dependent factored language models by utilizing the dependence between prosody and syntax. For notational convenience and clarity, we used bigram models for our derivation. The equations presented in this section can be easily extended to higher order n-gram models.

3.1 Prosody Dependent Factored Language Model

The semi prosody dependent bigram probability (the probability of observing a word w_j given the previous prosody dependent word label $[w_i, p_i]$) can be calculated from the prosody independent bigram probability $p(w_j | w_i)$ using the following equation:

$$\begin{aligned} & p(w_j | w_i, p_i) \\ & = \frac{p(p_i, w_j | w_i)}{p(p_i | w_i)} \\ & = \frac{p(p_i | w_j, w_i) p(w_j | w_i)}{p(p_i | w_i)} \\ & \approx \frac{\sum_{s_i, s_j} p(p_i | s_i, s_j) p(s_i, s_j | w_i, w_j) p(w_j | w_i)}{\sum_{w_j} \sum_{s_i, s_j} p(p_i | s_i, s_j) p(s_i, s_j | w_i, w_j) p(w_j | w_i)}, \end{aligned} \tag{6}$$

where s_i and s_j are the POS of w_i and w_j respectively. The approximation in equation (6) assumes that p_i (the prosody on the previous word) is dependent on the POS context but independent of the actual word context:

$$p(p_i | s_i, s_j) \approx p(p_i | s_i, s_j, w_i, w_j). \tag{7}$$

Similarly, the prosody dependent bigram probability (the probability of observing a prosody dependent word token $[w_j, p_j]$ given the previous prosody dependent word token $[w_i, p_i]$) can be calculated from the semi prosody dependent bigram probability $p(w_j | w_i, p_i)$:

$$\begin{aligned} &p(w_j,p_j \mid w_i,p_i) \\ &= p(p_j \mid w_j,w_i,p_i)p(w \mid w_i,p_i) \\ &= \sum_{s_i,s_j} p(p_j \mid s_j,s_i,w_j,w_i,p_i)p(s_j,s_i \mid w_j,w_i,p_i)p(w_j \mid w_i,p_i) \\ &\approx \sum_{s_i,s_j} p(p_j \mid s_j,s_i,p_i)p(s_j,s_i \mid w_j,w_i)p(w_j \mid w_i,p_i). \end{aligned} \tag{8}$$

The following approximations are required in deriving equation (8):

$$p(p_j \mid s_i,s_j,p_i) \approx p(p_j \mid s_i,s_j,w_i,w_j,p_i), \tag{9}$$

and

$$p(s_i,s_j \mid w_i,w_j) \approx p(s_i,s_j \mid w_i,w_j,p_i). \tag{10}$$

Equation (9) assumes that prosody is dependent on its syntactic context represented by the POS of current word and the previous word but independent of the actual words. Equation (10) assumes that prosody does not affect the probability distribution of POS given the actual word context. This assumption is plausible except for the cases where prosody is used to resolve syntactic ambiguities (Price et al., 1991). In this chapter, we assume that the use of prosody to resolve POS ambiguity is statistically rare.

Equations (6) and (8) provide an approach to calculate the prosody dependent bigram probability $p(w_j,p_j \mid w_i,p_i)$ based on the regular prosody independent bigram probability $p(w_j \mid w_i)$ and three additional probability mass functions: $p(p_i \mid s_i,s_j)$, $p(p_j \mid s_i,s_j,p_i)$, and $p(s_i,s_j \mid w_i,w_j)$. $p(s_i,s_j \mid w_i,w_j)$ describes the stochastic mapping between a word pair and the associated POS pair. In most cases, this probability is a delta function, meaning that a word pair can only be associated with a unique POS pair. In a few cases, it is possible for a word pair to have more than one associated POS pairs. The probability mass functions $p(p_i \mid s_i,s_j)$ and $p(p_j \mid s_i,s_j,p_i)$ describe the inter-dependence between prosody and parts-of-speech, and can be very robustly estimated from a small database due to the small cardinality of the POS set and the prosody set. Note that equation (8) is possibly more accurate than equation (6) because the approximations are made only in the numerator while equation (6) has approximations in both numerator and denominator.

3.2 Methods for Smoothing the Language Models

Two popular techniques can be used to smooth the resulting language model: the backoff scheme and linear interpolation. When a prosody dependent bigram can not be estimated from the training data, it can be backed off to a prosody dependent unigram using Katz's backoff scheme (Katz, 1987):

$$p_b(w_j,p_j \mid w_i,p_i) = \begin{cases} d_r p(w_j,p_j \mid w_i,p_i), & \text{if exists} \\ b(w_i,p_i)p(w_j,p_j), & \text{else} \end{cases}, \tag{11}$$

where $0 < d_r \leq 1$ is a constant discount ratio and the backoff weight $b(w_i,p_i)$ is computed to ensure that the bigram probabilities conditioned on $[w_i,p_i]$ sum up to 1:

$$b(w_i,p_i)=\frac{1-\sum_{j\in B}p(w_j,p_j\mid w_i,p_i)}{1-\sum_{j\in B}p(p_j\mid w_j)}, \tag{12}$$

where B is the set of all prosody dependent word labels $[w_j,p_j]$ whose bigram probabilities can be calculated from equations (6) and (8).

The bigram probabilities calculated from equations (6) and (8) can be interpolated with the bigram probabilities estimated directly from the data (equation (2)). Let p_c be the probabilities calculated by equation (6) and (8), and p_m the probabilities estimated by equation (2), the interpolated probability p_i can be obtained using:

$$\begin{aligned} &p_i(w_j,p_j\mid w_i,p_i)\\ &=\lambda p_c(w_j,p_j\mid w_i,p_i)+(1-\lambda)p_m(w_j,p_j\mid w_i,p_i), \end{aligned} \tag{13}$$

where λ is a constant weight optimized using an EM algorithm to minimize the cross entropy of the interpolated language model over an independent development-test set.

3.3 Joint Perplexity and Word Perplexity

The quality of a standard prosody independent language model $p(W)$ can be measured by its perplexity E over a test set $T=[w_0,w_1,\ldots,w_N]$:

$$E(T)=2^{H(T)}, \tag{14}$$

where the cross-entropy $H(T)$ can be calculated as:

$$H(T)=-\frac{1}{N}\sum_{k=1}^{N}\log_2 p(w_k\mid w_{k-1}). \tag{15}$$

Similarly, the quality of a prosody dependent language model $p(W,P)$ can be measured by its perplexity E_p over the test set $T_p=[w_0,p_0,w_1,p_1,\ldots,w_N,p_N]$ that contains the same word sequence as T does but is transcribed prosodically:

$$E_p(T_p)=2^{H_p(T_p)}, \tag{16}$$

where $H_p(T_p)$ can be calculated as:

$$H_p(T_p)=-\frac{1}{N}\sum_{k=1}^{N}\log_2 p(w_k,p_k\mid w_{k-1},p_{k-1}). \tag{17}$$

To avoid confusion, we name E the Word Perplexity, and E_p the Joint Perplexity. Obviously, E and E_p are not directly comparable because they are calculated over different hypothesis spaces: E is an estimate of how many possible words can appear in the next spot given current word history, while E_p is an estimate of how many possible prosody dependent word tokens can appear in the next spot given current word and prosody history.

To directly compare the quality of a prosody dependent language model with that of a prosody independent language model, we need to compute the word perplexity for the prosody dependent language model. Note that equation (15) can be expanded as

$$H(T)=-\frac{1}{N}\sum_{k=1}^{N}\log_2\frac{\sum_{W_{0,k-1}}\sum_{P_{0,k}}p(W_{0,k}P_{0,k})}{\sum_{W_{0,k-2}}\sum_{P_{0,k-1}}p(W_{0,k-1}P_{0,k-1})}, \quad (18)$$

where $W_{0,k}=[w_0,w_1,...w_k]$, $P_{0,k}$ includes all possible prosody paths that can be assigned to $W_{0,k}$, and $p(W_{0,k}P_{0,k})$ is calculated using the estimated prosody dependent language model. Note that equation (18) can be computed efficiently using the forward algorithm, one of the standard algorithms for HMM.

4. Experiments and Results

4.1 The Corpus

To train prosody dependent speech recognizers, a large prosodically labeled speech database is required. The Boston University Radio News Corpus is one of the largest corpora designed for study of prosody (Ostendorf et al., 1995). The corpus consists of recordings of broadcast radio news stories including original radio broadcasts and laboratory broadcast simulations recorded from seven FM radio announcers (4 male, 3 female). Radio announcers usually use more clear and consistent prosodic patterns than non-professional readers, thus the Radio News Corpus comprises speech with a *natural but controlled* style, combining the advantages of both read speech and spontaneous speech. In this corpus, a majority of paragraphs are annotated with the orthographic transcription, phone alignments, part-of-speech tags and prosodic labels. The part-of-speech tags used in this corpus are the same as those used in the Penn Treebank. This tag set includes 47 parts-of-speech: 22 open class categories, 14 closed class categories and 11 punctuation labels. Part-of-speech labeling is carried out automatically using the BBN tagger. The tagger uses a bigram model of the tag sequence and a probability of tag given word taken from either a dictionary or, in the case of an unknown word, based on features of the word related to endings, capitalization and hyphenation. The tagger was trained on a set of Wall Street Journal sentences that formed part of the Penn Treebank corpus. For the labnews stories (a subset of the Radio New Corpus recorded without noise in a phonetics laboratory), only 2% of the words were incorrectly labeled.

The prosodic labeling system represents prosodic phrasing, phrasal prominence and boundary tones, using the Tones and Break Indices (ToBI) system for American English (Beckman & Ayers, 1994). The ToBI system labels pitch accent tones, phrase boundary tones, and prosodic phrase break indices. Break indices indicate the degree of decoupling between each pair of words; intonational phrase boundaries are marked by a break index of 4 or higher. Tone labels indicate phrase boundary tones and pitch accents. Tone labels are constructed from the three basic elements H, L, and !H. H and L represent high tone, low tone respectively, while !H represents a high tone produced at a pitch level that is stepped down from the level of the preceding high tone. There are four primary types of intonational phrase boundary tones: L-L%, representing the pitch fall at the end of a declarative phrase or sentence; H-L%, representing a fall or plateau at a mid-level pitch such as occurs in the middle of a longer declarative dialog turn; H-H%, representing the canonical, upward pitch contour at the end of a yes-no question; and L-H%, representing the low-rising contour found at the end of each non-final item on a list. The contours !H-L% and !H-H% are down-stepped variants that may occur following a H* pitch accent and are less frequently observed. Seven types of accent tones are labeled: H*, !H*, L+H*, L+!H*, L*, L*+H and

H+!H*. The ToBI system has the advantage that it can be used consistently by labelers for a variety of styles. For example, if one allows a level of uncertainty in order to account for differences in labeling style, it can be shown that the different transcribers of the Radio News Corpus agree on break index with 95% inter-transcriber agreement (Ostendorf et al., 1995). Presence versus absence of pitch accent is transcribed with 91% inter-transcriber agreement.

In the experiments we report in this chapter, the original ToBI labels are simplified: accents are only distinguished by presence versus absence, word boundaries are distinguished by those in intonational phrase-final position, and those that are medial in an intonational phrase. Applying this simplification, we create prosody dependent word transcriptions in which a word can only have 4 possible prosodic variations: unaccented phrase medial (``um''), accented phrase medial (``am''), unaccented phrase final (``uf'') and accented phrase final (``af'').

4.2 Perplexity

The prosodically labeled data used in our experiments consist of 300 utterances, 24944 words (about 3 hours of speech sampled at 16Khz) read by five professional announcers (3 female, 2 male) containing a vocabulary of 3777 words. Training and test sets are formed by randomly selecting 85% of the utterances for training, 5% of the utterances for development test and the remaining 10% for testing (2503 words).

We first measured the quality of the language models in terms of their perplexity on the test set. Four language models are trained from the same training set: a standard prosody independent backoff bigram language model LPI, a prosody dependent backoff bigram language model LPDM computed using equation (2), a prosody dependent backoff bigram language model LPDC1 computed using equation (8) only, and a model LPDC2 computed using both equation (6) and equation (8). The difference between LPDC1 and LPDC2 is that in LPDC1, the semi prosody dependent bigram probabilities $p(w_j | w_i, p_i)$ required by equation (8) are estimated directly from training data using their maximum likelihood estimators; whereas in LPDC2 they are computed from the prosody independent bigram probabilities $p(w_j | w_i)$ using equation (6). The models LPDC1 and LPDC2 were linearly interpolated with LPDM using equation (13), with interpolation weights λ optimized over the development-test set. Table I lists the results of this experiment.

	LPI	LPDM	LPDC1	LPDC2
Joint Perp.		340	282	235
Word Perp.	130	60	54	47
Unseen bigrams	931	1244	1103	956
Total bigrams	12100	14461	37373	81950

Table 1. The joint perplexity, word perplexity, number of unseen bigrams in the test set and total number of estimated bigrams in the prosody independent language model (LPI), the prosody dependent language model estimated using the standard ML approach (LPDM) and the prosody dependent language model calculated using the proposed algorithm (LPDC1 and LPDC2).

Compare the performance among the prosody dependent language models: LPDM, LPDC1, and LPDC2. Both LPDC1 and LPDC2 have much smaller joint perplexity than LPDM: the joint perplexity of LPDC1 is 17% less than that of LPDM, while that of LPDC2 is 31% smaller. Factorial modeling increases the number of bigrams whose probabilities can be estimated more accurately than their backed-off unigrams: the number of total estimated bigrams increased by 2 and 7 times respectively in LPDC1 and LPDC2, and the number of unseen bigrams in the test data reduced by around 25%, approaching the number of unseen bigrams in LPI.

To compare the perplexity of the prosody dependent language models with the prosody independent language model LPI, we computed the word perplexity for the prosody dependent language models using equation (18). As can be seen in the third row of Table 1, word perplexity of LPDC2 is reduced by 64% relative to LPI. Note that the word perplexities of the prosody dependent language models are only weakly comparable with that of the prosody independent language models in terms of predicting the word recognition performance. The word recognition power of a prosody dependent language model is prominent only when it is coupled with an effective prosody dependent acoustic model.

4.3 Word Recognition

Encouraged by the great reduction in perplexity, we conducted word and prosody recognition experiments on the same training and test sets. Two acoustic models are used in this experiment: a prosody independent acoustic model API and a prosody dependent acoustic model APD. All phonemes in API and APD are modeled by HMMs consisting of 3 states with no skips. Within each state, a 3 mixture Gaussian model is used to model the probability density of a 32-dimensional acoustic-phonetic feature stream consisting of 15 MFCCs, energy and their deltas. The allophone models in APD contain an additional one-dimensional Gaussian acoustic-prosodic observation PDF which is used to model the probability density of a nonlinearly-transformed pitch stream, as described in (Chen et al, 2004; Chen et al, 2006). API contains monophone models adopted from the standard SPHINX set (Lee, 1990) and is unable to detect any prosody related acoustic effects. APD contains a set of prosody dependent allophones constructed from API by splitting the monophones into allophones according to a four-way prosodic distinction (unaccented medial, accented medial, unaccented final, accented final): each monophone in API has 4 prosody dependent allophonic variants in APD. Allophone models in APD that are split from the same monophone share a single tied acoustic-phonetic observation PDF, but each allophone distinctly models the state transition probabilities and the acoustic-prosodic observation PDF. The APD allophones are therefore able to detect two of the most salient prosody induced acoustic effects: preboundary lengthening, and the pitch excursion over the accented phonemes. The parameter count of the acoustic-phonetic observation PDF (195 parameters per state) is much larger than the parameter count of the acoustic-prosodic observation PDF (2 parameters per state) or the transition probabilities (1 parameter per state); since the acoustic-phonetic parameters are shared by all allophones of a given monophone, the total parameter count of the APD model set is only about 6% larger than the parameter count of API.

Five recognizers are tested: a standard prosody independent recognizer RII using API and LPI, a semi prosody independent recognizer RID using APD and LPI, a prosody dependent recognizer RDM using APD and LPDM, a prosody dependent recognizer RDC1 using APD and LPDC1, and a prosody dependent recognizer RDC2 using APD and LPDC2. The word recognition accuracy, accent recognition accuracy and intonational phrase boundary recognition accuracy of these recognizers over the same training and test set are reported in Table 2.

	RII	**RID**	**RDM**	**RDC1**	**RDC2**
AM	API	APD	APD	APD	APD
LM	LPI	LPI	LPDM	LPDC1	LPDC2
Word	75.85	76.02	77.29	78.27	77.08
Accent	56.07	56.07	79.59	79.71	80.26
IPB	84.97	84.97	85.06	85.80	86.62

Table 2. Percent word, accent, and intonational phrase boundary recognition accuracy for recognizers RII, RID, RDM, RDC, and RDC2.

Overall, the prosody dependent speech recognizers significantly improve the word recognition accuracy (WRA) over the prosody independent speech recognizer. RDM improved the word recognition accuracy by 1.4% over RII and 1.2% over RID. RDC1 further improved the WRA by 1% over RDM, apparently benefiting from the improved prosody language model LPDC1. The pitch accent recognition accuracy (ARA) and the intonational phrase boundary recognition accuracy (BRA) are also significantly improved. Since RII and RID classify every word as unaccented and every word boundary as phrase-medial, the ARA and BRA listed in RII and RID are the chance levels. RDM showed a great improvement in ARA but only slight improvement in BRA mostly due to the already high chance level 84.97%. RDC2 used the language model LPDC2 that has the smallest perplexity. However, it only achieved improvement over RDM on ARA and BRA (0.7% and 1.5% respectively), but not on WRA. The failure of LPDC2 to outperform the WRA of LPDC1 may not be meaningful: it is well known that perplexity does not always correlate with recognition performance. However, it is possible to speculatively assign some meaning to this result. The flexible class-dependent structure of LPDC2 is able to model a number of prosody-dependent bigrams that is seven times larger than the number observed in the training data (Table I). It is possible that the approximations in equation (6) do not accurately represent the probabilities of all of these bigrams, and that therefore the increased flexibility harms word recognition accuracy.

5. Conclusion

In this chapter, we proposed a novel approach that improves the robustness of prosody dependent language modeling by leveraging the dependence between prosody and syntax. In our experiments on Radio News Corpus, a factorial prosody dependent language model estimated using our proposed approach has achieved as much as 31% reduction of the joint perplexity over a prosody dependent language model estimated using the standard Maximum Likelihood approach. In recognition experiments, our approach results in a 1% improvement in word recognition accuracy, 0.7% improvement in accent recognition accuracy and 1.5% improvement in intonational phrase boundary (IPB) recognition accuracy over the baseline prosody dependent recognizer. The study in the chapter shows that prosody-syntax dependence can be used to reduce the uncertainty in modeling concurrent word-prosody sequences.

6. Acknowledgment

This work was supported in part by NSF award number 0132900, and in part by a grant from the University of Illinois Critical Research Initiative. Statements in this chapter reflect the opinions and conclusions of the authors, and are not endorsed by the NSF or the University of Illinois.

7. References

Arnfield, S. (1994). Prosody and syntax in corpus based analysis of spoken English, Ph.D. thesis, University of Leeds

Beckman, M. E. and Ayers, G. M. (1994). Guidelines for ToBI Labelling: the Very Experimental HTML Version, http://www.ling.ohio-state.edu/research/phonetics/E ToBI/singer tobi.html

Bellegarda, J. (2000). Exploiting latent semantic information in statistical language modeling, *Proceedings of the IEEE* 88, 8, 1279-1296

Chen, K., Borys, S., Hasegawa-Johnson, M., and Cole, J. (2003). Prosody dependent speech recognition with explicit duration modeling at intonational phrase boundaries, *Proc. EUROSPEECH*, Geneva, Switzerland

Chen, K. and Hasegawa-Johnson, M. (2004). How prosody improves word recognition, *Proc. ISCA International Conference on Speech Prosody*, Nara, Japan

Chen, K., Hasegawa-Johnson, M., and Cohen, A. 2004. An automatic prosody labeling system using ANN-based syntactic-prosodic model and GMM-based acoustic-prosodic model, *Proc. ICASSP*, Montreal, Canada

Chen, K., Hasegawa-Johnson, M., Cohen, A., Borys, S., Kim, S., Cole, J., and Choi, J. (2006). Prosody dependent speech recognition on radio news, *IEEE Trans. Speech and Audio Processing* 14(1): 232-245

Cho, T. 2001. Effects of prosody on articulation in English, Ph.D. thesis, UCLA

Cole, J., Kim H., Choi H., & Hasegawa-Johnson M. (2007). Prosodic effects on acoustic cues to stop voicing and place of articulation: Evidence from Radio News speech. *Journal of Phonetics* 35: 180-209

DeJong, K. (1995). The supraglottal articulation of prominence in English: Linguistic stress as localized hyperarticulation, *J. Acoust. Soc. Am* 89, 1, 369-382

Fougeron, C. and Keating, P. (1997). Articulatory strengthening at edges of prosodic domains, *J. Acoust. Soc. Am* 101, 6, 3728-3740

Hahn, L. (1999). Native speakers' reactions to non-native stress in English discourse, Ph.D. thesis, UIUC

Hasegawa-Johnson M., Chen K., Cole J., Borys S., Kim S., Cohen A., Zhang T., Choi J., Kim H., Yoon T., and Chavarria S. (2005). Simultaneous Recognition of Words and Prosody in the Boston University Radio Speech Corpus, *Speech Communication*, 46(3-4): 418-439

Heeman, P. and Allen, J. (1999). Speech repairs, intonational phrases and discourse markers: modeling speakers' utterances in spoken dialog, *Computational Linguistics* 25, 4

Hirschberg, J. (1993). Pitch accent in context: Predicting intonational prominence from text, *Artificial Intelligence* 63, 1-2

Katz, S. M. (1987). Estimation of probabilities from sparse data for the language model component of a speech recognizer, *IEEE Trans. Speech and Audio Processing* 35, 3 (Mar.), 400-401

Khudanpur, S. and Wu, J. (2000). Maximum entropy techniques for exploiting syntactic, semantic and collocational dependencies in language modeling, *Computer Speech and Language* 14, 355-372

Kim, J. H. and Woodland, P. C. (2001). The use of prosody in a combined system for punctuation generation and speech recognition, *Proc. EUROSPEECH*

Kirchhoff, K., Bilmes, J., Das, S., Duta, N., Egan, M., Jin, G., He, F., Henderson, J., Liu, D., Noamany, M., Schone, P., Schwartz, R., and Vergyri, D. (2003). Novel approaches to Arabic speech recognition: report from the 2002 Johns-Hopkins summer workshop, *Proc. ICASSP*, Hong Kong, China

Kompe, R. (1997). Prosody in Speech Understanding Systems, Springer-Verlag

Lee, K. F. (1990). Context-dependent phonetic hidden Markov models for speaker-independent continuous speech recognition, *IEEE Trans. Speech and Audio Processing* 38, 4 (Apr.), 599-609

Nakatani, C. H. and Hirschberg, J. (1994). A corpus-based study of repair cues in spontaneous speech, *J. Acoust. Soc. Am* 95, 3, 1603-1616

Ostendorf, M., Price, P. J., and Shattuck-Hufnagel, S. (1995). The Boston University Radio News Corpus, Linguistic Data Consortium

Price, P. J., Ostendorf, M., Shattuck-Hufnagel, S., and Fong, C. (1991). The use of prosody in syntactic disambiguation, *J. Acoust. Soc. Am* 90, 6 (Dec.), 2956-2970

Rosenfeld, R. (2000). Two decades of statistical language modeling: where do we go from here? *Proceedings of the IEEE* 88, 8, 1270-1278

Shriberg, E., Stolcke, A., Hakkani-Tur, D., and Tur, G. (2000). Prosody-based automatic segmentation of speech into sentences and topics, *Speech Communication* 32, 1-2 (Sep.), 127-154

Taylor, P., King, S., Isard, S., Wright, H., and Kowtko, J. (1997). Using intonation to constrain language models in speech recognition, *Proc. EUROSPEECH*

Waibel, A. (1988). Prosody and Speech Recognition, London: Pitman

19

Early Decision Making in Continuous Speech

Odette Scharenborg, Louis ten Bosch and Lou Boves
CLST, Department of Linguistics/Language and Speech, Radboud University Nijmegen
The Netherlands

1.Introduction

In everyday life, speech is all around us, on the radio, television, and in human-human interaction. Communication using speech is easy. Of course, in order to communicate via speech, speech recognition is essential. Most theories of human speech recognition (HSR; Gaskell and Marslen-Wilson, 1997; Luce et al., 2000; McClelland and Elman, 1986; Norris, 1994) assume that human listeners first map the incoming acoustic signal onto prelexical representations (e.g., in the form of phonemes or features) and that these resulting discrete symbolic representations are then matched against corresponding symbolic representations of the words in an internal lexicon. Psycholinguistic experiments have shown that listeners are able to recognise (long and frequent) words reliably even before the corresponding acoustic signal is complete (Marslen-Wilson, 1987). According to theories of HSR, listeners compute a word activation measure (indicating the extent to which a word is activated based on the speech signal and the context) as the speech comes in and can make a decision as soon as the activation of a word is high enough, possibly before all acoustic information of the word is available (Marslen-Wilson, 1987; Marslen-Wilson and Tyler, 1980; Radeau et al., 2000). The "reliable identification of spoken words, in utterance contexts, before sufficient acoustic-phonetic information has become available to allow correct identification on that basis alone" is referred to as early selection by Marslen-Wilson (1987).
In general terms, automatic speech recognition (ASR) systems operate in a way not unlike human speech recognition. However there are two major differences between human and automatic speech recognition. First of all, most mainstream ASR systems avoid an explicit representation of the prelexical level to prevent premature decisions that may incur irrecoverable errors. More importantly, ASR systems postpone final decisions about the identity of the recognised word (sequence) as long as possible, i.e., until additional input data can no longer affect the hypotheses. This too is done in order to avoid premature decisions, the results of which may affect the recognition of following words. In more technical terms: ASR systems use an integrated search inspired by basic Bayesian decision theory and aimed at avoiding decisions that must be revoked due to additional evidence. The competition between words in human speech recognition, on the other hand, is not necessarily always fully open; under some conditions an educated guess is made about the identity of the word being spoken, followed by a shallow verification. This means that the winning word might be chosen before the offset of the acoustic realisation of the word, thus while other viable competing paths are still available. Apparently, humans are willing to take risks that cannot be justified by Bayesian decision theory.

At a higher level, i.e., the level of human-human interaction, early decision making plays an eminent role as well. This is shown by the extremely efficient turn-taking processes, in which listeners take the turn after predicting the moment when turn-switching can take place (Garrod & Pickering, 2004), resulting in dialogues with minimal latencies between successive turns. Since current ASR systems do not recognise words before their acoustic offset, let alone that they would predict the end of an utterance, latencies in turn-taking in human-computer interaction are unavoidable, resulting in unnatural dialogues.

If one wants to build an ASR system capable of early decision making, one needs to develop an algorithm that is able to produce a measure analogous to the word activation measure - as used by human listeners - that can be computed on-line, as speech is coming in. It is important to note that since early recognition involves making decisions before all potentially relevant information is available, it introduces the risk of making errors (i.e., false alarms of other words than were actually spoken).

This chapter introduces a novel approach to speech decoding that enables recognising polysyllabic words before their acoustic offset. The concept behind this novel approach is 'early recognition', i.e., the reliable identification of spoken words before the end of their acoustic realisation, but after the uniqueness point (UP)[1] of the word (given a lexicon). The restriction to recognition at or after the uniqueness point allows us to focus on acoustic recognition, with the same impact of a language model as in conventional ASR systems, which would be comparable - but certainly not identical - to the contexts used in human word recognition in Marslen-Wilson's definition of 'early selection'.

Early recognition is dependent on the structure and the contents of the lexicon. If a lexicon contains many words that have a UP very late in the word (i.e., only differ in the last one or two phones), early recognition (on the basis of acoustic input) is more difficult than when the lexicon mainly consists of words which have an early UP (i.e., contain long phone sequences after the lexical uniqueness point). At the same time, it is evident that making decisions on the basis of only a few phones at the beginning of a long word is more dangerous than deciding on the basis of a longer string of word-initial phones. Therefore, we will investigate the impact of the number of phones before and after the UP on the decision criteria that must be applied for early recognition. This chapter will present experiments conducted to optimise the performance of a procedure for making decisions before all acoustic information is available and discuss the results.

2.The recognition system

For conventional speech recognition, it suffices to search for the best-scoring path in the search space spanned by the language model, the lexicon, and the acoustic input. In early recognition, on the other hand, an additional decision procedure is needed for accepting a word as being recognised if its local word activation fulfils one or more criteria. In Scharenborg et al. (2003, 2005), we presented a speech recognition system called SpeM (Speech-based Model of human word recognition), based on Shortlist (Norris, 1994), that is capable of providing on-line dynamically changing 'word activations' derived from the log-

---

[1] In a lexicon organised in the form of a prefix-tree, the uniqueness point is the phoneme after which a path does not branch anymore.

likelihood values in conventional ASR systems. SpeM was originally developed to serve as a tool for research in the field of HSR.

SpeM consists of three modules. The first module, the automatic phone recogniser (APR), generates a symbolic prelexical representation of the speech signal in the form of a (probabilistic) phone graph. The second module, the word search module, parses the graph to find the most likely (sequence of) words, and computes for each word its activation based on, among others, the accumulated acoustic evidence for that word. During the lexical search, SpeM provides a list of the most likely path hypotheses at every phone node in the phone graph. The third -decision- module is entered each time after a node in the phone graph is processed in the second module. This enables SpeM to recognise and accept words before the end of an utterance or phrase. The focus of this paper is on the third module, which makes decisions about accepting a word as being recognised if its local word activation fulfils one or more criteria.

The most important difference between SpeM and conventional ASR systems is that the search module in SpeM depends in a crucial manner on the availability of some kind of prelexical symbolic representation of the speech signal. Consequently, it is not straightforward to implement early recognition as presented here in conventional frame-based ASR systems, since in those systems a prelexical symbolic representation is deliberately lacking. This is not to say that computing on-line dynamically varying word activation scores is fundamentally impossible in decoders that avoid an explicit prelexical representation, but doing so would require a class of algorithms that differ very much from SpeM.

2.1 Material and evaluation

In our evaluation of SpeM's ability for early decision we focus on polysyllabic content words. The reasons for this are twofold. Firstly, function words and short content words that are not easy to predict from the (linguistic) context may not be identified by human listeners until the word following it has been heard (Grosjean, 1985). Secondly, short words are likely to have a UP that is not before the end of the word since they are often embedded in longer words (McQueen et al., 1995), making it a priori impossible to recognise the word before its acoustic offset on the basis of only acoustic evidence.

The training and test data are taken from the VIOS database, which consists of utterances taken from telephone dialogs between customers and the Dutch public automatic transport timetable information system (Strik et al., 1997). The material to train the acoustic models of the APR (AM training material) consists of 25,104 utterances in Dutch (81,090 words, corresponding to 8.9 hours of speech excluding leading, utterance internal, and trailing silent portions of the recordings).

A set of 318 polysyllabic station names is defined as focus words. From the VIOS database, 1,106 utterances (disjoint from the AM training corpus) were selected. Each utterance contained two to five words, at least one of which was a focus word (708 utterances contained multiple focus words). 885 utterances of this set (80% of the 1,106 utterances) were randomly selected and used as the independent test corpus. The total number of focus words in this test corpus was 1,463 (563 utterances contained multiple focus words). The remaining 221 utterances were used as development set and served to tune the parameters of SpeM (see also Section 2.3). The parameter settings yielding the lowest Word Error Rate (WER) on the development test set were used for the experiment. The WER is defined as:

$$WER = (\#I + \#D + \#S) / N \cdot 100\% \quad (1)$$

where #I denotes the number of word insertions; #D the number of word deletions, #S the number of word substitutions, and N denotes the total number of words in the reference transcription.

The lexicon used by SpeM in the test consisted of 980 entries: the 318 polysyllabic station names, additional city names, verbs, numbers, and function words. There are no out-of-vocabulary words in the test. For each word in the lexicon, one unique canonical phonemic representation was available. A unigram language model (LM; see also Section 2.3) was trained on the AM training data. This implies that the SpeM decoder only knew about the relative frequency of the 980 lexical entries (words), but that it had no means for predicting words from the preceding linguistic context - which is good for making the word competition as fair as possible.

2.2 The automatic phone recogniser

The APR used in this study was based on the Phicos ASR system (Steinbiss et al., 1993), but it is easy to build an equivalent module using open source software, such as HTK (Young et al., 2002). 37 context-independent phone models, one noise model, and one silence model were trained on the VIOS training set. All phone models and the noise model have a linear left-to-right topology with three pairs of two identical states, one of which can be skipped. For the silence model, a single-state hidden Markov Model is used. Each state comprises a mixture of maximally 32 Gaussian densities. The phone models have been trained using a transcription generated by a straightforward look-up of the phonemic transcriptions of the words in a lexicon of 1,415 entries (a superset of the 980 words in the recognition lexicon), including entries for background noise and filled pauses. For each word, the lexicon contained only the unique canonical (citation) pronunciation. Thus, potential pronunciation variation in the training corpus was ignored while training phone models.

The 'lexicon' used for the phone decoding by the APR consists of 37 Dutch phones and one entry for background noise, yielding 38 entries in total (in the lexicon, no explicit entry for silence is needed). During decoding, the APR uses a bigram phonotactic model trained on the canonical phonemic transcriptions of the AM training material.

The APR converts the acoustic signal into a probabilistic phone lattice without using lexical knowledge. The lattice has one root node and one end node. Each edge (i.e., connection between two nodes) carries a phone and its bottom-up evidence in terms of negative log likelihood (its acoustic cost). This acoustic cost is directly related to the probability $P(X|Ph)$ that the acoustic signal X was produced given the phone Ph.

2.3 The search module

The input of the search module consists of the probabilistic phone lattice created by the first module and a lexicon represented as a lexical tree. In the lexical tree, entries share common phone prefixes (called word-initial cohorts), and each complete path through the tree represents the pronunciation of a word. The lexical tree has one root node and as many end nodes as there are pronunciations in the lexicon. Nodes that are flagged as end nodes but also have outgoing edges indicate embedded words.

Like a conventional ASR system, SpeM searches for the best-scoring or cheapest path through the product graph of the input phone lattice and the lexical tree. It is implemented using dynamic programming (DP) techniques, and is time-synchronous and breadth-first.

SpeM calculates scores for each path (the total cost), and also a score for the individual words on a path (the word cost). The total cost of a path is defined as the accumulation along the path arcs of the bottom-up acoustic cost (as calculated by the APR) and several cost factors computed in the search module.

During the recognition process, for each node in the input phone graph, SpeM outputs N-best lists consisting of hypothesised word sequences and word activation scores (see Section 3) for each of the hypothesised words on the basis of the phones in the phone graph (thus the stretch of the acoustic signal) that have been processed so far. The order of the parses in the N-best list is determined by the total cost of the parses (thus not by the word activation scores). Each parse consists of words, word-initial cohorts, phone sequences, garbage, silence, and any combination of these, except that a word-initial cohort can only occur as the last element in the parse. So, in addition to recognising full words, SpeM is able to recognise partial words. In the N-best list, no identical parses exist: Word sequences on different paths that are identical in terms of phone symbols, but have different start and end time of the words, are treated as the same word sequence (thus timing differences are ignored). That is, we only take the order and identity of the words into account for pruning the N-best lists. The number of hypotheses in the N-best list is set to 10, so that SpeM will output the 10 most likely parses for each node in the input phone graph. Subsequently, the N-best list with the word sequences and their accompanying word activation scores is sent to the decision module that makes decisions about early recognition.

The current implementation of SpeM supports the use of unigram and bigram LMs, which model the prior probability of observing individual words and of a word given its predecessor. In the experiments reported in this paper, only a unigram LM is used. SpeM has a number of parameters that affect the total cost and that can be tuned individually and in combination. Most of these parameters, e.g., a word entrance penalty (the cost to start hypothesising a new word) and the trade-off between the weights of the bottom-up acoustic cost of the phones and the contribution of the LM, are similar to the parameters in conventional ASR systems. In addition, however, SpeM has two types of parameters that are not usually present in conventional ASR systems. The first novel parameter type is associated to the cost for a symbolic mismatch between the input lattice and the lexical tree due to phone insertions, deletions, and substitutions. Insertions, deletions, and substitutions have their own weight that can be tuned individually. Because the lexical search in SpeM is phone based, mismatches can arise between symbols in the input phone graph and the phonemic transcriptions in the lexical tree. It is therefore necessary to include a mechanism which explicitly adjusts for phone-level insertions, deletions, and substitutions. In mainstream ASR, on the other hand, the search space is usually spanned by a combination of the pronunciation variants in the system's dictionary and the system's language model, so that explicit modelling of insertions, deletions, and substitutions on the phone-level is not necessary. The second novel parameter type is associated to the Possible Word Constraint (PWC, Norris et al., 1997). The PWC determines whether a (sequence of) phone(s) that cannot be parsed as a word (i.e., a lexical item) is phonotactically well formed (being a possible word) or not (see also Scharenborg et al., 2003, 2005). The PWC evaluation is applied only to paths that do not consist solely of complete words. Word onsets and offsets, utterance onsets and offsets, and pauses count as locations relative to which the viability of symbol sequences that are no words (i.e., lexical items) are evaluated. If there is no vowel in the sequence between any of these locations and a word edge, the PWC cost is added to the total cost of the path. For example, consider the utterance "they met a fourth time", where the last sound of the word fourth is pronounced as [f]. Because *fourf* is not stored as a word in the lexicon, a potential parse by the recogniser is *they metaphor f time*. Since *f* is not a possible word in English, the PWC mechanism penalises this parse, and if the cost of the substitution of [θ] by [f] is less than the PWC cost, the parse yielding the word sequence *fourth time* will win. At the same time, it is worth mentioning that the PWC enables SpeM to parse input with broken words and disfluencies, since it provides a mechanism for handling arbitrary phone input (see Scharenborg et al., 2005, for more information).

All parameters in SpeM are robust: Even if they are not optimised in combination, SpeM's output does not change significantly if the value of the parameter that was optimised with fixed values of other parameters is changed within reasonable bounds. In this study, the parameters were tuned on the independent development set (see Section 2.1), and subsequently used for processing the test corpus.

3. The computation of word activation

An essential element for early decision making is the computation of word activation. The measure of word activation in SpeM was originally designed to simulate the way in which word activations evolve over time in experiments on human word recognition (Scharenborg et al., 2005, 2007). In the computation of the word activation, the local negative log-likelihood scores for complete paths and individual words on a path are converted into word activation scores that obey the following properties, which follow from the concept of word activation as it is used in HSR:

- The word that matches the input best, i.e., the word with the smallest *word cost* (see Section 2.3), must have the highest activation.
- The activation of a word that matches the input must increase each time an additional matching input phone is processed.
- The measure must be appropriately normalised: Word activation should be a measure that is meaningful, both for comparing competing word candidates, and for comparing words at different moments in time.

The way SpeM computes word activation is based on the idea that word activation is a measure related to the bottom-up evidence of a word given the acoustic signal: If there is evidence for the word in the acoustic signal, the word should be activated. Activation should also be sensitive to the prior probability of a word (even if this effect was not modelled in the original version of Shortlist (Norris, 1994)). This means that the word activation of a word W is closely related to the probability $P(W|X)$ of observing a word W, given the signal X and some kind of (probabilistic) LM, which is precisely the cost function that is maximised in conventional ASR systems. Thus, it is reasonable to stipulate that the word activation $Act(W|X)$ is equal to $P(W|X)$, and apply the same Bayesian formulae that form the basis of virtually all theories in ASR to estimate $P(W|X)$. This is why we refer to $Act(W|X)$ (or $P(W|X)$) as the 'Bayesian activation'. It is important to emphasise that the theory underlying word activation does not require that the sum of the activations of all active words should add to some constant (e.g., 1.0, as in probability theory). For the purpose of early recognition it suffices to normalise the activation value in such a manner that (possibly context dependent) decisions can be made. This too is reminiscent of what happens in conventional ASR systems.

Since we also want to deal with incompletely processed acoustic input (for early recognition of words), Bayes' Rule is applied to Act(W | X) in which both W and X are evolving over time t, and t-steps coincide with phone boundaries:

$$Act(W(n) \mid X(t)) = \frac{P(X(t) \mid W(n))P(W(n))}{P(X(t))} \tag{2}$$

where W(n) denotes a phone sequence of length n, corresponding to the word-initial cohort of n phones of W. So, W(5) may, for example, be /Amst@/, i.e., the prefix (or word-initial cohort) of the word 'amsterdam' (but also of other words that begin with the same prefix). X(t) is the gated signal X from the start of W(n) until time t (corresponding to the end of the last phone included in W(n)). P(X(t)) denotes the prior probability of observing the gated signal X(t). P(W(n)) denotes the prior probability of W(n).

As said before, in the experiments reported in this chapter, P(W(n)) is exclusively based on the unigram probability of the words and the word-initial cohorts (the unigram probabilities for word-initial cohorts are determined by summing over the unigram probabilities of all words in the cohort). The (unnormalised) conditional probability P(X(t) | W(n)) in equation 2, is calculated by SpeM as:

$$P(X(t) \mid W(n)) = e^{-aTC} \tag{3}$$

where TC is the total bottom-up cost associated with the word starting from the beginning of the word up to the node corresponding to instant t. TC includes not only the acoustic costs in the phone lattice, but also the costs contributed by substitution, deletion, and insertion of symbols (like the acoustic cost calculated by the APR, TC is a negative log likelihood score). The definition of the total bottom-up cost is such that TC > 0. The value of a determines the contribution of the bottom-up acoustic scores to the eventual activation values. The a weights the relative contribution of TC to Act(W(n) | X(t)), and therefore balances the contribution of P(X(t) | W(n)) and P(W(n)). Thus, a is similar to the 'language model factor' in standard ASR systems. a is a positive number; it's numerical value is determined such that the three properties of word activation introduced at the start of this section hold (for a more detailed explanation of a, see Scharenborg et al., 2007).

In contrast to conventional ASR systems, in SpeM, the prior P(X(t)) in the denominator of equation 2 cannot be discarded, because hypotheses covering different numbers of input phones must be compared. The problem of normalisation across different paths is also relevant in other unconventional ASR systems (e.g., Glass, 2003). Furthermore, the normalisation needed in SpeM is similar to the normalisation that has to be performed in the calculation of confidence measures (e.g., Bouwman et al., 2000; Wessel et al., 2001). In order to be able to compare confidence measures of hypotheses with unequal length, the normalisation must, in some way, take into account the duration of the hypotheses. In normalising equation 2, we followed the procedure for normalising confidence measures. However, instead of the number of frames, the number of phones is the normalising factor, resulting in a type of normalisation that is more phonetically oriented. The denominator of equation 2, then, is approximated by

$$P(X(t)) = D^{\#\,nodes(t)} \tag{4}$$

where D is a constant (0 < D < 1) and #nodes(t) denotes the number of nodes in the cheapest path from the beginning of the word up to the node associated with t in the input phone graph. In combination with a, D plays an important role in the behaviour over time of Act(W(n) | X(t)). Once the value of a is fixed, the value of D follows from two constraints: 1) the activation on a matching path should increase; 2) the activation on any mismatching path should decrease (for a more detailed explanation of D, see Scharenborg et al., 2007).

Our choice to normalise the Bayesian activation by the expression given by equation 4 is also based on another consideration. Given the Bayesian paradigm, it seems attractive to use a measure with the property that logarithmic scores are additive along paths. If X1 and X2 are two stretches of speech such that X2 starts where X1 ends, associated with two paths P1 and P2 in the phone lattice (such that P2 starts where P1 ends), then log(P(X1)) + log(P(X2)) = log(P(X1 : X2)) (where ':' means 'followed by'). By doing so the lengths of X1 and X2 are assumed to be independent, which is a plausible assumption.

4. Early recognition in SpeM

4.1 The performance of SpeM as a standard speech recognition system

In order to assess SpeM's ability for early decision, it is essential to know the upper-bound of its performance: First of all, if a word is not correctly recognised, it will be impossible to analyse its recognition point (RP); secondly, only if the RP of a word lies before the end of that word, it can, in principle, be recognised before its acoustic offset during the recognition process. In this paper, the RP is defined as the node after which the activation measure of a correct focus word exceeds the activation of all competitors, and remains the highest until the end of the word (after the offset of a word, the word's activation does not change). The RP necessarily lies after the UP (since prior to the UP, multiple words (in the word-initial cohort) share the same lexical prefix, and therefore cannot be distinguished on the basis of the acoustic evidence), and is expressed as the position of the corresponding phone in the phonemic (lexical) representation of the word.

In a first step, the performance of SpeM as a standard ASR system was investigated. The WER on the full test set and on the focus words was calculated by taking the best matching sequence of words as calculated by SpeM after processing the entire input and comparing it with the orthographic transcriptions of the test corpus. The WER obtained by SpeM on all words in the test material was 40.4%. Of the 1,463 focus words, 64.0% (936 focus words) were recognised correctly at the end of the word. Despite the mediocre performance of SpeM as an ASR system, we believe it is still warranted to investigate SpeM on the task of early decision, since there is a sufficiently large number of correctly recognised focus words. It should be noted that in this study no attempt has been made to maximise the performance of the acoustic model set of the APR. However, the results presented in Scharenborg et al. (2003, 2005) show that SpeM's performance is comparable to that of an off-the-shelf ASR system (with an LM in which all words are equally probable) when the acoustic model set used to construct the phone graph is optimised for a specific task. It is thus quite probable that improving the performance of the APR should allow SpeM to reach an ASR performance level comparable to a conventional ASR system on the VIOS data set (see Scharenborg et al., 2007).

Length-UP	#Types	#Tokens	Cumulative
0	10	30	1,463
1	44	190	1,433
2	50	182	1,243
3	63	450	1,061
4	50	271	611
5	39	186	340
6	38	82	154
7	17	57	72
8	3	11	15
9	2	4	4

Table 1. The distribution (in #types and #tokens) in number of phones between the UP and the length of a word (Length-UP); Cumulative: #focus word tokens that could in principle be recognised at position Length-UP.

4.2 Analysis of the recognition point

In a second step, to determine SpeM's upper-bound performance on the task of early decision, we investigate how many of the focus words have an RP that lies before the end of the word. Table 1 shows the distribution of the distance in number of phones between the UP and the end of a focus word. 'Length-UP' = 0 means that the UP is at the end of the word: Either the word is embedded in a longer word or the words only differ in their last phoneme. Columns 2 and 3 show the number of focus word types and tokens with 'Length-UP' phones between the end of the word and the UP. The column 'Cumulative' shows the number of focus word tokens that could in principle be recognised correctly at 'Length-UP' phones before the end of a word. For instance, at 8 phones before the end of a word, the only words that can in principle be recognised correctly are those that have a distance of 8 or more phones between the end of the word and the UP; at 0 phones before the end of a word, all words could in principle be identified correctly. From Table 1 it can be deduced that the UP of 85.0% of all focus word tokens (1,243/1,463) is at least two phones before the end of the word; only 2% of the focus word tokens (30/1,463) have their UP at the end of the word.
In our analysis of the RP, we only took those focus words into account that were recognised correctly, since, obviously, a word that is not recognised correctly does not have an RP. First, the path and word hypotheses were ranked using the Bayesian word activation score. Subsequently, for each correctly recognised focus word, the node after which the Bayesian word activation exceeds the Bayesian word activation of all its competitors, and remains the highest until the end of the word is determined. Of the focus words that were recognised correctly, 81.1% had their RP before the end of the word (759 of 936 correctly recognised focus words; 51.9% of all focus words).
To understand how much evidence SpeM needs to make an early decision about 'recognising' a word, the RP of all 936 correctly recognised focus words was related to the UP and the total number of phones of that word. The results are shown in the form of two histograms in Fig. 1. The frequency is given along the y-axis. In the left panel, the x-axis represents the distance (in phones) between the UP and the RP of the focus words. N = 0 means that the word activation exceeded all competitors already at the UP. In the right panel, the x-axis represents the position of the RP (in number of phones (N)) relative to the

last phone in the canonical representation of the word. Here, N = 0 means that the word activation exceeded the competitors only at the last phone of the word. The high frequency in the case of N = 3 in the right panel of Fig. 1 is due to an idiosyncratic characteristic of the data, which is irrelevant for the task. As can be seen in Table 1, there is a large set of words that have their UP three phones before the end of the word (450).

Combining the information in Fig. 1 and Table 1 shows that although only 2% of the focus words have their UP at the end of the word, 19.8% (185/936, see right panel of Fig. 1) of the words were only recognised at the end of the word. Apparently, SpeM is not always able to recognise a word before its acoustic offset, despite the fact that the UPs in the set of words were almost always at least one phone before the end of the word. More interestingly, however, from Fig. 1 it can also be deduced that 64.1% (sum of N = 0 and N = 1, see left panel of Fig. 1) of the total number of recognised focus words were already recognised at or maximally one phone after the UP. Taking into account that 85.0% of the focus words have at least two phones after their UP, this indicates that SpeM is able to take advantage of the redundancy caused by the fact that many words in the vocabulary are unique before they are complete.

As pointed out at the start of this chapter, psycholinguistic research (Marslen-Wilson, 1987) has shown that listeners are able to recognise long and frequent words before their acoustic offset. However, this does not imply that this always happens and for all words. There are still words (including frequent and long words) that can only be recognised by a listener after some of the following context has been heard. The SpeM results showed that the UP and RP do not coincide for all focus words that were recognised. SpeM, like listeners, occasionally needs information from the following context to make a decision about the identity of a word. This can be explained by the fact that a focus word that is correctly recognised at the end of an utterance may not match perfectly with the phone sequence in the phone graph. An analysis (see Scharenborg et al., 2007) showed that for 34.9% of the utterances, the canonical phone transcription of the utterance was not present in the phone graph. For these focus words, phone insertion, deletion, and substitution penalties are added to the total score of the word and the path. Competing words may have a phonemic representation that is similar to the phonemic representation of the correct word sequence. In these cases, it may happen that the best matching word can only be determined after all information of all competing words is available.

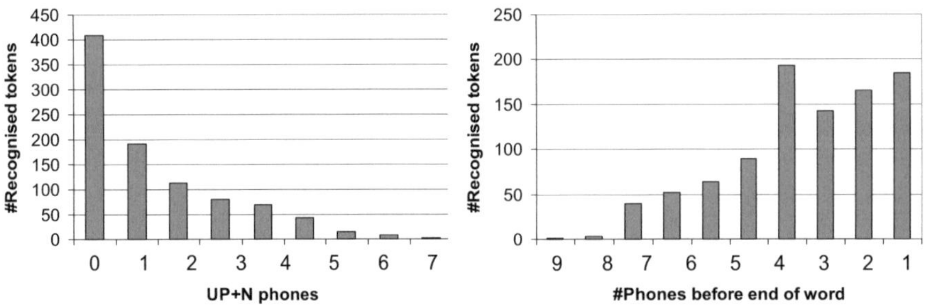

Figure 1. *Left panel:* histogram relating the RP to the UP. *Right panel:* histogram relating the RP to the total number of phones in the word for the 936 correctly recognised focus words.

5. Predictors for reliable on-line early decision making

In the previous analyses, the RP and thus SpeM's ability of early decision was investigated after the recognition process had taken place. This was done to determine the upper-bound of SpeM's performance on the task of early decision: 936 focus words were recognised correctly, while 2% of the focus words have their UP at the end of the word. It can be deduced from the right panel of Fig. 1 that, as an upper-bound, 751 (80.2%) correctly recognised focus words can be recognised before the acoustic offset of the word. Of course, in order to use the concept of early decision in an operational system in order to speed up for instance human-computer interaction, a procedure needs to be developed that accurately and reliably decides whether a word is considered as recognised before the end of its acoustic realisation.

As stated above, in comparison to integrated search approaches as used in mainstream ASR systems, early decision making introduces an additional decision problem that introduces additional errors and thus additional risks. Intermediate results are also computed in integrated search and therefore might be made available at the output interface of the search module, but because these results can still change later on in the recognition process, this is not usually done. One exception to this rule are dictation systems that show word hypotheses on the screen that are subsequently revised as the search progressed. In the case of early decision making as defined in this study, however, a decision made during the recognition process cannot be adapted, and is thus final. Early decision making is thus not synonymous with fast decision making; early decision making predicts the future.

The analyses presented in the previous section showed that the Bayesian word activation of many polysyllabic content words exceeds the activation of all competitors before the end of the words. However, this does not imply that the Bayesian word activation can be safely used to perform early decision. We created a decision procedure on the basis of the Bayesian word activation and experimented with a combination of absolute and relative values of the Bayesian word activation. Additionally, we investigated whether the reliability of early decision making is affected by the number of phones of the word that have already been processed and the number of phones that remain until the end of the word. The performance of that module will be evaluated in terms of precision and recall:

- *Precision*: The total number of *correctly* recognised focus words, relative to the total number of recognised focus words. Thus, *precision* measures the trade-off between correctly recognised focus words and *false alarms*.
- *Recall*: The total number of correctly recognised focus words divided by the total number of focus words in the input. Thus, *recall* represents the trade-off between correctly recognised focus words and *false rejects*.

As usual, there is a trade-off between precision and recall. Everything else being equal, increasing recall tends to decrease precision, while increasing precision will tend to decrease recall. We are not interested in optimising SpeM for a specific task in which the relative costs of false alarms and false rejections can be established, since in this paper we are mainly interested in the feasibility of early recognition in an ASR system. Therefore, we decided to refrain from defining a total cost function that combines recall and precision into a single measure that can be optimised.

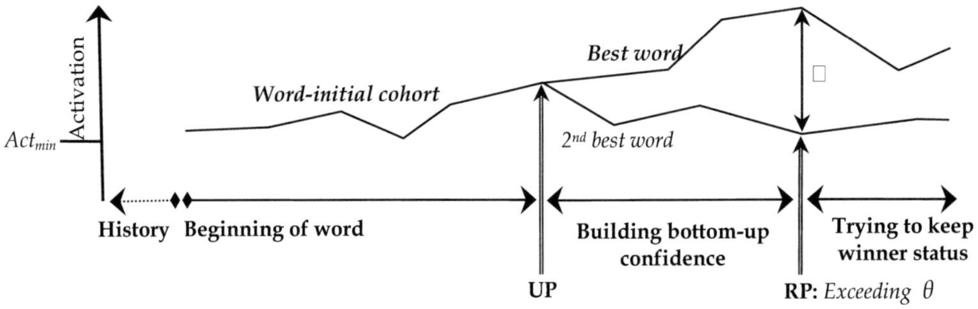

Figure 2. Schematic illustration of the process of early decision making.

5.1 Decision Module

For the task of early decision making, the SpeM model is expanded with a decision module. The input of the decision module consists of the N-best list with the word sequences and their accompanying Bayesian word activation scores as created by the search module at each point in time when a new symbol is added to the phone graph. The decision module only makes a decision about early recognition for focus words. For a focus word to be recognised by SpeM, the following three conditions have to be met:

1. The phone sequence assigned to the focus word is at or beyond the focus word's UP.
2. We do not want SpeM to accept a word that happens to have the highest activation irrespective of the absolute value of the activation. Therefore, the value of the Bayesian word activation of the focus word itself must exceed a certain *minimum activation* (Act_{min}). In the experiments described below, various values for Act_{min} were tested.
3. Since we do not want SpeM to make a decision as long as promising competitors are still alive, the *quotient* of the Bayesian word activation of the focus word on the best-scoring path and the Bayesian word activation of its closest *competitor* (if present) must exceed a certain threshold (□). In the experiments, various values for □ were tested.

In the SpeM search, two words are said to be in competition if the paths they are on contain an identical sequence of words, except for the word under investigation. Recall that we only look at the order and identity of the words (see Section 2.3). Thus, two word sequences on two different paths that are identical, but have a different start and end time of the words, are treated as the same word sequence, and so do not compete with each other. (Remember that we only look at the current word; it does not matter whether the paths on which the two competing words lie combine again later on.) Given our definition of 'competitor' it is not guaranteed that all words always have a competitor, because it is possible that all paths in the N-best list are completely disjunct - and so do not share the same history, as is required for being competitor in our definition of the term. Absence of a competitor makes the computation of □ impossible. To prevent losing all words without competitors due to a missing value, we accept all focus words without a competitor that appear at least five times (at the same position in the word sequence) in the N-best list.

Fig. 2 schematically depicts the process of early recognition. The Bayesian activation of words grows over time as matching evidence is added. Before the word's UP, several words are consistent with the phone sequence; the difference in activation of the individual words in the cohort is caused by the influence of the LM. After a word's UP, each word has its own Bayesian word activation. For the purpose of the experiments in this section, we define the decision point (DP) as the point at which a word on the first best path meets the three decision criteria described above.

5.2 □ and Act_{min} as predictors of early recognition

To determine the effect of the variables introduced in decision criteria 2 and 3, experiments were carried out in which their respective values were varied: The value of Act_{min} was varied between 0.0 and 2.0 in 20 equal-sized steps; the value of □ was varied between 0.0 and 3.0 in six equal-sized steps of 0.5. Fig. 3 shows the relation between precision (y-axis) and recall (x-axis) for a number of combinations of □ and 21 values of Act_{min}. For the sake of clarity, Fig. 3 is limited to three values of □, viz. □ = 0.5, 1.5, 2.5; all other values of □ show the same trend. The left-most symbol on each line corresponds to Act_{min} = 2.0; the right-most one corresponds to Act_{min} = 0.0.

The results in Fig. 3 are according to our expectation. Recall should be an inverse function of □: The smaller □ becomes, the less it will function as a filter for words that have a sufficiently high activation, but which still have viable competitors. Similarly for Act_{min}: For higher values of Act_{min}, fewer focus words will have an activation that exceeds Act_{min}, and thus fewer words are recognised. These results indicate that the absolute and relative values of Bayesian activation that were defined as decision criteria seem to work as predictors for the early recognition of polysyllabic words.

5.3 The effect of the amount of evidence for a word on precision and recall

As pointed out before, in our definition of early recognition a word can only be recognised at or after its UP. Thus, words that have an early UP can fulfil the conditions while there is still little evidence for the word. This raises the question what the effect is of the amount of evidence in support of a word (the number of phones between the start of the word and the DP) or of the 'risk' (in the form of the number of phones following the DP until the end of the word) on precision and recall. In the following analysis this question is investigated. For fixed values for Act_{min} and □, precision and recall are calculated for different amounts of evidence, thus different 'risk' levels, as a function of the number of phonemes between the start of the word and its DP and number of phones between the DP and the end of the word. The value for Act_{min} is set to 0.5, a value that guarantees that we are on the plateau shown in Fig. 3; □ was set at 1.625 (on the basis of results in Scharenborg et al., 2007). In these analyses, we are interested in the number of words that could in principle be recognised correctly at a certain point in time. The definitions of precision and recall are therefore adapted, such that they only take into account the number of focus word tokens that in principle could be recognised. For calculating recall, the total number of correctly recognised focus words is divided by the total number of focus words that could in principle have been recognised at that position in the word (accumulating to 1,463 focus words). Precision is calculated in the same manner: The total number of correctly recognised focus words so far is divided by the total number of recognised focus words so far.

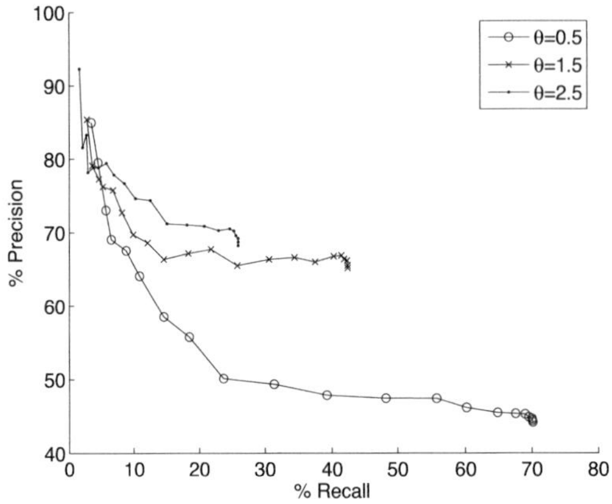

Figure 3. For three values of □, the precision and recall of 21 values of Act_{min} are plotted.

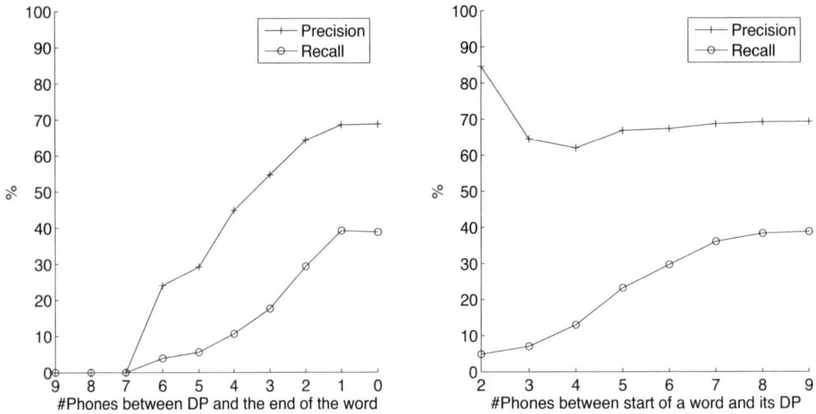

Figure 4.The x-axes show the number of phones between the DP and the end of the word (left panel) and between the start of the word and its DP (right panel); the y-axes show for □ = 1.625 and Act_{min} = 0.5 the percentage recall (solid lines with crosses +) and precision (solid lines with circles o), respectively.

Fig. 4 shows the results. In the left panel, the x-axis shows the number of phones between the DP and the end of the word; the y-axis shows the percentage recall (line with circles o) and precision (line with crosses +), respectively. The right panel of Fig. 4 shows on the x-axis the number of phones between the start of the word and its DP; the y-axis shows the percentage recall (line with circles o) and precision (line with crosses +), respectively. The left panel of Fig. 4 clearly shows that precision and recall increase if the number of phones remaining after the DP decreases. This is easy to explain, since mismatches in the part of the word that is as yet unseen cannot be accounted for in the activation measure, but the risk that future mismatches occur will be higher if more phones remain until the end of the word. At the same time, recall increases if the DP is later, so that more information in support of the hypothesis is available (see right panel of Fig. 4). This too makes sense, since one may expect that a high activation measure that is based on more phones is statistically more robust than a similarly high value based on a small number of phones. It should be noted, however, that the right panel of Fig. 4 suggests that precision is not dependent on the number of phones between the start of a word and its DP: The trade-off between the false alarms and the correctly recognised focus words does not change much.

5.4 Summary

We investigated a predictor related to the absolute and relative values of the word activation, Act_{min} and □, respectively, for deciding whether a word is considered as recognised before the end of its acoustic realisation. The results showed that the predictor functions as a filter: The higher the values for the predictor, the fewer words are recognised, and vice versa. In this paper, we only presented the results in a form equivalent to ROC curves. Selecting the best possible combination of the values of the predictor is straightforward once the costs of false alarms and false rejects can be determined. In the subsequent analyses, the effect on precision and recall of the amount of evidence for a word, in terms of the number of phones of the word that have already been processed and the number of phones that remain until the end of the word was investigated. Not surprisingly, the results showed that SpeM's performance increases if the amount of evidence in support of a word increases and the risk of future mismatches decreases if there are fewer phones left until the end of the word. These results clearly indicate that early recognition is indeed dependent on the structure and the contents of the lexicon. If a lexicon contains many (long) words that have an early UP, decisions can be made while only little information is known, at the cost of increasing the risk of errors. It is left to follow-up research to investigate whether the decision thresholds for □ and Act_{min} can be made dependent on the phonemic structure of the words on which decisions for early recognition must be made. Summarising, we observed that a word activation score that is high and based on more phones with fewer phones to go predicts the correctness of a word more reliably than a similarly high value based on a small number of phones or a lower word activation score.

6. Discussion

In the laboratory, listeners are able to reliably identify polysyllabic content words before the end of the acoustic realisation (e.g., Marslen-Wilson, 1987). In real life, listeners not only use acoustic-phonetic information, but also contextual constraints to make a decision about the identity of a word. This makes it possible for listeners to guess the identity of content words even before their uniqueness point. In the research presented here, we investigated an alternative ASR system, called SpeM, that is able to recognise words during the speech recognition process for its ability for recognising words before their acoustic offset - but after their uniqueness point - a capability that we dubbed 'early recognition'. The restriction to recognition at or after the uniqueness point allowed us to focus on acoustic recognition only, and minimise the impact of contextual constraints. The probability theory underlying SpeM makes it possible for an advanced statistical LM to emulate the context effects that enable humans to recognise words even before their uniqueness point. Such an LM would make SpeM's recognition behaviour even more like human speech recognition behaviour.
In our analyses, we investigated the Bayesian word activation as predictor for early recognition. The results in Section 5 indicate that the Bayesian word activation can be used

as a predictor for on-line early recognition of polysyllabic words if we require that the quotient of the activations of the two hypotheses whose scores with first and second rank (□) and the minimum activation (Act_{min}) of the word with the highest activity score both exceed a certain threshold. There was, however, a fairly high percentage of false alarms. In the subsequent analysis, we found that the amount of evidence supporting a decision affects the performance. If the decision point was later in the word, thus based on more acoustic evidence in support of a word, the performance in terms of precision and recall improved. Furthermore, the risk of future mismatches decreases with fewer phones between the end of the word and the decision point, which also improves the performance. The predictor we chose has its parallels in the research area that investigates word confidence scores. For instance, □ is identical to the measure proposed in Brakensiek et al. (2003) for scoring a word's confidence in the context of an address reading system, while □ and Act_{min} are reminiscent of the graph-based confidence measure introduced in Wessel et al. (2001). The definition of word activation in SpeM resembles the calculation of word confidence measures (e.g., Bouwman et al., 2000; Wessel et al., 2001) in that both word activation and word confidence require a mapping from the non-normalised acoustic and LM scores in the search lattice to normalised likelihoods or posterior probabilities. Conceptually, both word activation and word confidence scores are measures related to the 'probability' of observing a word given a certain stretch of speech (by the human and ASR, respectively). However, in contrast to the early decision paradigm presented in this chapter, most conventional procedures for computing confidence measures are embedded in an integrated search; therefore, they only provide the scores at (or after) a point in an utterance when no new data are available that might revise the original scores.

The capability of recognising words on the basis of their initial part helps listeners in detecting and processing disfluencies, such as self-corrections, broken words, repeats, etc. (Stolcke et al., 1999). The integrated search used in ASR systems makes it difficult to adequately deal with these disfluencies. The incremental search, however, used by SpeM to recognise a word before its acoustic offset, in combination with the concept of word activation proposed in this study, opens the door towards alternatives for the integrated search that is used in almost all current ASR systems. An incremental search combined with word activations will be able to detect and process potential problems such as disfluencies more accurately and faster. Furthermore, if an incremental search would be incorporated in a speech-driven application, the time needed to respond to a speaker can be much shorter. This will be beneficial for ease of use of speech-centric interaction applications.

7. Conclusions and future work

In this chapter, we showed that SpeM, consisting of an automatic phone recogniser, a lexical search module, and an early decision mechanism is able to recognise polysyllabic words before their acoustic offset. In other words, the results presented in this chapter showed that early decision making in an ASR system is feasible. This early decision making property of SpeM is based on the availability of a flexible decoding during the word search and on the availability of various scores along the search paths during the expansion of the search space that can be properly normalised to support decision making. The early recognition process is comparable to what human listeners do while decoding everyday speech: Making guesses and predictions on the basis of incomplete information.

For 81.1% of the 936 correctly recognised focus words (51.9% of all focus words), the use of local word activation allowed us to identify the word before its last phone was available, and 64.1% of those words were already recognised one phone after the uniqueness point. However, the straightforward predictors that we derived from the Bayesian word activation appeared to yield relatively many false alarms. Yet, we are confident that the predictive power of measures derived from word activation can be improved, if only by making decision thresholds dependent on knowledge about the words that are being hypothesised. Finally, the reason for starting the research on early recognition to begin with was the potential benefits that early recognition promises for improving the speed and naturalness of human-system interaction. So far, the results of our work are promising. However, our experiments have shown that substantial further research is needed to better understand the impact of all the factors that affect and support the 'informed guessing' that humans perform in day-to-day interaction, and that allows them to predict what their interlocutor is going to say and when (s)he will reach a point in an utterance where it is safe to take the turn.

8. Acknowledgements

The work of Odette Scharenborg was supported by a Veni grant from the Netherlands Organization for Scientific Research (NWO).

9. References

Bouwman, G., Boves, L., Koolwaaij, J. (2000). Weighting phone confidence measures for automatic speech recognition. *Proceedings of the COST249 Workshop on Voice Operated Telecom Services*, Ghent, Belgium, pp. 59-62.

Brakensiek, A., Rottland, J., Rigoll, G. (2003). Confidence measures for an address reading system. *Proceedings of the IEEE International Conference on Document Analysis and Recognition*, (CDROM).

Garrod, S. & Pickering, M.J. (2004). Why is conversation so easy? *Trends in Cognitive Sciences*, *8*, 8-11.

Marslen-Wilson, W.D. (1987). Functional parallelism in spoken word recognition. *Cognition*, *25*, 71-102.

Gaskell, M.G., Marslen-Wilson, W.D. (1997). Integrating form and meaning: A distributed model of speech perception. *Language and Cognitive Processes*, *12*, 613-656.

Glass, J.R. (2003). Probabilistic framework for segment-based speech recognition. *Computer Speech and Language*, *17*, 137-152.

Grosjean, F. (1985). The recognition of words after their acoustic offset: Evidence and implications. *Perception & Psychophysics*, *28*, 299-310.

Kessens, J.M., Wester, M., Strik, H. (1999). Improving the performance of a Dutch CSR by modelling within-word and cross-word pronunciation variation. *Speech Communication*, *29*, 193-207.

Kessens, J.M., Cucchiarini, C., Strik, H. (2003). A data-driven method for modeling pronunciation variation. *Speech Communication*, *40*, 517-534.

Luce, P.A., Goldinger, S.D., Auer, E.T., Vitevitch, M.S. (2000). Phonetic priming, neighborhood activation, and PARSYN. *Perception and Psychophysics*, *62*, 615-625.

Marslen-Wilson, W.D., Tyler, L. (1980). The temporal structure of spoken language understanding. *Cognition, 8*, 1-71.

Marslen-Wilson, W.D. (1987). Functional parallelism in spoken word recognition. *Cognition, 25*, 71-102.

McClelland, J.L., Elman, J.L. (1986). The TRACE model of speech perception. *Cognitive Psychology, 18*, 1-86.

McQueen, J.M., Cutler, A., Briscoe, T., Norris, D. (1995). Models of continuous speech recognition and the contents of the vocabulary. *Language and Cognitive Processes, 10*, 309-331.

Norris, D. (1994). Shortlist: A connectionist model of continuous speech recognition. *Cognition, 52*, 189-234.

Norris, D., McQueen, J.M., Cutler, A., Butterfield, S. (1997). The possible-word constraint in the segmentation of continuous speech. *Cognitive Psychology, 34*, 191-243.

Radeau, M., Morais, J., Mousty, P., Bertelson, P. (2000). The effect of speaking rate on the role of the uniqueness point in spoken word recognition. *Journal of Memory and Language, 42* (3), 406-422.

Scharenborg, O., ten Bosch, L., Boves, L. (2003). Recognising 'real-life' speech with SpeM: A speech-based computational model of human speech recognition. *Proceedings of Eurospeech*, Geneva, Switzerland, pp. 2285-2288.

Scharenborg, O., Norris, D., ten Bosch, L., McQueen, J.M. (2005). How should a speech recognizer work? *Cognitive Science: A Multidisciplinary Journal, 29* (6), 867-918.

Scharenborg, O., ten Bosch, L. Boves, L. (2007). 'Early recognition' of polysyllabic words in continuous speech. *Computer Speech and Language, 21* (1), 54-71.

Steinbiss, V., Ney, H., Haeb-Umbach, R., Tran, B.-H., Essen, U., Kneser, R., Oerder, M., Meier, H.-G., Aubert, X., Dugast, C., Geller, D. (1993). The Philips research system for large-vocabulary continuous speech recognition. *Proceedings of Eurospeech*, Berlin, Germany. pp. 2125-2128.

Stolcke, A., Shriberg, E., Tür, D., Tür, G. (1999). Modeling the prosody of hidden events for improved word recognition. *Proceedings of Eurospeech*, Budapest, Hungary. pp. 311-314.

Strik, H., Russel, A.J.M., van den Heuvel, H., Cucchiarini, C., Boves, L. (1997). A spoken dialog system for the Dutch public transport information service. *International Journal of Speech Technology*, 2(2), 119-129.

Wessel, F., Schlueter, R., Macherey, K., Ney, H. (2001). Confidence measures for large vocabulary continuous speech recognition. *IEEE Transactions on Speech and Audio Processing*, 9(3), 288-298.

Wester, M. (2003). Pronunciation modeling for ASR - knowledge-based and data-derived methods. *Computer Speech & Language*, 17(1), 69-85.

Young, S., Evermann, G., Kershaw, D., Moore, G., Odell, J., Ollason, D., Povey, D., Valtchev, V., Woodland, P. (2002). *The HTK book (for HTK version 3.2)*. Technical Report, Cambridge University, Engineering Department.

20

Analysis and Implementation of an Automated Delimiter of "Quranic" Verses in Audio Files using Speech Recognition Techniques

Tabbal Hassan, Al-Falou Wassim and Monla Bassem
Lebanese University
Lebanon

1. Introduction

With more than 300 audio recitations of the Holy Quran available free on the internet, there is an increasing need to synchronize textual information with the audio recitation. The synchronized text can contain simply the textual representation of the recited verses or more information like the translation to a foreign language and the meaning of difficult verses. The general approach used nowadays consists of manually marking the beginning and ending of every verse. Taking into account the special way to recite Quran : "The art of tajweed", the manual method required a lot of work and proved to be unable to adapt to new recitors .

The goal of this chapter is to try the applicability and effectiveness of a new approach that uses common speech recognition techniques to automatically find and delimit verses in audio recitations regardless of the recitor. "The art of tajweed" defines some flexible yet well-defined rules to recite the Quran creating a big difference between normal Arabic speech and recited Quranic verses, thus it is interesting to analyze the impact of this "art" on the automatic recognition process and especially on the acoustic model. The study uses the Sphinx Framework (Carnegie Mellon University) as a research environment.

2. The sphinx IV framework

Sphinx is an open source (since version 2) project, financed by DARPA and developed at the Carnegie Melon University CMU in Pittsburgh with the contribution of Sun Microsystems, Mitsubishi Electric Research Lab, Hewlett Packard, University of California at Santa Cruz and the Massachusetts Institute of Technology. The sphinx-4 framework is a rewrite in java of the original sphinx engine. It follows a modular and extensible architecture to suit the needs of the researchers (Sphinx Group,2004).

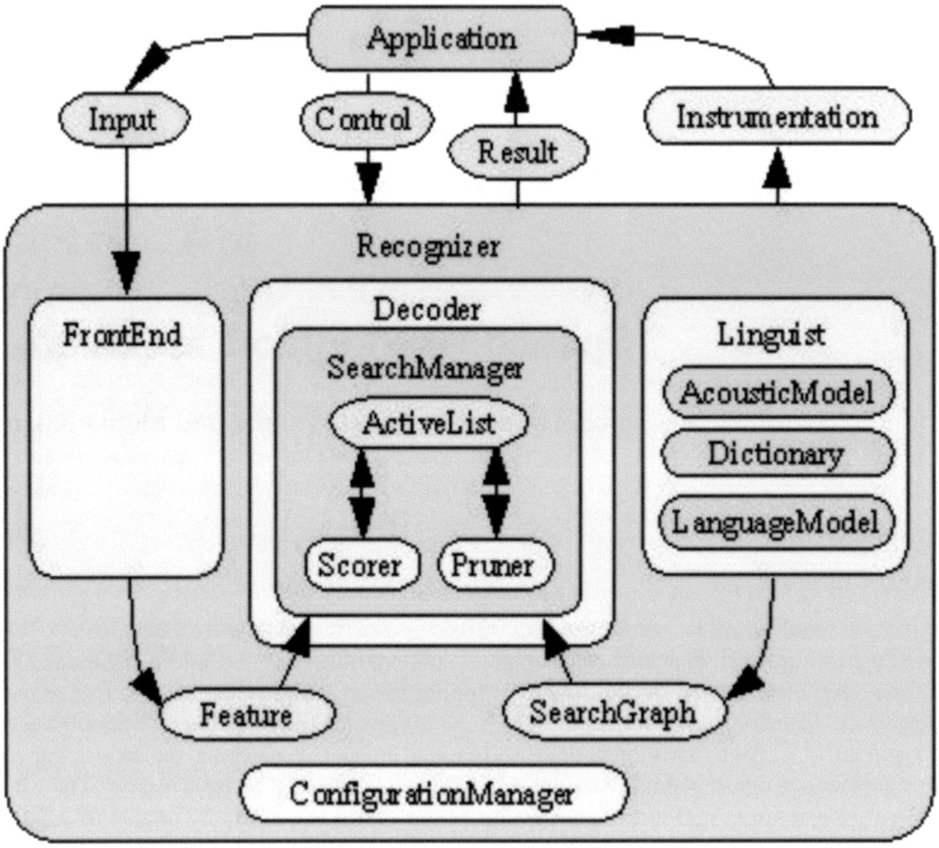

Figure 1. The functional bloc diagram of Sphinx-4

Sphinx-4 (Sphinx Group,2004) is based on HMM (Hidden Markov Model), and provides the researcher with a tool: SphinxTrain for the development of Acoustic models. The "Configuration Manager" uses an external configuration file to bind, at run-time, each part of the system with the corresponding algorithm. This flexibility makes it a practical choice for researchers because of the ability to test different algorithms or even develop new ones without the need of recompilation of the application. Once properly configured, the "FrontEnd" must either receive its input from audio files (batch mode) or directly from the microphone (live mode). Although not implemented yet, but the sphinx team envisaged the ability to switch between live mode and batch mode at run-time. The "frontend" generates the feature vectors (Cepstrum, delta cepstrum and delta delta cepstrum).The generated vectors will then be processed by the decoder that uses information from both the language model and the acoustic model to generate the search space for the HMM nodes. A number of search algorithms can be specified (Breadth-First, Beam Search, Viterbi, A*,…). The result of the decoding phase will then be returned to the calling application.

3. Holy Quran recitations and acoustic model

3.1 The "Art of Tajweed"

The recitation of the holy Quran differs from the normal reading of Arabic text due to a special art: "Fan al tajweed". "Tajweed" is considered as an art because not all recitors will perform the same verses in the same way. Furthermore, the same recitor may perform the same verses differently due to the flexibility of the laws of tajweed. Another word to describe the art of reciting Quran is "Tarteel". While obeying to the same laws of "tajweed", "tarteel" is generally identified by a faster reading pace in contrast with "tajweed" where reading is slower and where there is more focus on the artistic (musical) aspect of reading the holy Quran. "Tarteel" is the preferred reading style of recitors from Gulf countries while Syrian, Egyptian, Lebanese and other Middle Eastern recitors, prefers "tajweed".

There is 10 different law sets according to the 10 certified scholars[Hafs, Kaloun, Warsh,....] who teached the recitation of the Holy Quran (M.Habash,1998). Furthermore, recitors tend to vary the tone of their recitations according to musical "maqams" (The basic number of maqams is seven but there are other variations resulted from the combination of different maqams).

3.2 Impact of the "Art of Tajweed" on the acoustic model

The laws of "tajweed" introduce additional difficulties to the inherently difficult Arabic Speech Recognition problem. The most important part in our project was to identify what aspects of the laws of tajweed will affect the recognition phase and for which factors. After that analysis phase, we assumed that the seven "maqams" does not require any special treatment because of the statistical nature of the Hidden Markov Model (HMM). We considered only the laws of the art of Tajweed according to Hafs (used in 98% of the recitations) and found the following laws to have the most influence on the recognition of a specific recitation:

- Necessary prolongation of 6 vowels
- Obligatory prolongation of 4 or 5 vowels
- Permissible prolongation of 2,4 or 6 vowels
- Normal prolongation of 2 vowels
- Nasalization (ghunnah) of 2 vowels
- Silent unannounced letters
- Emphatic pronunciation of the letter R

Note that there is also the echoing sound that is produced with some unrest letters but we found that it has no effect on the recognition because the echo will be considered as noise and thus the noise-canceling filter will eliminate it.

In order to deal with these rules, we considered the prolongation as the repetition of the vowel n-corresponding times. The same consideration was used for the nasalization. The emphatic pronunciation of R led us to introduce another phoneme, or voice, that will also be used with other emphatic letters such as Kaf, Khaa when they are voweled by a fatha.

This conclusion can be verified by examining thoroughly the spectrogram of the Quranic recitations.

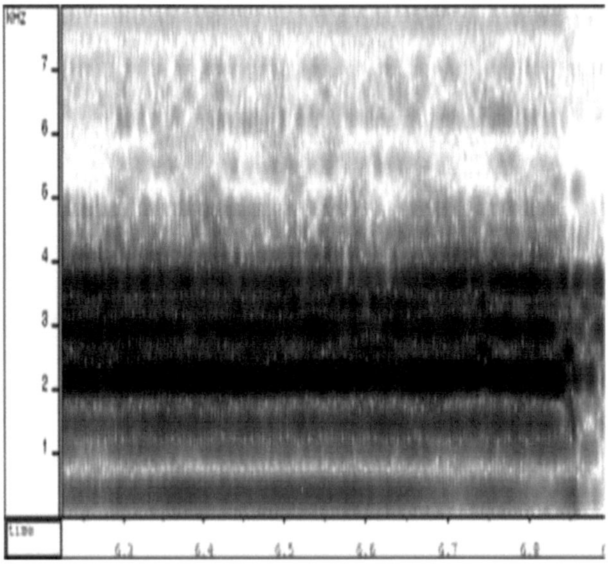

Figure 2. Spectrogram of a 6 vowels prolongation in "Bismillahi Al-Rahmani Al-Rahim"

The above spectrogram shows us that the six vowels prolongation of the "I" in "Al-Rahim" does not present so much variation, so considering it as the repetition of six "I" is a correct assumption.

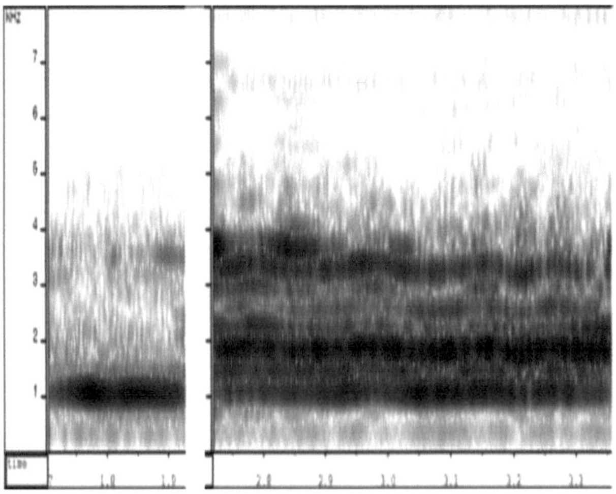

Figure 3. Comparaison between 2 "fatha" one emphatic with the letter R (left) and a normal with 2 vowels prolongation

If we compare the emphatic "fatha" and the normal "fatha", the differences between their spectrogram justifies the need to have two different phonemes representing each one of them. (All spectrograms were generated by the Open source tool WaveSurfer)
We can deduce from this study the following set of phonemes:

Symbol	Alphabet	Transliteration
AA	ء	Alef
B	ب	Ba'
T	ت	Ta'
TO	ط	Emph. Ta'
TH	ث	Tha'
J	ج	Jim
H	ح	Ha'
KH	خ	Emph. Kha'
D	د	Dal
DO	ض	Emph. Dad
DZ	ذ	Thal
DZO	ظ	Emph. Tha'
Z	ز	Zay
R	ر	Ra'
S	س	Sin
SH	ش	Shin
SO	ص	Emph. Sad
AIN	ع	Ayn
GAIN	غ	Ghayn
F	ف	Fa'
KO	ق	Emph. Kaf
K	ك	Kef
L	ل	Lam
M	م	Mim
N	ن	Noun
HI	ه	Ha'
W	و	Waw
Y	ي	Ye'
A	َ	Fatha
I	ِ	Kasra
E	َ مع مد أو ِ	Between kasra and fatha
AO	َ (مفخمة)	Emph. fatha
OU	ُ	Damma

Table 1. List of selected phonemes

The preceding set was then used to train the states of the HMM that corresponds to the acoustic model. About 1 hour of audio recitations of Sourate Al-Ikhlass for different recitors including normal (with no tajweed) and women performed recitations were used alongside with the corresponding dictionary mapping each word to the corresponding symbolic representation, to feed the sphinxTrain application that generated the corresponding Acoustic model for the application. It is recommended however to have a minimum of 8 hours of recorded audio in order to get efficient recognition, but we estimated that for the scope of our research, the use of only 1 hour is sufficient especially that we will be testing the system on a limited vocabulary(only sourate "Al-Ikhlass"). The following table shows an excerpt from the dictionary used for the training and recognition phases.

Bismi	B I S M I
Lahi	L L A HI I
Rahmani	R R AO HI M A N I
Rahim	R R AO HI I I M
Rahim(2)	R R AO HI I I I I I I M
Rahim(3)	R R AO HI I I I I M
Koul	KO OU L
Houwa	HI OU W A

Table 1. Excerpt from the dictionnary of Sourate Al-Ikhlass

4. Language Model

As with the majority of speech recognition solutions, a language model is used to increase the accuracy of the recognition process. The most important choices is either to create a statistical model of the words in a given language (or linguistic context) or to create a grammar file. The first approach is most suitable for large vocabulary applications while the latter is very well adapted to small ones. In the case of the holy Quran, Creating a statistical language model is the best approach but, in our research, we chose to use a grammar file based on the Java Speech Grammar Format JSGF specification that is well supported by Sphinx-4 because of the relatively small vocabulary that we chose for our test. Furthermore, It is imperative to have a high accuracy ratio based on an "all or none" paradigm meaning that if an "aya" could not be 100% recognized, it is better to drop it rather than filling it with garbage words because of the holiness of the Quran. These JSGF rules are similar to those used for conversational systems and are, actually, not suitable for large vocabulary continuous speech recognition but we generated them as such to reflect the structure of the "Sourat".

```
grammar Quran;

public <Ikhlass> = (Bismi  Lahi  Rahmani  Rahim |
        (Koul houwa llahou Ahad | Koul houwa llahou Ahadounil |Allahou
Samad |Lam Yaled wa Lam youlad |        wa Lam yakoun lahou koufouan
Ahad)
```

Listing 1. Excerpt from the grammar file

5. System Design

The core recognition process is provided automatically by the sphinx engine using the appropriate language and acoustic models. The sphinx framework must be configured using an xml based configuration file.

5.1. Data preparation

We configured our system with the following pipeline before being processed by the recognizer:

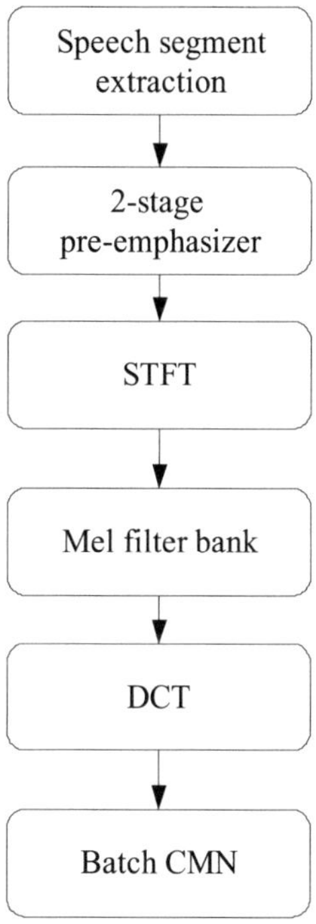

Figure 4. frontend pipeline of the system

The **Speech Segment Extraction** bloc labels speech frames as "speech" and "no speech" using a threshold that we set to -10db. The **pre-emphasis filter** consists of a digital network that flattens the signal:

$$\tilde{s}(n) = s(n) - as(n-1) \tag{1}$$

Where a is the pre-emphasis factor $0<a<1$

Although it is often enough to use one pre-emphasis filter, we have found that for some audio files the recognition ratio could be increased with the use of a 2-stage pre-emphasis filter with different factor values (0.92 and 0.97).

The **Short Time Fourier Transform STFT** bloc uses a raised cosine windower to apply the Fourier transform on detected speech blocs. We specified the number of point of FFT points to 512 points.

The **Mel Filter Bank** bloc transforms the frequency domain to the Mel frequency domain that mimics the sensitivity and perception of the human ear by transforming the frequency domain from a linear to a non-linear one. This goal is achieved by using a set of 30 triangular Mel filters where each filter is given by:

$$H_m(k)=\begin{cases}0 & k<f(m)\\ \dfrac{k-f(m-1)}{f(m)-f(m-1)} & f(m-1)\leq k\leq f(m)\\ \dfrac{f(m+1)-k}{f(m+1)-f(m)} & f(m)\leq k\leq f(m+1)\\ 0 & k>f(m)\end{cases}\quad \text{With m = 1,2,...30}$$

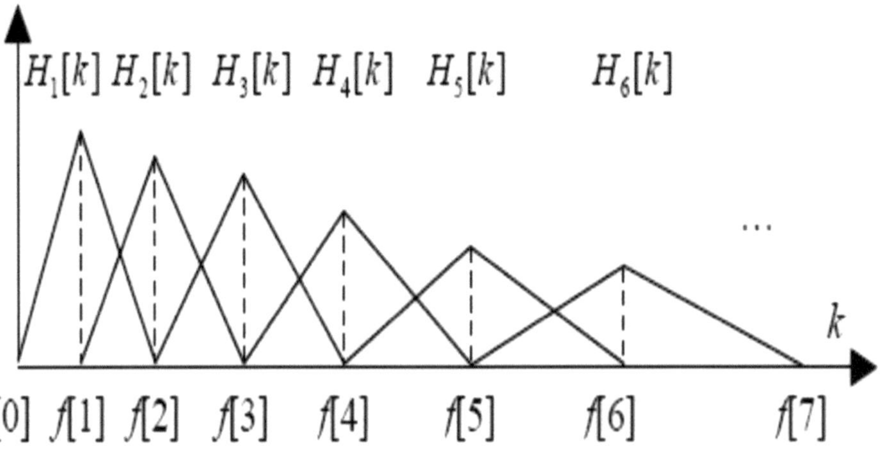

Figure 5. Representation of the Mel triangular filters

The **DCT** bloc applies the Discrete Cosine Transform on the result to extract the Mel Frequency Cepstral Coefficients MFCC (When all of the FFT coefficients are real values, DCT is often used to calculate the cepstras instead of the inverse FFT). The use of the MFCC has proven remarkable results in the field of speech recognition.

The final Cepstral Mean Normalization **CMN** operation is used to reduce the distorsion effect introduced by the transmission medium (microphone). It consists of subtracting the mean vector $\bar{x}$ from each vector x_t to obtain the normalized cepstrum vector. This is justified by recalling that the cepstral transformation transforms the convolution to addition due to the use of the logarithm, thus the mean of the cepstral holds the characteristic of the transmission medium (X. Huang, et al.,2001).

5.2. Application Design

The output of the front-end was then used to feed the sphinx core recognizer, which uses the Hidden Markov Models HMM as the recognition tool.

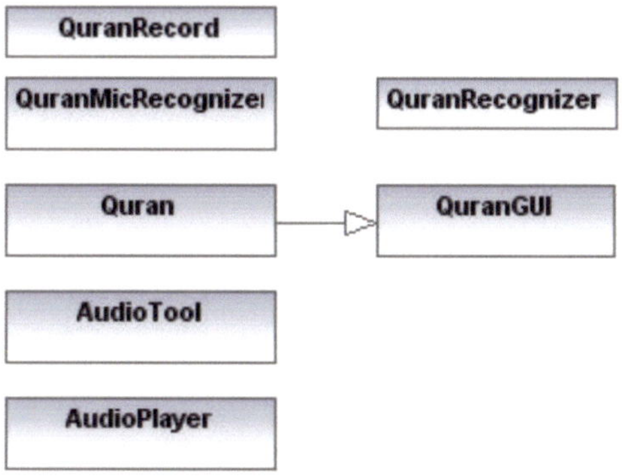

Figure 6. Class Diagram of the Quranic Recognizer application

The application uses a multithreaded architecture for better performance. **QuranRecognizer** takes audio files as an input and launches the recognition process. The result of the recognition is recorded in a list of type **QuranRecord** where each entry specifies the recognized word and its starting and ending time in the audio file. **AudioTool** and **AudioPlayer** are used for the playback of the audio files after the recognition process.
The internal application uses the **Observer** design pattern in order to notify the main application of each result of the detection process.

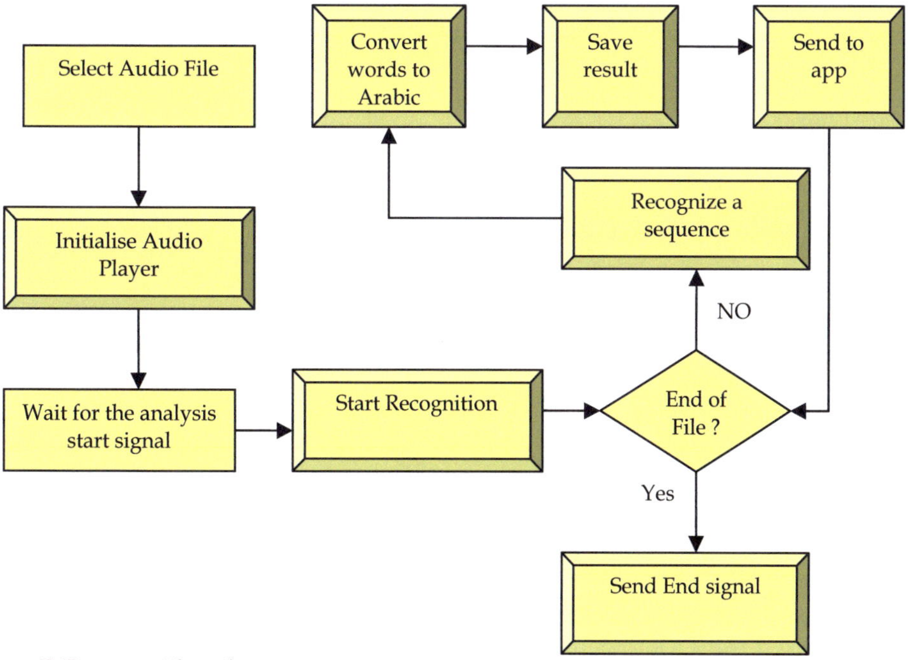

Figure 7. Program Flowchart

The version of SphinxTrain we used didn't support Unicode characters for text and thus we were forced to use transliteration for all the words in our dictionary. At the application level, we used a hash map to translate the results of the recognizer into common Arabic words. The search algorithm used in the decoder was the simple breadth first combined with the beam search. In the breadth first search algorithm, all the nodes on one level are examined before considering any node of the next level, it could thus take a longer time to reach the best solution if

6. Experiments and Results

We performed a large number of experiments on different individuals: each one was asked to recite sourat "Al-Ikhlass" several times and each time we recorded the number of ayates that were recognized correctly then a mean recognition ratio for each tester was calculated. The global mean is what we are showing in the following tables and the mean per individual represents the values shown in the graphs. The testers were chosen from different backgrounds without excluding women and children from them.

Type of Recitation	Number of Recitors	Mean Recognition Ratio
Tajweed	20	90%
Tarteel	20	92%

Table 2. Test results for professional recitors for sourate Al-Ikhlass

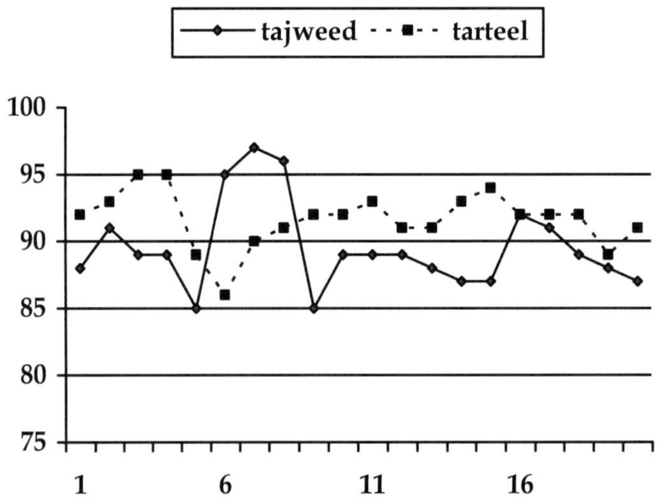

Figure 8. Chart illustrating the accuracy for both tarteel(dotted) and tajweed(plain) according to each recitor

The recognition ratio in the case of tarteel is slightly better than in the case of tajweed. One possible reason for this could be that the majority of the tarteel recitations available now follow the same monotony and the duration (in time) of each phoneme differ slightly from one recitor to another. There is also the extra noise that is caused by the compression of the audio files and the law quality of the recordings. Although we have anticipated this by using noisy audio files during the training, but the differences in compression ratios between the files add a lot of variety for the added noise and thus causing extra errors.

Gender of recitor	Number of Recitors	Mean Recognition Ratio
male	20	90%
female	20	85%

Table 3. Test results for normal arabic speaking people for Sourate Al-Ikhlass

When unskilled persons tested the system (we even tested it on children), it behaved astonishingly well even when the recitor was a woman, a case that cannot be encountered in real life because it not common to have a woman reciting the Holy Quran. There is also an interesting observation drawn from these tests: It is always recommended [6] to train the system with more than 500 different voices in order to reach speaker independence. But we didn't train our system with this relatively large number and still we were able to have remarkable speaker independence results.

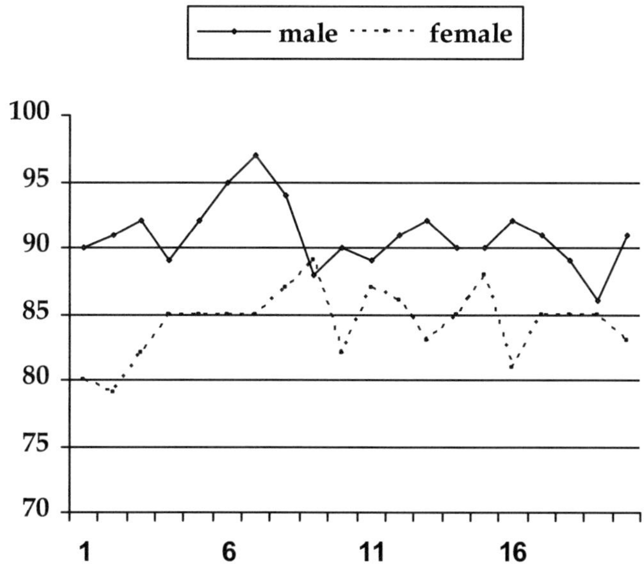

Figure 7. Chart illustrating the accuracy for male and female recitors (each tick on the x axis represents one recitor)

7. Conclusion

The system that we developed showed promising results although it was only tested against small Quran' chapters. We think that the incorporation of morphological knowledge of the Arabic language with a more sophisticated statistical model deduced from the full scope of the Holy Quran can lead to a robust universal recognizer for the Arabic language. The results that we obtained were far beyond our expectations: It behaved as well accurately with children and female voices as well as with male voices. The HMM is know to be poor in its representation of the time that the phoneme takes, however, time in our application was a very important factor and to resolve this issue, we were forced to represent all the variations of each pronunciation, this could prove to be very painful if it is to be applied to the whole Quran. Another approach based on a smarter representation of the duration of each phoneme may represent a better solution to this problem. But, overall, the system proved that it is possible to construct an Automatic delimiter of the verses of the Holy Quran; May be a search inside the audio files will emerge one day as an alternative and more versatile way to search the Holy Quran.

8. References

The Holy Quran.

M. Habash, "How to memorize the Quran" , Dar al-Khayr, Beirut 1986.

Sphinx group, "Sphinx-4: A flexible Open Source Framework for Speech Recognition", Sun Microsystems, 2004.

O. Kimball, "Recognition of Conversational and Broadcast Arabic Speech", BBN technologies.

R. Descout, "Applied Arabic linguistics and signal and information processing" , Hemisphere, 1987.

X. Huang, A. Acero, H. Hon, "Spoken language processing a guide to theory, algorithm and system design",Prentice Hall 2001.

21
An Improved GA Based Modified Dynamic Neural Network for Cantonese-Digit Speech Recognition

[1]S.H. Ling, [2]F.H.F. Leung, [2]K.F. Leung, [3]H.K. Lam, and [1]H.H.C. Iu
[1] *The University of Western Australia, WA, Australia*
[2]*The Hong Kong Polytechnic University, Hung Hom, Kowloon, Hong Kong*
[3] *Division of Engineering, King's College London, Strand, London, United Kingdom*

1. Introduction

An artificial Neural Network (ANN) is a well known universal approximator to model smooth and continuous functions (Brown & Harris, 1994). As ANNs can realize nonlinear models, they are flexible in modeling a wide variety of real-world complex applications, such as handwriting recognition, speech recognition, fault detection, medical inspection (Zhang, 2000), etc. ANNs being applied for pattern classification can be divided into two main categories: static and dynamic. Static pattern classification problems are usually tackled by multi-layer perceptron (MLP), radial basis feed-forward (RBF) networks and learning vector quantization (LVQ). However, limited by its structure of a traditional, a feed-forward network cannot model the correlation between the previous time frames and the current time frame. Thus, some dynamic applications, such as speech recognition, time varying prediction, dynamic control, etc. are difficult to be realized by static neural networks. Neither can feed-forward neural networks deal with problems without a fix dimension of input patterns. Recurrent Neural Network (RNN) (Engelbrecht, 2002; Kirschning et al., 1996; Zhang et al., 1993) and Time Delay Neural Network (TDNN) (Waibel et al., 1989) are used to overcome the limitations of feed-forward networks. They dynamically model time series cases; in other words, they are predictor networks that predict the next data frame from the current data frame.

ANNs operate in two stages: learning and generalization. Learning of a neural network is to approximate the behavior of the training data while generalization is the ability to predict well beyond the training data (Zhang, 2000). In order to have a good learning and generalization ability, a good tuning algorithm is needed. In this chapter, Genetic Algorithm (GA) is used as the tuning algorithm for training neural networks.

GA is a directed random search technique (Hanaki et al., 1999; Michalewicz, 1994; Pham & Karaboga, 2000) that is widely applied in optimization problems (Hanaki et al, 1999; Michalewicz, 1994; Pham & Karaboga, 2000). It is especially useful for complex optimization problems when the number of parameters is large and the analytical solutions are difficult to obtain. GA can help find out the globally optimal solution over a domain. It has been applied in different areas such as fuzzy control (Leung et al., 2004), path planning, modeling and classification (Setnes & Roubos, 2000), tuning parameters of neural/neural-fuzzy networks (Leung et al., 2003; Ling et al., 2003) etc. A lot of research efforts have been spent to improve the performance of GA. Different selection schemes and genetic operators have been proposed. Selection schemes such as rank-based selection, elitist strategies, steady-state election and tournament selection have been reported (Davis, 1991). There are two kinds of genetic operations, namely crossover and mutation. Apart from random mutation and crossover, other crossover and mutation mechanisms have been proposed. As the crossover mechanisms, two-point crossover, multipoint crossover, arithmetic crossover and heuristic crossover have been reported (Davis, 1991; Michalewicz, 1994; Srinivas & Patnaik, 1994). As the mutation mechanisms, boundary mutation, uniform mutation and non-uniform mutation can be found (Davis, 1991; Michalewicz, 1994; Srinivas & Patnaik, 1994).

In this chapter, a dynamic neural network tuned by an improved GA (Lam et al., 2004) is proposed. New genetic operations (crossover and mutation) will be introduced. Rules have been introduced to the crossover process to make offspring widely spread along the domain. A fast convergence rate can be reached. A different process of mutation has been applied. The proposed dynamic neural network of architecture shown in Fig. 1 consists of two modules: a tuner neural network (TNN) and a classifier recurrent neural network (CRNN). This specific architecture provides a one-input-one-rule property to the network. By using the TNN, some parameters can be determined from the input patterns and applied to the CRNN for further classification. In general, a traditional RNN can only have one set of fix parameters to model all different input patterns and their time variations owing to the limitation of its structure. In practice, consider the case depicted by Fig. 2; the data sets S1 & S2 belong to the class 1 but they are separated far apart, and the data set S3 belong to the class 2 in the spatial domain. When a traditional RNN with an inadequate number of parameters is used, the network will only be trained to recognize a data set R between S1 and S2. Then, S3 could be misclassified as class 1 as shown in Fig. 2(b). The recognition accuracy will then be lowered. However, if the number of parameters is large, the number of iteration required in the training process will be increased. In order to reduce the number of parameters of the network, we propose the dynamic NN. On using this network, when the input data belongs to S1, the TNN will provide the parameter set 1 for the CRNN to handle the data set S1. When the input data S2 is given, the parameter set corresponding to S2 will be used.

This chapter is organized as follows. The genetic algorithm with improved genetic operations will be briefly described in section 2. The specific structure of the proposed dynamic neural network will be presented in section 3. In section 4, a Cantonese-digit speech recognition system will be discussed. The results for recognizing thirteen Cantonese digits and a conclusion will be given in section 5 and 6 respectively.

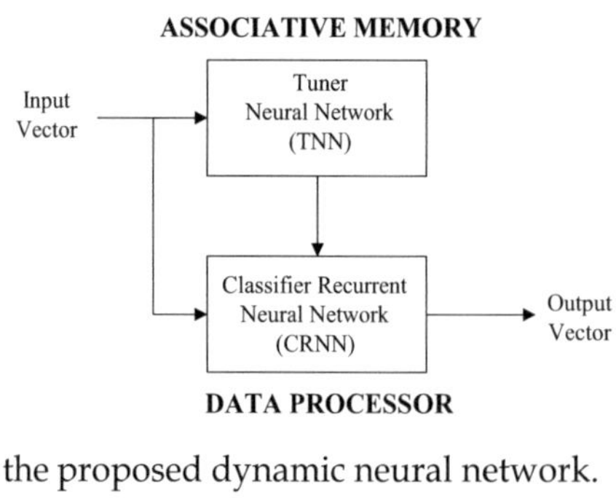

Figure 1. Architecture of the proposed dynamic neural network.

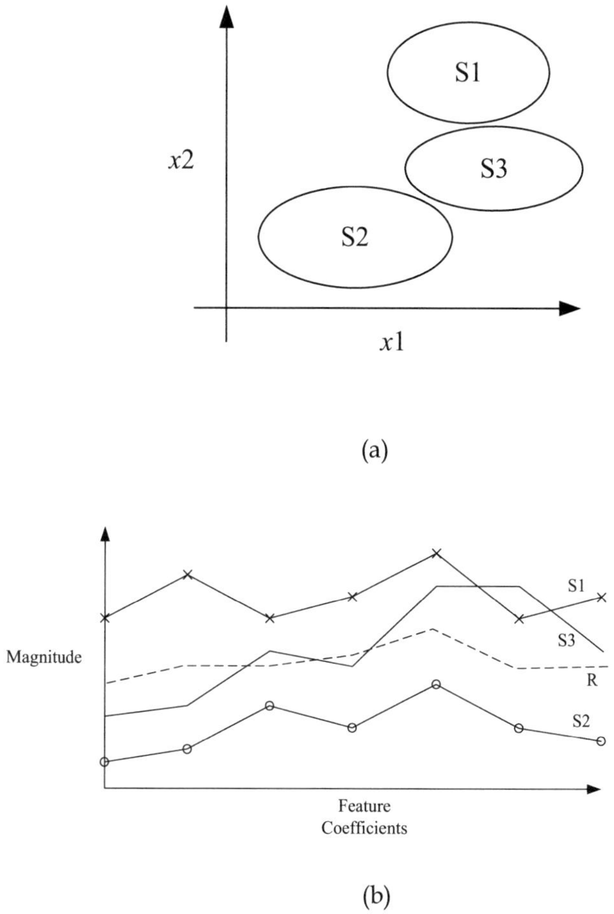

Figure 2. (a) Diagram showing 3 data sets in the spatial domain. (b) Diagram showing the feature curves of the 3 sets.

2. Genetic Algorithm with Improved Genetic Operations

Genetic algorithms (GAs) are powerful searching algorithms that can be used to solve optimization problems. The standard GA process (Michalewicz, 1994) is shown in Fig. 3. First, a population of chromosomes is created. Second, the chromosomes are evaluated by a defined fitness function. Third, some of the chromosomes are selected for performing genetic operations. Fourth, the genetic operations of crossover and mutation are performed. The produced offspring replaces their parents in the population. This GA process repeats until a user-defined criterion is reached. In this chapter, the standard GA is modified and new genetic operators are introduced to improve its performance. The improved GA process is shown in Fig. 4. Its details will be given as follows.

```
Procedure of the standard GA
begin
        τ → 0                      // τ: iteration number
initialize P(τ)                    //P(τ): population for iteration τ
        evaluate f(P(τ))           // f(P(τ)):fitness function
while (not termination condition) do
      begin
          τ→τ+1
          select 2 parents p1 and p2 from P(τ–1)
          perform genetic operations (crossover and mutation)
          reproduce a new P(τ)
          evaluate f(P(τ))
      end
end
```

Figure 3. Procedure of the standard GA

```
Procedure of the improved GA
begin
        τ → 0                      // τ: iteration number
initialize P(τ)                    //P(τ): population for iteration τ
        evaluate f(P(τ))           // f(P(τ)):fitness function
while (not termination condition) do
        begin
        τ→τ+1
        select 2 parents p1 and p2 from P(τ–1)
        perform crossover operation according to equations (7) - (10)
        perform mutation operation according to equation (14) to generate the offspring os
        // reproduce a new P(τ)
                if random number < pa   // pa: probability of acceptance
                        os replaces the chromosome with the smallest fitness value in the
                        population
                else if f(os) > smallest fitness value in the P(τ–1)
                        os replaces the chromosome with the smallest fitness value
                end
        evaluate f(P(τ))
        end
end
```

Figure 4. Procedure of the improved GA.

2.1 Initial Population

The initial population is a potential solution set **P**. The first set of population is usually generated randomly.

$$\mathbf{P} = \{\mathbf{p}_1, \mathbf{p}_2, \cdots, \mathbf{p}_{pop\_size}\} \tag{1}$$

$$\mathbf{p}_i = \begin{bmatrix} p_{i_1} & p_{i_2} & \cdots & p_{i_j} & \cdots & p_{i_{no\_vars}} \end{bmatrix},$$

$$i = 1, 2, \ldots, pop\_size; j = 1, 2, \ldots, no\_vars \quad (2)$$

$$para_{\min}^{j} \le p_{i_j} \le para_{\max}^{j} \quad (3)$$

where *pop_size* denotes the population size; *no_vars* denotes the number of variables to be tuned; p_{i_j}, $i = 1, 2, \ldots, pop\_size$; $j = 1, 2, \ldots, no\_vars$, are the parameters (genes) to be tuned; $para_{\min}^{j}$ and $para_{\max}^{j}$ are the minimum and maximum values of the parameter p_{i_j} respectively for all *i*. It can be seen from (1) to (3) that the potential solution set **P** contains some candidate solutions $\mathbf{p}_i$ (chromosomes). The chromosome $\mathbf{p}_i$ contains some variables p_{i_j} (genes).

2.2 Evaluation

Each chromosome in the population will be evaluated by a defined fitness function. The better chromosomes will return higher values in this process. The fitness function to evaluate a chromosome in the population can be written as,

$$fitness = f(\mathbf{p}_i) \quad (4)$$

The form of the fitness function depends on the application.

2.3 Selection

Two chromosomes in the population will be selected to undergo genetic operations for reproduction by the method of spinning the roulette wheel (Michalewicz, 1994). It is believed that high potential parents will produce better offspring (survival of the best ones). The chromosome having a higher fitness value should therefore have a higher chance to be selected. The selection can be done by assigning a probability q_i to the chromosome $\mathbf{p}_i$:

$$q_i = \frac{f(\mathbf{p}_i)}{\sum_{k=1}^{pop\_size} f(\mathbf{p}_k)}, i = 1, 2, \ldots, pop\_size \quad (5)$$

The cumulative probability $\hat{q}_i$ for the chromosome $\mathbf{p}_i$ is defined as,

$$\hat{q}_i = \sum_{k=1}^{i} q_k, i = 1, 2, \ldots, pop\_size \quad (6)$$

The selection process starts by randomly generating a nonzero floating-point number, $d \in [0 \quad 1]$. Then, the chromosome $\mathbf{p}_i$ is chosen if $\hat{q}_{i-1} < d \le \hat{q}_i$ ($\hat{q}_0 = 0$). It can be observed from this selection process that a chromosome having a larger $f(\mathbf{p}_i)$ will have a higher chance to be selected. Consequently, the best chromosomes will get more offspring, the average will stay and the worst will die off. In the selection process, only two chromosomes will be selected to undergo the genetic operations.

2.4 Genetic Operations

The genetic operations are to generate some new chromosomes (offspring) from their parents after the selection process. They include the crossover and the mutation operations.

A. Crossover

The crossover operation is mainly for exchanging information from the two parents, chromosomes $\mathbf{p}_1$ and $\mathbf{p}_2$, obtained in the selection process. The two parents will produce two offspring. First, four chromosomes will be generated according to the following equations,

$$\mathbf{o}_{\mathbf{s}_c}^1 = \begin{bmatrix} o_{\mathbf{s}_1}^1 & o_{\mathbf{s}_2}^1 & \cdots & o_{\mathbf{s}_{no\_vars}}^1 \end{bmatrix} = \frac{\mathbf{p}_1 + \mathbf{p}_2}{2} \tag{7}$$

$$\mathbf{o}_{\mathbf{s}_c}^2 = \begin{bmatrix} o_{\mathbf{s}_1}^2 & o_{\mathbf{s}_2}^2 & \cdots & o_{\mathbf{s}_{no\_vars}}^2 \end{bmatrix} = \mathbf{p}_{\max}(1-w) + \max(\mathbf{p}_1, \mathbf{p}_2)w \tag{8}$$

$$\mathbf{o}_{\mathbf{s}_c}^3 = \begin{bmatrix} o_{\mathbf{s}_1}^3 & o_{\mathbf{s}_2}^3 & \cdots & o_{\mathbf{s}_{no\_vars}}^3 \end{bmatrix} = \mathbf{p}_{\min}(1-w) + \min(\mathbf{p}_1, \mathbf{p}_2)w \tag{9}$$

$$\mathbf{o}_{\mathbf{s}_c}^4 = \begin{bmatrix} o_{\mathbf{s}_1}^4 & o_{\mathbf{s}_2}^4 & \cdots & o_{\mathbf{s}_{no\_vars}}^4 \end{bmatrix} = \frac{(\mathbf{p}_{\max} + \mathbf{p}_{\min})(1-w) + (\mathbf{p}_1 + \mathbf{p}_2)w}{2} \tag{10}$$

$$\mathbf{p}_{\max} = \begin{bmatrix} para_{\max}^1 & para_{\max}^2 & \cdots & para_{\max}^{no\_vars} \end{bmatrix} \tag{11}$$

$$\mathbf{p}_{\min} = \begin{bmatrix} para_{\min}^1 & para_{\min}^2 & \cdots & para_{\min}^{no\_vars} \end{bmatrix} \tag{12}$$

where $w \in \begin{bmatrix} 0 & 1 \end{bmatrix}$ denotes a weight to be determined by users, $\max(\mathbf{p}_1, \mathbf{p}_2)$ denotes the vector with each element obtained by taking the maximum among the corresponding element of p1 and p2. For instance, $\max(\begin{bmatrix} 1 & -2 & 3 \end{bmatrix}, \begin{bmatrix} 2 & 3 & 1 \end{bmatrix}) = \begin{bmatrix} 2 & 3 & 3 \end{bmatrix}$. Similarly, $\min(\mathbf{p}_1, \mathbf{p}_2)$ gives a vector by taking the minimum value. For instance, $\min(\begin{bmatrix} 1 & -2 & 3 \end{bmatrix}, \begin{bmatrix} 2 & 3 & 1 \end{bmatrix}) = \begin{bmatrix} 1 & -2 & 1 \end{bmatrix}$. Among $\mathbf{o}_{\mathbf{s}_c}^1$ to $\mathbf{o}_{\mathbf{s}_c}^4$, the two with the largest fitness value are used as the offspring of the crossover operation. These two offspring are put back into the population to replace their parents. One of the offspring is defined as,

$$\mathbf{o}_{\mathbf{s}} \equiv \begin{bmatrix} o_{s_1} & o_{s_2} & \cdots & o_{s_{no\_vars}} \end{bmatrix} = \mathbf{o}_{\mathbf{s}_c}^{i_{os}} \tag{13}$$

i_{os} denotes the index i which gives a maximum value of $f\left(\mathbf{o}_{\mathbf{s}_c}^i\right)$, $i = 1, 2, 3, 4$.

If the crossover operation can provide a good offspring, a higher fitness value can be reached in a smaller number of iteration. In general, two-point crossover, multipoint crossover, arithmetic crossover or heuristic crossover can be employed to realize the crossover operation (Michalewicz, 1994). The offspring generated by these methods, however, may not be better than that from our approach. As seen from (7) to (10), the potential offspring after the crossover operation spreads over the domain. While (7) and (10) result in searching around the centre region of the domain (a value of w near to 1 in (10) can move $\mathbf{o}_{\mathbf{s}_c}^4$ to be near $\frac{\mathbf{p}_1 + \mathbf{p}_2}{2}$), (8) and (9) move the potential offspring to be near the domain boundary (a small value of w in (8) and (9) can move $\mathbf{o}_{\mathbf{s}_c}^2$ and $\mathbf{o}_{\mathbf{s}_c}^3$ to be near $\mathbf{p}_{\max}$ and $\mathbf{p}_{\min}$ respectively).

B. Mutation

The offspring (13) will then undergo the mutation operation, which changes the genes of the chromosome. Consequently, the features of the chromosomes inherited from their parents can be changed. In general, various methods like boundary mutation, uniform mutation or non-uniform mutation (Michalewicz, 1994) can be employed to realize the mutation operation. Boundary mutation is to change the value of a randomly selected gene to its upper or lower bound. Uniform mutation is to change the value of a randomly selected gene to a value between its upper and lower bounds. Non-uniform mutation is capable of fine-tuning the parameters by increasing or decreasing the value of a randomly selected gene by a weighted random number. The weight is usually a monotonic decreasing function of the number of iteration. We propose a different process of mutation with details as follows. Every gene of the offspring os of (13) will have a chance to mutate governed by a probability of mutation, $p_m \in [0 \quad 1]$, which is defined by the user. This probability gives an expected number ($p_m \times$ no_vars $\times$ pop_size) of genes that undergo the mutation. For each gene, a random number between 0 and 1 will be generated such that if it is less than or equal to p_m, the operation of mutation will take place on that gene and updated instantly. The gene of the offspring of (13) is then mutated by:

$$\hat{o}_{s_k} = \begin{cases} o_{s_k} + \Delta o_{s_k}^U \text{ if } f(\mathbf{o}_\mathbf{s} + \Delta \mathbf{o}_{\mathbf{s}_k}^U) \geq f(\mathbf{o}_\mathbf{s} - \Delta \mathbf{o}_{\mathbf{s}_k}^L) \\ o_{s_k} - \Delta o_{s_k}^L \text{ if } f(\mathbf{o}_\mathbf{s} + \Delta \mathbf{o}_{\mathbf{s}_k}^U) < f(\mathbf{o}_\mathbf{s} - \Delta \mathbf{o}_{\mathbf{s}_k}^L) \end{cases}, k = 1, 2, \ldots, no\_vars \tag{14}$$

where

$$\Delta o_{s_k}^U = w_{m_k} r\left(para_{\max}^k - o_{s_k}\right) \tag{15}$$

$$\Delta o_{s_k}^L = w_{m_k} r\left(o_{s_k} - para_{\min}^k\right) \tag{16}$$

$$\Delta \mathbf{o}_{\mathbf{s}_k}^U = \begin{bmatrix} 0 & 0 & \cdots & \Delta o_{s_k}^U & \cdots & 0 \end{bmatrix} \tag{17}$$

$$\Delta \mathbf{o}_{\mathbf{s}_k}^L = \begin{bmatrix} 0 & 0 & \cdots & \Delta o_{s_k}^L & \cdots & 0 \end{bmatrix} \tag{18}$$

$r \in [0 \quad 1]$ is a randomly generated number; $w_{m_k} \in (0 \quad 1]$ is a weight governing the magnitudes of $\Delta o_{s_k}^U$ and $\Delta o_{s_k}^L$. The value of weight w_{m_k} is varied by the value of $\frac{\tau}{T}$ to serve a fine-tuning purpose. T is the total number of iteration. In order to perform a local search, the value of weight w_{m_k} should be very small as $\frac{\tau}{T}$ increases in order to reduce the significance of the mutation. Under this assumption, a monotonic decreasing function governing w_{m_k} is proposed to be,

$$w_{m_k} = w_f \left(1 - \frac{\tau}{T}\right)^{\frac{1}{w_\tau}} \geq 0 \qquad (19)$$

where $w_f \in [0 \quad 1]$ and $w_\tau > 0$ are variables to be chosen to determine the initial value and the decay rate respectively. For a large value of w_f, it can be seen from (15) and (16) that $\Delta o_{s_k}^U \approx r\left(para_{\max}^k - o_{s_k}\right)$ and $\Delta o_{s_k}^L \approx r\left(o_{s_k} - para_{\min}^k\right)$ initially as $\left(1 - \frac{\tau}{T}\right)^{\frac{1}{w_\tau}} \approx 1$, which ensure a large search space. When the value of $\left(1 - \frac{\tau}{T}\right)^{\frac{1}{w_\tau}} \approx 0$, it can be seen that the values of $\Delta o_{s_k}^U$ and $\Delta o_{s_k}^L$ are small to ensure a small search space for fine-tuning.

2.5 Reproduction

The reproduction process takes place after the genetic operations. The new offspring will be evaluated using the fitness function of (4). This new offspring will replace the chromosome with the smallest fitness value among the population if a randomly generated number within 0 to 1 is smaller than $p_a \in [0 \quad 1]$, which is the probability of acceptance defined by users. Otherwise, the new offspring will replace the chromosome with the smallest fitness value only if the fitness value of the offspring is greater than the fitness value of that chromosome in the population. p_a is effectively the probability of accepting a bad offspring in order to reduce the chance of converging to a local optimum. Hence, the possibility of reaching the global optimum is kept.

After the operation of selection, crossover, mutation and reproduction, a new population is generated. This new population will repeat the same process. Such an iterative process can be terminated when the result reaches a defined condition, e.g. the change of the fitness values between the current and the previous iteration is less than 0.001, or a defined number of iteration has been reached.

3. Modified Dynamic Neural Network

Recurrent Neural Network (RNN) is a dynamic network which is commonly used to tackle complex dynamic sequential problems, such as time series prediction, dynamic system identification and grammatical inference. With the specific network structure, the temporal information can be brought to the next time frame. As a result, the RNN can process static as well as time-varying information. Elman network, Jordan network (Rabiner & Juang, 1993), etc. are commonly used RNNs. They are constructed as closed-loop systems while the hidden node outputs or the network outputs are fed back to the network inputs as the dynamic information respectively. However, training a recurrent network to the desired behavior is not easy. It is because there is only a fix set of parameters representing both the temporal and static features of the input data sets.

In order to improve the classifying ability of a traditional RNN, a traditional 3-layer feed-forward neural network and a recurrent neural network can be combined together as a modified network. A traditional 3-layer feed-forward neural network provides a distinct solution to static pattern classification problems (Jang, 1997) and a recurrent network provides a solution to time-varying problems. The proposed neural network architecture employs a feed-forward neural network (rule-base neural network) to offer some rule information to the recurrent neural network (classifier recurrent neural network) with respect to the input patterns. Thus, the additional information provided by the rule-base neural network can compensate the limitation of the fixed parameter sets.

3.1 Model of the Modified Dynamic Neural Network

The proposed modified dynamic neural network consists of two parts, namely the Tuner Neural Network (TNN) and the Classifier Recurrent Neural Network (CRNN). The network architecture is shown in Fig.5.

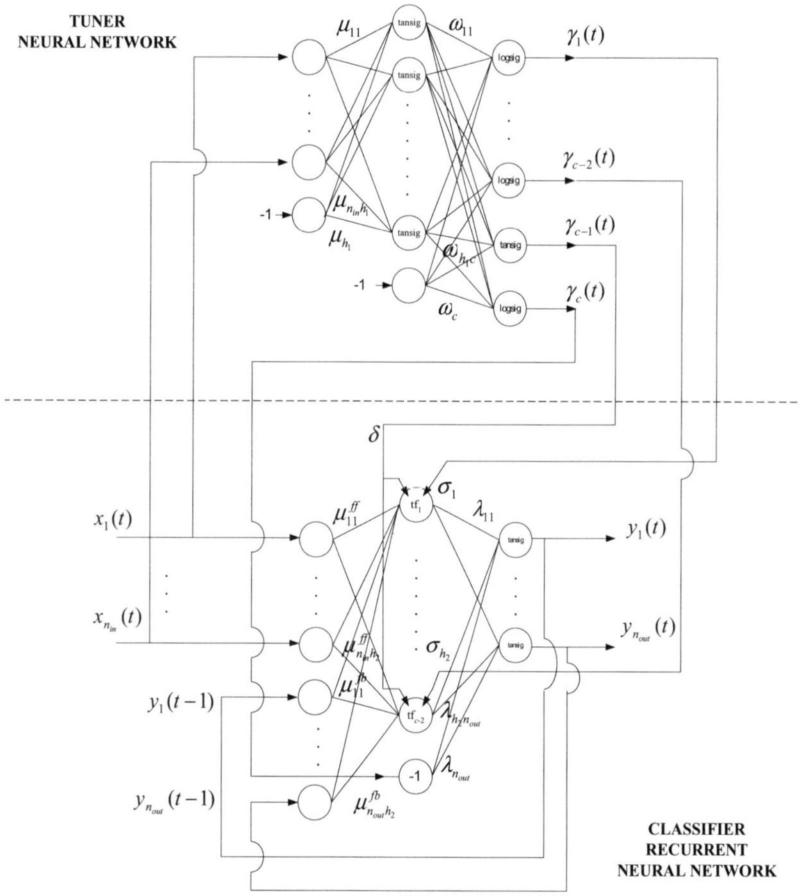

Figure 5. Modified dynamic neural network architecture.

A. Tuner Neural Network

The tuner neural network (TNN) is a traditional 3-layer feed-forward neural network that provides suitable parameters to the classifier recurrent neural network according to the input patterns. The input-output relationship of the TNN is defined as follows.

$$\gamma_g(t) = logsig\left[\sum_{j=1}^{h_1} \omega_{jg} tansig\left(\sum_{i=1}^{n_{in}} \mu_{ij} x_i(t) - \mu_j\right) - \omega_g\right] \quad (20)$$

$$\gamma_{c-1}(t) = tansig\left[\sum_{j=1}^{h_1} \omega_{jc-1} tansig\left(\sum_{i=1}^{n_{in}} \mu_{ij} x_i(t) - \mu_j\right) - \omega_{c-1}\right] \quad (21)$$

$$\gamma_c(t) = logsig\left[\sum_{j=1}^{h_1} \omega_{jc} tansig\left(\sum_{i=1}^{n_{in}} \mu_{ij} x_i(t) - \mu_j\right) - \omega_c\right] \quad (22)$$

where $\gamma_g(t)$, $\gamma_{c-1}(t)$, and $\gamma_c(t)$ are the outputs of the TNN for the t-th data frame; $tansig(\alpha) = \frac{2}{1+e^{-2\alpha}} - 1$, $\alpha \in \Re$, is the tangent sigmoid function; $logsig(\alpha) = \frac{1}{1+e^{-\alpha}}$, $\alpha \in \Re$, denotes the logarithmic sigmoid function; ω_{jg}, $j = 1, 2, \ldots, h_1$, denotes the weight of the link between the j-th hidden node and the g-th output; h_1 is a non-zero positive integer denoting the number of hidden nodes; μ_{ij}, $i = 1, 2, \ldots, n_{in}$, denotes the weight of the link between the i-th input node and the j-th hidden node; $x_i(t)$ denotes the i-th input of the TNN; μ_j, denotes the weight of the j-th bias term for the hidden layer; ω_g, ω_{c-1}, and ω_c are the link weights of the bias terms for the output layer; n_{in} and c denote the numbers of input and output respectively.

B. Classified Recurrent Neural Network

As shown in Fig. 5, the classifier recurrent neural network (CRNN) is a 3-layer recurrent network. It analyses the input patterns, recurrent information and the information provided by the TNN to produce the network outputs. The input patterns are tokens of short-time feature frames. The feature frames will be fed to the input of the network one-by-one. The outputs of the network will be fed back to the network inputs with one sampling-period delay. The input-output relationship of the CRNN is defined as follows.

$$y_k(t) = tansig\left[\sum_{j=1}^{h_2} \lambda_{jk} tf\left(\sum_{i=1}^{n_{in}} \mu_{ij}^{ff} x_i(t) + \sum_{q=1}^{n_{out}} \mu_{qj}^{fb} y_q(t-1)\right) - \lambda_k \gamma_c(t)\right], k = 1, 2, \ldots, n_{out} \quad (23)$$

where $y_k(t)$ denotes the k-th output of the CRNN for the t-th data frame; h_2 is a non-zero positive integer denoting the number of hidden nodes (excluding the bias node); λ_{jk}, $j = 1,2, \ldots, h_2$ denotes the weight of the link between the j-th hidden node and the k-th output; μ_{ij}^{ff}, $i = 1,2, \ldots, n_{in}$ denotes the weight of the link between the i-th input and the j-th hidden node; $\gamma_c(t)$ denotes the last output from the TNN; μ_{qj}^{fb}, $q = 1, 2, \ldots, n_{out}$ denotes the weight of the link between the q-th recurrent input and the j-th hidden node; λ_k denotes the link weight of the k-th bias term for the output layer; $tf(\cdot)$ denotes the hidden node activation function and is defined as follows.

$$tf(\chi_g; \delta, \sigma_g) = \frac{2}{1+e^{\frac{-(\chi_g-\delta)}{2\sigma_g^2}}} - 1, g = 1,2, \ldots, h_2 \quad (24)$$

χ_g, δ and σ_g denote the input and the two parameters of the activation function respectively. It should be noted that δ and σ_g are the outputs of the TNN. Thus, $\sigma_g = \gamma_g$, $g = 1, 2, \ldots, h_2$;

$h_2 = c - 2$, and $\delta = \gamma_c - 1$. These parameters are given by the TNN to guide the CRNN how to handle the input data. Owing to the dynamic structure of the proposed NN, both the static and dynamic properties of the data can be modeled. Different parameter values change the shape of the non-linear activation function (24). The CRNN performs dynamic adaptation to the input frame variations through the recurrent links. Each frame pattern will have its own parameter set. Owing to the structure of the modified RNN, both static (TNN) and dynamic (CRNN) changes of the data are classified at the same time.

C. Training of the Modified Dynamic Neural Network

An individual class network training process is employed. Every data class has its own network, where every network has the same structure. The training process is to train the network input frame(s) to match the network temporal output frame(s); where the output frame(s) of the network is equal to the network input frame(s). Thus, the highest fitness value can be obtained from the network by using the same class of input data set. All parameters in the modified RNN are trained by the improved GA (Lam et al., 2004).

4. Speed Recognition System

Electronic Book (eBook) provides a new trend of reading. By using eBook, traditional reading materials can be enriched. However, the input method for an eBook reader is typically realized by handwritten graffiti recognition through the touch-screen. In order to develop a more natural way for eBook inputs, speech recognition is proposed.

Speech recognition is a tool to make machines understand the sounds made by the human vocal tract, which is called speech. Speech is an acoustic signal that varies in time. Every speech has its unique characteristics in the frequency domain, called speech features. Although a speech frame is characterized by unique features, other factors such as background noise, words with similar spectral characteristics (especially common for Cantonese words) may affect the recognition accuracy. A good feature extraction method and a high-accuracy classification algorithm are needed to produce a high-performance speech recognizer.

Cantonese speech composes of a chain of mono-syllabic sound. Each Cantonese-character speech is a combined unit of a tone and a syllable. There are nine possible tones for a Cantonese syllable. Some Cantonese characters share the same vowel, e.g. the Cantonese character of "1" (/jat1/) and the Cantonese character of "7" (/cat1/) share the same vowel of /a/ (Markowitz, 1996). It is a difficult task to recognize Cantonese characters that requires the discrimination of not only characters with different syllable but also tones of the same syllable with high accuracy.

In general, speech recognition (Rabiner & Juang, 1993) is realized in two stages: speech preprocessing and classification. The preprocessing stage involves segmentation and feature extraction. Segmentation is used to define the boundaries of the temporal speech segments that represent the basic phonetic components. Then, the stationary properties of the individual segment can be modeled by some static classification approach. The dynamic properties of the temporal segments can be modeled by some dynamic classification approach. Feature extraction is a technique to find a good representation to a speech signal. Normally, the time-domain speech signals will be windowed into speech frames. From each speech frame, the fast Fourier transform is applied to obtain the frequency spectrum. Based on the frequency spectrum, digital signal analysis techniques will be applied to obtain the cepstral coefficients, which describe the features of the speech frame. Filter-bank analysis (Rabiner & Juang, 1993) is often used to analyze the speech frames for extracting features. By distributing different band-pass filters in the mel-scale of frequency, which models the characteristics of the human ears, the frames of speech feature coefficients can be obtained. Using the feature coefficients, we can perform the second step of classification..

Speech classification methods can be categorized into 3 types: template matching, acoustic-phonetic recognition and stochastic processing. For the template matching technique, reference speech units called templates are used to perform the matching process between the testing speech units and the templates. Thus, the testing speech units that produced close matching with the reference templates can be identified. The acoustic-phonetic recognition approach is a phoneme level speech recognition approach. By using this approach, the acoustic similarity among the phoneme combinations in a speech will be used to identify the input speech. The stochastic process for speech recognition is similar to the template matching process that requires the reference speech units for identifying the input speech. The main difference is that the stochastic process performs a statistical and probabilistic analysis matching process, which is not a direct mapping to the reference templates.

Two popular Cantonese speech recognition techniques are that using the Hidden Markov Model (HMM) and that using the Neural Network (NN) (Rabiner & Juang, 1993; Wu & Chan, 1993; Lee et al., 1998). HMM is one well-known statistical state-sequence recognizing approach for speech recognition (Markowitz, 1996). The states in a HMM structure represent the stochastic process, and the directional links between states indicate the transitions of flowing from one state to another. With a different states-and-transitions structure for each speech pattern, recognition can be done by matching the testing speech unit to the reference models. The Baum-Welch maximum-likelihood algorithm can be employed to compare the probability score between the testing and reference models as the likelihood index. Another verification process for HMM speech recognition is done by the Viterbi algorithm, which is a method to determine the nodes and sequence of the testing speech unit that closely match the reference models.

Recently, neural networks (NNs), especially the recurrent neural networks, are commonly used for speech recognition. Based on its connectionist modeling technique, non-linear functions can be modeled. Thanks to the capability of being a universal approximator through training, an NN can be trained to become a classifier for a certain input pattern.

On applying NNs to realize the classification of speech patterns, we can adopt a static or a dynamic pattern classification method. The static pattern classification method uses a conventional 3-layer feed-forward neural network to model each single-character Cantonese speech. The static properties of the speech frames can be analyzed. However, the input vector of the network contains no acoustic feature, and the network is only suitable for recognizing speech patterns with a single syllable.

Since the dynamic properties between speech frames are important for recognizing speech, we should consider using recurrent neural networks (RNNs) as the classifiers, and learn the relationships between speech frames through the training process. In practice, an RNN is suitable to classify speech with multiple syllables. However, an RNN consumes more computing power than a feed-forward NN. Owing to the recurrent information fed back, an

RNN needs a large number of network parameters so as to cope with the speech frame updates and the recurrent information updates for each speech pattern. As the number of parameters is large, a longer training time is needed for an RNN to converge.
It should be noted that one neural network, feed-forward or recurrent, is needed effectively to model one speech pattern. If we have to recognize a large number of recognition vocabularies, a standard structured NN is difficult to achieve a good performance. It is because the trained network parameters are used to model the features of the input patterns. When the number of input patterns is large and they are not sufficiently clustered into the same class, more network parameters are needed to model them. A complicated network structure will result. This will degrade the performance of the network in terms of computational power, convergence rate and recognition accuracy.

A. Speech feature extraction

The speech patterns are formatted in 8-bit PCM format sampled at 11kHz. The obtained time-domain speech vector $\mathbf{s}=[s(1) \;\; s(2) \;\; \cdots \;\; s(no\_sample)]$ is then windowed by the 128-sample sliding Hamming windows $wh(\tau)$ with 50% overlap to form speech frames. The zero-crossing rate and speech energy have to be found in order to determine whether the frames are voiced (sonorant) or unvoiced (non-sonorant). A speech frame with a high zero-crossing rate but low speech energy level is defined as the non-sonorant speech frame. Conversely, a sonorant speech frame will have a high speech energy level but low zero-crossing rate. The process is defined as follows.

$$E_n = \sum_{\tau=1}^{128} s(m_n+\tau)^2 \;\; ,n = 1, 2, \ldots, no\_frame \tag{25}$$

$$Z_n = \frac{1}{2\times 128}\sum_{\tau=1}^{127}\left[s_s(m_n+\tau)-s_s(m_n+\tau+1)\right],$$
$$n = 1, 2, \ldots, no\_frame \tag{26}$$

$$m_n = [64(n-1)] \;\; ,n = 1, 2, \ldots, no\_frame \tag{27}$$

$$s_s(\tau)=\begin{cases} 1, \text{when } s(\tau) >= 0 \\ -1, \text{when } s(\tau) < 0 \end{cases},$$
$$\tau = 1, 2, \ldots, no\_sample \tag{28}$$

where E_n denotes the speech energy of the n-th frame; m_n denotes the starting index of the n-th frame; *no_frame* denotes the number of frames for a speech signal; Z_n denotes the zero-crossing rate of the n-th frame; *no_sample* (= 128) denotes the number of time samples of a speech frame (i.e. the number elements of a speech frame vector). As shown in Fig. 6(a), G_1, G_2 and G_3 indicate the non-sonorant, sonorant and non-sonorant region of a single-syllable Cantonese-digit speech. The starting speech frame of a new group begins when the speech energy curve and the zero-crossing curve intersect, provided that the group has more than six speech frames (i.e. a duration longer than 40ms); otherwise, no group change will take place. Therefore, the speech signal as shown in Fig. 6(a) gets three groups. Five groups are obtained from a double-syllable Cantonese-number speech as shown in Fig. 6(b). G_1, G_3 and G_5 are the non-sonorant regions due to high zero-crossing rate and low speech energy level.

While G_2 and G_4 are the sonorant regions due to high speech energy level and low zero-crossing rate. Since a pause has been added after the first syllable, G_3 is obtained.

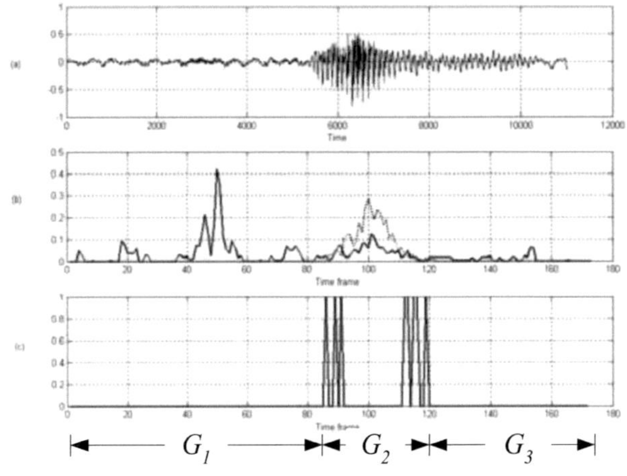

(a)

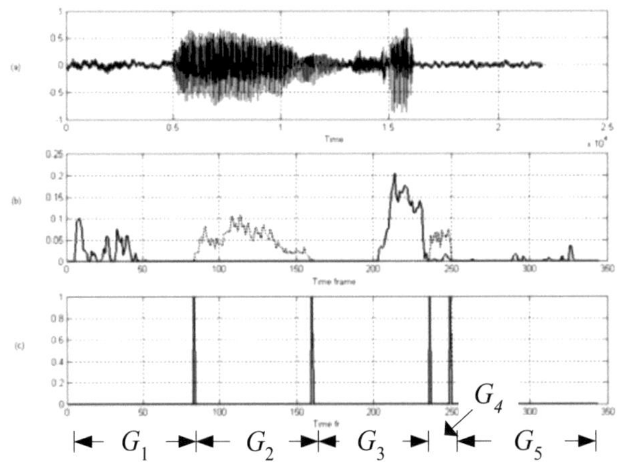

(b)

Figure 6. Acoustic feature groups of (a) single Cantonese digit, (b) double Cantonese digits.

Fast Fourier Transform (FFT) and uniform filter-bank filtering are then performed to each speech frame. The feature coefficients of each speech frame are defined as follows.

$$\mathbf{Sf}_n = [Sf_n(1) \quad Sf_n(2) \quad \cdots \quad Sf_n(128)] = Re\{FFT([wh(\tau)s_n(\tau)])\}, \ 1 \le \tau \le 128 \tag{29}$$

$$c_n^{\beta} = \frac{20\log_{10} \sum_{l=1}^{\alpha} Sf_n(\rho_\beta + l)wt(\rho_\beta + l)}{\alpha} \quad \beta = 1,2, \ldots, no\_filter \tag{30}$$

$$wt(l) = \begin{cases} \frac{2l-1}{\alpha}, & 1 \le l \le \frac{\alpha}{2} \\ \frac{2(\alpha - l + 1)}{\alpha}, & \frac{\alpha}{2} + 1 \le l \le \alpha \end{cases} \tag{31}$$

$$\alpha = floor\left(\frac{128}{no\_filter}\right) \times 2 \tag{32}$$

$$\rho_\beta = 0.5\alpha(\beta - 1),\ \beta = 1, 2, \ldots, no\_filter \tag{33}$$

$$\mathbf{D}_n = \begin{bmatrix} c_n^2 - c_n^1 & c_n^3 - c_n^2 & \cdots & c_n^{no\_filter} - c_n^{no\_filter-1} \end{bmatrix} \tag{34}$$

where $\mathbf{Sf}_n$ denotes the frequency spectrum of the n-th speech frame; $Re\{\cdot\}$ denotes the real part of the argument vector; $FFT(\cdot)$ denotes the fast Fourier transform function; $s_n = [s_n(1) \ \ s_n(2) \ \ \cdots \ \ s_n(128)]$ denotes the n-th speech frame in time-domain; $wt(\cdot)$ denotes the triangular window; α denotes the number of frequency components tackled by each band-pass filter; $floor(\cdot)$ denotes the floor function which is used to round up a floating point number; no_filter denotes the number of band-pass filters; ρ_β denotes the starting index of the β-th band-pass filter; c_n^{β} denotes the mean power output from the β-th band-pass filter for the n-th frame; $\mathbf{D}_n$ is a vector formed by the magnitude differences between two consecutive band-pass filter outputs.

The neighboring speech frames of the same nature, i.e. voiced/sonorant or unvoiced/non-sonorant frames, will be grouped together as shown in Fig. 6. The mean feature coefficient of all the speech frames in the same group will be calculated as follows.

$$\mathbf{scoeff}_\eta = \frac{\sum_{n=1}^{G_\eta} \mathbf{D}_n}{G_\eta},\ \eta = 1,2, \ldots, no\_group \tag{35}$$

where $\mathbf{scoeff}_\eta$ denotes η-th speech feature group; G_η denotes the number of speech frames in the η-th group; no_group denotes the number of groups that can be segmented from the speech. Thus, the acoustic feature sequence of the speech can be written as $\mathbf{Sp} = \begin{bmatrix} \mathbf{scoeff}_1 & \mathbf{scoeff}_2 & \cdots & \mathbf{scoeff}_{no\_group} \end{bmatrix}$, and each element vector is then normalized as input to the dynamic variable-parameter neural network in sequence to do the speech recognition.

B. Speech classification

The inputs of the modified RNN is defined as $\mathbf{x} = \frac{\mathbf{Sp}}{\|\mathbf{Sp}\|}$ where $\|\cdot\|$ denotes the l_2 vector norm.

The objective of the training process for each network is to adjust the parameters so as to minimize the error between the network outputs and the desired values, where the desired values are the inputs of the network. The performance of the network is governed by the value of fitness, which is a function the error value err :

$$fitness = \frac{1}{1+err} \tag{36}$$

$$err = \mathbf{e}_w sort\left(\left[\sum_{\eta=1}^{ng}\left|d_\eta^1 - y_\eta^1\right| \quad \sum_{\eta=1}^{ng}\left|d_\eta^2 - y_\eta^2\right| \quad \cdots \quad \sum_{\eta=1}^{ng}\left|d_\eta^{n_{out}} - y_\eta^{n_{out}}\right|\right]^T\right) \tag{37}$$

$$\mathbf{e}_w = \left[e_w^1 \quad e_w^2 \quad \cdots \quad e_w^k\right] = \left[\frac{1}{n_{out}} \quad \frac{2}{n_{out}} \quad \cdots \quad 1\right] \tag{38}$$

where err is governed by the sum absolute error between the desired output $\mathbf{d}_\eta = \left[d_\eta^1 \quad d_\eta^2 \quad \cdots \quad d_\eta^{n_{out}}\right]$ and the network output $\mathbf{y}_\eta = \left[y_\eta^1 \quad y_\eta^2 \quad \cdots \quad y_\eta^{n_{out}}\right]$; $\mathbf{e}_w$ denotes the error-weight vector, $sort(\cdot)$ returns a vector that has the argument vector's elements sorted in descending order; ng denotes the number of groups that can be segmented from the speech signal. It should be noted that the desired value will be equal to the input in the classification process. The fitness value will be optimized by the improved GA.

After the training process of each network has been done, m sets of parameters are obtained. In order to classify the target class to which an input pattern belongs, the input pattern will be tested simultaneously by all the networks. Therefore, m fitness values will be produced by the networks according to (36). The class of the network with the highest fitness value is the most likely class to which the input pattern belongs. In other words, the most likely word class is given by

$$dig_{\max} = \underset{1<dig<no\_pat}{\operatorname{argmax}}\ fitness(\mathbf{w}_{dig}, \mathbf{x}_\eta) \tag{39}$$

where dig denotes the word class; no_pat denotes the number of word classes; $fitness(\cdot)$ denotes the fitness value offered by the proposed NN with input $\mathbf{x}_\eta$ and the dig-th network weight set $\mathbf{w}_{dig}$.

5. Simulation Results

The Cantonese-digit speech recognition is processed as shown in Fig. 7. Speech signals are recorded from a male speaker with a low cost microphone. Eleven single Cantonese digits (0 to 10) and two double Cantonese digits (12 and 20) are used to test the performance of the proposed network, where the double Cantonese digits (12 and 20) are mainly used to test the sequential classification ability of the proposed recurrent network. The Cantonese syllables for the single digits can be found in "http://humanum.arts.cuhk.hk/Lexis/Canton/". The syllables of the two double

Cantonese digits (12 and 20) are the syllable combinations of (10, 2) and (2, 10) respectively. Each Cantonese digit is recorded with 20 repetitions as training data sets and 50 repetitions as testing data sets. The speech signals are then passed to the feature extractor.

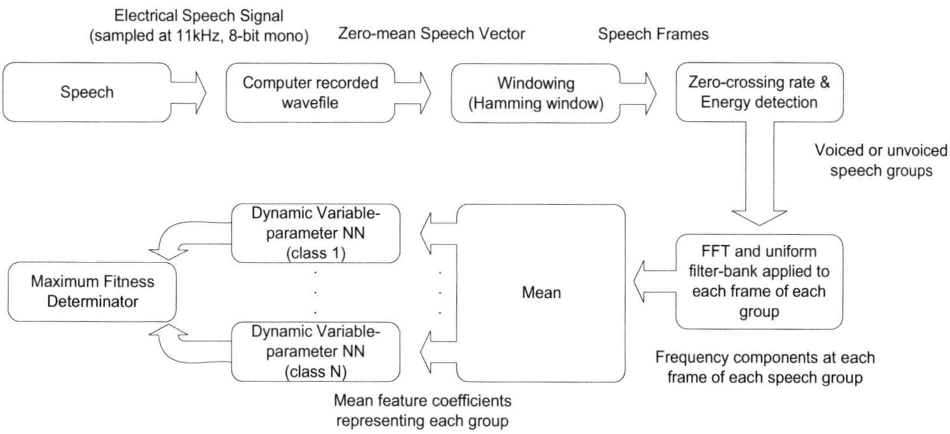

Figure 7. Block diagram of the Cantonese speech recognition system.

Firstly, the time domain speech signal will be windowed by the 128 hamming sliding window with 50% overlap. Zero-crossing rate and average energy of the speeches are calculated to obtain the acoustic speech frames using (25) to (28). If a speech frame has over 30% of its maximum zero-crossing rate and the average energy is less than 10% of its maximum energy level, the frame will be regarded as non-sonorant; otherwise, it is regarded as sonorant. FFT is then employed to obtain the frequency spectrum of each speech frame and the feature coefficients are extracted by using a uniform filter-bank. 12 feature coefficients will be obtained for each group using (29) to (34). Finally, the element vectors of the normalized acoustic feature sequence (**Sp**) will become the inputs of the modified RNN.

One network will be used to model one input class on doing the Cantonese digits recognition. The proposed network is a 24-inputs-12-outputs modified recurrent neural network. The element vectors of acoustic feature sequence are fed to the modified RNN one-by-one. Each group will have 12 parameters to represent the temporal speech feature. Hence, the network inputs are 12 feature coefficients given from the current speech frame and 12 parameters fed back from the outputs of the network at the previous state. The number of recurrent loop(s) is determined by the number of acoustic feature group(s) of the speech signal. The initial feedback values of the recurrent network are set to zeros. The improve GA is used to train all the linked weights, $[\mu_{ij} \quad b_{h_1} \quad \omega_{jg} \quad \mu_{ij}^{ff} \quad \mu_{qj}^{fb} \quad \lambda_{jk}]$ for all i, j, g, q, k, of the modified RNN. The vector of the linked weights is the chromosome of the improved GA. The control parameters w, p_m, w_f and w_{τ} for the improved GA are chosen to be 0.5, 0.02, 0.5 and 1 respectively. The upper and lower bound of the chromosome are 2.0 and –2.0 respectively. The number of iteration used for training is 2000. The initial values of the chromosomes are generated randomly. The number of hidden nodes used for the simulation were (3, 5), (5, 5), (5, 10), (10, 10), (10, 12) and (12, 12) where the first number inside the bracket is the number of hidden nodes used in the TNN and the second number inside the bracket is the number of hidden nodes used in the CRNN. The learning process is done by a personal computer with Pentium 4, 1.4GHz CPU and 256MB RAM. The simulation results of the 11 single-syllable Cantonese digits are tabulated in Table 1. The performance of sequence recognition is tabulated in Table 2. The overall performance of the proposed method is summarized in Table 3.

h_1,h_2		3,5	5,5	5,10	10,10	10,12	12,12
No. of parameters		259	299	509	634	728	782
Digit	Syllable	Performance (%)					
0 (零)	ling4	84	98	92	88	96	84
1 (一)	jat1	94	96	100	100	98	98
2 (二)	ji6	98	100	94	100	100	100
3 (三)	saam1	92	88	88	90	86	86
4 (四)	sei3	100	100	100	100	100	100
5 (五)	ng5	98	100	98	100	100	100
6 (六)	luk6	92	92	94	100	98	88
7 (七)	cat1	90	86	90	90	86	86
8 (八)	baat3	86	80	72	94	90	68
9 (九)	gau2	100	92	96	92	100	92
10 (十)	sap6	64	66	86	96	78	72

Table 1. Recognition performance of 11 Cantonese digits "0" to "10" (test data) by the proposed approach.

h_1,h_2		3,5	5,5	5,10	10,10	10,12	12,12
Digit	Syllable	Performance (%)					
2 (二)	ji6	98	100	94	100	100	100
10 (十)	sap6	64	66	86	96	78	72
12 (十二)	sap6, ji6	98	90	92	98	86	78
20 (二十)	ji6, sap6	88	90	98	94	98	96

Table 2. Recognition performance of the sequential Cantonese digits "2", "10", "12" and "20" (test data) by the proposed approach.

h_1,h_2	3,5	5,5	5,10	10,10	10,12	12,12
Testing Performance (%)	91.1	90.6	92.3	95.5	93.5	88.3
Training Performance (%)	98.5	99.6	98.8	99.2	99.2	98.8

Table 3. Overall recognition performance of 13 testing and training Cantonese digits by the proposed approach.

The results show that the proposed method provides a fast convergence rate. Only 2000 times of iteration for each Cantonese digit are sufficient for the training process to obtain about 99% accuracy models as shown in Table 3. This indicates that the structure of the TNN can provide useful information for the CRNN in order to reduce the number of iteration for training the network. In order to examine the effects of the network size to the network performance, we have tried different combinations of h1 and h2 values. Referring to the results shown in Tables 1 and 3, the best result is obtained when the numbers of hidden nodes (h_1, h_2) are set to (10,10). The recognition accuracy is 95.5%. The number of parameters used in each network at that setting is only 634. Apart from that, if the number of parameters used in each network is reduced to 259, i.e. 41% of the best setting, the recognition accuracy can still reach over 91%. The results demonstrate that the proposed network can use much fewer parameters for a drop of only 4% recognition accuracy. Considering the performance of the network to some Cantonese digits that have same vowel /a/ or /u/ (Lee et al., 1995), the Cantonese digits "1", "7", "8", "10" have the common vowel /a/ and "6", "9" have the common vowel /u/. By using the proposed method, they can be discriminated among each other with accuracy over 90% and 92% respectively. However, if the numbers of hidden nodes are set to (10, 12) and (12, 12), the accuracies of the network are then dropped to 93.5% and 88.3% respectively. This is because the numbers of parameters used for these two settings are increased to 728 and 782 respectively. Hence, there may be some redundant parameters affecting the network accuracy. Referring to Table 2, the sequence of the speech signals can be well determined by the propose method. By using the configuration that produces the best recognition accuracy from Table 1, the recognition accuracies of the four Cantonese digits "2", "10", "12", "20" are 100%, 96%, 98% and 94% respectively. Thus, the proposed network can produce high recognition accuracy for multi-syllable speech patterns although their syllables are similar. As a result, the static and dynamic feature of the Cantonese digits can be obtained effectively and classified clearly by the proposed method. The proposed recognition system is compared with one using a 3-layer fully connected neural network with recurrent paths as shown in Fig 8. The recognition system is trained by the improved GA with the same number of iteration for the proposed system. Besides that, the system is trained and tested by the same data patterns. The results produced by this network are tabulated from Table 4 to Table 6. As shown from the results, the recognition system produces the highest accuracy when the number of hidden node is equal to 22 (804 parameters). The overall recognition accuracy of this setting is 95.4%. By comparing the best performance of this recognition system to the proposed system in terms of the number of parameters used and the recognition accuracy, it can be seen that the proposed system requires a smaller number of parameters but offers similar recognition accuracy. It illustrates that the proposed network architecture can improve the recognition ability of the Cantonese-digit speech recognition application. In addition, the associative memory technique can improve the learning ability of the recurrent neural network from 98.8% (Table 6) to 99.2% (Table 3).

h_1		8	12	14	16	18	22
No. of parameters		300	444	516	588	660	804
Digit	Syllable	Performance (%)					
0 (零)	ling4	92	92	96	94	96	96
1 (一)	jat1	94	88	98	96	88	94
2 (二)	ji6	98	100	100	100	100	100
3 (三)	saam1	78	84	76	86	90	94
4 (四)	sei3	96	100	98	98	100	100
5 (五)	ng5	100	98	100	92	92	100
6 (六)	luk6	96	96	94	92	96	98
7 (七)	cat1	90	86	94	88	88	96
8 (八)	baat3	88	76	86	96	82	92
9 (九)	gau2	96	84	100	94	100	92
10 (十)	sap6	46	92	60	78	86	90

Table 4. Recognition performance of 11 Cantonese digits "0" to "10" (test data) by the 3-layer fully connected neural network with recurrent paths.

h_1		8	12	14	16	18	22
Digit	Syllable	Performance (%)					
2 (二)	ji6	98	100	100	100	100	100
10 (十)	sap6	46	92	60	34	86	90
12 (十二)	sap6, ji6	94	78	86	80	90	90
20 (二十)	ji6, sap6	94	98	96	98	88	98

Table 5. Recognition performance of the sequential Cantonese digits "2", "10", "12" and "20" (test data) by the 3-layer fully connected neural network with recurrent paths.

h_1	8	12	14	16	18	22
Testing Performance (%)	89.4	90.2	91.1	91.7	92	95.4
Training Performance (%)	99.6	98.5	98.8	98.8	99.6	98.8

Table 6. Overall recognition performance of 13 testing and training Cantonese digits by the 3-layer fully connected neural network with recurrent paths.

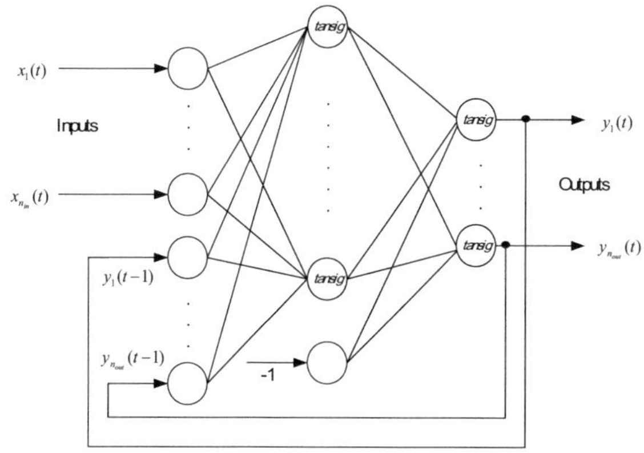

Figure 8. 3-layer fully connected neural network with recurrent paths.

6. Conclusion

A proposed Cantonese-digit speech recognizer by using a GA-based modified dynamic recurrent neural network has been developed. The structure of the modified neural network consists of two parts: a rule-base 3-layer feed-forward neural network and a classifier 3-layer recurrent neural network. The network parameters are trained by an improved GA. With this specific network structure, the dynamic feature of the speech signals can be generalized and the parameter values of the network can adapt to the values of the input data set. Cantonese digits 0 to 10, 12 and 20 have been used to demonstrate the merits of the proposed network. By using the proposed dynamic network, the dynamic and static information of the speech can be modeled effectively. Therefore, both single-syllable and multi-syllable Cantonese digits can be recognized.

7. Acknowledgement

The work described in this paper was substantially supported by The University of Western Australia, Australia, and a grant from the Centre for Multimedia Signal Processing, The Hong Kong Polytechnic University (Project No. A432).

8. References

Brown, M. & Harris, C. (1994). *Neuralfuzzy Adaptive Modeling and Control.* Prentice Hall, 1994.

Davis L. (1991). *Handbook of Genetic Algorithms.* NY: Van Nostrand Reinhold.

Engelbrecht, A.P. (2002). *Computational Intelligence: An Introduction*, John Wiley & Sons, Ltd, England.

Hanaki, Y., Hashiyama, T. & Okuma, S. (1999). "Accelerated evolutionary computation using fitness estimation," in *Proc. IEEE Int. Conf. Systems, Man, and Cybernetics*, 1999, vol. 1, pp. 643-648.

Jang, R.J.S. (1997). *Neural-Fuzzy and Soft Computing.* NJ: Prentice Hall.

Kirschning, I, Tomabechi, H., Koyama, M., & Aoe, J.I. (1996). "The time-sliced paradigm: a connectionist method for continuous speech recognition," *Information Sciences*, vol. 93, issues 1-2, pp. 133-158, Aug. 1996.

Markowitz, J.A. (1996). *Using Speech Recognition.* New Jersey, Prentice Hall.

Michalewicz, Z. (1994). *Genetic Algorithm + Data Structures = Evolution Programs*, 2nd extended ed. Springer-Verlag.

Lam, H.K., Ling, S.H., Leung, F.H.F., & Tam, P.K.S. (2004). "Function estimation using a neural-fuzzy network and an improved genetic algorithm," *International Journal of Approximate Reasoning*, vol. 30, no. 3, pp. 243-260, Jul. 2004.

Lee, T., Ching, P.C. & Chan, L.W. (1995). "Recurrent neural networks for speech modelling and speech recognition," *Acoustic, Speech and Signal Processing*, 1995 Int. Conf. on ICASSP-95, vol. 5, May 1995, pp. 3319-3322.

Lee, T., Ching, P.C. & Chan, L.W. (1998). "Isolated word recognition using modular recurrent neural networks," *Pattern Recognition*, vol. 31, no. 6, pp. 751-760, 1998.

Leung, F.H.F., Lam, H.K., Ling, S.H. & Tam, P.K.S. (2003). "Tuning of the structure and parameters of neural network using an improved genetic algorithm," *IEEE Trans. Neural Networks*, vol.14, no. 1, pp.79-88, Jan. 2003.

Leung, F.H.F., Lam, H.K., Ling, S.H. & Tam, P.K.S. (2004). "Optimal and stable fuzzy controllers for nonlinear systems using an improved genetic algorithm," *IEEE Trans. Industrial Electronics*, vol. 51, no. 1, pp.172-182, Feb. 2004.

Ling, S.H., Leung, F.H.F., Lam, H.K., & Tam, P.K.S. (2003). "Short-term electric load forecasting based on a neural fuzzy network," *IEEE Trans. Industrial Electronics*, vol. 50, no. 6, pp.1305-1316, Dec. 2003.

Pham, D.T. & Karaboga, D. (2000). *Intelligent Optimization Techniques, Genetic Algorithms, Tabu Search, Simulated Annealing and Neural Networks.* Springer.

Rabiner L., & Juang, B.H. (1993). *Fundamentals of Speech Recognition.* Englewood Cliffs, New Jersey, Prentice Hall.

Setnes, M. & Roubos, H. (2000). "GA-fuzzy modeling and classification: complexity and performance," *IEEE. Trans, Fuzzy Systems*, vol. 8, no. 5, pp. 509–522, Oct. 2000.

Srinivas, M. &. Patnaik, L.M. (1994). "Genetic algorithms: a survey," *IEEE. Computer*, vol. 27, issue 6, pp. 17-26, June 1994.

Waibel, A., Hanazawa, T., Hinton, G., Shikano, K., & Lang, K.J. (1989). "Phoneme recognition using time-delay neural networks," *IEEE. Trans. Acoust., Speech, Signal Processing*, vol.37, pp.328–339, Mar. 1989.

Wu, J., & Chan, C. (1993). "Isolated word recognition by neural network models with cross-correlation coefficients for speech dynamic," *IEEE. Trans. on Pattern Analysis and Machines Intelligence*, vol. 15, no. 11, Nov. 1993.

Zhang, L.P., Li, L.M. & Cai, C.N. (1993). "Speech recognition using dynamic recognition neural network," in Proc. *Computer, Communication, Control and Power Engineering, 1993 IEEE. Region 10 Conf.* (TENCON '93), vol. 3, 19-21 Oct 1993, pp 333-336.

Zhang, G.P. (2000). "Neural networks for classification: A survey," *IEEE Trans. on Sys. Man. and Cyber.*, part C, vol. 30, no. 4, Nov. 2000, pp 451-462.

22

Talking Robot and the Autonomous Acquisition of Vocalization and Singing Skill

Hideyuki Sawada
Kagawa University
Japan

1. Introduction

Voice is used as primary media in the human communication. It is employed not only in simple daily communication, but also for the logical discussions and the expression of emotion and feelings. Different vocal sounds are generated by the complex movements of vocal organs under the feedback control mechanisms using an auditory system. Vocal sounds and human vocalization mechanisms have been the attractive researching subjects for many researchers so far [1],[2], and computerized voice production and recognition have become the essential technologies in the recent developments of flexible human-machine interface studies.

Various ways and techniques have been reported in the researches of sound production. Algorithmic syntheses have taken the place of analogue circuit syntheses and became widely used techniques [2],[3]. Sound sampling methods and physical model based syntheses are typical techniques, which are expected to provide different types of realistic vocal sounds [4]. In addition to these algorithmic synthesis techniques, a mechanical approach using a phonetic or vocal model imitating the human vocalization mechanism would be a valuable and notable objective.

Several mechanical constructions of a human vocal system to realize human-like speech have been reported. In most of the researches [2],[5],[6], however, the mechanical reproductions of the human vocal system were mainly directed by referring to X-ray images and FEM analysis, and the adaptive acquisition of control methods for natural vocalization have not been considered so far. In fact, since the behaviours of vocal organs have not been sufficiently investigated due to the nonlinear factors of fluid dynamics yet to be overcome, the control of mechanical system has often the difficulties to be established.

The author has been developing a mechanical voice generation system together with its adaptive learning of the control skill for the realization of a talking robot which imitates human vocalization [7]-[11]. The fundamental frequency and the spectrum envelope determine the principal characteristics of a sound. The former is the characteristic of a source sound generated by a vibrating object, and the latter is operated by the work of the resonance effects. In vocalization, the vibration of vocal cords generates a source sound, and then the sound wave is led to a vocal tract, which works as a filter to determine the spectrum envelope.

A motor-controlled mechanical model with vocal cords, a vocal tract and a nasal cavity is constructed so far to generate a natural voice imitating a human vocalization. By introducing an auditory feedback learning with an adaptive control algorithm of pitch and phoneme, the robot is able to autonomously acquire the control method of the mechanical system to produce stable vocal sounds imitating human vocalization skill [7],[8]. In this chapter, the adaptive control method of mechanical vocal cords and vocal tract for the realization of a talking and singing robot is described, together with the singing performance with the use of acquired vocalization skill.

2. Human voice system and voice generation

Human vocal sounds are generated by the relevant operations of vocal organs such as the lung, trachea, vocal cords, vocal tract, nasal cavity, tongue and muscles. In human verbal communication, the sound is perceived as words, which consist of vowels and consonants. The lung has the function of an air tank, and the airflow through the trachea causes a vocal cord vibration as the source sound of a voice. The glottal wave is led to the vocal tract, which works as a sound filter as to form the spectrum envelope of the voice.

The fundamental frequency and the volume of the sound source is varied by the change of the physical parameters such as the stiffness of the vocal cords and the amounts of airflow from the lung, and these parameters are uniquely controlled when we speak or utter a song. On the other hand, the spectrum envelope or the resonance characteristics, which is necessary for the pronunciation of words consisting of vowels and consonants, is formed based on the inner shape of the vocal tract and the mouth, which are governed by the complex movements of the jaw, tongue and muscles. Vowel sounds are radiated by the relatively stable configuration of the vocal tract, while the short time dynamic motions of the vocal apparatus produce consonants generally.

The dampness and viscosity of organs greatly influence the timbre of generated sounds, which we may experience when we have a sore throat. Appropriate configurations of the vocal cords and vocal tract for the production of vocal sounds are acquired as infants grow by repeating vocalization and listening through trial and error.

3. Mechanical model for vocalization

3.1 Configuration of Mechanical Voice System

As shown in Figure 1, the mechanical voice system mainly consists of an air compressor, artificial vocal cords, a resonance tube, a nasal cavity, and a microphone connected to a sound analyzer, which correspond to a lung, vocal cords, a vocal tract, a nasal cavity and an audition of a human.

The air in the compressor is compressed to 8000 hpa, while the pressure of an air from lungs is about +200 hpa larger than the atmospheric pressure. A pressure reduction valve is applied at the outlet of the air compressor so that the pressure is reduced to be nearly equal to the air pressure through the trachea. The valve is also effective to reduce the fluctuation of the pressure in the compressor during the operations of compression and depression process. The decompressed air is led to the vocal cords via an airflow control valve, which works for the control of the voice volume. The resonance tube is attached to the vocal cords for the modification of resonance characteristics. The nasal cavity is connected to the resonance tube with a sliding valve between them. The sound analyzer plays a role of the auditory system. It realizes the pitch extraction and the analysis of resonance characteristics of the generated sound in real time, which are necessary for the auditory feedback control. The system controller manages the whole system by listening to the produced sounds and generating motor control commands, based on the auditory feedback control mechanism employing a neural network learning.

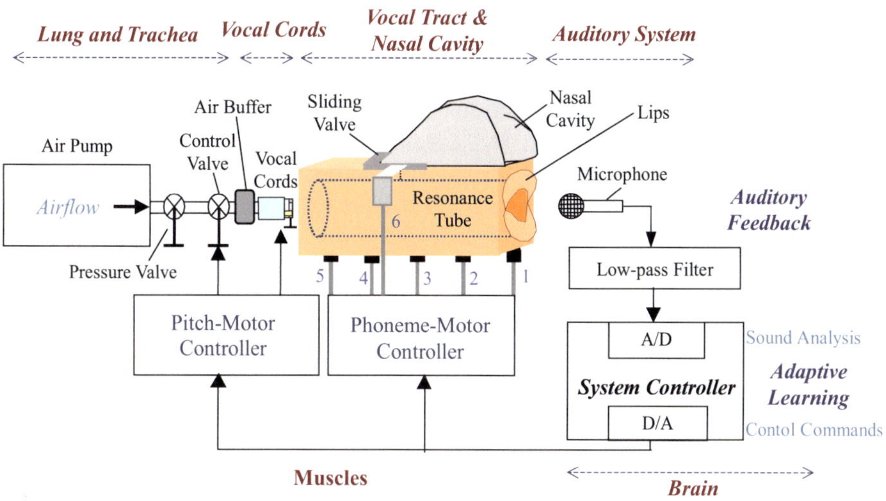

Figure 1. Configuration of the talking robot

3.2 Construction of Resonance Tube and Nasal Cavity

The human vocal tract is a non-uniform tube about 170mm long in man. Its cross-sectional area varies from 0 to 20cm^2 under the control for vocalization. A nasal tract with a total volume of 60 cm^3 is coupled to the vocal tract. Nasal sounds such as /*m*/ and /*n*/ are normally excited by the vocal cords and resonated in the nasal cavity. Nasal sounds are generated by closing the soft palate and lips, not to radiate air from the mouth, but to resonate the sound in the nasal cavity. The closed vocal tract works as a lateral branch resonator and also has effects of resonance characteristics to generate nasal sounds. Based on the difference of articulatory positions of tongue and mouth, the /*m*/ and /*n*/ sounds can be distinguished with each other.

In the mechanical system, a resonance tube as a vocal tract is attached at the sound outlet of the artificial vocal cords. It works as a resonator of a source sound generated by the vocal cords. It is made of a silicone rubber with the length of 180 mm and the diameter of 36mm, which is equal to 10.2cm^2 by the cross-sectional area as shown in Figure 2 and 3. The silicone rubber is molded with the softness of human skin, which contributes to the quality of the resonance characteristics. In addition, a nasal cavity made of a plaster is connected to the intake part of the resonance tube to vocalize nasal sounds like /*m*/ and /*n*/.

By actuating displacement forces by stainless bars from the outside, the cross-sectional area of the tube is manipulated so that the resonance characteristics are changed according to the transformations of the inner areas of the resonator. DC motors are placed at 5 positions x_j (j=1-5) from the intake side of the tube to the outlet side as shown in Figure 2, and the displacement forces $P_j(x_j)$ are applied according to the control commands from the motor-phoneme controller.

A nasal cavity is coupled with the resonance tube as a vocal tract to vocalize human-like nasal sounds by the control of mechanical parts. A sliding valve as a role of the soft palate is settled at the connection of the resonance tube and the nasal cavity for the selection of nasal and normal sounds. For the generation of nasal sounds /*n*/ and /*m*/, the sliding valve is open to lead the air into the nasal cavity as shown in Figure 4(a). By closing the middle position of the vocal tract and then releasing the air to speak vowel sounds, /*n*/ consonant is generated. For the /*m*/ consonants, the outlet part is closed to stop the air first, and then is open to vocalize vowels. The difference in the /*n*/ and /*m*/ consonant generations is basically the narrowing positions of the vocal tract.

In generating plosive sounds /*p*/ and /*t*/, the mechanical system closes the sliding valve not to release the air in the nasal cavity. By closing one point of the vocal tract, air provided from the lung is stopped and compressed in the tract as shown in Figure 4(b). Then the released air generates plosive consonant sounds like /*p*/ and /*t*/.

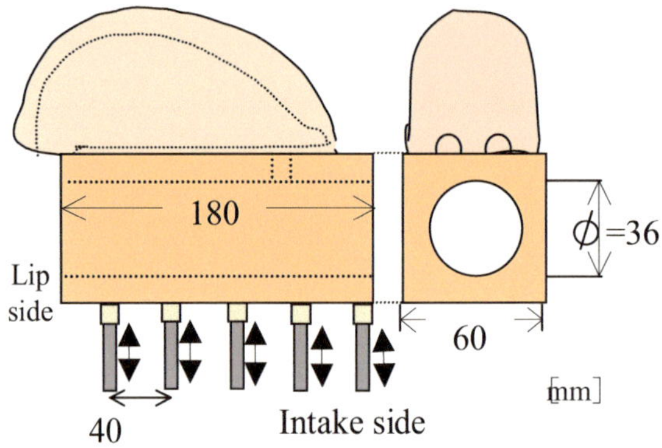

Figure 2. Construction of vocal tract and nasal cavity

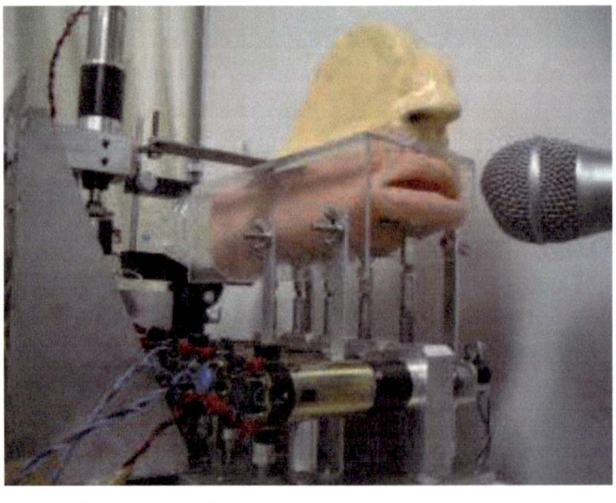

Figure 3. Structural view of talking robot

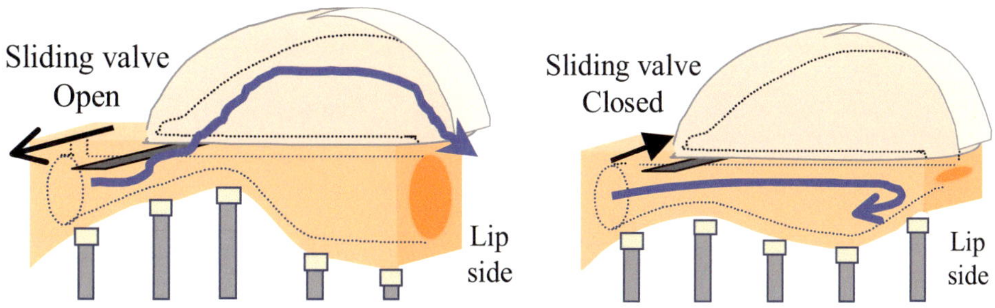

(a) Airflow Control for Nasal Sound /n/ (b) Airflow Control for Plosive Sound /p/

Figure 4. Motor control for nasal and plosive sound generation

3.3 Artificial Vocal Cords and its pitch control

(A) Construction of Artificial Vocal Cords

The characteristic of a glottal sound wave, which determines the pitch and the volume of human voice, is governed by the complex behavior of the vocal cords. It is due to the oscillatory mechanism of human organs consisting of the mucous membrane and muscles excited by the airflow from the lung. Although several researching reports about the computer simulations of these movements are available [12], the author have focused on generating the wave using a mechanical model [7].

In this study, we constructed new vocal cords with two vibrating cords molded with silicone rubber with the softness of human mucous membrane. Figure 5 shows the picture. The vibratory actions of the two cords are excited by the airflow led by the tube, and generate a source sound to be resonated in the vocal tract.

Here, assume the simplified dynamics of the vibration given by a strip of a rubber with the length of L. The fundamental frequency f is given by the equation

$$f = \frac{1}{2L}\sqrt{\frac{S}{D}}, \tag{1}$$

by considering the density of the material D and the tension S applied to the rubber. This equation implies that the fundamental frequency varies according to the manipulations of L, S and D.

The tension of rubber can be manipulated by applying tensile force to the two cords. Figure 6 shows the schematic figures how tensile force is applied to the vocal cords to generate sounds with different frequencies. By pulling the cords, the tension increases so that the frequency of the generated sound becomes higher. For the voiceless sounds, just by pushing the cords, the gap between two cords are left open and the vibration stops.

The structure of the vocal cords proved the easy manipulation for the pitch control, since the fundamental frequency can be changed just by giving tensile force for pushing or pulling the cords.

We constructed three vocal cords with different kinds of softness, which are hard, soft and medium. The medium one has two-layered construction: a hard silicone is inside with the soft coating outside.

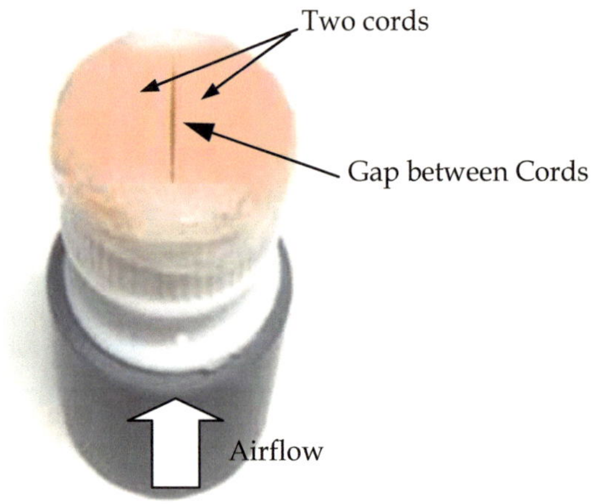

Figure 5. Vocal cords

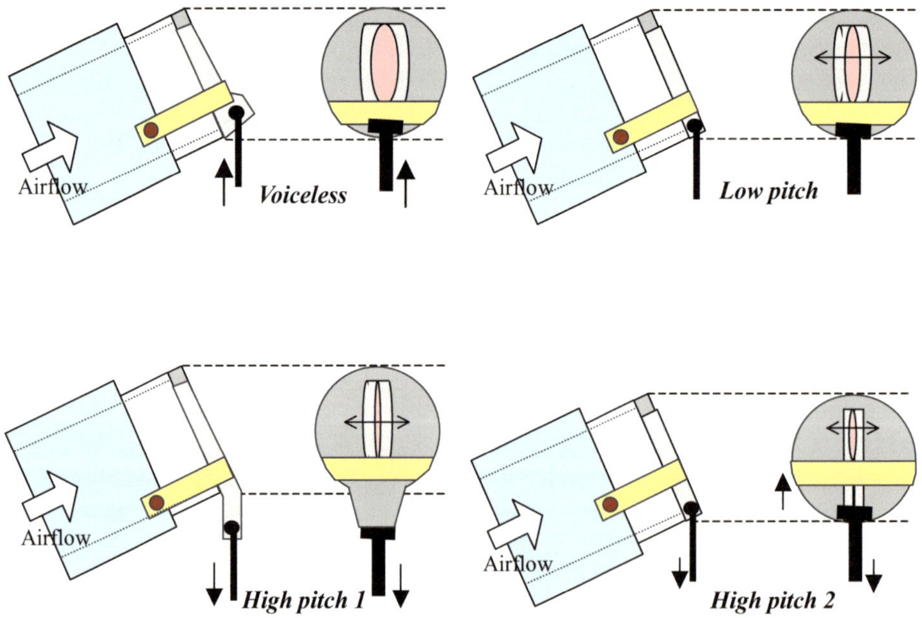

Figure 6. Different manipulations for pitch control

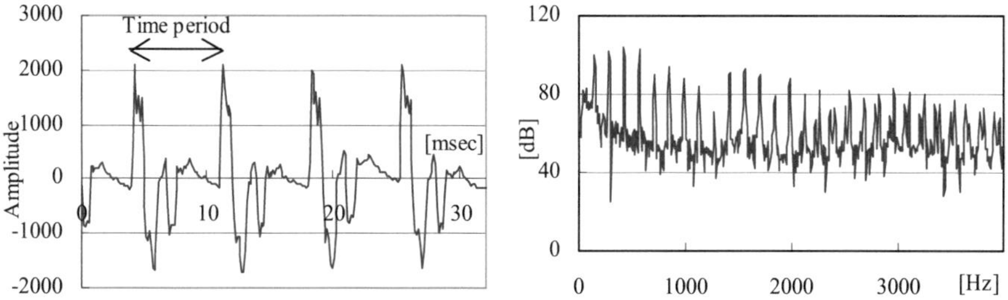

(a) Hard vocal cords

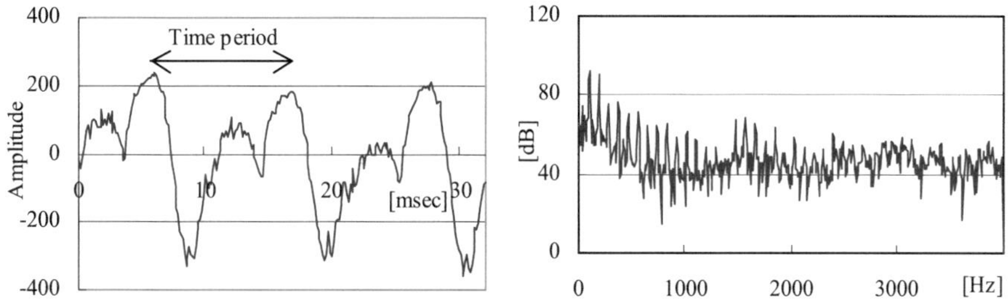

(b) Soft vocal cords

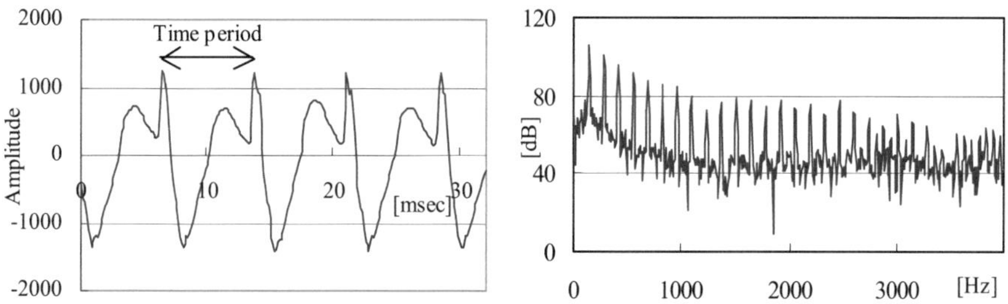

(c) Two-layered vocal cords

Figure 7. Waveforms and spectra of three vocal cords

Figure 7 shows examples of sound waves and its spectra generated by the three vocal cords. The waveform of the hard cords is approximated as periodic pulses, and a couple of resonance peaks are found in the spectrum domain. The two-layered cords generate an isolated triangular waveform, which is close to the actual human one, and its power in the spectrum domain gradually decreases as the frequency rises.

In this study, the two-layered vocal cords are employed in the mechanical voice system. Figure 8 shows the vocal cords integrated in the control mechanism.

(B) Pitch Control of Vocal Cords

Figure 9 shows experimental results of pitch changes using the two-layered vocal cords. The fundamental frequency varies from 110 Hz to 250 Hz by the manipulations of a force applying to the rubber.

The relationship between the applied force and the articulated frequency is not stable but tends to change with the repetition of experiments due to fluid dynamics. The vocal cords, however, reproduce the vibratory actions of human actual vocal cords, and are also considered to be suitable for our system because of its simple structure. Its frequency characteristics are easily controlled by the tension of the rubber and the amount of airflow.
For the fundamental frequency and volume adjustments in the voice system, two motors are used: one is to manipulate a screw of an airflow control valve, and the other is to apply a tensile force to the vocal cords for the tension adjustment.

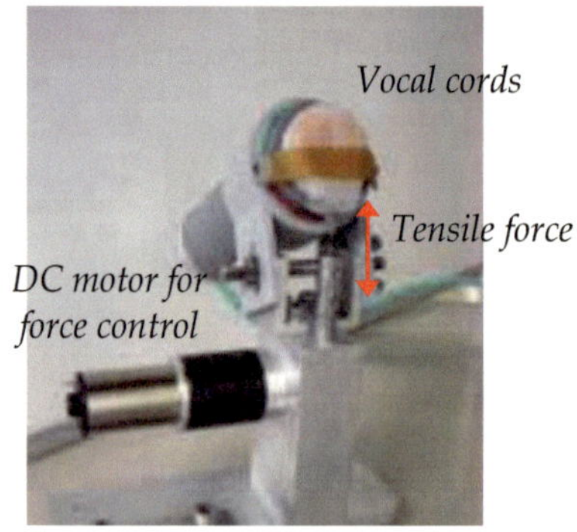

Figure 8. Vocal cords and control mechanism

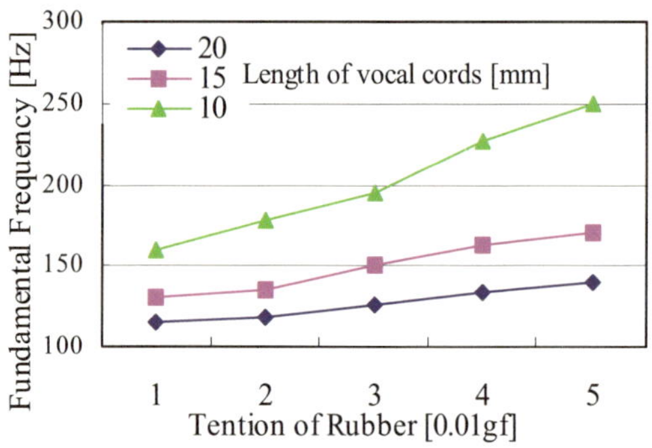

Figure 9. Relation between tensile force and fundamental frequency

(C) Adaptive Pitch Control

Not only adjusting but also maintaining the pitch of output sounds is not easy tasks due to the dynamic mechanism of vibration, which is easily disturbed by the fluctuations of the tensile force and the airflow. Stable output has to be obtained no matter what kind of disturbance applies to the system. Introducing an adaptive control mechanism would be a good solution for getting such robustness [7],[8].
An adaptive tuning algorithm for the production of a voice with different pitches using the mechanical voice system is introduced in this section. The algorithm consists of two phases. First in the learning phase, the system acquires a motor-pitch map, in which the relations

between the motor positions and the fundamental frequencies are described. It is acquired by comparing the pitches of output sounds with the desired pitches for the vocalization. Then in the performance phase, the robot utters words by referring to the obtained map while pitches of produced voices are adaptively maintained by hearing its own outputs.

Figure 10 shows a schematic diagram of the adaptive pitch learning in the learning phase. The algorithm simulates the pitch learning process of a human in practicing singing. The algorithmic process of the pitch acquisition in the system controller is shown in the dotted lines. The pitch-tuning manager manages the behaviors of all the other units presented in the boxes. The system starts its action by receiving a present-position vector v_p as a command to let the motors move. Actual values of the vector elements can be estimated by the work of calculations in the pitch-to-motor translator, which is trained in advance to output desired motor positions from pitches of produced sounds according to the relations between tensile force and fundamental frequency as shown in Figure 9.

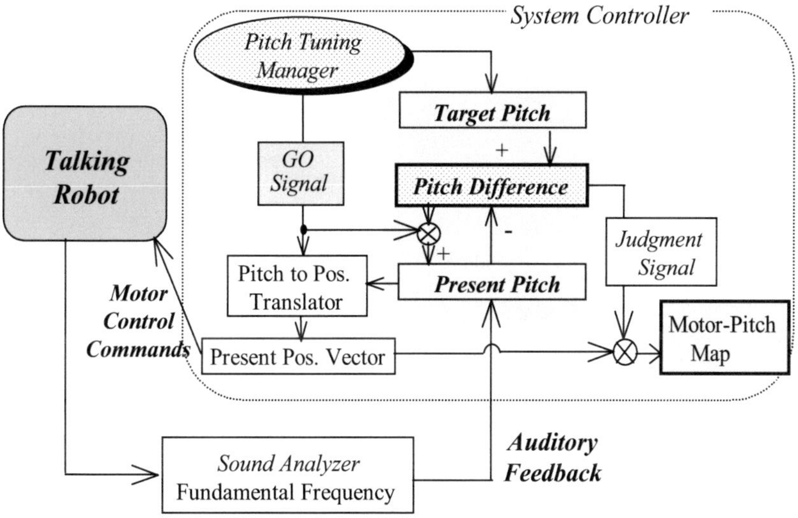

Figure 10. Adaptive pitch learning

First, the system controller starts with setting arbitrary values as a present-position vector to send to the vocal system. The fundamental frequency of the generated sound is calculated by the sound analyzer of the auditory system which realizes FFT calculations in realtime. Since the desired pitches of the produced sounds are assumed to be lower than 500 Hz in the vocal system, the sampling frequency is set to 1kHz. The analysis window of 1024 points are chosen and the frequency resolution is about 1Hz in this system. After applying the Hamming window, the produced sound wave data are fed to the FFT algorithm and the fundamental pitch is extracted. To compare with the desired pitch, the difference between the two pitches is obtained according to the tuning signal trigger generated by the tuning manager. The tuning signal, in the same instant, drives the pitch-to-motor translator to let the motors work. As the feedback process repeats, the pitch difference between the target pitch and the produced pitch decreases. When the pitch difference becomes smaller than a predetermined threshold value, which is currently set to 0.6 Hz, the judgment-signal unit arises, so that the present-position vector is associated with the target pitch and stored as the motor-pitch map.

The results of the pitch learning based on the auditory feedback are shown in Figure 11, in which the system acquired the sound pitches from C to G. The system was able to acquire vocal sounds with desired pitches.

3.4 Learning of Vowel and Consonant Vocalization

The neural network (NN) works to associate the resonance characteristics of sounds with the control parameters of the six motors equipped in the vocal tract and the nasal cavity, as shown in Figure 12. In the learning process, the network learns the motor control commands by inputting 10th order LPC cepstrum coefficients derived from vocal sound waves as teaching signals. The network acquires the relations between the sound parameters and the motor control commands of the vocal tract. After the learning, the neural network is connected in series into the vocal tract model. By inputting the sound parameters of desired sounds to the NN, the corresponding form of the vocal tract is obtained.

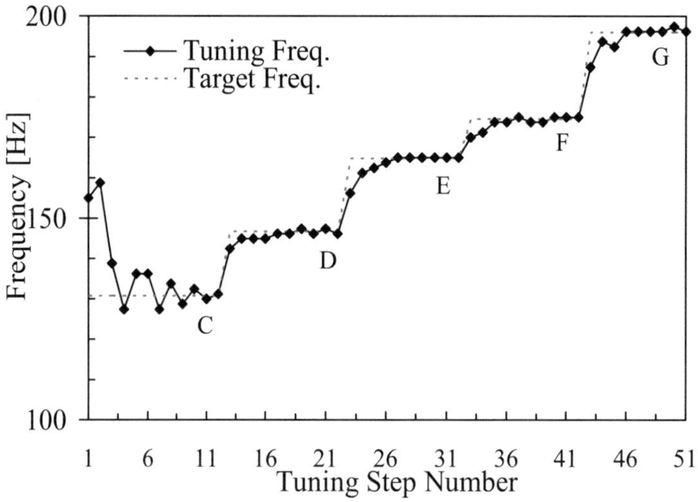

Figure 11. Experimental result of pitch tuning

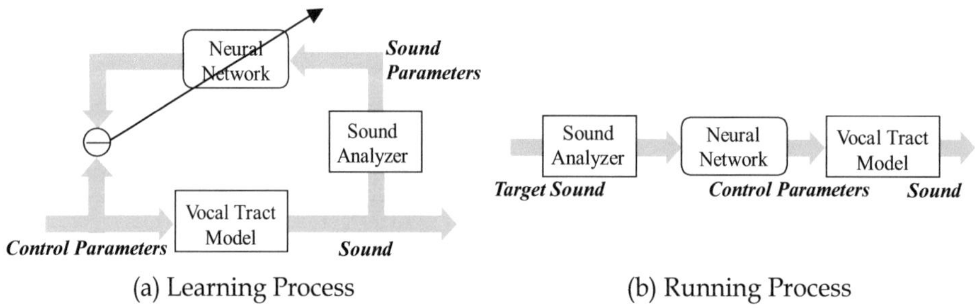

Figure 12. Neural network for vocalization learning

In this study, the Self-Organizing Neural Network (SONN) was employed for the adaptive learning of vocalization. Figure 13 shows the structure of the SONN consisting of two processes, which are an information memory process and an information recall process.

After the SONN learning, the motor control parameters are adaptively recalled by the stimuli of sounds to be generated.

The information memory process is achieved by the self-organizing map (SOM) learning, in which sound parameters are arranged onto a two-dimensional feature map to be related to one another.

Weight vector V_j at node j on the feature map is fully connected to the input nodes x_i [i =1, ... , 10], where 10th order LPC cepstrum coefficients are given. The map learning algorithm updates the weight vectors V_j-s. A competitive learning is used, in which the winner c as the output unit with a weight vector closest to the current input vector $\boldsymbol{x}(t)$ is chosen at time t in the learning. By using the winner c, the weight vectors V_j -s are updated according to the rule shown below;

$$\boldsymbol{V}_j(t+1) = \boldsymbol{V}_j(t) + h_{cj}(t)[\boldsymbol{x}(t) - \boldsymbol{V}_j(t)]$$
$$h_{cj}(t) = \begin{cases} \alpha(t) \cdot \exp\left(-\dfrac{\|r_c - r_j\|^2}{2\sigma^2(t)}\right) & (i \in N_c) \\ 0 & (i \notin N_c) \end{cases} \tag{2}$$

Here, $\| r_c - r_j \|$ is the distance between units c and j in the output array, and N_c is the neighborhood of the node c. $\alpha(t)$ is a learning coefficient which gradually reduces as the learning proceeds. $\sigma(t)$ is also a coefficient which represents the width of the neighborhood area.

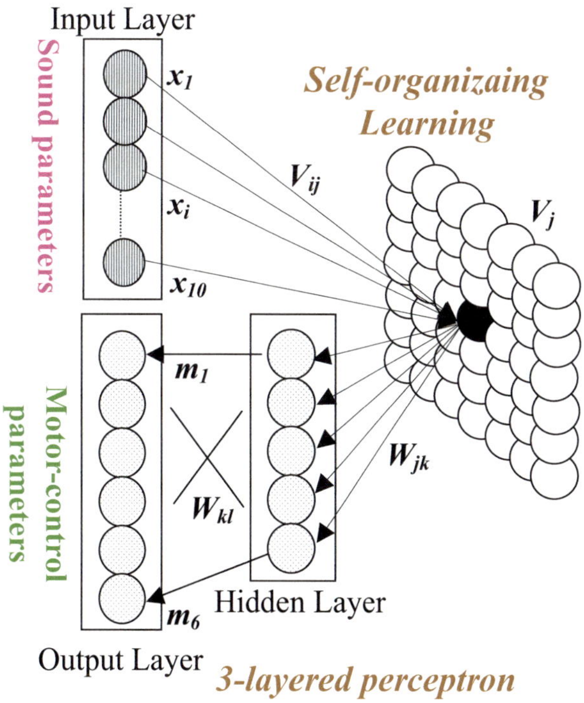

Figure 13. Structure of self-organizing neural network (SONN)

Then in the information recall process, each node in the feature map is associated with motor control parameters for the control commands of six motors employed for the vocal tract deformation, by using the three-layered perceptron. In this study, a conventional back-propagation algorithm was employed for the learning.
With the integration of the information memory and recall processes, the SONN works to adaptively associate sound parameters with motor control parameters.
In the current system, 20x20 arrayed map $\boldsymbol{V} = [V_1, V_2, ..., V_{20 \times 20}]$ is used as the SOM. For testing the mapping ability, 150 sounds randomly vocalized by the robot were mapped onto the map array. After the self-organizing learning, Japanese five vowels vocalized by six different people (No.1 to 6) were mapped onto the feature map, which is shown in Figure 14. Same vowel sounds given by different people were mapped close with each other, and five vowels were roughly categorized according to the differences of phonetic characteristics. We found that, in some vowel area, two sounds given by two different speakers fell in a same unit in the feature map. It means the two different sounds could not be separated although they have close tonal features with each other. We propose a reinforcement learning algorithm to optimize the feature map.

3.5 Reinforcement Learning of Japanese Five Vowels by Human Voices

SONN gave fairly good performance in the association of sound parameters with motor control parameters for the robot vocalization, however redundant sound parameters which are not used for the Japanese speech are also buried in the map, since the 150 inputted sounds were generated randomly by the robot. Furthermore, two different sounds given by two different speakers are occasionally fallen in the same unit. The mapping should be optimized for the Japanese vocalization.
The reinforcement learning was employed to establish the feature map optimized. After the SONN learning, Japanese five vowel sounds given by 6 different speakers were applied to the supervised learning as the reinforcement signal to be associated with the suitable motor control parameters for the vocalization.
Figure 15 shows the result of the reinforcement learning with Japanese 5 vowels. The distribution of same vowel sounds concentrates with one another, and the patterns of different vowels are placed apart.

3.6 Reinforcement Learning of Japanese Five Vowels by Human Voices

After the learning of the relationship between the sound parameters and the motor control parameters, we inputted human voices from microphone to confirm whether the robot could speak autonomously by mimicking human vocalization.
Figure 16 shows the comparison of spectra between human vowel vocalization and robot speech. The first and second formants F1 and F2, which present the principal characteristics of the vowels, were formed as to approximate the human vowels, and the sounds were well distinguishable by listeners.

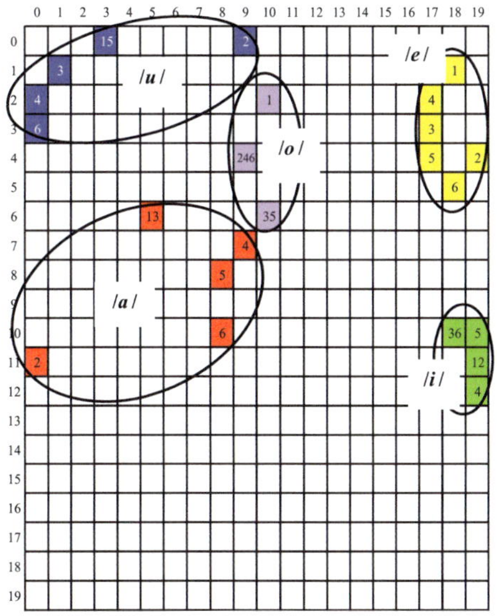

Figure 14. Experimental result of Japanese 5 vowel mapping by SONN

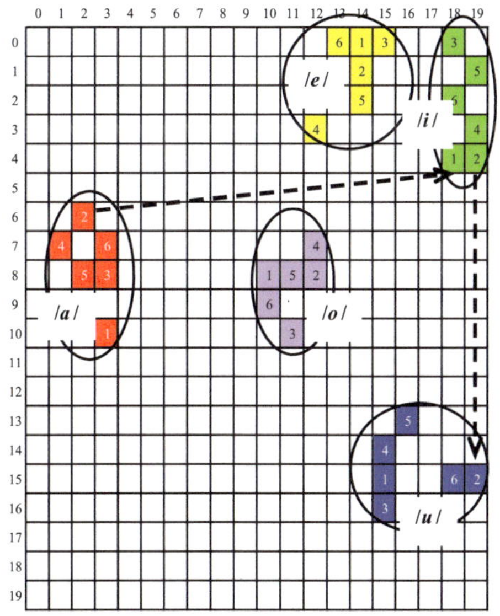

Figure 15. Result of reinforcement learning with Japanese 5 vowels

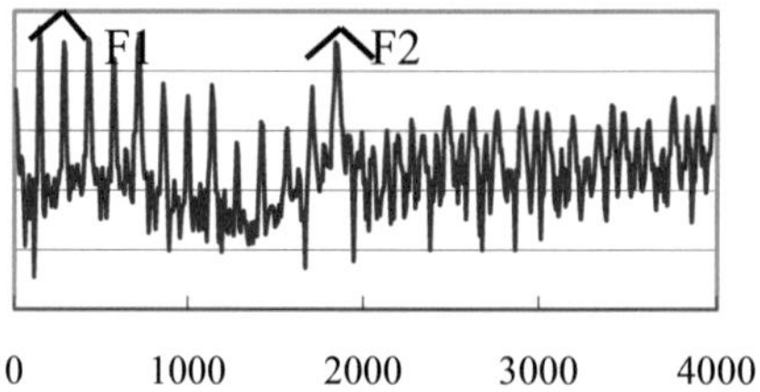

(*a*-1) Robot Speech /*i*/

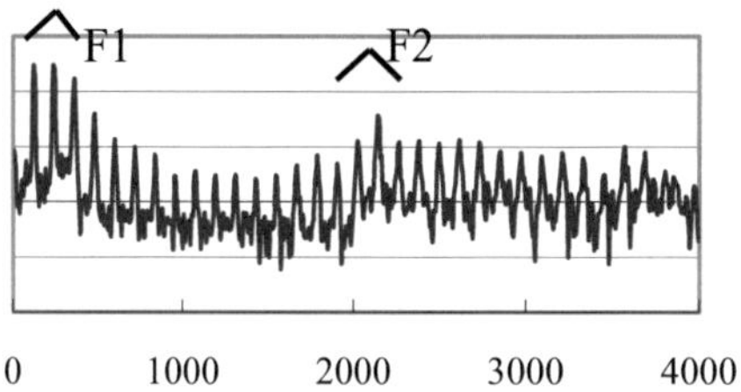

(*a*-2) Human Speech /*i*/

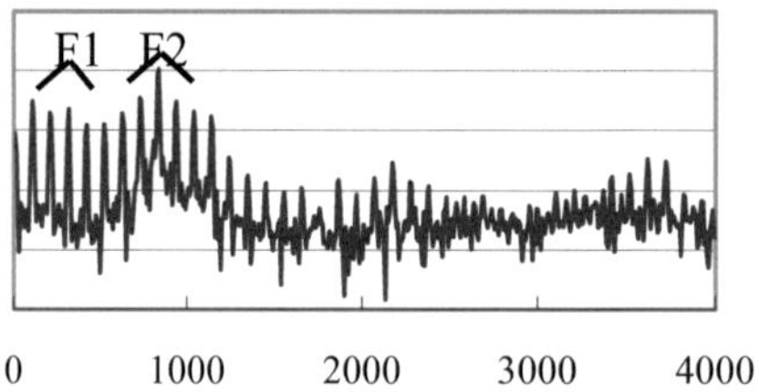

(*b*-1) Robot Speech /*o*/

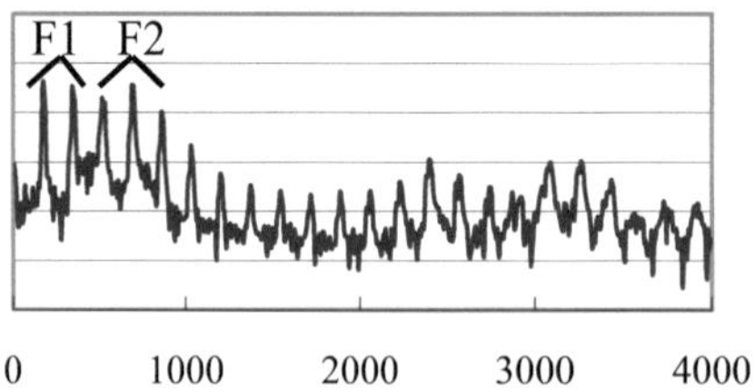

(*b*-2) Human Speech /*o*/

Figure 16. Comparison of spectra of Japanese /i/ and /o/ vowel

We also verified the robot's vocalization motion. In the /*a*/ vocalization, for example, the glottal side was narrowed while the lip side was open, which was the same way as a human utters the /*a*/ sound. In the same manner, features for the /*i*/ pronunciation were acquired by narrowing the outlet side and opening the glottal side.

The experiment also showed the smooth motion of the vocalization. The transition between two different vowels in the continuous speech was well acquired by the SONN learning.

Figure 17 shows two experimental results of the temporal motor control values of the vocal tract in the speech /*ai*/ and /*iu*/, where the motor values are autonomously generated by SOM as shown by the dotted arrows in Figure 15. The /*a*/ vocalization was transited to /*i*/ vocalization, then /*u*/ speech smoothly.
Nasal sounds such as /*m*/ and /*n*/ are generated with the nasal resonance under the control of the valve between the nasal cavity and the vocal tract. A voiced sound /*m*/ was generated by closing the lip and leading the sound wave to the nasal cavity, then by opening the lip and closing the nasal valve, the air was released to the mouth to vocalize /*o*/ sound.
Figure 18 shows generated sound waves in the vocalization of /*mo*/ and /*ru*/, where the smooth transition from consonant sounds to vowel sounds was achieved by the acquired articulations.

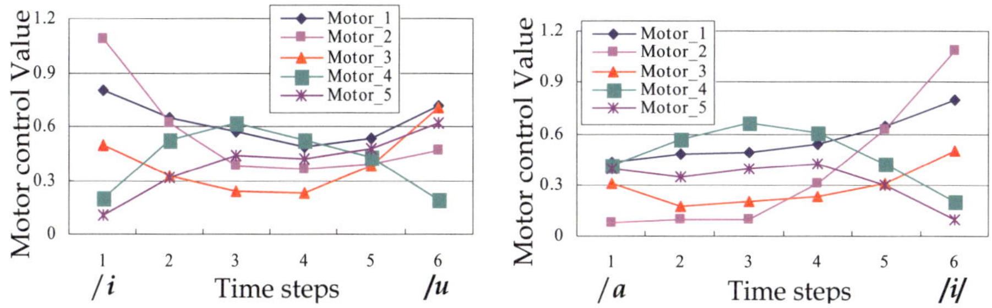

(*a*) Vocalization /*a*/ to /*i*/ (*b*) Vocalization /*i*/ to /*u*/

Figure 17. Transition of motor control values in vocalization

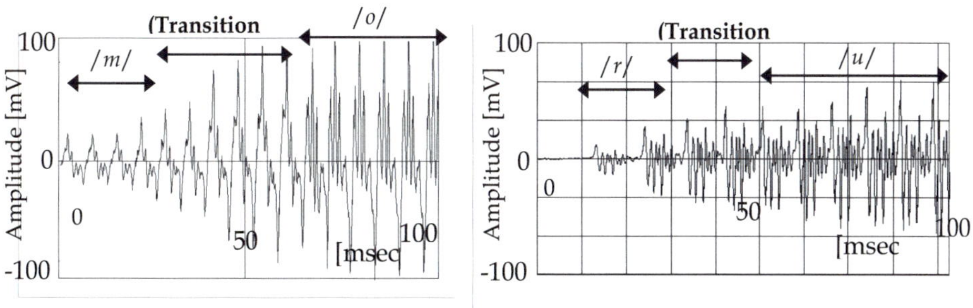

(*a*) /*ma*/ vocalization (*b*) /*ru*/ vocalization

Figure 18. Results of /*mo*/ and /*ru*/ vocalizations

4. Listening experiments

For the assessment of speech vocalized by the robot, listening experiments were conducted and voices were evaluated by questionnaires. 14 able-bodied subjects (9 males and 5

females) listened to 11 Japanese words and 1 English word given by the robot, while they were watching the motion of the robot vocalization, and answered what they thought it said. The results are shown in Table 1.
The words /Uma/ and /Ai/ were perfectly recognized by all the listeners, and 70.2 % recognition was achieved in average. The clarity of /r/ consonants was not enough to be distinguished, since the robot is not equipped with a flexible tongue to generate fricative sounds, and the sounds were often mis-recognized by the listeners as nasal sounds. Some listeners commented that the actual motion of the speech by the robot helped them to estimate what it speaks, although the speech itself was not clear enough.

Words	**Correct #**	**Listened as**
MonoMane	8	Mamomame, Mamamama
Raion	8	Airon, Naiyo, Nyanyane
Inu	9	Nna, Ushi
Uma	14	-
Momo	12	Oh-oh-
Remon	5	Imo, Ranran, Meron
Meron	9	Remon
Umi	9	Suna, Ume
Nami	12	Hami, Ii
Marimo	10	Mambo, Menzu, Mamma
Ai	14	-
Good-bye	8	Umai, Good-night
Average	**9.8**	**Recognition rate: 70.2%**

Table 1. Results of listening experiments

5. Singing Performance with Adaptive Control

The robot is able to sing a song by referring to the acquired maps for controlling its vocal organs. The schematic diagram of the singing performance is shown in figure 19. The performance-control manager takes charge of two tasks; one is for the performance execution presented by bold lines in the figure, and the other is for the adaptive control of pitches and phonemes with the auditory feedback during the performance. The score-information unit stores melody lines as sequential data of pitches, durations, phonemes and lyrics. Figure 20 shows one of the user interfaces , by which a user inputs musical score information for the singing performance.
The singing performance is executed according to the performance signals generated by the performance-control manager. The manager has the internal clock and makes a temporal

planning of note outputs with the help of the duration information in the score-information unit. The note information is translated into present-position vectors by referring to the motor-pitch map and the motor-phoneme map.

During the performance, unexpected changes of air pressure and tensile force cause the fluctuations of sound outputs. The adaptive control with the auditory feedback is introduced in this mechanical system by hearing the own output voices. The auditory units observe errors in the pitch and the phoneme so that the system starts fine tuning of produced sounds by receiving the tuning-signal trigger under the control of the performance manager. The motor-pitch / motor-phoneme maps are also renewed by the map-rewrite signal. The system is able to realize a stable singing performance under the adaptive mechanical control using the auditory feedback.

An experimental result of the singing performance is presented in Figure 21. In spite of the unexpected disturbances being applied or the drop of an air pressure in an air pump, the system was able to maintain the target pitch.

The system autonomously performs singing as a robot by generating performance signals which are governed by the internal clock in the computer. The robot also makes mimicking performance by listening and following a human singer. The auditory system listens to a human singer and extracts pitch and phonemes from his voice in realtime. Then the pitch and phonemes are translated into motor-control values to let the robot follow the human singer.

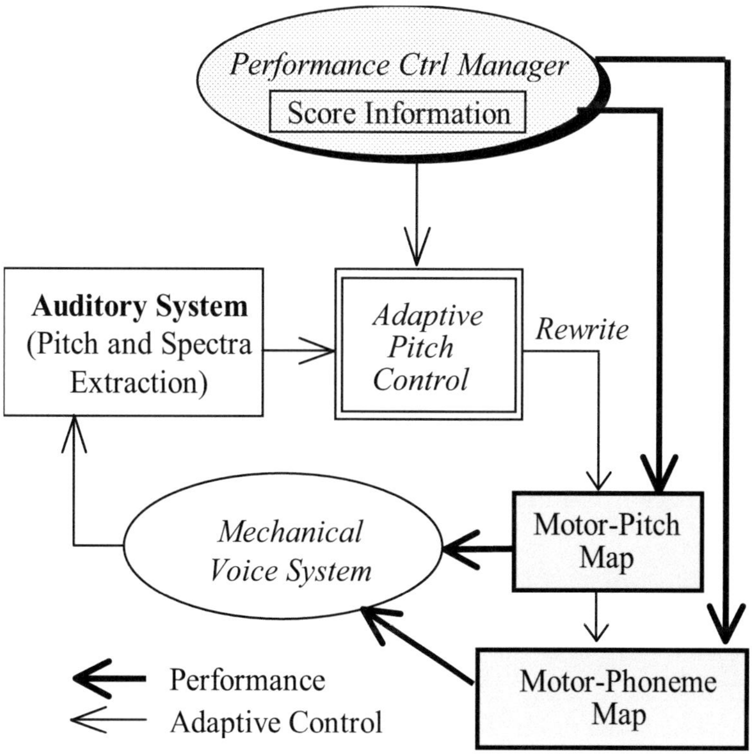

Figure 19. Singing performance with adaptive control

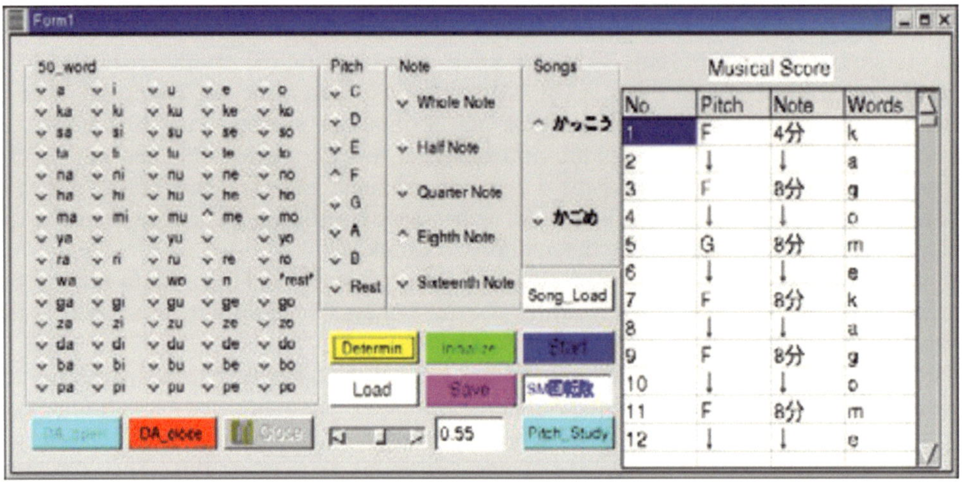

Figure 20. An interface for singing performance

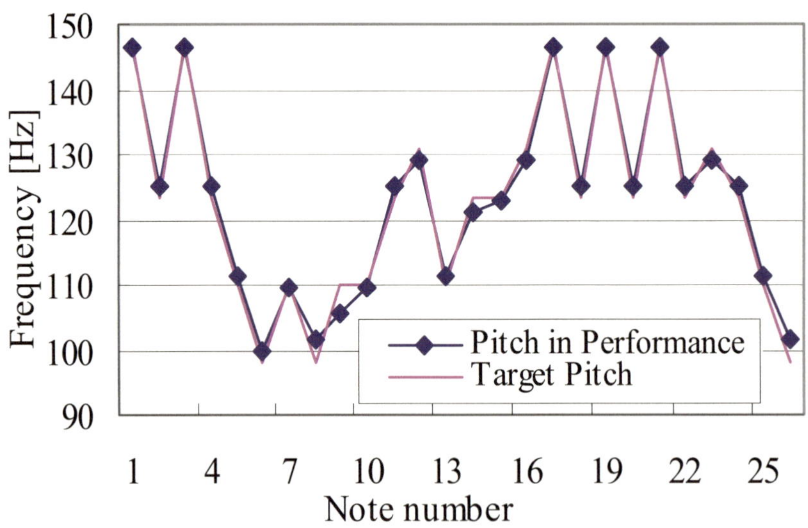

Figure 21. Result of singing performance

6. Conclusions

In this paper a talking and singing robot was introduced, which is constructed mechanically with human-like vocal cords and a vocal tract. By introducing the adaptive learning and controlling of the mechanical model with the auditory feedback, the robot was able to

acquire the vocalization skill as a human baby does when he glows up, and generate vocal sounds whose pitches and phonemes are uniquely specified.
The authors are now working to develop a training device for auditory impaired people to interactively train the vocalization by observing the robot motion. The mechanical system reproduces the vocalization skills just by listening to actual voices. Such persons will be able to learn how to move vocal organs, by watching the motions of the talking robot.
A mechanical construction of the human vocal system is considered not only to have advantages to produce natural vocalization rather than algorithmic synthesis methods, but also to provide simulations of human acquisition of speaking and singing skills. Further analyses of the human learning mechanisms will contribute to the realization of a speaking robot, which learns and sings like a human. The proposed approach to the understandings of the human behavior will also open a new research area to the development of a human-machine interface.

8. Acknowledgements

This work was partly supported by the Grants-in-Aid for Scientific Research, the Japan Society for the Promotion of Science (No. 18500152). The author would like to thank my students Mr. Toshio Higashimoto, Mr. Mitsuhiro Nakamura, Mr. Yasumori Hayashi and Mr. Mitsuki Kitani for their efforts for this research and study.

9. References

Y. Hayashi, "Koe To Kotoba No Kagaku", Houmei-do, 1979

J. L. Flanagan, "Speech Analysis Synthesis and Perception", Springer-Verlag. 1972

K. Hirose, "Current Trends and Future Prospects of Speech Synthesis", Journal of the Acoustical Society of Japan, pp. 39-45, 1992

J.O. Smith III, "Viewpoints on the History of Digital Synthesis", International Computer Music Conference, pp. 1-10, 1991

N. Umeda and R. Teranishi, "Phonemic Feature and Vocal Feature -Synthesis of Speech Sounds Using an Acoustic Model of Vocal Tract", Journal of the Acoustical Society of Japan, Vol.22, No.4, pp. 195-203, 1966

K. Fukui, K. Nishikawa, S. Ikeo, E. Shintaku, K. Takada, H. Takanobu, M. Honda, A. Takanishi: "Development of a Talking Robot with Vocal Cords and Lips Having Human-like Biological Structure", IEEE/RSJ International Conference on Intelligent Robots and Systems, pp2526-2531, 2005.

H. Sawada and S. Hashimoto, "Adaptive Control of a Vocal Chord and Vocal Tract for Computerized Mechanical Singing Instruments", International Computer Music Conference, pp. 444-447, 1996

T. Higashimoto and H. Sawada, "Vocalization Control of a Mechanical Vocal System under the Auditory Feedback", Journal of Robotics and Mechatronics, Vol.14, No.5, pp. 453-461, 2002

T. Higashimoto and H. Sawada: "A Mechanical Voice System: Construction of Vocal Cords and its Pitch Control", International Conference on Intelligent Technologies, pp. 762-768, 2003

H. Sawada and M. Nakamura: "Mechanical Voice System and its Singing Performance", IEEE/RSJ International Conference on Intelligent Robots and Systems, pp. 1920-1925, 2004

M. Nakamura and H. Sawada, "Talking Robot and the Analysis of Autonomous Voice Acquisition", IEEE/RSJ International Conference on Intelligent Robots and Systems, pp. 4684-4689, 2006

K. Ishizaka and J.Flanagan, "Synthesis of Voiced Sounds from a Two-Mass Model of the Vocal Chords", Bell Syst. Tech. J., 50, 1223-1268, 1972

23

Conversation System of an Everyday Robot Robovie-IV

Noriaki Mitsunaga[1], Zenta Miyashita[2,1], Takahiro Miyashita[1], Hiroshi Ishiguro[2,1] and Norihiro Hagita[1]
[1]*ATR Intelligent Robotics and Communication Laboratories*
[2]*Graduate School of Engineering, Osaka University*
Japan

1. Introduction

Robots are expected to play a much more active role in our daily lives in the near future. Since there are large differences in social aspects between short-term interaction in a laboratory and long-term interaction in real life, it is imperative to conduct experiments with a robot that interacts with people every day in their real daily lives to develop such robots in the future.

Jijo-2 (Matsui et al., 1997) was developed as an office-conversant robot that informs people where a person is, guides them to a room, and so on. Also, a museum guiding robot (Burgard et al. 1998) has been developed. They both interacted with people on a daily basis, and their interactions were designed to achieve tasks such as providing information about a person, guiding a visitor to a room, or explaining displays. However, communication is not just for achieving tasks but also for building social relationships. For example, when people chat with others, there may be no explicit intention to exchange information; it is just conversation. Although such kinds of interaction without explicit intention might seem unnecessary, we think they increase familiarity which serves as the basis of smooth communication to achieve tasks. This means we will prefer the robot most familiar to us when encountering two robots that are functionally identical.

We call such an interaction that increases familiarity and facilitates communication "social interaction." Our interest is in how to realize such interactions in a robot and what makes an interaction a social one. To investigate these issues it is necessary to perform experiments in daily life environments. For the first step of our research, we have developed a human-sized version of Robovie, Robovie-IV. Robovie-IV features interaction abilities including voice chats, which are intended to be "social interactions." Using Robovie-IV we conducted an experiment in which it interacted with people in their daily life in our office environment for six months.

This chapter is arranged as follows. In Section 2, we discuss how to implement daily interactions between a human and a robot, and then in Section 3 we discuss the requirements for a robot to carry out everyday communication. In Sections 4 and 5 respectively we briefly introduce the hardware and software architecture of Robovie-IV. Section 6 outlines the implementation of the base software for the daily interaction, and

Section 7 describes our experiment and observations. Finally, we discuss the results and offer conclusions in Section 8.

2. Daily interaction between humans and robots

Isbell et al. (Isbell et al., 2001) have realized an agent that can participate in a chat session over the Internet. The agent learns how to interact in a chat with rewards given by other human participants. Kubota et al. (Kubota et al., 2000), meanwhile, have created an agent that chats with people using a type of corpus based on exchanged E-mails on a mailing list that discusses drinks. These agents and the method to build the corpus are free from speech recognition, speech synthesis (text-to-speech), and so on since electrical texts are given.

It is still difficult, however, to dictate our daily conversations and to build a usable corpus by current voice recognition methods. Also, there are many differences between chats over the Internet and our daily face-to-face chats. To the best of our knowledge, there is no corpus presently usable for daily human-robot conversation. Consequently, we have decided to implement rule-based interactions between a human and a robot including chats.

There are four modes in human-robot interaction:

- Mode A) the human makes the first move and does not wait for the robot's reaction;
- Mode B) the human makes the first move and expects a reaction from the robot;
- Mode C) the robot makes the first move and does not wait for the human's reaction; and
- Mode D) the robot makes the first move and expects a reaction from the human.

Patting a robot's shoulder or head is an example of interaction Mode A. In the case where a human passes by without expecting a reaction from the robot, it is not necessary to explicitly implement interactions. Approaching, touching, talking to, and making a gesture to the other are examples of Modes B and D, while saying "hello" is an example of interaction Mode C. We regarded Mode D as most important and mainly implemented the interactions where the robot actively tries to talk with a human when the distances between them are within a certain range. For Mode B, we mainly implemented reactions in which a human touched the robot's skin.

We classify the interactions in Mode D into four types, according to sensor information:

- Type1) interactions in which a robot can continue to play regardless of the sensor values, without making people feel that there is something wrong with them;
- Type2) interactions that may comprise reactions that rely only on simple sensor information;
- Type3) interactions that need voice recognition, but mis-recognitions do not lead to severe discomfort; and
- Type4) interactions that need voice recognition, and mis-recognitions lead to severe discomfort.

Greetings and performances like a dance are examples of Type1 interactions, and giving responses is an example of Type2 interaction. When a person is drinking something, the robot might ask "What are you drinking?" Without recognizing the answer, the robot can say "I would like to drink it too," A Type2 interaction does not need voice recognition even if the communication type is a chat. Both Type3 and 4 interactions use the result of the voice recognition system; the differences are their required recognition accuracy. Suppose the robot says "Let's play," and fails to recognize the person's vocal response of "no," and it starts to play. The human may feel it is selfish but this is not serious problem. However, if

the voice recognition fails for a word used in the robot's response from the robot, the human will easily detect the failure.
We are mainly implementing Type2 and 3 interactions because too many Type1 interactions reduces humans' interest in the robot, and Type4 interactions disappoint the human if voice recognition fails. For Type4 interactions, we needed to carefully construct a voice recognition dictionary in order to reduce the number of failures.
To talk about current events, we prepared fixed-form rule-based chats that included sensing results, chat histories, dates and times, and information from the Internet. For example, how many people the robot met today, who it met, current weather, and so on. We incrementally added interaction rules to Robovie-IV since we incrementally learned what were expected interactions. Robovie-IV had 12 Type1, 11 Type2, 49 Type3, and 2 Type4 interactions at the end of the experiment.

3. Requirements for a communication robot

What capabilities are necessary for a communication robot? At least the following requirements are needed to achieve natural and effective human-robot communication. First of all, the robot should be self-contained. Although its computers, database systems, and even sensors can be outside its body, it should have mechanisms to perform both verbal and nonverbal communication by itself. Furthermore, it should be able to move around with no wires for smooth communication because the distance between a person and a robot cannot be ignored when attempting to achieve effective communication. Also, it should not have an outward appearance that frightens or discomforts people.
Second is the capability of haptic communication because haptic communication is as important as vision and voice. People who are familiar with each other often touch each other's hair or hug each other; such haptic interaction reinforces their familiarity. If a communication robot equipped with tactile sensors over its entire body could have the same haptic interaction capability as human do, the robot would become more familiar, thus shortening its communicative distance from people. To study haptic communication, we have previously developed two types of humanoid robots, Robovie-IIS and Robovie-IIF, that have tactile sensors embedded in a soft skin that covers the robot's entire body (Miyashita et al., 2005). These robots were developed based on Robovie-II (Ishiguro et al. 2001). Fig. 1 shows overall views of Robovie-IIS, Robovie-IIF, and a scene of communication with a human. Robovie-IV has tactile sensors based on the technique we used for these robots.

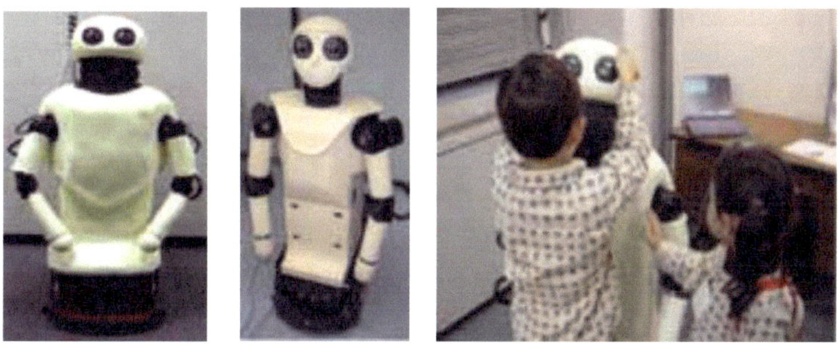

Figure 1. From left to right, Robovie-IIS, Robovie-IIF, and haptic interaction between children and Robovie-IIS.

Third is the locomotion mechanism that can generate involuntary motions. Human motion can be classified into two types: voluntary and involuntary motion (Bruno, 2002, Zheng, 1990, Wu 1991). Voluntary motions are a set of motions made to achieve given tasks or intentions. Going to a certain place, moving an arm forward for a handshake, vocalization to say hello, and reacting to a pat in order to know who did it are such examples. Involuntary motions, on the other hand, are a set of incidental motions such as feedback control arising in response to physical stimuli from the environment without prior planning or motivation. These motions do not correspond to tasks directly but instead consist of motions that make the robot appear to behave more naturally. Robovie-III was developed to enable involuntary motion for a robot (Miyashita & Ishigruro, 2004). It uses a wheeled inverted pendulum mechanism for locomotion. Since the inverted pendulum is controlled by feedback on its posture, involuntary motion of the whole body occurs. In addition to effecting involuntary motion, the wheeled inverted pendulum has a unique feature: When some external force is applied to the body from its front, it moves backwards. Since its wheels are controlled to maintain its posture, it moves backwards to keep the posture as it tilts backwards due to the applied force. We also adopt the wheeled inverted pendulum mechanism for Robovie-IV.

Fourth is human recognition. People expect a robot to be able to find and identify them. Many methods for human detection and identification using images have been proposed; however, with current computational power and video camera resolution and viewing angles, conditions under which those methods work are still limited. Consequently, we decided to use a laser range sensor to find human leg candidates and an optical/RF tag system for human identification. Robovie-IV finds leg candidates using a laser range sensor, verifies the results with its camera, and identifies the detected human with a tag.

Based on the above discussion, Robovie-IV is designed as a robot 1) whose height is the same as a child's; 2) whose whole body is covered with soft, light-colored skin for a soft look and touch; 3) with many tactile sensors are embedded in the soft skin; 4) which can move in two modes, one is a normal wheeled robot mode with passive casters, and the other is the inverted pendulum mode; and 5) which has optical and RF tag readers and laser range sensors for human identification.

4. The hardware Implementation

Fig. 2 shows front and side views of Robovie-IV. The height of the robot is about 1.1 m, which is smaller than the Robovie-II/II-S/II-F models (which are 1.2 m high). As the figure shows, it has two arms each with four degrees of freedom, one head with pan, tilt, and roll joints, four support wheels (passive casters), two drive wheels, and one jack to enable the inverted pendulum state. Robovie-IV is equipped with two video cameras with pan and tilt joints, one camera with an omni-directional mirror, a microphone (attached on the omni-directional mirror as in Fig. 3) and speaker, an optical tag reader (easily detachable, not shown in the figure), and an RF tag reader (the system is based on the active tag system called Spider by RF Code Inc.). Robovie-IV also features two laser range sensors in the front and back, two gyros that sense the same axes (we use two to take the average of their outputs in order to reduce random noise, and to detect failure so that the robot does not fall over), and 56 tactile sensors.

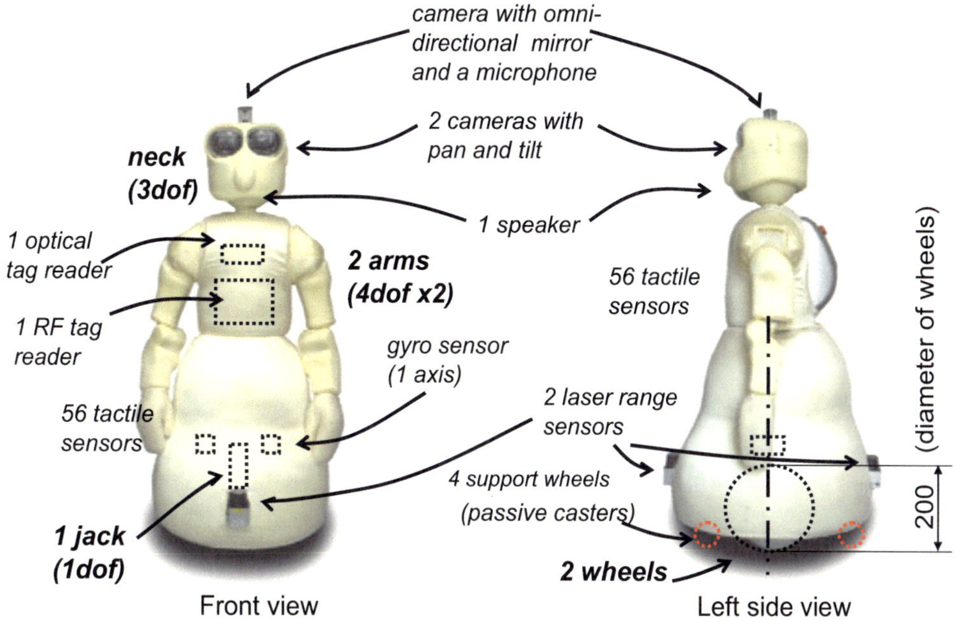

Figure 2. Front and left-side views of Robovie-IV. Fitted actuators and sensors are shown.

Figure 3. A microphone, attached on a omni-directional mirror, is located on top of the head

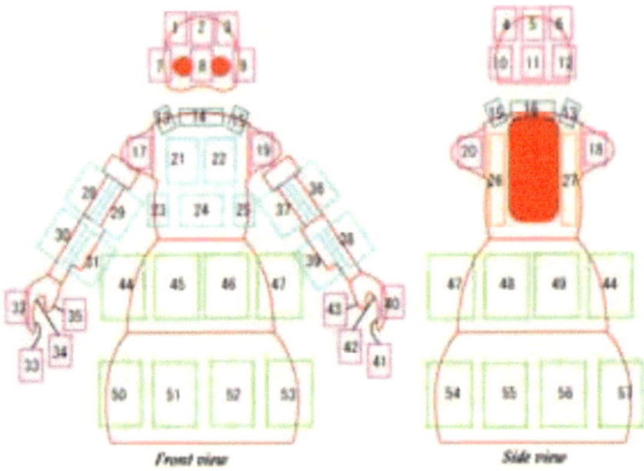

Figure 4. Arrangement of the skin sensor elements. There are 56 sensors in its soft skin (#16 is not implemented).

Fig. 4 displays the arrangement of the sensor elements that are embedded in the soft skin. The figure clearly shows that there are tactile sensors under the nose, ears, and in the thumbs for Robovie-IV to sense contact to those areas.

Fig. 5 shows Robovie-IV's hardware architecture. There are four PID motor controllers connected to a PC via RS-232 dedicated for wheels, left and right arms, and neck joints. The jack and the inverted pendulum are controlled by the motor controller. Two laser range sensors and optical and RF tag readers, and cameras with pan/tilt joints are also connected to the PC via RS-232. Signals from the tactile sensors are fed to five skin processors. The processed signals are then sent to the PC via the RS-422 bus. Images from three cameras are captured by a frame grabber installed on the PC. A speaker and a microphone are connected to the sound output and input of the PC. Each controller has a SH2 micro-processor (Renesas Technology Corp.) and the main computer has a Pentium-M processor that runs at 2 GHz. The PC can be connected to the sensors via a wireless LAN.

The flow of sound signals is shown in Fig. 6. The sound signal recorded by a microphone (monaural) is fed to two high-pass filters (f_c = 100Hz) followed by a low-pass filter (f_c=2kHz). The LPF's output is fed to the input of the PC's sound card. The two HPFs and the LPF are 2nd order active filters which consist of OP-amps. The HPFs are used to reduce wind noise. The sound signal from the microphone is sampled at a 16kHz sampling rate with 16 bits of accuracy by a speech recognition program. The output from the PC is amplified and fed to a speaker which is located in the head of Robovie-IV.

Fig. 7 shows the structure of a tactile sensor element embedded in the soft skin. As the figure illustrates, the soft skin consists of four layers. The outside layer is made of thin silicone rubber, and the middle layer is made of thick silicone rubber. We use these silicone rubber layers to realize humanlike softness. The inner layer is made of urethane foam, which has a density lower than that of the silicone rubber; the densities of the urethane foam and the silicone rubber are 0.03 g/cm^3 and 1.1 g/cm^3, respectively. The total density of the soft skin, including all layers, is 0.6 g/cm^3. Robovie-IV's tactile sensor elements are film-type piezoelectric sensors inserted between the thin and thick silicone rubber layers. These film-type sensors, consisting of polyvinylidene fluoride (PVDF) and sputtered silver, output a high voltage proportionate to changes in applied pressure. Since the middle and the inner layers deform easily upon human contact with the skin, the sensor layer can easily detect the contact.

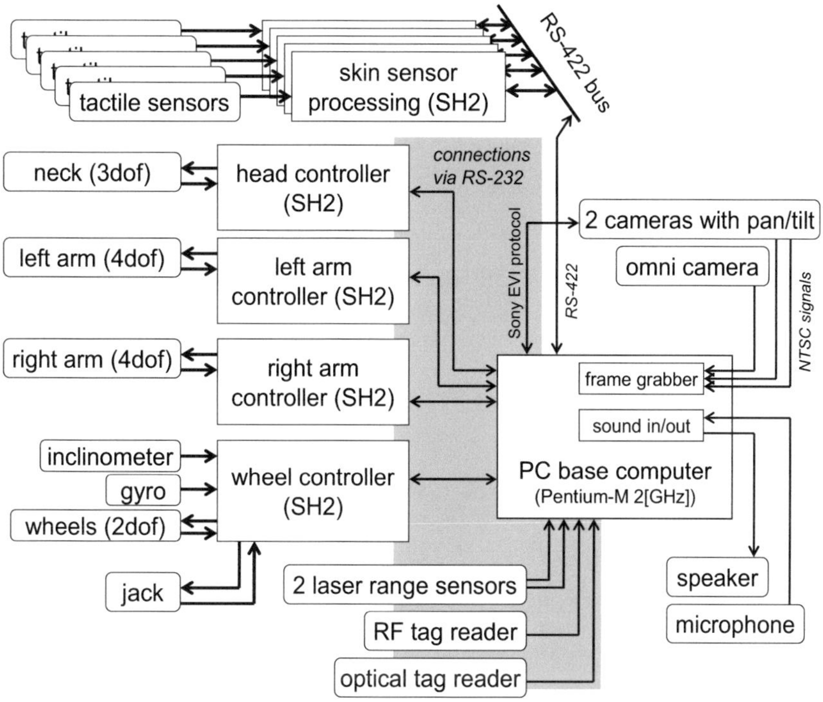

Figure 5. Robovie-IV's hardware architecture. There are four motor controllers, five skin processors, and one main computer.

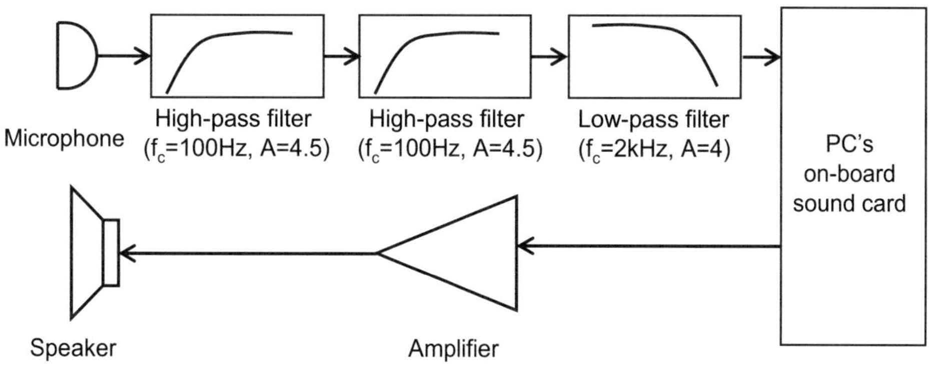

Figure 6. The flow of sound signals. The sound signal from a microphone is fed to the PC's on-board sound card via two HPFs and a LPF. The sound from the PC is amplified and fed to a speaker.

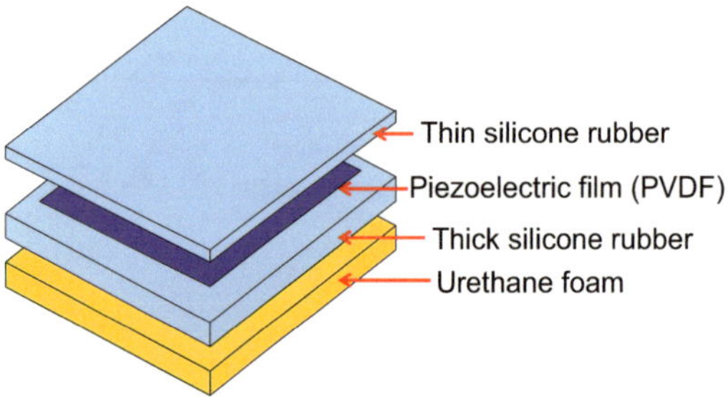

Figure 7. The skin's structure, which consists of four layers. The piezoelectric sensor is inserted between the outer and middle layers.

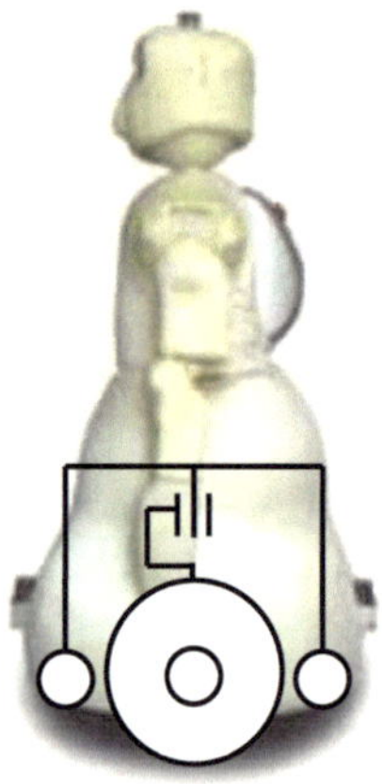

Figure 8. The drive wheels are connected by a jack to the main body and support wheels. The figure shows the inverted pendulum mode.

Fig. 8 illustrates how the drive wheels, the support wheels, and the jack are connected. The support wheels are connected to the main body directly, while the drive wheels are connected via the jack. Robovie-IV can select two locomotion modes, with or without support wheels, by controlling the jack. With the support wheels, Robovie-IV moves as a normal robot with two drive wheels, but without them, it moves in the inverted pendulum mode. We use the wheeled inverted pendulum controller proposed by Ha and Yuta (Ha & Yuta, 1994).

5. The Software Implementation

Fig. 9 presents an overview of Robovie-IV's software architecture. The PC's operating system is Linux, and a box with bold line in the figure indicates a process running on Linux. There are five processes, *robovie4, robobase4, robomap4, PostgreSQL,* and *Julian*. The processes are connected through named pipes, sockets, and shared memory. The process *robovie4* makes decisions for the robot from the internal state, information in the database, and the sensor information gathered and processed by the other processes. Processors on the motor controllers control motors as directed by a program called *robobase4* running on the PC. Process *robobase4* handles the communication between controllers and sensors while hiding the differences of the protocols from *robovie4*. Process *robomap4* is the one for self-localization. It receives information from the two laser range sensors and odometry from *robobase4* and compares this information with the map of the environment. The estimated position is returned to *robobase4* and sent to *robovie4*. The *PostgreSQL* (see http://www.PostgreSQL.org/) is a popular database engine. We use the database to store and recall co-experiences with humans.

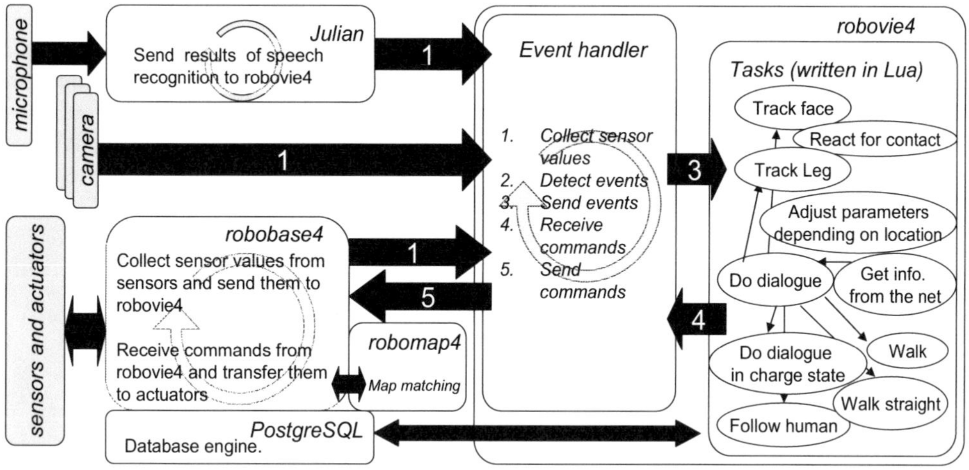

Figure 9. Robovie-IV's software architecture. The PC's OS is Linux. There are five processes *robovie4, robobase4, robomap4, PostgreSQL,* and *Julian.*

The *Julian* process is that of a grammar-based recognition parser called *"Julian." Julian* is a modified version of *Julius,* which is a high-performance, two-pass large-vocabulary continuous speech recognition (LVCSR) decoder software for speech-related researchers and developers. We have prepared manually designed deterministic finite automata (DFA) grammar as the language model and use it for the speech recognition by Julian. The *robovie4* process connects to the *Julian* process and commands dictionary selection and so on. The recognized words are sent back to *robovie4*.

We adopted a text-to-speech program called *CHATR* (Campbell & Black, 1996) to produce Robovie-IV's voice. The *robobase4* process calls *CHATR* when it is commanded to utter text by the *robovie4* process. The synthesized voice is fed to the speaker through the on-board sound card in the PC.

The *robovie4* process mainly consists of an event handler written in C++ and tasks written in Lua (see http://www.Lua.org/), which is a scripting language that can be embedded in a C or C++ program. Tasks written in Lua run in parallel by the collaborative multithreading supported by Lua. There are task threads to do dialogue, react to tactile events, track a human's face, track legs, and so on. The events from sensor values are detected in the event handler, negating the need to copy an event detection for each task thread. The event handler in *robovie4* continuously,

1. collects sensor values from *julian* and *robobase4;*
2. detects events;
3. sends events to task threads;
4. receives commands from task threads; and
5. sends commands to *robobase4* as in Fig. 9.

Each of the task thread continuously,

1. waits for events from the event handler;
2. reads sensor values sent from *julian* or *robobase4*; reads from and writes to the database; and
3. decides the next action.

The dialogue task is responsible for human-robot interactions and controls other task threads. In terms of the four modes of human-robot interaction defined earlier, the dialogue task does not react to Mode A (human-initiated non-waiting) interactions since no reaction is expected. It just records the event, such as someone patting the robot's head. When a Mode B (human-initiated waiting) interaction, such as a human approaching the robot, is detected, the task tries to take the initiative and move to the interaction Mode D (robot-initiated waiting) by initiating a dialogue. Although people may feel that the robot interacted in Mode C (robot-initiated non-waiting), no Mode C interaction is explicitly implemented.

An interaction in Mode D repeats the following until its end.

1. The robot speaks and makes a gesture,
2. the robot waits for an answer or reaction from the human, and
3. the robot reacts according to the answer.

The Type1 interactions do not have steps 2) and 3). The Type2 interactions do not use the result of *Julian* but just use the fact that the human utterance ends. The Type3 and Type4 interactions react according to the result of voice recognition. The Type3s do not repeat a word which the human uttered, while the Type4s directly include it in the robot's answer.

6. The daily interactions

Basically, Robovie-IV repeats (a) moving around, seeking a human to interact with; and (b) interaction with the found human until he or she quits the interaction as Fig. 10 shows. Robovie-IV detects humans by first finding leg candidates from front laser range-sensor values by background subtraction, large sound, or reading of RF-ID tag. The laser range sensor measures distances at the height of an ankle. Fig. 11 illustrates the readings of the range sensor plotted on the floor map. The circle on the right and the line indicates the position and the posture of Robovie-IV from self-localization data based on map matching. Clearly, the walls and cartoon boxes are detected by the sensor, whereas distant walls are not detected since the sensor's maximum range is 4 m. The two small circles in front of the circle representing the robot indicate detected legs. The circle on the left of the robot, however, is a falsely detected leg candidate. When a leg candidate is found, Robovie-IV rotates itself and gazes in the direction of the leg candidate. If a large skin-colored blob or a large blob in a differential image is detected by Robovie-IV's camera, or the tag reader detects a valid ID, it assumes the candidate to be a human leg. During interaction, it tracks the skin-colored blob at the shortest distance in the direction of the leg candidate and maintains that distance and posture with respect to the leg candidate. The tag reader's attenuator is adjusted to detect tags within 1.5m of Robovie-IV.

Fig. 12 shows the flow of one of Robovie-IV's typical interaction. Once it has detected a human (Fig. 12 (a)), it will try to interact with him or her. It will say "hi" in Japanese and wait for the response (Fig. 10 (a) and 12 (b)). If it does not detect a response it will begin to seek another human; otherwise, it will recognize the person as an interaction partner. Then it starts a dialogue as in Fig . 10 (b) and Fig. 12(c). It continues by selcting a topic and trying to chat with the person. In the chat, it repeats the following sequence of actions: 1) stop speech recognition, 2) do a gesture and/or say something, 3) change DFA grammar of *Julian* and start speech recognition (not for Type2 interactions), 4) wait for a reply, a reaction, or some time to elapse. The end condition of the chat is met when the person says "bye-bye" or goes away. Then, it says "bye-bye" and searches for the next person to talk with (Fig. 12 (d).)

Interaction rules are derived from the Lua program (functions), gestures, and DFA grammars for Julian. There are more than 70 interaction rules and Lua codes implemented, with more than 5,000 lines of code. There are three branches on average on the conditional branches of Type2, 3, and 4 interactions.

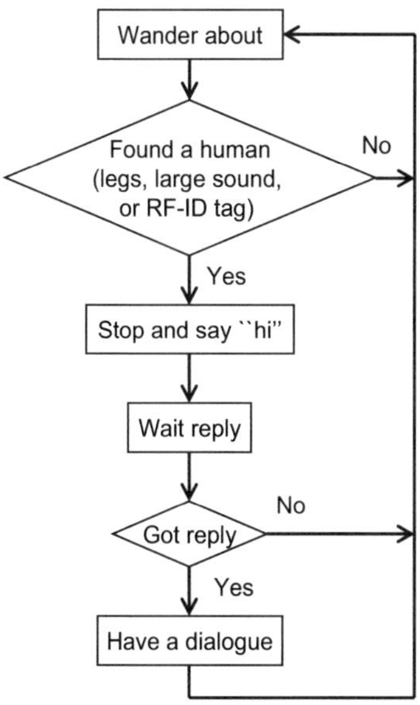

(a) flow of moving around and seeking a human to interact with

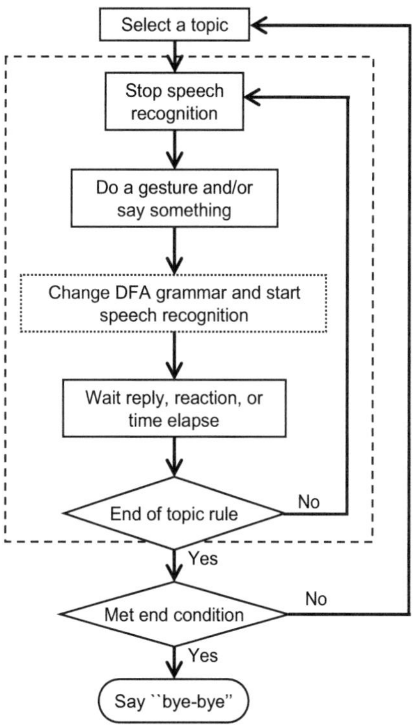

(b) flow of interaction with a human

Figure 10. Flow of Robovie-IV's daily interaction. Robovie-IV wander around to search for a human to talk with (a) and have a dialogue (b).

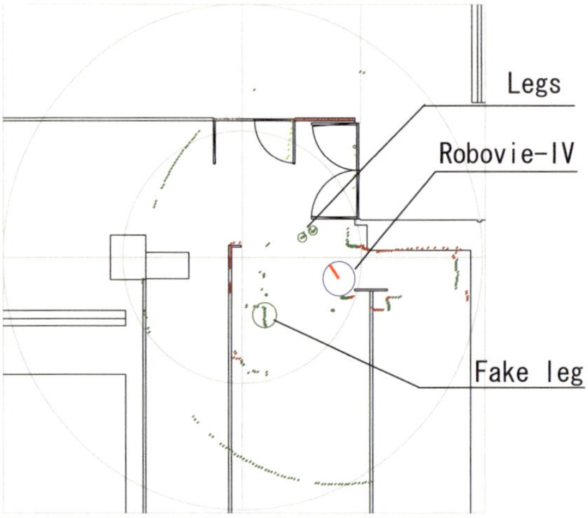

Figure 11. A depth image plotted on the floor map by a laser range sensor. A circle and a line on the right indicate Robovie-IV's position and posture. Two circles in front of the robot are detected legs. The larger circle to the left of the robot is a false detection.

1) search for a human to talk with

2) find a human and say "hi"

3) have a chat

4) say "bye-bye"

Figure 12. Flow of a typical interaction that Robovie-IV tries to do. 1) it searches for a human to talk with, 2) say "hi", 3) have a chat, and 4) say "bye-bye".

Robovie-IV records the results of interaction to the database. Examples of results include with whom it interacted, which rule it used, when the interaction rule started and finished being used, the response from the human, how long the human moved, how many times it met with a person, and so on. It also records the number of leg candidates, skin-colored blobs, and Ids detected by the tag reader in a certain interval. Robovie-IV uses the data in the database in order not to repeat same interaction, to say it has met many people today, and so on. It also talks about current weather based on the information from the Internet.

7. Observation of Daily Human Robot Interaction in an Office Environment

We have conducted a long-term experiment in our office at ATR's IRC laboratory for six months. Robovie-IV roamed around the office and interacted in our daily life. In the office there were about 100 people including researchers, engineers, and secretaries. The total length of the corridor in which Robovie-IV could move was about 150 meters. We implemented interactions resembling those of a child in an office who comes along with its parent, since the height of the Robovie-IV is about 1.1 m, similar to that of a child. We incrementally added interactions and updated other items of software during the experiment. Fig. 13 (a) and (b) show a scene in the office and an example of interaction.
Fig. 14 shows some scenes from the daily experiment, (a) Robovie-IV trying to communicate, (b) a person patting the robot's head while passing by, (c) two people talking to each other, one toying with the robot's nose, (d) a person covering the robot's eyes, and (f) Robovie-IV interacting with a person. In scene (e), following its usual human-seeking behavior, Robovie-IV moved into the middle of a conversation in progress. At this stage, of course, Robovie-IV is unable to meaningfully join such a conversation. Robovie-IV did not always interact with detected humans as in Fig. 14 (a) because the experimental environment was an office and people were busy with their jobs. Though the novelty of having Robovie-IV in the office had worn off, people still noticed it out of the corner of their eye while working, indicating that they were still aware of its presence, and that it was gradually changing its behavior. Robovie-IV is still under development, but it has become a robot that makes its presence felt by people.

(a) Robovie-IV is roaming in the office at ATR's IRC laboratory

(b) A person is communicating with Robovie-IV. The robot is asking if the person likes watching baseball

Figure 13. Scenes from the experiment in our office. (a) shows Robovie-IV and the office that it roamed around. (b) shows an example of interaction

(a)Robovie-IV trying to communicate

(b)A person patting the robot's head while passing by

(c) Two people talking to each other, one toying with the robot's nose

(d) A person covering the robot's eyes

(e) Robovie-IV moving into a conversation in progress

(f) Robovie-IV interacting with a person

Figure 14. Some scenes from the daily experiment.

There still remain some technical issues to be solved. One is the timing to say hello to a person passing by. There were cases that he or she would walk away before Robovie-IV started its greeting. The second issue is that there are people who are not getting used to conversing with Robovie-IV. *Julian* does not allow overlapping of human and robot voices without external sound processing. Also there is a sweet spot in the microphone where the success rate of recognition increases. We do not have answers to deal with these issues yet.

Furthermore, there are different feelings toward what a robot actually does. When Robovie-IV asks, "What are you drinking?", even if a person is not drinking, one would feel it is very strange that the robot does not understand the situation. The person might feel that is interesting, however, that the robot is making small talk, so he or she answers the question. What kinds of interaction increase familiarity and make communication smoother is still open question. We think this question will be answered by having more experiment and adding more types of interaction.

8. Fundamental Issues and Conclusions

An interaction robot communicating with people in everyday life is the key to revealing the social relationships of a robot among people. Long-term everyday interactions are necessary to observe and analyze the following;

- Influence of a robot on people's sense of time, e.g. whether a robot's behavior reminds us of the current time; for example, if the robot establishes a "habitual" routine of behaviors based on the time of day, could it serve to make people aware of the time?
- The relationship between a robot's task and its preferred social interactions, e.g. what kinds of interactions are necessary for a cleaning robot, a secretary robot, a guiding robot, or a robot that carries heavy objects in tandem with a human;
- Preferred types of human-robot dialogues according to the social relationship and the robot's task, e.g. whether simple statements are preferred, colloquial language is preferred, or new type of language emerges;
- The social role of a robot among people, e.g. whether a robot will be perceived to be "alive" in a way that is different from humans, plants, pets, inanimate objects, and so on, and what factors contribute to this perception;
- What kind of social behaviors would be acceptable to different communities.

We believe our daily experiment is the first step to reveal these fundamental issues.

In this chapter, we proposed a basic framework for analyzing the daily interactions between a human and a robot. We first discussed the daily interactions between a human and a robot. Human-robot interaction falls into four modes according to who initiates the interaction and whether he or she expects a reaction from the other. Then, we subdivided one mode of that interactions, which a robot initiates and expects a reaction from the human, into four types according to the sensor information the robot uses. We focused on the interactions which require voice recognition but for which misrecognitions do not lead to severe discomfort.

Next, we explained what is necessary for a communication robot and introduced the hardware and software architectures of Robovie-IV. Robovie-IV has been developed as a self-contained robot that fulfills the requirements of a communication robot. That is, it is as tall as a human child, its entire body is covered by a soft-skin containing 56 embedded tactile sensors, it moves by an inverted pendulum mechanism that causes involuntary motions, and it has sensors for human recognition. Finally, we briefly described the current status of our ongoing daily experiment in our office and discussed behaviors of the robot and how humans relate to it.

9. Acknowledgement

This research was supported by the Ministry of Internal Affairs and Communications.

10. References

Bruno, H. (2002). Repp.: phase correction in sensorimotor synchronization: nonlinearities in voluntary and involuntary responses to perturbations. *Human movement science*, Vol. 211, No. 1, (2002) (1-37)

Burgard, W.; Cremers, A. B., Fox, D. Haehnel, D. Lakemeyer, G. Schulz, D. Steiner, W., & Thrun, S. (1998). The interactive museum tour-guide robot, In *Proceedigns of the Fifteenth National Conference on Artificial Intelligence*, 1998

Campbell, W.N. & Black, A. (1996). Prosody and the selection of source units for concatenative synthesis, In: Progress in Speech Synthesis, van Santen, J. et al. (Ed.), Springer

Ha, Y. & Yuta, S. (1994). Trajectory tracking control for navigation of self-contained mobile inverse pendulum, In *Proceedings of the IEEE/RSJ/GI International Conference on Intelligent Robots and Systems 1994*, pp. 1875-1882, 1994

Isbell, C.; Shelton, C. R. Kearns, M. Singh, S. & Stone, P. (2001) A social reinforcement learning agent, In *Proceedings of the Fifth International Conference on Autonomous Agents*, pp. 377—384, Montreal, Canada, 2001, ACM Press

Ishiguro, H.; Ono, T. Imai, M. Maeda, T. Kanda, T. & Nakatsu R. (2001). Robovie: A robot generates episode chains in our daily life. In *Proceedings of the 32nd International Symposium on Robotics*, pp. 1356—1361, 2001

Kubota, H.; Nishida, T. & Koda, T. (2000). Exchanging tacit community knowledge by talking-virtualized-egos. In *Fourth International Conference on AUTONOMOUS AGENTS*, pp. 285—292, 2000

Lee, A.; Kawahara, T. & Shikano, K. (2001). Julius --- an open source real-time large vocabulary recognition engine, In *Proceedings of the European Conference on Speech Communication and Technology*, pp. 1691-1694, 2001

Matsui, T.; Asoh, H. Hara, I. & Otsu, N. (1997). An event-driven architecture for controlling behaviours of the office conversant mobile robot, Jijo-2, In *Proceedings of the 1997 IEEE International Conference on Robotics and Automation*, pp. 3367—3372, April 1997

Miyashita, T. & Ishiguro, H. (2004). Human-like natural behaviour generation based on involuntary motions for humanoid robots, *International Journal of Robotics and Autonomous Systems*, Vol. 48, (2004) (203-212)

Miyashita, T.; Tajika, T. Ishiguro, H. Kogure, K. & Hagita, N. (2005). Haptic communication between humans and robots, In *Proceedings of the 12th International Symposium of Robotics Research*, 2005

Wu, C. (1991). Analysis of voluntary movements for robotic control, In *Proceedings of the IEEE International Conference on Robotics and Automation*, pp. 326—331, 1991

Zheng, Y. (1990). A neural gait synthesizer for autonomous biped robots, In *Proceedings of the IEEE International Workshop on Intelligent Robots and Systems*, pp. 601—608, 1990

24

Sound Localization of Elevation using Pinnae for Auditory Robots

Tomoko Shimoda, Toru Nakashima, Makoto Kumon, Ryuichi Kohzawa, Ikuro Mizumoto and Zenta Iwai
Kumamoto University
Japan

1. Introduction

Humans perceive sound lags and differences in loudness between their two ears to ascertain the location of sounds in terms of azimuth, elevation and interval, etc. Humans and animals can determine the direction of sounds using only two ears, by making use of interaural time difference (ITD), interaural phase difference (IPD), interaural intensity difference (IID), etc. Robots can also use sound localization to detect changes in the environment around them; consequently, various sound localization methods for robots have been investigated. Since many animals have two ears, two ears seem to be the minimum requirement for determining sound localization.

While most robot's sound localization systems are based on microphone arrays that consist of three or more microphones, several researchers have attempted achieving binaural sound localization in robots. Nakashima (Nakashima and Mukai, 2004) developed a system that consisted of two microphones with pinnae and a camera that was only utilized in learning. By adopting a neural network that estimated the control command, he proposed a method utilizing sound signals for guiding the robot in the direction of a sound. Takanishi (Takanishi et al., 1993) achieved continuous direction localization of a sound source in the horizontal plane. They used the interaural sound pressure difference and the ONSET time difference as parameters and proposed a method for achieving two-step direction localization in a humanoid head using these parameters. Kumon (Kumon et al., 2003) approached the problem using an adaptive audio servo system based on IID as the control method for orientating the robots in the direction of the sound source in the horizontal plane by using two microphones.

This chapter describes the use of an audio servo of elevation for achieving sound localization using spectral cues caused by pinnae. Here, the term "audio servo" denotes a method for simultaneously localizing sound sources and controlling the robot's configuration, in contrast with conventional methods that are based on the "listen-and-move" principal. The audio servo is characterized by a feedback system that steers the robot toward the direction of the sound by combining dynamic motion of the robot with auditory ability. In order to achieve this, this chapter proposes a method for detecting instantaneous spectral cues, when these cues are not very accurate. Furthermore, controllers that compensate for the inaccuracy of the measured signal are also considered. In addition, this

chapter considers using sound source separation to detect spectral cues even in a noisy environment by attenuating the noise. Sound source separation is achieved using two microphones while spectral cues from only a single microphone and a pinna are utilized.
This chapter is organized as follows. In the next section (Section II) spectral cues caused by pinnae and artificial pinnae are briefly introduced. Then, in Section III a robust detection method for spectral cues is described. Methods for measuring spectral cues and a filter for investigating the relationships between the elevation angle and spectral cues are described. Modelling and identification with respect to the relationship between the elevation angle and the filtered spectral cues are also presented in this section. This section also describes sound source separation. Section IV describes the realization of an audio servo system that includes a controller for an auditory robot; its performance and results from experiments are also presented. Finally, Section V gives the conclusions and describes future projects.

2. Spectral Cues

This section briefly introduces spectral cues, pinnae and their frequency responses.

2.1 Spectral Cues

Generally, humans are considered to use frequency domain cues to estimate the elevation of a sound source (Garas, 2000). The frequency response varies with respect to the sound source direction as a result of the interference that occurs between the sound wave that enters the auditory canal directly and the sound wave reflected from the pinnae. In particular, spectral peaks and notches produced respectively by constructive and destructive interference contain information regarding the elevation of the sound source, making it possible to estimate the elevation of a sound source by analyzing them.

2.2 Robotic Pinnae

Spectral cues are dependent on the shape of the pinnae. In this chapter, logarithmic-shaped reflectors were used as pinnae (see Fig. 1). The pinnae had a depth of 6 (cm) (Lopez-Poveda and Meddis, 1996) and were made from 0.5 (mm) thick aluminum sheets. Figure 2 shows a photograph of experimental device with the pinnae attached. Figures 3 and 4 show a front view and a side view of the experimental device with the pinnae attached, respectively.

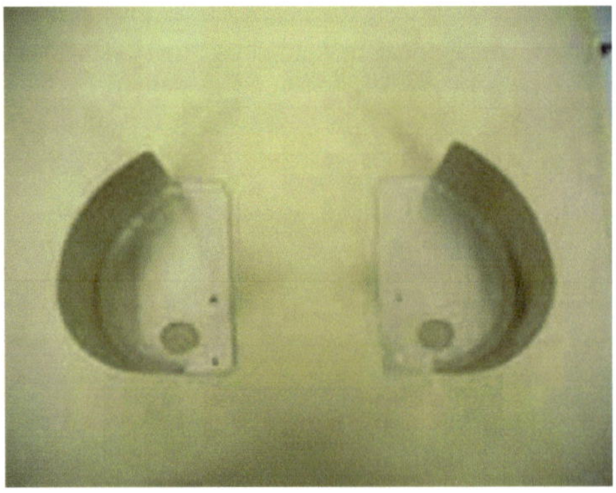

Figure 1. Developed Pinnae

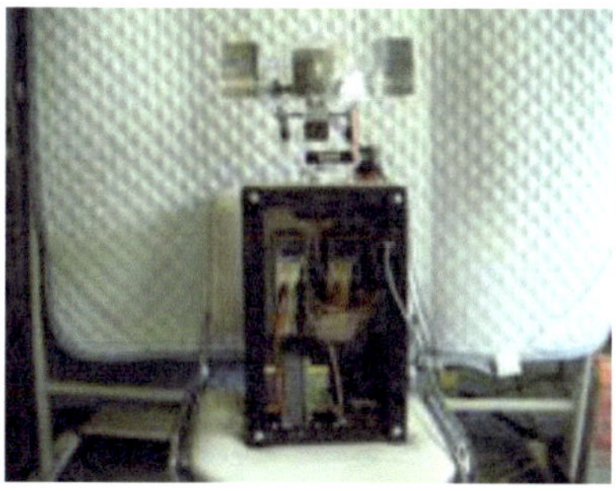

Figure 2. Photograph of robot with pinnae attached

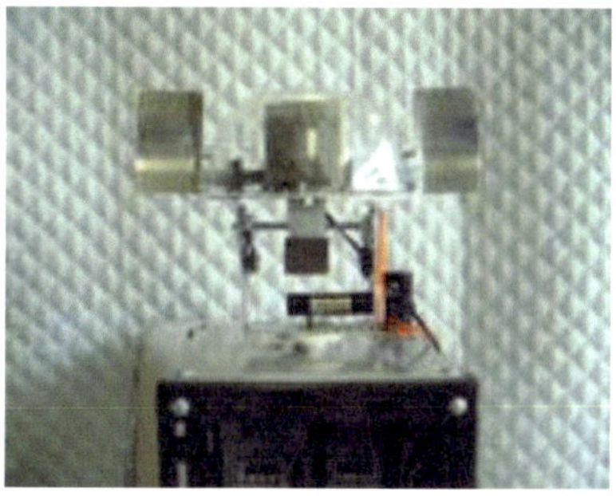

Figure 3. Front view of the robot with pinnae

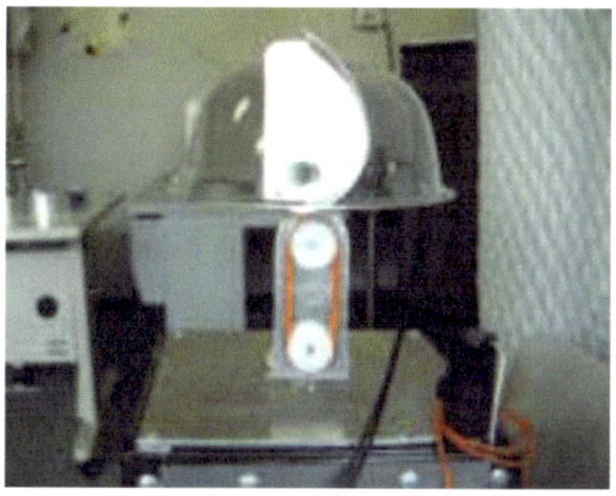

Figure 4. Side view of the robot with pinnae

The frequency response of the developed robotic pinna was measured to examine the relationship between spectral cues and sound source elevation. The robot's head was kept still while these measurements were made. A loudspeaker was positioned 0.5 (m) in front of the robot. The frequency characteristics of the pinnae were measured using time-stretched pulses (TSPs). The sound source direction is expressed as follows. The angle is defined as being 0 (deg) when the sound source is located directly in front of the robot. When the sound source is located below the robot's head, the angle is denoted by a positive value.

The results obtained using TSP are shown in Figs. 5(a) to (g). In these results, there are three sharp notches (labeled N1, N2 and N3) within the frequency range from 2 (kHz) to 15 (kHz) and these notches shift to lower frequencies as the robot turned its head upward. Thus, it can be concluded that it is possible to detect the elevation angle of a sound source using pinna cues.

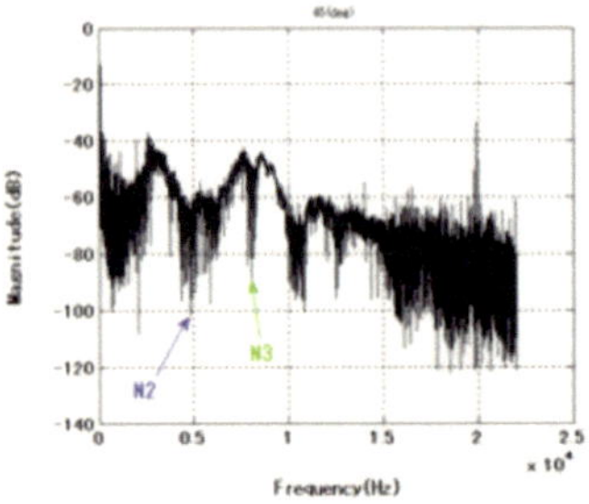

(a) 45 (deg)

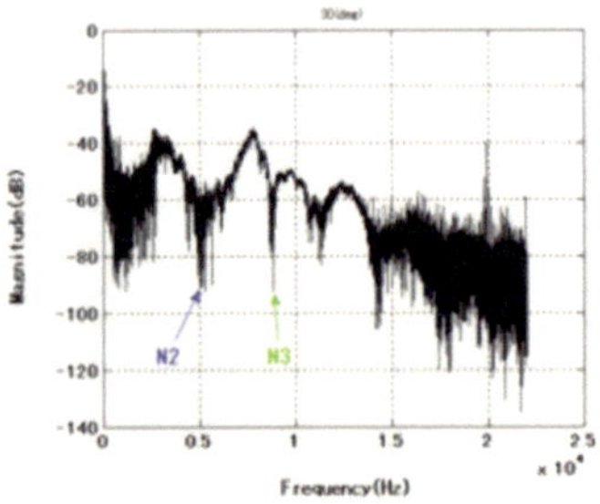

(b) 30 (deg)

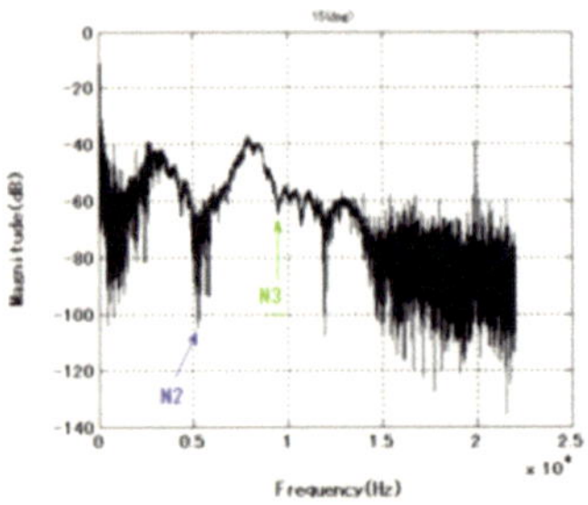

(c) 15 (deg)

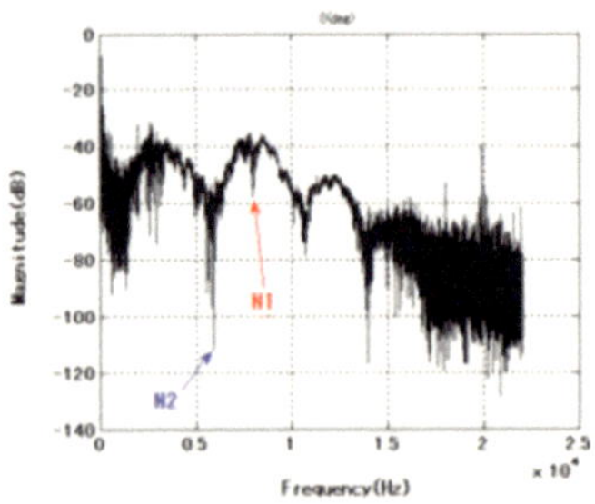

(d) 0 (deg)

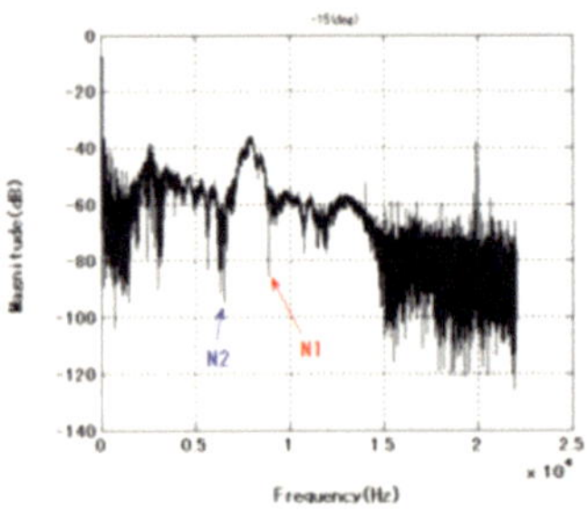

(e) -15 (deg)

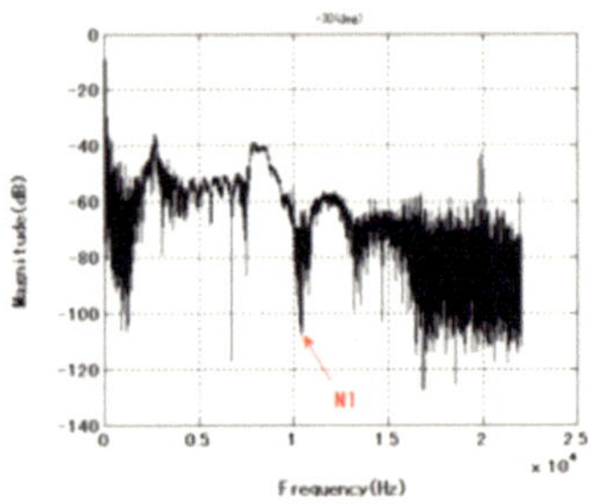

(f) -30 (deg)

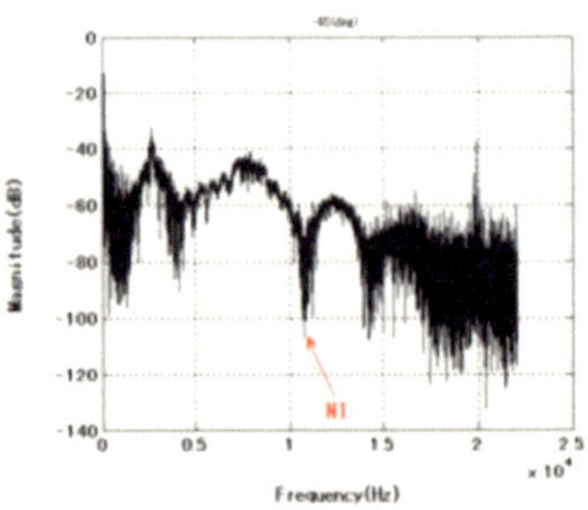

(g) -45 (deg)

Figure 5. Frequency responses of the developed pinnae

3. Spectral Cues Detection

3.1 Spectral Cues Extraction

In what follows, spectral cue candidates are defined as the center points between adjacent peaks and notches in a smoothed power spectrum; these candidates are simply referred to as spectral cues in this chapter. The following method is adopted to determine the frequency of a spectral cue. Firstly, the sound signal is transformed using short-time fast Fourier transformation (STFFT) and the frequency response is obtained for each instance of time (Fig. 5). Next, this frequency response is smoothed using a zero-phase low-pass filter (LPF).
An example of dynamic spectral cues is shown in Fig. 6. The ordinate axis represents frequency (Hz) and the abscissas axis represents time (s). Each of points represents a spectral cue. The sound source was fixed 0.5 (m) in front of the robot, as above, while the head was programmed to follow a triangular reference trajectory (Fig. 7). A white signal was utilized as the pilot signal instead of a TSP. Although multiple spectral cue candidates exist at every instant in Fig. 6, most of them varied with the head motion.
Unfortunately, not all of the detected candidates corresponded with the head motion, and there are some frequency bands in which spectral cues disappear for a specific direction. In addition, several adjacent cues had similar frequencies as each other. Hence it is difficult to immediately determine the sound source direction for these candidates. In particular, since sound signals in a short sampling time were employed, it is possible that the time frequency responses could have been degraded due to extraneous noises. Thus an improved robust cue detection method is required; such a method is described in following subsection.

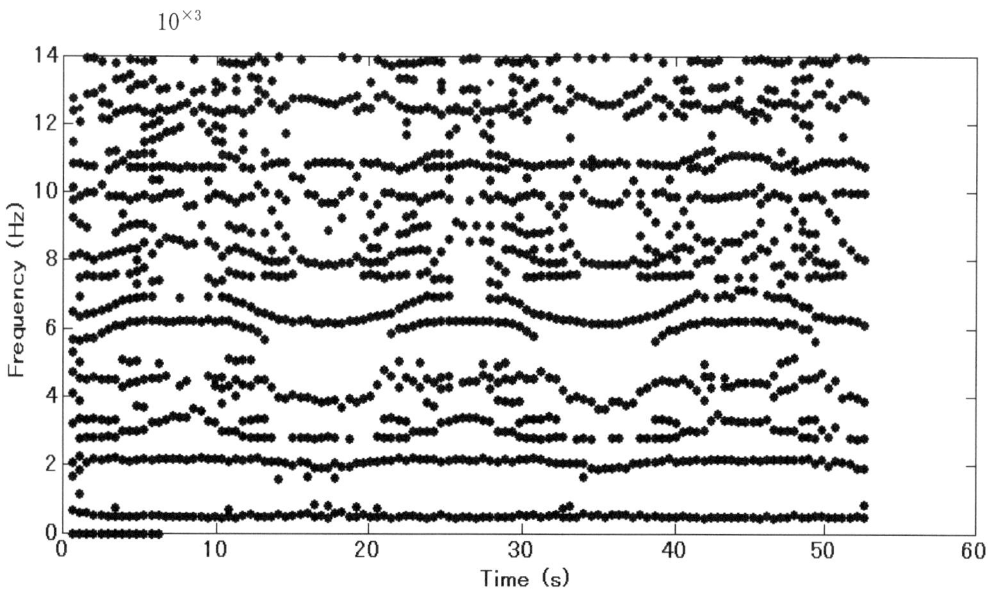

Figure 6. Spectral Cue Candidates obtained by experiment

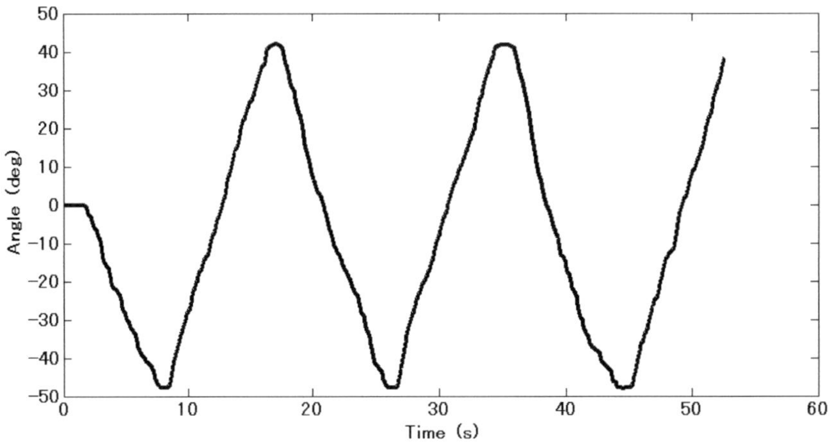

Figure 7. Head motion of the robot for the experiment in which the spectral cues of Fig. 6 were obtained

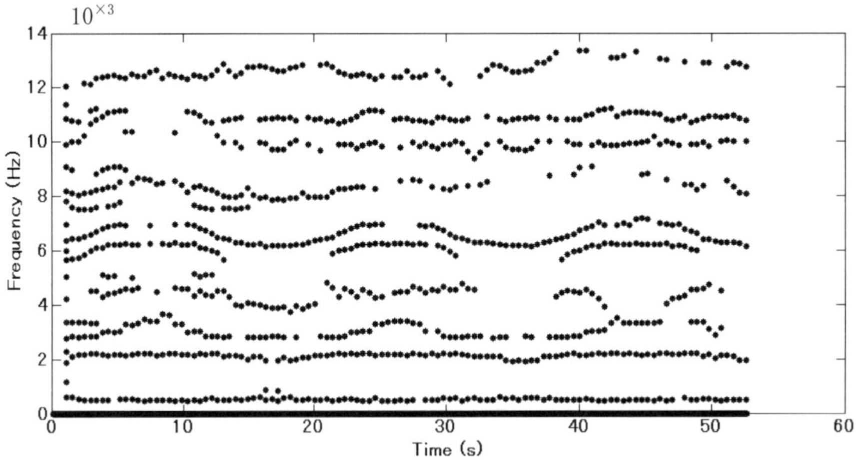

Figure 8. Clustered spectral cues produced by the proposed method (corresponds to Fig. 6)

3.2 Clustering

The robot's head motion is continuous owing to its dynamics. Since there is a relationship between the spectral cues and sound source direction, it is conceivable that the variation of spectral cues due to the motion of the robot's head is also continuous. Thus, given the values of the spectral cues at any particular moment, it should be possible to determine the spectral cues for the next time step by searching in their neighborhoods. Based on this supposition, a filter for detecting spectral cues from the frequency response for each instant was designed as follows.

Let $\boldsymbol{f}_k$ denote the vector whose elements represent the spectral cues' frequencies at time k; f_{kn} represents the n-th element of this vector. We assume that the frequency of a spectral cue remains within a certain range, which is referred to as the scope. The validity of the measured signal is stored in a vector of flags whose i-th element is denoted as d_{ki}. We assume that the number of cues is given and we denoted it by N_k. The proposed algorithm is given as follows.

<Spectral Cue Clustering>

1. Given spectral cues at time k.
2. Measure the frequency response at time $k+1$. Obtain the candidates of the spectral cues and denote them by the vector $\hat{f}_{k+1}$ whose n-th element ($\hat{f}_{(k+1)n}$) represents the frequency of the candidate.
3. Compute the assessment function $J_n(r)$ as follows.

$$J_n(r) = \begin{cases} C\Delta(n,r) & (\Delta(n,r) \geq 0), \\ -C\Delta(n,r) & (\Delta(n,r) < 0), \end{cases} \tag{1}$$

   where $\Delta(n,r) = f_{kn} - \hat{f}_{(k+1)r}$ and $0 < C < 1$.

   For each n, find r that minimizes $J_n(r)$ and let $f_{(k+1)n} = \hat{f}_{(k+1)r}$ as far as $\hat{f}_{(k+1)r}$ lies within the r scope. Otherwise, let $f_{(k+1)n}$ be f_{kn}.
4. If $f_{(k+1)n} = f_{(k+1)(n+1)}$, then replace $f_{(k+1)(n+1)}$ with $f_{(k+1)(n+1)}+\delta$, where δ represents a small positive constant.
5. If $\hat{f}_{(k+1)r}$ in step 3 lies outside of the scope, let the flag $d_{(k+1)i} = 0$. Otherwise let $d_{ki} = 1$. Note that d_{ki} will be also updated using the sound separation method described below.
6. Return to step 2 by incrementing k by 1.

Figure 8 shows the clustered spectral cues of Fig. 6 processed using the above method. The initial frequencies of cues were defined every 300 (Hz) from 0 (Hz) to 6000 (Hz). Scopes were given as ranges of 300 (Hz) around their initial frequencies.

3.3 Modeling

In the previous section, an algorithm for detecting spectral cues was proposed. Next, the relationship between the filtered spectral cues and the sound source detection is considered in order to localize the sound source direction correctly. The simplest model that determines the elevation angle from the frequency, the relationship between the filtered spectral cues and the sound source direction is introduced. Let θ_e be the angular difference between the sound source and the robot's head. Let the frequency of the filtered spectral cues and coefficients that are identified below be denoted by f_i, C_i and C_{i0}, respectively. The model is then expressed mathematically by:

$$\theta_e = \frac{\sum_i (C_i d_i f_i + C_{i0} d_i)}{\sum_i d_i}, \tag{2}$$

where d_i is 1 or 0.

3.4 Identification

Just as when measuring the characteristic of the pinnae, the sound source was fixed approximately 0.5 (m) in front of the robot. The white signal was generated while the robotic head was in motion. The data measured when d_i was not 0 were used to determine C_i and

C_{i0}. Using these extracted data, C_i and C_{i0} are determined such that they minimize the following squared residual,

$$\sum_{k \in K_i} (\theta(k) - (C_i f_i(k) + C_{i0}))^2, \tag{3}$$

where K_i represents a set of times when $d_i \neq 0$ and $\theta(k)$ defines the direction of the sound source computed using the angle of the robot's head data.
The elevation angles estimated by the above method with the identified coefficients are shown in Fig. 9. The ordinate axis represents the angle of the robot's head while the abscissas axis represents time. The solid line indicates the motion of the robot's head while the points indicate the computed angles; there is good agreement between the two. Figure 9 was produced using three spectral cues that correspond to the motion of the robot's head; this figure confirms the method used for estimating the elevation angle of the sound source.

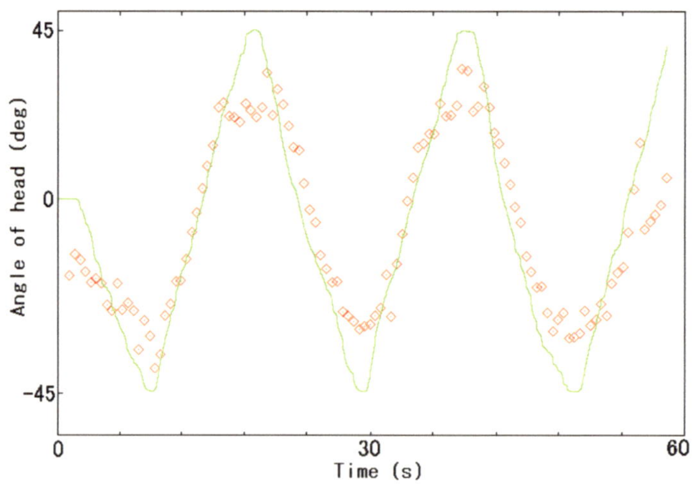

Figure 9. Elevation angle estimated by the model expressed by Eq. (2)

3.5 Sound Source Separation

In the previous sections, sound source localization was considered in order to adapt the method described above to cases when there is a lot of noise present. Accurate spectral information is critical for performing sound localization with spectral cues. In real applications, however, spectral information is often contaminated with extraneous noise. It is thus necessary to separate the extraneous noise from the target noise and to extract only the spectral cues from the target sound source.
In order to achieve this, horizontal sound source separation with two microphones is performed by assuming that the sound source and the extraneous noise do not originate from the same median plane. Although this assumption is rather strict, it is acceptable for many practical situations. In order to separate horizontal sound sources, Suzuki's method (Suzuki et al., 2005) was adopted; this method focuses on the proportional relationship that exists between the IPD and frequency.

3.5.1 Horizontal sound source separation (Suzuki et al., 2005)

Consider two microphones installed with a displacement *a*. When a planar sound wave with frequency *f* propagates in the direction ξ (see Fig. 10), the phase difference $\Delta\varphi(f)$ is given by

$$\Delta\phi(f) = \frac{a \sin\xi}{V} f, \tag{4}$$

where *V* represents the speed of sound. Therefore, the relationship between *f* and φ can be expressed by

$$f = \alpha\Delta\phi, \tag{5}$$

where α is given by *V/a* sinξ and is treated as a constant. Equation (5) for the case when there is only one sound source is depicted in Fig. 11. The ordinate and abscissas axes represent the frequency and the phase difference $(\Delta\phi, f)$, respectively. Each data point belongs to a line passing through the origin. Thus line detection can be utilized for separating sound sources.

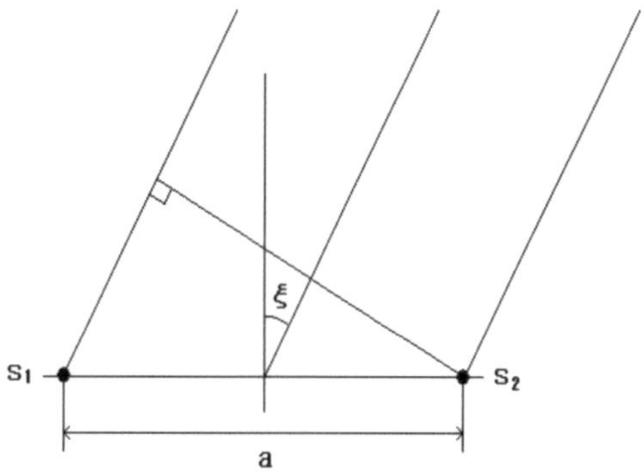

Figure 10. Diagram showing measurement of IPD using two microphones

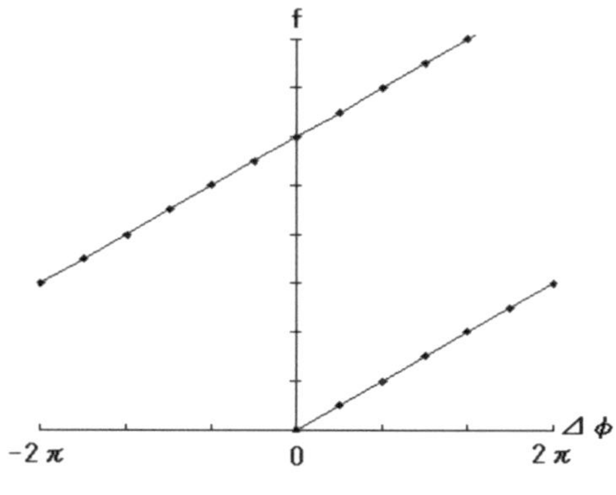

Figure 11. Signal from a single sound source depicted in frequency-IPD space

3.5.2 Line Detection

In line detection, the gradient ($\alpha = f/\Delta\phi$) is first computed at each measured point $(\Delta\phi, f)$. The angle (η_0) of the straight line connecting $(\Delta\phi, f)$ is defined as follows.

$$\eta_0 = \tan^{-1}\frac{f}{\Delta\phi}. \tag{6}$$

Since the phase difference is circular periodic, shifted values of α, $f/(\Delta\phi + 2\pi)$ and $f/(\Delta\phi - 2\pi)$ are also taken into consideration as shown in Fig. 12.

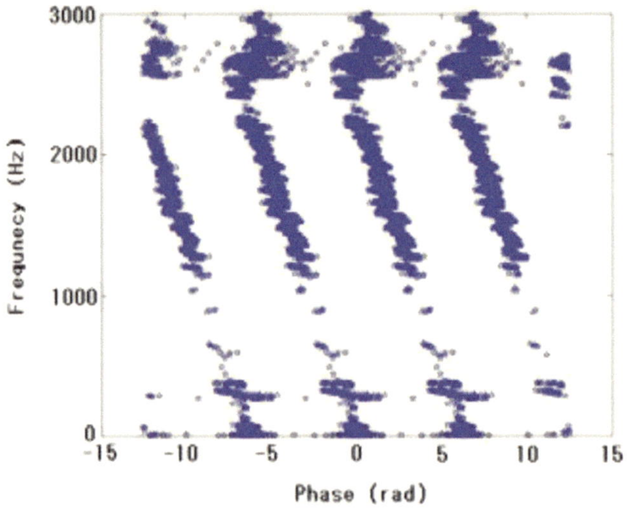

Figure 12. Measured response in frequency and IPD

In order to determine η_0, let us consider the relationship between f and $\Delta\phi$ of the measured data (Fig. 12). These data are plotted in two dimensions, where the ordinate axis represents frequency (f) and the abscissa axis represents phase difference ($\Delta\phi$). The space is discretized by dividing it into $2n$ fan-shaped regions whose vertical angles at the origin are given by $(\pi - 2\eta_{\min})/2n$. $\eta_{\min}$ is the vertical angle when the sound source is located just beside the robot, or when the phase difference is minimized.

The line of the sound source is computed by determining the region to which it belongs. This is done by counting the numbers of $(\Delta\phi, f)$ points that exist in each region. Region j is defined by the angle η_0, which satisfies the condition

$$\eta_{j-1} \le \eta_0 < \eta_j, \tag{7}$$

where

$$\eta_j = \eta_{\min} + j\frac{\pi - 2\eta_{\min}}{2n}.$$

Let *P(j)* represent the number of points in the region *j*. Given a point (ξ), *j* is expressed as follows.

$$j = \left\lceil \frac{2n}{\pi - 2\xi_{\min}} \left(\xi_0 - \xi_{\min}\right) \right\rceil + 1, \tag{9}$$

where $\lceil X \rceil$ represents the largest integer that is smaller than *X*. By using the above expressions, *P(j)* is counted for all data points. For simplicity, in this chapter, the region having the most points is taken to be the region of the sound source. Alternative selection algorithms are also possible and they should be investigated in the future.

Consequently, the region that contains spectral cues from the sound source can be determined by evaluating the frequency of points in the region having the most data points. If this region does not contain the above-mentioned detected spectral cue, then d_i is set to 0. Spectral cues from the sound source are extracted by determining d_i.

4. Audio Servo

As mentioned in the introduction, audio servo is a method for simultaneously achieving sound localization and configuration control. In this section, measured spectral cues are utilized in an audio servo system. The robotic controller is derived first and its performance is then evaluated. Finally, an experiment involving this controller and the results obtained are described.

4.1 Controller Design

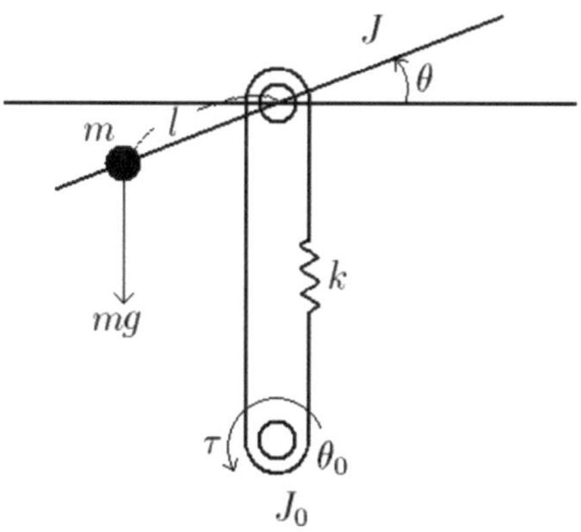

Figure 13. Dynamical model of the robot head.

Figure 13 shows the model for the robotic head; the equations of motion for this model are given as follows:

$$\begin{cases} J\ddot{\theta} = mgl\cos\theta - ksr - d\dot{\theta}, \\ J_0\ddot{\theta}_0 = ksr + \tau, \end{cases} \tag{10}$$

where J is the inertia of the upper pulley, J_0 is the inertia of the lower pulley, k is the elastic constant of the belt, m is the mass of the robot's head, g is the acceleration of gravity, l is the distance from the center of gravity, d is the coefficient of friction factor, and θ and θ_0 are the rotational angles of the robot's head and the motor shaft, respectively. s is given by $r\theta - r_0\theta_0$, where r and r_0 are the radii of the upper and lower pulleys, respectively.
The motor torque τ is modeled by

$$\tau = -K(\dot{\theta}_0 - u), \tag{11}$$

where K is the feedback gain of the servo system and u is the control input which is defined below.
The elevation angle of the sound source is denoted by θ_d and define $e = \theta - \theta_d$. The output is defined by $y = \hat{\theta} + \gamma\dot{\theta}_0$ and the state of the system as $\mathbf{x} = (\theta - \theta_d \quad \theta^{(1)} \quad \theta^{(2)} \quad \theta^{(3)})^T$. γ is an arbitrary positive value and it is given as a small constant below since its exact value is not critical. Assuming that $|e|\ll 1$ is small, the dynamic model of the robot can be approximated as:

$$\begin{cases} \dot{\mathbf{x}} = \mathbf{A}\mathbf{x} + \mathbf{b}u + \Delta, \\ y = \mathbf{C}\mathbf{x}, \end{cases} \tag{12}$$

where $\mathbf{A} \in \mathbf{R}^{4\times 4}$, $\mathbf{b} \in \mathbf{R}^4$ and $c \in \mathbf{R}^{4\times 1}$ represent matrices. Δ is a vector of nonlinear functions. Specifically,

$$A = \begin{pmatrix} 0 & 1 & 0 & 0 \\ 0 & 0 & 1 & 0 \\ 0 & 0 & 0 & 1 \\ 0 & a_1 & a_2 & a_3 \end{pmatrix}, b = \begin{pmatrix} 0 \\ 0 \\ 0 \\ a_6 \end{pmatrix}, c = (c_1 \quad \frac{r}{r_0}\gamma \quad \frac{d}{krr_0}\gamma \quad \frac{J}{krr_0}\gamma), \ \Delta = \begin{pmatrix} 0 \\ 0 \\ 0 \\ a_4\cos e + a_5 \sin e \end{pmatrix}$$

where

$$a_1 = -(\frac{Kkr^2 + krr_0 d}{JJ_0}), \quad a_2 = -\frac{kr(Jr_0 + J_0 r + Kd)}{JJ_0}, \quad a_3 = -\frac{d + KJ}{JJ_0},$$

$$a_4 = \frac{krr_0 mgl}{JJ_0}\cos\theta_d, \quad a_5 = -\frac{krr_0 mgl}{JJ_0}\sin\theta_d, \quad a_6 = \frac{Kkrr_0}{JJ_0}.$$

The dominant system (*A, b, c*) of (12) satisfies the almost strictly positive real (ASPR) condition which implies that it is possible to achieve high gain output feedback using the control objective (Wen, 1988, Kaufman, 1998). Hence, the control input u is given as,

$$u = -My, \tag{13}$$

where M is an appropriate positive constant. It should therefore be possible to align the robot with the sound source direction (Kumon et al., 2005).
Figure 14 shows the result of the experiment when sound separation was used. The ordinate axis represents angle from the horizontal plane (deg) and the abscissas axis represents time (s). The target sound source was located 16 (deg) above the horizontal plane. After about 10

(s), the robot was aligned in the direction of the sound source, although it oscillated about the true direction.

By way of comparison, Fig. 15 shows the result of the experiment when sound separation was not employed. It demonstrates that it is necessary to determine the frequency domain which contains the spectral cues of the sound source.

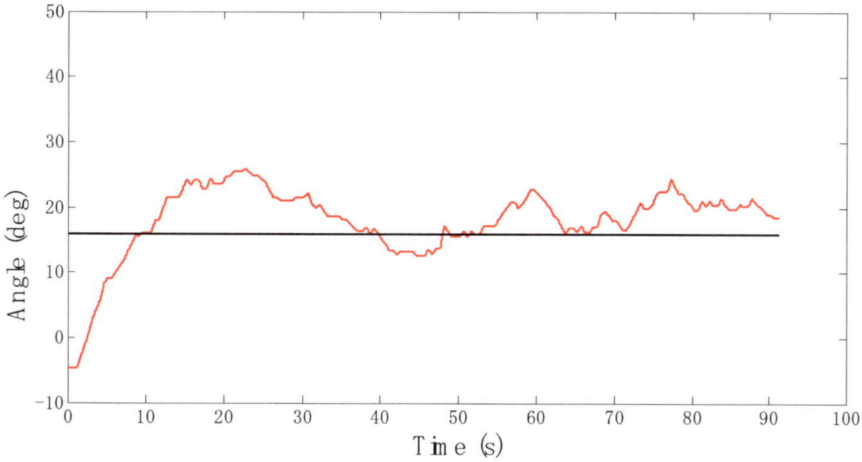

Figure 14. Motion of the robot's head with sound separation

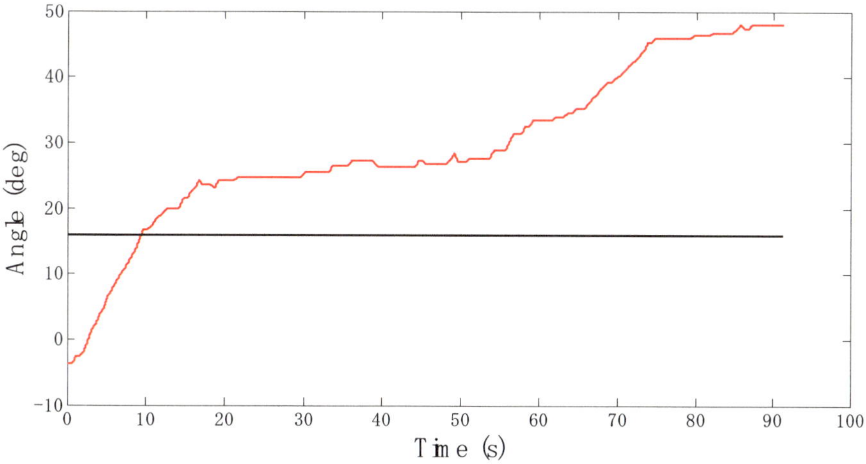

Figure 15. Motion of the robot's head without sound separation

4.2 Controller performance

In the above experiment, the robot head oscillated about the correct orientation; this aspect needs to be improved. When controlling robots based on the location of sound sources, it is clearly desirable to precisely locate cues and to accurately determine the relationship between cues and physical quantity. However, it is impractical to rely on sufficient measurement accuracy when the number of microphones is restricted and when external noise is present. We therefore evaluated the performance of the audio servo controller by accounting for inaccurate measurements. The performance of the audio servo controller was evaluated after the structure of the controller had been modified (13) in order to attenuate the effect of noise.

4.2.1 Controller

When the effect of observation noise is considered, the system is modeled using the following set of equations rather than that of (12),

$$\begin{cases} \dot{\mathbf{x}} = \mathbf{A}\mathbf{x} + \mathbf{b}u + \Delta, \\ y = \mathbf{C}\mathbf{x} + h, \end{cases} \tag{14}$$

where h is the observation noise and it is assumed to be bounded. When observation noise h is present, using a higher feedback gain M in (13) does not necessarily improve control performance, since it also increases the sensitivity to the observation noise h.

The dead zone is one control technique that can be applied to noisy output signals; it disregards the output, or error, if magnitude of the output is smaller than a given threshold. The following modified controllers were evaluated by applying the dead zone:

$$u = \begin{cases} -My & (|\, y_0 \,| < y) \\ 0 & (|\, y_0 \,| > y) \end{cases} \tag{15}$$

$$u = \begin{cases} -M(y - y_0) & (y > y_0) \\ 0 & (|\, y_0 \,| > y) \\ -M(y + y_0) & (y < -y_0) \end{cases} \tag{16}$$

$$u = \begin{cases} L & (y > y_0) \\ 0 & (|\, y_0 \,| > y) \\ -L & (y < -y_0) \end{cases} \tag{17}$$

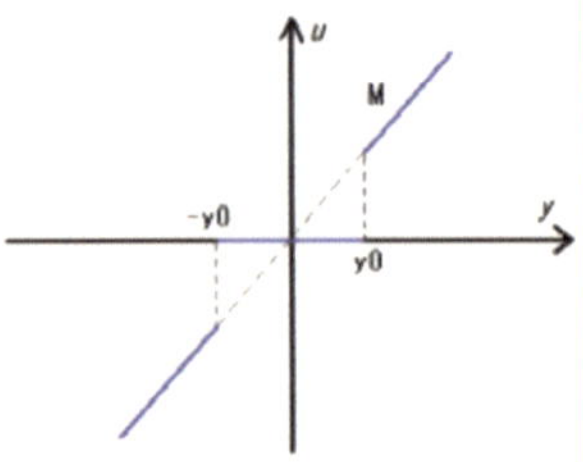

Figure 16. Controller (15)

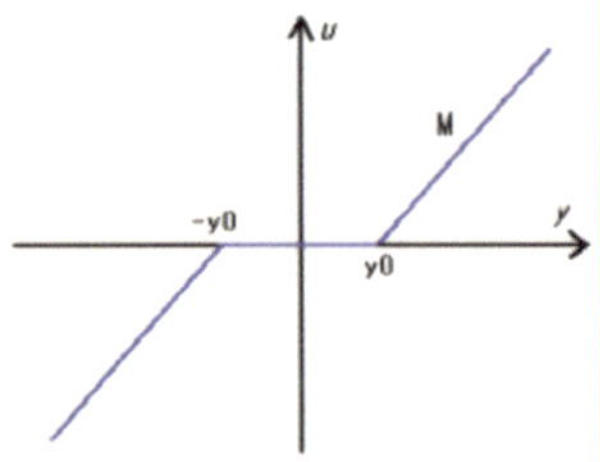

Figure 17. Controller (16)

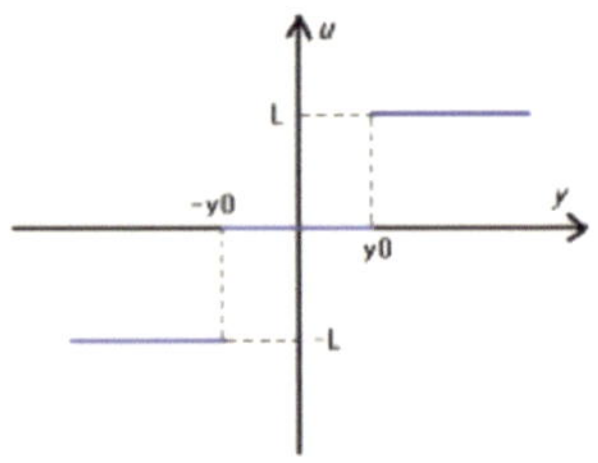

Figure 18. Controller (17)

4.2.2 Experiment and Performance

The proposed controllers were implemented in the robot and their performances were evaluated. In the experiment, the sound source was positioned in front of the robot. The initial elevation angle of the sound source was approximately 16 (deg) above the horizontal plane. A white signal was generated for about 3 (min), which included the duration of the experiment. Three different gains were used for each of the three controllers, namely M=0.1, 0.5, 1.0 for (15) and (16), and L=10, 50, 100 for (17).

Figures 19, 20 and 21 show the motion of the robot's head in these experiments when the parameters of the controllers were M=0.5, L=50 and y_0=3 (deg), respectively. In all these figures, the ordinate axis is the angle of the robot's head (deg) and the abscissa axe is time (s).

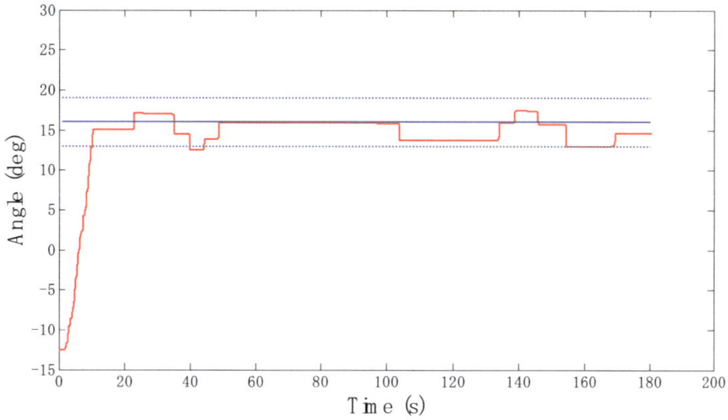

Figure 19. Result with Controller (15)

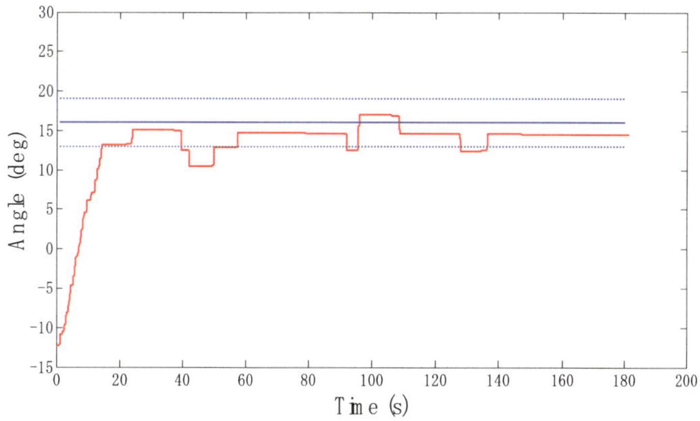

Figure 20. Result with Controller (16)

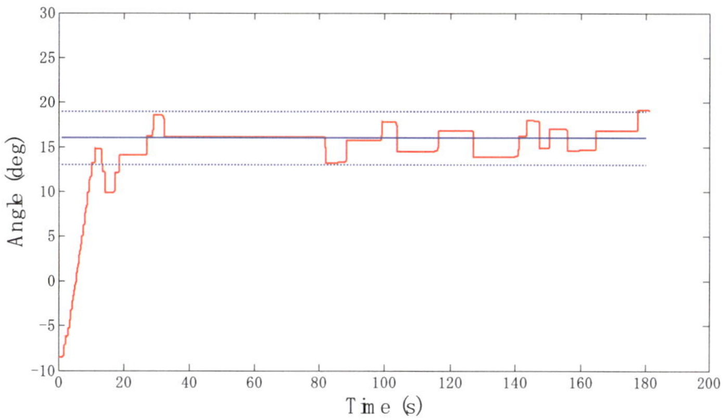

Figure 21. Result with Controller (17)

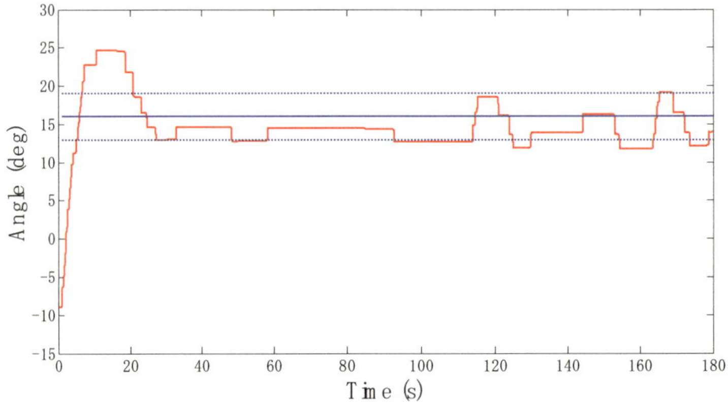

Figure 22. Result of Controller (16) for high gain (M=1.0)

Controller	Gain	Transient Period (s)	Means Error (deg)	Standard Deviation (deg)
(13) with sound separation	1.0	8.6	1.6	57.4
(15)	1.0	9.9	4.5	2.2
(15)	0.5	10.1	0.7	1.2
(15)	0.1	47.8	3.3	1.1
(16)	1.0	5.4	1.0	3.1
(16)	0.5	14.1	1.8	1.5
(16)	0.1	78.0	0.8	0.8
(17)	100	7.2	1.8	2.3
(17)	50	10.0	0.5	1.6
(17)	10	50.0	2.3	2.2

Table 1. Transient Period Error Variance

All of the results show that the robot's head was stably oriented toward the sound source. However, as the gains M, L increase, oscillations were observed with all the controllers. For instance, Fig. 22 shows the case when gain M is 1.0. The mean error angle and variance after the robot's head had been stably oriented toward the target are also shown in this figure.

Table 1 shows the transient period (s), mean error (deg) and standard deviation (deg) for each combination of controller and gain used. When the robot's head was oriented towards the sound source, the estimated angle had a standard deviation 2.1 (deg).

From Table 1, it can be concluded that all controllers succeeded in controlling the robot's head so that it was oriented toward the sound source and that the dead zone technique was effective in attenuating the vibration. However, if a high gain is used to achieve faster response, the control performance deteriorates since the robot moves in an oscillating manner. On the other hand, if a *gray* gain is used, it is possible to achieve a better response speed and convergence performance. In particular, it is noteworthy that the deviation achieved is better than that for the uncontrolled case.

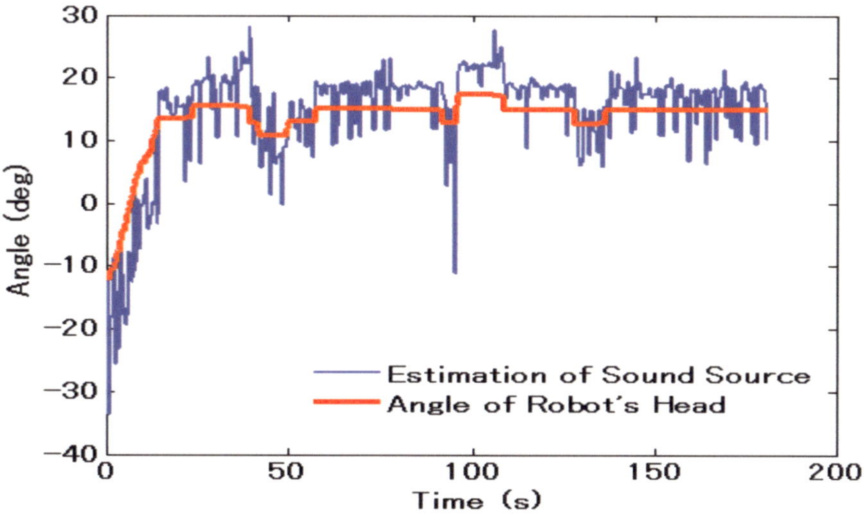

Figure 23. Estimation of Sound Source and Angle of Robot's Head

Figure 23 shows the comparison of the estimated sound source direction and the angle of robot's head. The blue line shows the estimated angle of the sound source and it has a standard deviation of 5.0 (deg), while the red line shows the angle of robot's head and it has a standard deviation of 1.5 (deg). Thus the performance of the sound source localization is improved if the angle of the robot's head is utilized rather than the direct estimated signal, confirming the effectiveness of the technique.

In summary, even when the robot's auditory sensing is inaccurate to some extent, it has been demonstrated that the performance of audio servo can be improved by using it in combination with an appropriately designed control system. If the use of an actual robot head is possible, this technique could be used to improve its sound localization ability by using an audio servo.

5. Conclusion

In this chapter, by using a system consisting of two microphones and one pinna, a method for sound localization using spectral cues was considered. In particular, a robust spectral cue detection method was considered and a method for orientating the robot's head toward a sound source was proposed. In addition, this chapter considers the use of sound source separation in order to attenuate the effect of noise. The conclusions of this present study are summarized as follows:

- Real robotic pinnae were designed and a robot using the pinnae was developed.
- In order to realize sound localization with vertical displacement, an algorithm for detecting spectral cues using the developed pinnae was proposed.
- Spectral cue detection was made robust by considering their frequency continuity with respect to time. A model for determining the sound elevation angle by measuring spectral cues was introduced.

- Horizontal sound separation was considered for extracting the sounds of interest in a noisy environment so that the robot would recognize the spectral cues of only the sound source.
- Controllers were designed to realize an audio servo using the derived spectral cues by the proposed algorithm.
- The performances of the audio servo controllers were evaluated by accounting for the need to allow measurement error when designing the controllers.
- Experiments were conducted with the developed robot. The results demonstrated the ability of the system to orientate the robot's head in the direction of the sound source.

While the proposed method was able to localize the sound source vertically, higher precision sound localization is needed. In order to achieve this, we intend to extend our research as follows:

- Online identification of coefficients C_i and C_{i0} is required for practical applications.
- Determination of optimal gains and parameters is also required.
- In this chapter, a white signal was used as the target. However, sound localization of other sound sources, such as a human voice, is also needed.
- In this chapter, sound localization in only the vertical direction is described. In future work, sound localization should also include lateral and distance detection, thus making it possible to work in three-dimensional space.

6. References

J.Garas, (2000). Adaptive 3D Sound Systems, Kluwer.

H.Kaufman, I.Bar-Kana and K.Sobel, (1998) Direct Adaptive Control Algorithms: Theory and Application.

M.Kumon, T.Sugawara, K.Miike, I.Mizumoto, and Z.Iwai, (2003). Adaptive audio servo for multirate robot systems, *Proceeding of 2003 International Conference on Intelligent Robot Systems,* pp.182-187.

M.Kumon, T.Shimoda, R.Kohzawa, I.Mizumoto, and Z.Iwai, (2005). Audio Servo for Robotic Systems with Pinnae, *IEEE/RSJ International Conference on Intelligent Robots and Systems,* pp.885-890.

E.A.Lopez-Poveda and R.Meddis, (1996). A physical model of sound diffraction and reflections in the human concha, The Journal of the Acoustical Society of America, vol.100, no.5, pp.3248-3259.

H.Nakashima, T.Mukai, (2004). The Sound Source Localization Learning System for a Front Sound Source, *22nd Annual Conference of the Robotics Society of Japan.*

K.Suzuki, T.Koga, J.Hirokawa, H.Ogawa, and N.Matsuhira, (2005). Clustering of sound-source signals using Hough transformation, and application to omni-directional acoustic sense for robots, Special Interest on AI Challenges Japanese Society for Artificial Intelligence, pp.53-59 (In Japanese).

A.Takanishi, S.Masukawa, Y.Mori and T.Ogawa, (1993). Study on Anthroporomorphic Auditory Robot ~Continuous Localization of a Sound Source in Horizontal Plane, *11th Annual Conference of the Robotics Society of Japan,* pp.793-796.

H.T.Wen, (1988). Time Domain and Frequency Domain Conditions for Strict Positive Realness, *IEEE Transaction on Automatic Control,* 33-10, pp.988-992.

25

Speech Recognition Under Noise Conditions: Compensation Methods

Angel de la Torre, Jose C. Segura, Carmen Benitez, Javier Ramirez, Luz Garcia and Antonio J. Rubio
University of Granada
Spain

1. Introduction

In most of the practical applications of Automatic Speech Recognition (ASR), the input speech is contaminated by a background noise. This strongly degrades the performance of speech recognizers (Gong, 1995; Cole et al., 1995; Torre et al., 2000). The reduction of the accuracy could make unpractical the use of ASR technology in applications that must work in real conditions, where the input speech is usually affected by noise. For this reason, robust speech recognition has become an important focus area of speech research (Cole et al., 1995).

Noise has two main effects over the speech representation: it introduces a distortion in the representation space, and it also causes a loss of information, due to its random nature. The distortion of the representation space due to the noise causes a mismatch between the training (clean) and recognition (noisy) conditions. The acoustic models, trained with speech acquired under clean conditions do not model speech acquired under noisy conditions accurately and this degrades the performance of speech recognizers. Most of the methods for robust speech recognition are mainly concerned with the reduction of this mismatch. On the other hand, the information loss caused by noise introduces a degradation even in the case of an optimal mismatch compensation.

In this chapter we analyze the problem of speech recognition under noise conditions. Firstly, we study the effect of the noise over the speech representation and over the recognizer performance. Secondly, we consider two categories of methods for compensating the effect of noise over the speech representation. The first one performs a model-based compensation formulated in a statistical framework. The second one considers the main effect of the noise as a transformation of the representation space and compensates the effect of the noise by applying the inverse transformation.

2. Overview of methods for noise robust speech recognition

Usually the methods designed to adapt ASR systems to noise conditions are focused on the reduction of the mismatch between training and recognition conditions and can be situated in one of these three groups (Gong, 1995; Bellegarda, 1997):

- Robust representations of speech: if speech is represented with a parameterization that is minimally affected by noise, we can assume that the mismatch between training and recognition conditions can be ignored.
- Compensation of the noisy speech representation: if we know how the speech representation is affected by noise, the effect of the noise over the representation of the speech can be compensated, and a clean version of the speech representation can be processed by the recognizer.
- Adaptation of the clean speech models to the noise environment: taking into account the noise statistics, the speech models (trained in the reference clean environment) can be adapted to the recognition noisy conditions and the recognition can be performed using the noisy speech representation and the models adapted to noise conditions.

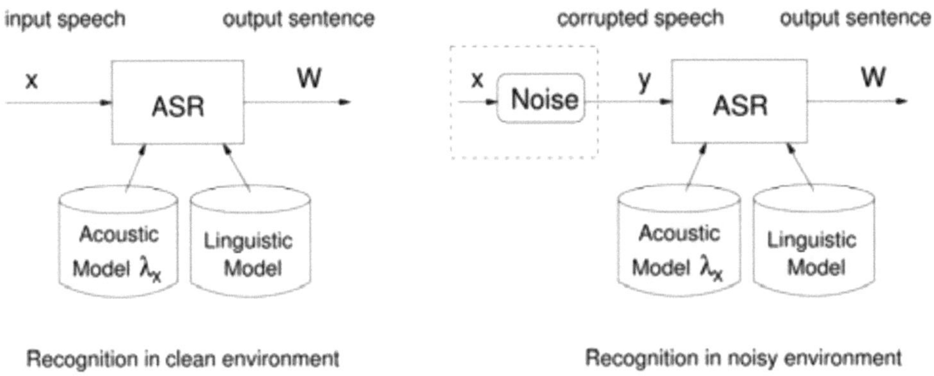

Figure 1. Block diagram of a speech recognition system processing clean or noisy speech with clean speech models

If we denote with x the clean speech representation, the effect of the noise produces a distortion and converts x into y. As shown in figure 1, the noise produces a mismatch between training and recognition conditions since corrupted speech y is recognized using clean models λ_x. According to the above classification, methods based on robust representation assume that x K- y, which minimizes the impact of recognizing noisy speech y using clean models λ_x. Compensation and adaptation methods assume that noisy speech y is a distorted version of the clean speech $y = T(x)$, where T(-) models the distortion caused by noise. Compensation methods estimate for the inverse distortion function T^{-1} (•), and provide an estimation of the clean speech as:

$$\hat{x} = \hat{T}^{-1}(y) \tag{1}$$

and recognition is performed using the estimation of the clean speech x and the clean models λ_x. On the other hand, adaptation methods apply the estimated distortion function T(-) to the models:

$$\hat{\lambda_y} = \hat{T}(\lambda_x) \tag{2}$$

and recognition is performed using the noisy speech y and the estimation of the noisy models $\hat{\lambda}_y$.

2.1 Robust parameterizations

For those methods included in this category, speech parameterization is assumed to be independent of the noise affecting the speech. In order to improve robustness against noise a variety of methods have been proposed:

- Application of liftering windows: In LPC-cepstrum based representations, cepstral coefficients are not equally affected by noise. For this reason, the application of liftering windows to reduce the contribution of low-order coefficients (i.e. those more affected by noise) increases robustness against noise (Junqua & Wakita, 1989; Torre et al., 1997).
- Methods based on auditory models: Some authors have designed parameterizations based on human auditory models in order to increase robustness. In this group we can find, for example, PLP analysis (Perceptually-based Linear Prediction) (Hermanski et al., 1985; Junqua & Haton, 1996), the EIH model (Ensemble-Interval Histogram) (Ghitza, 1992; Ghitza 1994; Rabiner & Juang, 1993), or the synchronous auditory models like the Seneff auditory model 0ankowski et al., 1995) and the SLP (Synchronous Linear Prediction) proposed by Junqua 0unqua & Haton, 1996). Compared to LPC-cepstrum, parameterizations based on auditory models provides better recognition results under noise conditions, where auditory masking or lateral inhibition play an important role in speech perception.
- Mel-scaled cepstrum: The Mel-Frequency Cepstral Coefficients (MFCC) (Davis & Mermelstein, 1980) provide significant better results than LPC-cepstrum under noise conditions, and similar results to those provided by parameterizations based on auditory models, even though with significantly lower computational load (Jankowski et al., 1995). For this reason, high resolution auditory models are not considered for speech recognition applications that must work in real time, and MFCC parameterization is one of the most commonly used speech representations for robust speech recognition (Moreno, 1996).
- Discriminative parameterizations: Parameterizations based on discriminative criteria enhance those features containing more discriminative information, and this improves separability among classes. This improves recognition in both, clean and noisy conditions. In this group, Linear Discriminant Analysis (LDA) (Duda & Hart, 1973; Fukunaga, 1990) has been successfully applied for robust speech recognition (Hunt et al., 1991). Some comparative experiments shows that IMELDA representation (Integrated MEL-scaled LDA) are more robust to noise than LPC-cepstrum or MFCC. Discriminative Feature Extraction (Torre et al., 1996) has also been successfully applied to robust speech recognition (Torre et al., 1997).
- Slow variation removal: Most noise processes varies slowly in time (compared to the variations of the speech features). High-pass filtering of the speech features tends to remove those slow variations of the feature vectors representing speech, which increases accuracy of speech recognizers under noise conditions. RASTA processing (RelAtive SpecTrAl) performs this high-pass filtering of speech parameterization either in the logarithmically scaled power spectra (Hermanski et al., 1993) or in the cepstral domain (Mokbel et al., 1993). Some experiments show that RASTA processing reduces error rate when training and recognition conditions are very different, but increases it when conditions are similar (Moreno & Stern, 1994). An efficient and simple way to remove slow variations of speech parameters is the Cepstral Mean Normalization (CMN). CMN provides results close to those of RASTA processing without the

undesired degradation observed when training and recognition conditions are similar (Anastasakos et al., 1994). Currently, the use of CMN is generalized for robust speech parameterizations (Moreno, 1996; Young et al., 1997).

- Inclusion of time derivatives of parameters: Dynamic features or time derivatives (i.e. delta-cepstrum and delta-delta-cepstrum) (Furui, 1986) are usually included into the speech parameterization since they are not affected by slow variations associated to noise. The inclusion of the dynamic features improves the recognizer performance in both, clean and noisy conditions (Hernando & Nadeu, 1994).

2.2 Compensation of the noise

Compensation methods provide an estimation of the clean speech parameterization in order to reduce the mismatch between training (clean) and recognition (noisy) conditions. This way, the clean version of the speech is recognized using models trained under clean conditions. In this category, we can find the following methods:

- Parameter mapping: Based on stereo speech observations (the same speech signal acquired under both, clean and noisy conditions) this method estimates a mapping that transforms clean into noisy speech parameterizations. Linear mapping assumes that mapping is a linear function that is estimated based on minimum mean squared error criterion over the stereo speech observations. Usually stereo observations are obtained by adding noise to some clean speech observations (Mokbel & Chollet, 1991). Some authors have proposed non linear mappings (Seide & Mertins, 1994) or mapping based on neural networks (Ohkura & Sugiyama, 1991). The effectiveness of this method is limited because in practice there is no stereo speech material available for the estimation of the transformation, and clean speech must be contaminated with an estimation of the noise in the recognition environment.
- Spectral subtraction: Assumed that noise and speech are uncorrelated signals, and that noise spectral properties are more stationary than those of the speech, the noise can be compensated by applying spectral subtraction, either on the spectral domain, or in the filter-bank domain (Nolazco & Young, 1994). The effectiveness of spectral subtraction strongly depends on a reliable estimation of the noise statistics.
- Statistical enhancement: Clean speech can be considered a function of the noisy speech and the noise, where the noise parameters are unknown and randomly variable. Under this assumption, clean speech parameterization can be estimated in a statistical framework (Ephraim, 1992). Maximum A-Posteriori (MAP) methods computes the noise parameters maximizing the a-posteriori probability of the cleaned speech given the noisy speech and the statistics of the clean speech. Minimum mean squared error methods estimate noise parameters minimizing the distance between cleaned speech parameters and clean speech models, given the noisy speech observations. Usually, statistical enhancement based on an explicit model of the probability distributions of clean speech and noise involves numerical integration of the distributions, which implies practical problems for real time implementations.
- Compensation based on clean speech models: Under some approaches, compensation is formulated from a clean speech model based on a vector quantization codebook (Acero, 1993) or a Gaussian mixture model (Moreno, 1996; Stern et al., 1997). Under methods like CDCN (Codeword-Dependent Cepstral Normalization) (Acero, 1993) and RATZ (Moreno, 1996; Stern et al., 1997; Moreno et al., 1998) the transformation associated to

noise is computed for each Gaussian (or each region of the vector quantizer). Clean Gaussians and the corresponding noisy Gaussians provide an estimation of the clean speech from the noisy speech. The VTS (Vector Taylor Series) approach (Moreno, 1996; Moreno & Eberman, 1997) computes the correction for each Gaussian taking into account its parameters and the statistics of the noise, and performs the compensation taking into account the clean and the corresponding noisy Gaussian mixture models.

2.3 Adaptation of the models

The aim of adaptation methods is, as in the previous case, to minimize the mismatch between training (clean) and recognition (noisy) conditions. However, in this case, the mismatch is minimized by adapting the clean models to noise conditions.

- HMM decomposition: Under this approach, also called Parallel Model Combination (PMC) (Gales & Young, 1993; Gales, 1997), noisy speech is modeled with a hidden Markov model (HMM) with N X M states, where N states are used to model clean speech, and M are used to model the noise. This way, a standard Viterbi algorithm is applied to perform simultaneous recognition of speech and noise. In the case of non-stationary noises, several states M can be used to model the noise. In the case of stationary noises, one state would be enough to represent the noise. The probability distribution of the combined model at each state must take into account that one of the clean speech model and the one corresponding to the noise. One of the main drawback of this method is the computational load.
- State dependent Wiener filtering: Hidden Markov models allow segmentation of the speech signal into quasi-stationary segments corresponding to each state of the HMM. This adaptation method includes, for each state of the HMM, a Wiener filter to compensate for the noise effect in the recognition process, or alternatively, a correction of the probability distribution to implement the Wiener filtering (Vaseghi & Milner, 1997).
- Statistical adaptation of HMMs: This methods adapts the hidden Markov models to noisy conditions under a statistical formulation. Usually, mean and variances of the Gaussians are adapted taking into account stereo speech observations (if available) by iteratively maximizing the probability of the noisy speech being generated by the adapted models (Moreno, 1996).
- Contamination of the training database: Training with noise speech is obviously the most efficient way for adapting models to noise conditions. However, this cannot be done in practice because a-priori knowledge of the noise statistics is not available during recognition, and perform retraining with noisy speech would require estimation of the noise in the sentence to be recognized, contamination of the training database with such noise and training the recognizer with the noisy database. Training is a time consuming process and this procedure cannot be implemented in real time. However, recognition results under retrained conditions can be obtained in laboratory conditions. This kind of experiments provides an estimation of the upper limit in performance that can be obtained with the best method for robust speech recognition. Training with a specific type and level of noise significantly improves recognition performance when the speech to be recognized is affected for this kind and level of noise, but usually the performance degrades if the training and recognition noises do not match. Usually, if training is performed with a variety of noises, robustness improves and performance

under noise condition significantly improves. This is the philosophy of multi-condition training proposed in the standard Aurora II (Hirsch & Pierce, 2000).

3. Effect of the noise over the speech representation

3.1 MFCC speech representation

The effect of the noise depends on the speech representation and the type and level of noise. Currently, most of the representations for ASR are based on Mel Frequency Cepstral Coefficients (MFCC). Standard MFCC parameterization usually includes: (1) Pre-emphasis of the speech signal, in order to enhance high frequencies of the spectrum. (2) Segmentation of the signal into frames, typically with a duration from 20 to 40 msecs, using a Hamming window. (3) Using a Filter Bank, the output power in logarithm scale is obtained for each filter. These coefficients are known as Filter Bank Outputs (FBO). Usually, the Filter-Bank is composed of triangular filters distributed in the Mel frequency scale. (4) By applying a Discrete Cosine Transform (DCT), the FBO coefficients are transformed into the cepstral coefficients (the MFCC). In the MFCC domain, the correlations among the different coefficients is small. Also, high order MFCC parameters are removed in order to ignore the fine structure of the spectral shape. (5) Finally, coefficients describing the evolution in time of the MFCC parameters (Δ-cepstrum and ΔΔ-cepstrum) can be included in the parameterization. Additionally, the energy of the frame (and the Δ and ΔΔ associated parameters) are usually be included in the feature vectors representing the speech signal.

3.2 Additive noise in M FCC-based representations

(A) Distortion in the log-filter-bank domain: Let x_i and n_i be the samples of the speech signal and an additive noise, and $y_i = x_i + n_i$ the samples of the noisy speech. The energy of a frame can be written as:

$$E_y = \sum_{i=1}^{I} y_i^2 = \sum_{i=1}^{I} (x_i^2 + n_i^2 + 2x_i n_i) \quad (3)$$

and assuming statistical independence of the noise and speech signals:

$$\sum_{i=1}^{I} x_i n_i = 0 \quad \Rightarrow \quad E_y = E_x + E_n \quad (4)$$

This result can be applied to whatever parameter representing an energy of the noisy signal, and in particular, to the output energy of each filter of the filter-bank. Let $X_b(t)$, $Nb(t)$ and $Yb(t)$ be the output energy of the filter b at frame t corresponding to the clean speech, the noise and the noisy speech, respectively. The relationship among them is described by:

$$Y_b(t) = X_b(t) + N_b(t) \quad (5)$$

and for the logarithmically scaled output of the filter-bank ($x_b(t)$ =log($X_b(t)$)):

$$y_b(t) = \log[\exp(x_b(t)) + \exp(n_b(t))] \quad (6)$$

This equation describes how additive noise affects log-filter-bank outputs in MFCC based parameterizations. Figure 2 represents the effect of the additive noise in this domain. One can observe three effects associated to additive noise:

- Additive noise produces a non-linear distortion of the representation space.
- For those regions where noise level is greater than speech level, the log-energy of the noisy speech is similar to that of the noise. In that case, speech signal is masked by noise.

For those regions where speech level is greater than noise level, the noisy speech is only slightly affected by noise.

Since MFCC representation is obtained by a linear transformation (usually a discrete cosine transform) of the log-filter-bank energies, the above described effects are also present in MFCC domain.

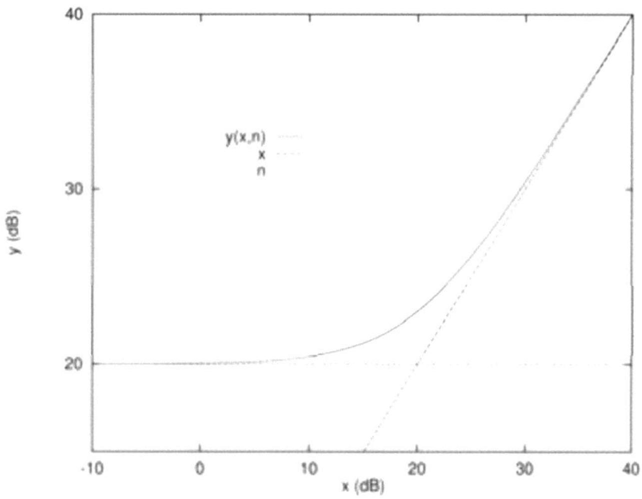

Figure 2. Distortion of the logarithmically scaled energy when a noise with constant level of 20 dB is added

(B) Distortion of the probability distributions: The previously described distortion of the representation space caused by additive noise also transforms the probability distributions. Let $p_x\ (x_b)$ be a probability density function (pdf) in the clean domain, and n_b the noise level affecting the clean speech. The pdf in the noise domain can be obtained as:

$$p_y(y_b) = p_x(x_b(y_b, n_b))\frac{\partial x_b}{\partial y_b} \tag{7}$$

where xb(yb, nb) and the derivative can be calculated from equation (6):

$$x_b(y_b, n_b) = y_b + \log(1 - \exp(n_b - x_b)) \tag{8}$$

$$\frac{\partial x_b}{\partial y_b} = \frac{1}{1 - \exp(n_b - y_b)} \tag{9}$$

Figure 3 represents a Gaussian probability distribution representing clean speech (mean 15dB; standard deviation 2dB) and the corresponding noisy pdf when speech is contaminated with noise with different levels (0 dB, 5 dB, 10 dB, 15 dB). The following effects of the noise over the pdf can be observed:

- The additive noise causes a displacement of the mean.
- The standard deviation is reduced because the compression caused by noise is not uniform (is more important for the region of low energy).
- Due to the non-linear effect of the noise, the noisy pdf is distorted and it is not a Gaussian.

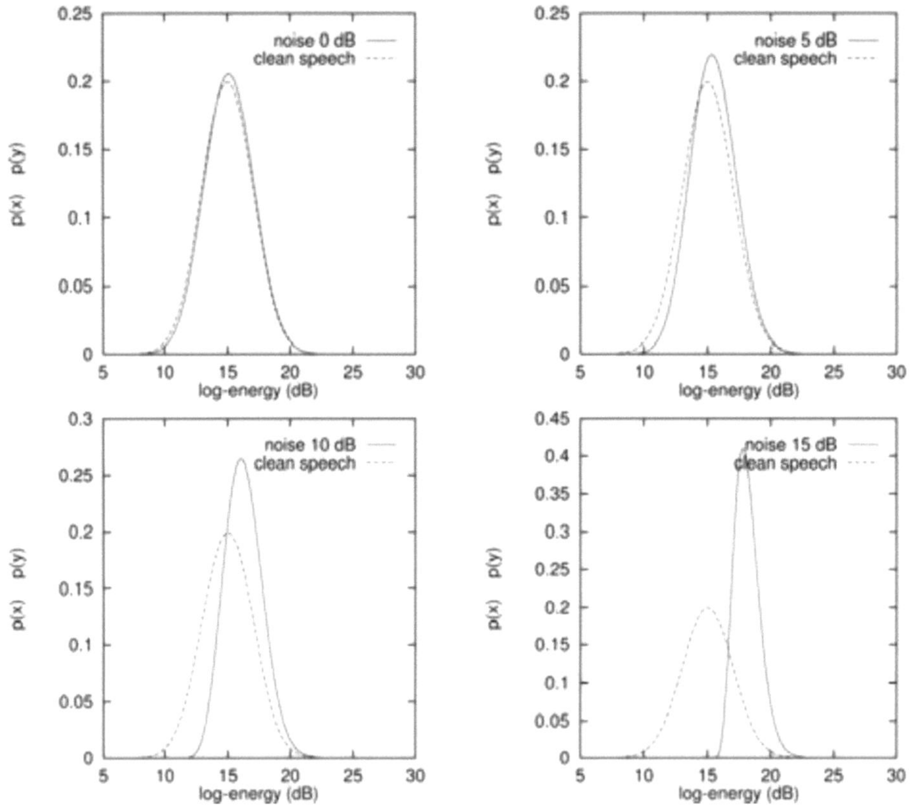

Figure 3. Distortion of the probability distributions caused by additive noise. Clean Gaussian with μ_x=15dB and σ_x=2dB. Noise with constant level OdB, 5dB, lOdB and 15dB

The impact of the mismatch caused by noise over classification is evident. Due to the distortion of the representation space caused by noise, the pdfs representing clean speech do not represent appropriately noisy speech. Let $p_x\ (x|\lambda_1)$ and $p_x\ (x|\lambda_2)$ be two pdfs representing class λ_1 and class λ_2 in the clean domain respectively. Due to the noise, both pdfs are distorted, and both clases would be represented by $p_y\ (y|\lambda_1)$ and $p_y\ (y|\lambda_2)$ in the noisy domain (that can be obtained by equation (7)). As illustrated in figure 4 the optimal boundaries are different in the clean and noisy representations. Mismatch is produced because noisy speech observations are classified using clean pdfs (and therefore boundary associated to clean pdfs), which increases the probability of classification error. In order to avoid this mismatch, the noise should be compensated on the speech representation (by applying the inverse transformation according to equation (6)) in order to obtain the clean

speech x_b, or alternatively, the models should be adapted (by applying equation (7)) in order to classify noisy speech with noisy models.
In figure 5 the area associated to the classification error in the previous example is shown. When the clean boundary is used to classify noisy speech, there is an increment in the error probability (this increment is associated to the mismatch). However when the noisy boundary is used, the probability error is exactly the same as in the case of clean speech.
(C) Randomness of noise: If noise was a constant level Uf,, the problems of noise compensation or noise adaptation would be easy to be solved. Using equation (6), an exact clean version of the speech would be obtained (or using equation (7) an exact noisy model could be used to classify noisy speech). In both cases, the probability of error would be independent of the noise level and similar to that obtained for clean speech (as can be observed in figure 4).
However, noise is a random process and therefore, the transformation is a function of random and unknown parameters. The energy of the noise cannot be described as a constant value n_b but as a pdf p_n (n_b), and therefore, for a given value of the clean speech x_b the noisy speech is not a value y_b, but a probability distribution given by:

$$p_y(y_b|x_b) = p_n(n_b(y_b, x_b))\frac{\partial n_b}{\partial y_b} \tag{10}$$

where n_b (y_b, x_b) and the partial derivative are given by equation (6):

$$n_b(y_b, x_b) = y_b + \log(1 - \exp(x_b - y_b)) \tag{11}$$

$$\frac{\partial n_b}{\partial y_b} = \frac{1}{1 - \exp(x_b - y_b)} \tag{12}$$

Figure 6 shows a Monte Carlo simulation representing how clean speech observations x_b are transformed into noisy speech observations y_b when noise is considered a random process described by a Gaussian distribution with different standard deviations. This figure illustrates the effects of the noise due to its randomness:

- For each value of clean speech x_b we do not obtain a value of noisy speech y_b but a probability distribution $p_y(y_b \mid x_b)$.
- For high energies of the clean speech (greater than the noise level) the noisy speech distribution is narrow.
- For low energies of the clean speech (compared to the noise level) the noisy speech distribution is wider.
- From a noisy speech observation y_b an estimation of the corresponding clean speech x_b is not possible. In the best case we could estimate the probability distribution p_x $(x_b \backslash y_b)$ and from it, the expected value x_b = $E[x_b \mid y_b]$ and the corresponding standard error. *In* other words, due to the randomness of the noise, there is an information loss that will increase the classification error.
- The information loss is more important as x_b is more affected by noise (for x_b with low energy compared to the noise).
- The information loss is more important as the noise level increases.

When the noise is described as a pdf, the probability distribution of the noisy speech can be computed as:

$$p_y(y_b) = \int_{-\infty}^{\infty} p(y_b, x_b)dx_b = \int_{-\infty}^{\infty} p(y_b|x_b)p_x(x_b)dx_b \qquad (13)$$

and taking into account equations (10), (11) and (12):

$$p_y(y_b) = \int_{-\infty}^{\infty} p_n(n_b(y_b, x_b)) \frac{1}{1 - \exp(x_b - y_b)} p_x(x_b)dx_b \qquad (14)$$

Figure 7 shows the effect of considering the randomness of the noise over the distribution of the noisy speech, obtained by numerical integration of equation (14). It can be observed that distributions are wider as the distribution of the noise pdf is wider. This increment in the width of $p_y(y_b)$ increases the error probability and causes the information loss associated to the randomness of the noise.

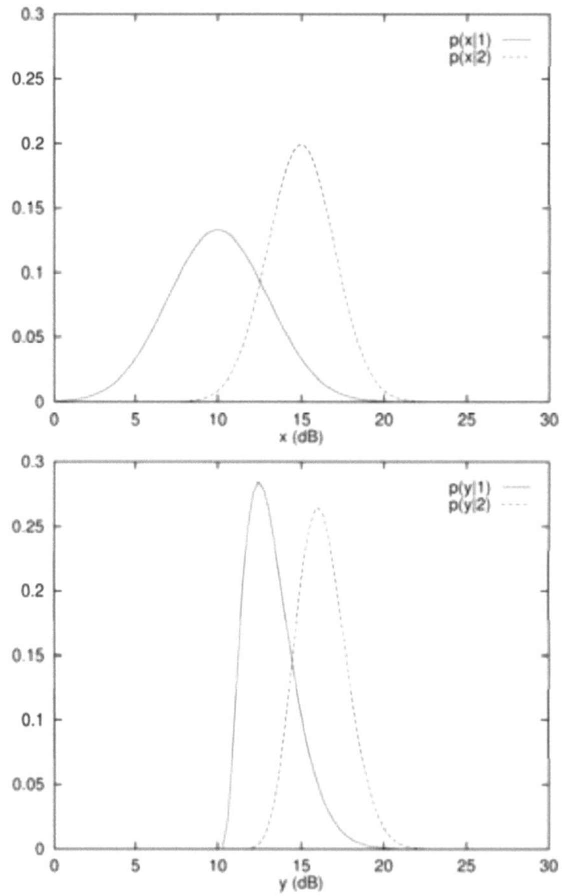

Figure 4. Displacement of the optimal decision boundary due to the noise. Clean distributions are Gaussians with μ_1=10dB, σ_1=3dB, μ_2=15dB, σ_1=2dB. Clean distributions are contaminated with a constant noise of lOdB. Optimal clean boundary at x_b =12.5317dB; optimal noisy boundary at y_b =14.4641dB

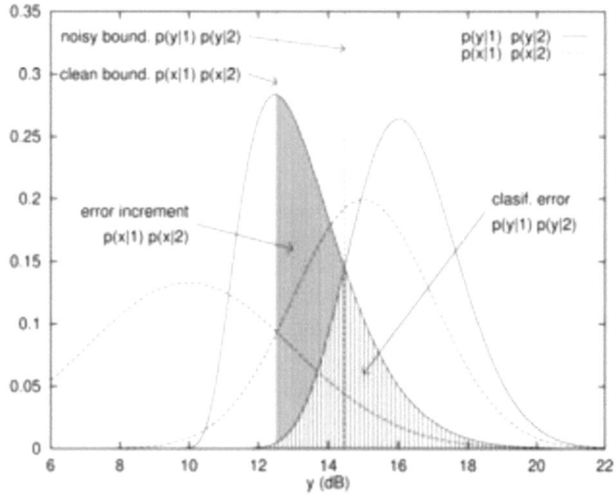

Figure 5. Classification error for noisy distribution using the optimal decision boundary y_b, and error increment when clean optimal decision boundary x_b is used

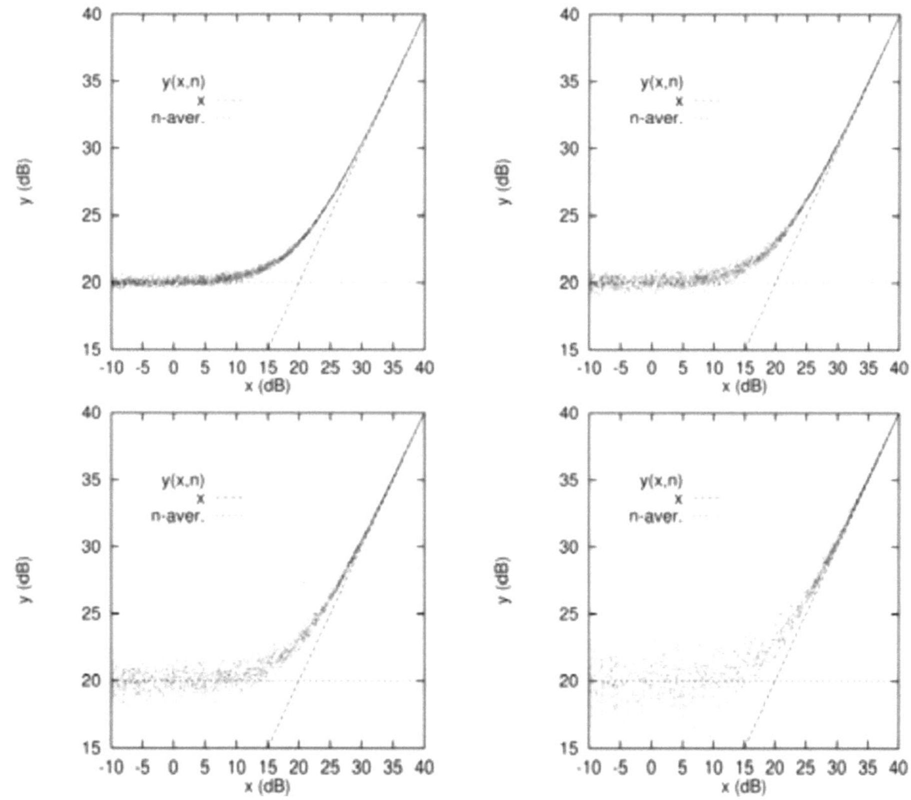

Figure 6. Transformation of clean observations into noise observation when contaminated with a noise with Gaussian distribution with $/z_n$=20dB and u_n equal to 0.25dB, O.SdB, IdB and 2dB

3.3 Effects of the noise over recognition performance

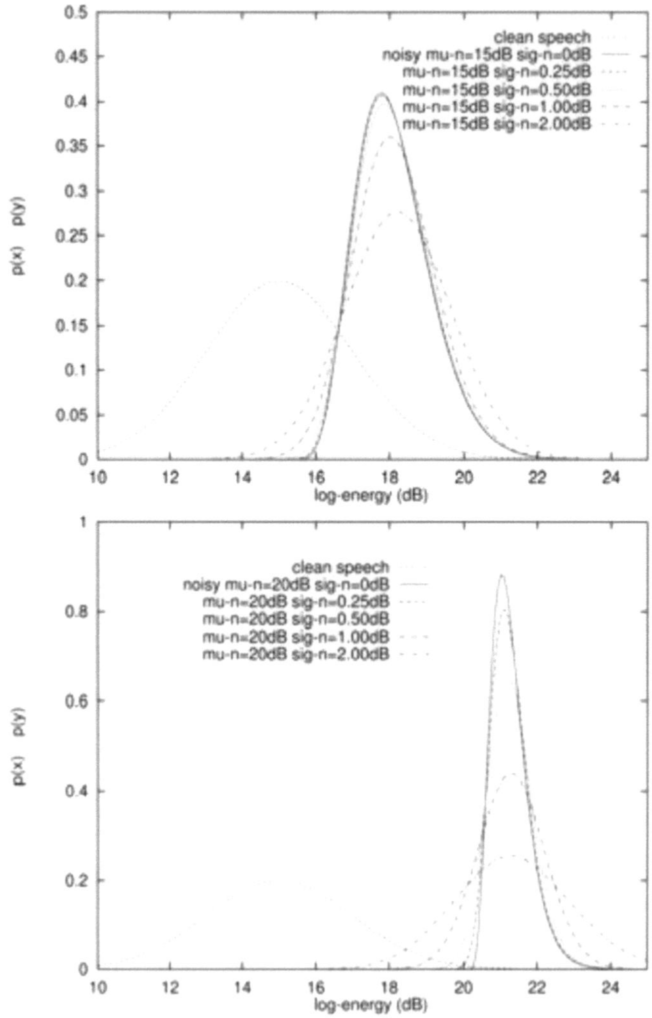

Figure 7. Effect of the randomness of noise over the probability distribution of the noisy speech: as the standard deviation of the noise increases, the noisy speech presents a wider distribution

According to the previous analysis, additive noise has two effects over speech recognition performance. On one hand, the distortion of the representation space produces a mismatch between training and recognition environments. On the other hand, the noise causes an information loss due to its implicit randomness. In order to study the role of each one over the error rate, recognition experiments can be performed using clean speech models and speech models retrained (using speech contaminated with the same noise affecting in the recognition environment). The increment of the error rate in the retrained conditions represents the degradation associated to the information loss caused by noise, while the increment of the error rate when using clean speech models represent the degradation due to both, the mismatch and the information loss.

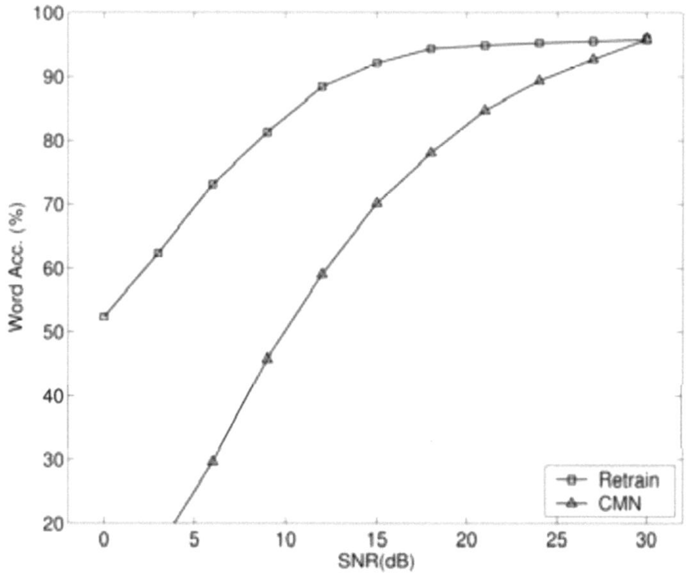

Figure 8. Reference recognition results (word accuracy versus SNR) for the baseline system (MFCC with CMN, clean training) and the retrained system

Figure 8 shows recognition performance for both, clean training and retraining conditions, for a connected digit recognition task (database of Spanish connected digits "DIGCON" (Torre et al., 2001)). The speech, represented with MFCC (including Δ and ΔΔ associated parameters and CMN) has been artificially contaminated with additive Gaussian white noise for SNRs ranging from 30 dB to -3 dB. Recognition experiments were carried out using a 256 Gaussians Semi-Continuous HMM speech recognizer. As observed in the figure, noise degrades performance of speech recognizer, due to both, the mismatch between training and recognition conditions and the information loss. The recognition results obtained under retraining conditions approaches the best results that could be achieved in the case of optimal compensation of speech representation or adaptation of speech models.

4. Model based compensation of the noise effects

4.1 Statistical formulation of noise compensation

Compensation of the noise effect can be formulated in a statistical framework, taking into account the probability distribution of the clean speech from a clean speech model. This way, the estimation of the clean speech could be obtained as the expected value of the clean speech, given the observed noisy speech, the model describing the clean speech and the model describing the noise statistics:

$$\hat{x}_b = E[x_b | y_b, \lambda_x, \lambda_n] \tag{15}$$

As clean speech model λx, a Gaussian mixture model (GMM) in the log-filter-bank domain can be trained using clean speech. The model describing the noise λn must be estimated from the noisy speech to be recognized. Usually the noise is represented as a Gaussian pdf in the log-filter-bank domain, and the parameters of the Gaussian are estimated from the first frames of the sentence to be recognized, or using the silence periods identified with a Voice Activity Detector (VAD). Different methods have been proposed to provide the compensated clean speech under a statistical formulation. In the next section we describe the Vector Taylor Series (VTS) approach (Moreno, 1996; Moreno et al, 1997).

4.2 Vector Taylor Series approach

The effect of additive noise, described by equation (6), can be rewritten as:

$$y_b(t) = x_b(t) + g_b(t) \tag{16}$$

representing that noisy speech $y_b(t)$ is obtained by applying a correction $g_b(t)$ to the clean speech $x_b(t)$, where the correction is:

$$g_b(t) = \log(1 + \exp(n_b(t) + x_b(t))) \tag{17}$$

Let us ignore the frame index t for simplicity. We can define two auxiliary functions f_b and h_b as:

$$f_b \equiv \frac{1}{1 + \exp(x_b - n_b)} \tag{18}$$

$$h_b \equiv (1 - f_b)f_b \tag{19}$$

verifying that:

$$\frac{\partial g_b}{\partial x_{b'}} = -\frac{\partial g_b}{\partial n_{b'}} = -f_b \delta_{b,b'} \tag{20}$$

$$\frac{\partial^2 g_b}{\partial x_{b'} \partial x_{b''}} = \frac{\partial^2 g_b}{\partial n_{b'} \partial n_{b''}} = -\frac{\partial^2 g_b}{\partial x_{b'} \partial n_{b''}} = -h_b \delta_{b,b'} \delta_{b,b''} \tag{21}$$

$$\begin{aligned} y_b \approx\ & x_b + g_0 + f_0[-(x_b - x_0) + (n_b - n_0)] + \\ & \frac{1}{2} h_0[(x_b - x_0)^2 + (n_b - x_0)^2 - 2(x_b - x_0)(n_b - n_0)] \end{aligned} \tag{22}$$

where g_o, f_o and h_o are the functions g_b, f_b and h_b evaluated at x_O and n_O.

Using the Taylor series approach, we can describe how a Gaussian pdf in the log-filter-bank domain is affected by additive noise. Let us consider a Gaussian pdf representing clean speech, with mean $\mu_x(b)$ and covariance matrix $\Sigma_x(b, b')$, and let us assume a Gaussian noise process with mean $\mu_n(b)$ and covariance matrix $\Sigma_n(b, b')$. Taylor series can be expanded around $x_O = \mu_x(b)$ and $n_O = \mu_n(b)$. The mean and the covariance matrix of the pdf describing the noisy speech can be obtained as the expected values:

$$\mu_y(b) = E[y_b] \tag{23}$$

$$\Sigma_y(b, b') = E[(y_b - \mu_y(b))(y_{b'} - \mu_y(b'))] \tag{24}$$

and can be estimated as a function of $\mu_x(b)$, $\Sigma_x(b, b')$, $\mu_n(b)$ and $\Sigma_n(b, b')$ as:

$$\mu_y(b) \approx \mu_x(b) + g_0(b) + \frac{1}{2} h_0(b)[\Sigma_x(b, b) + \Sigma_n(b, b)] \tag{25}$$

$$\begin{aligned} \Sigma_y(b, b') \approx\ & (1 - f_0(b))(1 - f_0(b'))\Sigma_x(b, b') + f_0(b)f_0(b')\Sigma_n(b, b') + \\ & \frac{1}{2} h_0(b)(\Sigma_x(b, b') + \Sigma_n(b, b'))\delta_{b,b'} \end{aligned} \tag{26}$$

where $g_o(b)$, $f_o(b)$ and $h_o(b)$ are the functions g_b, f_b and h_b evaluated at $x_0 = \mu_x(b)$ and $n_o = \mu_n(b)$. Therefore, the Taylor series approach gives a Gaussian pdf describing the noisy speech from the Gaussian pdfs describing the clean speech and the noise.

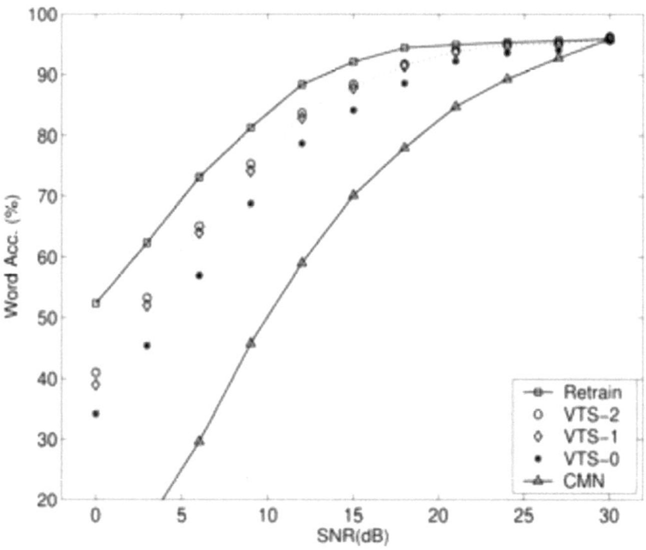

Figure 9. Recognition results obtained with VTS for different orders (0, 1 and 2) in Taylor series expansion

If the clean speech is modeled as a mixture of K Gaussian pdfs, the Vector Taylor Series approach provides an estimate of the clean speech vector $\hat{\mathbf{x}}$ given the observed noisy speech $\mathbf{y}$ and the statistics of the noise (μ_n and Σ_n) as:

$$\hat{\mathbf{x}} \approx \mathbf{y} - \sum_{k=1}^{K} P(k|\mathbf{y})\mathbf{g}(\mu_{x,k}, \mu_n) \tag{27}$$

where $n_{x,k}$ is the mean of the kth clean Gaussian pdf and $P(k \mid y)$ is the probability of the noisy Gaussian k generating the noisy observation, given by:

$$P(k|\mathbf{y}) = \frac{P(k)\mathcal{N}(\mathbf{y}, \mu_{y,k}, \Sigma_{y,k})}{\sum_{k'=1}^{K} P(k')\mathcal{N}(\mathbf{y}, \mu_{y,k'}, \Sigma_{y,k'})} \tag{28}$$

where $P(k)$ is the a-priori probability of the kth Gaussian and $\mathcal{N}(\mathbf{y}, \mu_{y,k}, \Sigma_{y,k})$ is the kth noisy Gaussian pdf (with mean $\mu_{y,k}$ and covariance matrix $\Sigma_{y,k}$) evaluated at $\mathbf{y}$. The mean and covariance matrix of the kth noisy Gaussian pdf can be estimated from the noise statistics and the kth clean Gaussian using equations (25) and (26). This way, under VTS approach, the compensation process involves the following steps:

1. A Gaussian mixture model (GMM) with K Gaussians in the log-filter-bank domain is previously trained using clean speech
2. The noise statistics are estimated for the sentence to be compensated.
3. The clean GMM is transformed into the noisy GMM using equations (25) and (26).

4. The probability of each Gaussian generating each noisy observation $P(k \mid y)$ is computed using the noisy GMM (equation (28)).
5. The correction function *g(/J-x,ki M"n)* associated to each Gaussian of the GMM is computed.
6. The expected value of the clean speech is then computed for each frame using equation (27).

Figure 9 shows recognition results for the previously described connected digit task when VTS (K=V2&) is applied as noise compensation method. The reference plots correspond to the baseline clean trained and retrained systems. The other plots represent the error rate obtained when Oth, 1st and 2nd order VTS approach is applied for noise compensation. As can be observed, VTS significantly improves recognition performance, even though results are below that of the retrained system. Performance improves as the order in the expansion increases.

5. Non-linear methods for noise compensation

5.1 Limitations of model-based compensation

Model-based methods for noise compensation provide an appropriate estimation of the clean speech. They benefit from an explicit modelling of the clean speech and noise distributions as well as from an explicit modelling of the mechanism of distortion. Other effective way to face the noise compensation is to focus on the probability distribution of the noisy speech and apply the transformation that converts this distribution into the one corresponding to the clean speech. This approach does not take into account the mechanism of distortion, and only assumes that the compensated speech must have the same distribution as the clean speech. This can be considered as a disadvantage with respect to model based procedures (which would provide a more accurate compensation). However, if the mechanism of distortion if not completely known, a blind compensation procedure that is not restricted by a model of distortion can be useful. That is the case of Cepstral Mean Normalization (CMN) or Mean and Variance Normalization (MVN) (Viiki et al., 1998) that provides some compensation of the noise independently of the noise process and independently of the representation space where they are applied. This way, CMN compensates for the effect of channel noise, but is also able to partly reduce the effect of additive noise (since one side effect of additive noise is the displacement of the mean of the Gaussian pdfs). MVN allows compensation of mean and variance of the distributions, and therefore provides a more accurate compensation of additive noise than CMN.

One of the limitations of CMN and MVN is that they apply a linear transformation to the noisy noisy speech representation, and, as described in figure 2 the distortion caused by the noise present a non-linear behavior. In order to compensate for the non-linear effect of the noise, an extension of CMN and MVN methods has been formulated in the context of histogram equalization (HEQ) (Torre et al., 2005).

5.2 Description of histogram equalization

Histogram equalization was originally proposed in the context of digital image processing (Russ, 1995). It provides a transformation $x_1 = F(x_0)$ that converts the probability density function $p_0(x_0)$ of the original variable into a reference probability density function $p_1(x_1) = p_{ref}(x_1)$. This way, the transformation converts the histogram of the original variable into the reference histogram, i.e. it equalizes the histogram, as described below.

Let x_0 be an unidimensional variable following a distribution $p_0(x_0)$. A transformation $x_1(x_0)$ modifies the probability distribution according to the expression,

$$p_1(x_1) = p_0(x_0(x_1))\frac{\partial x_0}{\partial x_1} \tag{29}$$

where $x_0(x_1)$ is the inverse transformation of $x_1(x_0)$. The relationship between the cumulative probabilities associated to these probability distributions is given by,

$$\begin{aligned} C_0(x_0) &= \int_{-\infty}^{x_0} p_0(x_0')dx_0' = \int_{-\infty}^{x_0(x_1')} p_0(x_0(x_1))\frac{\partial x_0}{\partial x_1}dx_1' = \\ &= \int_{-\infty}^{x_0(x_1)} p_1(x_1')dx_1' = C_1(x_1(x_0)) \end{aligned} \tag{30}$$

and therefore, the transformation $x_1(x_0)$ which converts the distribution $p_0(x_0)$ into the reference distribution $p_1(x_1) = p_{ref}(x_1)$ (and hence converts the cumulative probability $C_0(x_0)$ into $C_1(x_1) = C_{ref}(x_1)$) is obtained from equation (30) as,

$$x_1(x_0) = C_1^{-1}[C_0(x_0)] = C_{ref}^{-1}[C_0(x_0)] \tag{31}$$

where $C_{ref}^{-1}[C]$ is the reciprocal function of the cumulative probability $C_{ref}(x_1)$, providing the value x_1 corresponding to a certain cumulative probability C. For practical implementations, a finite number of observations is utilized and therefore cumulative histograms are utilized instead cumulative probabilities, and for this reason the procedure is named histogram equalization rather than probability distribution equalization.

The histogram equalization method is frequently utilized in Digital Image Processing in order to improve the brightness and contrast of the images and to optimize the dynamic range of the grey level scale. The histogram equalization is a simple and effective method for the automatic correction of too bright or too dark pictures or pictures with a poor contrast.

5.3 Noise compensation based on histogram equalization

The histogram equalization method allows an accurate compensation of the effect of whatever non-linear transformation of the feature space assumed that (1) the transformation is mono-tonic (and hence does not cause an information loss) and (2) there are enough observations of the signal to be compensated for an accurate estimation of the original probability distribution.

In the case of Digital Image Processing, the brightness and contrast alterations (mainly due to improper illuminations or non-linearities of the receptors) usually correspond to monotonic non-linear transformations of the grey level scale. On the other hand, all the pixels in the image (typically between several thousands and several millions) contribute to an accurate estimation of the original probability distributions. This makes the histogram equalization very effective for image processing.

In the case of automatic speech recognition, the speech signal is segmented into frames (with a frame period of about 10 ms) and each frame is represented by a feature vector. The number of observations for the estimation of the histograms is much smaller than in the case of image processing (typically several hundreds of frames per sentence) and also an independent histogram equalization should be applied to each component of the feature vector. If the method is applied for noise compensation, one should take into account that the more speech is considered for the estimation of the histograms the more accurate transformation is obtained for the noise compensation. Additionally, the histogram equalization is intended to correct monotonic transformations but the random behavior of the noise makes the transformation not to be monotonic (which causes a loss of information in addition to the mismatch). The noise compensation based on histogram equalization (like the rest of the methods for noise compensation) can deal with the mismatch originated by the noise but not with the loss of information caused by the random behavior of the noise, and this limits the effectiveness of the noise compensation based on histogram equalization (like for other compensation methods).

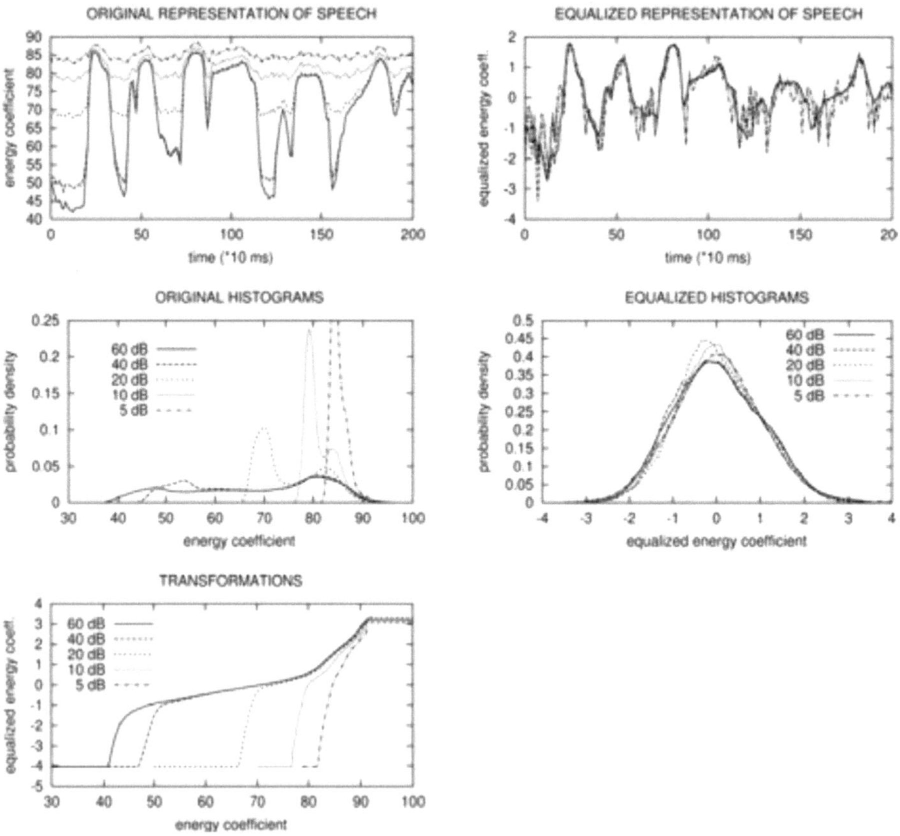

Figure 10. Effect of the histogram equalization over the representation of the speech for the energy coefficient. In the first row, the evolution over time of the energy (at different SNRs) is represented before (left) and after (right) histogram equalization, for a sentence. Histograms are represented in the second row. Transformations provided by histogram equalization procedure are represented in the last row

Compared to other compensation methods, the histogram equalization presents the advantage that it does not require any a-priori assumption about the process affecting the speech representation and therefore it can deal with a wide range of noise processes and can be applied to a wide range of speech representations. We have applied the histogram equalization to each component of the feature vector representing each frame of the speech signal. As reference probability distribution, we have considered a normal probability distribution for each component. The histogram equalization is applied as a part of the parameterization process of the speech signal, during both, the training of the acoustic models and the recognition process. In Figure 10 we show how the histogram equalization method compensates the noise effect over the speech representation. We have contaminated the speech signal with additive Gaussian white noise at SNRs ranging from 60 dB to 5 dB. In the figure we have represented the effect of the noise and the histogram equalization for the energy coefficient. As can be observed, the noise severely affects the probability distributions of the speech causing an important mismatch when the training and recognition SNRs do not match. Histogram equalization significantly reduces the mismatch caused by the noise. However, it cannot remove completely the noise effect due to its random behavior.

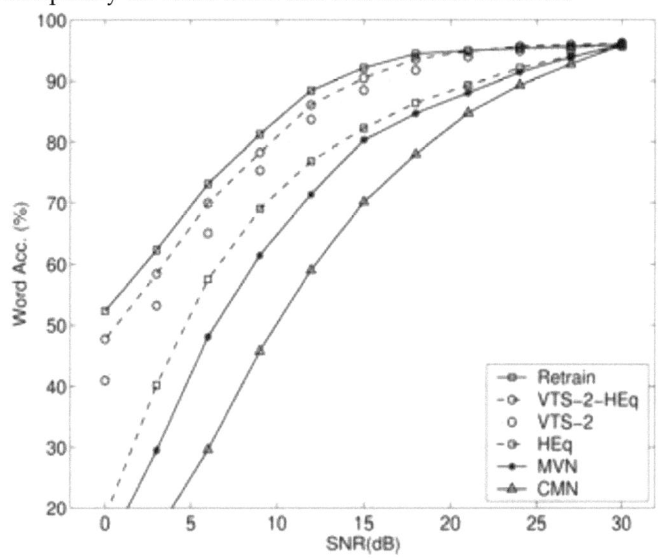

Figure 11. Recognition results obtained with different compensation methods, including 2nd order VTS (VTS-2), histogram equalization (HEq), and the combination of both (VTS-2-HEq). Compensation based on mean and variance normalization has also been included as reference

5.4 Application of histogram equalization to remove residual noise

One of the main features of histogram equalization is that no assumption is made with respect to the distortion mechanism. This reduces its effectiveness with respect to methods like VTS. However, this allow to use histogram equalization in combination with other methods. Usually, after applying a compensation method (for example, VTS, spectral subtraction, Wiener filtering, etc.) a residual noise is still present. This residual noise is difficult to be modeled because the mechanism of distortion becomes more complex than for additive or channel noise. In this case, histogram equalization can be applied since no assumption is required about the distortion process, and the compensation is performed taking only into account the probability distributions of the clean an noisy speech representations.

In figure 11 recognition results are presented for the previously described recognition task, including the reference results (clean training and retraining), histogram equalization, VTS and the combination of both. Results applying Mean and Variance Normalization (MVN) have also been included as reference. As can be observed, histogram equalization provides better results than reference (CMN) and also better than MNV. This is consistent with the fact that histogram equalization can be considered an extension of CMN and MVN. Results provided by histogram equalization are worse than those of VTS, which shows that a model-based compensation method provides a more accurate compensation of the noise noise (particularly in these experiments, where additive Gaussian white noise was artificially added and therefore noise distortion match with the model proposed for VTS noise compensation). One can also observe that the combination of both, VTS and histogram equalization, provides an improvement with respect to VTS, showing that after VTS there is a residual noise that can be reduced by histogram equalization.

6. Conclusions

In this chapter, we have presented an overview of methods for noise robust speech recognition and a detailed description of the mechanism degrading the performance of speech recognizers working under noise conditions. Performance is degraded because of the mismatch between training and recognition and also because of the information loss associated to the randomness of the noise. In the group of compensation methods, we have described the VTS approach (as a representative model-based noise compensation method) and histogram equalization (a non-linear non-model-based method). We have described the differences and advantages of each one, finding that more accurate compensation can be achieved with model-based methods, while non-model-based ones can deal with noise without a description of the distortion mechanism. The best results are achieved when both methods are combined.

7. Acknowledgements

This work has received research funding from the EU 6th Framework Programme, under contract number IST-2002-507943 (HIWIRE, Human Input that Works in Real Environments) and SR3-VoIP projects (TEC2004-03829/TCM) from the Spanish government. The views expressed here are those of the authors only. The Community is not liable for any use that may be made of the information contained therein.

8. References

Acero, A. (1993). Acoustical and environmental robustness in automatic speech recognition, Kluwer Academic Publishers, 1993.

Anastasakos, A.; Kubala, E; Makhoul, J. & Schwartz, R. (1994). Adaptation to new microphones using tied-mixture normalization. Proceedings ofICASSP-94,1994.

Bellegarda, J.R. (1997). Statistical techniques for robust ASR: review and perspectives. Proceedings of EuroSpeech-97, Rhodes, 1997.

Cole, R.; Hirschman, L.; Atlas, L.; Beckman, M.; Biermann, A.; Bush, M.; Clements, M.; Cohen, J.; Garcia, O.; Hanson, B.; Hermansky, H.; Levinson, S.; McKeown, K.; Morgan, N.; Novick, D.G.; Ostendorf, M.; Oviatt, S.; Price, P.; Silverman, H.; Splitz, J.; Waibel, A.; Weinstein, C.; Zahorian, S.; & Zue, V (1995). The challenge of spoken language systems: research directions for the nineties. IEEE Trans, on Speech and Audio Processing, 3,1,1995,1-21.

Davis, S.B. & Mermelstein, P. (1980). Comparison of parametric representations for monosyllabic word recognition in continuosly spoken sentences. *IEEE Trans, on Acoustic,Speech and Signal Processing,* 28,4,1980,357-366.

Duda, R.O.; Hart, RE. (1973). *Pattern Classification and Scene Analysis,* J. Wiley and Sons, 1973.

Ephraim, Y. (1992). A bayesian estimation approach for speech enhancement using hidden Markov models. *IEEE Trans, on Acoustic, Speech and Signal Processing,* 40, 4, 1992, 725-735.

Fukunaga, K. (1990). *Introduction to Statistical Pattern Recognition,* Academic Press, 1990.

Furui, S. (1986). Speaker-independent isolated word recognition using dynamic features of speech spectrum. *IEEE Trans, on Acoustic, Speech and Signal Processing,* 34,1986,52-59.

Gales, M.F.J. & Young, S.J. (1993). HMM recognition in noise using parallel model combination. *Proceedings ofEuroSpeech-93,*1993.

Gales, M.F.J. (1997). 'Nice' model-based compensation schemes for robust speech recognition. *Proceedings ofESCA-NATO Tutorial and Research Workshop on Robust Speech Recognition for Unknown Communication Chanels,* 1997.

Ghitza, O. (1992). Auditory nerve representation as a basis for speech processing. In: *Advances in Speech Signal Processing,* 453-486, Dekker, 1992.

Ghitza, O. (1994). Auditory models and human performance in tasks related to speech coding and speech recognition. *IEEE Trans, on Speech and Audio Processing,* 2,1,1994,115-132.

Gong, Y. (1995). Speech recognition in noisy environments: A survey. *Speech Communication,* 16,3,1995,261-291.

Hermanski, H.; Hanson, B.A. & Wakita, H. (1985). Low dimensional representation of vowels based on all-pole modeling in the psychophysical domain. *Speech Communication,* 4, (1-3), 1955,181-188.

Hermanski, H.; Morgan, N. & Hirsch, H.G. (1993). Recognition of speech in additive and convolutional noise based on RASTA spectral processing. *Proceedings ofICASSP-94,* 1994.

Hernando, J. & Nadeu, C. (1994). Speech recognition in noisy car environment based on OSALPC representation and robust similarity measuring techniques. *Proceedings of ICASSP-94,*1994.

Hirsch, H.G. & Pierce, D. (2000). The AURORA experimental framework for the performance evaluation of speech recognition systems under noise conditions. *ISCAITRW ASR2000, Automatic Speech Recognition: Challenges for the Next Millenium,* 2000.

Hunt, M.J.; Richardson, S.M.; Bateman, D.C. & Piau, A. (1991). An investigation of PLP and IMELDA acoustic representations and their potential for combination. *Proceedings of ICASSP-91,*1991.

Jankowski, C.R.; Hoang-Doan, J. & Lippmann, R.P. (1995). A comparison of signal processing front ends for automatic word recognition. *IEEE Trans, on Speech and Audio Processing,* 3, 4,1995, 286-293.

Junqua, J.C. & Wakita, H. (1989). A comparative study of cepstral lifters and distance measures for all pole models of speech in noise. *Proceedings ofICASSP-89,*1989.

Junqua, J.C. & Haton, J.P. (1996). *Robustness in automatic speech recognition,* Kluwer Academic Publishers, 1996.

Mokbel, C. & Chollet, G. (1991). Speech recognition in adverse environments: speech enhancement and spectral transformations. *Proceedings of ICASSP-91,*1991.

Mokbel, C.; Monn, J. & Jouvet, D. (1993). On-line adaptation of a speech recognizer to variations in telephone line conditions. *Proceedings ofEuroSpeech-93,*1993.

Moreno, P.J.; Stern, R. (1994). Source of degradation of speech recognition in telephone network. *Proceedings oflCASSP-94,*1994.

Moreno, P.J. (1996). *Speech Recognition in Noisy Environments,* PhD thesis, Carnegie Mellon University, Pittsburgh, Pennsylvania, 1996.

Moreno, P.J.; Eberman, B. (1997). A new algorithm for robust speech recognition: the delta vector taylor series approach. *Proceedings of EuroSpeech-97,*1997.

Moreno, P.J.; Raj, B. & Stern, R. (1998). Data-driven environmental compensation for speech recognition: a unified approach. *Speech Communication,* 24, 4,1998,267-288.

Nolazco-Flores, J.A. & Young, S. (1993). *CSS-PMC: a combined enhancement/compensation scheme for continuous speech recognition in noise,* Cambridge University Engineering Department. Technical Report CUED/F-INFENG/TR.128,1993.

Ohkura, K. & Sugiyama, M. (1991). Speech recognition in a noisy environment using a noise reduction neural network and a codebook mapping technique. *Proceedings oflCASSP-91,*1991.

Rabiner, L.R. & Juang, B.H. (1993). *Fundamentals of Speech Recognition,* Prentice-Hall, 1993.

Russ, J.C. (1995). *The Image Processing Handbook,* CRC Press, 1995.

Seide, F. & Mertins, A. (1994). Non-linear regression based feature extraction for connected-word recognition in noise. *Proceedings oflCASSP-94,*1994.

Stern, R.; Raj, B. & Moreno, P.J. (1997). Compensation for environmental degradation in automatic speech recognition. *Proceedings of ESCA-NATO Tutorial and Research Workshop on Robust Speech Recognition for Unknown Communication Chanels,* 1997.

Torre, A.; Peinado, A.M.; Rubio, A.J.; Sanchez, V.E. & Diaz, J.E. (1996). An application of Minimum Classification Error to feature space transformations for speech recognition. *Speech Communication,* 20,3-4,1996,273-290.

Torre, A.; Peinado, A.M.; Rubio, A.J. & Garcia P. (1997). Discriminative feature extraction for speech recognition in noise. *Proceedings ofEuroSpeech-97,* Rhodes, 1997.

Torre, A.; Fohr, D. & Haton, J.P. (2000). Compensation of noise effects for robust speech recognition in car environments. *Proceedings oflCSLP 2000,* Beijing, 2000.

Torre, A.; Peinado, A.M.; Rubio, A.J. (2001). *Reconocimiento automdtico de voz en condiciones de ruido,* University of Granada, 2001.

Torre, A.; Peinado, A.M.; Segura, J.C.; Perez-Cordoba, J.L.; Benitez, C. & Rubio, A.J. (2005). Histogram equalization of the speech representation for robust speech recognition. *IEEE Trans, on Speech and Audio Processing,* 13,3,2005,355-366.

Vaseghi, S.V. & Milner, B.P. (1997). Noise compensation methods for hidden Markov model speech recognition in adverse environments. *IEEE Trans, on Speech and Audio Processing, 5,*1,1997,11-21.

Viiki, O.; Bye, B. & Laurila, K. (1998). A recursive feature vector normalization approach for robust speech recognition in noise. *Proceedings oflCASSP-98,*1998.

Young, S.; Odell, J.; Ollason, D.; Valtchev, V. & Woodland, P. (1997). *The HTK Book,* Cambridge University, 1997.